SPANISH ISLAM

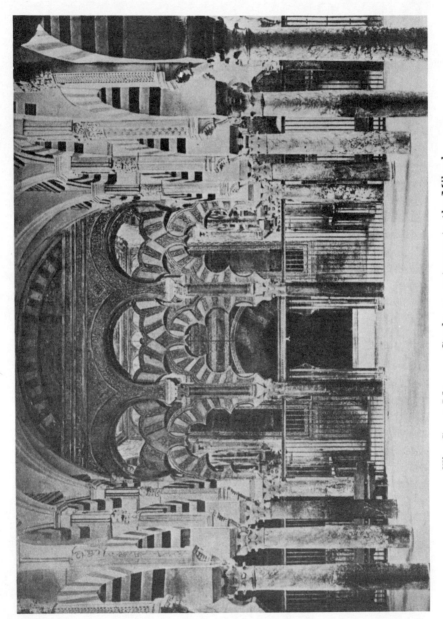

The Great Mosque, Cordova : entrance to the Mihrab

SPANISH ISLAM : A HISTORY OF THE MOSLEMS IN SPAIN BY REINHART DOZY: TRANSLATED WITH A BIOGRAPHICAL INTRODUCTION AND ADDITIONAL NOTES BY FRANCIS GRIFFIN STOKES

DARF PUBLISHERS LIMITED

LONDON

1988

FIRST PUBLISHED 1913
NEW IMPRESSION 1988

ISBN 1 85077 180 4

Printed and bound in Great Britain
by A. Wheaton & Co. Ltd, Exeter, Devon

TO

THE MEMORY OF

ERNEST BRUCE IWAN-MÜLLER

THIS ENGLISH VERSION

OF A WORK WHICH HE HELD IN HIGH ESTEEM

IS AFFECTIONATELY DEDICATED

BY HIS FRIEND

THE TRANSLATOR

CONTENTS

BOOK III

THE KHALIFATE

CONTENTS

BOOK IV

THE PETTY TYRANTS

ERRATA

Page 27, line 2, *for* 'Ommayads' *read* 'Omayyads.'
  „ 27,   „ 15, *for* 'Ommayad' *read* 'Omayyad.'
  „ 76,   „ 15, *for* 'Âmir' *read* 'Amr.'
  „ 209,   „ 22, *for* 'Moghîra' *read* 'Mughîra.'
  „ 265,   „ 30, *for* 'Debonnaire' *read* 'Débonnaire.'
  „ 535,   „ 22, *for* 'Massarîa' *read* 'Masarrîa.'
  „ 684,   „ 40, *for* 'Jaumin' *read* 'Yaumin.'

TRANSLATOR'S PREFACE

THIS volume presents, for the first time, an English version of a notable work which has remained for half a century the standard authority upon an important and fascinating branch of medieval history.

Notwithstanding an assertion to the contrary which has found its way into several leading works of reference, Reinhart Dozy's *Histoire des Musulmans d'Espagne*—originally published in 1861—has never been reprinted, and, having consequently become scarce and costly, is little known except to historical specialists. The reason why no second edition was issued of a book at once so brilliant and so profound will be made apparent in the Biographical Introduction ; it is here only necessary to record the fact. In 1874, however, a German translation of the *Histoire* was made under the direction of Dr. Wolf Wilhelm, Graf von Baudissin, and this version, to which Dozy contributed some emendations of the original, has frequently been consulted during the preparation of the present volume : a Spanish version (by F. de Castro, late Professor of Spanish History in the University of Seville), published in 1877, has also occasionally been found useful for purposes of reference.

In 1881, two years before the historian's death, there appeared the Third Edition—corrected and considerably enlarged—of his *Recherches sur l'Histoire et la Littérature de l'Espagne pendant le moyen âge :* from this work, which is of the highest value to the student of early Spanish history, supplementary notes have been selected, and in some cases additions and corrections thence derived have been embodied in the text.

The present translation is entirely unabridged, and aims at being faithful without being baldly literal : the footnotes have been modified by the omission of those which appealed essentially to Arabic scholars, and the substitution of others of more general interest—selected mainly from the historian's own works and more recent sources.

Lists of authorities are appended to each chapter (with one or two necessary exceptions), while the full titles of the printed works cited in an abbreviated form, together with precise references to the manuscripts consulted by the author, are fully set forth in an Appendix.

In the transliteration of Oriental names—which, of course, had to be undertaken afresh—certain inconsistencies, incidental to a compromise, will be observed. After careful consideration, I determined to omit the diacritical marks, distinguishing allied consonants from one another. While they are needless for the Arabic scholar, there is little doubt, on the other hand, that the uninitiated reader regards them with something of the resentful perplexity with which decimal points are said to have inspired a famous statesman. The use of consonantal compounds for the same purpose is also not without its drawbacks. Simplicity, after all, has its charms, and even Hajjâj, the introducer of diacritics, would probably have admitted that his name thus written conveys as near an approach to its true pronunciation as the " Chaddschâdsch " of the German version. I have, further, unhesitatingly preserved forms which, though anomalous, have become familiarized to English eyes ; but since this practice has been condoned by sundry eminent authorities, for old friends such as " Mohammed," " Mecca," " Koran," " Kady," and " Almanzor," I trust no formal apology is needed.

The Map, which has been specially designed for the work, is mainly based on Maps No. 15 and 16 of the *Spruner-Menke* Historical Atlas ; it indicates some additional places and omits irrelevant names. (A considerable number of places mentioned by the early chroniclers cannot, however, now be identified.)

I desire gratefully to acknowledge my obligations to Sir W. Muir's *Life of Mohammad* (New Edition, by T. H. Weir, 1912), M. Clément Huart's *History of Arabic Literature* (1903), and more especially Mr. R. A. Nicholson's *Literary History of the Arabs* (1907), which I have had constantly at my side. (In one instance I have appropriated, almost inevitably, Mr. Nicholson's version of a sentence from the *Histoire*.)

In the preparation of the Biographical Introduction I have mainly relied, for the facts, upon the sketch of the historian's life presented by M. J. de Goeje to the Royal Academy of Sciences, at Amsterdam (*Jaarboek van de Koninklijke Akademie van Weten-schappen gevestigd te Amsterdam*, 1883, pp. 12–52), and translated into French by M. Victor Chauvin. M. Gustave Dugat's *Histoire des Orientalistes de l'Europe* (1870) has also been of service : the writer was a personal friend of Dozy, who undoubtedly supplied him with information relating to his early years. I have also had the advantage of consulting, for genealogical details, the admirable Family History, by a kinsman of the historian, which has been very recently published.

The Index has been compiled afresh, and is much fuller than that appended to the original work.

That there are no material errors to be detected in the execution of an undertaking which has proved by no means a light task I scarcely venture to hope, and I can only trust that they are not numerous. Any corrections with which I may be favoured will be heartily welcomed.

F. G. STOKES.

London, 1913.

BIOGRAPHICAL INTRODUCTION

VALENCIENNES, and the adjoining districts of Hainault, witnessed much fierce fighting during the second half of the sixteenth century. Though defended by strong ramparts and deep moats, the fortress was captured by Philip de Noircarmes in 1567, and delivered up to the vengeance of his troops. Five years later it was wrested from the Spaniards, only to fall again immediately into their hands. But notwithstanding its vicissitudes as a strong-' old, Valenciennes was looked upon as a harbour of refuge by the peasants and villagers of its environs. Harassed by the depredations of a brutal soldiery, and exposed to savage outrages of every kind, the hapless country-folk flocked within its walls to seek comparative security, and many of the refugees who settled there became thrifty and industrious burghers who adopted surnames reminiscent of their ancestral homes.

If it cannot be rigorously proved that from a family of these refugees the immediate forefathers of the historian of Moorish Spain were descended, it is at least extremely probable that such was their origin.

The connecting link is ready at hand. At a short distance from Valenciennes, between Cambrai and Douai, lay the seigneury of Oisy. In a Gazetteer published early in the eighteenth century [1] it is recorded that the hamlet even then contained seventy-eight inhabitants, and that the domain of Oisy formerly gave its name to a noble family which supplied the hereditary Constable of Cambrai. That many of the inhabitants of the village betook themselves to the town in the troublous times we have referred to, and were still proud to speak of themselves as " Oisy folk," seems a reasonable inference. The conjecture, moreover, is supported by a very apposite fact, for it is certain that in 1603 there was living in Valenciennes one François Dozy, or Doizy [d'Oisy], from whom Dr. G. J. Dozy has traced, in an erudite genealogical work

---

[1] *Dictionnaire Universel de la France ancienne et moderne et de la Nouvelle France.* Paris, 1726.

recently published,[1] the descent of the numerous branches of the family now flourishing in the Netherlands.

It must suffice here to add that in 1647 the family quitted Valenciennes for Holland, and may thenceforth be claimed by the land of their adoption.

On February 21, 1820, Sara Maria (*née* Van Lelyveld), wife of François Jaques Dozy, physician, of Leyden, bore him a son who was christened " Reinhart Pieter Anne," but who, as the title-pages of his chief works testify, usually contented himself in after life with his first baptismal name. His mother having died when he was nine years old, the boy's early education was entrusted to Heer Van Veen at Wassenaar, whence he was removed to a school at Hattem. He made such good progress that at the age of fourteen he became a pupil of Dr. J. J. de Gelder, in order to be prepared for a university career, and so well had the boy employed his time at the preparatory schools that his tutor has recorded that he already had a competent knowledge of French, German, and English.

De Gelder was accustomed to teach the elements of Arabic to those of his pupils who studied Theology, and, observing young Dozy's aptitude for languages, he offered to instruct him in that tongue. The lad eagerly grasped the opportunity thus afforded him, and studying the subject, as a mere *parergon*, in his spare time, outstripped all his fellows. For the rest, it may be recorded that he displayed a linguist's healthy distaste for mathematics, but that his interest in other branches of knowledge was so wide that his tutor feared lest—in emulation of Whewell, and to the sacrifice of sound scholarship in a limited field—omniscience might become his foible.

In September, 1837, Dozy entered the University of Leyden, and in the Faculty of Letters at once attracted the attention of Professor Weijers, a young and brilliant philologist, who with great zeal devoted all his time to his pupils, and hence, while doing admirable work as an able and stimulating lecturer, was not destined to achieve literary fame. No teacher could have been

[1] *De Familie Dozy Genealogie en Geschiedenis*, door Dr. Gualtherus Jacob Dozy. s-Gravenhage, 1911.

[2] The historian's pedigree may thus be summarised, the names of the wives being given in italics, and (;) being used to divide successive generations :

François Dozy (living in 1603) ; Pierre Dozy (*d.* 1647) ; François Dozy (1619–1670), *Jeanne de l'Espine* ; Pierre Dozy (1648–1712), *Esther Drolenvaux* ; Jacques Dozy (1686–1766), *Maria de Pla* ; Abraham Hendrik Dozy (1726–1778), *Titia Kiers* ; Pieter Dozy (1762–1836), *Anna van Dijk* ; François Jaques Dozy (1793–1874), *Sara Maria van Lelyveld* ; Reinhart Pieter Anne Dozy.

better suited to curb Dozy's tendency to dilettantism than Weijers, who had a passion for minute accuracy as well as a lucid precision of exposition which had no tinge of pedantry, and the master's insistence on the supreme importance of exactitude had a lifelong influence on the pupil, with whom he read Arabic, Hebrew, Chaldee, and Syriac.

The ardent student of eighteen desired, however, to scale forthwith the alluring heights of Oriental poetry. But Weijers, who looked upon the matter with the eyes of a philologist and a grammarian, dissuaded Dozy from pursuing his too fascinating dream, and suggested Arabian history as a preferable subject for him to attack.

The young student, soon growing wearied and bewildered over the barren chronicle of countless battles and the shifting scenes of transient dynasties, not unnaturally became disheartened. Casting about, therefore, for a more congenial outlet for his energies, he was attracted by the subject of lexicography. Freytag's *Lexicon Arabico-Latinum*, though an esteemed work, was meagre and unsatisfactory for European students, since it was a mere compilation from Arabic dictionaries, and, being confined to the " classical " language of the Koran, its pages might be ransacked in vain for a multitude of words used by later writers. To enlarge his vocabulary, Dozy accordingly took up the works of Étienne Marc Quatremère and studied them with great thoroughness, giving especial attention to the valuable notes, which he learnt almost by heart.

In December, 1841, the Royal Institute proposed as a subject for competition a thesis thus specified :

De vestibus, quibus Arabes utriusque sexus diversis temporibus et in diversis terris usi sunt, aut etiam nunc utuntur, sic exponatur, ut, post brevem de universis disputationem, singulæ secundum ordinem litterarum Arabicarum deinceps recenseatur, earumque forma, materia atque usus explicentur.

In short, a monograph on Arabian costume was demanded. The subject instantly appealed to young Dozy's restless intellect. Yet the preliminary labour would be very severe if intrinsically valuable results were to be reached. A mass of manuscripts must be consulted, the most intricate researches must be made, and there was little more than a year in which to carry them out. Quite undaunted, however, by the difficulties which confronted him, and undeterred by the warnings of friends, the enthusiastic

b

student flung himself into the task. So exceptional were the demands which he consequently made upon the resources of the University Library that the authorities—amongst whom was Weijers—were at last constrained to inform Dozy that the supply must be cut short unless he could give a satisfactory reason for his inordinate requisitions. The question was a most embarrassing one ; strict anonymity was imposed on the competitors— and Weijers was one of the adjudicators. Dozy promptly cut the Gordian knot, and informed Weijers, " unofficially," of his intention. The Professor was not a little astonished at his pupil's audacity ; he did not, however, attempt either to dissuade or encourage him, but merely gave him permission to use the library as freely as he desired. The months flew by, but with the aid of a friendly amanuensis the essay, or rather treatise, was ready just in time.

On November 20, 1843, the prize was awarded to the youth of twenty-three. The conditions under which the treatise had been written naturally prevented it from being as complete as its author desired ; but he immediately undertook to remedy its deficiencies, and in 1845 there appeared Dozy's first published book : *Dictionnaire détaillé des noms des vêtements chez les Arabes*—a valuable and brilliant piece of lexicographical work displaying great acumen and an immense width of reading. The foundation-stone of Dozy's reputation as a profound scholar was securely laid.

Weijers had given a good deal of attention to the writings of the Arabs of Spain, and he early introduced José Antonio Conde's *Historia de la dominacion de los Árabes en España* to his former pupil's notice. This work must be more fully referred to later ; it suffices here to mention that Dozy speedily recognised that it was hopelessly uncritical and teemed with errors. Forthwith he threw himself with ardour into the study of Spanish. In a letter dated 1841 he had asked for a grammar and dictionary of the language, and an edition of *Don Quixote ;* " for," he adds, " Spanish I must learn ! " Two years later he writes : " I give up all the time I can spare to Spanish. Thanks to my London correspondent, I have already formed the best Spanish library in the place. Before collecting the *belles-lettres*, however, I must get together the books relating to the Middle Ages. . . . This will not, I hope, take me long."

This extract can scarcely fail to suggest what was indeed the case, namely, that Dozy possessed that inestimable advantage

for the ambitious scholar—a well-filled purse.[1] He never seems
to have made the slightest allusion to

> "That eternal want of pence
> Which vexes public men."

Perhaps he regarded too lightly this boon which Fortune had
accorded him. The poet may, conceivably, soar the higher if
not encumbered by a superfluity of pelf ; the novelist may evolve
romance from his own empty larder—but one of the historian's
most inspiring volumes should be his bankers' pass-book. An
impecunious Gibbon is almost unthinkable.

Dozy's Spanish studies seem to have given him transient
thoughts of writing a book upon Lope de Vega. The unparalleled
mental activity of the prodigy who composed fifteen hundred plays,
and could toss off an Epic, in twenty books, as a mere interlude,
doubtless had its attraction for a student of Dozy's untiring industry ; but his energies were fortunately diverted into another
channel. He had for some time meditated writing an accurate
history of some episode of the Moslem dominion in Spain, and,
having accumulated valuable materials from hitherto unexplored
sources, by the time he had completed his prize essay he had
selected a very promising subject, namely, the strange and
romantic history of the family of the 'Abbâdids, who reigned in
Seville after the downfall of the Omayyad Khalifs (A.D. 1023–1091).

In 1844, Dozy—who had just proceeded to the degree of
Doctor—married Maria Carolina van Goor den Oosterlingh. Of
her it must suffice here to record that she proved an excellent and
sympathetic wife to the student whose lifelong companion she
was destined to be. (She died in 1901, having survived her
husband for eighteen years.)

Though one of the most important events of the scholar's
placid life, Dozy's marriage scarcely interrupted his literary
pursuits. The honeymoon was spent in Germany, and the bridegroom seized the opportunity thus afforded him of making the
acquaintance, at Leipsic, of the eminent Orientalist Heinrich
Fleischer—thus initiating a friendship which lasted, with one
unfortunate lapse, for nearly forty years ; he also made careful
researches in sundry libraries for manuscripts bearing on the
'Abbâdids.

---

[1] " Il n'était pas obligé de considérer le science comme un gagne-pain, ce qui a
été le triste sorte de tant d'autres ; car dans ce cas il se mêle toujours un peu de
sang aux sueurs du savant pauvre."—G. Dugat, *Hist. des Orientalistes de l'Europe*,
1870, i. 46.

His investigations were unexpectedly rewarded. In a manuscript at Gotha—wrongly described as a fragment of al-Makkarî's *History of Spain*, but really a portion of Ibn Bassâm's *Dzakhîra* (A.D. 1109)—he discovered a valuable document bearing on the Cid Campeador. This included a letter from an Arab taken prisoner by the Cid at Valencia, and since Ibn Bassâm's work was written only ten years after Rodrigo's death, it is anterior by thirty-two years to the Latin Chronicle, written in the south of France, which had hitherto been regarded as the earliest source. As Mr. H. E. Watts has remarked, "this document settled for ever the question of the Cid's identity." Dozy instantly recognised the importance of his discovery, and great was his satisfaction when he was permitted to take the precious manuscript away with him for further examination. From this event dates the rise of his wider project of a comprehensive history of Moorish Spain.

In the Spring of 1845 Dozy visited Oxford, to make extracts from Oriental MSS., and in the Bodleian Library reaped an abundant harvest. It may be mentioned that, ever on the alert, he incidentally discovered there two medieval Dutch poems hitherto unknown.

On his return to Leyden, Dozy planned the issue of a series of Arabic texts, to be published by subscription. The first volume, which appeared in 1846, was the *Commentaire historique d'Ibn-Badroun sur le poeme d'Ibn-Abdoun ;* this was accompanied by a complete apparatus of introduction, notes, glossary and index. The historical interest of this volume lies in the fact that Ibn Badrûn—who lived at Seville in the twelfth century—in his Commentary on Ibn Abdûn's poem, which had for its subject the fall of the Aftas family, throws important light on the period of the Almoravide invasion of Spain.

During the same year Dozy was appointed *Adjutor Interpretis legati Warneriani*, and was entrusted with the compilation of a catalogue of Oriental MSS., a task which, as might have been expected, was admirably executed. In 1847, at the expense of the (London) Society for the Publication of Oriental Texts, there appeared, in English, *The History of the Almohades by Abdo'l-wâhid al Marrékoshí, preceded by a sketch of the History of Spain, from the times of the conquest till the reign of Yusof Ibn-Táshifín, and of the history of the Almoravides.* This history of the African dynasty which succeeded the Almoravides, by 'Abd al-wâhid of Morocco, was edited by Dozy from a MS. in the Leyden library. In the same year the industrious scholar published the first part of his *Notices sur quelques manuscrits arabes*—a work which was completed in 1851—and in 1848 the first volume of Ibn Adhârî's *History of Africa and Spain* (*Al-Bayân al-Mughrib*)—with notes, glossary and introduction—followed.

The more Dozy studied the Arab historians, the more impressed he was by the grave defects of Conde's much belauded work, and he eventually made up his mind, in the interests of historical science, to prick the bubble of the Spaniard's reputation. But though Conde, who died in 1820, had long been immune from personal attacks, the fame of his posthumous *Historia de la dominacion de los Árabes* was firmly established, and to assail a work of European celebrity with any hope of success it was necessary to be armed at all points. Dozy accordingly devoted several months to further researches amongst the somewhat jejune pages of the Christian chroniclers, and then—feeling the ground firm beneath his feet—he published his *Recherches sur l'histoire politique et littéraire de l'Espagne pendant le moyen âge.* This volume, which appeared in 1849, fell like a thunderbolt on Conde's followers. As a critic, Dozy—especially in his earlier days—could be not only severe but merciless upon occasion, and never did he wield his weapons more ruthlessly than in the present instance. Conde, according to his assailant, knew little more of Arabic than the alphabet: " Bringing an imagination of extreme fertility to the aid of a knowledge scarcely elementary, he has, with unparalleled impudence "—we are told—" forged dates by the hundred, and invented facts by the thousand—always under the false pretence that he is faithfully translating Arabic texts. In the words of Pierre Corneille :

> ' Vois que fourbe sur fourbe à nos yeux il entasse,
> Et ne fait que jouer des tours de passe-passe ! '
> *Le Menteur*, v. 7."

" How strange it is," he continues, " that even eminent Orientalists should have allowed themselves to be tricked into following such a Jack-a-lantern ! "

Dozy's attack upon the Spanish historian speedily carried conviction to the minds of those who were best qualified to form a judgment upon the subject. The fallen idol was trampled upon by its former worshippers. Ernest Renan, for instance, in an article contributed to the *Journal des Débats*, endorses Dozy's strictures in scathing terms. "Conde's History," he writes, "swarms with blunders, and passages of sheer nonsense. He makes two, or even three, persons out of a single individual. In his pages,

men die twice—and sometimes before they are born : Arabic
infinitives become the names of populous cities : non-existent
characters play imaginary parts. In making use of Ibn al-Abbar's
Biographical Dictionary, Conde did not observe that certain
sheets had been misplaced by a book-binder's error ; he consequently jumbles at random the lives of eminent men of the fourth
and fifth centuries of the Mohammedan era, and triumphantly
extricates himself from the resulting welter by the aid of cock-
and-bull stories of the most diverting kind ! "

And yet a counsel for the defence could have pleaded not a
few extenuating circumstances on the luckless Conde's behalf.
Appointed interpreter to Joseph Bonaparte, and henceforward
regarded as little else than a traitor to his country, he was exiled
from Spain by the Government of Ferdinand VII, and his name
was erased from the list of members of the Spanish Academy and
of the Academy of History. Deprived of his post as Librarian
of the Escorial, he was, moreover, cut off from access to the
Oriental manuscripts there treasured. In 1813, he took refuge
in France, and on his return he was not allowed to visit Madrid
until 1816. Four years later he died in such abject poverty that
his friends alone saved him from the indignity of a pauper's burial.
The first volume only of his History had been corrected by its
author ; the other two were compiled from the manuscript by the
scarcely qualified hand of Don Juan Tineo. It may be added
that the American writer George Ticknor, in the Preface to his
History of Spanish Literature, gracefully acknowledges the assistance afforded him by Conde, and speaks of him as " a retired,
gentle, modest scholar," who had already " tasted the bitterness
of political exile and had been reduced to honourable poverty."

But it did not enter into the head of the prosperous scholar of
Leyden to make allowances for the difficulties under which the
Spanish historian laboured. Historical inaccuracy was in Dozy's
eyes a crime—and the slipshod historian, a criminal.

Of late years a more lenient view of Conde's delinquencies has
prevailed. It is recognised that he was, after all, a pioneer—
ill-equipped, doubtless, for his great undertaking, but, for all
that, a zealous and strenuous explorer. Few would now be inclined to go beyond Mr. Stanley Lane-Poole's temperate judgment
of the *Historia*, as being " a book of considerable literary merit
but very slight historical value, and the source of most of the
errors that are found in later works." In short, if Conde's book
had been regarded by his immediate successors as a bold but
rough sketch, needing much modification and correction before

being worked up into a picture, all would have been well : but it was extolled by writers unable to check his treatment of the original authorities, as a work of impeccable erudition, and the ultimate catastrophe might have been foreseen.

Conde, however, was not the only historian who fell under the critic's lash in the *Recherches*. Dozy treated none too tenderly the translation by his own friend Don Pascual de Gayangos of al-Makkarî's *History of the Mohammedan Dynasties in Spain* (London, 1843), and in this case the acerbity of his tone is much less excusable. Don Pascual's work, it is true, is not free from inaccuracies, but it is none the less of great value to the student who is unacquainted with Arabic, and the elaborate notes, as Mr. Lane-Poole observes, present a mass of valuable material which can be obtained nowhere else. It may here pertinently be remarked that learned Spain felt no grudge against the foreign critic, for in 1851 Dozy was elected Corresponding Member of the Academy of History, of Madrid, and in 1853 the dignity of Commander of the Order of Charles III was conferred on him.

Ten years later, materials for a Second Part of the *Recherches* had been accumulated, and since the earlier volume was nearly out of print, Dozy simultaneously reissued it. But in this revised edition, although the pith of the original preface was reproduced, the bitterly polemical portions of the original text found no place. The writer's motives for their omission were probably twofold. In the first place, as he himself tells us, he felt that his criticisms of Conde, having done their deadly work once for all, were no longer needed ; while with regard to Don Pascual, a feeling of something like compunction for the writer's acrimony may safely be inferred.

On Peerlkamp's resignation of the Professorship of History at Leyden, in 1850, Dozy was appointed to the vacant chair. On the very day of his nomination he received perhaps the only severe blow that ever marred the unruffled calm of his domestic happiness, in the death of a fondly loved little son. " La science," writes the historian characteristically, " elle aussi, doit me venir en aide, tout autant que l'amour et l'amitié."

Dozy's new post gave a new direction to his studies, and enlarged his outlook. No better preparation, in fact, could have been devised for the historical masterpiece which was to see the light eleven years later. At the outset, it is true, he had to devote a great part of his time to his official duties. It is whispered that there have been Professors who have looked upon their lectures as irksome formalities to be perfunctorily discharged : how differently Dozy regarded his responsibilities may, however, be gathered from a letter to M. de Vries written in the Spring of his first year of office. " In the Long Vacation," he says, " I hope to tackle Swedish and Icelandic—I already know enough Danish to read historical works—for I wish next year to lecture on the history of the Normans in Europe." Each year, in fact, he chose a fresh period for his discourses, and it was ever his aim to inspire his pupils with a genuine taste for historical studies ; but his immense range of reading and prodigious memory facilitated his task.

During five or six years, beginning with 1854, Dozy was at intervals engaged—as a collaborator with G. Dugat, L. Krehl, and W. Wright of Cambridge—in the preparation of an edition of the *Nafh al-Tíb* of al-Makkarî. This important work, written in the seventeenth century, is the chief authority for the literary history of Spanish Islam. It was primarily intended as the Biography of a famous Vizier of Granada, but the elaborate " Introduction " constitutes a vast mine of information on literary and political matters, and it is this portion of Makkarî's book which Dozy and his colleagues issued, in five parts, under the title of *Analectes sur l'Histoire et la Littérature des Arabes d'Espagne* (1855–61).

In his attack on Conde, Dozy had undoubtedly rendered an important service to students of history, but the effect of his criticism had been mainly destructive : he had demolished a false and misleading picture, but he had left an empty frame. The nobler work of construction was now to be his, and year after year he laboured assiduously at a task the fulfilment of which seemed to him almost a debt of honour. During these strenuous years the only published productions of Dozy's pen, apart from his share in the *Analectes*, were a few articles in *De Gids* (Amsterdam), one of the principal literary periodicals of the Netherlands—mere sparks from the workman's anvil—on such varied subjects as the Chansons de Geste of the cycle of Guillaume d'Orange ; Russia in the seventeenth century ; Spain under Charles III ; together with occasional excursions into contemporary politics.

At length the formidable task was completed, and in 1861 there appeared, in four octavo volumes, *Histoire des Musulmans d'Espagne jusqu'à la Conquête de l'Andalousie par les Almoravides* —the work here presented to English readers.

The four volumes corresponded to the four somewhat over-lapping sections into which, with excellent judgment, Dozy divided his subject. A chronologically continuous narrative would have entailed confusion rather than perspicuity.

The materials with which the historian had to deal were of the utmost complexity and diversity. Broadly, the facts to be dealt with were these : Spain, originally a Province of Rome, had, during the decline of the Empire, been overrun by Barbarian invaders—Alans, Vandals, Suevi, and finally Visigoths. Each of these inroads, which occurred in rapid succession, had left its mark upon the inhabitants of the Peninsula, but the Visigothic dominion proved enduring, and lasted for two centuries, during which the simple and hardy invaders gradually succumbed to the same causes of corruption and decadence as had their Roman predecessors. Early in the eighth century a fresh invasion took place, of a wholly different character. Across the Straits of Gibraltar there poured a strange host from the South and East —a multitude of dark-skinned warriors from Arabia, Syria, Egypt, and Northern Africa, who found Spain an easy prey. Fired by religious fervour and the lust of conquest, the Moslem hordes spread rapidly over all save the extreme north of the Iberian Peninsula, and, passing the Pyrenees, threatened all Western Europe until checked by the great Christian victory of Tours.

But in Spain itself their dominion seemed destined to endure, fostering, as it did, a civilization in many respects higher than Europe then knew. It is true that Charles the Hammer had repulsed the Saracenic invasion of France, but the blow he dealt tended rather to consolidate the Moorish Empire in Spain. It was internal decay, and not the pressure of external foes, which was to cause that Empire to crumble into dust. For even when the invaders landed, the germs of dissolution were present in their midst. Centuries before, in the deserts of Arabia, fierce inter-tribal feuds had existed—unending because inexplicable. These animosities had been transferred from the arid heights of Nejd and the kindlier soil of " Araby the Blest " to the banks of the Guadal-quiver and the Ebro—and thereby the West was saved.

To trace the history of these fatal feuds from their misty origins to their tragic and far-reaching consequences—to indicate the part played by the religious fervour of Christian zealots and Khârejite fanatics as well as by the philosophic scepticism of the true Arab—to narrate the dissensions between Berbers and Bedawin, and the bitter rivalries between the Christian States even when threatened by a common foe—such are some of the tasks which confront the historian who seeks to unravel the tangled skein of the history of Medieval Spain. And this dis-entanglement Dozy effected with consummate art. In the First Book he sketches, in bold strokes, the character of the pre-Islamic Arabs, the blood-feuds of Yemenites and Ma'addites, the career of the Prophet, the rapid spread of the Moslem Empire—the occupation of Spain by Arabs and Berbers, and the resulting jealousies and rivalries which arose between them. The Second Book deals primarily with the conquered people ; it takes us back to the Visigothic dominion, relates the Conquest in another aspect, describes the settlement of the country, the gallant but ineffectual efforts of Christians and Renegades to cast off the Moslem yoke, the thrilling episode of the Martyrs of Cordova, and the attainment to supreme power of the great Khalif 'Abd-er-Rahmân III. The Third Book continues the history of Spain under the Omayyad Khalifs. The scholarly and peace-loving Hakam II is succeeded nominally by the boy-Khalif Hishâm, but actually by the great Prime Minister Almanzor, who makes his authority absolute. Almanzor's domestic policy and victorious campaigns against the Christians of the North are described in seven vivid chapters. The rest of this Book deals with the disastrous reigns of the " puppet Khalifs " who in rapid succession ascended the throne after the death of Almanzor, and brings the history of the country down to the year A.D. 1030. In the Fourth, and last, Book, the tangled story of the republics, and dynasties of petty princes—the *Reyes de Taifas* of Spanish historians—which arose upon the ruins of the Khalifate, is unravelled with great skill : the revival of inter-tribal jealousies, the rapid and inevitable decay of the Moslem power, the fatal invitation sent to the Almoravides, the second African invasion which resulted, and its inevitable results, are vividly set forth—the work aptly closing with the strange and romantic history of al-Mu'tamid of Seville, which, as Dr. Nicholson has remarked, " reminds one of a sentence frequently occurring in the *Arabian Nights :* ' Were it graven with needle-gravers upon the eye-corners, it were a warner to whoso would be warned.' "

Dozy's *magnum opus* challenges comparison with the best specimens of historical literature. In the words of a writer eminently qualified to sit in judgment upon it, it is " at once judicious and profound, and equally pleasing to the literary and historical sense." There have been, and perhaps still are, critics who grudge to admit the compatibility of historical profundity and literary artifice. " Give us hard facts," they say, in effect, " and no word-painting. It is the historian's duty to efface himself, to supply the student with an abundance of bricks, and to allow him to be his own architect." These pages are clearly not the place for a discussion of this theory ; it is enough to say that it was not Dozy's.

He delighted, on the contrary, in literary architecture, and attached, moreover, considerable importance to the removal of all scaffolding and débris from the finished building—with the result that the grace and lightness of the edifice suggest, perhaps, but faintly the immense labour expended on the discovery and accumulation of its materials. It cannot be denied that a lucid and vivacious style may convey an impression of superficiality to the unreflecting student : but the fault, which lies with the reader, is excusable. When we admire the placid flow of a noble river in its lower reaches, we seldom think of the cataracts over which it has dashed, of the rocky obstacles through which it has forced its way, and still less of the countless affluents which have contributed to its flood. Yet, as Dozy reminds us in his Preface, the result of the labour of weeks was often compressed into a paragraph of the History—or, not seldom, was wholly rejected, as lying beyond the scope of the work as he conceived it.

To the objection that Dozy relies mainly on Arab sources, and therefore lacks impartiality, the reply is obvious. He was compelled to rely on such sources when all others were lacking. But he consulted every available authority, and if the Christian annals of the epoch are bald and scanty, he made the fullest possible use of these meagre documents. A glance at the list of Authorities given in the Appendix to the present volume will suffice to show how deeply Dozy delved in that mine of Spanish History, the *España Sagrada*. The Chronicles—often mere fragments—of Isidorus Pacensis, Sebastian of Salamanca, the Monks of Silos and Albelda, and twenty others, are frequently, and respectfully, cited — and if these barren chronicles cannot compare for copiousness and literary charm with the full-blooded narratives of the Arab historians, no more blame attaches to Dozy than to the struggling monastic writers who did their best to hand on the flickering torch of learning in those dark and stormy days.

Nor are the personal anecdotes and romantic episodes, here and there introduced in the very words of contemporary annalists and poets, to be scorned by the purely scientific historian. Imagination may have coloured them ; yet Southey's advice to his brother, who contemplated a *History of the Crusades,* is of the soundest : " Omit," says he, " none of those little circumstances which give life to narration, and bring old manners, old feelings, and old times before your eyes."

It might be supposed that a work of such power and originality speedily won its way to popularity and placed its writer in his true position amidst the ranks of eminent historians. Yet—if the plain truth be told—in Holland it attracted very slight attention, and won neither popular esteem nor the eulogies of the learned. The reason for this paradoxical neglect is, however, easily explicable. Two years after its publication the History was worthily reviewed in *De Gids* (1863, ii. pp. 411–462) by Professor Veth. In the course of a long and appreciative criticism the writer makes the cause of the " boycott "—for to this the treatment accorded the work by literary Holland amounted—perfectly plain. Veth gives the book the highest praise ; he points out the immense labour undertaken by Dozy, and the art with which he has concealed it ; he makes it clear that the historian had to make a *tabula rasa* of all that had previously been written on the subject ; and he goes on to record his opinion that had the book been written in Dutch it would instantly have been hailed as one of the glories of the national literature.

Having thus furnished the clue to the mystery, the reviewer emphasizes the cause of the slighting reception of the book by bluntly pointing out that the publication of a work so important, by a Dutchman, in a foreign language, was held by his fellow-countrymen to be flagrantly unpatriotic. Such a sentiment on the part of a small but proud nationality is natural and wholly excusable : it is well known that Gibbon seriously contemplated composing *The Decline and Fall* in French : the effect this would have had upon its popularity in England can scarcely be doubtful. Yet the difficulty which confronted Dozy is obvious. If he had published his History in Dutch, however loudly it might have been applauded in Holland, it would indubitably have been neglected by the rest of Europe ; but knowing, on the other hand, that most educated Hollanders were acquainted with French, he underestimated the chilling effect upon national sentiment produced by the appearance of a *Histoire* when a *Historie* was looked for. A century or two earlier such a work might conveniently have been written in Latin—more or less canine—but that device being inadmissible, Dozy chose as his medium a language perhaps unrivalled for its universality, with the unfortunate and unexpected result that no second edition of the original work has ever appeared.

The historian was soon able to make some amends for the apparent slight which he had cast on his national tongue, for in 1863 he enriched Dutch literature by an excellent book, *Het Islamisme*—an essay on the History of Mohammedanism. This work—a contribution to a collection of histories of the principal religions of the world—attained considerable popularity, being reprinted, in 1880, and translated into French by M. Victor Chauvin.

In the course of writing the last-named treatise Dozy arrived at certain results which he regarded as somewhat astonishing, and in his Preface he promised to pursue the subject further. In 1864 there accordingly appeared, also in Dutch, a volume entitled *Israeliten te Mekka*, " The Israelites at Mecca." Of this work M. Gustave Dugat remarks that it is " considered by some to be the best, and by others, the worst of all Dozy's books. No book gained him more praise in Holland—or more bitter criticism, especially at the hands of the Jews of Germany." It aimed at proving that the ancient sanctuary of Mecca was founded in the reign of Saul by a body of exiled Israelites of the tribe of Simeon —that these Israelites there established the Great Festival of Mecca—and that at the time of the Babylonian captivity a second column of Israelites proceeded thither. The writer further argued that the primitive worship of Israel was that of Baal and not of Yahveh. An extended account of this theory must be sought elsewhere : it attracted much attention at the time, and Bishop Colenso was found among its supporters.

The duties of the professorial chair, though, as we have seen, taken with due seriousness by its occupant, did not prevent him from undertaking further labours. In 1866 there appeared *Description de l'Afrique et de l'Espagne*, containing the Arabic text of al-Idrîsî, based on the Paris and Oxford manuscripts, together with a translation, notes, and glossary. This valuable section of the Moorish geographer's great work had been taken in hand by Dozy before 1864, and was now completed with the collaboration of M. de Goeje. In the following year Dozy issued, under the title of *Oosterlingen*, a list of Dutch words derived from Arabic, Hebrew, Persian, and other Oriental sources, and this was followed, in 1869, by a corrected and greatly enlarged edition of W. H. Engelmann's *Glossary of Spanish and Portuguese words derived from the Arabic*. This was awarded the Volney Prize by the French " Academie des Inscriptions et belles-lettres," July 16, 1869.

On retiring from his post as Rector, early in the same year, Dozy chose as the subject of his farewell oration : " De causis cur Mohammedanorum cultura et humanitas præ ea quæ Christianorum est, imminuta et corrupta sit." This important and suggestive discourse was immediately published. In 1869 an article, which is a masterpiece of criticism, on De Slane's translation of Ibn Khaldûn's *Prolegomena*, appeared from Dozy's pen in the *Journal asiatique*, and seemed to indicate that he had quitted the field of History for that of Philology.

Dozy's pugnacity as a scholar, and ruthlessness as a critic, might have been expected to furnish materials for an additional chapter—not devoid of piquancy—in the *Quarrels of Authors ;* as a matter of fact, however, none of his controversies seem to have led to a breach of amity, save in a single instance, and that, strangely enough, in the case of his old and valued friend Fleischer. Since this serious misunderstanding severed for some years the friendship of two eminent scholars, and was the origin of by no means the least important of Dozy's works, a brief account of the source of the trouble will not be out of place. It was the practice of the famous Leipsic Orientalist to read critically new and important texts, and to send to their editors any corrections or comments which occurred to him. This he had done in the case of the *Analectes*, and in the fifth part of this, which appeared in 1861, many observations over Fleischer's signature were included in the *Additions and Corrections*. In the Preface, moreover, the Professor was especially thanked for having devoted so much of his valuable time—stolen from his special studies—to Makkarî, and was assured that his labour was by no means lost. It is possible that Fleischer detected in these remarks a slightly acid suggestion that he was straying outside his province ; at any rate, in the Preface to the first part of his *Corrections* (1867)—published in the Reports of the Royal Academy of Sciences of Saxony [1]—he made it clear that he was not pleased with the way in which his emendations had been treated—alleging that the arguments put forward in support of many of them had been suppressed ; that several due to himself had no indication of their origin, and that some had been ignored. Now in Fleischer's own view all his comments were, without exception, valuable ; and since, on re-reading the text and collating it with some sources which the editors seemed to have treated with scant respect, he had been able to add to his list, he resolved on an independent publication. There was apparently no cause of offence in this, but it happened that ten years previously Dozy had entered into a quite informal correspondence with Fleischer on the subject of the emendations in that part of the *Analectes* for which he was especially responsible, and Fleischer, by what seems a singular lapse in taste and judgment, treated these often tentative letters as though they had

---

[1] *Berichte der Kön. sächs. Gesellschaft der Wissenschaften,* Phil. Hist. Class., t. xix–xxi.

been published, and also—which was worse—as though they represented Dozy's final views upon the subject.

Such procedure would have nettled a man much more patient of injustice than was the Leyden professor. He was seriously aggrieved. In his almost forgotten letters he had advanced more than one opinion which he would have retracted or modified if he had given its subject further reflection ; and these opinions were cited as though his matured judgments—and refuted ! Dozy accordingly relinquished the work upon which he was then busily employed, burnished his weapons, and in 1871 published his brilliant *Lettre à M. Fleischer contenant des remarques critiques et explicatives sur le texte d'al-Makkarí*. In this work he wields the rapier rather than the bludgeon. In polished and courteous phrases he upbraids the veteran of Leipsic for his manifest unfairness, reminding him, in the words of the Abbé Bargés, that " ten years in a man's life represent more than a century in the life of a society," and adding : " Would you have had no cause for complaint if I, in turn, had printed those conjectures of your own which I refuted long ago and which you are careful no longer to advance ? " After a few more pages of expostulation Dozy plunges into technicalities, and, in minutely criticising Fleischer's notes and conjectures, incidentally confers a solid boon on students of Oriental literature and history. The breach between the two eminent Orientalists lasted, as we have mentioned, several years, but it is satisfactory to be able to record that ultimately, in the words of Fleischer's biographer : " the misunderstanding was cleared up in a way that reflects credit on both scholars ; " [1] and, as will immediately become apparent, their friendship was established on a firmer basis than ever.

Ever since 1867, Dozy had been sedulously amassing materials for the book which was, perhaps, to furnish in the eyes of Orientalists his chief title to fame—under the title of *Supplément aux dictionnaires arabes*. In 1873, he found himself in a position to commence the work of construction, and on this he laboured, with few intermissions, for eight years. He had become conscious, it appears, of a failure in health, which his friends had not observed, but which warned him that if he would successfully carry out his great design, to it he must henceforth devote all his remaining energies. In 1881 the *Supplément* was finished. A personal reference in the Preface will speak for itself : " The accomplishment

---

[1] *Memoir of Heinrich Leberecht Fleischer*, by Professor A. Müller. Washington, 1892.

of my task," he writes, " fills me with gratitude. The labour has been long protracted : the quotations—some of them noted forty years ago—have all been verified, and had I foreseen that the mere arrangement of the materials would occupy eight years, I should perhaps have abandoned my project. In hours of pain and sickness I have feared that I might not live to accomplish it ; but, thanks be to God ! my fears were groundless ; life and strength have sufficed. . . . This fulfilment of the hope of my youth has caused me the liveliest satisfaction."

Before the *Supplément* was finished fresh distinctions had been conferred upon its author. Already Member of the Royal Academy of Sciences of Copenhagen, in 1878 he was made Corresponding Member of the Academy of Sciences of St. Petersburg ; in the following year, Honorary Member of the *Deutsche Morgenländische Gesellschaft ;* and in 1880, Foreign Correspondent of the *Accademia dei Lincei* of Rome and Honorary Professor of the *Institucion libre de Enseñanza* of Madrid—his name being linked, in the last case, with those of Charles Darwin and John Tyndall.

And yet, as M. de Goeje observes, Dozy valued above all these honours the judgment of the veteran Fleischer — now happily restored to his friendship—who hailed the *Supplément* as " the greatest work of Oriental lexicography which has appeared since Lane's great (but unfinished) dictionary of classical Arabic," and congratulated the author on having been enabled to achieve " such a triumph both in matter and form, by dint of the width of his reading, his indefatigable zeal, his profound knowledge of the language, and his oft-proved perspicacity."

Little did the octogenarian scholar, seemingly endowed with the vigour of eternal youth, suspect that the illness referred to by the friend who was more than twenty years his junior was the precursor of a fatal disease. But so it was : no sooner had the *Supplément* been safely launched than its author experienced a grave premonition of ebbing vitality—for the first time in his life he did not know what next to turn his hand to. This feeling of lassitude passed off to some extent, but he undertook no fresh labours. He corrected his *History of the Almohades,* a second edition of which had been called for, and corresponded on technical points with his friends Fleischer and De Goeje ; but the most gratifying event of the closing years of his life was the reception accorded to the third edition of his *Recherches,* which contained numerous additions and a few corrections. These volumes, published in 1881, are of the highest value to the student of Moslem Spain who desires to investigate more fully certain matters necessarily touched upon briefly in the *Histoire;* and, though the work consists of disconnected notes and dissertations, so lucid and attractive is its style that Gottfried Buist well said of it that whoever dipped into its pages to verify a reference read the whole article.

This was Dozy's last book: on the twenty-ninth of April, 1883, he died. His uneventful career calls for no judicial summing-up: its simple record suffices. Reinhart Dozy was essentially and entirely a man of letters. Literature—in the widest sense, including Philology and History—satisfied all his ambitions. In the unwearied service of literature he spent forty strenuous years, and he left the world the richer for his labours.

F. G. S.

AUTHOR'S PREFACE

THE history of Spain, and especially of Moorish Spain, has been the congenial study which has unceasingly occupied my attention for twenty years, and before commencing the present work I had devoted no small part of a lifetime to accumulating materials—scattered throughout almost all the libraries of Europe —to examining and collating relevant documents, and to editing not a few.

Nevertheless, it is with extreme diffidence that I give this History to the world. In it I traverse ground hitherto untrodden, for—as I have elsewhere tried to demonstrate [1]—existing treatises on the subject are wholly valueless. They are all, in fact, based on the labours of Conde—on the labours, that is to say, of a writer who had but scanty materials at his disposal, who was unable, from the inadequacy of his linguistic attainments, to understand the documents to which he had access, and who lacked the historic sense. The task which confronted me was therefore not merely that of exhibiting in a truer light facts misinterpreted by my predecessors, or of announcing fresh discoveries ; I found it necessary, on the contrary, to delve to the roots of the subject if I would make the Moslems of Spain, for the first time, live in the pages of History ; and while the very novelty of the subject-matter constituted one of its attractions, it has proved the source of many and various difficulties.

I believe I can justly claim to have examined nearly all the manuscripts extant in Europe which bear upon the history of the Moors, and I have wittingly neglected no aspects of the subject. Since, however, it has not been my intention to compile an arid and severely scientific treatise, destined only for a limited class of readers, I have refrained from overloading my pages with excess of detail. To the extent of my ability, I have, moreover, conformed to the literary canons which prescribe that in historical composition prominence should be given to facts of a specific class, to which all others should be made ancillary ; hence I have often been obliged not only to condense in a few lines the labours

---

[1] In the first edition of my *Recherches sur l'histoire et la littérature de l'Espagne pendant le moyen âge.*

of weeks, but to pass over in silence many matters by no means devoid of special interest, the inclusion of which, however, did not square with my general design.

On the other hand, I have aimed at setting forth very fully events which appear to me vividly to characterize their epochs; and I have not hesitated, upon occasion, to enliven the drama of political history with interludes of personal adventure ; for, in my opinion, it is too often forgotten that without the relief afforded by picturesque details and the side-lights thrown by them upon contemporary manners, all history is apt to be colourless and insipid. The methods of those historians who seek to exhibit in the foreground, not so much public men, as the ideas or tendencies of which they are held to be representative, and who deal mainly with wide generalisations, are, I apprehend, unsuited to my subject.

Further, although I have spared no pains to endow this History with precision and actuality, I am convinced that an undue display of erudition would not tend to add vivacity or lucidity to its pages ; I have therefore refrained from the lavish use of notes, references, and quotations. But though I hold that in a work of this character results alone should find a place, disengaged from the scientific apparatus by which they have been attained, I have throughout been careful to indicate the authorities upon which my statements are based.

It is right to mention that portions of the present book were written before the publication of certain recent contributions to historical criticism. The opening chapters of the first volume, for instance, were completed before the appearance in the *Revue des deux Mondes* of the able article on " Mohammed and the Origins of Islamism " by my learned and excellent friend M. Renan : many of our conclusions are identical, but we have reached them independently.

There remains for me the pleasant duty of thanking those of my friends—notably MM. Mohl, Wright, Defrémery, Tornberg, Calderon, De Slane, and Dugat—who have either placed manuscripts at my disposal, or, with the utmost courtesy and kindness, supplied me with extracts and collations.

Leyden, *February* 1861.

BOOK I

THE CIVIL WARS

A

SPANISH ISLAM

CHAPTER I

THE BEDAWIN

WHILST Europe, century after century, treads the path of progress and development, the abiding characteristic of the numberless tribes that wander with their tents and flocks over the vast and arid deserts of Arabia is their immutability. What they are to-day, such they were yesterday, and such they will be to-morrow: they know neither advance nor variation: the Bedawy preserves, in all its purity, the spirit which animated his ancestors in the days of Mohammed, and the best commentaries on the history and the poetry of the Pagan Arabs are the descriptions given by modern travellers of the manners, customs, and modes of thought of the Bedawin amongst whom they have sojourned.[1]

And yet this race lacks neither the intelligence nor the energy necessary for enlarging its borders and bettering its condition, if such were its desire. If the Arab does not advance, if he remains a stranger to the very idea of progress, it is because, being indifferent to the ease and material pleasures procured by civilization, he has no wish to change his lot. The Bedawy's pride assures him that he embodies the consummate pattern of created beings; he despises other nations simply because they are unlike Arabs; and he believes himself infinitely happier than the civilized man. Every condition of life has its inconveniences and advantages; but the arrogance of the Bedawin is easily intelligible: guided, in fact, not by philosophic principles but by a kind of instinct, they have

---

[1] " I believe that, not only in manners and mode of life, but even in dress and speech, the sons of Ishmael are now what they were in the days of the Patriarchs." E. H. Palmer, *The Desert of the Exodus* (1871), p. 78. See also G. R. Lees, *The Witness of the Wilderness* (1909), p. 34; and C. R. Conder, *Tent Work in Palestine* (1885), p. 337.

put in practice, from time immemorial, the inspiring watch-
words of the French Revolution—"Liberty, Equality,
Fraternity."

Of liberty, no man on earth has inherited a fuller share
than the Bedawy. "I acknowledge no master," he boasts,
"save the Lord of the Universe!" And the freedom he
enjoys is trammelled by so few limitations that in face of
it the doctrines of our most advanced Radicals read like
maxims of despotism. In civilized States government of
some kind is a necessary and inevitable evil—an evil
which is an essential condition of good: the Bedawin
simply dispense with it. It is true that each tribe has a
chief, chosen by itself; but this chief is merely influential;
he is respected, and deference is paid to his advice, especially
if he is a ready speaker, but he is not entitled to issue
commands: far from receiving emoluments, he is expected,
and even forced by public opinion, to provide for the
sustenance of the poor, to share with his friends the
baksheesh which he receives, and to offer to strangers a
hospitality more lavish than other members of the tribe
could afford. He is obliged at every turn to consult the
tribal council, which is composed of the heads of the com-
ponent families of the clan. Without the assent of this
assembly, war cannot be declared nor peace concluded—
even the camp cannot be struck.[1]

The title of *Sheik* bestowed by a tribe upon one of its
members is often little more than an empty compliment—
a public testimony of the esteem in which he is held—a
formal avowal that the recipient is the ablest, the bravest,
the most generous man amongst them, and most devoted to
the welfare of the community. "We confer this dignity on
no man," said an Arab of old, "unless he hath given us all
that he possesseth, unless he hath allowed us to trample
under foot all that he holdeth dear and in honour, and hath
rendered to us the services that we look for in a slave."[2]

Often, indeed, the authority of the chief is so meagre,
that it is almost imperceptible. Arâba, a contemporary of
Mohammed, was once asked how he had come to be made
Chief of his tribe. He at first denied that he occupied this
position, but on the question being pressed, he replied: "If
misfortunes have befallen my fellow-tribesmen, I have

---

[1] Burckhardt, *Notes on the Bedouins,* pp. 66–7; Sir R. F. Burton, *Pilgrimage to
El Medinah and Meccah,* iii. 85.
[2] Mubarrad, p. 71.

given them money; if one of them has committed a fault,
I have paid the penalty for him; I have established my
authority by reliance on the kindliest of my tribe. Those
of my comrades who cannot do as much are held in less
respect; those who can do the like are my equals; and those
who can do more are more highly esteemed."[1] Then, as
now, a chief was sometimes deposed if he could not maintain his position, or if a braver and more bountiful man
could be found among his fellows.[2]

Although absolute equality is not to be found even
in the desert, it is there more nearly attained than anywhere
else. The Bedawin neither admit disparity in their social
relations—for they all live the same lives, wear the same
dress, and partake of the same food—nor is a plutocracy
conceivable amongst them, for, in their eyes, riches confer
no title to public esteem.[3] To despise wealth, and to live
from hand to mouth on booty captured by his own valour,
after having squandered his patrimony in lavish hospitality—
such is the ideal of an Arab cavalier.[4] Disdain for riches is,
doubtless, evidence of magnanimity and philosophic calm,
but it must be borne in mind that wealth has not the same
importance for a Bedawy as for another man, since his
property is held on an extremely precarious tenure and
flits with surprising alacrity. "Wealth cometh in the
morning, and ere the evening it hath departed," writes an
Arab poet; and in the desert this is literally true.

Since he is ignorant of agriculture, and owns not a
foot of soil, the Bedawy's only wealth consists in his camels
and horses; and these are riches on which he cannot reckon
for a single hour. When enemies attack his tribe—an
everyday occurrence—and carry off his all, the rich man
of yesterday finds himself to-day in poverty. But to-
morrow he will take his revenge and become wealthy once
more.[5]

Absolute equality, however, can only exist in a state
of nature—and "a state of nature" is a mere abstraction.
Up to a certain point the Bedawin live on a footing of
mutual equality, but their levelling principles by no means
extend to humanity at large: they deem themselves the

---

[1] Mubarrad, p. 71; cf. Ibn Nubâta, cited by Rasmussen, *Additamenta ad
Historiam Arabum*, p. 18 (text).
[2] Burckhardt, *op. cit.*, p. 68; Caussin, ii. p. 634.
[3] Burckhardt, p. 41.
[4] Caussin, ii. pp. 555, 611.
[5] Burckhardt, p. 40.

superiors, not only of their slaves, and of the artisans who
work for their living in the camps, but of all other men
whatsoever; they claim to have been moulded from quite
other clay than the rest of the human race. Natural in-
equalities, however, bring social distinctions in their train,
and, if riches confer no consideration or importance on the
Bedawy, generosity, hospitality, courage, poetical talent,
and eloquence [1] bring him so much the more. " Men may
be divided into two classes," said Hâtim; [2] "the grovellers
that take pleasure in heaping up riches, and the exalted
souls that seek the glory conferred by generosity."

The aristocracy of the desert—the " kings of the Arabs,"
in the phrase of the Khalif 'Omar—are the orators and poets,
and all those who practise the Bedawy virtues; the plebeians
are the mean and vicious who practise them not. The
Bedawin have never known either privileges or titles—
unless we regard as a title the surname of " The Perfect,"
(al-Kâmil), given of old to the man who to poetic talent
added courage, liberality, knowledge of writing, and ability
to swim and bend the bow. Nevertheless, nobility of birth
—which, rightly understood, imposes high responsibility,
and binds together successive generations—exists even among
the Bedawin. The rank and file are filled with veneration
for the memory of great men, whom they worship after a
fashion. The descendants of men of mark are treated with
esteem and affection, provided that, although they may not
have received from heaven the same gifts as their ancestors,
they preserve in their hearts admiration and love of noble
deeds, of talent and of virtue. In pre-Islamic days that man
was deemed right noble who was the chief of the tribe, and
whose father, grandfather, and great-grandfather had successively occupied the same position. Nothing more natural
—for since the title of *Sheik* was never conferred save on the
most distinguished, it was reasonable to suppose that the
Bedawy virtues had become hereditary in a family which
for four generations had provided a leader for their tribe. [3]

All the Bedawin of the same tribe are *brothers;* such

[1] " Nalegha, a poet, writes thus : ' O God, preserve me from being silenced in
conversation!'" Syed Ahmed Khan Bahadur, *Manners and Customs of the pre-
Islamic Arabs* (1870), p. 5.

[2] Hâtim of the tribe of Tai, famous for his unbounded generosity. His *Dîwán*
has been translated by F. Schulthess (1897).

[3] " The glories that have grown up with the grass can match not those inherited
of old." *Hamâsa*, 679 ; R. A. Nicholson, *A Literary History of the Arabs* (1907),
p. 100.

indeed is the term applied by fellow-tribesmen of the same age to one another. An old man speaking to a young one calls him "my brother's son." If need be, a Bedawy will slaughter his last sheep to supply food for a poverty-stricken *brother* who craves for aid, while he will resent an affront shown to a *brother* by a man of an alien tribe as a personal injury, and will not rest until he has avenged it.

It is difficult to give an adequately vivid and distinct idea of this *'asabiyya* as it is called—this deep, limitless, steadfast fidelity of the Arab to his fellow-clansman ; this absolute devotion to the interests, the prosperity, the honour and glory of the community wherein he was born and will die. The sentiment is not paralleled by Patriotism, as we understand that term—for that is an emotion which appears to the fiery Bedawy but lukewarm—it is a fierce and over-powering passion, and at the same time the first and most sacred of duties ; in a word, it is the true religion of the desert.[1]

The Arab will make any sacrifice for his tribe ; for it he is ever ready to risk his life in those dangerous enterprises in which faith and enthusiasm can work miracles ; for it he will fight till his body is crushed out of human semblance beneath the feet of the foe. " Love thy tribe," sings a poet, " for to it thou art bound by firmer bonds than is a husband to his wife."[2] Such, then, is the meaning which the Bedawy gives to " Liberty, Equality, Fraternity." These blessings suffice him : he desires, he dreams of no others—he is content with his lot. Europe is never content with hers, or only for the moment. Our feverish activities, our thirst for political and social improvements, our ceaseless endeavours to better our conditions—are they not in truth at once symptoms and an implicit confession of the weariness and restlessness which in the Western World gnaw at the roots of society ? The idea of progress, extolled *ad nauseam* from professorial chairs as well as from the political platform, is the fundamental principle of modern social systems—but do men prate ceaselessly of change and improvement when their condition is healthy and when happiness is theirs ? In our unending yet fruitless pursuit

---

[1] This devotion to the tribe was not incompatible with the fact that "the genealogical unity of the tribe was a fancy often superimposed on what in origin was a local unity, or union of emigrants under a single leader, or some other fortuitous combination." See D. S. Margoliouth, *Mohammed*, 2nd ed., p. 4, and the works there cited.

[2] Mûbarrad, p. 233.

of felicity—pulling down to-day what we built yesterday, proceeding from illusion to illusion, from disappointment to disappointment—we end by despairing of mankind : we exclaim, in our moments of dejection and weakness, that the destiny of man is not bound up with the fate of common-wealths, and we thirst for unknown blessings in an unseen world.   But the Bedawy feels none of these vague and morbid aspirations after a happier future : his buoyant spirit, expansive, heedless, serene as the sky, participates in none of our cares, our sorrows, or our shadowy hopes.   But to us —our limitless ambitions and importunate yearnings fanned by imagination—the aimless life of the desert would appear insupportable in all its monotony and uniformity, and we should soon prefer our wonted excitements, our cares and hardships, our political perplexities, even the throes of our travailing civilization, to all the advantages enjoyed by the Arabs in their changeless existence.

There subsists, indeed, a fundamental difference between the European and the Arab.   Our imagination is too fertile to allow us mental repose ; yet we owe our progress to this faculty, and derive from it our relative superiority.   Where imagination is lacking progress is impossible ; to perfect our social life and develop the mutual relations of men, it is necessary first to present to the mind an image of a society more nearly perfect than that which exists.   But the Arabs, despite a widespread belief to the contrary, possess very little imagination.   Their blood is more impetuous than ours, their passions are more ardent, but they are at the same time the least inventive of races.   To recognise this fact we have only to glance at their religion and their literature. Before their conversion to Islam, they had, it is true, their gods—typical of the celestial bodies—but, unlike the Hindus, the Greeks, and the Scandinavians, they had no mythology.   Their deities had no legendary history, and no poet dreamed of fabricating one.   The religion preached by Mohammed—a simple Monotheism, with an accretion of certain institutions and ceremonies borrowed from Judaism and the ancient pagan worships—is incontestably the simplest and least mysterious of all positive religions ; the most reasonable and the purest, indeed, in the eyes of those who exclude the supernatural as far as possible, and who would banish ritual and ornament from worship.   In their literature we find the same absence of originality, the same predilection for the actual and positive.   Other races have produced epics, in which the supernatural plays an important part. Arab literature contains no epic—not even a narrative poem; exclusively lyrical and descriptive, its verse has never aimed at depicting more than the poetic side of actuality. The Arab poets describe what they see and feel, but they create nothing : if now and then they show a spark of imagination, their own critics, far from praising them, bluntly call them liars. Aspirations after the infinite and the ideal are unknown to the Bedawin, and from the earliest ages accuracy and elegance of expression—the merely technical side of poetry—has appeared all-important in their eyes.[1] Invention is indeed so rare in Arab litera- ture, that when we find traces of it in some fanciful poem or tale, we can almost always be sure that we are dealing with a translation, and not an Arab original. Thus in the *Thousand and One Nights* all the stories of enchantments, the delightful offspring of a fresh and exuberant imagination, which charmed us in our youth, are of Persian or Indian origin :[2] in the whole of this immense collection the only portions truly Arabian are pictures of manners, and anec- dotes derived from real life.

Finally, when the Arabs, established in vast provinces conquered at the point of the sword, turned their attention to the sciences, they manifested the same lack of creative power. They translated and commented on the writings of the ancients ; they enriched certain branches of science by their patient, accurate, and minute observations ; but they made no capital discoveries, and we are not indebted to them for a single great and fruitful idea.

Such, then, are the deep-seated differences which exist between the Arabs and ourselves. It may be that they have more elevation of character and true greatness of soul, with a keener sense of the dignity of man ; but they do not possess within them similar germs of development and pro- gress ; and such are their passionate cravings for personal liberty and their complete lack of political instinct, that they seem incapable of submitting to social laws. Nevertheless, they made the endeavour : torn from their deserts by a prophet, and launched forth by him to conquer the world,

---

[1] For an account of pre-Islamic poetry, see Nicholson, *op. cit.*, chap. iii.

[2] " An Arabization of the Persian *Hazár Afsânah*, or Thousand Tales." Burton, *Arabian Nights* (Terminal Essay, p. 68, 1887).

" It is probable that this Persian archetype included the most finely imaginative tales in the existing collection." Nicholson, *op. cit.*, p. 458.

they filled it with the glory of their deeds. Enriched by the spoils of twenty provinces, they learnt the pleasures of luxury ; through contact with the subjugated races they were led to cultivate the sciences, and attained to as great a height of civilization as was possible for them. Yet after the days of Mohammed, long years elapsed before the Arabs lost their national characteristics. When they landed in Spain they were still true children of the desert, and it was but natural that beside the banks of the Tagus or the Guadalquiver they dreamed only of carrying on the intertribal conflicts begun in Arabia, Syria, or Africa. These inveterate feuds must first claim our attention ; and rightly to understand them we must go back to the days of the Prophet.

CHAPTER II

THE PROPHET

IN the days of Mohammed, the population of Arabia consisted of a multitude of tribes—some settled, but the majority constantly nomadic—without community of interests, owning no central authority, and usually at war with one another. Could mere bravery make a people invincible, such the Arabians would assuredly have been. Nowhere was the warlike spirit more generally diffused. Without fighting there could be no booty, and booty formed the Bedawin's livelihood. Moreover, they found an intoxicating pleasure in wielding the pliant bamboo lance, or the flashing sword—in cleaving the skulls or severing the necks of their enemies—in crushing a hostile tribe, " as a millstone crusheth the corn "—in immolating victims, " not as offerings pleasing to heaven." [1]

Valour in the fight conferred the highest claim to the eulogy of poets and the love of women. The latter had imbibed not a little of the martial spirit of their brothers and their husbands. Following with the rear-guard, they tended the wounded and encouraged the warriors by chanting verses instinct with relentless ferocity. [2] " Courage !" they would cry, " Courage ! defenders of women ! Smite with the edge of your swords ! . . . We are the daughters of the morning-star ; soft are the carpets we tread beneath our feet ; our necks are adorned with pearls, and our tresses are perfumed with musk. The brave who confront the foe we will clasp to our bosoms, but the dastards who flee we will spurn—not for them our embraces ! " [3] Nevertheless it would have been easy for an attentive observer to recognise the intrinsic weakness of the nation—a weakness consequent upon its utter lack of unity, and the ceaseless rivalry between the different tribes. Arabia would indubitably

---

[1] *The Seven Poems*, transl. by Capt. F. E. Johnson, R.A. : London (1894), pp. 142-4. *The Seven Golden Odes of Pagan Arabia*, transl. by Lady A. and W. S. Blunt (1903), p. 40.
[2] *Cf.* D. S. Margoliouth, *Mohammed*, 2nd ed., p. 30.
[3] *The Seven Golden Odes*, ut supra, p. 43.

have fallen a prey to a foreign conqueror if she had not been too poor to be worth conquering.

" What doth thy land contain ? " asked a king of Persia of an Arabian prince who had begged him for troops, and offered him in return a large province : " What doth it contain ? A few sheep and camels ! Never will I, for such trifling guerdon, risk a Persian army in your deserts."

The day came, nevertheless, which saw the conquest of Arabia ; but she was conquered by a child of her own—an extraordinary man—the Arab Mohammed.[1]

Perhaps the Messenger of God—for such he called himself—was not superior to his fellows, but it is certain that he did not in the least resemble them. Of a delicate, impressionable, and highly nervous constitution, inherited from his mother ; endowed with inordinate and morbid sensibilities ; melancholy, silent, loving aimless roving and self-communion by twilight in lonely valleys ;[2] for ever haunted by a vague disquietude, weeping and sobbing like a woman in his hours of sickness, subject to fits of epilepsy,[3] lacking in martial courage,[4] his character was in strange contrast with that of normal Arabs—hardy, vigorous, warlike men, who knew nothing of reveries, and who looked upon tears as a shameful weakness in a man, even though wrung from him by the loss of the dearest objects of his affection. Furthermore, Mohammed was endowed with a more vivid imagination than his compatriots, and a profoundly pious mind. Before dreams of earthly ambition arose to sully the original purity of his heart, religion was his all-in-all—it absorbed his every thought and mental faculty. It was preeminently in this respect that he stood apart from his compatriots.

It is with races as with individuals : some are constitutionally religious, others the reverse. For some men religion is the basis of their lives : so needful is it for them that when their reason revolts against the creed into which

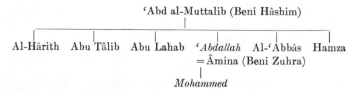

[1]

'Abd al-Muttalib (Beni Hâshim)

Al-Hârith	Abu Tâlib	Abu Lahab	'Abdallah	Al-'Abbâs	Hamza
			=Âmina (Beni Zuhra)		

Mohammed

[2] *Cf.* Muir, *Life of M.* (1912), p. 37.
[3] *Cf.* D. S. Margoliouth, *op. cit.*, pp. 45–6.
[4] "Care for his life and safety was invariably his first consideration." *Ibid.*, p. 65.

they are born, they will devise some philosophic system much more irrational and mysterious than that creed itself. Whole nations have similarly lived for and by religion, and have found in it their only hope and consolation. But the Arabs are not naturally religious, and there is in this respect a vast difference between them and the other races who have embraced Islamism. Nor is this strange. In its very essence religion has a firmer hold upon the imagination than upon the intellect, and, as we have seen, in the Arab the imagination by no means dominates. Take the Bedawin of to-day. Although nominally Moslems, they pay but little heed to the precepts of Islam : instead of praying five times a day, as their religion enjoins, they never pray at all.[1] Burckhardt, a traveller who knew them well, has testified that they are the most tolerant people in Asia ; and their tolerance is of long standing, for a race so jealous of liberty is little given to condone tyranny even in matters of faith. Marthad, King of Yemen in the fourth century, used to say, " I rule over persons, not over opinions. I require my subjects to submit to my authority : but their doctrines I leave to the judgment of God their Creator." The Emperor Frederick II could have said no more. Such tolerance, however, verges upon indifference and scepticism. Marthad's son and successor first embraced Judaism, then Christianity, and ended by drifting dubiously between these two faiths.

In Mohammed's time three religions shared Arabia— Judaism, Christianity, and a vague form of Polytheism. The Jewish tribes alone, perhaps, were sincerely attached to their faith, and were alone intolerant. In the early history of Arabia persecutions are rare, and when they occur it is usually the Jews who are to blame. Christianity could count but few adepts, for most of those who professed the faith had but a very superficial knowledge of its tenets. The Khalif 'Alî scarcely exaggerated when he said, speaking of a tribe[2] in which that religion had taken the deepest root, " The Taghlib are not Christians ; all they have borrowed from that Church is the practice of wine-bibbing." [3]

[1] Palmer, while defending the Bedawin from the charge of irreligion and profanity, adds : " Professedly [they] are Mohammedans, but few of them know any more of that religion than the name." *Desert of the Exodus* (1871), p. 94, *sq. Cf.* D'Escayrac de Lauture, *Le Desert et le Soudan*, p. 340 : " L'Arabe est naturellement et par essence le plus sceptique et le plus irréligieux de tous les nomades."
[2] For an account of the Beni Taghlib, established in the N.E. of Arabia, see Nicholson, *Lit. Hist. of the Arabs* (1907), pp. 55–60.
[3] Baidâwî, *Commentary on the Koran*, Sura V, v. 7.

Christianity, in fact, involved too many miracles and mysteries to commend itself to so sceptical and derisive a race. Certain bishops who, about the year 513, tried to convert Mundhir III, King of Hîra,[1] were made to realize this. After the king had listened to them attentively, one of his officers whispered a word in his ear. Immediately Mundhir assumed an aspect of the deepest sorrow, and when the prelates respectfully asked him the cause of his grief he replied, "Alas! I have heard melancholy tidings. Michael the Archangel is dead!" "Nay, Prince, thou must be mistaken; angels are immortal!" "Immortal!" cried the King; "and ye have been trying to convince me that God Himself died!"

The idolaters, who formed the majority of the nation, recognised deities peculiar to each tribe, and almost to each family, but admitted the existence of a supreme God, Allah, before whom the other gods were mediators. These pagans had a certain respect for their soothsayers and their idols, but they would slay the former if their predictions failed, and would cheat their idols by sacrificing a gazelle when they had promised a sheep, or abuse them when they did not gratify their hopes or desires.

When Imru'u'l-Kais[2] set out to take vengeance on the Beni Asad for their murder of his father, he halted at the temple of the idol Dhu-'l-Khalasa to consult the oracle by means of three arrows typifying respectively "Proceed," "Abandon," "Delay."[3] Having drawn forth "Abandon" he once more made trial. Thrice did "Abandon" appear. Then, breaking the arrows, and hurling the fragments at the idol, Imru'u'l-Kais cried, "Wretch! Had it been thy father who was murdered, thou wouldst not have forbidden me to avenge him!" Whatever religion the Arab professed, it usually occupied a place of little importance in his life, absorbed as he was in worldly interests, in fighting, gambling, love, and wine. "Let us enjoy the present day," sang the poets, "for soon death will overtake us;"[4] and this, indeed, was the Bedawy's motto. The same men who waxed enthusiastic over a gallant deed or a beautiful poem remained, as a rule, cold and indifferent when religion was touched

---

[1] Near the site of ancient Babylon ; founded about A.D. 200 by Arab tribes.

[2] One of the Mu'allakât poets.

[3] This form of divination was denounced by Mohammed : " Wine and gambling and statues and divining arrows are only an abomination of the devil's making." *Sura* v., 4 and 92.

[4] Cf. *The Seven Poems*, ut sup., p. 11.

upon: to it, the poets, faithful interpreters of the national sentiments, scarcely ever allude. Listen to the words of Tarafa:[1]

"In the morning at thy coming I will hand thee a goblet brimming with wine. If thou hast already drunk deeply, it matters not; with me thou shalt drink again. My boon-companions are noble youths whose faces shine as the stars. Each evening a singing-girl attired in a striped robe and a tunic of saffron graces our company. Her vestment is open at the neck: without reproof amorous hands fondle her charms. . . . My life is surrendered to wine and pleasures; I have sold all my possessions; I have squandered the wealth I gained, as well as my patrimony. But thou, O Censor, who blamest my passion for carousal and the fray, canst thou make me immortal? If in thy wisdom thou canst not ward off the fatal moment, suffer me to lavish all in enjoyment before Death hath me in his clutch. The man of generous impulses quaffs deeply while he liveth. To-morrow, harsh reprover, when thou and I are dead, we shall see which of us twain is consumed by burning thirst."

A few facts, however, have come to light which show that the Arabs, and especially the settled tribes, were not altogether inaccessible to religious enthusiasm. For instance, twenty thousand Christians in the town of Nejrân, having to choose between death and Judaism, preferred to perish in the flames rather than abjure their faith.[2] But zeal was the exception: complete indifference, if not lukewarmness, was the rule.

It is evident, therefore, that in declaring himself a prophet Mohammed undertook a task of twofold difficulty. He could not confine himself to a mere demonstration of the truth of the doctrines which he preached. It was necessary for him to overcome the mental torpor of his fellow-country-men—to awaken the religious sentiment in their hearts—to persuade them that religion was not a matter of indifference, a thing which might be ignored. In a word, he had to mould, to metamorphose, a sensual and sceptical people—a nation of scoffers. An enterprise so formidable would have dismayed a man less convinced of the truth of his mission. Mohammed reaped on all sides nothing but jeers and insults. His fellow-townsmen in Mecca either pitied him or flouted him. Some thought him a poet inspired by a *jinni;* others, a soothsayer,[3] a magician, or a madman. "Here cometh the son of 'Abdallah with his news from

[1] Tarafa ibn al-'Abd ; *flor. c.* A.D. 550.
[2] A.D. 523. This unique persecution of Christians by Jews led to an Abyssinian invasion in aid of the former: this was followed by the establishment of Abyssinian rulers in S. Arabia. *See* Muir, *Mohammed* (1912), p. xciii.
[3] Ar. *Kâhin.*

heaven!" they would cry when they saw him approaching. Some proposed, with apparent benevolence, to provide physicians at their own expense, who should try to cure him. Others threw filth at him. He would find the path before his dwelling strewn with thorns. He was assailed on all sides with such epithets as "knave" and "cheat." He had met with no better fortune elsewhere. At Tâ'if he had expounded his doctrines to the assembled chiefs. There also he had been derided.[1] "Could not God find a better apostle than thee?" asked one. "I will hold no discussion with thee," said another; "if thou art a prophet, thou art a being too exalted for me to bandy words with; and if thou art an impostor, thou deservest not to be addressed." With despairing heart Mohammed left the assembly, followed by the hoots and insults of the populace as they pursued him and pelted him with stones.

In this manner more than ten years passed. The sect remained small in number, and everything pointed to the speedy disappearance of the new religion, leaving no trace behind, when Mohammed found unhoped-for champions in the Aus and the Khazraj, two tribes which towards the end of the fifth century had wrested Medina from the dominion of the Jews.[2] The people of Mecca and of Medina hated one another because they sprang from antagonistic stocks. Arabia contained two such races— the Yemenites and the Ma'addites. The Medinese belonged to the former, and were not only detested but despised by the Meccans. In the eyes of an Arab, who considered the pastoral life and commerce to be the only occupations worthy of free men, the cultivation of the soil was a derogatory calling. Now, the Medinese were agriculturists, and the Meccans, traders. Moreover, a large number of Jews still lived in Medina, and many families of the Aus and Khazraj had adopted the religion which the former masters of the city, although reduced to the grade of dependents, still preserved. Consequently, although the majority of both these tribes seem to have been idolaters like the Meccans, the latter looked upon the whole population as Jewish, and disdained them accordingly. Mohammed, for his part, shared the prejudices of his fellow-

[1] Tâ'if is some 60 miles from Mecca. "He could not have made a worse choice," writes Prof. Margoliouth; "the people of Tâ'if were no less devoted to their goddesses than the Ephesians to Artemis." *Mohammed*, 2nd ed., p. 178.
[2] The two tribes formed the bulk of the population of Medina. See D. S. Margoliouth, *op. cit.*, pp. 186–190, and Burton, *Pilgrimage* (1855), ii. 120 *sq.*

townsmen against Yemenites and husbandmen. It is
related of him, that hearing some one recite this verse:
" I am a Himyarite ;[1] my ancestors sprang neither from
Râbi'a nor from Mudar ! " he cried, " So much the worse
for thee ! Thine origin cuts thee off from God and from
His prophet ! " It is also said that on observing a plough-
share in the house of a Medinese, he remarked to the owner,
" Whenever such a thing enters a house, shame enters with
it." Nevertheless, despairing of winning over to his doctrines
the merchants and nomads of his own race, and believing
his life in danger after the death of his uncle and protector,
Abû Tâlib, Mohammed was constrained to lay aside his
prejudices, and accept help from whatever side it came.
He therefore joyfully received the overtures of the Arabs
of Medina, to whom the annoyance and persecution he had
endured at the hands of the Meccans formed his highest
recommendation and the best title to their hospitality.
The "great oath of al-'Akaba" permanently united the
fortunes of the Medinese and Mohammed.[2] Snapping a
bond which the Arabs respected more than any other, he
abandoned his tribe, settled in Medina with his Meccan
disciples, who were henceforth known as the *Refugees*,[3]
unleashed against his fellow-tribesmen the Medinese poets
with their mordant wit, and proclaimed a Holy War.
Animated by burning zeal, and despising death because
sure of Paradise if they fell at the hands of the idolaters, the
Aus and Khazraj, henceforth classed together as the *Helpers*,[4]
performed prodigies of valour. The strife between them
and the pagans of Mecca lasted for eight years. During
this period the terror spread far and wide by the Moslems'
arms induced many tribes to adopt the new faith : but of
spontaneous, sincere, and lasting conversions there were but
few. At last the capture of Mecca put the seal upon
Mohammed's power. The day had come on which the
Medinese had vowed to make the haughty traders pay
dearly for their insufferable disdain. " To-day is the day
of slaughter ! " cried the chief of the Khazraj, "the day
when none will be spared ! " But the hopes of the Medinese

---

[1] The Himyarites were a younger branch of the Sabæans, in S.W. Arabia.
Râbi'a and Mudar were legendary descendants of 'Adnân, through whom the
Northern Arabs claimed descent from Ishmael.

[2] On this occasion seventy pilgrims from Yathrib (Medina) made oath, at the
foot of the hill of 'Akaba, to defend the new faith with the sword.

[3] " Muhâjirûn."

[4] " Ansâr " : also termed " Defenders."

were dashed: Mohammed deprived their chief of his command, and ordered his generals to use the greatest moderation. The Meccans silently witnessed the destruction of the idols in their temple—which was literally a Pantheon, containing three hundred and sixty divinities [1] worshipped by as many tribes—and with rage in their hearts, they acknowledged Mohammed to be the Messenger of God, inwardly vowing to avenge themselves some day both on the Medinese boors and on the Jews, who had had the impudence to vanquish them.

After the capture of Mecca, the remaining pagan tribes soon found further resistance useless, and the threat of a war of extermination induced them to embrace Islamism—which was preached to them by Mohammed's generals, with the Koran in one hand and a sword in the other.

A somewhat remarkable instance of conversion was that of the Thakîf, a tribe who lived in Tâ'if, and who had formerly pelted the Prophet from their coasts with stones. A deputation from this tribe declared that they were ready to become Moslems on condition that they might keep their idol, al-Lât,[2] for three years, and that they should not be required to pray. " Three years of idolatry !" replied Mohammed ; "that is too long ! Moreover, what is religion without prayer?" Thereupon the deputies lowered their demands, and at last, after much haggling, the two contracting parties agreed to the following conditions: that the Thakîf should not pay the tithe, should not be required to take part in the Holy War, should not prostrate themselves in prayer, should keep Lât for a year, and at the end of that period should not be compelled to destroy the idol with their own hands. But Mohammed still felt some scruples; he was afraid of public opinion. " Do not let that consideration stand in your way," said the deputies ; "if the Arabs ask you how you came to make such a treaty, you have only to tell them that it was in obedience to God's command." This argument appeared to the Prophet conclusive, and he forthwith proceeded to dictate a formal covenant, as follows: " In the name of the Compassionate

[1] One, apparently, for each day of the year. Little is certainly known about pre-Islamic idolatry, but there is evidence of the worship of the heavenly bodies side by side with mere fetishism. " Goddesses" seem to have been numerous.

[2] Al-Lât, Manât, and al-'Uzzà, the moon-goddesses, or "the three daughters of Allah." *Cf.* R. A. Nicholson, *Lit. Hist. of the Arabs* (1907), p. 135. Herodotus mentions that the Arabians called Urania " Alilat" (iii. 8).

and Merciful God! It is hereby agreed between Mohammed, the Messenger of God, and the Thakîf, that the latter shall not be obliged to pay tithes, nor to take part in a Holy War, nor "—but, as he uttered these words, shame and remorse caused Mohammed to break off. "Nor to prostrate themselves at prayer," prompted one of the deputies. Then, as Mohammed still kept silence, the Thakîfite, addressing the scribe, added, "Write that down: it hath been agreed upon." The scribe looked at the Prophet and awaited his commands. But the fiery 'Omar,[1] who had been a mute spectator of this scene, so wounding to the honour of the Prophet, sprang up, and drawing his sword cried, "Thou hast defiled the Prophet's heart! May God fill thine with fire!" "Our words are not addressed to thee," remarked the Thakîfite deputy imperturbably; "we are holding converse with Mohammed." "Nay," said the Prophet at last, "I will make no such covenant. Ye must either embrace Islamism unconditionally, and observe all its precepts, without exception, or—prepare for war!" "Permit us, at least, to keep Lât for six months," pleaded the disappointed Thakîfites. "Nay!" "For but a single month, then." "Not for an hour!"

So the deputies returned to their clan, accompanied by Moslem soldiers, who destroyed Lât amidst the lamentations and despairing tears of the women.[2] This strange conversion turned out to be the most lasting of all. When in later years Arabia as a whole abjured Islamism, the Thakîfites remained faithful. The sincerity of other conversions may hence be estimated.

Apostasy began before the death of Mohammed. Several provinces could not even wait for that event: a rumour of Mohammed's failing health sufficed to kindle a revolt in Nejd, in Yemâma, and in Yemen. Each of these three provinces had a self-styled prophet of its own,[3] an imitator and rival of Mohammed, who learned upon his

---

[1] Afterwards the second Khalif. His conversion seems to have been due to his sister Fàtima, wife of a proselyte. Impetuous, cruel, and of great bodily strength, he soon became one of the Prophet's chief adherents. "I, Abû Bakr, and 'Omar" was a phrase often used by Mohammed, who said that Satan himself would avoid an encounter with the last. "It is said," writes Burton, "that he laughed once, and wept once. The laugh was caused by recollecting how he ate his dough-gods (the idols of the Hanifah tribe) in The Ignorance. The tears were drawn by remembering how he buried alive his baby daughter, who, while the grave was being dug, patted away the dust from his hair and beard." *Arabian Nights* (1887), ii. 158 n.

[2] Sprenger, *Life of Mahomet*, p. 186.

[3] Tolheiha, Museilima, and al-Aswad, respectively.

deathbed that in Yemen the leader of the insurrection, al-
Aswad, the " Veiled Prophet "—a chieftain who possessed
vast wealth in addition to seductive eloquence—had expelled the Moslem officers, and taken Nejrân, San'a, and
finally the whole province. The vast edifice was, indeed,
already tottering when Mohammed breathed his last (A.D.
632). His death was the signal for a formidable and almost
universal insurrection. Everywhere the insurgents got the
upper hand; every day there arrived at Medina Moslem
officials, Refugees and Helpers, who had been expelled
from their districts by the rebels, and the neighbouring
tribes made ready to lay siege to Medina.

But the Khalif, Abû Bakr,[1] worthy to be the successor of
Mohammed, and full of confidence in the destiny of Islamism,
did not hesitate for an instant in the midst of these great
perils. He was without an army. Faithful to Mohammed's
behest, he had sent it into Syria, despite the protests of the
Moslems, who, foreseeing the dangers which threatened, had
besought him to postpone the expedition. " I will not re-
voke an order given by the Prophet," he had said; " Though
Medina were exposed to an invasion by wild beasts, these
troops must do what Mohammed willed." If he had consented to bargain with them, the Khalif by certain concessions might have purchased the neutrality, or even the
alliance, of many tribes in Nejd, for their deputies had informed him that if he would exempt them from paying
tithes, they would continue to offer the orthodox prayers.
The principal Moslems were of opinion that the deputies
should not be rebuffed. Abû Bakr alone scouted the idea
of bargaining, as unworthy of the holy cause which was
theirs to defend. " The law of Islamism," he said, " is one
and indivisible; no distinction can be admitted between its
precepts." " He has more faith than all of us put together,"
observed 'Omar bluntly. The remark was just: there lay
the secret of the first Khalif's greatness and strength.
According to the testimony of Mohammed himself, all his
disciples had shown momentary hesitation before acknowledging his mission, except Abû Bakr. Without
being endowed with exceptional originality, without being
a very great man, Abû Bakr was best fitted to be master of
the situation: he possessed that which had formerly given

---

[1] Father of Mohammed's wife Ayesha. "*Bikr* is the usual form, but *Bakr*,
primarily meaning a young camel, is metaphorically applied to human youth.
(*Lane's Lexicon*, s.v.) . . . The Persians, who hate him, call him ' Pir-i-Kaftâr,
the old she-hyæna." Burton, *Arabian Nights* (1887), ii. 167 *n*.

the victory to Mohammed himself, and which his enemies lacked—a steadfast faith.

There was but little concert in the attack of the insurgents ; they were already at discord among themselves, and were murdering one another. Abû Bakr, who had armed every man able to take the field, seized the opportunity of crushing the neighbouring clans. Later, when the loyal tribes of the Hijâz[1] had furnished their contingents of men and horses, and the main army had returned from the north, bringing with them no little booty as the result of their foray, he boldly assumed the offensive, dividing his army into many divisions, which, although at the outset severally consisting of but a handful of men, grew as they marched, by the accession of crowds of Arabs whom the fear, or hope, of pillage attracted to the Moslem standards.

In Nejd, Khâlid,[2] bloodthirsty and bold, attacked the hordes of Toleiha, and the latter, who was previously " worth a thousand men to an army," on this occasion—forgetting his duty as a warrior and only mindful of his rôle as prophet—wrapped in his cloak awaited inspiration from heaven, at some distance from the battlefield. For a long time he waited in vain, but when his men began to waver, the inspiration came. " Follow me—if ye can ! " he cried to his comrades, and vaulting on his horse he fled at top speed. That day the victors made no prisoners. " Slay the apostates pitilessly, by the sword, by fire, by every kind of torture ! " Such were the instructions which Abû Bakr had given to Khâlid.

Preceded by the fame of his victories and his cruelties, Khâlid marched against Museilima, the prophet of Yemâma, who had just defeated two Moslem armies in succession. The conflict was terrible. At first the rebels gained the upper hand, and penetrated as far as Khâlid's tent. The general, however, succeeded in driving them back to the plain which lay between the two camps. After several hours of stubborn resistance the insurgents were worsted on all sides. " To the garden ! To the garden ! " arose the cry, as they retreated to a spacious orchard, surrounded by a thick wall, and provided with massive gates. Drunk with slaughter, the Moslems pursued them. With unexampled boldness two of them clambered astride the rampart and let

---

[1] The western plateau on which stand Mecca and Medina.
[2] " The Sword of Allah," son of al-Walîd ; his savagery had more than once been rebuked by the Prophet. Before his conversion he had been instrumental in defeating Mohammed at Ohod.

themselves drop within the enclosure in order to open the
gates. One of them, riddled with wounds, instantly fell
dead; the other, more fortunate, snatched the key and hurled
it over the wall to his comrades. The gates flew open and
the assailants entered in a torrent. A horrible massacre ensued in this arena, whence escape was impossible. Within
"The Garden of Death" the rebels, to the number of ten
thousand, were slain to the last man.

Whilst the fierce Khâlid was thus quenching the insurrection in Central Arabia with rivers of blood, the other
generals were doing like deeds in the southern provinces.
In Bahrein the camp of the Bakrites was surprised during
an orgy, and they were put to the sword. A few, however,
who found time for escape, reached the sea-coast and sought
safety in the island of Dârîn.[1] But the Musulmans were
soon upon their track,[2] and slew them all. The like
carnage took place in 'Omân, in Mahra, in Yemen, and in
Hadramaut. Here, the remnant of the forces of al-Aswad,
after having in vain implored the Moslem general for
quarter, were exterminated; there, the commander of a
fortress could only obtain as the price of surrender the
promise of an amnesty for ten persons—all the rest of
the garrison being decapitated; in yet another district an
entire caravan route was for a long time rendered pestiferous
by exhalations from the innumerable decaying bodies of the
rebels.

If the Arabs were not altogether convinced by these
torrents of blood that the religion preached by Mohammed
was true, they at any rate recognised in Islamism an irresistible, and to some extent a supernatural, power. Decimated by the sword, overwhelmed with terror and amazement,
they resigned themselves to becoming Moslems—at least
ostensibly; and the Khalif, that they might have no time
to recover from their dismay, forthwith hurled them against
the Roman Empire and Persia—two nations ripe for
conquest, because for many years rent by intestine discord,
enervated by slavery, and cankered by all the vices of
decadence. Boundless wealth and vast domains compensated the Arabs for their submission to the Law of the
Prophet of Mecca. Apostasy was unknown, it was unthinkable, it meant death—upon this point the law of
Mohammed is inexorable—but sincere piety and zeal for

[1] In the Persian Gulf.
[2] The sea having been miraculously dried up, according to the legend.

the faith were almost equally rare. By the most horrible and atrocious means the outward conversion of the Bedawin had been effected; that was much; it was indeed all that could fairly be looked for on the part of these unfortunate people, who had witnessed the death of their fathers, brothers, and children beneath the sword of Khâlid or the other pious executioners who were his rivals.

For a long time the Bedawin, neutralising by a passive resistance the efforts made by zealous Moslems to instruct them, neither learnt the principles of the faith nor had the least desire to learn them. During the Khalifate of 'Omar I, an old Arab made an agreement with a young man to lend him his wife every other night, the young man in return undertaking to tend the other's flock. This singular compact having reached the ears of the Khalif, he summoned the two men to his presence and asked them whether they did not know that Islamism forbade a husband to make such a bargain. They declared that they knew of no such law. Another man had wedded two sisters. " Is it possible," demanded the Khalif, " that you were unaware that such an act is not permitted by our religion ? " " Yea," replied the man, " I knew nothing of the sort; and I confess that I see nothing blameworthy in the act you censure." " Nevertheless, the law is quite explicit on the point : instantly repudiate one of these sisters, or you lose your head ! " " Dost thou speak seriously ? " " Very seriously ! " " Well, it is a hateful religion to forbid such things, and I have gained nothing by having adopted it ! " So complete was the poor wretch's ignorance, that he never suspected that in speaking thus he ran the risk of being executed as a blasphemer, or even an apostate. A century later, none of the Arab tribes settled in Egypt knew what had been permitted or forbidden by the Prophet. They would dilate enthusiastically on the good old times, and on the wars and heroes of pagan days—but, as for religion, it was never mentioned. At about the same epoch the Arabs quartered in the north of Africa were in a similar case. These worthy fellows drank their wine without suspecting the least in the world that Mohammed had prohibited that beverage. They were not a little astonished when missionaries, sent by the Khalif 'Omar II, arrived, to make them acquainted with the fact. There were even Moslems whose sole knowledge of the Koran consisted in the words, " In the name of

the Compassionate and Merciful God."[1]   It is possible, but
by no means certain, that there would have been greater
zeal for the faith, generally, if the means adopted for effecting conversion had been less detestable.   It has always been
extremely difficult to overcome the Bedawin's lukewarmness
in matters of religion.   In our own days, the Wahhâbis,[2]
that grim and puritanical sect which seeks to wipe out the
luxury and superstitious ritual with which in the course of
time Islamism became tainted—the sect which takes for its
motto " The Koran and nothing but the Koran," just as
Luther took for his, " The Bible and nothing but the Bible "
—the Wahhâbis have endeavoured, but in vain, to wean
the Bedawin from their religious indifference.   They have
seldom resorted to force, and they have found devoted
adherents among the settled Arabians, but not among the
Bedawin, who have preserved the true Arab character unalloyed.   Although they sympathised with the political
views of the innovators, although the tribes immediately
under the control of the Wahhâbis were obliged to observe
their religious duties with greater strictness, and although
some of them, to serve their own interests, assumed an
appearance of zeal, and even of fanaticism—still, these
Bedawin did not become truly religious.   As soon as the
Wahhâbi power had been broken up by Mohammed 'Alî
they lost no time in dropping a ceremonial which mortally
wearied them.   " To-day," wrote Sir R. F. Burton, " there
is little or no religion to be met with in the desert : no one
troubles himself about the laws of the Koran."

The Arabs, therefore, although they accepted the revolution as an accomplished fact which it was impossible to undo,
did not forgive those who had brought it about, and would
not submit to the hierarchical sway which resulted from it.
Their opposition, at length, took another form : a conflict
concerning principles became a personal struggle.

In a certain sense, the noble families—using that term to
mean those which for several generations had supplied chiefs
to tribes—lost nothing through the revolution.   It is true
that Mohammed wavered in his opinions with regard to the
nobility.   Sometimes he preached absolute equality, sometimes he recognised a ruling class.   He had cried, " No more

---

[1] Nöldeke, *Gesch. des Qorâns*, p. 204.   This formula prefaces each *Sura* of the
Koran, with one exception.
[2] Still existing in India and elsewhere, and repeatedly guilty of treasonable
practices.

pagan arrogance! No more pride of birth! All men are
Adam's children, and Adam was made of the dust of the
earth: the worthiest man in God's eyes, is he who fears Him
most!" And again, "All men are equal, as are the teeth
of a comb; bodily strength alone makes some superior to
others." But he had also declared, "Let those who were
nobles under paganism remain nobles under Islamism, provided that they pay homage to the True Wisdom"—that is
to say, provided they become Moslems. Mohammed had
been, indeed, at times desirous of abolishing the Arab
aristocracy; but either he was unable, or did not dare, to
carry out his wish. The nobility therefore still existed;
they maintained their privileges and acted as tribal chieftains;
for Mohammed, far from indulging in the vain dream of
welding the Arabs into a nation, had maintained the tribal
organization (which he even declared to be of Divine
origin),[1] and each of these petty societies continued to live
only for itself, was engrossed in its own concerns, and took
no interest in matters that did not directly affect it. In war
they formed so many different bands, each with its standard,
borne by the sheik or a warrior appointed by him;[2] in the
towns each tribe had its own quarter, its own caravanserai,
and even its own cemetery. Strictly speaking, the right of
appointing chiefs lay with the Khalif, but we must distinguish between this theoretical right and actual usage.
Originally the Khalif could only confer the chieftainship of
a tribe on one of its members, for the Arabs would obey
a stranger very reluctantly—or not at all. Mohammed
and Abû Bakr, accordingly, almost always conformed to this
practice, and delegated their authority to men whose personal influence was already acknowledged; while under
'Omar it appears that the Arabs claimed as a right the
appointment of none but their fellow-tribesmen as chiefs.
Usually, however, the tribes elected their own sheiks, and
the Khalifs were content with confirming their choice; this
custom was indeed observed by the Wahhâbi leader in the
nineteenth century. The old nobility, therefore, had maintained its position: but a more influential class had been
created. Mohammed, as well as his two immediate successors, had conferred the most important offices—such as the

---

[1] *Koran, Sura.* xlix. 13.

[2] In later days the chiefs bore the standards in the Musulman armies, so that
"standard-bearer" and "chieftain" became synonymous. *Recherches* (1881), i.
81 *n.*, where authorities are cited.

command of armies and the government of provinces—upon
veteran Moslems, both Refugees and Helpers. He had but
little choice in the matter; for these were almost the only
sincere Islamites, and the only men upon whom the Government—at once temporal and spiritual—could rely. What
confidence could be placed in tribal chiefs, never orthodox
and sometimes atheistic, such as 'Oyeina, chief of the
Fezâra, who said, " If there were a God, I should swear in
His name that I believed not in Him."

The preference accorded to the Refugees and Helpers
was, therefore, natural and legitimate enough; but it was
none the less galling to the pride of the sheiks to see town-
folk, husbandmen, and other nonentities placed over their
heads. Their tribesmen, who always identified the honour
of their chiefs with their own, were equally indignant; they
impatiently awaited a favourable opportunity to enforce by
arms their leaders' claims and to make an end of the
fanatics who had slain their kinsfolk. Similar sentiments of
envy and implacable hatred animated the aristocracy of
Mecca, at the head of whom were the Omayyads. In their
pride and arrogance, they had seen with ill-dissembled wrath
the original Moslems alone summoned to the Council of the
Khalif. Abû Bakr, it is true, had been inclined to let them
share in its deliberations, but 'Omar had strongly opposed
the plan, and his advice had prevailed. We shall see that
the Arab aristocracy at first tried to recover influence without having recourse to violence, but it might easily have
been foreseen that, if they failed in their attempt, they would
find eager allies against the Refugees and Helpers in the
sheiks of the Bedawin tribes.

[AUTHORITIES: Burckhardt, pp. 41, 160, 295; Burton, *Pilgrimage*, ii. 86,
    109; Caussin, i. 111, 114; ii. 78, 281, 391; iii. 99, 231, 288, 507;
    Raihân, f. 105; Ibn Khaldûn, *Proleg.* (xvi.) 243; (xvii.) 296; Al-
    Basrî, pp. 37–9, 45, 77, 161–2, 198, 200, 208–9, 237–9; Ibn
    Adhârî, i. 34; *Kartâs*, p. 25; Istakhrî, p. 26; Ahmad ibn Abî
    Ya'kûb, ff. 52–3, 64; Ibn Kutaiba, p. 121; Tabarî, i. 80, 110; ii.
    4, 110, 164, 206, 208, 210, 224; Abû 'l-Mahâsin, i. 343.]

CHAPTER III

RISE OF THE OMMAYADS

THE Khalif 'Omar, mortally wounded by the dagger of a Christian artisan,[1] had, when at the point of death, named as electors of his successor the six senior Companions of Mohammed; amongst these the most conspicuous were 'Alî, 'Othmân, Zubair, and Talha. When 'Omar had breathed his last, the six electors sat in conclave for two days, without arriving at any result, each member being engrossed in emphasizing his own qualifications and disparaging those of his colleagues. On the third day it was agreed that the nomination of the Khalif should rest with one of the electors, who had renounced his own claims.[2] To the great disappointment of 'Alî, Zubair, and Talha, he named 'Othmân, the Ommayad (A.D. 644).

The choice was scarcely justified by 'Othmân's personality. He was, it is true, both wealthy and liberal, and had made pecuniary sacrifices on behalf of Mohammed and his followers; but when it is added that he was diligent in prayer and fasting, and that he was the personification of good-nature and diffidence, almost all his merits have been enumerated. His intellect, never very powerful, had been enfeebled by the approach of old age—he had reached three-score years and ten—and so great was his timidity, that when he mounted the *minbar* for the first time, courage and words alike failed him. "A first attempt is a very difficult thing," he muttered with a sigh, as he descended from the pulpit. Unfortunately for himself, this kindly old man had an excessive partiality for his family—and his family belonged to that Meccan aristocracy who for twenty years had insulted, persecuted and opposed

---

[1] One Feroze, or Abû Lulû, a native of Kûfa. See Muir, *Annals of the Early Caliphate* (1883), p. 278.
[2] The other two electors were Sa'd ibn Abû Wakkâs and 'Abd-er-Rahmân ibn 'Awf; the latter renounced his claim.

Mohammed.[1] The Khalif was in complete subjection to them. His uncle Hakam, and to a still greater degree Merwân, son of the latter, soon became *de facto* rulers, leaving to 'Othmân little else than the title of Khalif, and the responsibility for all compromising measures, of which, notwithstanding, he was usually kept in ignorance. The orthodoxy of these two men, especially that of the father, was by no means above suspicion. Hakam was only converted upon the day of the capture of Mecca—and later, having betrayed certain secrets confided to him by Mohammed, the Prophet had laid his curse upon him and sent him into exile. Abû Bakr and 'Omar had confirmed this sentence. 'Othmân, on the other hand, recalled the banished reprobate, and presented him with a hundred thousand pieces of silver, in addition to certain lands which were not his to give, but were the property of the State; furthermore the Khalif appointed Merwân his secretary and Vizier, gave him one of his daughters in marriage, and enriched him from the spoils of Africa. Eager to improve the opportunity, other Omayyads, able and ambitious young men, the sons withal of Mohammed's most implacable enemies, secured the most lucrative posts, and this to the great delight of the vulgar, who were only too glad to exchange elderly devotees, harsh and austere, for jovial and witty nobles, but much to the chagrin of devout Moslems, who conceived a profound aversion to the new provincial governors. Who was there that did not shudder at the recollection that Abû Sufyân— father of that Mu'âwiya whom 'Othmân had appointed Governor of all Syria—had been in command of the army which defeated Mohammed at Ohod, and of that which besieged him in Medina? Leader of the Meccans, he did not yield until he saw that his cause was lost, and that ten thousand Moslems were ready to overwhelm him and his adherents; even then, when called upon by Mohammed to acknowledge him as the Messenger of God, he replied,

[1]

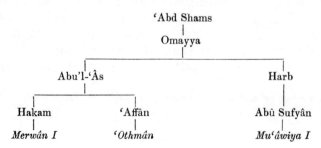

"Pardon my candour—but I still feel some doubt upon that point." "Bear witness to the Prophet, or your head falls," was the reply. Convinced by this final argument, Abû Sufyân became a Moslem; but so short was his memory, that a moment later he had forgotten his conversion.

Who, again, was there who did not remember Hind, Mu'âwiya's mother—the atrocious woman who had made necklaces and bracelets of the ears and noses of the Moslems slain at Ohod—the woman who had ripped open the body of Hamza, the Prophet's uncle, and tearing thence the liver had rent it with her teeth?[1] Offspring of such a father and such a mother, "son of the Liver-eater" as he was called—was it possible that Mu'âwiya could be a true Moslem? His enemies boldly declared that he was not.

The case of the Governor of Egypt, 'Othmân's foster-brother,[2] was still worse. His courage was indisputable, for he had defeated the Greek Governor of Numidia, and had gained a brilliant victory over the Greek fleet, though greatly superior in number to his own; but he had been Mohammed's amanuensis, and when the Prophet dictated to him his Revelations, he had tampered with the words and perverted the meaning. His sacrilege having been detected, he took flight and fell back into idolatry.[3]

On the day of the capture of Mecca, Mohammed gave orders that he should be slain, upon his being found hidden behind the hangings which covered the Ka'ba. The apostate placed himself under the protection of 'Othmân, who led him to the Prophet and besought his clemency. Mohammed for a while remained silent: at last he muttered, "I pardon him"; but when 'Othmân had retired with his protégé, the Prophet, casting an angry glance upon his guards, cried, "Why are ye so slow of understanding? I kept silence that one of you might leap forth and slay that man!" And the man was now governor of one of the fairest provinces of the Empire.

Walîd, half-brother of the Khalif, was made Governor of Kûfa.[4] He suppressed the revolt in Azerbâijân when that

---

[1] Probably as a charm. Dr. Frazer (*The Golden Bough* (1900), ii. 357), states that certain tribes in S.E. Africa eat the liver of an enemy who has behaved with conspicuous bravery, since it is considered "the seat of valour." *Cf.* Sir S. Baker, *Ismailia*, ii. 354.

[2] ('Abdallah ibn Sád ibn) Abi Sarh.

[3] *Sura* vi. 93 was believed to have been aimed against him : "Is any more wicked than he who deviseth a lie of God, or saith, 'I have had a revelation,' when nothing was revealed to him?"

[4] Sa'd had been deposed.

province tried to regain its independence; his troops, in co-operation with those of Mu'âwiya, captured Cyprus, and his prudent rule was praised throughout the province. Never-theless, Walîd's father, 'Okba, had spat in the Prophet's face, and at another time had nearly strangled him; later, upon being made prisoner by Mohammed and condemned to death, when 'Okba cried despairingly, " Who will care for my children when I am gone ? " the Prophet replied, " The fire of Hell ! " The son, who came to be known of as " the Child of Hell," seemed to have taken some pains to justify the prediction. Once, after a carousal which, under the incentives of wine and the charms of beautiful singing-girls, had been prolonged till dawn, Walîd heard the muezzin proclaiming the hour of the morning prayer from a minaret. With a brain still heated by the fumes of wine, and clad only in his tunic, he proceeded to the mosque and there recited, with less titubancy than might have been expected, the customary prayer, which, indeed, occupies but three or four minutes. This ended, he turned to the congregation, and cried, probably to prove that he was per-fectly sober, " Shall I recite yet another ? " " By Allah," cried a pious Moslem in the first rank behind him, " I will tarry for no other from such a man as thou! I should never have believed that such a governor could have been sent to us from Medina," and forthwith he began to tear up the pavement of the mosque. His example was followed by equally zealous bystanders, and Walîd, to escape stoning, fled in haste. He re-entered his palace, reeling, and shout-ing a verse from a pagan poet : " Where wine and song abound, there you will find me ! Mine is no heart of flint, insensible to good cheer ! " The famous poet al-Hutay'a[1] seems to have looked upon the adventure as an inspiring one. " On the Day of Judgment," he sings, " al-Hutay'a will certify that Walîd in no way deserves the obloquy heaped on him. What was his fault when all is related ? When the prayer was ended he but cried, ' Are ye minded to hear it again ? ' He was merry with wine, and perchance knew not very well what he said. It was providential, Walîd, that someone checked you, else peradventure you would have continued in prayer until doomsday ! " It must, however, be admitted that al-Hutay'a, though a poet of the highest rank, was a reprobate who by turns embraced

[1] " The Dwarf "; surname of Jarwal ibn Aus. See C. Huart, *Arabic Literature* (1903), p. 44.

and abjured Islamism. There were, moreover, at Kûfa a
few persons, perhaps in the pay of the holy men of Medina,
who were by no means of his mind. Two of these betook
themselves to the Capital and denounced Walîd. At first
'Othmân refused to receive their depositions; but 'Alî
intervened, and, to the great regret of the Arabs of Kûfa,
Walîd was deprived of his governorship. But the aged
Khalif was reproached by the orthodox party not only for
his choice of governors. He was further taxed with having
ill-treated many companions of the Prophet, with having
revived a pagan custom abolished by Mohammed, with
purposing to take up his residence in Mecca, and—most
unpardonable offence of all—with having caused a new
edition of the Koran to be prepared, not by its most learned
students—even he whom Mohammed had indicated as the
best " Reader " of the Koran was not consulted—but by his
own most devoted adherents:[1] to make matters worse, this
version was declared to be the only authentic one, the Khalif
having ordered all the others to be burnt. Determined to
tolerate no longer such a state of affairs, 'Othmân's former
rivals, 'Alî, Zubair, and Talha—who, thanks to their having
appropriated funds intended for the poor, had become so
wealthy that they reckoned their money by the million—
scattered their gold lavishly in all directions in order to stir
up revolts. They were, however, only partially successful:
sporadic risings took place, but the bulk of the people remained faithful to the Khalif. At last, relying on the
temper of the Medinese, the conspirators introduced into
the Capital a few hundreds of those Bedawin of gigantic
stature and swarthy complexion who were always ready to
commit murder for hard cash. These so-called avengers of
outraged religion, after having maltreated the Khalif in the
mosque, proceeded to besiege him in his palace, which was
defended by only five hundred men, mostly slaves, under
Merwân's command. It was hoped that 'Othmân would
abdicate voluntarily, but this expectation was not fulfilled.
Believing that no one would dare to attempt his life, or
perhaps reckoning on Mu'âwiya's assistance, the Khalif displayed much firmness. Extreme measures therefore became
necessary. After a siege of several weeks, the ruffians broke

---

[1] 'Othmân, in 651, entrusted Zaid ibn Thâbit (a former amanuensis of the
Prophet) with the preparation of a revised version in association with three
Kurashites. See Muir, *Life of Mohammad* (1912), xxi. *sq.*; Nicholson, *Lit. Hist. of
the Arabs* (1907), p. 142; Margoliouth, *Mohammedanism* (1911), pp. 69-70.

into the palace from a neighbouring house; assassinated the venerable octogenarian as he was piously reading the Koran;[1] and, to crown all, proceed to pillage the public treasury. Merwân and the other Omayyads had time to escape (A.D. 656). The Medinese, or "Defenders"—for this name passed from the Companions of Mohammed to their descendants—had stood aloof, and the house from which the assassins had entered the palace actually belonged to the Beni Hazm, a family of Defenders, who later on became conspicuous for their hatred of the Omayyads. This untimely neutrality, only too closely resembling complicity, was made a subject of stern reproach by their poet Hassân ibn Thâbit,[2] who had been a devoted adherent of 'Othmân, and who had good grounds for fearing that the Omayyads would revenge themselves upon his fellow-tribesmen for their kinsman's death. " When the venerable old man," he said, "saw death staring him in the face, the Defenders did not lift a hand to save him. Alas! soon will your walls ring with the cry: 'God is great! Vengeance, vengeance for 'Othmân!'"

'Alî,[3] raised to the Khalifate by the Defenders, dismissed all 'Othmân's governors and replaced them by Moslems of the old school, for the most part also Defenders. The orthodox party were victorious; they proceeded to re-establish themselves in power, to crush the tribal nobility and the Omayyads—those converts of yesterday who aimed at being the pontiffs and doctors of the morrow. Their triumph was of short duration. Dissensions broke out even in the Council-chamber. Each of the triumvirs, in hiring the murderers of 'Othmân, had felt the Khalifate within his grasp. Baffled in their hopes, Talha and Zubair, compelled at the point of the sword to swear allegiance to their fortunate rival, quitted Medina to join the ambitious and treacherous Ayesha. The Prophet's widow had formerly conspired against 'Othmân, but she now incited the populace to avenge him and to revolt against 'Alî, whom she hated with all the bitterness of wounded pride: had he not,

---

[1] When the insurgents burst in he was reading *Sura* iii. 174, which refers to the battle of Ohod, and contains the words: "When men said to them, 'Verily the Meccans have mustered against you; therefore fear them!' it only increased their faith, and they said, 'Our sufficiency is in God; and excellent the Guardian!'"

[2] Formerly Mohammed's court poet. D. S. Margoliouth, *Mohammed* (1905), p. 287.

[3] Son of Abù Tâlib, and husband of Fâtima, the Prophet's daughter.

during her husband's lifetime, once dared to asperse her virtue ?[1]

No foresight could anticipate the issue of the struggle Ayesha was entering upon. The forces of the confederates were as yet but few in number : 'Alî could reckon beneath his banner none but 'Othmân's assassins and the Defenders. It was for the nation at large to decide between the rivals. But it remained neutral. At the tidings of the murder of the good old man a cry of indignation had rung through all the provinces of the widespread Empire, and if the complicity of Zubair and Talha had been less well known, they might perhaps, as opponents of 'Alî, have enlisted the sympathy of the masses. But their participation in the crime was patent to all. " Must we show thee, then," cried the Arabs to Talha, in the Mosque at Basra, " the letter in which thou incitedst us to rise against 'Othmân ? " And Zubair was reminded that he had urged the men of Kûfa to rebel. There was indeed scarcely a man to be found who would draw the sword on behalf of either of these hypocrites, who were equally held in contempt.

Meanwhile, it was deemed desirable to maintain, as far as possible, the organization established by 'Othmân, as well as the Governors whom he had appointed. Accordingly, when the officer upon whom 'Alî had conferred the government of Kûfa approached his destination, he was met by the Arabs of that town, who bluntly told him that they demanded the punishment of 'Othmân's murderers, that they intended to keep their existing Governor, and that, as for himself, they would cleave his skull if he did not instantly turn back. The Defender appointed to the command in Syria was stopped at the frontier by a band of horsemen. " Wherefore comest thou ? " was the leader's challenge. " To be thy Emir." " If any man save 'Othmân sent thee it were well for thee to retrace thy steps." " Know ye not what has happened at Medina ? " " We know it but too well, and therefore we counsel thee to return whence thou camest." The Defender prudently took the proffered advice.

At length 'Alî found opportune friends and useful servants in the Arabs of Kûfa. These he won over to his cause, not without difficulty, by promising to take up his abode in their city and thus render it the capital of the Empire. With their aid proving victorious in what is

[1] See Muir, *Life of Mohammad* (1912), pp. 299 *sq.*

C

known as the " Battle of the Camel," [1] he rid himself of his
rivals. Talha was mortally wounded; Zubair was assassinated as he fled; Ayesha besought and obtained pardon.
The glory of the victory rests with the Defenders, who
formed the larger part of the cavalry.

Henceforth 'Alî was master of Arabia, 'Irâk, and Egypt,
in the sense that his authority was not flagrantly disputed
in those provinces; nevertheless, his rule was endured
frigidly, and even with manifest aversion. The Arabs of
'Irâk, whose co-operation was of the greatest importance,
never failed to find an excuse for not taking the field at his
orders; in the winter it was too cold, and in the summer it
was too hot. [2]

Syria, however, alone persistently refused to recognise
'Alî. Mu'âwiya could not have submitted, even had he
wished it, without tarnishing his honour. Even in our own
days the Egyptian fellah, degenerate and oppressed as he is,
will avenge a relative's murder, though he knows that
vengeance will cost him his life. Could Mu'âwiya then
leave unpunished the assassination of a kinsman? [3] Could
he submit to a man who counted murderers among his
generals? Moreover, even if he was not stirred by the
call of blood, he was actuated by ardent ambition. Had
he so desired, he might probably have saved 'Othmân by
marching to his aid. But this would have conferred no
benefit on Mu'âwiya himself, who while 'Othmân lived
must have remained what he was—Governor of Syria. He
acknowledged that ever since the Prophet had said to him,
" If thou obtainest the sovereignty, acquit thyself well," his
mind had been set upon no other object, he had aimed at
no other goal, save the Khalifate.

And now circumstances were wholly in his favour; he
hoped for all, he was ready to dare all. His ambition was
about to be realized! He would cast aside every restraint
and every scruple! His cause was just, and he could rely
upon the Arabs of Syria; they were his, body and soul.
Cultured, amiable, generous, with a profound knowledge
of the human heart, clement or severe as circumstances
demanded, Mu'âwiya had discovered how to gain their
respect and affection by his personal qualities. Between

[1] Fought near Basra, A.D. 656. So called from Ayesha's camel, which was a
rallying-point.
[2] 'Alî's own expression; see Reiske, *Anmerkungen zu Abûlfeda,* i. 67. Cf. *Koran,*
Su. ix. 82.
[3] Second cousin; see p. 28 *n.*

them and himself, moreover, community of views, sentiments, and interests formed an additional bond. For the
Syrians, Islamism was but a dead-letter, a vague and confused formula to which they did not even try to attach a
meaning; the duties and ceremonies prescribed by that
religion were irksome to them; they felt an inveterate
hatred against the upstart nobles who had no other title
to rule them than that of having been Companions of
Mohammed, and they regretted the bygone sway of the
tribal chiefs. At a word they would have marched straight
upon the two Holy Cities to pillage and burn them and
to massacre their inhabitants. The son of Abû Sufyân and
Hind shared their desires, their fears, their resentments, and
their hopes. Such were the true causes of the sympathy
which subsisted between the prince and his subjects, and
which was later exhibited in an affecting manner when
Mu'âwiya, after a long and glorious reign, had drawn his
last breath and was accorded his last honours. The Emir
to whom Mu'âwiya had entrusted the Government until
Yazîd, the heir to the throne, should arrive at Damascus,
ordered that the coffin should be borne by the kinsmen of
the illustrious dead; but on the day of the obsequies, as the
procession started, the Syrians cried to the Emir: "Whilst
the Khalif lived we took part in all his expeditions; his joys
and sorrows were ours. Permit us, therefore, to-day also to
play our part." Their request having been granted, they
pressed forward with such eagerness to touch, if it were
but with the tips of their fingers, the bier on which lay the
remains of their beloved prince, that the pall was torn to
pieces.

It was evident to 'Alî, from the very first, that the
Syrians identified Mu'âwiya's cause with their own. He
was told that every day a hundred thousand men came to
mourn at the Mosque before 'Othmân's blood-stained shirt,
having made a solemn oath to avenge him. Six months
had elapsed since the murder, when 'Alî, victor on the
"Day of the Camel," for the last time summoned Mu'âwiya
to make submission. Thereupon Mu'âwiya, displaying to
the Arabs assembled in the Mosque the bloody garment,[1]
besought their advice. He was listened to in solemn and
respectful silence, and when he had made an end, one of the
nobles, acting as spokesman for the rest, replied with pro-

---

[1] Together with the severed fingers of 'Othmân's faithful wife Nâila, who tried
to save him. See Muir, *The Caliphate* (1891), p. 248.

found deference: "Prince, it is for thee to counsel and command, and for us to hearken and to do!" Proclamation was forthwith made that every man able to bear arms must betake himself without delay to the banner of his clan, and that whosoever should be found absent from his post after three days would be condemned to death. Not a man was missing at the appointed time. The enthusiasm was as sincere as it was universal: it was for a truly national cause that they were about to fight. Syria alone furnished Mu'âwiya with more soldiers than all the other provinces together supplied to 'Alî. The latter sorrowfully compared the zealous devotion of the Syrians with the lukewarmness of his Arabs of 'Irâk. "Willingly would I exchange ten of you for one of Mu'âwiya's soldiers," he said: "By Allah, the Son of the Liver-eater will triumph!"

It seemed probable that the quarrel would be fought out ¡on the plains of Siffîn, near the right bank of the Euphrates.[1] However, after the two opposing armies had come within touch of one another, several weeks were spent in ineffective negotiations and in sanguinary but indecisive skirmishes. Both sides avoided a general engagement. At length, however, when all attempts at conciliation had failed, the battle was joined. The veteran Companions of Mohammed fought with the fanatical fury of the days when they compelled the Bedawin to choose between Islamism and death. In their eyes the Arabs of Syria were virtually pagans. "My oath, my oath!" cried Ammâr,[2] then more than ninety years old. "Naught is more meritorious in God's sight than to do battle with these infidels! If I am slain by their spears, I am a martyr for the true faith! Follow me, Companions of the Prophet! The Gates of Heaven open for us, the Houris await our coming!" Throwing himself into the thickest of the fray, he fought like a lion, till, riddled with wounds, he fell dead. For their own part, the Arabs of 'Irâk, seeing that their honour was at stake, fought more bravely than might have been anticipated, and 'Alî's cavalry executed so vigorous a charge that the Syrians fell back. Fearing that the battle was lost, Mu'âwiya had already put his foot in the stirrup with a view to taking flight, when 'Amr, son of al-'Âs, came up to him. "Ha!" cried the prince, "thou art ever boasting of thy

---

[1] To the west of Ricca (Nicephorium), at the confluence of the Euphrates and the Belik. See Muir, *op. cit.*, p. 270.

[2] Formerly Governor of Kûfa, and one of the assassins of 'Othmân.

craft in overcoming difficulties; hast thou found some way of escape from the disaster which threatens us? Thou rememberest that I promised thee the Government of Egypt if I proved victorious. Counsel me, then, what to do." 'Amr, who had maintained communications with 'Alî's army, thereupon advised Mu'âwiya to order all those of his soldiers who possessed copies of the Koran to fasten them to the points of their lances. "Then," he continued, "declare that you leave the issue to be decided by the Book itself. I will take upon myself full responsibility for this advice: I know it to be sound." 'Amr, in fact, in anticipation of eventual defeat, had previously arranged this *coup de théâtre* with several of the enemy's leaders, amongst whom the chief was Ash'ath, the greatest traitor living. Ash'ath, indeed (who when he was yet a pagan and sheik of the Beni Kinda, had boldly assumed the title of King), had but little reason to be well-disposed to Islamism or its founder, for when he abjured Islamism under Abû Bakr he had seen the whole of the garrison of his fortress of Nojair decapitated by the Moslems. Mu'âwiya followed 'Amr's advice, and gave orders that the Korans should be affixed to the spears. The sacred book was rare among this army of eighty thousand men: scarcely five hundred copies were forthcoming, but these sufficed in the eyes of Ash'ath and his friends, who crowded around the Khalif, and cried: " We bow to the decision of God's Book; we call for an armistice!"

"It is a ruse!" said 'Alî, trembling with rage: "an infamous trick. Those Syrians scarce know what the Koran is: their every action violates its precepts!" "But since we are fighting for God's Book, how can we refuse its arbitrament?" "Nay, we are fighting to constrain these men to submit to God's laws: they have rebelled against the Almighty; they have rejected his sacred Book. Think ye that Mu'âwiya, or 'Amr, or the Child of Hell and the rest care aught for religion or the Koran? I know them better than ye: I have known them as children, and I have known them as men; and, men or children, they have ever been workers of iniquity." "Nevertheless," was the reply, "they appeal to God's Book, and thou appealest to the sword."

" Alas, too well I see that ye are determined to abandon me. Depart then; join yourselves to the remnants of the confederacy made of yore against our Prophet! Depart,

MS–C*

and ally yourselves with these men, who cry, ' God and his prophet '—all a cheat and a lie ! " " Recall Ashtar from the field," they cried—he was in command of the cavalry— " or the fate of ' Othmân awaits thee."

Knowing that they would not hesitate to carry out their threat if necessary, 'Alî yielded. He sent the order for retreat to the victorious general then closely pursuing the enemy. Ashtar refused to obey. The tumult burst forth afresh. 'Alî repeated his orders. " Can the Khalif know that the victory is ours ? " cried the gallant Ashtar. " Must I turn back at the very moment when the enemy is on the point of utter defeat ? " " What boots your victory," replied one of the messengers, an Arab of 'Irâk, " if meanwhile 'Alî is murdered ? " With a heavy heart, the General ordered the retreat to be sounded. That day the erstwhile King of the Kinda tasted the sweets of revenge : he it was who initiated the ruin of those pious Moslems who had stripped him of his kingship and had slain his fellow-tribes-men at Nojair. 'Alî sent him to Mu'âwiya to inquire in what way he proposed to decide the dispute by the Koran. " 'Alî and I," replied Mu'âwiya, " will each appoint an umpire. These two umpires will then decide, in accord-ance with the Koran, which of us twain hath the better right to the Khalifate. For my part, I select 'Amr, son of al-'Âs."

When Ash'ath reported this reply to 'Alî, the latter wished to nominate his cousin 'Abdallah, son of 'Abbâs. This, however, was held to be inadmissible : so near a kins-man could not be impartial. When 'Alî next proposed his brave general Ashtar, the cry was raised : " Who is it that has set the world on fire, if it is not Ashtar ? " " We will have no one else as arbitrator except Abû Mûsâ," said the treacherous Ash'ath. " But that man oweth me a grudge," cried 'Alî, " ever since I deprived him of the governorship of Kûfa : he hath played me false, he hath hindered the Arabs of 'Irâk from following me to the field ; how can I entrust my interests to him ? " " We will accept none other ! " and the reply was followed by a renewal of fierce threats. At last 'Alî, as the price of peace, gave his assent. Twelve thousand soldiers immediately deserted his banner, after having called upon him in vain to annul the covenant which he had just made, and which they regarded as sacrilegious, inasmuch as the settlement of the quarrel rested with God alone, and not with men. There was at least one

traitor among them, if, as alleged, Ash'ath was of their
number; but they were for the most part pious Readers of
the Koran, honest men, strongly attached to their religion,
highly orthodox—but what they held to be orthodoxy was
not that of 'Alî and the Medinese nobility. For a long
time, indignant at the depravity and hypocrisy of the Companions of Mohammed—who used their religion to further
the ends of their worldly ambition—these "Nonconformists" had determined to cut themselves adrift from the
official Church at the earliest opportunity.[1] Republicans
and democrats to a man, in religion as well as in politics—
austere moralists withal, seeing that they ranked grave sins
with infidelity—they present many points of resemblance
with those adherents of Cromwell, the English Indepen-
dents of the seventeenth century.

Some chroniclers hold that the arbitrator nominated
by 'Alî was outwitted by his colleague; others, that he
betrayed his master. At any rate the war broke out afresh.
'Alî encountered disgrace after disgrace, defeat after defeat.
His victorious rival bereft him successively of Egypt and
Arabia. Master of Medina, the Syrian general, ascending the
throne, exclaimed: " Aus and Khazraj! What hath be-
come of the venerable old man who used to be seated here?
By heaven! if it were not that I feared the wrath of
Mu'âwiya, my master, not one of you should be spared!
Yet, take the oath of allegiance to Mu'âwiya without reser-
vation and ye shall be pardoned." The majority of the
Defenders were absent, in 'Alî's army, but the oath was
wrung from the rest.

Not long afterwards 'Alî fell victim to the vengeance of
a young Khârejite maiden, whose father and brother he had
caused to be beheaded,[2] and who as the price of her hand in
marriage to her cousin[3] had demanded of him the head of
the Khalif (A.D. 661).

'Alî's son, Hasan,[4] inherited his claims to the Khalifate.
He was ill-suited to be leader of a party: indolent and
sensual, he preferred an easy, uneventful life of opulence
to glory, power, and the cares of a throne. The true head
of the party was henceforth the Defender Kais, son of Sa'd,

[1] *Ar.* Khawâridj: "Khârejite" meaning probably "one who leaves his home
among unbelievers for God's sake" (*Koran,* iv. 101). See R. A. Nicholson, *Lit.
Hist. of the Arabs* (1907), p. 209.
[2] At Nehrwân. See Muir, *Annals* (1883), p. 412.
[3] Ibn Muljam, of the tribe of Beni Taym.
[4] Nicknamed "The Divorcer"; see Muir, *The Caliphate* (1891), p. 302.

a man of gigantic stature and athletic frame, a splendid
type of physical force, and distinguished by his bravery in
twenty battles. His piety was exemplary : if need were he
would perform his religious duties at the peril of his life.
One day when he was engaged in prayer, he saw a large
serpent coiled upon the spot where he was about to lay his
forehead. Too scrupulous to interrupt his prayer, he continued it, and placed his head calmly by the side of the
reptile. The serpent coiled itself around his neck, without
doing him any harm. Not until he had finished his devo-
tions did he seize the creature and throw it to a distance.
This pious Moslem hated Mu'âwiya, not only because he
regarded him as the enemy of his fellow-tribesmen in
general and of his family in particular, but also because he
deemed him an infidel. Kais would, indeed, never admit
that Mu'âwiya was an Islamite. To such a pitch did the
mutual hatred of these two men attain, that while Kais was
Governor of Egypt, under 'Alî, they entered into correspondence solely for the pleasure of loading each other with
insults. One would begin his letter with "Jew, son of a
Jew!" and the other would retaliate with "Pagan, son
of a pagan! Thou adoptedst Islamism grudgingly, under
compulsion, but thou hast rejected it with right goodwill.
Thy faith, if thou hast any, is of yesterday, but thy hypocrisy is inveterate." From the first, Hasan's pacific aims
were but ill-concealed. "Stretch forth thy hand," said Kais
to him ; "I will swear allegiance to thee when thou hast
first made oath to obey God's Book as well as the laws
ordained by the Prophet, and to draw the sword upon
our foes." "I swear," replied Hasan, "to submit to the
Eternal, and to obey God's Book, and the laws of the
Prophet ; but thou shalt engage on thy part to bear
obedience to me ; to fight against those to whom I declare
war, and to sheathe the sword when I make peace." Kais
took the oath, but the Khalif's words had produced an ill
effect. "He is not the man we need," folk murmured ;
"he will never make war." For the Defenders, all would
be lost if Mu'âwiya got the upper hand. Their fears were
speedily realized. For several months Hasan, although he
had no inconsiderable forces at his disposal, remained inactive at Medâin :[1] he had probably entered into negotiations with Mu'âwiya. At last he sent Kais against the

---

[1] On the Tigris, called the "Twin City" since it occupied the site of the more
ancient Ctesiphon and Seleucia.

Syrian frontier, but with too small a force, and the brave
Defender was overwhelmed by superior numbers. The
fugitives on reaching Medâin in great confusion maltreated
Hasan, who, if he had not actually betrayed them to the
enemy, had laid himself open to grave suspicion. Hasan
thereupon, on the condition of resigning all claim to the
Khalifate, concluded peace with Mu'âwiya. The latter
guaranteed him a magnificent pension, and promised an
amnesty to his followers.

Kais, however, still had under his command five thousand
men, all of whom after 'Ali's death had shaved their heads
in token of mourning. With this little army he was desirous
of carrying on the war, but being by no means sure that his
soldiers shared his own glowing ardour, he addressed them
thus : " If it is your desire, we will continue to fight, and will
die to the last man rather than surrender ; but if ye elect to
sue for terms, so be it. Make your choice ! " The soldiers
chose peace.

Kais, accompanied by his chief fellow-tribesmen, accordingly sought the presence of Mu'âwiya, craved pardon for
himself and his men, and reminded him of the words of the
Prophet, who upon his deathbed had commended the Defenders to the other Moslems, saying : " Honour and respect
those who gave shelter to the Prophet in his flight, and firmly
established the foundations of his cause."

In conclusion, Kais gave Mu'âwiya to understand that
the Defenders would cheerfully place their services at his
disposal : for, in spite of their devoutness, and their repugnance to serving an unbeliever, they could not reconcile
themselves to the loss of important and lucrative posts.
Mu'âwiya replied to this effect: "I know not, Defenders,
what title ye have to my clemency. By heaven ! ye have
been my implacable foes. It was ye who, at the battle of
Siffîn, came near to overwhelming me when your glittering
spears wrought havoc amongst my men. The satires of your
poets have stung me to the quick. And now that God has
established that which ye sought to overthrow, ye come to
me and say, ' Pay heed to the Prophet's words.' Nay ! union
between us is scarcely conceivable."

Kais, with wounded pride, changed his tone. " Our title
to thy clemency," said he, " consists in our being good
Moslems : that alone suffices in the sight of God. It is
true that the men who are in league against the Prophet
have other claims which weigh with thee : we do not envy

them.   It is true that we have been thine enemies in the field ;
but had it been thy desire, thou couldst have prevented the
war.   Our poets may have provoked thee with their satires ;
in so far as these are false, they will be forgotten, but the
truths that they contain will abide. Thy power is established;
with regret we admit the fact.   In the battle of Siffîn, when
we came near to overthrowing thee, we fought under the
banners of a man who believed that he was fulfilling God's
will.   As for the Prophet's exhortation, every true believer
will follow it ; but since thou declarest that there is incom-
patibility between us, God alone can henceforth preserve
thee from doing ill, O Mu'awiya ! "   " Begone ! and that instantly," cried the Khalif, indignant at such audacity.

The Defenders had succumbed.   Power naturally returned to the tribal chiefs—the old nobility.   Nevertheless
the Syrians were not satisfied ; they had hoped to enjoy to
the full an all-embracing revenge.   Mu'âwiya, in his moderation, would not permit this : but they well knew that the
day would come when the conflict would blaze forth once
more, and then there would be a struggle to the death.
As for the Defenders, they gnawed their hearts in anger
and vexation.   While Mu'âwiya lived, the power of the
Omayyads was so firmly established that it was useless for
them to challenge it ; but Mu'âwiya was not immortal, and
far from giving way to despair, the Medinese prepared for a
future struggle.

During this interval of enforced inaction, the task of the
warriors devolved upon the poets on both sides ; bloodthirsty
satires gave vent to their mutual hatred.   They attacked
one another without respite ; there were daily broils, and
ceaseless bickerings.   While the Syrians and the Omayyad
princes lost no opportunity of showing their hatred and scorn
of the Defenders, the latter never failed to pay them back
in their own coin.

[AUTHORITIES: Mas'ûdî (MS. 127), pp. 185, 194, 204–6, 231–2, 277–8 ;
(MS. 537), pp. 141, 159 ; Tabarî, ii. pp. 250, 252 ; Ibn Badrûn,
p. 148 ; Nawawî, p. 565 ; Raihân, ff. 138–140, 197, 200 ; Sharastânî,
pp. 85–6 ; Mûbarrad, pp. 278, 304–5 ; Abû 'l-Mahâsin, i. p. 113.]

CHAPTER IV

YAZÎD I

MU'ÂWIYA, shortly before his death, counselled his son Yazîd to keep a watchful eye on Husain, 'Alî's second son,[1] and on the Refugee 'Abdallah, son of that Zubair who had disputed the throne with the Prophet's son-in-law. These two men were dangerous. They both resided at Medina, and on Husain's informing 'Abdallah that he had good reason to believe that the Khalif was dead, 'Abdallah sounded him as to his intentions. "Never will I acknowledge Yazîd as my sovereign," exclaimed Husain; "he is a wine-bibber, and a profligate, and has an infatuation for the chase." 'Abdallah made no reply, but Husain's opinion was his own.

Yazîd I possessed neither his father's moderation nor his refinement of manners, nor did he share his love of ease and comfort. He was a faithful image of his mother, Maysûn, a mettlesome Bedawy lady, who, as she herself had declared in spirited verse, preferred the whistling of the breeze in the Desert to the strains of the most talented musicians, and a crust of bread eaten in the shadow of a tent to all the dainties set before her in the gorgeous halls of Damascus. Trained under his mother in the desert of the Beni Kelb, Yazîd brought to the throne the qualities expected in a young tribal chief rather than in a monarch and hierarch. He despised ceremony and etiquette; affable to all,[2] jovial, generous, eloquent, no mean poet, a lover of the chase, the dance, wine and song—his sympathy with the frigid and austere religion at the head of which chance had set him, and against which his grandfather had unsuccessfully fought, was lukewarm indeed. The devoutness—often insincere, and the rectitude—often feigned, of the veterans of Islamism,

---

[1] The eldest son, Hasan "The Divorcer," was dead, having being poisoned by one of his wives. The Shî'ites believe that the deed was instigated by Mu'âwiya. See *The Miracle Play of Hasan and Hosein*, by Sir L. Pelly; with notes by Sir A. N. Wollaston (1879).

[2] "Nullam umquam sibi regalii fastigii causa gloriam appetivit, sed cum omnibus civiliter vixit." Isid. c. 18.

were abhorrent to his frank nature; he did not attempt to
conceal his preference for the days which the theologians
called "The Ignorance";[1] he indulged, without scruple,
in pleasures forbidden by the Koran; he yielded to every
caprice of his whimsical and volatile disposition; and he
stood upon ceremony with no man. He was detested at
Medina; but in Syria he was adored.[2]

As usual, the old Moslem party had a superabundance
of officers and no troops. Husain, who after he had eluded
the vigilance of the too credulous Governor of Medina,
had sought refuge, together with 'Abdallah, on the sacred
soil of Mecca, was overjoyed to receive letters from the
Arabs of Kûfa, urging him to place himself at their head.
They pledged themselves to recognise him as Khalif, and
to induce the whole population of 'Irâk to declare for him.
Messengers from Kûfa followed one another in quick succession; the last brought a petition of prodigious length,
the appended signatures filling no fewer than a hundred and
fifty leaves. In vain did clear-sighted friends implore him
not to plunge rashly into so perilous an enterprise, but to
mistrust the promises and factitious enthusiasm of a people
who had deceived and betrayed his father. Husain, however, proudly exhibiting the innumerable petitions which
he had received—amounting, so he boasted, to nearly a
camel-load—preferred to listen to the baneful promptings of
his ambition. He bowed to destiny, and set out for Kûfa,
to the great satisfaction of his pretended friend 'Abdallah,
who, while generally believed quite incapable of opposing
the Prophet's grandson, inwardly rejoiced at seeing him
deliberately march to his doom, and spontaneously offer his
head to the executioner.

Religious sentiment did not enter into the devotion displayed to Husain's cause in 'Irâk. This province was exceptionally circumstanced. Mu'âwiya, although a Meccan
by birth, had founded a dynasty essentially Syrian. Under
his reign Syria had become the preponderating province.
Damascus was henceforth the capital of the Empire: under
the Khalifate of 'Alî, Kûfa had held the post of honour.
Wounded in their pride, the Arabs of 'Irâk evinced from

---

[1] Ar. *Jâhiliyya*, "The Age of Barbarism."
[2] "Vir nimium gratissime habitus." Isid. The observations of this almost
contemporary writer on the character of the Omayyads possess peculiar interest,
for he expresses the opinions of the Syrians of Spain, while more recent Arab
chroniclers usually judge these princes from the point of view of the Medinese.
See also the elegy on the death of Yazîd in Wright, *Opuscula Arabica*, pp. 118–19.

the first a turbulent, seditious, anarchical, and, in a word,
a very Arab spirit. The province soon became a focus for
political firebrands—the haunt of brigands and assassins.
Mu'âwiya thereupon entrusted the Government to Ziyâd,
his natural brother.[1] Ziyâd was not content with keeping
hotheads in check ; he exterminated them. Patrolling the
country with an escort of soldiers, lictors, and executioners,
he put down with an iron hand the slightest attempt to stir
up political or social disorder. His stern and even ruthless
administration soon established security throughout the province; but it was precisely for this reason that 'Irâk was
ready to welcome Husain.

The inhabitants of the province were, however, held more
firmly in the clutches of terrorism than they themselves
were aware. Ziyâd was no more, but he had left a son
worthy of him—by name 'Obaidallah. It was to him that
Ziyâd entrusted the task of stifling the conspiracy at Kûfa
when Nu'mân ibn Bashîr, Governor of the town, had shown
a moderation which the Khalif deemed suspicious. Setting
out from Basra at the head of his troops, 'Obaidallah halted
at some distance from Kûfa. Then, veiling his face, he
entered the town at nightfall accompanied by only ten of
his soldiers. In order to probe the intentions of the populace, he posted some of his men to acclaim him as he passed
by, as though he had been Husain. Forthwith many
citizens of high rank offered him hospitality. The pretended Husain declined their invitations, and surrounded
by an excited crowd shouting " Long live Husain ! " he
rode straight to the citadel. Nu'mân instantly ordered the
gates to be shut. " Open ! " cried 'Obaidallah, " and admit
the Prophet's grandson ! " " Return whence thou camest ! "
replied Nu'mân ; " I foresee thy fate, and I would not have
it said that Husain, Son of 'Alî, was slain in Nu'mân's
castle." Satisfied by this reply, 'Obaidallah threw off his
veil. Recognising him, the crowd immediately dispersed,
terror-stricken, while Nu'mân respectfully saluted him and
begged him to enter the citadel. Next day 'Obaidallah declared to the populace assembled in the mosque that he
would be a father to the well-disposed, but a sword to the
wicked. A disturbance ensued, but it was quelled. Henceforth no one dared to speak of rebellion.

Tidings of these disastrous events reached the unfor-

---

[1] Ziyâd's paternity was doubtful, but Mu'âwiya acknowledged him as son of
Abû Sufyân.

tunate Husain when he was not far from Kûfa. With him
there were scarcely a hundred men, for the most part his
own kinsfolk. Nevertheless he continued his advance : the
blind and fatuous credulity which seems to throw a spell
over pretenders did not fail him : he was convinced that as
soon as he appeared before the gates of Kûfa the citizens
would take up arms in his cause. Near Kerbelâ he found
himself confronted by a body of troops sent by 'Obaidallah,
with instructions to bring him in, alive or dead. Summoned
to surrender, Husain began to parley. The commander of
the Omayyad troops[1] did not adhere strictly to orders, but
wavered. He was a Kurashite—son of one of Mohammed's
first disciples—and the idea of shedding the blood of a son
of Fâtima revolted him. He therefore applied to his chief
for fresh instructions, and informed him of Husain's proposals. Upon receiving the message, 'Obaidallah himself
felt momentary hesitation. But Shamir,[2] a Kûfan noble
and general in the Omayyad army—an Arab of the Arabs,
as was his grandson whom we shall meet later in Spain—
inspired him with fresh resolution. " What! " he cried,
" Hath fortune delivered thine enemy into thy hands, and
wilt thou spare him ? It is unthinkable ! He must surrender at discretion." 'Obaidallah sent his officer orders to
this effect. But though Husain refused to surrender except
on terms, still no onslaught was made upon him. 'Obaidallah
thereupon sent fresh troops, under the command of Shamir,
with these instructions: " If the Kurashite persists in his
inaction, cut off his head and assume the command in his
place." [3] But upon Shamir's reaching the camp, the
Kurashite, without further hesitation, gave the signal for
attack. In vain did Husain cry: " If ye believe the religion founded by my grandfather, how can ye justify your
conduct at the Last Day ? " In vain were Korans fastened
to the spears of his followers : Shamir gave the word to his
men—they fell upon Husain, sword in hand, and slew him.[4]
Almost all his companions, after selling their lives dearly,
were left dead upon the field (Oct. 10, 680).

Posterity—ever prone to wax sentimental over the fate
of unsuccessful pretenders, and often unmindful of justice,
national peace, and the horrors of a civil war that is not

[1] 'Amr ibn S'ad.
[2] Shamir ibn Dhi'l-Jawshan.
[3] Ibn Badrûn, p. 164.
[4] According to other accounts, he was pierced by an arrow.

checked at the outset—has regarded Husain as the victim
of an atrocious crime. Persian fanaticism has completed
the picture: it has delineated a saint, in the place of a mere
adventurer hurried to destruction by strange mental aberration and an almost insane ambition.[1] The great majority of
his contemporaries viewed Husain in a very different light:
they looked upon him as a man forsworn, and guilty of
high treason, seeing that he had taken an oath of fealty to
Yazîd in Mu'âwiya's lifetime, and could not make good his
right or title to the Khalifate.

Husain's death gave an opening to another pretender
who was more prudent and, in his own eyes, more capable
than his predecessor. This was 'Abdallah, son of Zubair.
He had posed as Husain's friend, but his true sentiments
had been self-evident to Husain himself and his adherents.
"Set your mind at ease, Ibn Zubair!" exclaimed 'Abdallah
ibn 'Abbâs, when he had bade farewell to Husain, after
vainly urging him not to proceed to Kûfa; and reciting a
popular triplet, he continued: "For thee, skylark, the
heaven is free! Lay thine eggs, warble, preen, as thy heart
listeth! . . . Husain departs for 'Irâk, and all the Hijâz is
thine!" Nevertheless, though Ibn Zubair had secretly
assumed the title of Khalif as soon as Husain's departure
had left a clear stage, he professed the deepest grief when
the news of the tragedy reached the holy city, and he
hastened to deliver a pathetic panegyric of the deceased.
'Abdallah was a born orator: none was more eloquent,
none possessed to the same degree the great art of concealing and feigning sentiments, none could more effectually
cloak devouring greed for riches and power under the fair-
sounding names of duty, virtue, religion, and piety. This
was the secret of his influence; thus it was that he imposed
upon the multitude. Now that Husain no longer stood in
his way, 'Abdallah declared him to have been the rightful
Khalif, vaunted his virtues and his piety, lavished vitupera-
tions upon the treacherous and villainous Arabs of 'Irâk,
and concluded with a peroration which Yazîd might apply
to himself if he thought fit: "Never did that saintly man
prefer strains of music to the reading of the Koran—or
effeminate ditties to compunction caused by the fear of
Allah—or wine-bibbing to fasting—or the pleasures of the
chase to pious discourses. . . . Soon will the wicked reap
the fruits of their evil deeds."[2]

---

[1] See Sir L. Pelly, *op. cit.*   [2] *Nouv. Journ. asiat.*, ix. 332.

It was of the first importance for 'Abdallah to win over
the most influential Refugees to his side. He feared that
they could not be hoodwinked as easily as the common
people with regard to the true motives of his rebellion ; and
he foresaw opposition, especially from 'Abdallah, son of the
Khalif 'Omar, a man wholly disinterested and sincerely
pious, as well as singularly discerning. However, Ibn
Zubair was not fainthearted nor easily discouraged. The
son of 'Omar had a wife whose piety was only equalled by
her credulity. With this lady Ibn Zubair was convinced
that he must begin. He visited her, and expatiated with
his wonted glibness on his zeal for the Helpers, the Refugees,
the Prophet, and Allah, and when he saw that his unctuous
phrases had wrought a deep impression, he begged her to
persuade Ibn 'Omar to acknowledge him as Khalif. She
promised to do her best, and that night, when she served
supper to her spouse, she spoke enthusiastically of Ibn
Zubair, and concluded her eulogy with the words, " In very
truth, he seeketh after naught save the glory of the Eternal !"
" Thou rememberest," replied her husband drily, " the
magnificent retinue which used to follow in Mu'âwiya's
train when he went on pilgrimage—especially the goodly
white mules, adorned with purple housings, on which were
seated damsels in dazzling attire, crowned with pearls and
diamonds ? Thou canst not have forgotten them ? Well,
those mules are what thy saintly friend seeketh after !"
So saying, he resumed his supper and would listen no longer
to his simple-minded wife.[1]

Ibn Zubair had now been for a year in revolt against
Yazîd, and yet the latter took no heed of him. This indifference seemed strange in a ruler who could not boast of
patience and meekness as prominent among his virtues.
But, in the first place, Yazîd did not consider 'Abdallah
very dangerous, since, more prudent than Husain, he had
not quitted Mecca ; and, further, he had no wish, except in
case of absolute necessity, to stain with blood a region
which, even in pagan times, enjoyed the privilege of affording inviolable sanctuary to man and beast. Such an act of
sacrilege, he was well aware, would fill up the measure of
his iniquity in the eyes of the devout.

But at last his patience was exhausted. He summoned
'Abdallah, for the last time, to acknowledge him. Ibn
Zubair refused. The Khalif, in a rage, thereupon made a

---

[1] *Aghâni*, i. 18 ; *cf.* Ibn-Badrûn, p. 199.

vow that the rebel should not take the oath of allegiance save at the foot of the throne, with chains upon his neck and wrists. But when the first access of his anger had passed, Yazîd with habitual good-nature regretted his vow. As he could not break it, he devised a means of keeping it, without wounding 'Abdallah's pride. He resolved to send him a silver chain, and with it a splendid mantle, which would conceal the costly fetters from view.

The Khalif appointed ten persons to convey these singular gifts to Ibn Zubair. At the head of the mission was the Helper Nu'mân, son of Bashîr, the usual intermediary between the ultra-orthodox party and the Omayyads: his less conciliatory colleagues were chiefs of various Syrian tribes. The deputation arrived at Mecca. 'Abdallah, as might have been expected, declined to accept the Khalif's gifts; but Nu'mân, far from being discouraged by this refusal, tried to bring him to reason by judicious persuasion. The frequent interviews between the two—which after all proved fruitless—were confidential, and aroused the suspicions of one of the other deputies, Ibn Idhâh, chief of the Ash'arites, the most numerous and powerful tribe at Tiberias.[1] "After all, this Nu'mân is a Helper," he said to himself; "and one who is a traitor to his party and to his tribe is quite capable of betraying the Khalif." One day, meeting 'Abdallah, he accosted him: "Ibn Zubair," he said, "I can swear to you that Ibn Bashîr has received no instructions from the Khalif other than those which were given to the rest of us. He is head of the mission; that is all. But, by Allah, I must confess that I know not what to make of this hugger-mugger. Helpers and Refugees are birds of a feather, and Allah alone knows whether there is not some plot afoot."

"What concern is this of thine?" replied 'Abdallah with supreme disdain. "While I am here I shall do as I will. I am inviolable as that dove yonder which is protected by the sanctity of the place. Thou darest not kill it, for that would be a crime—a sacrilege."

"Thinkest thou that I have any such scruples?" replied Ibn Idhâh: then, turning to the page who carried his weapons, he added, "Boy, give me my bow and arrows!" The page obeyed; the Syrian sheik, choosing an arrow, fitted it to his bow, and taking aim at the dove, exclaimed: "Dove! is Yazîd son of Mu'âwiya a wine-bibber? Say

---

[1] Ahmad ibn Abî Yakûb, f. 62.

'Yes,' if thou darest, and this arrow shall transfix thee.
Dove, plannest thou to dethrone the Khalif Yazîd, to exclude him from Mohammed's flock, and countest thou on
impunity because this is a sanctuary? Say that this is in
thine heart, and this shaft shall pierce it!"

"Thou knowest that the bird cannot reply," said
'Abdallah, with an air of pity, but trying in vain to conceal
his uneasiness.

"That is true: the bird cannot reply—but thou canst,
Ibn Zubair! Hearken; I swear that thou shalt take the
oath of allegiance to Yazîd, either freely or by force, else
shalt thou see the banner of the Ash'arites[1] floating in this
valley, and in that case little heed shall I pay to the sanctity
thou pratest of!" At this threat 'Abdallah's cheek grew
pale. He had never dreamed of such impiety, even in a
Syrian, and he ventured to ask, in a voice tremulous with
fear: "Wouldst thou indeed dare to commit the sacrilege
of shedding blood upon this holy ground?"

"I would dare," replied the Syrian imperturbably; "and
the guilt would lie upon the head of him who made choice
of holy ground on which to conspire against the Commander
of the Faithful."[2]

Perhaps, if 'Abdallah had been more firmly convinced
that this sheik interpreted truly his compatriots' sentiments,
many calamities to Islam and to himself might have been
avoided; but Ibn Zubair was doomed to perish, as the son-
in-law and grandson of the Prophet had already perished, as
all the Moslems of the old school, sons of companions and
friends of Mohammed, would perish. To suffer unparalleled
misfortunes, calamity following calamity, such was the fate
in store for them.

For 'Abdallah, however, the fatal hour had not yet
struck. Destiny had decreed that unhappy Medina should
first expiate by her utter ruin—by the exile and massacre of
her children—the fatal honour of having offered asylum to a
fugitive Prophet, and of having produced the true founders
of Islamism—those fanatical warriors, who conquering
Arabia in its name, bestowed on the new-born faith a
blood-stained cradle.

[1] Of whom Ibn Idhâh was the chieftain.
[2] *Aghânî*, i. 18.

CHAPTER V

THE SACK OF MEDINA

IT was the year of grace 682. The sun had just set behind the mountain-range which lies to the west of Tiberias. The former splendour of the town is to-day hinted only by its ruins, but at the epoch of which we write it was the Capital of the province of Jordan,[1] and the temporary residence of the Khalif Yazîd I. The minarets of the mosques, and the towers on the battlements, illumined by the silver rays of the moon, began to be mirrored in the placid waters of the lake—that Sea of Galilee which recalls so many sacred memories to the Christian—when a little caravan, profiting by the coolness of the night, emerged from the town and directed its course towards the south. The nine travellers who rode at the head of the cavalcade were clearly men of rank, but there was nothing in their appearance to indicate that they were courtiers, for the Khalif rarely admitted to his intimacy persons of so ripe an age, or of a mien so austere —not to say surly.

For some time not a word was spoken. At last one of the travellers broke silence. " Well, brothers," said he, " what think ye of him ? We must at least admit that he hath shown us liberality. To thee he gave a hundred thousand pieces, did he not, son of Handhala ? "[2]

" Such is the sum," replied the person addressed : " but he drinketh wine and deemeth it no sin ; he playeth on the lute ; his companions in the daytime are his hunting-dogs, and at night, brigands. He liveth in incest with his sisters and his daughters, he never prayeth—in short, it is manifest that he is wholly without religion. What shall we do, brother ? Think ye that it is possible for us to tolerate such a man any longer ? We have, perchance, already shown unjustifiable forbearance, and if we continue in the same course,

---

[1] Roughly including central Palestine to the W. of the river. The five *Junds*, or districts, were Damascus, Hims, Kinnasrîn, Jordan, and Filastîn. See G. le Strange, *Palestine under the Moslems* (1890), pp. 24 *sq.*

[2] 'Abdallah ; see below, p. 53.

I fear me that stones will fall from heaven to destroy us.[1]
What is thy counsel, son of Sinân?"[2]

"I will tell thee," was the reply. "Upon our return
to Medina let us solemnly vow not to obey this profligate,
and son of a profligate; and thereafter we should do well to
render homage to the son of a Refugee." While he was
thus speaking a man journeying in the opposite direction
passed the caravan. The lowered hood of his cloak would
have hidden his face from the travellers, even if their attention had not been absorbed by a conversation which every
moment grew more animated. When the horsemen were
out of earshot the hooded man halted. Even to have
encountered him was an ill-omen according to Arab ideas,
for he was one-eyed.[3] Moreover, hatred and ferocity were
displayed in the terrible glance which his remaining orb
darted after the travellers now fading in the distance, while
he muttered deliberately and solemnly: "I swear that if
ever I meet with thee again where I can slay thee, I will
not spare thee, thou son of Sinân—Companion of Mohammed
though thou art!"

The travellers may, perhaps, have been already recognised
as Medinese. They were, indeed, notables of that city—
Helpers or Refugees, almost to a man. The circumstances
which had brought them to the Khalif's court may be briefly
recounted.

Signs of rebellion had shown themselves at Medina, and
serious quarrels had arisen with reference to the arable
lands, and plantations of date-trees, which Mu'âwiya had
formerly bought from the inhabitants, but which the latter
now reclaimed, on the ground that he had forced them to sell
these lands for a hundredth part of their true value. 'Othmân,
the Governor—who flattered himself that his kinsman the
Khalif would easily find some way of composing these
differences, and would moreover ingratiate himself with the
Medinese nobles by his affable manners and well-known
generosity—had suggested that a mission should be sent
to Tiberias, and his advice had been taken. But although
actuated by the best intentions, the Governor had committed
not merely an act of imprudence, but an unpardonable

[1] See *History of the Caliphs*, by *Jalál'uddín a's Suyúti*, transl. by Major H. S.
Jarrett, Calcutta (1881), p. 213.

[2] Ma'kil; see p. 58 *infra*.

[3] "This prejudice extends all over the East: the Sanscrit saying is 'Kvachit
kaná bhaveta sádhus'—now and then a monocular is honest. The left eye is the
worst." Burton, *Arabian Nights* (1887), iv. 194.

blunder. Could he have been blind to the fact that the nobles of Medina wished for nothing better than to be able to recount, as eye-witnesses, his cousin's impieties, in order to excite their fellow-citizens to revolt? Instead of suggesting a visit to the Khalif's court, it should have been his policy to thwart it at all costs.

The event might have been easily foreseen. Yazîd had, it is true, offered a hospitality to the deputies which was both cordial and courteous; he had treated them with lavish generosity; he had presented the Helper 'Abdallah—the son of Handhala, a noble and valiant warrior who had fallen at Ohod fighting for Mohammed—with a hundred thousand pieces of silver; and he had given ten or twenty thousand pieces to each of the other deputies, according to their rank;[1] but nevertheless, since Yazîd was no respecter of persons and his court was not a pattern of temperance and propriety, his licentious habits, added to his liking for the Bedawin—who, it must be admitted, were little better than brigands on occasion—had greatly scandalized the austere and puritanical citizens, natural enemies of the Sons of the Desert.[2]

Upon their return to Medina, the deputies, far from extenuating the Khalif's impieties, made disclosures which perhaps exaggerated what they had seen or heard. Their denunciations, glowing with pious wrath, made, indeed, so great an impression on hearts already disposed to believe unquestioningly the worst that could be reported of Yazîd, that an extraordinary scene was enacted in the Mosque. When the Medinese were assembled, one of the deputies shouted, " I cast off Yazîd as I cast off this turban!" and, so saying, he dashed his head-dress to the ground. " Yazîd has loaded me with gifts," he continued, " I admit it: but he is a drunkard and an enemy of God!" " As for me," cried another, " I cast off Yazîd as I cast off my sandal!" A third broke in with, " I cast him off as I cast off this cloak!" A fourth added, " I cast him off as I do this shoe!" The rest followed their example, and soon the unusual spectacle was seen of a mosque everywhere littered with turbans, cloaks, shoes, and sandals. Having in this fashion decreed the deposition of Yazîd, the Medinese next

[1] Weil, i. 326. The tenth deputy, Mundhir ibn Zobair, did not accompany his colleagues on their return to Medina, for he had obtained permission from Yazîd to visit 'Irâk.

[2] For an account of Yazid, see *History of the Caliphs, by Jalál'uddín a's Suyúti,* transl. by Major H. S. Jarrett, Calcutta (1881), pp. 209–215.

determined to expel from the city all the Omayyads to be found therein. The latter were accordingly ordered to depart without delay, but not until they had made oath not to aid any soldiers that might be marching against the city, but, on the contrary, to repel them—or, if this were beyond their power, not to re-enter the city with the Syrian troops. 'Othmân, the Governor, tried unsuccessfully to make the rebels realize the danger they would incur if they expelled him. " Ere long," he said, " a mighty army will come here to overwhelm you, and then you would have good reason to congratulate yourselves if you could plead that, at least, you had not driven out your Governor. Wait until you have gained the victory before dismissing me. I give you this advice for your own sake and not for mine; I would fain prevent, if possible, the shedding of your blood." Far from yielding, however, to these words of wisdom, the Medinese loaded the Governor, as well as the Khalif, with curses. " We shall begin with thee," they cried, " and the expulsion of thy kinsfolk will soon follow thine own !" The Omayyads were infuriated. " What a wicked business is this ! And what a detestable religion !" cried Merwân, who had been successively the Khalif 'Othmân's Minister and Governor of Medina, but who, notwithstanding, now found no small difficulty in finding some one to whom he could entrust his wife and children. But circumstances were too strong for the Omayyads. Having taken the prescribed oath they set out, followed by the derisive shouts of the populace, some of whom even cast stones at them, while a freedman, Horaith the Leaper—so called because he had been deprived of one foot by a former Governor, and made his way in a series of hops—goaded without intermission the animals on which rode the luckless exiles, driven like the vilest criminals from the city where they had so long held sway. At last the exiles reached Dhû Khoshob, where they were to await further orders.

Their first care was to send a messenger to Yazîd with tidings of their misfortunes and a request for help. This became known to the Medinese. Fifty horsemen immediately set out to chase the Omayyads from their halting-place. " The Leaper " did not fail to take advantage of this new opportunity of glutting his revenge. Aided by one of the Beni Hazm (a family of Helpers who had abetted the murder of the Khalif 'Othmân by placing their house at the disposal of the rebels), he goaded Merwân's camel so sharply that it was on the point of throwing its rider. Half in fear and half in pity, Merwân dismounted, and cried to the animal, "Go thy way, and save thyself!" When they reached a hamlet named Sowaida,[1] Merwân met one of his clients,[2] who lived there and who asked him to share his meal. "The Leaper and his worthy comrades will not suffer me to stay," replied Merwân; "Please heaven, we shall one day have this fellow in our power, and then it will not be our fault if his hand does not share the fate of his foot!" On reaching Wadi 'l-kura[3] the Omayyads were at last allowed to rest.

In the meantime, discord was on the point of breaking out among the Medinese themselves. So long as there was only a question of expelling the Omayyads, of abusing them and maltreating them, perfect unanimity reigned among the inhabitants of the city, but matters were otherwise when it came to electing a new Khalif. The Kuraish would not have a Helper, and the Helpers would not have a Kurashite. However, as the necessity of concord was manifest, it was resolved to postpone this burning question, and to choose provisional chiefs. A new Khalif could be elected after Yazîd had been dethroned. The messenger sent by the Omayyads[4] duly informed the Khalif of what had occurred. When Yazîd heard the news, he was more surprised and indignant at the feebleness of his kinsmen than incensed against the rebels.

"Could not the Omayyads have mustered a thousand men by calling up their freedmen?" he asked.

"Certainly," replied the messenger, "they could have mustered three thousand without difficulty."

"Yet with such considerable forces they did not even attempt to hold out against the rebels for an hour!"

"The insurgents were too numerous; resistance would have been futile."

Had Yazîd been influenced solely by just indignation against men who had rebelled after accepting large sums from him without scruple, he would have forthwith despatched an army to chastise them; but he still wished,

---

[1] About 60 miles N.W. of Medina.
[2] A client was a manumitted slave, who, by adoption, might become an actual member of his master's clan.
[3] 20 miles N. of Sowaida. (For further details concerning "Horaith Saltator" see *Aghânî*, pp. 234–5).
[4] His name was Habib.

if possible, to avoid embroiling himself with the fanatics.
Perhaps he remembered the saying of the Prophet : "The
curse of God, of angels and of men will rest upon him who
draws the sword against the Medinese!" At any rate, for
the second time he showed a moderation which was all the
more remarkable since it was not characteristic. Still
wishing, therefore, to adopt mild measures, he sent the
Helper Nu'mân, son of Bashîr, on a mission to Medina. It
was all in vain. The Helpers, it is true, did not remain
altogether insensible to the prudent advice of their fellow-
tribesman, who pointed out that they were far too weak,
and too few in numbers, to be able to resist the armies of
Syria; but the Kuraish were all for war, and their chief,
'Abdallah, son of Motî, exclaimed to Nu'mân, "Begone!
for thou art come only to destroy the amity which, thanks
be to God, at present reigns amongst us!" "Thou art
bold enough, and brave enough just now," replied Nu'mân,
"but I know well what thou wilt do when the army of
Syria is at the gates of Medina! Then thou wilt flee to
Mecca mounted on thy swiftest mule, and thou wilt
abandon to their fate these luckless Helpers, whose throats
will be cut in the streets, in the mosques, and at the
thresholds of their own homes!"

At last, seeing the uselessness of all his efforts, Nu'mân
returned to Yazîd, and related to him the ill-success of his
mission.

"Be it so, then," replied the Khalif: "I must needs
trample them beneath the hoofs of my Syrian cavalry."

The expeditionary force, ten thousand strong, to be sent
to Hijâz was intended to reduce the other holy city, Mecca,
as well as Medina. Since the general to whom Yazîd had
entrusted its command had just died, the other generals,
eager to destroy once for all the upstart aristocrats, were
contending for the honour of taking his place.[1] Yazîd had
not definitely decided which of the rival candidates he would
select, when a man of ripe experience in warfare entered the
lists. This was none other than the one-eyed wayfarer
whom we saw upon the highway near Tiberias.

There was perhaps no better representative of days gone
by and the old pagan principles than the veteran warrior

[1] Certain ecclesiastical historians have asserted that two of the generals—
'Obaidallah ibn Ziyâd, and 'Amr ibn Sa'îd—refused, from religious scruples, to
attack the holy cities. The early chroniclers know nothing of this. On the other
hand, both these generals had personal grievances against Yazîd; cf. Weil, i. 330.

Moslim, son of 'Okba, of the tribe of Muzaina.[1]   On him
there rested not even the shadow of the Mohammedan faith ;
all that Musulmans held sacred was naught in his eyes.
Mu'âwiya knew his sentiments, and appreciated them ; he
had recommended him to his son as the most suitable man
to undertake the subjugation of the Medinese in the event
of their revolting.   If, however, Moslim had no faith in the
divine mission of Mohammed, he believed none the less
firmly in the superstitions of Paganism—in prophetic dreams,
and in mysterious words proceeding from the *gharkad*,[2] a
species of large thorn-bush which in the days of paganism
was held in certain parts of Arabia to be oracular.   This
mental trait of Moslim's became manifest when, presenting
himself before Yazîd, he said : " Any other man whom you
might send against Medina would fail.   I alone can conquer.
In a dream I saw a thorn-bush, and from it a voice proceeded
saying, ' By the hand of Moslim.'   Then I drew nigh to the
place whence the voice proceeded, and I heard these words :
' It is thou who shalt avenge 'Othmân upon the men of Medina,
his murderers ! ' "   Convinced that Ibn 'Okba was the man
whom he needed, Yazîd accepted him as general, and gave
him his orders as follows : " Before attacking the Medinese,
grant them three days in which to surrender ; if they refuse
to submit, and you gain the victory, give the city up to
pillage for three days ; all the money, food and arms which
your soldiers find therein shall be theirs.   Then make the
Medinese swear to be my bondsmen, and behead every man
who refuses to take the oath."

   The army—which included Ibn Idhâh, chief of the
Ash'arites, whose conversation with the son of Zubair has
been related—arrived without casualties at Wadi 'l-Kura,
where the Omayyads who had been expelled from Medina
had taken up their abode.   Moslim ordered them to be
brought before him, one after the other, in order to consult
them as to the best means of making himself master of the
city.   A son of the Khalif 'Othmân refused to violate the
oath which the Medinese had compelled him to take.   " If
thou wert not 'Othmân's son," cried the fiery Moslim, " I
would have thee beheaded ; and, while I spare thy life, I
will not spare a single other Kurashite who refuseth me his
aid and his advice."   Merwân's turn came.   He, too, was

---

[1] 'Okba was the founder of Kairwan (*c.* A.D. 677).
[2] The cemetery selected by Mohammed near Medina was known as the Bakî,
al-Gharkad.

assailed by scruples of conscience; on the other hand, he
feared for his life, for with Moslim it was " a word and a
blow "—besides, the ex-minister's hatred of the Medinese
was too bitter for him to lose an opportunity of gratifying
it.   Fortunately, it occurred to Merwân that it was not impossible to compromise with heaven, and that an oath might
be broken in effect without being violated in the letter.
He accordingly gave full instructions to his son, 'Abd al-
Malik, who had not taken the oath.   " Precede me," he
added; "perchance Moslim will ask me no questions when
he hath heard what thou hast to say."   'Abd al-Malik, having been ushered before the general, counselled him to advance his troops to the nearest groves of palm-trees, to
bivouac there for the night, and on the following morning
to march to Harra—which lay to the east of Medina—so
that the Medinese, who would not fail to sally forth to the
attack, might have the sun in their eyes.   ' Abd al-Malik
also hinted to Moslim that his father would contrive to
communicate with certain Medinese who, perhaps, when the
battle had begun, would betray their fellow-citizens.   Well
satisfied with what he had just heard, Moslim remarked
with a sneer, " Of a truth, an estimable man—thy father ! "
and, without requiring Merwân to commit himself personally,
he carefully followed 'Abd al-Malik's counsels, encamped
to the east of Medina on the high-road leading to Kûfa, and
informed the Medinese that he would give them a respite of
three days in which to bethink themselves.   The three days
elapsed, and the Medinese sent word that they refused to
surrender.   As Merwân had foreseen, the citizens, instead of
awaiting the attack of the enemy behind their walls, which
they had fortified as far as possible, sallied forth to meet
them (Aug. 26, 685), divided into four columns comprising
three different classes of citizens.

The Refugees were under the command of Ma'kil, son of
Sinân, a Companion of Mohammed, who at the head of his
tribe—the Ashja'—had assisted at the capture of Mecca, and
who must have been highly esteemed at Medina, since the
Refugees had conferred the command upon him although he
was not of their tribe.   Those of the Kuraish who were not
included among the Refugees, but who had at different times,
after the capture of Mecca, taken up their abode at Medina,
were divided into two detachments, one of which was commanded by 'Abdallah, the son of Motî, and the other by a
Companion of the Prophet.   The fourth, and largest column,

that of the Helpers, was led by 'Abdallah, son of Handhala.
In profound silence the Medinese set out towards Harra,
where the impious pagans whom they were about to attack
were drawn up. The general of the Syrian army was
dangerously ill; nevertheless he caused himself to be borne
on a chair to a position a little in front of the ranks, and entrusting his banner to a gallant Greek page, he cried to his
soldiers: "Arabs of Syria! now show that you can defend
your general! Set on!"

The battle began. The Syrians fell upon the foe with
such impetuosity that three Medinese divisions—those,
namely, of the Refugees and the Kuraish—gave way; but
the fourth—that of the Helpers—drove back the Syrians
and compelled them to rally round their commander.

On both sides the battle was stubbornly contested, when
the intrepid Fadl, who commanded a troop of twenty horse
under the banner of 'Abdallah, son of Handhala, said to
his chief: " Put the whole of the cavalry under my orders,
and I will strive to cut my way through to Moslim. If
I succeed either he or I will fall!" 'Abdallah consented,
and Fadl charged so vigorously that the Syrians again fell
back. " One more such gallant onset, dear friends!" he
cried, " and, by Allah, if I descry the General, for one
of us this day will be the last! Forget not that victory
is to the brave!" The cavalry renewed their attack with
redoubled courage, broke the ranks of the Syrian horse, and
forced their way to the spot where Ibn 'Okba sat. Five
hundred foot-soldiers defended him with lowered lances,
but Fadl, hewing a way for himself with his sword, urged
his horse straight towards Moslim's banner, aimed at the
page who bore it a blow which cleft both helmet and skull,
and cried, " By the Lord of the Ka'ba, I have slain the
tyrant!" "Thou liest," cried Moslim, who, ill as he was,
instantly seized the banner and reanimated the Syrians by
his words and his example. Fadl, covered with wounds,
fell dead by his enemy's side.

At the very moment when the Medinese saw the divisions
under Ibn Idhâh and the rest preparing to charge them
once more, they heard the walls of the city resounding with
the shout of victory—the cry "God is great!" They had
been betrayed. Merwân had kept his word to Moslim.
Seduced by glittering promises, the Beni Hâritha, a family
numbered among the Helpers, had by stealth admitted
Syrian soldiers into the town. It lay in the enemy's power;

all was lost; the Medinese found themselves between hammer and anvil. The greater number sought to rush back into the town to save the women and children; some, among whom was 'Abdallah, son of Moti, fled in the direction of Mecca; but 'Abdallah, son of Handhala, resolving not to survive the fatal day, cried to his clansmen: "The victory rests with the foe! In less than an hour all will be over. Pious Musulmans—men of a city which gave asylum to the Prophet—one day all of us must die, and the fairest death is that of a martyr. Let us then perish to-day! To-day God giveth us the opportunity of dying in a sacred cause!"

The Syrian arrows began to rain on them from all sides, and 'Abdallah once more shouted, "Those who would straightway enter Paradise, follow my banner!" All followed him and fought with the strength of despair, resolved to sell their lives dearly. 'Abdallah urged his sons, one after the other, into the thickest of the fray, and saw them all perish. Whilst Moslim had promised gold to every man who brought him the head of an enemy, 'Abdallah himself made heads fall on the right hand and on the left, and the firm belief that a much more terrible fate awaited his victims beyond the grave yielded him a savage joy. As was the wont of the Arabs, he chanted verses as he fought. They breathed the spirit of the fanatic who clings to his faith and revels in hatred. "Thou diest," he cried to every victim, "thou diest, but thy sins outlive thee! Allah has told us: in His Book he hath said it, Hell is prepared for the unbelievers!" At last he was overcome. His half-brother fell mortally wounded at his side. "Since I die by the swords of these men," he cried, "I am surer of Paradise than if I had fallen at the hands of the pagan Dailamites!"[1] These were his last words. The carnage was horrible: among the slain were seven hundred persons who knew the Koran by rote,[2] and eighty who were clothed in sanctity as Companions of Mohammed.[3] None of the venerable elders who had fought at Badr, where the Prophet gained his first victory over the Meccans, survived this fatal day. The exulting victors entered the city after their general had given them permission to sack it for three consecutive

---

[1] See C. Huart, *Arabic Literature* (1903), p. 59.

[2] Such persons now have the title of *Hâfiz*.

[3] The original "Companions," *As-hâb;* their followers were known as *Tâbi'ûn,* or "Successors."

days. Hampered by their horses, the cavalry galloped to the
Mosque to stable them there.   At that moment it contained a solitary Medinese, Sa'îd, son of Mosaiyab, the most
learned theologian of his day.   He saw the Syrians burst
into the Mosque, and tether their horses in the space between the chair of Mohammed and his tomb—a sacred
spot which the Prophet had called the Garden of Paradise.[1]
At the sight of this horrible sacrilege, Sa'îd, believing the
Universe to be threatened by some dread calamity, remained
motionless and plunged in stupor.   " Behold this imbecile
doctor!" cried the Syrians scornfully; but, in their eagerness to begin pillaging, they did him no hurt.   None else was
spared.   The children were carried away as slaves or were
massacred.   The women were violated, and later there were
seen a thousand wretched mothers of as many outcasts—
branded for ever as " Children of Harra." [2]

Among the prisoners was Ma'kil, son of Sinân.   He
was tortured by thirst, and bitterly bewailed his condition.
Moslim sent for him, and received him with as benevolent
an aspect as it was possible for him to assume.   " Thou
thirstest, son of Sinân, dost thou not?" he asked.   " Yes,
General."   " Give him to drink of this wine which the
Khalif has supplied us with," said Moslim to one of his
soldiers.   The order was obeyed, and Ma'kil drank.   " Thy
thirst is ended?" inquired Moslim.   " My thirst is ended."
" Thou sayest well!" said the General, with a sudden change
of voice and expression: " thou hast drunk for the last time !
Prepare to die."   The old man threw himself upon his
knees and begged for mercy.   " Who art thou, to hope for
mercy?   Did I not pass thee on the road near Tiberias,
that night when thou settedst out for Medina with the
other deputies?   Was it not thou whom I heard loading
Yazîd with insults ?   Was it not thou whom I heard saying:
' As soon as we have reached Medina let us solemnly make
oath no longer to obey this profligate and son of a profligate; and thereafter we should do well to render homage
to the son of a Refugee'?   Know then, that at that
moment I swore that if ever again I encountered thee, and
had thee in my power, I would slay thee.   Before God, I
will keep my oath !   Let this man be put to death!"   The
order was instantly obeyed.

When the pillage was at an end, those Medinese who
still remained in the city—for most of the inhabitants had

[1] See Muir, *Mohammad* (1912), p. 198.   [2] See H. S. Jarrett, *op. cit.*, p. 213.

MS-D

already sought safety in flight—were called upon to take
an oath to Yazîd. It was, however, far different from the
ordinary oath — that, namely, by which obedience was
vowed to the Khalif, to the Koran, and to the laws of
Mohammed. The Medinese were required to swear to be
the slaves of Yazîd, "slaves whom he could enfranchise or
sell at his good pleasure"—thus ran the formula; they
were compelled to admit his absolute power over all that
they possessed—their wives, their children, even life itself.
The penalty of death awaited those who refused to take
this dreadful oath. Two Kurashites, however, boldly
declared that they would only take the oath in its accustomed form. Moslim forthwith ordered them to be beheaded.
Merwân, himself a Kurashite, ventured to demur to this
sentence, but Moslim, striking his belly with his staff, said
roughly: "By heaven, if thou hadst said what these wretches
have dared to say, thy head would have fallen." Nevertheless, Merwân once more ventured to plead for another
"non-juror" who was a connection of his. The Syrian
general refused to yield. But the case was altered when a
Kurashite whose mother belonged to the tribe of Kinda
refused the oath; for when one of the chiefs of the Syrian
forces who belonged to the Sakûn (a branch of the tribe
of Kinda) cried, "Our sister's son cannot take such an
oath!" Moslim excused him.

The Arabs of Syria had settled an old score with the
sons of the fanatical sectaries who had deluged Arabia with
their fathers' blood. The old nobility had wiped out the
upstarts. Yazîd, as representative of the earlier Meccan
aristocracy, had avenged the murder of the Khalif 'Othmân
and the defeats which the Medinese—although then fighting
under Mohammed's banner—had inflicted upon his grandfather. The reaction of pagan principles against orthodoxy was cruel, terrible, and inexorable. The Helpers
never recovered from this deadly blow; their power was
broken for ever. Their almost deserted city long remained
abandoned to dogs, and the adjacent region to antelopes;
for most of the inhabitants, seeking new homes and a
happier lot in a distant land, departed to join the army of
Africa. Those who remained were much to be pitied; the
Omayyads let slip no opportunity of crushing them beneath
the weight of their disdain, of showing their contumely and
implacable hatred, and of overwhelming them with bitter
mortifications.

Ten years after the battle of Harra, Hajjâj, Governor of the province, caused many of the sainted old men who had been Companions of Mohammed to be branded. In his eyes every Medinese was a murderer of 'Othmân, as if that crime—even supposing the Medinese to have been more implicated in it than they were—had not been sufficiently atoned for by the slaughter at Harra and the sack of Medina! Hajjâj is reported to have cried, on quitting the town, "God be praised, in that he has permitted me to depart from this the vilest of all cities, which hath ever requited the favours of the Khalif with treachery and rebellion! By Allah, if my sovereign had not urged me in all his letters to spare these miscreants, I would have razed their town and laid them groaning around the Prophet's seat!" When these words were reported to one of the old men whom Hajjâj had dishonoured, he said, "A dreadful punishment awaits him in the next life! His words are worthy of Pharaoh!"

Alas, the belief that their oppressors would be tormented in eternal flames was henceforth the sole hope and consolation of these unhappy men. And in this consolation they indulged themselves freely. Prophecies by the Companions of Mohammed, prophecies by Mohammed himself, miracles worked on their behalf—all these they accepted with eager and insatiable credulity. The theologian Sa'îd, who had been present in the Mosque when the Syrian horsemen turned it into a stable, related to all who would listen to him, how that when he was left alone in the holy place, he heard a voice proceeding from Mohammed's tomb uttering solemn words prophetic of that hour. In the formidable Moslim, the man of Muzaina, the Medinese saw the most hideous monster that the earth had ever beheld; they believed that he would find no rival until the last days— and then in the person of another man of his own tribe: they used to relate that the Prophet had declared: "The last to rise at the resurrection will be two men of the Muzaina. They will find the earth uninhabited. They will come to Medina, where they will meet with naught but wild deer. Thereupon two angels will descend from heaven and dash them prone upon the ground; then in this posture they will drag them to the place where all mankind is assembled."

Oppressed, exposed to every outrage, trampled under foot, the only course which seemed left to the Medinese was to follow the example set by their fellow-citizens who had been enrolled in the army of Africa. This they did. From Africa they proceeded to Spain. Almost all the descendants of the Helpers were included in the army with which Mûsâ crossed the Straits.[1] In Spain, they settled for the most part in the West and East, where their tribe became the most numerous of all. Medina knows them no more. In the thirteenth century a traveller who visited that city was induced by curiosity to inquire whether any descendants of the Helpers still remained there. A man and a woman were alone pointed out to him, both of an advanced age.

It is permissible, therefore, to be sceptical with regard to the alleged illustrious origin of the few poor families,[2] living in the suburbs of Medina, who as late as last century claimed descent from the Helpers.

But even in Spain the Helpers were not sheltered from the hatred of the Syrian Arabs. We shall see later the strife bursting out afresh upon the banks of the Guadalquiver when Spain was under the governorship of a Kurashite, who in the disastrous battle of Harra had fought in the ranks of the Medinese and after their defeat had fled to join the army of Africa.

But at present our attention must be directed to a conflict of a different nature, which was also perpetuated in the Spanish Peninsula. In relating this we shall have occasion to refer once again to 'Abdallah, son of Zubair, and it will become apparent that the fate of this other Companion of Mohammed was no less unhappy than that of the men of Medina.

---

[1] A.D. 712.

[2] Twelve at the date of Burckhardt's visit (1814) ; see *Travels in Arabia*, ii. 237. Burton gives the number as four, in 1853 (*Pilgrimage*, ii. 254).

[AUTHORITIES: Ibn Khaldûn, ii. 169–70; Samhûdî, ff. 30–2; *Raihân*, ff. 200–1 ; Fâkihî, f. 400; Ibn al-Athîr, iii. 78–9 ; iv. 17 ; Nawawî, p. 567 : Ibn Kutaiba, pp. 152, 201; Makkarî, i. 187 ; *Aghânî*, i. pp. 18–21.]

CHAPTER VI

YEMENITES AND MA'ADDITES

WITH the exception of antagonisms arising from the clash of those fundamental principles which ever have been, and ever will be, in dispute amongst mankind, no form of strife has been more persistent, whether in Europe or Asia, among Moslems or Christians, than that resulting from racial antipathies. Such antipathies, perpetuated through centuries, long survive all political, social, and religious revolutions.

We have already had occasion to mention, incidentally, that the Arab race comprised two distinct and mutually hostile branches, and we now propose to give greater precision to this statement, and to point out the far-reaching consequences of the fact in some detail.

In accordance with the Oriental custom of tracing the origin of a nation to an eponymous personage, the most ancient of the two branches claimed descent from a certain Kahtân, whom the Arabs, when they became acquainted with the Hebrew Scriptures, identified with Joktan, one of the descendants of Shem according to Genesis.[1] Kahtân's posterity, they asserted, had invaded Southern Arabia many centuries before the Christian Era, and subjugated the people, of uncertain origin, who then inhabited that region.

The Kahtânids were usually called Yemenites—a name borrowed from that of the most flourishing province of the South—and as such we shall henceforth speak of them.

The other race, who claimed as their ancestor 'Adnân, a descendant of Ishmael, inhabited the more northerly districts comprising Hijâz—a province extending from Palestine to Yemen, in which both Mecca and Medina are situated—and Nejd, that vast plateau, broken by a few undulations, which forms Central Arabia. These people are variously called Ma'addites, Nizârites, Mudarites, and Kaisites—names which are applied to certain subdivisions as well

---

[1] *Gen.* x. 25.

as to the whole race, Kais having been a descendant of Mudar, the son of Nizâr, the son of Ma'add. We shall term them Ma'addites.

European history shows us nothing analogous to the mutual hatred—sometimes stifled, more often inflamed— existing between these two races, ever ready to fly at each other's throats on the most trivial pretexts. The district of Damascus, for instance, was for two years the scene of relentless warfare because a Ma'addite had plucked a melon growing in a Yemenite's garden;[1] and in Murcia blood flowed in torrents for seven years because a Ma'addite, as he passed a Yemenite's field, had chanced thoughtlessly to tear off a vine-leaf. Strong racial antipathies have from time to time existed in Europe, but they have at any rate arisen as a natural consequence of the relations between victors and conquered. In Arabia, on the other hand, neither race could claim sway over the other. It is true that in days of old the Ma'addites of Nejd had recognised the King of Yemen as their overlord and had paid him tribute; but they had done this of their own free will, since a ruler of some kind had become a necessity if these fanatical hordes were to be preserved from self-destruction, while a chieftain chosen from any one of their own clans would be obeyed by none of the rest. Whenever these Ma'addite tribes, after having been temporarily united under a chief of their own choice, reasserted their independence—as frequently happened—civil war soon compelled them to seek another ruler. Being thus driven to make choice between anarchy and foreign domination, the tribal chiefs, after a long inter-necine struggle, took counsel together. "There is nothing left for us to do," they agreed, "but once more to place the King of Yemen over us: let us pay him a tribute of sheep and camels, and he shall in return prevent the strong from oppressing the weak."[2] In later years, when Yemen had been conquered by the Abyssinians, the Ma'addites of Nejd were only too glad to confer on another prince of Yemenite origin—the King of Hîra—the mild authority which they had formerly granted to the King of Yemen. But there is a wide gulf between purely spontaneous submission such as this, and subjection to a foreign people.

In Europe diversity of language and customs has before now raised an insurmountable barrier between two races whom conquest has forcibly brought together within

---

[1] Abû 'l-Fidâ, ii. 64.   [2] Caussin, ii. 285.

the same territory. But this was not the case in the Moslem Empire. Long before Mohammed's days, the Yemenite or Himyaritic dialect,[1] as it is called—a mixture of Arabic with the language of conquered tribes—had given place to pure Arabic, as spoken by the Ma'addites, who had acquired in some sort an intellectual pre-eminence. Save for a few dialectal divergences, the two races, therefore, spoke the same tongue, and it appears that in the Moslem armies a Ma'addite never had any difficulty in understanding a Yemenite.[2] They had, moreover, the same predilections and customs, and the great majority of both races were nomads. Finally, when they both embraced Islamism they had the same religion. In short, the difference between them was much less appreciable than that which existed between one Teutonic tribe and another when the barbarians invaded the Roman Empire. Nevertheless, though the reasons which account for racial antipathy in Europe did not exist in the East, such antipathy there evinced a tenacity unknown to Western lands. For three or four hundred years ancestral hostility has disappeared in Europe, but among the Bedawin the blood-feud has endured for twenty-five centuries ; it can be traced back to the earliest historical times, and is far from extinct to-day. " Ancestral enmity," writes an ancient poet, " is a heritage from our forefathers, and while their descendants exist, it will abide." Never, moreover, in Europe has this animosity led to such atrocities as in the East: among our ancestors it never stifled the most tender and sacred sentiments of nature : we do not hear of a son despising and hating his mother on the sole ground that she did not belong to his father's stock. A Yemenite who was making the ceremonial circuit of the Ka'ba at Mecca was asked why, though he prayed for his father, he never prayed for his mother. " For my mother ! " cried the Yemenite disdainfully, " How could I pray for her ? She is a daughter of Ma'add ! "

Of this mutual hatred, handed down from generation to generation in spite of community of language, laws, customs, modes of thought, religion, and, to some extent, of origin—since both races were Semitic—we can only say that its causes are inexplicable, but that " it is in the blood " :

[1] Known only from inscriptions, knowledge of which has been much extended during the last forty years.
[2] In Mahra (the extreme S.E. of Arabia) the ancient tongue, however, lingered, and was scarcely intelligible to other Arabs.

probably the Arabs of the seventh century would have been as little able to give an account of its origin, as are the Yemenites who to-day wander over the deserts of the province of Jerusalem, and who, when asked by travellers why they are sworn foes of the Kaisites (Ma'addites), of the province of Hebron, reply that all they know about the matter is that the mutual hatred has existed from time immemorial.[1] Islamism, far from diminishing this instinctive aversion, gave it a strength and keenness which it had never reached before.   While glaring at one another defiantly, Yemenites and Ma'addites were compelled henceforth to fight beneath the same banner, to live side by side, to share the fruits of victory; and this close association and daily intercourse seemed but to engender fresh disputes and affrays.   The feud, indeed, was destined to assume an interest and importance which it did not possess when it was confined to an almost unknown corner of Asia.   In the years to come it would drench Spain and Sicily, the deserts of Atlas and the banks of the Ganges, with blood.   Ultimately this strange antipathy determined the fate, not only of conquered nations, but of the Latin and Teutonic races as a whole, for it alone arrested the Moslems in their conquering path at the moment when they menaced France and all Western Europe.

Although throughout the whole extent of the Musulman Empire the two races were at strife, that empire was so vast, and co-operation between tribes was so imperfect, that no widespread conflict broke out directed towards predetermined ends.   Every province had its own intestine war, and the names of the opposing forces, borrowed from those of the two tribes who happened to be locally the most numerous, everywhere differed.   In Khorasan, for instance, the Yemenites were called Azdites, and the Ma'addites, Temîmites, because the tribes of Azd and Temîm were respectively the most important.   In Syria—the province with which we shall be principally concerned—the two parties were the Kelbites and the Kaisites; the former, of Yemenite origin, formed the majority of the Arab population, for under the Khalifate of Abû Bakr and 'Omar, when most of the Yemenite tribes migrated to Syria, the Ma'addites preferred to settle in 'Irâk.

[1] "No person of whom we inquired, could tell the origin or nature of this distinction; except that it goes back beyond the memory of man and does not now pertain in any degree to religious worship or doctrine." E. Robinson, *Biblical Researches in Palestine* (1867), ii. 17–18.

Kelbites and Kaisites were equally attached to Mu'âwiya, whose wise and prudent policy established a certain equilibrium between them, and gained him the affection of both. He could not, however, notwithstanding his well-devised measures, prevent their mutual hatred from blazing up at times; during his reign the Kelbites and the Fezâra (a Kaisite tribe) actually fought a pitched battle at Banât-Kain,[1] and later, the Kaisites raised difficulties when Mu'âwiya wished them to acknowledge Yazîd as his successor, on the ground that his mother was a Kelbite; for she was daughter of Mâlik ibn Bahdal, chief of the tribe,[2] and in the eyes of the Kaisites, Yazîd, brought up amongst his mother's folk in the desert of Semâwa, was a Kelbite simply, and not an Omayyad. The mode in which Mu'âwiya overcame their opposition is not known; at any rate the Kaisites ultimately recognised Yazîd as heir presumptive to the throne, and remained loyal to him throughout his reign. This lasted but three years. He died in November 683, two months and a half after the battle of Harra, at the early age of thirty-eight. At his death the vast empire found itself without a master. It was not that Yazîd died leaving no son; he left several; but the Khalifate was elective and not hereditary. This important principle had not been laid down by Mohammed—who had come to no decision on the point—but by the Khalif 'Omar, who was not, like the Prophet, wholly lacking in political foresight, and who wielded undisputed authority as legislator. He it was who declared, in an allocution pronounced in the Mosque at Medina, that "if any man shall be proclaimed sovereign, without the suffrages of all Islam, such nomination shall be null and void."[3] It is true that application of this principle had always been evaded, but though Yazîd himself had not been popularly elected, his father had at least taken the precaution to cause allegiance to be sworn to him as successor to the throne. Yazîd, however, had not taken this step ; death claimed him in the prime of life, and his eldest son—named Mu'âwiya after his grandfather—had thus no real right to the Khalifate. It is probable, nevertheless, that he would have succeeded in gaining recognition, if the Syrians, the effective makers of Khalifs at this epoch, had agreed in supporting him. But they did not agree, and it was rumoured that Mu'âwiya himself had no hanker-

---

[1] Wüstenfeld, *Tables généalogiques*, p. 265.
[2] See p. 43 *supra*.
[3] Cf. *Journal des savants* (1832), p. 542.

ings after sovereignty. This young man's true sentiments
are shrouded in profound mystery. If we are to believe
Moslem historians, Mu'âwiya resembled his father in no
respect : in his eyes, right was on the side of the Medinese ;
and when he heard of the victory of Harra, the sack of
Medina, and the death of the Companions of Mohammed,
he shed tears. But these historians, prejudiced by theological leanings, have sometimes falsified history, and
they are contradicted by an almost contemporary Spanish
chronicler, who, writing practically at the dictation of the
Syrians settled in Spain, declares that the young Mu'âwiya
was a counterpart of his father. Be this as it may, the
Kaisites would not bow down to a prince whose grandmother and mother were both Kelbites, nor would they
submit to the authority of the Kelbite, Hassân ibn Mâlik
ibn Bahdal, Governor of Palestine and the district of
Jordan, who had taken up the reins of government in his
great-nephew's name. The Kaisites everywhere assumed a
hostile attitude, and one of their chiefs, Zofar of the tribe
of Kilâb, raised the standard of revolt in the district of
Kinnisrîn, whence he expelled the Kelbite governor, Sa'îd
ibn Bahdal. Since it had become necessary to set up a
rival candidate, Zofar declared for 'Abdallah ibn Zubair—
in whose cause, however, the Kaisites took not the slightest
interest. The orthodox party hence gained a strange ally.
Since he was about to uphold the interests of the sons of
the Prophet's Companions, Zofar thought it his duty to
deliver an edifying harangue from the pulpit. But,
although a facile orator and poet, after the manner of the
pagan Arabs, he was unfortunately not well primed with
religious phrases, and was ill-fitted for an unctuous discourse.
He broke down in the midst of his first sentence, and his
brethren in arms shook with laughter.

Mu'âwiya II survived his father for forty days, or perhaps
for two or three months—the period is uncertain and unimportant. Anarchy followed. The provinces, weary of
being treated by the Syrians as conquered countries, threw
off the yoke. In 'Irâk, a Khalif or an Emir was chosen one
day and deposed the next. Ibn Bahdal had not made up
his mind whether to declare himself Khalif, or—seeing that
he would be acknowledged by none but the Kelbites—to
avow his readiness to obey any Omayyad chosen by the
people. But so small was any individual's chance of success
that it was not easy to find an Omayyad willing to come

forward as candidate. Walîd, grandson of Abû Sufyân and former Governor of Medina, had consented to do so, but while praying over the corpse of Mu'âwiya II he was stricken by pestilence and died. Ibn Bahdal would have liked to see Khâlid—brother of Mu'âwiya—Khalif, but since he was only sixteen, and the Arabs would tolerate none but an adult, the idea was impracticable. He accordingly approached 'Othmân,[1] but the latter, believing his family's cause a lost one, refused, and gave his support to the more fortunate Ibn Zubair, whose party was now daily increasing. In Syria all the Kaisites declared for him. Already supreme in Kinnisrîn, they soon became masters of Palestine, and the Governor of Emesa—Nu'mân ibn Bashîr, the Helper—also espoused Ibn Zubair's cause. Ibn Bahdal, on the other hand, could reckon only on Jordan, the least important of the five districts of Syria. There the people had sworn to obey him, on the single condition that he would not confer the Khalifate on any of Yazîd's sons, since they were too young. In Damascus, the most important district of all, the Governor, Dhahhâk, of the tribe of Fihr,[2] maintained neutrality. He could not, in fact, make up his mind. Formerly in command of the guard, he had been one of the most intimate confidants of Mu'âwiya I, and he could not countenance a Meccan candidate. But as a Ma'addite, he was loath to make common cause with the Kelbite chief: hence his irresolution. In order to test the intentions of the Governor and people of Damascus, Ibn Bahdal sent the former a letter to be read in the Mosque on a Friday. This letter was full of adulation of the Omayyads and invectives against Ibn Zubair; but Ibn Bahdal, fearing that the Governor would refuse to read it in public, took the precaution of entrusting a copy to the messenger, with the injunction that if Dhahhâk did not read the original to the Arabs of Damascus he was to read them the copy himself. It turned out as he had expected. On Friday, when Dhahhâk mounted the pulpit, he did not make the slightest reference to the letter which he had received. Thereupon Ibn Bahdal's messenger stood up and read it before the people. Scarcely had he made an end before shouts arose on all sides. " Ibn Bahdal's words are true ! " cried some ; " Nay ! he lieth ! " cried others. A prodigious tumult ensued, and the sacred

---

[1] Former Governor of Medina ; see p. 54.

[2] The Kurashites of the environs of Mecca, as opposed to those of the city.

precincts, which, as in all Moslem countries, served as a place
for political deliberations as well as religious ceremonies, rang
with the abuse levelled at one another by Kaisites and Kelbites.
At last Dhahhâk procured silence and brought the service
to a close, but as to his own opinions vouchsafed not a word.

Such was the situation in Syria when Moslim's soldiers
returned to their native country. But Ibn 'Okba no longer
led them. The events which had taken place in the meantime may be briefly narrated. After the capture of Medina,
Moslim, who was grievously ill at the time of the battle of
Harra, adhered no longer to the strict regimen imposed by
his physicians. " Now that I have chastised the rebels," he
said, " I can die content : and since I have slain 'Othmân's
murderers, Allah will pardon me my sins." When he
arrived with his army within three days' journey of Mecca,
and felt his end approaching, he sent for his general Husain,
who had been designated by Yazîd commander-in-chief in
the event of Moslim's death. Husain was of the tribe of
Sakûn and therefore, like Moslim, a Kelbite ; but the latter
despised him, for he doubted his ability and tenacity. Addressing Husain with that brutal candour which characterised
him, he blurted out : " Thou are about to succeed me, ass
that thou art ! I have no confidence in thee, but the Khalif's
will must be done. Hearken, however, to my advice : thou
hast need of it, for I know what thou art. Be on thy guard
against the wiles of the Kurashites, close thine ears to their
honeyed words, and remember that when thou arrivest before
Mecca thou hast but three things to do—fight valiantly,
take captive the inhabitants, and return to Syria." So saying, he breathed his last.

Husain in besieging Mecca behaved as though it were his
chief business to prove Moslim's prejudices against him to
be baseless. Far from being deficient in boldness, or from
allowing himself to be checked by religious scruples, he exceeded in sacrilege Moslim himself. His catapults first
rained huge stones upon the Ka'ba and smashed its columns :
then by his orders a Syrian horseman cast, during the night,
a torch fastened to a spear upon Ibn Zubair's tent, which
was pitched in the courtyard of the Mosque ; the tent
instantly caught fire, and—the flames spreading to the hangings of the temple—the holy Ka'ba, the most sacred of all
Mohammedan shrines, was burnt to the ground.[1]

[1] There are other traditions as to the cause of this fire ; the earliest and most
trustworthy authority, Al-Fâkihî, in his *History of Mecca* is here followed.

For their part, the Meccans—aided by a multitude of Nonconformists who, forgetting for the time their hatred of the orthodox, flocked enthusiastically to defend the sacred territory—sustained the siege with much courage, until tidings of Yazîd's death suddenly changed the whole aspect of affairs. To Ibn Zubair the news caused unspeakable joy: to Husain it was a thunderbolt. This general, cold, calculating and selfish—unlike Moslim, who had been devoted body and soul to the masters whom he served— was too well aware of the tension between parties in Syria not to foresee the outbreak of civil war, and being under no delusion with regard to the weakness of the Omayyads, it appeared to him that submission to the Meccan Khalif was the only remedy against anarchy, and the only means of safety both for his army, which was gravely compromised, and for himself, who was still more so. He therefore invited Ibn Zubair to an interview on the following night at a specified place. Ibn Zubair made his appearance, and Husain said to him in a whisper, inaudible to the Syrian bystanders :

" I am prepared to recognise thee as Khalif on condition that thou proclaimest a general amnesty, and exactest no vengeance for the blood shed at the siege of Mecca and the battle of Harra."

" Nay," replied Ibn Zubair, in a loud voice, " I should not rest content if I had slain ten of my enemies for each of my dead comrades ! "

" Cursed be he who henceforth regardeth thee as a man of sense," cried Husain. " I trusted in thy discretion ; but when I whisper to thee thou repliest in a loud voice ! I offer thee the Khalifate, and thou threatenest me with death ! "

Knowing that reconciliation with Ibn Zubair was henceforth impossible, Husain set out with his army for Syria. On the march he met Merwân. Returning to Medina after the battle of Harra, Merwân had again been expelled thence by Ibn Zubair's orders, and had proceeded to Damascus. There he found the cause of his family wellnigh desperate, and in an interview with Dhahhâk he undertook to visit Mecca and inform Ibn Zubair that the Syrians were ready to obey his orders. This seemed the best way of ingratiating himself with his former enemy. He was on his way from Damascus to Mecca when Husain met him. The General, after assuring Merwân that he did not recognise the Meccan claimant, declared that if the latter had the courage to raise the Omayyad banner he could count on his support. Merwân accepted the proposal, and they resolved to convoke a kind of Diet, at Jâbia, for the purpose of deliberating on the choice of a Khalif.

Ibn Bahdal and his Kelbites duly attended this assembly. Dhahhâk had also promised to be present, and to explain his recent conduct. He had indeed set out with his men, but on the way the Kaisites—persuaded that the Kelbites would vote for the candidate allied to their own tribe, Khâlid, younger brother of Mu'âwiya II—refused to go further. Dhahhâk therefore retraced his steps and encamped on the plain of Râhit, to the east of Damascus. The Kaisites realized that their quarrel with the Kelbites must be fought out before long, and the nearer the decisive day approached, the more clearly they saw the anomaly of acting in concert with the chief of the pietist party. As they had much more sympathy with Dhahhâk, former brother in arms of Mu'âwiya I, they said to him, "Why dost thou not declare thyself Khalif? Thou art as good a man as Ibn Bahdal or Ibn Zubair!" Flattered by these words, and only too glad to have the means of escape from his false position, Dhahhâk did not demur, and administered the oath of allegiance to the Kaisites.

The deliberations of the Kelbites at Jâbia lasted for no less than forty days. The Kaisites had judged rightly: Ibn Bahdal and his friends wished to make Khâlid Khalif, and Husain could not get his candidate Merwân accepted. In vain he exclaimed: "Our enemies put forward an old man: should we put forward one who is still almost a child?" The reply was that Merwân was too powerful. "If Merwân became Khalif," they said, "we should be his slaves: he hath ten sons, ten brothers, and ten nephews." Moreover, they looked upon him as a foreigner. The branch of the Omayyads to which Khâlid belonged was naturalised in Syria, but Merwân and his family had always resided in Medina. Ibn Bahdal and his friends, however, at length yielded; they accepted Merwân, but impressed upon him the fact that they were showing him a great favour in granting him the Khalifate, and they added hard and humiliating conditions. Merwân had to engage solemnly to confer upon Kelbites all the more important posts, to govern in accordance with their advice, and to pay them a considerable sum annually.[1]

Ibn Bahdal further stipulated that the youthful Khâlid should be Merwân's successor, and that in the meanwhile he should be Governor of Emesa. All having been settled, one of the chiefs of the tribe of Sakûn, Mâlik son of Hubaira, a keen partisan of Khâlid, said to Merwân with an arrogant and threatening air : " We shall not take the oath to thee which is properly taken to a Khalif, as successor of the Prophet, for in fighting under thy banner we have in view only this world's goods. If thou treatest us well, as did Mu'âwiya and Yazîd, we will aid thee; if not, thou wilt find to thy cost that we have no more esteem for thee than for any other Kurashite."

The Diet of Jâbia having closed, at the end of June, 684—more than seven months after Yazîd's death—Merwân, accompanied by the Kelbites, Ghassânids, Saksakites, Sakû-nites, and other Yemenite tribes, marched against Dhahhâk, to whom the three governors who sided with him had sent contingents. Zofar commanded in person the troops of his own province, Kinnisrîn. During his advance Merwân received news as unexpected as it was agreeable : Damascus had declared for him. A Ghassânid chief, instead of repairing to Jâbia, had lain in hiding in the Capital. Assembling the Yemenites as soon as he heard of Merwân's election, he seized Damascus by a *coup de main*, and compelled the Governor, Dhahhâk's nominee, to seek safety in so precipitate a flight that he was unable to remove the public treasure. The bold Ghassânid thereupon hastened to inform Merwân of the success of his enterprise, and to send him money, arms, and troops.

After the two armies, or rather the two nations, came face to face upon the field of Râhit, twenty days were spent in skirmishes and single combats. A general engagement followed. " So bloody a battle had never been fought before," writes an Arab historian, and the Kaisites, after losing eighty of their sheiks, amongst whom was Dhahhâk himself, were utterly routed.[2]

---

[1] Compare the "capitulation" (*haandfæstning*) sworn to by the elected kings of Denmark. C.-F. Allen, *Hist. de Danemark* (1878), i. 185–7.

[2] According to some chroniclers, Merwân gained the victory by treacherously breaking a truce. But earlier writers, who would not have failed to reproach their opponents for such perfidy, say nothing on the subject. Cf. *Abulfedae Annales Moslemici* (Transl. Reiske), 1754, p. 117, where it is stated that Merwân forbade the pursuit of the fugitives.

This Battle of Marj Râhit was never forgotten by Kelbites or Kaisites, and seventy-two years later it was fought
afresh, so to speak, in Spain. It was the favourite subject
for poets of both the rival peoples: inspiring them with
chants of joy and victory, or, on the other hand, with
lamentations, and cries of vengeance. Just as the rout
became general, Zofar had beside him two chiefs of the
tribe of Sulaym. His charger was the only one which
could compete in speed with the pursuing Kelbites, and his
two companions, seeing the enemy on the point of over-
taking them, cried, "Flee, Zofar, flee! We are dead men!"
Spurring his horse, Zofar escaped, and his two friends were
slain.

"How can I know happiness," he lamented later, "since I abandoned
Ibn 'Âmir and Ibn Ma'n, and Hammâm is no more? Never had any man
seen me lacking in courage; yet on that fatal evening, when I was pursued
—when encompassed by the foe none came to my rescue—I abandoned my
two friends, like a dastard, to save myself! Shall one act of weakness blot
out all my exploits, all my deeds of daring? Shall we leave the Kelbites
at peace? Shall not our spears pierce them? Our brethren fell at Râhit,
shall they not be avenged? The grass will grow again on the upturned
soil which covers their bones; but we shall never forget them, and implacable is our hatred of the foe. Wife, give me my arms! Would that
the war might never end! Verily the battle of Râhit hath opened an abyss
between Merwân and ourselves."

A Kelbite poet replied in a poem of which only two
verses are extant:

"Verily since the battle of Râhit Zofar hath been stricken with a cureless
malady. Never will he cease to mourn over the tribesmen of Sulaym, 'Âmir
and Dhubyân, slain in the fray: baulked of his dearest hopes, he will
ceaselessly renew by his verses the sorrows of widows and orphans."

Another Kelbite poet celebrated the victory of his
fellow-tribesmen. He gloats over the shameful flight of
the Kaisites, when, in their haste they flung away their
standards, which fell "like thirsty birds which circle in the
air before they settle upon the water." He enumerates one
by one the Kaisite chiefs—every tribe has its own to lament:

"Cowards! they were all wounded in the back! Verily, there were
upon the Plain those who leaped for joy! Those, namely, who cut off the
noses, hands and ears of the Kaisites, and unmanned them as they lay!"

[AUTHORITIES: Hamâsa, pp. 72, 317–19, 658–9; Hamâsa (Bukturî),
ff. 34–5; Ibn Khaldûn, ii. 170–2; Fâkihî, f. 400; Ibn al-Athîr,
iii. 84; Ibn Badrûn, p. 185; Ibn Adhârî, ii. 84; Istakhrî,
pp. 13–14, 37; Mûbarrad, p. 195; Tabarî, ii. 254; Raihân, ff. 187,
201–2; Isid., c 18.]

CHAPTER VII

KHÂREJITES AND SHÎʿITES

WHILE Merwân—made master of Syria by his victory on the Field of Râhit—was preparing to subdue Egypt, Zofar, henceforth leader of his party, threw himself into Kirckesia, a fortress in Mesopotamia, lying to the east of Kinnisrîn at the confluence of the Khabûr and the Euphrates. Kirckesia became by degrees the headquarters of the Kaisites. Hostilities on a large scale being impracticable, they confined themselves to a war of ambushes and night attacks—but nevertheless waged it ruthlessly. Led by Zofar's lieutenant ʿOmair ibn Hobâb, they pillaged the Kelbite encampments in the desert of Semâwa, giving no quarter, and in their savagery even ripping up the women. When Zofar saw the marauders returning laden with booty and covered with blood, he cried in exultation: " Now is your time of adversity, O ye Kelbites! Vengeance is ours, yours the punishment. No longer is there safety for you in the desert of Semâwa: flee thence and take with you the sons of Bahdal! Go, seek safety where vile slaves drudge in the olive-groves!"[1]

Nevertheless the Kaisites were then only of secondary importance. Kirckesia, it is true, was the terror and the scourge of the surrounding districts, but it was, after all, little more than a den of robbers which could not cause Merwân serious uneasiness. His chief concern now was the conquest of ʿIrâk, and the formidable foes that he had to attack were of a far different order.

ʿIrâk in those days presented a curious and complex spectacle. The strangest and most extravagant doctrines contended for popularity: succession and election, despotism and liberty, divine right and the sovereignty of the people, fanaticism and indifferentism, struggled for the mastery; victorious Arabs and conquered Persians, rich and poor, visionaries and sceptics, were everywhere at odds. First, there was the moderate party, who loved neither the

---

[1] Cf. *Nouv. Journ. asiat.*, xiii. 301.

Omayyads nor Ibn Zubair. Scarcely a man in 'Irâk felt respect for the character of the latter, or sympathy with the principles he represented; and yet, since every attempt to establish a national government at Basra or Kûfa had failed, the Moderates ended by acknowledging him, inasmuch as they believed him the only man able to maintain some semblance of order in the land. One section of the party consisted of Moslems whose faith was lukewarm, and whose ideal was to live a pleasant and indolent life: the rest, still more heedless of the morrow, preferred doubt to enthusiasm and negation to hope. They worshipped and sacrificed to only one god. That god was pleasure—the mere gratification of the senses. The graceful and witty pen of 'Omar ibn Abî Rabî'a,[1] the Arab Anacreon, has written their liturgy. The two most eminent and influential nobles of Basra, Ahnaf and Hâritha, were exactly representative of the two shades of the party. The name of the former occurs frequently in the history of this period, but merely as that of an adviser: he was for ever talking but never acting. As chief of the Temîm, he was, however, held in such unbounded esteem by the tribe, that Mu'âwiya I was wont to say: "If he were to fly into a rage, a hundred thousand Temîmites would share his anger without asking its cause." Fortunately, he was incapable of wrath: his forbearance was proverbial; even when he summoned his tribe to arms it was understood that it was merely to please the beautiful Zabrâ, his mistress, who ruled him tyrannically: "Zabrâ is in an ill humour to-day!" the soldiers would remark. Since Ahnaf was moderate in all things, his religion steered a middle course between fervour and indifference. He did penance for his sins, but the penance was not severe. In expiation for each misdeed he would pass his finger swiftly through a lamp-flame, and exclaim, with a little cry of pain, "Wherefore didst thou commit that sin?" To be guided by a cautious but unswerving egoism, not descending to duplicity or crime; to preserve an attitude of party neutrality as far as he could; to acknowledge the existing government, even if illegitimate, without censure or flattery, and without seeking favours from it—such was the line of conduct which he had marked out for himself in his youth, and from which he never swerved. Ahnaf's character was devoid of sympathy, piety, and magnanimity; yet, while this narrow and selfish opportunist was as incapable of inspiring enthusiasm as

[1] See C. Huart, *Arabic Literature* (1903), pp. 46-7.

of feeling it, he was universally admired for his good nature, his unvarying affability, and his conciliatory disposition.

A brilliant and witty representative of the old pagan nobility, Hâritha passed for a deep drinker and did not demur to the imputation. Whenever he had choice of a prefecture he always preferred one which produced the richest wines. His religious sentiments were no mystery to his friends. "A strange sight truly," remarked a poet who was his kinsman, "to see Hâritha assisting at public worship, while he has no more faith than a chimera!"[1] His courtesy, however, was exquisite, and his conversation was lauded as being at once sprightly and instructive—furthermore, he was distinguished among his fellow-countrymen for his bravery. If the truth be told, the men of 'Irâk were, as a rule, incredible cowards. During 'Obaidallah's governor-ship, two thousand of them, sent to subdue some forty Khârejites, durst not attack them. "I have little desire," said their commander, "to have my funeral oration pro-nounced by 'Obaidallah: I prefer his censure."

The other two great parties—namely the Khârejites and the Shî'ites—were composed of sincere and ardent believers. But these two sects, though they had the same starting-point, diverged as they advanced, and ended by regarding both religion and government from wholly different points of view.

The Khârejites were noble and ardent souls, who, in a self-seeking age, preserved their religious purity, whose hearts were not set upon earthly things, and who had too lofty an idea of God to do him mere lip-service and to drowse in conventional and sluggish piety. They were true disciples of Mohammed—but of Mohammed such as he was in the early years of his mission, when virtue and religion alone filled his soul with enthusiasm; while the orthodox of Medina were the disciples rather of that other Mohammed —the conscious impostor whose insatiable ambition thirsted to subjugate the world with the sword. In the days when civil war was cruelly ravaging the provinces of the vast empire, when each tribe alleged its noble origin as a claim to power, the Khârejites held fast to the beautiful words of the Koran: "All Moslems are brothers." "Do not ask us," said they, "whether we descend from Kais or from Temîm; we are all children of Islam, we worship the unity of God, and God is best pleased with him who best shows his grati-

---

[1] A proverbial expression: cf. Al-Maidâni, ii. 384.

tude." If they laid stress on equality and fraternity, it was
because their ranks were recruited rather from the working-
classes than from the aristocracy. Justly indignant at the
corruption of their contemporaries—who gave themselves
up, without scruple and without shame, to every form of
vice and licentiousness, in the belief that in order to blot out
all their sins it sufficed to attend public prayers and make
pilgrimage to Mecca—the Khârejites preached that faith
without works is dead, and that sinners as well as unbelievers
will be damned. Extravagant ideas, in fact, prevailed as to
the absolving power of faith: and yet the faith was then
often little else than mere deism. Wits of lax morality,
if they ever thought of heaven, counted on easily gaining
entrance there. "What preparation hast thou made for
such a day as this?" asked the pious theologian Hasan[1]
of the poet Farazdak[2] who stood beside him at a funeral.
"The witness that I have borne for sixty years to the unity
of God," replied the poet calmly.[2] The Khârejites inveighed
against this theory. "If this be true," they urged, "Satan
himself will escape damnation. Doth not he believe in the
unity of God?"

In the eyes of a fickle, frivolous, sceptical, and semi-
pagan society, a religion so impassioned, combined with
morality so austere, constituted a heresy. Its extirpation
was demanded; for scepticism sometimes proscribes piety in
the name of philosophy, just as piety sometimes proscribes
rationalism in the name of God. The Government, for
their part, were naturally alarmed at these democrats and
levellers. The Omayyads might have ignored them, or
even patronised them, if they had confined themselves to
declaring that the founders of the orthodox party, the self-
styled saints of Islamism—such as Talha, Zubair, 'Alî, and
Ayesha the Prophet's widow—were ambitious hypocrites:
but they went much further. Following the example of the
orthodox at Medina, they classed the Omayyads among unbelievers, they disputed the exclusive claim of the Kurashites
to the Khalifate, they boldly denied that the Prophet had
declared spiritual and temporal authority to belong to that
tribe alone. Every man, they said, is eligible for the Khalifate, whatever his standing—whether he belongs to the
highest nobility, or to the lowest ranks of society—be he

[1] Of Basra.
[2] *Nouv. Journ. asiat.*, xiii. 543. Hammâm ibn Ghâlib al-Farazdak died A.D.
728, as also did Hasan. Farazdak was known as "The Profligate."

Kurashite or slave : a dangerous doctrine, which cut at the very root of the constitution.   Nor was this all : dreaming of a perfect State, these simple folk—such was their passion for liberty—preached that a Khalif was only necessary to curb ill-doers, and that true believers, being virtuous men, could very well dispense with one.   The Government and the aristocracy of 'Irâk accordingly determined to crush, by a combined effort, the Khârejites and their doctrines—just as the Syrian nobility had aided the Omayyads in their conflict with the Companions of the Prophet.   A ruthless and cruel persecution, directed by 'Obaidallah, was set on foot. The sceptical philosopher, the man who had compassed the death of the Prophet's grandson, shed in torrents the blood of those whom in his heart he must have regarded as Mohammed's true disciples.   Moreover, they were, just then, far from formidable ; vanquished by 'Ali in two sanguinary battles, they no longer preached publicly, but secluded themselves, and had even deposed their chief because he disapproved of their inaction and of their intercourse with Arabs of other sects.   Nevertheless, fire, as their enemies well knew, yet smouldered beneath the ashes, ready to be fanned into a flame.   The Nonconformists secretly disseminated their principles, with a fiery eloquence which was irresistible because it sprang from the heart.   " This heresy must be destroyed root and branch," replied 'Obaidallah to those who urged that the sectaries were not dangerous enough to warrant such extreme measures : " These men are more formidable than you suppose ; their lightest words kindle the souls of men, as a tiny spark ignites a heap of rushes."

The Khârejites endured the terrible ordeal with wholly admirable constancy.   Self-possessed and resigned, they walked with a firm step to the scaffold, reciting prayers and verses of the Koran ; and glorifying God, they received the fatal blow.   Never did they seek to save their lives by breaking their word.   An agent of the Government arrested one of them in the street.   " Let me enter my house for a moment," said the Khârejite, "that I may purify myself and pray."   " Who will answer for your return ? "   " God," replied the Khârejite, who did not fail to surrender.   Another, undergoing imprisonment, astonished even his jailer by his exemplary piety and persuasive eloquence.   " Your doctrines seem lofty and holy," said the jailer, " and I will render you a service.   I will permit you to visit your family during the night, if you will promise me to return hither at daybreak."

F *

"I promise," said the prisoner, and henceforth the jailer released him every day at sunset. One night, while the Khârejite sat with his family, some friends came in with the news that the Governor, exasperated at the assassination of one of the executioners, had ordered all the heretics then incarcerated to be beheaded. In spite of the entreaties of his friends, and the tears of his wife and children, who besought him not to deliver himself up to certain death, the Khârejite returned to the prison. "Could I stand before God's face," he said, "if I had broken my word?" On entering his cell he saw a troubled expression on the worthy warder's face. "Make thy mind easy," said the prisoner, "I know thy master's decree." "Thou knowest it! and yet thou hast returned!" cried the jailer, lost in amazement and admiration.

The courage of the women rivalled that of the men. The pious Baljâ, warned that 'Obaidallah had the day before pronounced her name—which from his lips was equivalent to a sentence of death—refused to take her friends' advice and conceal herself. "If he arrests me," she said, "so much the worse for him, for God will punish him: but I would not that one of our brethren should be disquieted on my behalf." With calmness and resignation she awaited the executioners, who, after they had cut off her hands and feet, cast her body into the market-place.

Such transcendent heroism and piety excited the sympathy and admiration of all just men, and sometimes inspired the very executioners with respect. At the sight of the wan and emaciated enthusiasts, who scarcely ate or slept, and seemed clad in an aureole of glory, a divine dread seized the arm uplifted to strike. Soon, however, it was fear rather than reverence that made the executioners hesitate. The persecuted sect evolved a secret society whose members acted in unison. On the morrow of every execution a headsman was found assassinated. This was a beginning of armed resistance, but it did not satisfy the zealots of the party. It must be remembered that in the eyes of the sect, as well as of Moslems in general, meek resignation to punishment was regarded rather as a weakness than a merit. The Mohammedan, as well as the Catholic Church, is essentially a Church militant, if in a different sense. The extremists therefore reproached the more moderate for their intercourse with "robbers and infidels," and for what they termed their supineness and cowardice, while the poets,

joining in these reproaches, issued a call to arms when it
was noised abroad that Moslim was about to attack the
Holy Cities. This crisis was pregnant with the fate of the
sect, of which Nâfi' ibn Azrak was then the most
eminent member. Collecting his friends, he rushed to the
defence of the sacred soil, and Ibn Zubair—who had declared
that in fighting against the Arabs of Syria, he would accept
aid from Dailamites, Turks, pagans, and barbarians—received
him with open arms, and even assured him that he was a
convert to the new doctrines. So long as the siege of
Mecca lasted the Khârejites performed prodigies of valour,
but they afterwards became convinced that between the
head of the orthodox Church and themselves union was
impossible. They accordingly returned to Basra, and later,
profiting by the universal disorder, settled in the province
of Ahwâz,[1] whence they drove out the government officials.

Henceforth, the Khârejites—or at any rate those of
Ahwâz, whom the Arabs called Azrakites, after the father
of Nâfi'—were no longer content with avoiding all communication with Arabs who were not of their sect, and with
declaring that it was a sin to dwell among them, or to eat
animals slain by them, or to intermarry with them. Exasperated by many years of persecution, and thirsting for
vengeance, their character grew cruel and ferocious; they
pushed their principles to the most rigorous conclusions,
and found in the Koran—which they interpreted much as
certain English and Scottish sects in the seventeenth century
interpreted the Bible—arguments to justify and sanctify their
implacable hatred. All other Arabs were either unbelievers
or—which came to the same thing—sinners; they must
therefore be extirpated if they refused to accept the creed
of God's people, for Mohammed left the pagan Arabs no
alternative to Islamism save death. None ought to be
spared, neither women nor infants at the breast, for in the
Koran Noah saith: "Lord, leave not one single family of
Infidels on the Earth: for if thou leave them they will
beguile thy servants and will beget only sinners, infidels."[2]

Their extermination had been desired: in turn they
longed to exterminate their persecutors. Martyrs no longer,
they had become executioners. Soon, marking their route
in torrents of blood, they advanced on Basra. Unspeakable
terror reigned in the town. The inhabitants, who, as we have
seen, confessed their cowardice with revolting cynicism, had

---

[1] Khûzistân.   [2] Koran, Su. lxxi. 27-8.

only their own troops and their own courage to rely upon, for they had just shaken off their Omayyad rulers and had not yet acknowledged Ibn Zubair. To make matters worse, they had been so ill-advised as to place the Kurashite Babba [1] at the head of the government—a man of immense corpulence, but otherwise a mere nonentity. Nevertheless, since their property, their families, and their lives were at stake, the very gravity of the danger imparted to them some energy, and they sallied forth to meet the foe with more alacrity and courage than they usually displayed when there was fighting toward. They came in touch with the enemy near Dûlâb, and hostilities continued for a month. Nâfi‘ was slain in a skirmish, and the Arabs of Basra lost three commanders in succession; at last, wearied by so long a campaign, discouraged by the indecisive results of so many combats, and exhausted by their unaccustomed exertions, they felt that they had mistaken their strength, and returned to their homes. ‘Irâk would thereupon have been overrun by the fierce sectaries, if Hâritha had not barred the way at the head of his fellow-tribesmen the Ghoddânites. " Undying disgrace will be ours," he cried to his companions in arms, " if we abandon our brethren at Basra to the brutal rage of the Khârejites; " and, fighting as a volunteer, without official rank, he saved ‘Irâk from the terrible scourge which threatened her. But the danger remained imminent: Hâritha might be defeated any day, and then nothing would prevent the enemy from penetrating to Basra. The inhabitants accordingly saw no other means of safety except to join their forces with Ibn Zubair's and to acknowledge him as Khalif. This they did, and Ibn Zubair sent them a Governor. The latter appointed his brother, ‘Othmân by name, commander-in-chief. On taking the field, and finding that he had the advantage in point of numbers over the enemy, ‘Othmân exclaimed to Hâritha, who had joined him : " What! is that their army?"

" Thou little knowest them," replied Hâritha ; " they will give thee enough to do, I will answer for it."

" By Allah! " replied ‘Othmân disdainfully, " I will make proof of their prowess ere I dine! "

" Bear in mind, General, that when those men are once in battle array they never retreat."

" I know the men of ‘Irâk, that they are cowards. And

---

[1] On the origin of this name see Al-Tha‘âlibi, *Latâ'if al-Ma‘ârif* (ed. De Jong), p. 27.

as for thee, Hâritha, what knowest thou of fighting? Thou hast had more practice in another matter. . . ."

'Othmân accompanied these words with a significant gesture, and Hâritha, furious at having been subjected by this pietistic foreigner to the twofold reproach of cowardice and drunkenness, withdrew his men, and took no part in the engagement.

A victim to his own presumption, 'Othmân, after seeing his troops in full retreat, perished upon the field. The Khârejites were about to reap the fruits of their victory, when Hâritha, raising the fallen standard, and putting his tribesmen in battle array, checked the onset of the enemy. "If Hâritha had not been there," remarks a poet, very justly, "not a man of 'Irâk would have survived that fatal day. When it is asked who saved the country, Ma'addites and Yemenites answer with one accord, 'Hâritha!'"

Unfortunately, the pietists whom Ibn Zubair sent in succession as Governors of 'Irâk failed to appreciate the only man who, amidst general cowardice, had shown courage and energy. They looked upon him as a wine-bibber and an infidel, they stubbornly refused to grant him the official position he demanded, and they did not send him the reinforcements which were absolutely necessary for holding the enemy in check. At length the gallant warrior, hard pressed, was compelled to save the remnant of his forces by a retreat which resembled a flight. Pursued by the enemy, they reached the Little Tigris, and hastily crowded into boats to cross the river. The boats were already in mid-stream when Hâritha heard cries of distress from a gallant Temîmite, who had reached the river too late, and was almost overtaken by the enemy. Hâritha ordered the boatman to return; he obeyed, but the bank was very steep, and the Temîmite, heavily armed, flung himself down into the boat. The impact capsized it, and all its occupants perished in the stream. 'Irâk had lost its last defender. The advance of the enemy continued: they were already engaged on the construction of a bridge over the Euphrates. Many of the inhabitants had quitted Basra to seek safety elsewhere, others prepared to follow them, and the fear inspired by the terrible "Round-heads" was so acute and widespread that the Governor could not find another commander for the army. Then, as though by inspiration from heaven, one thought flashed through every mind, one cry burst from every mouth—"Muhallab alone can save us!" And

Muhallab saved them.   He was undoubtedly an exceptional
man, worthy in all respects of the enthusiastic admiration
shown for him by a Christian hero, the Cid, when in his
palace at Valencia he read of the gallant deeds wrought by
the doughty knights of Islam.[1]

Nothing escaped Muhallab's clear-sightedness; he saw
from the outset that a war of this kind called for something
besides military genius in the General, and that to subdue
these fanatics ever ready to conquer or die—who though
transfixed by lances would rush upon the foe shouting : " Oh
Lord, to thee we come ! "—it was necessary to oppose to
them soldiers, not merely hardened and disciplined, but
equally animated by religious enthusiasm.   And Muhallab
worked   a   miracle.   He   succeeded   in   transforming   the
sceptical men of 'Irâk into zealous believers ; he persuaded
them that the Khârejites were the Eternal's bitterest foes,
he inspired them with longings for the martyr's crown.
When their courage wavered, he boldly put in Mohammed's
mouth words promising them victory—for, strange to say,
his talent for imposture equalled his lofty courage.   Henceforth his troops showed no sign of wavering, and victory was
theirs because they were convinced that it had been assured
them by heaven.   This war, which lasted for nineteen years,
was one long rivalry in fanatical hatred ; it is impossible to
say which party showed itself the most fiery, stubborn, and
furiously implacable.   " Were I to see the pagan Dailamites
on the one side, and the Khârejites on the other," said
one of Muhallab's soldiers, " I would fling myself upon
the latter, for he who dieth at their hands will wear in
Paradise among the martyrs a crown of tenfold glory ! "

While Basra needed all its men and all its resources to
repel the Khârejites, another sect, that of the Shî'ites, caused
keen alarm to the Omayyads as well as to Ibn Zubair.

If the doctrines of the Khârejites necessarily tended to
democracy, those of the Shî'ites led straight to despotism of
the worst kind.   Refusing to admit that the Prophet had
had the imprudence to leave the choice of his successor to
the multitude, they relied on certain highly ambiguous expressions of Mohammed as proving that he had expressly
named 'Alî to succeed him, and that the family of Fâtima's
husband had an hereditary right to the Khalifate.   They
therefore regarded as usurpers, not only the Omayyads, but
Abû Bakr, 'Omar, and 'Othmân, and at the same time they

---

[1] *Recherches* (1881), ii. 23.

deified the Khalif, alleging him to be incapable of sin, and
to share none of the frailties and imperfections of humanity.
Premising the Khalif's divinity, the dominating sect of those
days—which had been founded by Kaisân,[1] one of 'Alî's
freedmen—reached logically the melancholy conclusion that
faith, religion, and virtue consisted solely in passive submission and unquestioning obedience to the commands of a
man-god. This strange and monstrous doctrine, uncongenial
to the Arab character, had been hatched in the brains of the
ancient disciples of Zoroaster, who—being accustomed to see
in their kings and priests descendants of the gods, or of divine
and celestial beings—transferred to the heads of the new religion the veneration which they had previously accorded to
their monarchs.[2]   For the Shî'ites were essentially a Persian
sect,[3] and were recruited for the most part from the freedmen—in other words, from the Persians.   Hence too it resulted that the creed of the sect assumed the formidable
aspect of a blind and furious war against society : hating the
dominant race, and envying their riches, these Persians demanded their share of earthly wealth.   Their leaders nevertheless were usually Arabs, who turned to account the
credulity and fanaticism of the sectaries.   At the period we
now speak of they were under the leadership of Mukhtâr—
a man at once violent and subtle, heroic and unprincipled,
a tiger in his wrath and a fox in his craftiness.   By turns
Khârejite, orthodox—Zubairite, as the phrase went—and
Shî'ite, he had belonged to every party, from that which
embodied democracy to that which preached absolutism ;
and to justify these frequent changes—calculated, as they
were, to raise doubts as to his sincerity and good faith—he
created a God after his own image, a deity essentially fickle,
who would think, will, and ordain to-morrow the opposite
of that which he thought, willed, and ordained yesterday.
This grotesque doctrine had a further advantage, for, while
Mukhtâr prided himself on his prophetic powers, his presentiments and visions were thereby sheltered from adverse
criticism ; since if they were not justified by events, he
would simply remark, " God hath changed his mind ! "

[1] Wrongly identified by some Arab writers with Mukhtâr, of whose body-guard
he became captain.
[2] De Sacy, *Exposé de la religion des Druzes*, I. xxvii., and Dozy, *Essai sur
l'histoire de l'Islamism* (Chauvin's transl.), pp. 219 *sq.*
[3] Though their dogmas were probably of Jewish origin, through the Saba'ites,
whose founder seems to have been a Jew. See Nicholson, *Lit. Hist. of the Arab*
(1907), p. 215.

Nevertheless, in spite of appearances to the contrary, none was less inconsistent or less variable than Mukhtâr. If he changed, it was merely with regard to the means which he employed. All his actions had a single motive power—an unbridled ambition; all his efforts were directed to a single end—supreme power. He despised all that other men feared or venerated. His proud spirit contemplated with disdainful indifference all political systems and religious creeds. He looked upon them as so many snares set to entrap the multitude, or prejudices which an able man could manipulate to serve his own purposes. But although he played every part with equal skill, that of chief of the Shî'ites was the most congenial to him. No other sect was so simple and credulous, or possessed that character of passive obedience, so gratifying to his imperious temper.

By a bold stroke he captured Kûfa from Ibn Zubair, and then marched to meet the Syrian army despatched against him by the Khalif 'Abd al-Malik, who had lately succeeded his father Merwân. The inhabitants of Kûfa, who had submitted with rage and indignation to the yoke placed on them by this impostor and his Persians—their slaves, as they called them—had only waited for such a juncture to rise in revolt. But Mukhtâr contrived to gain time by seductive promises and protestations, and he profited by the delay to send his general, Ibrâhîm, orders to return immediately. At a moment when they least expected it, the rebels saw Ibrâhîm and his Shî'ites rushing upon them sword in hand. When the insurrection had been drowned in blood, Mukhtâr caused two hundred and fifty men—most of whom had fought against Husain at Kerbelâ—to be arrested and beheaded. Husain's death served him as a pretext, but his real object was to deprive the Arabs of any desire to repeat their attempt. In this he was successful. To escape the despotism of the sword they emigrated in great numbers.

In giving orders to his troops to march once more against the Syrian army, Mukhtâr neglected no means of stimulating their enthusiasm and fanaticism. Before they set out he exhibited an old chair, bought from a carpenter at the modest price of two pieces of silver, but now covered with silk and alleged to be the throne of 'Alî. "This throne," he exclaimed to the soldiers, "shall be to you what the Ark of the Covenant was to the children of Israel. Bear it into the thick of the fray, place it where the carnage is greatest, and defend it. If the victory is yours it will be because God hath aided you; but be not faint-hearted if perchance you meet with a reverse, for it hath been revealed to me that in such a case, God will send angels to succour you, and ye shall see them flying in the clouds after the similitude of white doves."

Mukhtâr had, as a matter of fact, deposited with some trusty agents a number of pigeons reared in Kûfa, with orders to release them if an unfavourable issue was to be feared. The appearance of the birds would therefore warn Mukhtâr that the moment had arrived for him to consult his own safety, and at the same time would stimulate his credulous soldiers to do their utmost to turn defeat into victory.

The battle was fought on the borders of Khâzir, not far from Mosul (August, 686). The Shî'ites were at the outset repulsed. Thereupon the pigeons were released. The sight of the birds renewed the courage of the troops, and whilst, in fanatical exaltation, they flung themselves upon the foe with unbridled fury, crying " The angels! the angels!" another shout was heard on the left wing of the Syrian army, which was entirely composed of Kaisites, under the command of 'Omair, formerly Zofar's lieutenant. On the preceding night he had had an interview with the Shî'ite general. Now, lowering his standard, he cried : " Vengeance, vengeance, for the fatal field of Râhit ! " Henceforth the Kaisites became inert, but not indifferent, spectators of the fray, and by nightfall the Syrian army, having lost its commander-in-chief, 'Obaidallah, was utterly defeated.

While Mukhtâr was still elated by his victory, the fugitives from Kûfa urged Mus'ab, Ibn Zubair's brother and Governor of Basra, to try conclusions with the impostor, assuring him that as soon as he showed himself, all intelligent men in Kûfa would declare for him. Yielding to their request, Mus'ab recalled Muhallab to Basra, marched with him against the Shî'ites, gained two victories over them, and besieged Mukhtâr, who had withdrawn into the Citadel of Kûfa. Mukhtâr, seeing the ruin of his party to be inevitable, resolved not to survive it. " Let us fall upon the besiegers," he cried. " It is better to die like brave men than to perish here of hunger, or be slaughtered like lambs!" But his prestige was at an end. Out of six or seven thousand men only twenty answered to his appeal. These sold their lives dearly. As for the rest, their cowardice profited them nothing. They were declared brigands and assassins, and the pitiless Mus'ab put them all to the sword (A.D. 687). But he did not long enjoy his success. Unwillingly, he had rendered a notable service to his brother's rival, since he had rid him of his most formidable enemies, the Shî'ites, and 'Abd al-Malik, having henceforth nothing to fear from them, made vast preparations to attack the Zubairites in 'Irâk. Lest the enemy should threaten him in the rear, he began operations by besieging Kirckesia, where Zofar played a very ambiguous part, now pretending to fight for Zubair, now supplying the Shî'ites with provisions and proposing to march with them against the Syrians. All enemies of the Omayyads, however different their aims, were his friends and allies. When besieged by 'Abd al-Malik—who, acting on the advice of the Kelbites, prudently removed his Kaisite troops from the fighting line —Zofar defended his stronghold stubbornly; once, indeed, his men made so vigorous a sortie that they penetrated to the Khalif's tent. Since he was desirous of ending the siege in order to march against Mus'ab, 'Abd al-Malik then entered into negotiations—which, however, he broke off when the fall of four towers revived the hope of storming the town, and renewed when the assault failed. By the judicious distribution of money amongst the Khalif's soldiers, Zofar eventually obtained very honourable terms; namely, an amnesty for his brothers in arms, and the governorship of Kirckesia for himself.[1] As a salve to his pride, moreover, he stipulated that he should not be compelled to swear allegiance to an Omayyad Khalif during Ibn Zubair's lifetime. Finally, to ratify their reconciliation, it was agreed that Maslama, the Khalif's son, should marry Zofar's daughter. Upon the conclusion of peace, Zofar presented himself before 'Abd al-Malik, who received him with great courtesy and bade him sit beside him on the throne. The spectacle of these two men, enemies for so long a time, exchanging assurances of brotherly amity was assuredly a touching one! But appearances were deceitful. To convert 'Abd al-Malik's newborn friendship for Zofar into burning hate all that was needed was a poetical quotation. A noble Yemenite, Ibn Dhî 'l-Kalâ, entered the tent, and on seeing the place of honour occupied by Zofar he shed tears. The Khalif inquired the cause of his grief. " Commander of

---

[1] Cf. *Nouv. Journ. asiat.*, xiii. 305.

the Faithful," said he, " how can I refrain from bitter tears, when I look upon that man, but lately in revolt against thee, whose sword still drips with the blood of my kinsmen, victims of their loyalty to thee—when I see this murderer of my family seated beside thee, while I stand at the foot of the throne ? "

" In bidding him sit beside me," replied the Khalif, " I had no wish to place him above thee ; but he speaks my tongue, and his conversation interests me."

The poet al-Akhtal,[1] who was drinking wine in another tent, was told of the reception accorded to Zofar by the Khalif. He hated and loathed the brigand of Kirckesia, who had been more than once on the point of exterminating his tribe, the Beni Taghlib. " I will smite him a blow that Ibn Dhî 'l-Kalâ could not deal," said he. Thereupon he entered the Khalif's presence, and after gazing at him fixedly for a few moments declaimed these verses :

" The wine which filleth my cup sparkles like the bright and eager eye of a game-cock. It exalteth the spirits of the drinker. He who quaffeth three goblets thereof unmixed with water, feeleth a desire of bestowing benefits arise in his heart. He swayeth daintily in his walk, like a lovely daughter of the Kuraish, and suffereth the skirts of his raiment to flutter in the breeze."

" Wherefore dost thou recite these verses ? " asked the Khalif. " Doubtless some fancy passeth through thy mind."

" Verily, Commander of the Faithful," replied al-Akhtal, " many ideas crowd in upon me when I see seated beside thee on the throne the man who said but yesterday : ' The grass will grow again on the upturned soil which covereth the bones of our brothers ; but we shall never forget them, and implacable is our hatred of the foe !' "

At these words 'Abd al-Malik started up as though a wasp had stung him. Furious, panting with rage, his eyes sparkling with savage hate, he kicked Zofar violently on the chest, and flung him to the foot of the throne. Zofar afterwards confessed that he never thought himself nearer death than at that moment.[2]

The days of sincere reconciliation were not yet, and it was not long before the Kaisites gave the Omayyads fresh proof

---

[1] Ghiyàth ibn Ghawth, a Christian. "His religion, however, was less a matter of principle than of convenience, and to him the supreme virtue of Christianity lay in the licence which it gave him to drink wine as often as he pleased." Nicholson, *op. cit.*, p. 240.

[2] Cf. *Nouv. Journ. asiat.*, xiii. 304–7.

of their inveterate animosity.   Zofar had reinforced the army
of 'Abd al-Malik, when he took the field against Mus'ab,
with a division of Kaisites under his son Hudhail; but as
soon as the two armies came in sight of each other, the
Kaisites went over to the enemy with their arms and
munitions.   This desertion, however, did not produce, like
'Omair's, disastrous consequences.   Fortune, on the contrary, smiled on 'Abd al-Malik.   Fickle and light-hearted,
the men of 'Irâk had already forgotten their grievances
against the Omayyads.   Never very eager for warfare, and,
naturally, having no desire to die for a pretender whom
they despised, they had lent a willing ear to 'Abd al-Malik's
emissaries, who overran 'Irâk, scattering gold and promises
of the most tempting kind.   Mus'ab was therefore surrounded by generals already bought by the Omayyads, and
when the battle was joined, he soon discovered their real
sentiments.   " I refuse," replied one who was ordered to
attack, "to immolate my tribe for a cause which toucheth
them not."   " What!" cried another in an insolent and
derisive tone, " Thou orderest me to charge ?   But none of
my men will follow me; and charging alone I should cut a
ridiculous figure ! "

There was but one course open to a man so brave and
proud as Mus'ab.   Addressing his son 'Îsâ, he said : " Go,
and tell thy uncle that the perfidious men of 'Irâk have
betrayed him ; and bid adieu to thy father, who hath but
a few moments to live."

" Nay, my father," replied the young man, "never shall
the Kurashites reproach me for having deserted thee in
the hour of danger."   Father and son then rushed into the
thick of the fight, and a little later their heads were laid
before 'Abd al-Malik (A.D. 690).

All 'Irâk now swore allegiance to the Omayyad.   Muhallab, while ignorant of Mus'ab's death, which was already
known to the Khârejites, had declared during a conference
with the chiefs of that body, that Mus'ab was his lord
in this world and the next, and that it was the duty of
every good Musulman to resist 'Abd al-Malik, son of the
accursed one.   But on receiving from the Omayyad Khalif
a diploma confirming him in all his offices and titles,
Muhallab followed the example of his countrymen.   Such
was the meaning which even the best of the men of 'Irâk
attached to honour and loyalty !

" Decide for yourselves whether we or ye are in the

wrong," cried the justly indignant Khârejites, "but at least have the honesty to acknowledge that ye are this world's thralls, and that for lucre ye will serve and flatter any ruler —brethren of Satan that ye are!"

[AUTHORITIES: Mûbarrad, *Kâmil*, 575–7, 588–90, 623, 647–704, 736; Sharastânî, *Kitâb*, 87–91; 108–10, &c.; Ibn Khaldûn, ii. 171– 183; *Raihân*, f. 187; Ibn Khallikân (ed. Slane), i. 322 *sqq.*, (ed. Wüst.) fasc. ix. 48; Ibn Kutaiba, p. 203; Ibn Badrûn, p. 189; Mas'ûdî, f. 125.]

CHAPTER VIII

KELBITES AND KAISITES

'ABD AL-MALIK neared the goal of his ambition. To secure unquestioned sovereignty over the Musulman world, he had but to capture Mecca, the residence and last refuge of his rival. It is true that the attack would be a sacrilege, and 'Abd al-Malik would have shuddered with horror at the mere suggestion had he preserved the pious sentiments which characterised him in his early years. But he was no longer the ingenuous and ardent youth who, in an outburst of pious indignation, had called Yezîd the foe of the Eternal, for daring to send a force against Medina, the Prophet's city. Lapse of years, commerce with the world, and the exercise of power, had impaired his youthful frankness and simple faith, and it is related that on the day of his cousin Ashdak's death—that day on which 'Abd al-Malik had dishonoured himself with the twofold crime of perjury and murder—he had shut God's Book, with a cold and gloomy air, muttering, "Henceforth we have naught in common." Since his religious sentiments were well known, the news that he was about to despatch an army against Mecca was no cause of surprise, but far otherwise was the Khalif's astonishing choice of commander for such an important expedition. He appointed a man of the meanest extraction, one Hajjâj,[1] who had formerly followed the humble calling of schoolmaster at Tâ'if in Arabia, thinking himself fortunate if at the end of a day spent in teaching little children to read he had earned the price of a crust of bread. Later, he had become publicly known merely as having established some sort of discipline in 'Abd al-Malik's body-guard, as having commanded a division in 'Irâk (when the enemy, by their defection, deprived him of the opportunity of showing bravery or the reverse), and as having been beaten by the Zubairites in Merwân's reign. He owed his appointment to a singular circumstance. When he ventured to solicit the honour of

---

[1] Hajjâj ibn Yûsuf, d. 714.

commanding the army against Ibn Zubair, the Khalif exclaimed disdainfully, " Keep silence, fellow ! " But by one of those inconsistencies to which the human mind is so prone, 'Abd al-Malik's general scepticism was tempered by a firm faith in oneiromancy, and Hajjâj skilfully turned this fact to account. " I dreamed," he said simply, " that I was flaying Ibn Zubair." The Khalif forthwith conferred on him the coveted command.

Ibn Zubair himself had received with calmness and resignation the news of the loss of 'Irâk and of his brother's death. As a matter of fact he had been not wholly easy with regard to the ultimate designs of Mus'ab—who, in his opinion, was inconveniently disposed to play the sovereign —and he consoled himself the more readily since his brother's death gave him the opportunity of displaying his rhetorical talents in a funeral oration which to us may seem cold and forced, but which he doubtless deemed highly edifying. He declared naïvely that Mus'ab's death had inspired him at once with sorrow and joy; sorrow, because he was thereby " bereft of a friend whose loss had caused a poignant wound in his sensitive heart, which patience and resignation alone could alleviate ; " and joy, " because Allah, in granting his brother the glory of martyrdom, had been pleased to give him testimony of his gracious favour." [1]

But when the day came for fighting rather than preaching—when he saw Mecca beleaguered and threatened with all the horrors of famine—Ibn Zubair's courage failed. It is not that he was lacking in the ordinary bravery, which every soldier who is not a mere poltroon shows upon the battlefield, but he was lacking in moral strength. He sought counsel of his mother, a woman with the noble spirit of a Roman matron, despite her hundred years.

" Mother," he exclaimed, " all have abandoned me, and the enemy offer me favourable terms. What, thinkest thou, is my duty ? "

" To die," said she.

" But I fear," he replied piteously, " I fear that if I fall at the hands of the Syrians, they will glut their vengeance on my corpse ! "

" What is that to thee ? Doth the slaughtered sheep suffer when it is flayed ? "

'Abdallah flushed with shame at these trenchant words,

---

[1] *Nouveau Journ. asiat.*, x. 140.

and hastened to assure his mother that he shared her sentiments and had but sought their confirmation. Very soon he stood before her, fully armed, to bid her a last farewell. She drew him to her breast, and her hand fell upon a coat of mail.

" A man prepared for death hath no need of this," she said.

" I did but don this armour to inspire thee with a spark of hope," he replied, somewhat disconcerted.

" I have abandoned hope : strip thyself of it."

He obeyed. Then, after some hours spent in prayer at the Ka'ba, this unheroic hero rushed upon the foe, and won in his death more honour than in his life. His head was sent to Damascus, and his body was hung feet upwards on a gibbet (A.D. 692).

Throughout the six or eight months that the siege of Mecca lasted, Hajjâj displayed great courage, indefatigable activity, indomitable perseverance, and, it must be owned, an indifference for sacred things, which theologians have never forgiven, but which proved him to be devoted body and soul to his master's service. No scruple embarrassed him : he respected neither the immemorial sanctity of the Temple, nor what seemed to others a manifestation of the wrath of heaven. One day, when the Syrians were hurling stones upon the Ka'ba, a sudden tempest arose and twelve soldiers were struck by lightning. Seized with superstitious dread, the Syrians one and all refused to renew their attack ; Hajjâj accordingly girded up his loins, placed a stone in the catapult, and adjusting the ropes, remarked carelessly : "That imports nothing : I know this country ; I was born here : these storms are not unusual." Such striking devotion to the Omayyad cause merited commensurate reward. 'Abd al-Malik appointed Hajjâj Governor of Mecca, and, a few months later, of all Hijâz. Since he was by birth a Kaisite, his promotion would doubtless have inspired the Kelbites with suspicion and alarm had he been a man of noble ancestry instead of an insignificant upstart.

Moreover, the Kelbites also could plume themselves on having rendered important services at the siege of Mecca : they could claim, for instance, that the fatal stone which laid Ibn Zubair low, had been launched by one of their number—Humaid ibn Bahdal. But what completely reassured them was that the Khalif took delight in praising their valour and loyalty, that he flattered their leader in prose and verse, that he conferred offices upon them to the exclusion of their adversaries, and finally that they could rely on many princes such as Khâlid, son of Yazîd I, and 'Abd al-'Azîz—brother of the Khalif, and son of a Kelbite woman.

The Kaisites, however, were not without friends at court. Bishr especially, also the Khalif's brother, whose mother was a Kaisite, had espoused their interests and their quarrel, and as he never lost an occasion of declaring that they surpassed the Kelbites in valour, his boasting one day roused Khâlid's wrath to such a pitch that he said to certain Kelbites : " Is there none among you who will make a foray into the Desert of the Kaisites ? It is needful to humble the pride of those princes who have Kaisite mothers, for they cease not to assert that in every encounter, before and after the days of the Prophet, the Kaisites gained the advantage over us."

" I will gladly undertake the affair," said Ibn Bahdal, " if you can guarantee that the Sultan will not punish me." " I will answer for that." " Unfold, then, your plan." " Nothing could be simpler. You know that since Ibn Zubair's death the Kaisites have not paid tithe to the Khalif. I shall accordingly give you an order authorizing you to levy the tithe among the Kaisites, and this 'Abd al-Malik will be supposed to have written. Hence you will easily contrive an opportunity of treating them as they deserve."

Ibn Bahdal set out. In order to arouse no suspicions, his retinue was a small one, but he knew he should find recruits wherever he lighted upon his fellow-tribesmen. Arriving amongst the Beni Abd-Wadd and the Beni Olaim —two Kelbite clans who dwelt in the Desert, to the south of Dûma and Khabt—he unfolded to them Khâlid's scheme, and the bravest and most resolute men in the two clans having assured him that they asked for nothing better than to be his followers, he plunged into the Desert, after having made them swear to give the Kaisites no quarter.

One of the Beni Fezâra, a sub-tribe of the Kaisites, was their first victim. He came of rich and powerful lineage— his great-grandfather, Hudhayfa ibn Badr, had been the leader of the Dhubyân in the famous War of Dâhis [1]—but since he had the misfortune to be born of a slave mother,

[1] A long and fierce struggle, waged at the end of the fifth century A.D., arising from a race between the horse Dâhis and the mare Ghabrà, in which it was alleged that the former was defeated by foul play.

his proud fellow-tribesmen despised him to such a degree
that they had refused to give him even one of their daughters
in marriage (so that he had perforce chosen a wife from a
Yemenite tribe), and being unwilling to associate with him,
they had assigned him a place in the outskirts of the camp.
It was the custom of this unfortunate outcast to recite his
morning prayers in a loud voice; and this proved his
undoing.   Guided by the sound, the Kelbites fell upon him,
slew him, and adding robbery to murder, drove off his
camels to the number of a hundred.   Later, falling in with
five families also descended from Hudhayfa, they attacked
them.   A desperate fight followed, which lasted till the
evening; but at nightfall all the Kaisites lay stretched upon
the battlefield and their enemies believed them dead.   Such,
however, was not the case.   Their wounds, though numerous,
were not mortal, and thanks to the sand, which driven by
a strong west wind soon covered them, the bleeding was
stanched and they all escaped death.

Pursuing their journey throughout the night, the Kelbites
met, next morning, another of Hudhayfa's descendants, named
'Abdallah.   This old man was journeying with his family,
and was accompanied by no one capable of bearing arms
except his son Jad: the latter, when he saw the Kelbite
band approaching, seized his spear, mounted his horse, and
rode some distance apart.   When the Kelbites had alighted
'Abdallah asked them who they were.   They replied that
they were tithe-collectors sent by 'Abd al-Malik.

"Canst thou show me an order in proof of what thou
sayest?" asked the old man.

"Assuredly," replied Ibn Bahdal, "behold the order:"
and he showed him a document bearing the Khalif's seal.

"And what may be the tenour of these words?"

The document was read aloud: "'Abd al-Malik, son of
Merwân, to Humaid ibn Bahdal, greeting.   The aforesaid
Humaid ibn Bahdal is hereby commanded to levy tithe from
all the Bedawin whom he shall meet with.   Whosoever
payeth his tithe, and hath his name inscribed in this
register, will be deemed an obedient and faithful subject;
but whoso refuseth shall be held a rebel to God, to his
Prophet, and to the Commander of the Faithful."

"It is well: I am ready to obey, and pay the tithe."

"But that is not all.   There remaineth somewhat else.
We require thee to seek out all the members of thy tribe,
to collect the tithe from each of them, and to appoint a

place where we may meet thee and receive the money at thy hands."

" Nay, that may not be ! The Beni Fezâra are scattered far and wide over the Desert; I am no longer young, but am well stricken in years; I cannot fare so far, and I have with me one only of my sons. But ye who have come from afar, and are inured to long journeys, will discover my fellow-tribesmen more readily than I; each day you may light upon their encampments, for they halt wherever they find good pasturage."

" All this we know well; but it is not to seek good pasturage that they are scattered abroad over the Desert— it is to avoid payment of the tithe. They are rebels ! "

" I can swear to you that they are loyal subjects: it is but to seek for good pasturage—— "

" Enough ! Do thou that which we bid thee."

" I cannot ! Here is the tithe which is the Khalif's due; take it ! "

" Thy obedience is insincere. Thy son yonder, mounted on his horse, regardeth us disdainfully."

" Thou hast naught to fear from my son: take my tithe and depart ; if ye are, of a truth, tithers."

" Thy conduct showeth that we were told but too truly that thou and thy tribesmen fought for Ibn Zubair."

" Nay, that we did not. We paid him tithe, it is true, since we Bedawin meddle not with state matters, but pay the tithe to him who ruleth over the land."

" Prove the truth of thy words by bidding thy son dismount."

" What would ye with my boy ? The youth is fearful, seeing armed horsemen."

" Bid him dismount ; he hath naught to fear."

The old man approached his son, and bade him alight from his horse. " Father," pleaded the young man, " I read it in their pitiless eyes—they mean to slay me ! Give them what thou wilt, but suffer me to defend myself."

Returning to the Kelbites, 'Abdallah said to them: " The young man feareth for his life ; take my tithe, and leave us in peace."

" We will accept nothing while thy son remaineth in his saddle."

" He will not hearken to my words ; moreover, of what avail would this thing be to you ? "

" Enough: thou provest thyself a rebel. Slave, my

writing-gear! Our business here is at an end. We have
but to send word to the Commander of the Faithful that
'Abdallah, grandson of 'Oyeina, hath hindered us in the
execution of our mission to the Beni Fezâra."

" Do not so, I beseech thee, for I am innocent of such
conduct."

Paying no heed to the old man's supplications, Ibn
Bahdal wrote a letter and handed it to a horseman, who
immediately rode off in the direction of Damascus.
Thunderstruck at this proceeding, 'Abdallah cried : " Accuse
me not thus unjustly! I adjure you in Allah's name not
to write me down a rebel to the Khalif—I am ready to
obey his every command ! "

" Cause thy son to dismount, then."

" We have been taught to mistrust you : promise, therefore, that no evil shall happen to him."

The Kelbites having promised this in the most solemn
manner, 'Abdallah cried to his son: " May I be accursed
of Allah if thou alightest not from thy horse ! "

Jad thereupon obeyed, and throwing away his spear,
advanced slowly towards the Kelbites. " This will be an
ill day for thee, my father!" he said. As the tiger toys
with the victim he holds in his claws, before despatching it,
so the Kelbites began by insulting and scoffing at the young
man : then they bound him on a rock, the better to slay
him. In his death agony the poor boy cast upon his father
one last look, in which were mingled sorrow, resignation,
and reproach.

The Kelbites, savages though they were, felt constrained
to respect the old man's white hair : not venturing to shed
his blood as they had shed his son's, they beat him with
bludgeons, and left him for dead upon the sand. After a
while he recovered ; but gnawed by remorse he never ceased
to mutter: " If I were to forget all my calamities, never
would my son's glance, after I had delivered him to his
murderers, depart from my remembrance."

Jad's horse refused to quit the spot where the bloody
deed had been wrought. With its eyes fixed intently on
the ground, the faithful creature, ever and anon pawing the
sand still stained with its master's blood, awaited death by
starvation.

Other murders succeeded those already committed—
among the victims was Borda, son of Halhala an illustrious
sheik—and the bloodthirsty Kelbites did not return to

Damascus until the Kaisites, enlightened as to their real object, eluded their blind fury by seeking the remotest wilds of the Desert.

All the Kelbites were intoxicated with joy and pride, and a poet of the Joheina, a tribe which, as well as the Kelbites, were descended from Kodâ'a, has expressed their feelings with remarkable vigour and fanatical zeal:

" Know ye, my brethren, ye who are the allies of the Beni Kelb—know ye that Humaid ibn Bahdal the valiant hath brought joy and health to the Kelbites? Know ye that he hath covered the Beni Kais with shame and forced them to abandon their encampments? Terrible must their over-throw have been that they should thus flee! The victims of Humaid ibn Bahdal lie unburied on the sands of the Desert; the Kaisites pursued by their vanquishers cannot stay to bury them. Rejoice therefore, my brethren! The victories of the Beni Kelb are ours; they and we resemble the two hands of the same body; and when in the fight the right hand hath been severed, it is the left hand that wieldeth the sword."

There was great joy, moreover, amongst those of the Omayyad princes whose mothers were Kelbites. As soon as tidings of what had happened reached his ears, 'Abd al-'Azîz said to his brother Bishr, in the presence of the Khalif: " Knowest thou yet how my maternal uncles have treated thine ? "

" What have they done ? " he asked.

" The Kelbite horsemen have attacked and destroyed a Kaisite camp."

" Impossible! Thy maternal uncles are too sluggish and too cowardly to measure swords with mine ! "

Next morning, however, Bishr discovered that his brother had spoken truly. Halhala, Sa'îd, and another chief of the Fezâra reached Damascus, without cloaks, bare-footed, and with tattered garments; throwing themselves on their knees before Bishr, they entreated him to succour them and espouse their cause. He yielded to their request, and ap-proaching his brother the Khalif, pleaded the cause of his protégés so eloquently, that 'Abd al-Malik, notwithstanding his aversion to the Kaisites, promised to deduct the pecuniary compensation due to the Fezâra from the Kelbites' pay. But this decision, though in conformity with the law, did not satisfy the Fezâra. They thirsted, not for money but for blood. Upon their refusing the proffered terms of settle-ment, the Khalif said: " The public exchequer shall pay you forthwith half of the sum due to you, and if henceforth you remain loyal—which I much doubt—I will pay you the other half." Nettled by this insulting suspicion—the more since they could not deny that it was well-founded— and eager withal for retaliation, the Fezârites were on the point of again refusing the offer, when Zofar took them aside and advised them to accept the money, and with it to purchase horses and arms. The suggestion met with their approval, they consented to receive compensation, and after laying it out on their equipment, they set their faces towards the Desert.

On reaching the camp, they summoned a tribal council. In this assembly Halhala with burning words sought to excite his tribesmen to wreak vengeance on the Kelbites. His sons supported his appeal, but there were some present who, less blinded by hatred, judged such an expedition rash and dangerous. "Thine own family," urged one who differed with Halhala, "is too weak at present to take part in the fray. The Beni Kelb, hyenas that they are, have slain most of thy fighting men and pillaged all thy wealth. Of a surety in such circumstances thou wouldst not accompany us." "Son of my brother," replied Halhala, "I will set out with the rest, for my heart is on fire."—"They have slain my son, my Borda whom I loved so dearly!" he added in a hollow voice; and the bitter memory throwing him into one of those fits of fury habitual to him since his son's death, he began to utter loud and piercing cries, resembling rather the bellowing of a hind deprived of her fawn, than the accents of a human voice. "Who hath seen Borda?" he cried; "Where tarrieth he? Bring him to me; he is my son, my well-beloved, the pride and hope of his lineage!" Then he began deliberately to enumerate the names of all who had perished under the swords of the Kelbites, and after each name he cried: "Where is he? Where is he? Vengeance! Vengeance!"

The whole assembly, even those who a little while before had shown prudence and had opposed the project, suffered themselves to be won over by the fascination of this wild and savage eloquence. An expedition against the Beni Kelb was determined upon, and the Fezâra set out for Banât-Kain, where there was a Kelbite camp. Towards morning they fell upon their enemies unawares with shouts of "Vengeance for Borda! Vengeance for Jad! Vengeance for our brethren!" The reprisals were as cruel as the outrages which provoked them. A single Kelbite escaped, thanks to his fleetness of foot : all the others were massacred, and the Fezâra carefully examined their bodies, to mock the agonies of any that showed signs of life, and to despatch them.

Upon receiving tidings of this foray, Bishr took his revenge. In the Khalif's presence he said to his brother 'Abd al-'Azîz : " Knowest thou yet how my maternal uncles have treated thine ? " " Can it be," cried 'Abd al-'Azîz, " that they have made a raid after peace hath been concluded and the Khalif hath indemnified them ? " The Khalif, deeply angered at what he heard, but determined to await more precise information before coming to a decision, imposed silence on the brothers in a tone which admitted of no reply. Soon afterwards, a Kelbite, without his cloak, bare-footed, and with rent garments came in haste to 'Abd al-'Azîz, who immediately led him into the Khalif's presence and exclaimed : " Wilt thou suffer, O Commander of the Faithful, those whom thou hast taken under thy protection to be outraged, thine orders to be set at naught, thy gold to be stolen and used against thyself, and thy subjects to be murdered ? " The Kelbite then related all that had happened. Beside himself with rage, the Khalif resolved on extreme measures. Determined to make the Kaisites feel the whole weight of his displeasure and inveterate hatred, he instantly sent orders to Hajjâj, then Governor of all Arabia, to put every adult Fezârite to the sword.

Although this tribe was allied to his own, Hajjâj did not hesitate to obey. He was strongly attached to his race, but at the same time his ambition was insatiable. It was clear that by his party and himself there was but one attitude to be assumed, one course to be followed. His sound logical faculty taught him that opposition would be fruitless, that he must endeavour to regain the Khalif's goodwill, and that to this end he must bow without scruple or reservation to all his orders—even if he were commanded to destroy the holiest of sanctuaries or put a kinsman to death. And yet his heart was heavy. " When I shall have exterminated the Fezâra," he said, as he put himself at the head of his troops, " I shall be dishonoured, and my name will be held in abhorrence as that of the most unnatural Kaisite who ever trod the earth." The task before him, moreover, was one of great difficulty. The Beni Ghatafân, allies of the Fezâra, had sworn to help them, and a similar oath had been taken by all the Kaisite tribes. The first act of hostility would therefore be the signal for a ferocious civil war, the issue of which it was impossible to foresee. Hajjâj still hesitated when the arrival of Halhala and Sa'îd relieved his embarrassment. These two chieftains, satisfied with having wreaked their vengeance at Banât-Kain, and aghast at the thought of the outbreak of a war which might have for their people the most fatal consequences, sacrificed themselves, with a noble devotion, in order to avert the calamity which threatened their tribesmen. Love for their tribe, in fact, now possessed their minds as strongly as had, formerly, hatred for the Kelbites. Placing their hands on that of Hajjâj, they said to him: " Wherefore bearest thou ill-will towards the Beni Fezâra? We two alone are guilty." Rejoiced at this unlooked-for solution of his difficulty, the Governor, having put them in arrest, instantly wrote to the Khalif informing him that he had not ventured to make war upon the united Kaisite tribes, and urging him at the same time to rest content with the surrender of the two chiefs. The Khalif entirely approved his conduct, and bade him return to Damascus with his two prisoners.

When the Kaisites were led into the great hall where sat the sovereign surrounded by Kelbites, the guards ordered them to do obeisance. Halhala, however, instead of making salaam, began to recite, in a stentorian voice, some verses borrowed from a poem of his own:

"Salutation to the 'Adî, the Mâzin, the Shamkh,[1] and above all to Abû Wahb,[2] my faithful friend! I can welcome death, now that I have quenched my consuming thirst for Kelbite blood. What joy hath been mine! I have slain all those who encountered my sword; since they perished my heart hath been at rest."

To requite insolence with insolence, the Khalif in addressing him purposely mispronounced his name, as if it had been that of a man too obscure to deserve the honour of being correctly designated. He called him Halhal, but the chief instantly corrected him: " Halhala is my name," he said. " Halhal, surely," continued the Khalif. " Nay! it is Halhala; my father called me so, and it seemeth to me that he must have known it better than all else." " Well, Halhala—if Halhala it be—thou hast outraged those whom I, the Commander of the Faithful, took under my protection, thou hast ignored my orders, and thou hast stolen my money."

---

[1] Three sub-tribes of Fezâra. [2] One of the Mâzin.

"I have done none of these things: but I have fulfilled my vow, gratified my hatred, and glutted my vengeance."

"And God hath now delivered thee to the avenging hand of justice."

"I am guilty of no crime, O thou son of Zarkâ!" (The use of this name was an insult to 'Abd al-Malik, for it recalled a grandmother of scandalous memory.) The Khalif delivered him up to Soair, a Kelbite who laid to his charge the death of his father, slain at Banât-Kain.

"Tell me, Halhala," asked Soair, "when didst thou last see my father?" "At Banât-Kain," was the unconcerned reply: "and, poor wretch, he was trembling from head to foot!" "By Allah, I will slay thee!" cried Soair. "Thou? Thou liest! By Allah, thou art too vile and too cowardly for such a task! I know that I am about to die, but that is because it is the good pleasure of the son of Zarkâ." So saying, he walked to the place of execution with perfect equanimity and almost insolent gaiety, reciting ever and anon some snatch of the old Desert poetry, and having no need of the encouraging words addressed to him by Prince Bishr, who had desired to be present at his death and took great pride in his buoyant fortitude. As Soair raised his sword, Halhala said, "Try to strike me as fair a blow as that which I dealt thy father!" His comrade Sa'îd, whom the Khalif had handed over to another Kelbite, met his fate with a contempt for life equally profound.

[AUTHORITIES: Suyûtî, pp. 216–17; Mûbarrad, ff. 635–6, 870; Ibn Kutaiba, pp. 201–2, 272; Ibn Khallikân (ed. Slane), i. 182; Fâkihî, f. 401; Hamâsa, pp. 260–4, 658; Raihân, f. 204; Aghânî, i. 27.]

CHAPTER IX

KELBITES AND KAISITES (*continued*)

WHILE the Syrians pillaged and slew one another, the men of 'Irâk, a graceless and ungovernable race, indulged in like violence, and long afterwards the turbulent nobles of Kûfa and Basra recalled with regret this period of anarchy—the good old days when, accompanied by a score or so of clients, they would swagger through the streets, with heads held high and menacing glances, ever ready to draw their scimitars should another noble's mien be judged a trifle aggressive. If they chanced to stretch an opponent or two in the kennel, they well knew that the Governor was far too indulgent to punish them. Their Governors, however, left them not only unpunished but unprotected, for in their envy and hatred of Muhallab, they allowed 'Irâk to remain exposed to the incursions of the Khârejites, who were still formidable, despite their many defeats. It must be admitted that for their envy there was some cause. The people of 'Irâk regarded Muhallab as their country's greatest general, and also as her saviour. No other name was as popular as his, and, since he had made his own terms before consenting to assume the command, he had amassed a colossal fortune, which he spent with splendid prodigality.[1] He thus threw all the Governors into the shade by his luxury, his princely wealth, and his boundless liberality, as well as by his military renown.

"The Arabs of this city have no eyes save for that man," sadly observed the Omayyad Khâlid, the first Governor of Basra after the Restoration. He accordingly recalled Muhallab from the scene of his exploits, and condemned him to inaction by giving him the governorship of Ahwâz and conferring the command of the army, thirty thousand strong, on his own brother 'Abd al-'Azîz. This young man was as vain as he was inexperienced, and exclaimed with an arrogant gesture: "The people of Basra imagine that no one but

---

[1] It is said that he gave 100,000 silver pieces to the reciter of a poetical panegyric, and a like sum to its alleged author.

Muhallab can bring this war to a close : they shall see ! "
He expiated his foolish presumption by suffering a terrible
and sanguinary defeat. Despising the prudent advice of his
officers, who tried to dissuade him from pursuing a squadron
that feigned flight, he fell into an ambush, lost all his generals,
a vast number of his troops, and even his young and lovely
wife—he himself escaping as by a miracle the swords of a
score of the enemy who followed on his heels.

This disaster was no surprise to Muhallab. Expecting
something of the kind, he had instructed an agent to send
him a journal of all that happened in the army. After the
defeat the agent came to him in person.

" What tidings bringest thou ? " cried Muhallab, as soon
as he saw him.

" I bring thee news to gladden thine heart : *he* hath
suffered defeat, and his army is utterly routed ! "

" What ! thou wretch, thinkest thou that I rejoice to
near that a Kurashite hath been defeated, and that a Moslem
army is routed ? "

" Whether it giveth thee joy or not mattereth little : it
sufficeth that the news is true."

Resentment against the Governor was bitter throughout
the province : " See what comes of sending against the
enemy a young man of unproved courage instead of the
noble and loyal Muhallab—that hero, who, thanks to his long
experience of war, foresees dangers and knows how to avoid
them." Such reproaches Khâlid had to endure, as well as
the consciousness of his brother's disgrace ; but he was not
over-sensitive on points of honour : in revenge he clung to
his post, as well as to his life, but awaited with ever-increasing anxiety the arrival of a messenger from Damascus.

Craving, as is the wont of weak men, reassurance from a
stronger nature than his own, he sent for Muhallab. " What
thinkest thou 'Abd al-Malik will do ? " asked the Governor.

" Depose thee," replied the General laconically, owing him
too bitter a grudge to wish to alleviate his anxiety.

" Must I not look for something still more humiliating,
though I am the Khalif's kinsman ? "

" Undoubtedly," replied Muhallab coldly, " for he will no
sooner learn that thy brother 'Abd al-'Azîz has been defeated
by the Khârejites of Persia, than he will also hear that thy
brother Omayya hath been routed by those of Bahrain."

The dreaded messenger arrived at last, bearing a letter
from the Khalif to Khâlid. In this letter 'Abd al-Malik

bitterly reproached the Governor for his inept and culpable conduct, announced his dismissal, and ended with these words: "Were I to punish thee after thy deserts, thou wouldst feel my resentment much more heavily; but I am mindful of our kinship, and therefore confine myself to depriving you of office."

The Khalif replaced Khâlid by his own brother Bishr, then Governor of Kûfa, ordering the latter to give the command of the army to Muhallab and to reinforce it by eight thousand men from Kûfa.   It was impossible, in the circumstances, to have made a worse choice.   An extreme and violent Kaisite, as we have already seen, Bishr embraced all the Yemenite tribes in a common hatred, and detested Muhallab as the natural chieftain of that race in 'Irâk.   Accordingly when he received the Khalif's letter he fell into a rage and swore he would have Muhallab's life.   His Prime Minister, Mûsâ ibn Nusayr—the future conqueror of Spain [1]—soothed him with great difficulty and immediately despatched a letter to the General, urging him to be very circumspect—to mingle with the crowd and welcome Bishr when he arrived at Basra, but not to be present at the audience.   Muhallab acted upon this advice.

Upon reaching the palace at Basra, Bishr gave audience to the notables of the town, and, remarking Muhallab's absence, inquired its cause.   He was informed that the General had saluted him from among the crowd in the street, but that he felt too unwell to be able to pay his respects in person at the palace.   Bishr saw in the General's indisposition an excellent pretext for not giving him the command of the army.   His flatterers did not fail to assure him that, as Governor, he had a perfect right to nominate his own general, but not daring to disobey the Khalif's formal order, he hit upon the plan of sending 'Abd al-Malik a deputation with a letter informing him that Muhallab was ill, but that there were plenty of other generals in 'Irâk quite capable of taking his place.

When this deputation arrived at Damascus, 'Abd al-Malik had a private conversation with its head, Ibn Hakîm. "I know," said he, "that you are a wholly upright and very intelligent man; tell me therefore frankly who, in your

---

[1] At first a Zubairite, Mûsâ had been present at the Battle of Marj Râhit. Proscribed by Merwân, he had been taken under the protection of 'Abd al-'Azîz, son of the Khalif.   He was thenceforth one of the firmest supporters of the Omayyads.   Ibn Asakir, *Hist. de Damas* (MS. in the Bibl. d'Aatif, Constantinople).

opinion, is the general that possesses the talent and qualities
necessary for bringing this war to a successful issue?" Ibn
Hakîm, though not a Yemenite, replied without hesitation
that it was Muhallab. "But he is ill," said the Khalif.
"It is not his illness," replied Ibn Hakîm with a meaning
smile, "which prevents his receiving the command." "Ah!
I understand," said the Khalif: "Bishr intends to follow
in Khâlid's footsteps!"

'Abd al-Malik accordingly sent the Governor peremptory
orders to entrust Muhallab, and none other, with the command of the army. Bishr obeyed, but with a bad grace.
Muhallab having sent him a list of soldiers whom he wished
enrolled, the Governor struck out the names of the bravest,
and then summoning Ibn Mikhnaf, general of the Kûfan
auxiliary troops, said to him: "You know that I esteem
and trust you. If you would retain my friendship, do what
I now bid you: disobey every order given you by this barbarian from 'Omân, and contrive that all his plans may mis-
carry." Ibn Mikhnaf bowed; Bishr thought this signified
assent, but he had mistaken his man. Ibn Mikhnaf was of
the same race, and what was more, of the same tribe, as
Muhallab, and he had not the least intention of playing the
odious part suggested to him by the Governor: on leaving
the palace he remarked to his friends: "Assuredly the boy
must be crazy to suppose me capable of treachery towards
the illustrious chief of my tribe!"

The army took the field, and Muhallab, though deprived
of his best officers and bravest soldiers, had nevertheless
driven back the Khârejites successively from the Euphrates,
from Ahwâz, and from Râm Hormuz[1]—when his brilliant
series of victories was suddenly interrupted by news that
Bishr was no more. What this blunderer had failed to
accomplish while living was effected by his death. The
army fell into terrible confusion. Believing—such was
their selfishness—that the war concerned only the Arabs
of Basra, the Kûfan soldiers under Ibn Mikhnaf mutinied,
and deserting in a body, set out for home. Most of the
soldiers from Basra followed their example. Never during
the long struggle had such imminent danger threatened.
'Irak was a prey to utter anarchy: not a semblance of
authority or discipline remained. Bishr's lieutenant at Kûfa
threatened the deserters with death if they did not return to
their posts: their only reply was to go to their homes, and

[1] About 100 m. N.E. of Basra.

there was no question of punishing them. Soon the Khârejites overwhelmed the handful of brave men who had remained faithful to Muhallab's standard, burst through all
the former barriers, and poured into 'Irâk. The unfortunate
wretches who on the occasion of the defeat of 'Abd al-'Azîz
had fallen into the hands of these fanatics, had been loaded
with chains, thrown into dungeons, and suffered to die of
hunger: who could be sure that the Khârejites had not prepared a similar fate for all the " pagans " of the province ?
Much depended on the new Governor. If the Khalif's choice
was a bad one, as it had been on each previous occasion,
'Irâk was lost.

'Abd al-Malik appointed Hajjâj. The latter, who was
at Medina when he received his nomination, immediately
started for Kûfa with only twelve companions (December,
A.D. 694). Upon his arrival he proceeded straight to the
Mosque, where the populace, who had been warned of his
approach, were assembled. He entered girt with a sword,
and carrying a bow in his hand, his face being half concealed
by the voluminous folds of his turban. Ascending the
pulpit, he directed his weak and wandering gaze—for he was
short-sighted—at the congregation for some time, without
uttering a word. Taking this prolonged silence for a sign of
timidity, the townsmen grew indignant, and since they were,
if not valiant in deeds, at any rate insolent in speech—
especially when an opportunity arose of insulting a Governor
—they had already begun to say one to another: " May
Allah confound these Omayyads, who entrust the Government of our province to imbeciles ! " and one of the boldest
had even proposed to hurl a stone at his head, when Hajjâj
suddenly broke the silence which he had so obstinately maintained. A daring innovator in oratory, as well as in state-
craft, he did not begin with the customary prelude in honour
of God and the Prophet. Putting aside the turban which
screened his face, he began by reciting this verse of an ancient
poet: [1]

" I am the rising sun. I surmount every obstacle. To
be known, it sufficeth that I unveil myself." Then he continued in slow and solemn accents: " Known to me are
the heads ripe for the harvest.—And the reaper ? I am the
reaper.—Between turbans and beards that sweep the breast,
I see blood—blood !"

Then with slowly rising animation he went on: " By

[1] Suhaym ibn Wathil ; see Nicholson, *Lit. Hist. of the Arabs* (1907), p. 202.

Allah, ye men of 'Irâk, I am not one that fleeth at a
threatening look. I am not like a camel that gallopeth
away at full speed, terrified by the drumming of an empty
water-skin. Just as a horse's mouth is scanned to discover
his age and his fitness for work—mine hath been scanned,
and my wisdom teeth have been seen. The Commander
of the Faithful hath drawn his arrows from his quiver—he
hath spread them out—he hath examined them one by one,
heedfully, carefully. He hath made proof of them all, he
hath chosen the keenest and the toughest—that arrow is
myself. This is why he hath sent me among you. For a
long time ye have trodden the paths of anarchy and rebellion; but—hear my oath!—I will treat you as thorn-
bushes which men gather for fuel, and which they faggot
with cords ere they cut them in bundles—I will buffet you
as the herdsmen bethwack the camels that linger in the
pasturage when the others wend to the tethering. Mark
this well—what I say, I do; what I design, I accomplish;
once I have traced out the sole of a sandal, I cut the
leather true."

"The Commander of the Faithful hath ordered me to
give you your pay and to conduct you to the seat of war,
there to fight under Muhallab. I give you three days for
preparation, and I swear by all that is most holy that when
they are at an end, I will behead every man who doth not
set out. And now, young man, read the Khalif's letter."
The youth addressed read the words: "'Abd al-Malik,
Commander of the Faithful, sendeth greeting to all the
Musulmans of Kûfa——"

It was customary for the people to reply to this formula
with the words: "Greeting to the Commander of the
Faithful!" But on this occasion the assembly maintained
a sullen silence. Although they felt instinctively that they
had found their master in this orator whose style was so
harsh and abrupt, withal so picturesque and vigorous, they
could not yet admit it to themselves.

"Stay!" cried Hajjâj to the reader. Then, addressing
the people once more, "The Commander of the Faithful
greeteth you," he exclaimed, "and ye make no response?
By Allah! must I give you a lesson in courtesy? Begin
again, young man!"

As he uttered these simple words Hajjâj threw into his
gesture, into his glance, into the sound of his voice, an expression so threatening and terrible, that when the reader

repeated the words "sendeth greeting," the whole assembly
cried with one voice, "Greeting to the Commander of the
Faithful!"

A like method was adopted, with similar success, at
Basra. Many inhabitants of that town, informed of what
had happened at Kûfa, did not even await the arrival of
the new Governor before setting out to join Muhallab's
force, and that general, agreeably surprised at the unwonted
zeal of the men of 'Irâk, cried in a transport of joy, "God
be praised! At last there is a *man* in 'Irâk!"[1] Woe to
him who dared to show any hesitation, or the slightest hint
of resistance, for human life was of little account in the
eyes of Hajjâj. Two or three persons discovered this to
their cost.

If, however, Hajjâj thought that the game was won, he
was mistaken. Recovering somewhat from their first terror,
the men of 'Irâk blushed at having allowed themselves to
be stunned and intimidated like schoolboys in the presence
of a severe pedagogue, and just as Hajjâj was setting out
with a division to join Muhallab, a dispute with regard to
pay proved the signal for an outbreak which soon assumed
the aspect of a formidable revolt. The rallying cry was,
"Away with the Governor!" The rebels swore that they
would force 'Abd al-Malik to recall him, threatening that
in case of refusal they would depose him themselves. Abandoned by all except his relatives, his intimate friends, and
his household servants, Hajjâj saw the rebels pillage his
tent and carry off his wives: had they not been restrained
by fear of the Khalif, he would himself have been slain.
Yet not for an instant did he lose courage. Indignantly
rejecting the advice of his friends, who wished him to parley
with the rebels, he exclaimed boldly, and as though master
of the situation: "Never! until they have handed over to
me the ringleaders." In all probability he would have paid
for his inflexible pertinacity with his life, had not the Kaisites
at this critical juncture come over to his side. They had
already recognised in him their hope, their support, their
leader; they had grasped the idea that by following the
line of conduct Hajjâj had traced out for them they might
raise themselves from their humiliation and return to power.
Three Kaisite chiefs—amongst whom the gallant Kotaiba
ibn Moslim was conspicuous—rushed to his rescue; one of
Muhallab's tribesmen, and a Temîmite sheik not in sympathy

[1] Weil, i. 433.

with the rebels, followed their example, and as soon as Hajjâj saw six thousand men mustered under his standard he forced the insurgents to join battle. At one moment his defeat seemed imminent, but he succeeded in rallying his men, and the rebel leader having been killed by an arrow, he gained a victory which he rendered complete and decisive by his clemency towards the vanquished, who were not pursued, but were granted an amnesty. Hajjâj contented himself with sending the heads of nineteen rebel leaders, who had fallen in the fight, to Muhallab, to serve as a warning to any who might feel mutinous sentiments rising in their hearts.

The Kaisites, heretofore abettors of every rebellion, found themselves for the first time on the side of authority, and having once entered upon this path, they pursued it, recognising that it was the only way to reinstate themselves in the Khalif's favour.

Order having been restored, Hajjâj had but one care, namely to arouse and spur on Muhallab, whom he suspected of unduly protracting the war in his own interest. The Governor's natural impetuosity led him to adopt both wise and unwise measures. He sent the General letter after letter, bitterly reproaching him with what he termed his tardiness, his inactivity, his cowardice—even going so far as to threaten him with death, or at the least with deprivation. Besides this, he sent commissaries, one after another, to the field. Belonging to the same race as the Governor, and possessed with a mania for giving advice, especially unasked advice, these commissaries sometimes caused disorder in the army, but on the day of battle were conspicuous by their absence. Nevertheless, the end was gained. Two years had not elapsed since Hajjâj had been appointed to the government of 'Irâk before the Khârejites laid down their arms.[1]

Nominated viceroy of all the eastern provinces, as a reward for his faithful and valuable services, Hajjâj had yet many a revolt to deal with; but he quelled them all; and while he rendered his sovereign's crown more stable, he raised his tribe from the state of deep humiliation into which they had sunk, and endeavoured to reconcile them to the Khalif. He succeeded without great difficulty. Since the Khalif was obliged to rely either on the Kelbites or on the Kaisites, his choice could not, indeed, be doubtful.

---

[1] Towards the end of A.D. 696.

H

Monarchs usually have little liking for those who, having contributed to their elevation, have a just claim on their gratitude.   The services rendered by the Kelbites had inspired them with an arrogance which had become irksome; they were for ever reminding the Khalif that if it had not been for them neither he nor his father would have ascended the throne; they looked upon him as their dependant— even as their creature and property.   The Kaisites, on the other hand, desiring at all costs to make 'Abd al-Malik forget that they had been the foes of his father and himself, solicited his favour on their knees, and unquestioningly obeyed his every word and gesture.   They thus won him over and supplanted their rivals.

The discarded Kelbites were loud in their protests.   The Khalif's power was too firmly established at this period for them to attempt a revolt against it; but their poets bitterly reproached him with his ingratitude, and did not refrain from threats.   Witness the following verses by Jauwâs, the father of that Sa'd whose death in Spain as victim of Kaisite hatred we shall hear of later :

"'Abd al-Malik!   Thou hast not requited us, though we fought bravely for thee, and gained for thee the enjoyment of this world's pleasures. Rememberest thou that which happened at Jâbia in the Jawlân? If Ibn Bahdal had not stood by thee at the assembly there held thou wouldst live inglorious, and none of thy family would recite public prayer in the Mosque.   And yet, now that thou hast obtained the supreme power, and findest thyself without a rival, thou turnest thy back upon us, and art not far from treating us as enemies.   Art thou all unmindful that time may bring about its revenges?"

In another poem he reiterates his complaint :

"The Omayyads have made us stain our spears in the blood of their foes, and now they deny us any share in their good fortune!   Family of Omayya!   Legions numberless of doughty warriors, whose battle-cry was not yours, we have fought against with sword and spear; from you have we warded off the danger which menaced.   Perchance God will reward us for our services, inasmuch as with our arms we have established the throne; but of a surety the family of Omayya will not reward us.   Ye are strangers, who come from Hijâz, from a land that the Desert divideth wholly from ours, and whom Syria knoweth not.[1]   Time was when the Kaisites marched against you; their eyes flashing with hatred, and their standard flapping in the breeze. . . ."

Another Kelbite poet, one of those who had formerly

---

[1] The branch of the Omayyads to which Merwân belonged had settled at Medina.

sung the victory of Râhit, addressed these verses to the Omayyads :

"Ere ye had attained to sovereignty, we drove from the throne of Damascus those who had dared to occupy it, and gave it to you. On many a field we have proved our devotion, and at the Battle of Marj Râhit you owed the victory wholly to our valour. Repay not our good and loyal services with ingratitude ; formerly you smiled upon us ; take heed that you play not the tyrant towards us. Before Merwân's time, when care, like a thick veil, shrouded the eyes of an Omayyad Emir, we tore that veil away so that he saw the light ; when he was on the verge of defeat and gnashed his teeth, we saved him, so that he cried in his joy, 'God is great!' When the Kaisite plays the boaster, remind him of the valour which he displayed in Dhahhâk's camp to the east of Jaubar![1] There no Kaisite showed himself a man of mettle : all, mounted on their chestnut steeds,[2] took refuge in flight!"

But reproaches, murmurs, threats, availed the Kelbites nothing. Their ascendancy had passed, and passed for ever. It was true that the policy of the Court might change—as in fact later on it did change—it is also true that the Kelbites had still no unimportant part to play, especially in Africa and Spain, but they never regained the proud position they held under Merwân, that of being the paramount tribe among the Yemenites. That rank was henceforth held by the Beni Azd ; the family of Muhallab had supplanted that of Ibn Bahdal. At the same time the tribal conflict, while losing none of its bitterness, spread over a vaster field : henceforth Kaisites were everywhere at enmity with Yemenites.

In the reign of Walîd, who in 705 succeeded his father 'Abd al-Malik, the power of the Kaisites culminated. "My son," said 'Abd al-Malik upon his deathbed, "ever hold Hajjâj in the most profound respect ; it is to him that thou owest the throne, he is thy sword and thy right arm, and thou hast more need of him than he of thee." Walîd never forgot this counsel. "My father," he said, "was accustomed to declare that Hajjâj was the skin of his brow ; but I say that he is the skin of my face."[3] These words epitomize Walîd's whole reign, which was indeed more fertile than any other in conquests and military glory : in it the Kaisite Kutaiba planted the Moslem standard on the walls of Samarcand ; Mohammed ibn Kâsim, cousin of Hajjâj, conquered

---

[1] *I.e.* at the Battle of Râhit.

[2] "The Prophet has said, 'If I were to gather together all the horses of the Arabs, and make them race against one another, it is the chestnut that would outstrip the rest.'" 'Abd al-Kader, in E. Daumas, *The Horses of the Sahara* (1862), p. 136.

[3] *Hist. Khalifatus al-Walîdi* (ed. Anspach), p. 13.

India to the foot of the Himalayas; while at the other
extremity of the empire, the Yemenites, after achieving the
conquest of the north of Africa, annexed Spain to the vast
fabric of which the Prophet of Mecca had laid the foundation.
Nevertheless this was a disastrous period for the Yemenites,
and especially for the two most prominent, though not the
most estimable, men of that party, Yazîd, son of Muhallab,
and Mûsâ, son of Nusayr.   Unfortunately for himself, Yazîd
—head of his house since his father's death—had given
Hajjâj very good grounds for animosity against him.   Like
the rest of his family, which was the most open-handed of
all under the Omayyads—just as the Barmicides were, under
the 'Abbâsids—Yazîd scattered money wherever he went,
and with a view to being happy himself and making everyone
else happy, squandered his fortune on pleasure, on the arts,
and on the reckless outpourings of his princely munificence.
It is related that once, when making pilgrimage to Mecca,
he gave a thousand pieces of silver to a barber for shaving
him.   Amazed at receiving so large a sum, the barber
exclaimed in his joy : " With this I will ransom my mother
from slavery ! "   Touched by this instance of filial affection,
Yazîd gave him another thousand pieces.   " May I put
away my wife," cried the barber, " if I shave another man
so long as I live ! "   Whereupon Yazîd gave him yet two
thousand pieces more.   Many similar stories are told of him,
which at least tend to show that gold flowed like water
between his spendthrift fingers ; but since no fortune, however vast, could hold out against prodigality thus pushed
to the verge of insanity, Yazîd, to escape ruin, had been
tempted to encroach on the Khalif's treasure.   Upon
being condemned by Hajjâj to repay six millions to the
exchequer, and being unable to find more than half of this
sum, Yazîd was thrown into a dungeon and cruelly tortured.
After four years he succeeded in escaping, with two of his
brothers who had shared his captivity.   Hajjâj believed
that he had fled to Khorasan, to stir up an insurrection
there, and sent messengers to Kutaiba urging him to be on
his guard, and to nip in the bud any symptoms of revolt.
The fugitives, however, crossing the desert of Semâwa, with
a Kelbite guide, sought the protection of Sulaimân—the
Khalif's brother, and head of the Yemenite party—who was
heir to the throne by virtue of the provisions made by 'Abd
al-Malik.   Sulaimân swore that so long as he lived Muhallab's sons would have nothing to fear ; he further offered to

repay to the treasury the three millions which Yazîd had
been unable to find, and sought pardon for the latter. This
he obtained with much difficulty, and by a kind of *coup de
théâtre*. Yazîd thenceforth lived in his protector's palace,
awaiting the moment of his party's return to power. When
asked why he did not purchase a house for himself, he
replied : " Wherefore ? I shall soon find a permanent lodging :
a governor's palace, if Sulaimân becomes Khalif, and a prison
if he doth not."

The other Yemenite—the future conqueror of Spain—was
not, like Yazîd, of a noble stock. He was a freedman, and he
was only attached to the party then in disgrace, in the sense
that his patron 'Abd al-'Azîz—brother of the Khalif 'Abd
al-Malik, and Governor of Egypt—was, as we have seen, a
warm supporter of the Kelbites because his mother belonged
to that tribe. Already, during the reign of 'Abd al-Malik,
Mûsâ, when collector of taxes at Basra, had been guilty of
malversation. The Khalif, upon being informed of this,
ordered Hajjâj to arrest him. Warned in time, Mûsâ escaped
to Egypt, where he implored his patron's protection. The
latter not only accorded this, but betook himself to Court to
settle the matter. The Khalif demanded an indemnity of
a hundred thousand pieces of gold : 'Abd al-'Azîz paid him
half this sum, and afterwards nominated Mûsâ to the
Governorship of Africa—an appointment at that time in the
gift of the Governor of Egypt. Even after the conquest of
Spain, Mûsâ, though laden with riches, continued to make
free with the Khalif's property as impudently as before. It
is true that peculation from the public funds was almost
universal in those days : Mûsâ's fault consisted in his being
more daring than others, while it was his misfortune not to
belong to the dominant party. Walîd had kept a watchful
eye over the Governor, and after some time summoned him
to Syria to render an account of his administration. Mûsâ
evaded the order as long as he could, but at last perforce
obeying it, he quitted Spain, and on arriving at the Court,
endeavoured to disarm the Khalif's wrath by splendid gifts.
It was in vain. The long accumulated hatred of his companions, Târik, Mughîth and others, burst forth : they loaded
Mûsâ with accusations which were only too readily believed,
and the faithless Governor was ignominiously expelled from
the audience-chamber, before the council ended. The Khalif
had determined to put him to death, but some influential
courtiers, whom Mûsâ had won over by aid of his wealth,

succeeded in saving his life in consideration of his being mulcted in a very heavy fine.

Not long after this Walîd died, leaving the throne to his brother Sulaimân. The ruin of the Kaisites immediately followed, and was complete. Hajjâj was no more. " Allah, grant that I may die before the Commander of the Faithful, and let me not be subject to a sovereign who will show me no pity ! "[1] Such had been his prayer, and God had granted it ; but his clients, his creatures, and those of his friends who still held office were instantly dismissed and replaced by Yemenites. Yazîd Ibn Abî Moslim, freedman and secretary of Hajjâj, lost the Governorship of ʿIrâk and was thrown into a dungeon—whence he emerged five years later, on the accession of the Kaisite Khalif Yazîd II, to become Governor of Africa : in those days such sudden changes of fortune were not infrequent.

Less fortunate than Ibn Abî Moslim, the valiant Kutaiba was beheaded ; the illustrious conqueror of India, Mohammed ibn Kâsim, cousin of Hajjâj, expired under torture ; while Yazîd, son of Muhallab, who in the preceding reign had narrowly escaped the same fate, enjoyed unlimited power, as Sulaimân's favourite. Mûsâ alone failed to profit by the triumph of the party to which he belonged ; for in the vain hope of conciliating Walîd, he had grievously offended Sulaimân. Just as Mûsâ reached Syria Walîd was so dangerously ill that his death was daily expected, and his brother, who hankered after the rich presents which Mûsâ had offered the Khalif, requested the Governor to slacken his pace, so as not to reach Damascus until the Khalif's death had placed Sulaimân himself upon the throne. Mûsâ did not yield to this request, and Walîd's sons inherited the splendid gifts made to their father. Sulaimân consequently owed Mûsâ a grudge, and would not remit any portion of his fine : this, as a matter of fact, he could easily pay with the help of his many clients in Spain, and of members of the Beni Lakhm—his wife's tribe. But Sulaimân did not push his revenge further. A multitude of legends, some more affecting than others, have sprung up with regard to Mûsâ's fate ; they are the invention of romancists of an epoch when the position of parties in the eighth century had been entirely forgotten, and when all that was certainly known was that Mûsâ enjoyed —as an ancient and trustworthy writer [2] relates—the protection and friendship of Yazîd, son of Muhallab, the all-

---

[1] Weil, i. 553.   [2] Balâdhurî, p. 270.

powerful favourite of Sulaimân. There is not even plausible
ground for accepting the worthless legends referred to;
they rest on no trustworthy authority, and are directly
opposed to the circumstantial narrative of a contemporary
chronicler.[1]

Sulaimân's successor, 'Omar II, presents a singular exception in the history of the Omayyads. He was not a
partisan, but a venerable hierarch—a saintly man who held
in abhorrence the clamours of discord and hatred, who
thanked God that he had not lived in the days of the
saints of Islam, when 'Alî, Ayesha, and Mu'âwiya had
struggled for the victory, and who even forbade that unhappy
strife to be spoken of. Entirely absorbed in the interests
of religion and the propagation of the Faith, he reminds us
of that excellent and venerable pontiff who exclaimed to the
Florentines : " Be ye neither Guelphs nor Ghibellines, but
Christians and fellow-citizens !" But 'Omar II was as far
from realizing his generous dreams as was Gregory X.
Yazîd II, who succeeded him, and who had married a niece
of Hajjâj, was a Kaisite. Then Hishâm ascended the
throne. He at first favoured the Yemenites, and having
replaced by men of that party [2] many governors nominated
by his predecessor, he allowed those who succeeded to
power cruelly to persecute those whom they supplanted :
but when, for reasons to be explained later, he threw over
the Yemenites, the Kaisites took their revenge, especially
in Africa and Spain.

Since their Arab population was almost exclusively
Yemenite, these countries were usually tranquil when ruled
by men of that party; while, under Kaisite governors, they
became the scene of the most frightful outbreaks. This is
what happened on the death of the Kelbite Bishr, Governor
of Africa. Bishr, on his deathbed, had entrusted the
government of the province to one of his tribesmen, who,
it would appear, flattered himself that the Khalif Hishâm
would formally confirm him in his office. His hope was not
fulfilled, for Hishâm appointed 'Obaida, a Kaisite, of the
tribe of Sulaym. The Kelbite, on being informed of this,
believed himself strong enough to maintain his position by
force of arms.

It was a Friday morning, in the month of June or July,

---

[1] Namely, Isidore of Beja.
[2] In Khorasan, e.g. the Kaisite Moslim al-Kilâbî was replaced by the Yemenite
Asad al-Kasrî.

A.D. 728. The Kelbite Governor was duly attired and was about to set out to the Mosque to preside over public prayers, when his friends rushed into his chamber crying : "The Emir! The Emir 'Obaida is about to enter the town!" Thunderstruck, the Kelbite, at first silent and stupefied, only recovered his voice to exclaim : "God alone is powerful! The hour of the Last Judgment will come thus unlooked for!" His limbs refused to support him ; frozen with terror he fell to the ground.

'Obaida had recognised that to establish his authority, he must take the Capital by surprise. Fortunately for him, Kairwan had no walls, and marching silently with his Kaisites through byways he had entered unawares, while the townsfolk supposed he was still in Egypt or Syria. Once master of the Capital he treated the Kelbites with unparalleled cruelty. After casting them into dungeons he put them to torture, and to gratify his sovereign's cupidity mulcted them in exorbitant fines.

Spain's turn came.[1] Her Governor was at that time nominated by the Governor of Africa, but thus far she had been subject but once to a Kaisite. Having failed in his first attempts, 'Obaida sent thither, in April, 729, the Kaisite Haitham, one of the tribe of Kilâb, at the same time threatening the Arabs of Spain with condign punishment if they dared to resist the commands of their new governor. The Yemenites murmured—perhaps they even plotted against Haitham ; at any rate the latter thought so, and acting upon 'Obaida's secret instructions, he threw the chief men of the party into prison, wrung from them by atrocious tortures confession of a conspiracy, and put them to death. Among his victims was a Kelbite, who by reason of his noble origin, his riches, and his eloquence, was held in high esteem. This was Sa'd, son of that Jauwâs[2] who had in his verses so vigorously reproached the Khalif 'Abd al-Malik for his ingratitude towards those Kelbites who at the Battle of Râhit had decided the fate of the Empire and gained for Merwân a throne. At Sa'd's execution the Kelbites trembled with indignation, and some of them—including Abrash, Hishâm's secretary—who had not lost all influence at Court, used it to such good purpose that they

---

[1] The conquest of Spain is narrated in Book II.

[2] Called Zat (Sad) simply, by Isidore, but that he was son of Jauwâs may be inferred : see Chap. XII, p. 149.

induced the Khalif to send to Spain a certain Mohammed with instructions to punish Haitham and give the government of the province to the Yemenite 'Abd-er-Rahmân al-Ghâfikî, who enjoyed great popularity. Upon his arrival at Cordova, Mohammed could not find 'Abd-er-Rahmân, who was hiding to escape the tyrant's persecution; but having arrested Haitham, he ordered him to be beaten and his head to be shaved—as a brand of disgrace; afterwards the ex-Governor, loaded with chains and mounted on an ass, with his face to the tail and his hands tied behind him, was to be led through the streets of the city. This sentence having been duly carried out, Haitham was sent to Africa, in order that the Governor of that province might pass judgment on him. But 'Obaida could scarcely be expected to punish, in his turn, a man who had merely carried out his chief's orders. The Khalif, for his part, considered that he had given the Kelbites ample satisfaction, although their demands went further, since, according to Arab notions, Sa'd's death could only be expiated by that of his murderer. Hishâm accordingly sent such ambiguous orders to 'Obaida that the latter was able to interpret it to Haitham's advantage. This was highly disappointing to the Kelbites, but they would not be discouraged, and one of their most illustrious chieftains, Abu 'l-Khattâr, who had been Sa'd's intimate friend, and who when thrown into prison by 'Obaida had nursed his hatred against the tyrant and the Kaisites in general, composed a poem destined for the Khalif's ears:

"Thou sufferest the Kaisites to shed our blood, O son of Merwân; but if thou refusest to do us justice we will appeal to the righteous judgment of God. It seemeth that thou hast forgotten the Battle of Râhit, and rememberest not those who then gave thee the victory; know, thou, that it was by our breasts that thou wert shielded from the spears of the enemy, and that thou hadst no horse or foot but us. But since thou hast attained the object of thy ambition, and, thanks to us, swim in pleasures, we are beneath thy notice; yet, so long as we have known thee, we have gone hand in hand. Beware therefore of yielding to a fancied security when war breaketh out again; when thy foot slippeth upon the rope-ladder mayhap the cords that thou deemest so firmly twisted will untwist. Many a time hath this been seen."

The Kelbite Abrash, Hishâm's secretary, undertook to recite these verses to the Khalif, and the threat of a civil war had such an effect upon Hishâm that he instantly decreed 'Obaida's dismissal, exclaiming in real or feigned wrath: "May the curse of Allah light upon this son of a Christian who heedeth not my commands!"

[AUTHORITIES: Mûbarrad, pp. 46, 220–1, 740–66, 785; Ibn Khallikân (ed. Wüst.), fasc. ix. 51; x. 105–15; Ibn Kutaiba, pp. 201–2; *Hamâsa*, pp. 656–9; Suyûtî, p. 221; Ibn Khaldûn, ff. 186, 196; Isid., c. 38, 40, 57; Ibn Habîb, p. 153; *Akbâr majmûʿat*, 62; Abû 'l-Mahâsin, i. 288; Ibn al-ʿAbbâr, 47–9; Makkarî, ii. 10; *Notices*, pp. 47–9, 257; Ibn Adhârî, i. 24–5, 36–7.]

CHAPTER X

THE BERBERS

THE strife between Yemenites and Kaisites was not without its influence upon the conquered races, with regard to whom the two parties held widely divergent views, especially as concerned payment of tribute. It was Hajjâj who had laid down the policy to be followed by his own party. The Law provided that Christians and Jews who came under Mohammedan rule, and who embraced Islamism, were exempted from payment to the Treasury of the poll-tax [1] exacted from those who adhered to the faith of their ancestors. Thanks to this bait offered to avarice, the Mohammedan Church daily received into her bosom a multitude of converts who, without being entirely convinced of the truth of her doctrines, were devoted to the pursuit of wealth and worldly advantages. Divines rejoiced at this rapid spread of the faith, but the Exchequer lost heavily. The contribution from Egypt, for instance, rose during the Khalifate of 'Othmân to twelve millions; but a few years later, under Mu'âwiya, when most of the Copts had been converted, it fell to five millions. Under 'Omar II it fell still lower. This caused the pious monarch no uneasiness, and when one of his vicegerents warned him that ere long all the *Zimmies* [2] in Egypt would be converted, and the revenues which they brought to the State Treasury would be lost, his reply was: " I shall rejoice if all the *Zimmies* become Moslems, for God sent His Prophet to be an apostle and not a tax-collector." [3]

Hajjâj thought otherwise. He was not keenly interested in the propagation of the Faith, and he was obliged, in order to retain the Khalif's good graces, to replenish the Treasury. He had therefore not granted exemption from the poll-tax

---

[1] Tribute from unbelievers was called *Kharâj* or *Jazia,* as opposed to the tithe, *Zakât.*

[2] Protected subjects, confirmed in their holdings on payment of tribute. See Muir, *Early Caliphate* (1883), p. 194.

[3] *Journ. asiat.,* IVe série, xviii. 433.

to the new Musulmans of 'Irâk.[1] The Kaisites imitated
faithfully the example thus set them; indeed, they went
further, and treated all the vanquished with insolence and
excessive harshness. The Yemenites, on the other hand, if
they did not always treat the conquered with justness and
mildness when they were in power, at any rate when they
were in opposition joined their voices with those of the
oppressed in protest against the grasping policy of their rivals.
The conquered naturally looked for halcyon days when the
Yemenites returned to power; but they met with frequent
disappointments, for the Yemenites were neither the first
nor the last Liberals who have discovered that though it is
easy, when in opposition, to declaim against taxes, to demand financial reform, and to promise it upon their return
to office, it is nevertheless difficult, when that event takes
place, to fulfil their pledges.   " I find myself in a somewhat
embarrassing position," said the Yemenite chieftain, Yazîd
ibn Muhallab, upon being appointed Governor of 'Irâk by
Sulaimân ; " All the people of the province rest their hopes
upon me: they will curse me, as they cursed Hajjâj, if I
compel them to pay the same tribute as heretofore—and on
the other hand I shall incur Sulaimân's displeasure if he
does not receive as much at my hands as his brother received
when Hajjâj was Governor."   To escape from the dilemma
he had recourse to an ingenious expedient.   Having declared
to the Khalif that he could not undertake to collect the imposts, he entrusted this odious duty to a member of the
party that had lately fallen.

　　It must, moreover, be admitted that there were among
the Yemenites men of much pliability, who compounded with
their principles without difficulty, and who to keep their
posts served their master, whether he were Yemenite or
Kaisite, with undeviating devotion and docility.   The
Kelbite Bishr may be regarded as a type of this class, a
class which grew more numerous as morality grew laxer and
the love of the tribe yielded to ambition and a thirst for
wealth.   Appointed Governor of Africa by the Kaisite
Yazîd II, Bishr sent one of his tribesmen, Anbasa by name,
to Spain to collect a double tribute from the Christians of
that country; but when the Yemenite Hishâm ascended the
throne, Bishr sent Yahyâ, another of his tribesmen, with
orders to restore to the Christians all that had been unjustly
wrung from them.   A Christian writer of that day goes

---

[1] *Journ. asiat.*, IIIe série, xi. 580.

so far as to say that this "terrible Governor used cruel means" to compel the Musulmans to disgorge that which did not belong to them.

In general, however, the Yemenites were milder than their rivals in their treatment of the vanquished, by whom they were consequently less hated. The people of Africa especially—that agglomeration of heterogeneous elements which the Arabs found established from Egypt to the Atlantic and to which the name of Berbers is applied—had a marked predilection for the Yemenites. Strabo long ago pointed out that the Berbers in many respects resembled the Arabs.[1] Nomadic within fixed limits, like the sons of Ishmael, their method of warfare coincided with those of the Bedawin, as Mûsâ ibn Nusayr, who played so large a part in their subjugation, has recorded. Like the Arabs, the Berbers had been accustomed to immemorial independence— for the authority of Rome was practically confined to the coast—and they possessed a political organization similar to that of the Bedawin, namely a democracy tempered by the influence of patrician families. It followed that the Arabs found in the Berbers foes far more formidable than the mercenary troops and oppressed subjects of Persia and the Byzantine Empire. A victory was invariably paid for by a sanguinary defeat. No sooner had the Arab conquerors traversed the entire country and reached the shores of the Atlantic than their forces were surrounded and cut to pieces by hordes innumerable as the sands of the desert.[2] "The conquest of Africa is impossible," wrote a Governor to the Khalif 'Abd al-Malik ; "scarcely has a Berber tribe been exterminated when another comes to take its place." Nevertheless the Arabs, in spite of the difficulty of the enterprise—perhaps even by reason of the obstacles which they met at every step, and which honour bade them to surmount at all costs—resolved on conquest, with admirable courage and unparalleled pertinacity. After seventy years of murderous war the Africans submitted, in the sense that they agreed to lay down their arms on the understanding that there should be no taunting them with rights of conquest, that their irascible pride should be humoured, and that they should be treated not as a vanquished people, but as equals and brothers. Woe to the man who was so imprudent as to offend them ! With foolish pride the

[1] ii. 18.
[2] The furthest point reached by 'Okba was the Sûs el Adna (Northern Morocco).

Kaisite Yazîd Ibn Abî Moslim, formerly secretary to Hajjâj, would have treated them as slaves ; they assassinated him, and the Khalif Yazîd II, Kaisite though he was, had prudence enough not to demand the punishment of the assassins, but to send a Kelbite to govern the province.

Less sagacious than his predecessor, Hishâm provoked a terrible insurrection, which spread from Africa to Spain. A Yemenite at the beginning of his reign, and therefore not unpopular,[1] Hishâm ended by declaring for the Kaisites, because he deemed them ready to gratify his ruling passion —the love of gold. Handing over to them, therefore, the provinces they knew so well how to grind, he drew a larger revenue than any of his ancestors. In 734, a year and a half after 'Obaida's dismissal, Hishâm entrusted the government of Africa to a Kaisite, 'Obaidallah.

Though grandson of a freedman, 'Obaidallah was not a man to be despised. He had received a sound and even brilliant education, and knew by rote the classic poems and ballads of the warlike days of old. His attachment to the Kaisites inspired him with a noble and generous idea. Finding only two small Kaisite tribes in Egypt, he introduced into that country thirteen hundred poor families of the Kaisite race, and took great pains to make the colony prosperous.[2] 'Obaidallah's respect for his patron's family was touching in its intensity. Amidst the pomps of office, and at the height of his power, far from blushing at his humble origin, he openly proclaimed his obligations to Hajjâj, who had enfranchised his grandfather. When Governor of Africa, upon the occasion of 'Okba, son of Hajjâj, visiting him, 'Obaidallah made him sit by his side, and showed him so much deference that his sons, with the arrogance of upstarts, grew indignant. When alone with their father they took him to task : " You made this Bedawy," they said, " sit beside you, in the presence of nobles and Kurashites, who will certainly take offence thereat, and bear you a grudge. Since you are old, no one will treat you ill, and doubtless death will soon protect you from all hostility ; but we, your sons, have reason to fear that the shame of this proceeding will recoil upon us. What, moreover, will happen if this reaches the Khalif s ears ? Will not his wrath be kindled when he learns that

---

[1] "Qui Hiscam primordis suae potestatis satis se modestum ostendens." Isid., c. 55.

[2] Al-Makrîzî, *Des tribus arabes venues en Egypte* (ed. Wüstenfeld), pp. 39–40.

you have paid more honour to this fellow than to the Kuraish?" "What you say is just, my sons," replied 'Obaidallah, "I have no excuse to offer: I will not again merit your reproaches." Next morning he summoned 'Okba and the nobles to his palace. He treated them all with respect, but gave the place of honour to Ibn Hajjâj, at whose feet he seated himself. He then sent for his sons. As they entered the hall and gazed in astonishment at the sight presented to them, 'Obaidallah arose, and after glorifying God and His Prophet, he related to the nobles all that his sons had said to him the day before. "I call Allah and yourselves to witness," he continued, "though Allah alone sufficeth, that this man is 'Okba, son of that Hajjâj who released my grandfather from slavery. My sons have been led astray by Eblis, who hath inspired them with insane pride, but I desire to testify before God that I at least am not guilty of ingratitude, and that I know what I owe to the Eternal as well as to this man. I make this declaration publicly, fearing that my sons may lose God's blessing by disclaiming this man and his father as their patrons; whence it would assuredly follow that they would incur the curse of God and man, for I have heard that the Prophet hath said: 'Cursed be he who pretendeth to belong to a family to which he is a stranger; cursed be he who denieth his patron.' I have heard, too, that Abû Bakr hath said: 'To disavow even a distant kinsman, or to claim to have sprung from a family to which thou art not allied, is to be ungrateful to God.' My sons, since I love you as myself, I would not have you exposed to the malediction of God and man. Ye told me that the Khalif would be wroth with me if he learnt what I had done. Be of good comfort; the Khalif—to whom may Allah grant long life—is more magnanimous; he knoweth too well his duty towards God and man for me to fear that I shall excite his wrath by requiting my friends; on the contrary, I am persuaded that he will approve of my conduct." Cries of: "He speaketh well! Long live our Governor!" arose on all sides, but the sons of 'Obaidallah, overcome with shame at so great a humiliation, maintained a gloomy silence. Then turning to 'Okba, 'Obaidallah went on: "Sir, it is my duty to obey thy commands. The Khalif hath entrusted a vast territory to my care; choose, then, for thyself whatsoever province thou wilt." 'Okba chose Spain. "My greatest desire," he said, "is to take part in the Holy War; in Spain I can gratify it."

In spite, however, of the loftiness of his character, and although he possessed all the virtues of his race, 'Obaidallah also manifested in a marked degree the profound contempt felt by that race for all who were not Arabs.   In his eyes, Copts, Berbers, Spaniards, and all the conquered peoples— whom he scarcely regarded as men—had no other destiny upon earth than to enrich, by the sweat of the brow, the race which Mohammed had declared to be pre-eminent. In Egypt, where he had been Commissioner of Taxes, he had increased by a twentieth the tribute payable by the Copts, and this people, usually most pacific, who had never appealed to arms since they had lived under Musulman domination, had been so greatly exasperated by this arbitrary measure, that they rose in revolt.[1]   On his appointment as Governor of Africa, 'Obaidallah made it his duty to indulge the tastes and caprices of the lords of Damascus at the expense of the Berbers.   Since the wool of Merino lambs, from which raiment of dazzling whiteness was made, was in great request in the Capital, the Governor took by force the sheep from the Berbers, and slaughtered them indiscriminately, though often but a single lamb with the true wool was found in a flock of a hundred sheep, all the rest being what were called "smooth" lambs, devoid of wool and therefore useless for the Governor's purpose.   Not content with depriving the Berbers of their flocks, the principal source of their wealth—or, rather, their sole livelihood—'Obaidallah also carried off their wives and daughters, and sent them to replenish the harems of Syria; for the Arab nobles highly esteemed the Berber women, who have always had the reputation of excelling those of Arabia in beauty.

For more than five years the Berbers suffered in silence; they murmured, and stored up treasures of hatred in their hearts, but the presence of a large army kept them in check. An insurrection was, however, impending.   It was to assume a religious rather than a political character, and missionaries and priests were to be its leaders; for in spite of many striking points of resemblance between the Berber and the Arab, there was this profound and essential difference between the two races—that one was pious, with a strong leaning to superstition and filled with blind veneration for the priesthood, while the other was a nation of sceptics and scoffers, allowing scarcely any influence to ministers of

---

[1] Al-Makrîzi, *Hist. des Coptes* (ed. Wüstenfeld), p. 54 (note).

religion. Even in modern times the African Marabouts[1] have limitless power in political matters. They alone have the right of intervention when two tribes fall out. When chiefs are to be elected it is the Marabouts who designate the most worthy candidates: when some grave crisis calls for a tribal assembly, it is they who ascertain the various opinions of the people, and then, after discussing them in private, make known their decision. Their common dwellings are provided and maintained by the people, who anticipate all their wishes. Further, it is a remarkable fact that the Berbers have more veneration for their priests than for the Almighty Himself. A French author who conscientiously studied the manners of this people, tells us that "the name of God, invoked by a poor wretch in danger of being robbed, affords him no protection; but that of a revered Marabout will save him."[2] The Berbers have, indeed, never played an important part in the world except when instigated by their religious teachers. The Marabouts laid the foundation of the vast empire of the Almoravides as well as that of the Almohades. In their war with the Arabs, the Berbers of the mountains were for a long time led by a prophetess whom they believed to possess supernatural powers; but the Arab general, 'Okba ibn Nâfi', who understood better than his colleagues the character of his opponents, speedily realized that to vanquish them he too must work upon their superstition, and appeal to their imagination by the miraculous. He therefore boldly played the part of a sorcerer and a Marabout; he would charm serpents, and claim to hear celestial voices, and puerile and absurd though such methods may appear to us, they were so successful that a multitude of Berbers, impressed by the miracles which 'Okba worked, and convinced that it would be vain to resist him, laid down their arms and were converted to Islamism.

At the epoch with which we are now dealing Islamism was already dominant in Africa. Under the rule of the pious 'Omar II it had made rapid progress, and an ancient chronicler goes so far as to say that under 'Omar not a Berber remained who was not a Musulman—an assertion which will not appear extravagant when we remember that conversions were not altogether spontaneous, and that self-interest played an important part in bringing them about. In 'Omar's view the propagation of the Faith was the chief

[1] Ar. *morâbit*, a devotee or ascetic.	[2] Daumas, *La grande Kabylie*, 53-6.

I

object of his life ; he employed every means likely to multiply proselytes, and a "convert" had merely to pronounce the words: "There is only one God, and Mohammed is His Prophet," to be relieved from payment of poll-tax, without being required to conform strictly to the precepts of Islamism. The Governor of Khorasan once wrote to 'Omar, complaining that many who had ostensibly embraced the Faith had done so merely to escape the poll-tax, and adding that he had certain knowledge that they had not been circumcised ; but the Khalif merely replied: "God sent Mohammed to call men to the true Faith, and not to circumcise them." 'Omar looked to the future; beneath the rank vegetation he inferred a rich and fertile soil in which the Divine Word would germinate and bear fruit; he foresaw that if the newly-made Musulmans were liable to the reproach of lukewarmness, their sons and grandsons, born and bred in Islamism, would one day surpass in zeal and devotion those who had doubted the orthodoxy of their fathers.

The event justified his foresight, especially in the case of the Africans. Islam, repugnant and even odious as it was at first in their eyes, became by degrees endurable, and finally, all in all to them. But this religion, as they understood it, was not the cold official creed—a dreary compromise between deism and scepticism—which the missionaries preached without unction, insisting always upon the duty of subjects towards their Khalif, and never on the Khalif's duty towards them: the Berbers' faith was the stern and passionate religion preached to them by the Khârejites. For the Nonconformists, hunted down in the East like deer, and compelled to assume various disguises and feigned names to escape capture,[1] had at last, after passing through a thousand perils, found an asylum in the burning deserts of Africa, where they henceforth propagated their doctrines with unexampled success. Nowhere had these zealous and convinced teachers found their tenets so fervently embraced: the Calvinists of Islam had at last found their Scotland. The Arabs had rejected their doctrines, not through any repugnance to their political principles—which, on the contrary, accorded well with the republican instincts of the race—but because they would neither take their religion seriously, nor accept the intolerant Puritanism by which these sectaries were distinguished. On the other hand the

---

[1] The strange adventures of the nonconformist poet Imrân ibn-Hittân have been related by al-Mûbarrad (*Kâmil*, pp. 579 *sq.*).

inmates of squalid African huts accepted their teachings with indescribable enthusiasm. Simple and ignorant, they doubtless understood nothing of the speculations and dogmatic subtleties which were the delight of more cultivated minds. It would therefore be unprofitable to inquire what particular sect they gave a preference to—whether they were Harûrites, or Sofrites, or Ibâdites—for the chroniclers are not agreed upon this matter. At any rate they understood enough of the Khârejites' doctrines to assimilate their revolutionary and democratic principles, to share the fanciful hopes of universal levelling which their teachers aroused, and to be convinced that their oppressors were reprobates whose destiny was hell-fire.

Since all the Khalifs, from 'Othmân downwards, had been, in their view, merely infidel usurpers—far from its being a crime to revolt against the tyrant who robbed them of their property and their wives, it was a right, or rather, a duty. Since the Arabs had hitherto restrained the Berbers from any exercise of power—except that which necessarily pertained to tribal government—the latter readily came to believe that the doctrine of the sovereignty of the people— a doctrine which in their savage independence they had professed from time immemorial—was altogether Mohammedan and orthodox, and that the humblest Berber might, under universal suffrage, be raised to the throne. And yet this cruelly oppressed people—excited by fanatics who were half priests and half warriors, and who themselves had old scores to settle with the so-called orthodox—were about to shake off the yoke in the name of Allah and his Prophet, and in the name of that sacred book upon which the others relied were about to found a terrible despotism! Strange indeed are the destined uses of religious codes, those formidable arsenals which furnish every cause with weapons—now vindicating burners of heretics and preachers of absolutism, and now supplying arguments to champions of liberty of conscience, who behead a king and found a republic.

All minds were in fermentation, and the Berbers were but awaiting a favourable opportunity for taking up arms, when, in the year 740, 'Obaidallah despatched a large proportion of his troops on an expedition to Sicily. When this force had embarked it was obvious that an insurrection might break out on the most trifling pretext, and yet the Governor of Tingitana had the imprudence to select that very moment for the application of the Kaisite system, and to order the Berbers of his district to pay double tribute, just as though they had not been Moslems. They promptly flew to arms, shaved their heads, fastened the Koran to their spear-heads, after the manner of the Khârejites, and entrusted the command to Maisara, one of the most zealous of the sectaries, who was at once priest, soldier, and demagogue. They attacked the town of Tangier, captured it, and put to death the Governor and every other Arab they could find, applying their doctrines with such inhuman rigour as to spare not even little children. From Tangier Maisara marched towards the province of Sûs, then governed by Ismâ'îl, son of 'Obaidallah. Without waiting for his arrival, the Berbers rose in a body, and the Governor of Sûs was assassinated. The Arabs in vain attempted resistance; beaten at all points, they were obliged to evacuate the country, and in a few days all the West, the conquest of which had cost them years of sacrifice, was lost to them. The Berbers proceeded to elect a Khalif, and so democratic was the spirit of the revolution, that their choice fell, not upon a noble, but upon the brave Maisara himself, who had formerly been a water-seller in the market of Kairwan.

Thus taken unawares, 'Obaidallah ordered 'Okba, Governor of Spain, to make a descent upon the coast of Tingitana. 'Okba accordingly despatched some troops thither, but they were defeated. He then embarked in person with a larger force, landed in Africa, and put to the sword every Berber who fell into his hands, but he could not suppress the revolt.

'Obaidallah, when giving instructions to 'Okba, at the same time sent orders to the Fihrite Habîb, the leader of the Sicilian expedition, to return as quickly as possible to Africa with his troops, the Spanish fleet meanwhile keeping the Sicilians in check. In view, however, of the swiftly growing danger—for the insurrection was spreading with alarming rapidity—he deemed it imprudent to delay until the arrival of this force, and having assembled all the available troops, he placed them under the command of the Fihrite Khâlid, promising to reinforce him with Habîb's men as soon as they landed. Khâlid set out, encountered Maisara near Tangier, and gave him battle. After a stubborn but indecisive struggle, Maisara retired within Tangier, where he was assassinated by his soldiers—either because, after having come to regard victory as a matter of course, they could not brook the least lack of success, or because since his promotion the demagogue had turned traitor to the democratic principles of his sect. The Arab chroniclers allege the latter reason, and in that case the Berbers were merely acting within their rights and doing their duty, since their doctrines commanded them to depose, or even slay, a chief or Khalif who swerved from the principles of the Faith.

The Berbers, having elected a new leader, again assumed the offensive, and this time with more success: at the height of the battle which ensued, a division commanded by Maisara's successor fell upon the rear of the Arabs, who finding themselves in danger of being hemmed in, fled in confusion: but Khâlid and the nobles of his staff, too proud to survive the shame of such a defeat, rushed upon the enemy, and selling their lives dearly, perished to a man. This fatal combat, in which fell the flower of Arab chivalry, has been called the Battle of the Nobles.

Habîb had now returned from Sicily and advanced to the outskirts of Tahort, but hearing of Khâlid's disaster he did not dare to attack the Berbers. Africa soon resembled a ship that drifts without sail or pilot, for 'Obaidallah had been deposed by the Arabs themselves, who accused him, not unreasonably, of having brought these direful misfortunes on their heads. The Khalif Hishâm trembled with rage and grief when he heard of the Berber revolt and the defeat of his army. "By Allah!" he cried, "I will show them what the wrath of an Arab of the old stamp is! I will send against them an army such as they have never seen: its van shall be upon them before the rear-guard has left Damascus!" Four districts of Syria were ordered to provide six thousand soldiers each; the fifth, that of Kinnisrîn, three thousand. These twenty-seven thousand men were to be joined by three thousand Egyptian troops and all the African forces. Hishâm entrusted the command of this army, as well as the Governorship of Africa, to an experienced Kaisite General, Kulthûm of the tribe of Koshair. In the event of Kulthûm's death his nephew[1] Balj was to succeed him, and should Balj die, the command was to devolve upon Thalaba, a Yemenite of the tribe of Amila and leader of the troops of Jordan. Determined to inflict exemplary punishment on the rebels, the Khalif gave the General permission to behead all that fell into his hands, and to pillage every captured town.

[1] Or, according to some authorities, his cousin.

Guided by two officers, Hârûn and Mughîth, clients of the Omayyads, who knew the country, Kulthûm arrived in Africa in the summer of 741. The Arabs of that country by no means welcomed the Syrians, who treated them with arrogant harshness and whom they regarded as invaders rather than allies. The gates of the towns were shut against Kulthûm's force, and when Balj, who commanded the advanced guard, imperiously ordered them to be opened and announced that he intended to settle permanently with his soldiers in Africa, the townsfolk wrote to Habîb, who was still encamped near Tahort, to inform him of the fact. Habîb immediately sent a letter to Kulthûm to this effect: " Your nephew, madman that he is, has dared to boast that he will settle in this country with his soldiers, and has gone so far as to threaten the inhabitants of our towns. I warn you that if your force does not leave them at peace, we will turn our arms against you." Kulthûm made excuses, and told Habîb that he would shortly join forces with him at Tahort. This he did: but the Syrian and the African soon fell out, and Balj, who had warmly espoused his uncle's cause, cried: " That is the man who dared to threaten that he would turn his arms against us!" "Heed it not, Balj," replied 'Abd-er-Rahmân, Habîb's son; " my father is ready to give you satisfaction if you are offended." The two armies were only too eager to join in the quarrel; the cry " To arms!" was raised by the Syrians on the one hand, and on the other by the African and Egyptian troops. A conflict was prevented with great difficulty, and the reconciliation which was effected was apparent only. The army, now seventy thousand strong, advanced to a place named Bakdûra, or Nafdûra, where the Berber army barred the way. Seeing the numerical superiority of the enemy, the two Omayyad clients who had acted as guides advised Kulthûm to intrench himself, and, avoiding an engagement, to be content with sending detachments of cavalry to raid the neighbouring villages. Kulthûm was inclined to follow this prudent counsel, but the fiery Balj indignantly rejected it. " Distrust their advice," he said to his uncle, " and fear not the Berbers, for though numerous, they have neither weapons nor garments." This was not far from the truth, for the Berbers were ill-armed, and drawers of cotton formed their only apparel; moreover, they were badly provided with horses; but Balj forgot that religious enthusiasm and love of liberty doubled their strength. Kulthûm, accustomed to defer to his nephew, took his advice, and having resolved to join battle, gave Balj the command of the Syrian horse, entrusted the African troops to Hârûn and Mughîth, and personally led the Syrian infantry.

Balj began the engagement. He flattered himself that such an undisciplined multitude could not for a moment stand against his cavalry; but the enemy had discovered an effectual means of defence. They hurled bags filled with pebbles at the horses' heads, and this device was crowned with success; taking fright, the chargers of the Syrians reared and brought many of their riders to the ground. The Berbers then let loose against the infantry a number of unbroken mares, maddened by water-skins and large pieces of leather attached to their tails, and much confusion was thus caused in the ranks. Balj, however, who remained mounted with about seven thousand of his men, returned to the attack. This time he succeeded in breaking the Berbers' ranks, and in a furious charge penetrated to the rear of their army; but some Berber divisions faced about and prevented his return, while the others attacked Kulthûm so successfully that Habîb, Mughîth, and Hârûn were slain, and the Arabs of Africa, deprived of their leaders, and ill-disposed towards the Syrians, took to flight. Kulthûm, with the Syrian infantry, still maintained his ground. An eye-witness relates that the general, when scalped by a sabre-cut, replaced the skin with marvellous coolness. As he struck right and left he chanted from the Koran verses suitable for raising the courage of his comrades. "God," he cried, "buyeth from believers their goods and their persons, and Paradise is the price he payeth! A man dieth only when God willeth it; and the days of his life are written beforehand in the Book!" But when the nobles who fought by Kulthûm's side were all slain, and he himself fell to the ground covered with wounds, the Syrians were utterly routed. The Berbers' pursuit was so ruthless, that by the admission of the vanquished, a third of the great army perished, and another third were taken prisoners.

In the meanwhile, Balj, separated with his seven thousand horse from the main body, had been defending himself bravely, and wrought much carnage among the Berbers; but his opponents were so numerous that they heeded not the number of their slain, and now that many divisions, after having defeated his uncle's forces, turned their attention to him, he was on the point of being overwhelmed by an

immense multitude.	Retreat or annihilation were the only
alternatives open to him, and he decided to seek safety in
flight: but since the enemy blocked the road to Kairwan
taken by the other fugitives, he was obliged to flee in the
opposite direction.	Pursued without intermission by the
Berbers, who were mounted on the horses of their slain,
enemies, the Syrian cavalry arrived at Tangier, worn out
with fatigue.	After vainly endeavouring to enter Tangier,
they followed the road to Ceuta, and having gained possession of this town they collected some provisions—a matter of
no great difficulty, thanks to the fertility of the surrounding
district.	The Berbers attacked the place five or six times,
but as they were ignorant of the methods of beleaguering
a fortress, and the besieged defended themselves with the
courage of despair, they decided that they could never
succeed in taking by assault their enemies' last refuge.
They therefore resolved to reduce it by famine, and laid
waste the surrounding region so effectually that it became a
desert, two days' march in radius.	The Syrians were reduced
to living upon the flesh of their horses, but even this supply
began to fail, and if the Governor of Spain persisted in withholding the assistance which their deplorable situation demanded, they knew that they must die of hunger.

[AUTHORITIES : Ahmed ibn Abî Ya'kûb, f. 69 ; Ibn Khallikân (ed. Wüst.),
fasc. x. 116 ; Ibn Khaldûn, ff. 199, 202 ; *Hist. des Berbers*, i. 150–1
(text) ; *Hist. de l'Afrique* (ed. Noel des Vergers), pp. 10–11 (text) ;
Isid., c. 52–63 ; Ibn al-Kûtiyya, f. 6 ; *Akhbar majmû'at*, ff. 60–64 ;
Ibn Adhârî, i. 38–43, ii. 20.]

CHAPTER XI

SYRIANS AND MEDINESE IN SPAIN

THE Arabs who had now for thirty years been settled in Spain would in no circumstances have felt disposed to provide the Syrians, shut up within the walls of Ceuta, with ships to convey them to the Peninsula. The insolence with which their brethren in Africa had been treated by these troops, who had loudly proclaimed their intention of settling in that country, had warned the Arabs of Spain of the dangers they would run if such dangerous rivals were enabled to cross the Straits. And if the Syrians would thus in any case have had but little chance of obtaining assistance, in existing circumstances they had none—for, in Spain the Medinese were now predominant.

After having maintained against the Syrian Arabs— pagans as they called them—a long and stubborn conflict, the sons of the founders of Islamism, both Helpers and Refugees, had been overwhelmed at the fatal battle of Harra, and had seen their Holy City pillaged, their Mosque turned into a stable, and their wives violated. Moreover, as if these sacrileges and atrocities—which recall the sack of Rome by the savage soldiers of the Constable and the fanatical Lutherans of Georg von Frundsberg [1]—did not suffice, they had been compelled to swear that henceforth they would be the Khalif's slaves—" slaves whom he could enfranchise or sell at pleasure." They had therefore abandoned their formerly revered city, as we have already recorded, to the wild beasts of the desert, and enrolling themselves in the army of Africa crossed over with Mûsâ to Spain, and settled there. If their religious zeal—which had always been leavened with hypocrisy, pride, and worldly ambition—had somewhat cooled on the way, they still nourished in their hearts, and transmitted to their children, an implacable hatred against the Syrians, and a rooted con-

---

[1] Frundsberg himself, who had been previously struck by apoplexy, was not responsible for the atrocities.

viction that since they themselves had the honour to be the
descendants of the illustrious Companions of the Prophet,
political power was manifestly theirs of right.   Already upon
one occasion, when the Governor of Spain had fallen in the
famous battle which he fought against Charles Martel, in
October 732, the Medinese had elected as ruler of the Peninsula the most influential member of their party, 'Abd al-
Malik, son of Katan, who forty-nine years before had fought
at Harra.   'Abd al-Malik, however, was guilty of acts of
grave injustice, according to the unanimous testimony of
both Arabs and Christians, and mercilessly oppressed the
province; he had consequently fallen from power as soon as
Africa had regained its rightful authority over Spain, that
is, upon the appointment of 'Obaidallah as Governor of the
West.   'Obaidallah, as we have seen, entrusted the Peninsula to his patron 'Okba.   The new Governor on arriving
in Spain imprisoned 'Abd al-Malik and transported to Africa
the leaders of the Medinese party, whose restless and turbulent disposition troubled the peace of the country.   The
Medinese, however, were not discouraged, and a little later,
when the great Berber revolt had extinguished the African
Governor's authority over Spain, 'Okba fell so dangerously
ill that he was not expected to recover, and the Medinese
either persuaded or compelled him to name 'Abd al-Malik
as his successor (Jan. 741).

   It was therefore to 'Abd al-Malik that Balj had to apply
for the means of crossing the Straits, and there was no man
less likely to look with favour on the request.   In vain did
Balj endeavour to touch his heart by reminding him in his
letters that he and his comrades were dying of hunger at
Ceuta, and that after all they were Arabs equally with 'Abd
al-Malik himself.   The old Medinese chieftain, far from
pitying their distress, rendered thanks to heaven for having
permitted him to enjoy, at the age of ninety years, the inex-
pressible luxury of revenge.   They would soon perish of
famine—these children of the reprobates who at Harra
had slain his friends, and his kinsfolk, and had come near to
piercing his own body with their swords!   Had they not
sacked Medina and profaned the temple of the Prophet?
Yet the sons of these monsters dared to nourish the insane
hope that he would show pity upon them in their distress—
as if the revengeful spirit of an Arab could pardon such
offences; as if the torments of a Syrian could inspire a
Medinese with compassion!   'Abd al-Malik had but one

desire, one care, and that was to prevent others, less hostile
than himself to the Syrians, from supplying them with provisions. In spite of his precautions a compassionate noble,
of the tribe of Lakhm, succeeded in eluding his vigilance,
and sent to Ceuta two vessels laden with corn. 'Abd al-
Malik no sooner heard of this than he arrested the generous
noble, and inflicted on him seven hundred strokes of the
bastinado. Then, on the pretext that he was instigating a
revolt, the Lakhmite was deprived of sight, and afterwards
beheaded. His corpse was hung on a gibbet, and by his
side a dog was crucified, to complete the ignominy of his
fate.

But just as the Syrians seemed doomed to die of hunger,
an unforeseen event suddenly compelled 'Abd al-Malik to
change his cruel policy.

The Berbers settled in Spain, although, as it seems, not
actually oppressed, shared the jealous hatred of their brethren
in Africa against the Arabs. They had been the true conquerors of the country. Mûsâ and his Arabs had merely
reaped the fruits of the victory gained by Târik and his
twelve thousand Berbers over the army of the Visigoths:
the Arabs from the moment they had landed on the shores
of Spain had little to do except to occupy certain towns
which surrendered at the first summons. And yet when it
came to dividing the fruits of the conquest, Mûsâ's men had
secured the lion's share—appropriating the greater part of
the spoils, the government of the country, and the most
desirable territories. Keeping for themselves the fair and
fertile Andalusia, they banished Târik's followers to the
barren plains of La Mancha and Estremadura, or to the
bleak mountains of Leon, Galicia, and Asturia, where constant fighting with the partly subjugated Christians was
their lot. Though the Arabs had themselves but little
respect for the rights of property, they displayed inexorable
severity where the Berbers were concerned. When the
latter took upon themselves to exact ransom from certain
Christians who had surrendered upon terms, the Arabs,
after punishing their allies with the lash and with torture,
left them to groan, laden with chains, and scarcely covered
with verminous rags, in foul and pestilential dungeons.

The fortunes of Spain were, moreover, too intimately
linked with those of Africa for events on one side of the
Straits not to have their echo on the other. The proud and
valiant Monûsa, one of the four principal Berber chieftains

who accompanied Târik to Spain, had once raised the standard of revolt in La Cerdaña because he heard that his
brethren in Africa were being harshly treated by the Arabs,
and he had been supported by Eudes, Duke of Aquitaine,
whose daughter he had married.[1]   Upon the present occasion
the insurrection of the Berbers in Africa found a prodigious
echo in Spain.   The Berbers of the Peninsula had received
with open arms the Khârejites who came from Africa not
only as missionaries but to stimulate them to take up arms
and exterminate the Arabs.   An insurrection, which like
that in Africa was partly religious and partly political, broke
out in Galicia, and spread through all the North, with the exception of Zaragoza—the only northern district in which the
Arabs were in a majority.   Everywhere the Arabs were
routed and expelled ; the expeditions sent by 'Abd al-Malik
against the insurgents were defeated one after the other.
The Berbers of Galicia, Merida, Coria, Talavera and other
places then combined, elected an Imâm as a leader, and
formed their army into three divisions, one of which was to
besiege Toledo, another to attack Cordova, and the third to
proceed to Algeciras, with the object of seizing the fleet in
the roadstead, crossing the Straits, exterminating the Syrians
in Ceuta, and bringing back to Spain a multitude of Berbers
from Africa.

The plight of the Arabs in Spain had therefore become
so alarming that 'Abd al-Malik, much against the grain,
found himself driven to solicit help from the very Syrians
whom hitherto he had ruthlessly abandoned to their miserable fate.   However, he took precautions : he promised to
send them transports on condition that they would evacuate
Spain as soon as the revolt was quelled, and that ten chiefs
of each division should be handed over to him, to be kept
on an island as hostages for the due fulfilment of the compact.
The Syrians for their part stipulated that 'Abd al-Malik
should not separate them when they were taken back to
Africa, and that they should be landed on a part of the coast
not under Berber domination.

These conditions having been mutually accepted, the
Syrians disembarked at Algeciras, famished, and clad only in
miserable rags.   They were supplied with food and welcomed
by their fellow-tribesmen in Spain, who undertook to furnish

---

[1] Isidore, who gives details of this revolt, says that it took place when 'Abd-er-
Rahmân al-Ghâfiki was Governor of Spain.   Arab writers place it in the time of
Haitham, al-Ghâfiki's predecessor.

them with equipment, each according to his means: one wealthy chieftain provided garments for a hundred of the new-comers, others of smaller fortune, for ten, or even for but one. Since it was before all things necessary to check the advance of the Berber division then marching on Algeciras, which had already reached Medina Sidonia, the Syrians —reinforced by some Spanish-Arabian troops—attacked it, and fighting with all their old bravery, put it to rout and gained rich booty. The second Berber army, which had marched against Cordova, defended itself more stubbornly, and inflicted serious losses on the Arabs; it was, however, forced to retreat. There remained the third army, the most numerous of all, which had been besieging Toledo for twenty-seven days. This marched against the enemy, and the battle, which took place on the banks of the Guazalate, ended in the total defeat of the Berbers. Henceforth the rebels were chased like wild beasts throughout the Peninsula, and the Syrians, yesterday but beggars, amassed spoils in such abundance that they found themselves suddenly richer than they had ever dared to hope.

Thanks to these intrepid soldiers, the Berber revolt, which at first had seemed so formidable, had been quelled as though by magic; but 'Abd al-Malik no sooner found himself rid of his enemies, than he had to devise means of also ridding himself of the auxiliaries whom he now feared as well as hated. He therefore lost no time in reminding Balj of his compact, and insisting that he should quit Spain. But Balj and his Syrians had no wish to return to a country where they had suffered reverses and hardships of every kind; they had become enamoured of the beautiful land which had been the scene of their latest exploits and where they had reaped so rich a harvest. It is therefore not surprising that disputes and quarrels arose between hereditary foes whose interests, in the circumstances, were wholly antagonistic.

Since hatred is a bad counsellor, 'Abd al-Malik made matters worse, and opened all the old wounds, by refusing to convey the Syrians in a body to Africa, on the pretext that they now had so many horses and slaves, and so much baggage, that his ships did not suffice to carry out this clause of the agreement. Further, when the Syrians desired to embark from the coast of Elvira (Granada) or Tadmir (Murcia), 'Abd al-Malik declared that this was impossible, since all his ships were at Algeciras, and he could not remove them from that part of the coast lest the Berbers should be tempted to make a raid there. At last, no longer taking pains to conceal his treacherous designs, he had the effrontery to suggest transporting the Syrians back to Ceuta. This proposal aroused indescribable indignation. " It were better that we were thrown into the sea than delivered to the Berbers of Tingitana ! " cried Balj, and he bitterly reproached the Governor for having been on the point of abandoning him and his men to death by famine at Ceuta, and for having so infamously gibbeted the magnanimous Lakhmite who had sent them food. Deeds soon took the place of words. Taking advantage of a moment when 'Abd al-Malik had but a few troops at Cordova, the Syrians expelled him from the palace, and proclaimed Balj Governor of Spain (Sept. 20, 741).

Now that their passions had been unchained it was unlikely that the Syrians would rest content with this measure, and the fear of further reprisals was speedily justified. Balj's first care was to set at liberty the Syrian chiefs who had been kept as hostages, and whom 'Abd al-Malik had confined on the little island of Omm-Hakîm, opposite Algeciras. These chiefs reached Cordova in great wrath. They declared that the Governor of Algeciras, acting under 'Abd al-Malik's orders, had kept them short of food and water, and that a noble of Damascus, one of the Beni Ghassân, a Yemenite tribe, had actually perished of thirst : they demanded 'Abd al-Malik's death in expiation for the Ghassânid's. This relation of their sufferings, and the death of a respected chief, filled up the measure of the Syrians' hatred against 'Abd al-Malik : they declared that for his perfidy his life was forfeit. Balj, who did not sympathise with the extreme party, endeavoured to appease them by attributing the Ghassânid's death to accidental neglect rather than to premeditation. " Respect 'Abd al-Malik's life," he urged, " for he is a Kurashite, and moreover an aged man." But his appeal was fruitless : the Yemenites thirsted to avenge their kinsman, and suspected that Balj wished to save 'Abd al-Malik because they were both Ma'addites. They accordingly persisted in their demand, and Balj, who, like most of the nobles, only retained his leadership on condition of yielding to the wishes and passions of the soldiers, could not resist their clamours, but suffered them to seize 'Abd al-Malik in his house in Cordova, whither he had retired when deprived of office.

Drunk with rage, the Syrians dragged to execution the

old man of ninety years, whose long white hair—to use the
quaint but picturesque simile of the Arab chronicler—made
him resemble a young ostrich. " Dastard ! " they cried,
" thou escapedst our swords at Harra. To avenge thy
defeat thou hast suffered us to eat hides and the flesh of
dogs. Thou wouldst have betrayed us, or sold us—the army
of the Khalif—to the Berbers." Halting near the bridge,
they beat 'Abd al-Malik with bludgeons, plunged their
swords through his heart, and fastened his body to a cross.
On his left hand they crucified a dog, and on his right, a
swine.

A murder so brutal, a punishment so infamous, cried
aloud for vengeance. War broke out, and arms would
decide whether the Arabs of the first, or those of the second
invasion—Medinese or Syrians—were to remain masters of
the Peninsula.

The Medinese had for their leaders the sons of 'Abd al-
Malik, Omayya and Katan, one of whom had sought refuge
at Zaragoza and the other at Merida, when their father was
deposed. Their former enemies, the Berbers, made common
cause with them, intending later to turn their arms against
the Arabs of Spain, but longing in the first instance to take
vengeance on the Syrians. The Medinese had, besides these,
other allies. These were the Lakhmite 'Abd-er-Rahmân
ibn 'Alkama, Governor of Narbonne, and 'Abd-er-Rahmân
the Fihrite, son of the African general Habîb. The latter
had escaped to Spain, with a small force, after the terrible
defeat in which his father had been slain, but before the
arrival of the Syrians in the Peninsula.[1] He had quarrelled
with Balj, and was now his sworn enemy ; he had stirred up
the hate of the aged 'Abd al-Malik against the Syrians by
relating to him the acts of insolence which they had perpetrated in Africa, and had confirmed him in his resolve not to
send them ships, but rather to let them perish of hunger.
He thought himself, moreover, obliged to avenge the murder
of his tribesman 'Abd al-Malik, and since his lineage was
illustrious, he aspired to the Government of the Peninsula.

The confederates were numerically superior to their
opponents—their army amounting to forty thousand men
according to some, and to a hundred thousand according to
others—while Balj could not put more than twelve thousand
in the field, although he had been reinforced by a consider-

[1] Ibn Adhârî, i. 43 ; other chroniclers with less probability state that 'Abd-er-
Rahmân ibn Habîb arrived in Spain with Balj.

able number of Syrians who had re-crossed the Straits after several futile attempts to return to their own country. To augment his force he enrolled a multitude of Christian slaves —tillers of the soil for both Arabs and Berbers—and then awaited the enemy near a village called Aqua Portora.

An engagement was fought in August 742, and the Syrians defended themselves so bravely that they repulsed all the attacks of the confederates. Thereupon it occurred to 'Abd-er-Rahmân, Governor of Narbonne—then reputed the bravest and most accomplished warrior in Spain—that the death of the enemy's commander might decide the fate of the battle. " Point out Balj to me ! " he cried ; " I swear that I will slay him or myself be slain ! " " Behold him yonder," was the reply, " mounted on a white horse, and bearing the standard." 'Abd-er-Rahmân charged so impetuously with his frontier troopers that the Syrians fell back. At the second attempt he smote Balj upon the head, but being instantly attacked by the cavalry of Kinnisrîn he was beaten back, and in his precipitate retreat the entire confederate army was involved. Their rout was complete ; they lost ten thousand men, and the Syrians, who had scarcely lost a thousand, re-entered Cordova as victors.

Balj, however, had been mortally wounded ; a few days later he expired, and the Yemenite Thalaba, to whom the Khalif had entrusted the command in the event of Balj's death, was proclaimed by the Syrians Governor of all Spain. The Medinese had no reason to congratulate themselves. Balj had at least endeavoured, though fruitlessly, to restrain the bloodthirstiness of the Syrians, but his successor made no such attempt. Whether it were that he sought popularity, and felt that to gain it he must give them a free hand, or that he recognised in the mournful cry of some night-fowl a well-beloved voice reminding him that he yet had to avenge upon the Medinese the death of a near kinsman,[1] or perhaps his father—it is at any rate certain that his resolve to show no pity to the Medinese gained him the hearts of his soldiers, and that he became more popular than Balj had ever been.

Thalaba, however, began inauspiciously. Attacking the Arabs and Berbers who were assembled in strong force near

---

[1] "The souls of those slain without vengeance became owls that flew at night about the grave crying *iskûnî, iskûnî*—'Give me to drink, give me to drink !' When the blood of vengeance was shed, the thirst of the owl was quenched, and he ceased to cry." C. J. Lyall, *Trans. of Ancient Arabian Poetry* (1885), p. 67 *n.*

Merida, he was repulsed and obliged to retire into the chief town of the district, where his situation soon became very perilous. He had despatched an order to his lieutenant at Cordova to come to his aid with as many troops as possible, when a stroke of good fortune saved him. On a day of festival, when the besiegers were dispersed and had not taken sufficient precautions against a surprise, Thalaba profited by their carelessness: he attacked them unawares, did great execution, and having secured a thousand prisoners, and compelled the rest to seek safety in precipitate flight, he carried their wives and children into slavery.

Such an outrage was unprecedented, for the Syrians themselves had hitherto never ventured on such an act of barbarity. Under the leadership of Balj they had respected the immemorial usage—perpetuated amongst the Bedawin of modern times—of granting liberty to the women and children of the enemy (in internal wars), and even treating them with courtesy. But when Thalaba, with his ten thousand prisoners, returned to Andalusia, he proceeded from bad to worse. Encamping at Mosâra, near Cordova, one Friday in May 743, he ordered the prisoners to be put up for sale. In order to humble, once for all, the pride of the Medinese, many of whom were included among the captives, the Syrians with brutal humour agreed among themselves to sell them not to the highest, but to the lowest bidder. A Medinese for whom one Syrian had bid ten pieces of gold, was knocked down to another who offered a dog; a young goat was the price of a second, and so forth. Never before, even at the dreadful sack of Medina, had the Syrians inflicted such insult and ignominy on the sons of the founders of Islam. But while this scandalous scene was being enacted an event occurred which Thalaba and the enthusiasts of his party had not foreseen.

The more moderate and intelligent men on either side, labouring under the evils produced by civil war, indignant at the horrible excesses committed by both parties, and fearing lest the Christians of the North might take advantage of the strife between the Moslems and extend their borders, entered into communication with the Governor of Africa, Handhala the Kelbite, begging him to send a Governor capable of restoring order and tranquillity. Handhala thereupon sent the Kelbite Abu 'l-Khattâr to Spain, who arrived with his troops at Mosâra at the very moment when Arabs were being bartered for goats and dogs. Abu

'l-Khattâr produced his commission, and since he was a
noble of Damascus the Syrians could not refuse to recognise
him. The Arabs of Spain hailed him as their deliverer, for
his first care was to set at liberty the ten thousand captives who were being ignominously bartered. By prudent
measures the new Governor re-established tranquillity. He
granted an amnesty to Omayya and Katan, the two sons of
'Abd al-Malik, and to all their partisans, except the ambitious 'Abd-er-Rahmân ibn Habîb, who nevertheless succeeded in reaching the coast and crossing over to Africa,
where a brilliant career awaited him. Handhala exiled from
Spain a dozen of the most turbulent chieftains, including
Thalaba himself, telling them that while they were disturbers
of the peace in the Peninsula, their fiery valour would find
better scope in warring against the Berbers of Africa. Since
it was of primary importance that the Capital should be
freed from the embarrassing presence of the Syrians, Handhala gave them the public lands in fee, ordering the serfs
who tilled the soil henceforth to make over to the Syrians
that third part of the crops which they had hitherto yielded
to the State. The Egyptian division[1] was settled in the
districts of Oksonoba, Beja, and Tadmir; the division of
Emesa, in Niebla and Seville; that of Palestine, in the
district of Sidona and Algeciras; that of Jordan, in the
district of Regio; that of Damascus, in the district of
Elvira; and, finally, that of Kinnisrîn, in the district of Jaen.

The important but unhappy part played by the sons of
the *Helpers* of Mohammed here came to an end. Schooled
by so many reverses and calamities, they seem at last to
have become convinced that their ambitious hopes could
never be realized. Abandoning politics to others, they
retired into the background to live privately on their
domains, and when, at long intervals, the name of a Medinese chief crops up in Arab annals, it is always in connexion
with purely personal interests, or as a supporter of some
party other than his own. Although both numerous and
wealthy, they had scarcely any influence on the future
history of their country. Among the descendants of the
Governor 'Abd al-Malik, one branch, the Beni 'l-Jad, became
rich proprietors at Seville; another, the Beni Kâsim, possessed large estates near Alpuente, in the province of
Valencia, where a village (Benicasim) still bears their name,
but neither branch emerged from its relative obscurity. It

[1] Ar. *djond* (*jund*).

is true that in the eleventh century the Beni Kâsim were
the independent rulers of a petty State; but this does not
seem to have extended beyond the limits of their own
domains; moreover, this was at an epoch when, the Cordovan
Khalifate having fallen, every landed proprietor set up as a
petty sovereign.   It is also true that, two centuries later,
the Beni 'l-Ahmar, descended from the Medinese Sa'd ibn
'Obâda—one of the most illustrious of Mohammed's companions, and nearly chosen as his successor—ascended the
throne of Granada; but old pretensions and old grudges
had by that time been buried in oblivion; the very existence
of a Medinese party had been forgotten; the Arabs had
lost their national characteristics, and through Berber influence had become deeply religious.   The reign of the Beni
'l-Ahmar only lasted long enough for them to see all their
fortresses captured in succession by the Kings of Castile—
and to the days when, in the words of the Spanish romance,
" the cross entered Granada by one gate while the Koran
left it by another, and the *Te Deum* resounded within walls
still echoing to '*Allah Akbar!*"

A living image of the destiny of the Medinese, this family
of Sa'd ibn 'Obâda, whose name is linked to the greatest
names of history both in the East and in the West—Mohammed and Abû Bakr, Charlemagne and Isabella the Catholic
—has left behind it an ineffaceable and glorious memory, but
was always dogged by misfortune.   It commenced with
Sa'd and ended with Boabdil.   An interval of eight centuries
and a half separate these two names, and those who bore
them both died in exile, mourning their past greatness.   A
valiant champion of Islamism in all the battles which
Mohammed had waged against the pagans, Sa'd, " the
Perfect," was on the point of being elected Khalif by the
Helpers when the Meccan Refugees claimed this right for
themselves.   Through the treachery of some Medinese, and
still more through the arrival of a tribe entirely devoted
to the Refugees, the latter bore Sa'd into the midst of a
tumultuous crowd, where, as he lay grievously ill upon
a litter, he was cruelly insulted by 'Omar and nearly
crushed to death in the press.   Vowing that he would never
recognise Abû Bakr, and unable to endure the sight of his
enemies' triumph, he withdrew to Syria, where he met with
a mysterious death.   In a remote and desolate spot—so
ran the popular tradition—he was slain by the Jinn, and
his sons were informed of his death by some slaves, who

SPANISH ISLAM

told them that they had heard a voice proceeding from a
well, crying: "We have slain the chief of the Khazraj,
Sa'd ibn 'Obâda: we discharged two arrows at him which
found their way to his heart."[1] Boabdil, too, when he had
lost his crown, went to end his days in a far-off and inhospi-
table land. From the summit of a high rock, still bearing
its poetical name of *El ultimo sospiro del Moro*, "the Moor's
last sigh," he cast one long look of farewell upon his well-
beloved Granada—a city without her equal in the world.

[1] Rationalistic historians, however, aver that Sa'd died from the bite of a
venomous reptile.

[AUTHORITIES: Isid., c. 44, 58–67; Makkarî, i. 145; ii. 11–14; Sebast.,
c. 11; Ibn Adhârî, ii. 27, 30–4; Ibn al-'Abbâr, 51; *Akhbâr
majmû'at*, 65–9; Ibn al-Kûtiyya, 7–8; Ibn al-Khatîb (MS. G.),
f. 176; Tabarî, i. 6–12, 32–42; Nawawî, 274; Ibn Kutaiba, 132.]

CHAPTER XII

SUMAYL IBN HÂTIM

IN the early days of his governorship, Abu 'l-Khattâr treated all parties with equitable impartiality, and although he was a Kelbite, the Kaisites themselves, of whom there were many among the troops that accompanied Balj to Spain, had no complaint against him. But such moderation was exceptional in an Arab, and his natural antipathies soon displayed themselves. On two scores he had an account to settle with the Kaisites: in Africa he had himself been a victim of their tyranny, and in Spain they had put to death his tribesman Sa'd, son of Jauwâs—a man of whom he used to say: " I would gladly cut off my hand to recall him to life." He could at least avenge him, and this he did only too effectually. He acted, indeed, with such rigour towards the Kaisites whom he suspected of being concerned in his friend's death, that he was able to say in one of his poems:

" I would that the son of Jauwâs could learn with what ardour I have taken his cause in hand. To avenge his death I have slain ninety men: they lie on the ground like palm-trees uprooted by a torrent."

Such indiscriminate retribution naturally tended to rekindle civil war. The Kaisites, however—less numerous in Spain than the Yemenites—were in no hurry to extricate themselves forcibly from a situation which had become intolerable to them; their pent-up hatred did not burst its barriers until the honour of their chief had been compromised. A man of the Ma'addite tribe of Kinâna, having a dispute with a Kelbite, came before the Governor to plead his cause. He had right on his side, but the Governor, with flagrant partiality, decided against him. The Kinânite protested against this iniquitous decision before the Kaisite chief Sumayl,[1] of the Beni Kilâb, who immediately proceeded to the palace, and reproaching the Governor for showing bias in favour of his own tribesman, demanded

---

[1] Sumayl ibn Hâtim: Isidore transliterates the name " Zumahel."

justice for the Kinânite. The Governor returned a rough
answer; Sumayl retorted in a similar tone, whereupon he
was buffeted and thrust out. The chieftain suffered these
indignities uncomplainingly, and with calm disdain; but in
consequence of the treatment he had endured he left the
palace with disordered headgear. A bystander at the gate
exclaimed : " What has befallen your turban, Abû Jawshan ?
It is all awry ! " " If I have any fellow-tribesmen," replied
the Kaisite chief, " they will set it to rights." This was a
declaration of war. Abu 'l-Khattâr had made a dangerous
and implacable enemy of one who was no ordinary man,
either for good or evil. Sumayl's naturally generous—yet
haughty and vindictive—soul was torn by two potent influences, of equal power but contrary tendencies. He was
a man of strong but ill-balanced character—uncultured and
fickle, swayed by instinct, and the sport of chance—and in
his breast opposing impulses came into strong conflict. Of
persevering activity when his passions were aroused, he re-
lapsed into indolence and indifference, which seemed still
more natural to him, as soon as his stormy emotions had
subsided. His liberality—a virtue more highly appreciated
than any other by his compatriots—was boundless; in
order not to ruin him, his poet—for every Arab chief maintained a poet, as every Scottish chief his minstrel—visited
him but twice a year, on the occasion of two great religious
festivals, Sumayl having made an oath to give him all the
money in his possession whenever he saw him. And yet
Sumayl's education had been but slender : in spite of his
love of poetry—especially if it flattered his vanity—and
although he now and then composed verses himself, he
coûld not read, and the Arabs themselves considered him
behind the times. On the other hand, his good breeding
was such that even his enemies were obliged to acknowledge
him to be a model of courtesy. In the laxity of his morals
and his indifference towards religion he followed the type of
the nobles of earlier days, libertines who were Moslems only
in name. In defiance of the Prophet's prohibition, he
drank wine like any Pagan Arab ; indeed, he seldom went to
bed sober. The Koran was almost unknown to him, and he
had little desire to become acquainted with a book the
levelling tendencies of which wounded his Arab pride. It
is said that one day, hearing a schoolmaster, who was teaching children to read the Koran, enunciate this verse : " We
send failure and success in turn among men," Sumayl ex-

claimed, "Nay, it should be, 'among Arabs.'" "Pardon
me, Sir," replied the teacher, "it is, 'among men.'" "Doth
the verse run so?" "Assuredly." "How unfortunate for
us! In that case power doth not belong to us alone;
peasants, serfs, slaves, may share it." If, however, he was
a bad Moslem, he could lay the blame on heredity. His
grandfather was that Shamir, of Kûfa, of whom we have
already related that when general of the Omayyad army he
had not felt a moment's hesitation when it came to putting
the Prophet's grandson to death, while his colleagues,
sceptics though they were, recoiled from such a sacrilege.
This grandfather, who had carried Husain's head to Yazîd I,
had also been the direct cause of Sumayl's coming to Spain.
The Shî'ite Mukhtâr had beheaded Shamir, and thrown his
carcase to the dogs, when, as master of Kûfa, he avenged
Husain's murder by horrible reprisals; and Hâtim, Sumayl's
father, fleeing from the fury of the triumphant party, sought
refuge in the district of Kinnisrîn. There he settled with
his family, and when Hishâm was raising in Syria the army
intended to quell the Berber revolt, Sumayl had been
chosen by lot to join it. Later, he crossed the Straits with
Balj, and the Kaisites of Spain came to regard him as their
leader.

Sumayl upon returning to his house summoned a meeting of the most influential Kaisites that night. When they
were assembled, he related to them the insults to which
he had been subjected, and asked for their advice. "Lay
before us thine own plan," they exclaimed; "we approve
of it beforehand, and are ready to execute it." "By
Allah!" replied Sumayl, "I am firmly resolved to wrest
the power from the hands of this Arab; but we Kaisites in
this country are too weak to resist the Yemenites unaided,
and I would not expose you to the perils of so hazardous an
enterprise. We can doubtless count upon all those who
were worsted at the Battle of the Plain, and it will be well
also to form an alliance with the Lakhmites and Judhâmites,[1]
and confer the Emirate on one of them; or, rather, they
shall ostensibly enjoy the hegemony which will in reality
rest with us. I shall therefore immediately leave Cordova
to visit the chiefs of these tribes and induce them to take
up arms. Do you approve of my plans?" "We approve,"
replied one of the assembly, "but take heed that you broach
not the matter to our tribesman, Abû 'Atâ, for you may be

[1] Two Yemenite tribes.

sure that he will not co-operate with us." Now, Abû 'Atâ, who lived at Ecija, was chief of the Beni Ghatafân: Sumayl's commanding influence over men's minds had inspired this chieftain with violent jealousy; it is therefore not to be wondered at that, when the question was put to the vote, the Kaisites unanimously endorsed the advice which had just been given. A single individual, however, did not seem to share the general opinion. But since he was very young, and modesty forbade him to vote against his seniors, he merely showed his disapproval by silence, until Sumayl emboldened him by asking why he had not declared his opinion openly like the rest. " I have but one comment to make," replied the young man, " namely, that if you do not seek Abû 'Atâ's aid, we are lost; but that if you do, he will forget his animosity and be guided solely by the love he has for his race. You may be certain that he will support us vigorously." After a moment's reflection, Sumayl simply replied, " I believe you say well," and starting from Cordova before dawn he proceeded first of all to Abû 'Atâ. As the youthful Ibn Tufayl had foreseen, Abû 'Atâ promised to aid him, and he kept his word. From Ecija, Sumayl went to Moron, where dwelt Thoâba, chief of the Judhâmites, who had already had differences with Yûsuf. The two chiefs entered into a compact, and Thoâba having been proclaimed leader of the allies, the Kaisites, the Judhâmites, and the Lakhmites joined forces, in the district of Sidona (April, A.D. 745).

Abu 'l-Khattâr no sooner heard of these warlike preparations than he marched against the insurgents with the troops then at Cordova. During the battle which ensued beside the Gaudalete, the wisdom of the advice given by Sumayl to his tribesmen at the council became manifest. In concluding an alliance with two powerful Yemenite tribes, and granting one of them the supremacy, he had but followed an Eastern usage, by which tribes too weak themselves to resist their enemies, were wont to confederate with tribes allied to their opponents.[1] Alliances of this kind, besides strengthening weak tribes, yielded the further advantage that they, to some extent, disarmed the enemy, who were almost always reluctant to fight against tribes

---

[1] For, instance, in Khorasan and in 'Irâk, the Yemenites, who were in a minority in both provinces, leagued with the Rabî'a, a Ma'addite tribe, in order to cope with the Beni Temîm, who were also Ma'addites. *Cf.* Al-Sukkari's Commentary on the Dîwân of Ferazdak (Bodl. MS. f. 93 v.).

of their own race, especially when the latter held the hegemony. This is what happened at the battle of the Guadalete. Abu 'l-Khattâr's Yemenites, after contending half-heartedly with the Judhâmites and Lakhmites—with whom they had already come to an understanding, and who for their part spared them as much as possible—allowed themselves to be routed, and took to flight. Left alone with the Kelbites on the battlefield, Abu 'l-Khattâr was soon obliged to follow their example, after having seen many of his tribesmen killed; but, with three members of his family, he was captured by his pursuers. There were some in the victorious army who would have put him to death, but other counsels prevailed. He was merely loaded with fetters, and Thoâba, Governor of Spain by right of conquest, took up his residence in the Capital. The Kelbites, however, did not consider themselves vanquished, and one of their chiefs, 'Abd-er-Rahmân ibn Nu'aym, formed the bold resolution of attempting to deliver Abu 'l-Khattâr from captivity. Accompanied by thirty or forty horse, and two hundred foot, he entered Cordova in the darkness of the night, attacked unawares the soldiers who kept guard over Abu 'l-Khattâr, dispersed them, and conducted the former Governor to the Kelbites in the vicinity of Beja.

Thus restored to liberty, Abu 'l-Khattâr assembled some Yemenites under his banner and marched against Cordova, in the hope that this time the army would show more zeal for his cause. Thoâba and Sumayl set out to meet him, and the two opposing armies encamped in sight of one another. At nightfall a Ma'addite left Thoâba's camp, and, approaching Abu 'l-Khattâr's, cried at the top of his voice: "Yemenites, why fight ye against us, and why have ye set Abu 'l-Khattâr free ? Fear ye that we shall put him to death ? When we had him in our power, we spared his life and forgave him all. Ye might have had a plausible pretext for warring against us if we had chosen an Emir of our own race; but we have chosen one of yours. Reflect, therefore, we pray you, on what ye are about to do. It is not fear, I swear to you, which makes us speak to you thus: but we would, if possible, avoid bloodshed." These words, in which it is easy to recognise Sumayl's suggestion, made such an impression on Abu 'l-Khattâr's men, that carrying off their unwilling Emir, they struck their camp that night and marched homewards, and when dawn whitened the mountain-tops which formed the horizon, they were already several

leagues distant. In these civil wars the tribesmen did
not fight in the interests of an individual, but for supremacy.
Upon the death of Thoâba, which took place a year later,
Spain was once more plunged into anarchy. Two chiefs,
both Judhâmites, claimed the Emirate. These were 'Amr,
son of Thoâba, who considered that he was his father's
rightful successor, and Ibn Horaith, the son of a negress
but sprung from a family long settled in Spain. The latter
felt such fierce hatred for the Syrians, that he was wont to
say : " If one bowl contained the blood of all the Syrians,
I would drain it to the dregs!" Sumayl, a Syrian himself,
could not allow Spain to be governed by such an implacable
enemy of his race ; but he objected just as strongly to the
son of Thoâba. While not desiring the title of Governor
himself—since he believed the Kaisites were too weak to
support him—Sumayl aimed at conferring the post on some
nominee—a puppet, through whose agency he could actually
rule. He had already hit upon a man who fulfilled the
necessary conditions. This was the Fihrite Yûsuf,[1] a man
of inoffensive mediocrity, who possessed, however, qualifications recommending him to the suffrages of Arabs of
every race. He was old enough to please those who doted
on a gerontocracy—for he had attained the age of fifty-seven ;
he sprang from a noble and illustrious line—for he was
descended from 'Okba, the famous general who had conquered a great part of Africa; finally, he was a Fihrite—
and the Fihrites[2] were regarded as second in rank only to
the pure Kuraish ; it was natural to see them at the head of
affairs, and they were regarded as above faction. By dint
of trumpeting these advantages, Sumayl succeeded in procuring his candidate's nomination ; Ibn Horaith was consoled
with the prefecture of Regio, and in January A.D. 747 the
chiefs elected Yûsuf Governor of Spain.

Henceforth Sumayl, whose passions had hitherto been
kept in check by Thoâba's counterbalancing influence, was
the sole master of Spain, and he set his mind on making
Yûsuf, who was as wax in his hands, an instrument of his
vengeance. Confident that he could rely upon all the
Ma'addites, Sumayl no longer shrank from making war
against the combined Yemenites. His first step was to
break faith with Ibn Horaith, by depriving the Judhâmite
of his prefecture. This was the signal for hostilities.
Ibn Horaith, in great wrath, offered his alliance to Abu

[1] Yûsuf 'Abd-er-Rahmân al-Fihri.   [2] See above, p. 71 n.

'l-Khattâr, who was eating his heart among his tribesmen. The two chiefs had an interview which very nearly proved fruitless, since Abu 'l-Khattâr reasserted his right to the Emirate, while Ibn Horaith claimed it on the ground that his tribe was more numerous in Spain than Abu 'l-Khattâr's. The Kelbites themselves, who felt that in order to wreak vengeance on the Kaisites they needed the co-operation of their whole race, compelled Abu 'l-Khattâr to give way. Ibn Horaith was therefore acclaimed Emir, and the Yemenites flocked to his banner from all quarters. The Ma'addites, for their part, rallied round Yûsuf and Sumayl. Neighbours of different races everywhere took leave of one another with the courtesy and goodwill beseeming a calm and courageous people—at the same time firmly resolved to measure each other's strength upon the battlefield. Neither army was a large one, and the struggle upon which they were entering —confined as it was to the south of Spain—resembled a duel on a large scale, rather than a war, though those who took part in it were the bravest and noblest of their race.

The encounter took place near Secunda, an old Roman walled town, on the left bank of the Guadalquiver, opposite to Cordova and afterwards included among the suburbs of the Capital. After the morning prayer the horsemen attacked each other as though at a tourney; then when their spears were shattered, and the sun was high, a cry arose that the time had come to fight hand to hand. Leaping from their horses, and each man selecting his adversary, they fought till their swords were broken. Then every man used whatever weapon fell to his hand; one a bow, another a quiver; others threw sand in their enemies' eyes, or beat them with their fists, or tore out their hair. "Shall we summon the army which we left in Cordova?" asked Sumayl of Yûsuf, when this furious conflict had lasted till the evening, without decisive result. "What army?" asked Yûsuf in surprise. "The market folk," replied Sumayl. It was strange for an Arab, especially for an Arab of Sumayl's stamp, to seek the intervention of bakers, butchers, chapmen, and peasants in such a fray, but since he had conceived the idea, it is reasonable to suppose that he feared his side might yield at any moment. Be this as it may, Yûsuf as usual acquiesced in his friend's suggestion, and despatched two messengers to Cordova to summon this strange reinforcement. About four hundred citizens thereupon marched out, almost unarmed. A few had managed to provide themselves with swords or spears, and the butchers had their knives, but the rest carried cudgels only. Nevertheless, since Ibn Horaith's soldiers were half dead with fatigue, the arrival of this improvised national guard upon the field decided the fate of the battle, and the Ma'addites made a large number of prisoners, including Abu 'l-Khattâr himself. The Kelbite chief knew the doom which awaited him, and made no attempt to escape it, but he at least determined to give himself the satisfaction of seeing it shared by his so-called ally, Ibn Horaith, that implacable enemy of the Syrians, who had ousted him from his Emirate. He had marked Ibn Horaith crouching beneath a mill, and pointed out his hiding-place to the Ma'addites: then, seeing him made prisoner and condemned to death, he exclaimed, in allusion to the blood-thirsty phrase so often upon Ibn Horaith's lips : " Son of a negress, remaineth there one drop in thy bowl ? " Both of them were decapitated (A.D. 747). The Ma'addites dragged their other prisoners to the cathedral of Cordova, which was dedicated to S. Vincent.[1] There Sumayl acted at once as their prosecutor, their judge, and their executioner. He did prompt and terrible justice ; each doom which he pronounced and executed was a sentence of death. He had already beheaded seventy persons, when his ally Abû 'Atâ, sickened by the hideous scene, wished to end it. " Abû Jawshan," he cried, starting up, "return thy sword to thy scabbard ! " " Sit thee down again, Abû 'Atâ," replied Sumayl, in a murderous frenzy ; " this is a glorious day for thee and for thy people ! " Abû Atâ resumed his seat, and Sumayl continued his bloody work. At last Abû 'Atâ could restrain himself no longer. Frozen with horror at the carnage, at the murder of so many poor wretches who, though Yemenites, were Syrians, he saw in Sumayl the enemy of his countrymen, the descendant of the warriors of 'Irâk who, under 'Alî, had fought against Mu'âwiya's Syrians at the battle of Siffîn. Rising once more he cried : " Arab ! If thou takest so atrocious a pleasure in slaughtering my countrymen, it is because thou rememberest Siffîn. Stay thy murderous hand, or I will make the cause of thy victims that of the Syrians." Then, and not till then, did Sumayl replace his sword in its scabbard.

After the battle of Secunda, Yûsuf's authority was undisputed, but since he was merely a titular Governor, while Sumayl actually ruled, he grew weary of the subordinate

[1] Martyred under Diocletian ; a native of Zaragoza, put to death at Saguntum.

position to which the Kaisite had condemned him, and with
a view to ridding himself of his master, he offered him a kind
of viceroyship as Governor of the district of Zaragoza.
Sumayl did not reject this offer, but the chief motive which
led him to accept it was the fact that the district was inhabited by Yemenites. He looked forward to gratifying his
hatred by oppressing them. But events took an unexpected
turn. Accompanied by his clients, his slaves, and two
hundred Kurashites, Sumayl arrived at Zaragoza (A.D. 750),
just as Spain began to be devastated by a dearth which
lasted for five years. So grievous was the famine that communications were interrupted by the death of nearly all the
couriers, and the Berbers settled in the North emigrated in
a body to Africa. The widespread want and suffering so
greatly touched the Governor's heart that, by one of those
accesses of kindness, which in his character seemed to alternate with the most savage brutality, he forgot all his grievances and grudges, and making no distinction between friend
and foe, Ma'addite and Yemenite, he gave money to some,
slaves to others, and bread to all. In a man so compassionate, so charitable, it was hard indeed to recognise the butcher
who had made so many heads fall on S. Vincent's pavement.

Two or three years thus passed by, and if a good understanding between Kaisites and Yemenites had been possible,
if Sumayl could have become reconciled to his enemies by
dint of kindness, the Arabs of Spain would have enjoyed
repose after years of sanguinary warfare. But no actions of
Sumayl could win him forgiveness for his pitiless executions: he was always believed to be ready to recommence
them at the first opportunity, and hatred was too deeply rooted
in the hearts of the leading men on both sides to render the
apparent reconciliation anything more than a brief truce.
The Yemenites, moreover, who believed that Spain belonged
to them of right, could not tamely endure the supremacy of
the Kaisites, and were firmly resolved to regain, upon the
first favourable occasion, their lost dominion. Certain of the
Kurashite chiefs also murmured. Belonging to a tribe
which since Mohammed's days had been regarded as the most
illustrious, they could not with equanimity see Spain ruled
by a Fihrite—a mere Kurashite of the environs, whom they
naturally looked down upon.

A coalition between these two parties of malcontents
might have been predicted, and it was not long delayed.
There was at that time in Cordova an ambitious Kurashite

noble, 'Âmir by name, whom Yûsuf, who disliked him, had
deprived of the command of the army which from time to time
operated against the Christians of the North. Eager to
avenge this affront, and aspiring to the dignity of Governor,
'Âmir cherished the design of turning the discontent of the
Yemenites to his advantage and placing himself at their
head under the pretence that the 'Abbâsid Khalif had nominated him Governor of Spain. He began by building a fortress
on a domain which he owned to the west of Cordova. Upon
the completion of this he intended to attack Yûsuf, which he
might do with good prospect of success, since the Governor
had at his disposal only a body-guard of some fifty horse.
Even if he met with a reverse, 'Âmir could retire to his
fortress and await the arrival of the Yemenites, with whom
he had already come to an understanding. Yûsuf got wind
of the Kurashite's hostile intentions, and tried to arrest him ;
but he saw that 'Âmir was on his guard, and, moreover, he
did not dare to resort to extreme measures without seeking
the advice of Sumayl—whom he consulted on all points, in
spite of his remoteness from the Capital. He accordingly
wrote to Sumayl, asking him how to act. The Governor
of Zaragoza in his reply, urged the immediate assassination
of 'Âmir. Fortunately for the latter, he was warned of his
imminent danger by a spy in the Governor's palace. Mounting his horse without a moment's delay, he took the road
to Zaragoza, for he deemed the Yemenites of Syria too
much enfeebled by the battle of Secunda to be relied upon,
and was convinced that those of the North-East would afford
him surer aid. By the time 'Âmir reached the district of
Zaragoza, another Kurashite, Hobâb by name,[1] had already
raised the standard of revolt. 'Âmir having proposed that
they should join forces against Sumayl, the two chiefs met
and agreed to call the Yemenites and Berbers to arms against
both Yûsuf and his lieutenant, whom they dubbed usurpers
on the pretext that 'Âmir had been nominated Governor of
Spain by the 'Abbâsid Khalif. The Yemenites and Berbers
responding in large numbers to this summons, they defeated
the forces sent against them by Sumayl, and then proceeded
to lay siege to Zaragoza (A.D. 753-4).

    After appealing in vain for aid to Yûsuf, who was re-
duced to such helplessness as to be unable to muster any
troops, Sumayl applied to the Kaisites who formed part of
the divisions of Kinnisrîn and Damascus and were settled

----

[1] Or, Habhâb.

in the territories of Jaen and Elvira. He described the
perilous position in which he was placed, but added that at a
pinch he would be content with a small reinforcement. His
requisition was difficult to comply with. Sumayl's friend,
however, the Kilâbite 'Obaid—who next to him was the
most powerful chief among the Kaisites—traversed the
region inhabited by the two divisions, summoning on his way
all those on whom he could rely, to arm themselves and be
prepared to march on Zaragoza. The tribes of Kilâb,
Mohârib [1] Sulaym, Nasr, and Hawâzin also volunteered to
join the expedition; but the Ghatafân, who were without a
chief—Abû 'Atâ having died and his successor having not
yet being elected—were undecided, and put off from day to
day a definite reply. The tribe of the Ka'b ibn 'Âmir, on the
other hand, from petty jealousy, wished for nothing better
than to see Sumayl perish for lack of help.[1] Urged by
'Obaid, the Ghatafân, however, at last promised their support, whereupon the K'ab ibn 'Âmir thought that, all things
considered, they had better throw in their lot with the rest.
They realized, in fact, that by standing aloof, they would
attract general animosity without gaining their object, for
Sumayl would be rescued in any case, and could easily dispense with their aid. In the end, therefore, all the Kaisite
tribes supplied slender contingents : the number of infantry
is unknown, but of horsemen there were barely three hundred
and sixty. Seeing their united forces so weak, the Kaisites
began to be demoralised, when one of their number banished
their hesitation with burning words: " We must not," he
cried at the end of his harangue, "abandon to his fate a
chieftain such as Sumayl : rather let us lay down our lives to
save him!" Their wavering courage returned, and they set
out on their march to Toledo. Ibn Shihâb, chief of the
Ka'b ibn 'Âmir, was entrusted with the command of the
expedition. His appointment was due to the advice of
'Obaid, who, though himself entitled to the post, preferred,
generous and devoted friend that he was, to yield it to the
chief of the tribe which had shown itself most opposed to
the enterprise, in the hope that it would thereby become
firmly attached to Sumayl's cause. The expedition set out
at the beginning of the year 755.

Upon reaching the banks of the Guadiana, the Kaisites

---

[1] This tribe, including the three sub-tribes of Koshair, Osail, and Harish, were
discontented because the supremacy which had been theirs when Balj the
Koshairite had commanded all the Syrians in Spain, had now passed to the Kilâb,
to which tribe both Sumayl and 'Obaid belonged.

found there the Bakr ibn Wâ'il and the Beni 'Alî, two tribes which, although not Kaisites, at least belonged to the Ma'addite race. These sympathised with the expedition, and supplied a reinforcement of more than four hundred horse. Thus strengthened, the force arrived at Toledo, where information reached it that the siege was being prosecuted with such vigour that Sumayl would soon be compelled to surrender. Fearing to arrive too late, and wishing to inform the besieged of their approach, the Kaisites despatched one of their number to Zaragoza, with injunctions to slip through the besiegers and throw over the rampart a pebble wrapped in paper on which were written two verses:

"Rejoice, ye besieged, for succour arriveth, and soon the siege will be raised. Illustrious warriors, children of Nizâr, come to rescue you, mounted on well-bridled mares of the breed of Awaj."

The messenger carried out his orders adroitly. The missive was picked up and carried to Sumayl, who read it and hastened to revive the courage of his soldiers by communicating to them the joyful news which he had received. The operations came to an end without a blow being struck: upon the mere rumour of the approach of the Ma'addites the siege was raised, for 'Âmir and Hobâb feared to find themselves surrounded. The Kaisites with their allies thereupon entered the city, and Sumayl lavishly rewarded them for the services they had rendered him.

Among the auxiliaries were thirty clients of the family of Omayya, belonging to the Damascus division, settled in the province of Elvira. The Omayyads [1] had long been distinguished for their attachment to the Ma'addite cause, and at the battle of Secunda they had fought so bravely under Yûsuf and Sumayl that they had won the high esteem of those two chiefs. On the present occasion, however, the thirty horsemen had accompanied the Kaisites on their march to the relief of Sumayl, less because they regarded the latter as their ally, than because they wished to confer with him upon matters of high importance. To explain the nature of their business, we must revert to pregnant events which had taken place five years before.

[1] According to Arab usage the name was applied not only to members of the family, but also to their clients.

[AUTHORITIES: *Akhbâr majmú'at*, ff. 72–8, 81; Makkarî, Bk. vi.; Ibn Adhârî, ii. 35–8, 43–5; Ibn al-'Abbâr, 46–50, 52, 54; Isid., c. 68, 70, 75; Ibn al-Khatîb (MS. E.), Art. "Somail"; Ibn al-Kûtiyya, ff. 16–17; Ibn Khaldûn, ii. f. 177, *et passim*.]

CHAPTER XIII

'ABD-ER-RAHMÂN'S WANDERINGS

WHEN, in the year 750, Merwân II, the last Omayyad Khalif, met his death in Egypt, where he had sought refuge, a cruel persecution arose against his numerous family, whom the 'Abbâsids, usurpers of the throne, thirsted to exterminate. A grandson of the Khalif Hishâm was deprived of a hand and a foot, and thus mutilated was led on an ass through the towns and villages of Syria accompanied by a herald, who exhibited him as though he were a strange beast, crying: "Behold Abân, son of Mu'âwiya, the most renowned cavalier of the house of Omayya!" This punishment was only terminated by the victim's death. The princess Abda, Hishâm's daughter, upon refusing to reveal where she had hidden her treasures, was forthwith slain. But the persecution failed through its very violence. Many Omayyads succeeded in escaping, and sought concealment among Bedawy tribes. Seeing their victims slipping from their grasp, and realizing that they could not complete their bloody work except by a stratagem, the 'Abbâsids issued a treacherous proclamation, in the name of their Khalif Abu 'l-'Abbâs, in which it was admitted that they had gone too far, and an amnesty was promised to all the surviving Omayyads. More than seventy fell into the snare, and were beaten to death.

Two brothers, Yahyâ and 'Abd-er-Rahmân, grandsons of the Khalif Hishâm, escaped this horrible massacre. When the proclamation appeared, Yahyâ said to his brother: "Let us wait awhile; if all goes well we can at any time join the army of the 'Abbâsids when it is in our neighbourhood, but at present I have no great confidence in the promised amnesty. I will send an emissary to the camp, who will report to us how our kinsfolk have fared."

After the massacre Yahyâ's messenger brought him the fatal news with all speed; but he was closely followed by soldiers who had been ordered to put both Yahyâ and 'Abd-er-Rahmân to death, and before the former, paralysed with terror, could devise means of escape, he was seized and slain. 'Abd-er-Rahmân was out hunting at the time, and his absence saved him. Informed by trusty servants of his brother's fate, he profited by the darkness of the night to return home, and telling his two sisters that he would seek refuge in a village near the Euphrates—where he owned a house— he bade them join him there, as soon as possible, with his son and younger brother.

The Prince reached the village in question without accident, and was soon joined by his family. He had no intention of remaining long in this retreat, and resolved to proceed to Africa, but believing that his enemies would not easily discover his hiding-place, he waited until he could undertake his long journey without undue peril.

One day, when 'Abd-er-Rahmân, who was suffering from an affection of the eyes, lay in a darkened room, his son Sulaimân, then four years of age, who had been playing at the threshold of the house, ran in, terror-stricken and weeping, to throw himself upon his father's breast. " Nay, little one," said 'Abd-er-Rahmân, " thou knowest that I am sick. But what aileth thee? What hath frightened thee?" The child once more hid his face in his father's breast, with tears and sobs. " What can it be? " cried the Prince, starting up, and opening the door. But on looking out he saw in the distance black flags. The child had also seen them, and remembered that on the day when those flags had appeared before his father's former home, his uncle had been slain. 'Abd-er-Rahmân scarcely had time to put a few pieces of gold into his purse and to bid his two sisters farewell. " I must flee," he said; " bid my freedman Badr follow me; he will find me in such and such a place; tell him to bring me what I shall have need of, if it please God to save my life."

Whilst the 'Abbâsid horsemen, after having surrounded the village, searched the house which had served as a retreat for the Omayyad family—to find in it only two women and a child, whom they did not harm—'Abd-er-Rahmân and his brother, a youth of thirteen years, concealed themselves at some distance from the village: they found but little difficulty in doing this, for the country was well wooded. Upon Badr's arrival the two brothers set out, and reached the banks of the Euphrates. There the Prince confided in a man of his acquaintance, and giving him money begged him to procure provisions and horses. The man, promising to execute his commission, departed with Badr. Unfortu-

nately, a slave had overheard all that had passed.   In hopes
of a large reward, the traitor ran as fast as he could to tell
the 'Abbâsid captain where the fugitives were hidden.   The
latter were suddenly alarmed by the sound of horses' hoofs.
As they rushed to seek concealment in a garden, the troopers
espied them, and proceeded to surround the place ; it seemed
that in another moment the two brothers would be slain.
One last chance of escape remained—to throw themselves
into the Euphrates and endeavour to swim across it.   The
river was very wide ; the attempt would be fraught with
great danger, but in their despair they did not hesitate, and
plunged headlong into the stream.   " Come back ! " cried
the troopers, who saw the prey escaping which they had
thought was in their grasp, " Come back, and we will do
you no hurt ! "   'Abd-er-Rahmân, who knew the worth of
such a promise, only swam the faster.   Reaching mid-stream,
he stayed for an instant, and shouting to his brother, who
lagged behind, urged him to hasten.   But the poor boy,
who was not so strong a swimmer as 'Abd-er-Rahmân, was
in fear of drowning, and believing the soldiers' words, had
already turned back.   " Follow me, brother dear !   Follow
me !   Have no faith in their promises ! " cried 'Abd-er-
Rahmân—but he cried in vain.   " We have lost the other
one ! " exclaimed the soldiers, and one of them, bolder than
the rest, prepared to strip and essay the passage of the
Euphrates, but the width of the river deterred him.   'Abd-
er-Rahmân, therefore, was not pursued, but on gaining the
opposite bank he had the anguish of witnessing his brother's
decapitation.

Reaching Palestine in safety, he was rejoined by his
faithful servant Badr, and by Sâlim, a freedman of one of
his sisters, who brought him money and jewels.   The three
then set out for Africa, where the authority of the 'Abbâsids
had not been recognised, and where many Omayyads had
found refuge.   The journey was accomplished in safety,
and had 'Abd-er-Rahmân so desired, he could doubtless have
found in Africa tranquillity and repose.   But he was not
a man to resign himself to a humdrum and obscure existence.   Ambitious dreams thronged the brain of this youth
of twenty.   Tall, vigorous, brave, very carefully educated,
and possessed of remarkable talents, he felt instinctively
that he was destined for a brilliant career.   His spirit of
adventure and enterprise was nourished by recollections of
his childhood, which had been vividly renewed since he had

been condemned to a wandering life of poverty.   There was
a widespread belief among Arabs that the destiny of every
man is written on his countenance, and 'Abd-er-Rahmân
held this belief more firmly than most, since a prediction
made by his great-uncle Maslama, who was reputed an
accomplished physiognomist, tallied with his most ardent
desires.   At the age of ten—his father Mu'âwiya being
then dead—he was one day taken, with his brothers, to
Rosâfa.   This was a splendid mansion in the district of
Kinnisrîn, and the usual residence of the Khalif Hishâm.
The children had just reached the gateway when Maslama
happened to ride up.   Reining in his horse, he asked who
they were.   On learning that they were the sons of
Mu'âwiya, Maslama's eyes filled with tears.   " Poor
orphans ! " he exclaimed, and bade the children be presented to him two by two.   'Abd-er-Rahmân seemed to
please him most, and taking the boy on the pummel of
his saddle, Maslama affectionately caressed him.   Just then
Hishâm emerged from his palace.   " What child is this ? "
he asked his brother.   " It is Mu'âwiya's son," replied
Maslama, and then bending down he whispered in his
brother's ear—in a tone loud enough, however, for 'Abd-
er-Rahmân to hear—" The great event is at hand, and
this child will become the man you wot of."   " Canst thou
be sure of this ? " asked Hishâm.   " Yea, I can swear it,"
replied Maslama : " on his face and on his neck I have read
the tokens ! "

'Abd-er-Rahmân also remembered that ever since that
day his grandfather had shown a great predilection for him—
often sending him gifts in which his brothers had no share,
and inviting him every month to his palace.

'Abd-er-Rahmân did not precisely know the meaning
of Maslama's mysterious words, but at the time when they
were uttered many predictions of a like nature were current.
The power of the Omayyads had been rudely shaken, and
in their disquietude, these princes—superstitious as are all
orientals to some extent—importuned soothsayers, astrologers, physiognomists, and others who pretended to raise
in any way the veil which shrouded the future.   Not wishing to deprive of all hope credulous patrons who loaded
them with gifts, nor to delude them with expectations which
might soon be falsified, the adepts in occult sciences took
a middle course, and while declaring that the throne of the
Omayyads would fall, predicted that a scion of that illustrious

house would somewhere re-establish it.   Maslama seems to
have shared this idea.

'Abd-er-Rahmân, therefore, believed himself destined to
ascend a throne, but in what country he knew not.   The
East was lost: in that quarter there was nothing to hope
for.   There remained Africa and Spain, and in both of these
countries a Fihrite dynasty sought to establish itself.

In Africa—or, rather, in that part of the province which
was still under Arab domination[1]—there reigned a man
whom we have already met with in Spain, where he had
unsuccessfully endeavoured to be proclaimed Emir.   This
was 'Abd-er-Rahmân ibn Habîb, the Fihrite, a relative of
Yûsuf, Governor of Spain.   Ibn Habîb, who had not recognised the 'Abbâsids, hoped to hand down Africa to his
descendants as an independent principality, and with anxious
curiosity consulted the soothsayers concerning the future
of his family.   Some time before the young 'Abd-er-Rahmân
arrived at his Court, a Jew, initiated in the occult sciences
by the prince Maslama, from whose Court he came, predicted
that a descendant of the royal family, 'Abd-er-Rahmân by
name, and wearing a curl on each temple, would found a
dynasty which would reign over Africa.[2]   Ibn Habîb replied
that, in that case, since he was himself named 'Abd-er-
Rahmân and was master of Africa, he had merely to cultivate two locks of hair to fulfil the conditions.   " Nay,"
replied the Jew, " You are not the person designated, since
you are not of the blood-royal."   Afterwards, when Ibn
Habîb saw 'Abd-er-Rahmân, he observed that the young
man wore his hair in the manner indicated, and sending for
the Jew, he said to him : " So this is the man whom destiny
points out as the master of Africa,[2] since he possesses all
the necessary attributes.   But it matters not : he will not
deprive me of my province,'for he will shortly be assassinated."
The Jew, who was deeply attached to the Omayyads, his
former masters, shuddered at the thought of his prediction
furnishing a pretext for the murder of a young man who
claimed his regard, but without losing his presence of mind,
replied : " I admit, my lord, that this young man fulfils the
required conditions.   But since you rely on my prediction,
of two possible consequences one must follow : either this

---

[1] The western regions having at this time thrown off the yoke.
[2] The MSS. here have " Spain," which is clearly an error.   Probably the Jew
named Africa, but the event having falsified the prediction, " Spain " was substituted.

'Abd-er-Rahmân is not the man—and in that case if you slay
him you will commit a useless crime—or, he is the predicted
ruler of Africa, and in that case, whatever you do, you
cannot deprive him of life, since destiny is immutable."

Recognising the soundness of the Jew's logic, Ibn Habîb
postponed his attempt on the young prince's life; nevertheless, mistrusting not only 'Abd-er-Rahmân, but all the
other Omayyads who were then refugees in his province—
in whom he saw pretenders who might any day become
dangerous—he dogged their steps with ever-increasing
anxiety.   Among these princes were two sons of the Khalif
Walîd II.   Sons worthy of a father who lived only for
pleasure, who sent his mistresses to preside in his place at
public prayer, and who when practising archery used the
Koran as a target, they lived a dissolute life in the land of
their exile.   One night as they sat carousing together, one
of them exclaimed : " What folly ! Doth Ibn Habîb really
suppose that he will remain Emir of this land, and that we,
sons of a Khalif, will tamely suffer him to reign undisturbed ? "

Ibn Habîb, who listened at the door, heard these words.
Determined to rid himself, secretly, of his dangerous guests,
he awaited a favourable opportunity to compass their death
in such a way that it might be attributed to accident, or
private revenge.   He therefore made no change in his
demeanour towards them, and when they came to pay their
respects to him, received them with his usual affability.
He did not, however, conceal from his confidants the fact
that he had kept a watch upon the sons of Walîd, and heard
them use imprudent words.   One of these confidants was
a secret partisan of the Omayyads, and he counselled the
princes to flee the Emir's resentment.   They forthwith took
his advice; but Ibn Habîb, informed of their hasty departure,
and ignorant of its cause, feared that they were about to
incite some Arab or Berber tribe to revolt, and sent horsemen
in pursuit, who captured them and brought them back.
Thereupon the Emir, considering their flight and the words
which he had heard ample proofs of their criminal intentions,
ordered them to execution.   Ibn Habîb then determined to
rid himself of all the other Omayyads, but they, warned by
their friends, sought safety among the independent Berbers.

Wandering from tribe to tribe, and from town to town,
'Abd-er-Rahmân traversed the north of Africa from end to
end.   At one time he lay hid at Barca; then he sought

asylum at the Court of the Beni Rostem, Kings of Tâhort;
then he implored the protection of the Berber tribe of
Miknesa. Five years passed in this manner, and there is
no evidence that during this period 'Abd-er-Rahmân ever
thought of trying his fortune in Spain. It was Africa that
this ambitious youth, though penniless and friendless, hankered after. For ever intriguing, trying at all costs to gain
partisans, he was, however, expelled by the Miknesa, and
journeyed to the neighbourhood of Ceuta, a district inhabited
by the Berber tribe of Nafza, to which his mother belonged.
Convinced at last that no good fortune awaited him in
Africa, 'Abd-er-Rahmân turned his thoughts to the other
side of the Straits. He possessed some information about
Spain, gleaned from Sâlim, one of the two freedmen who
had shared the vicissitudes of his wandering life. Sâlim had
visited Spain in Mûsâ's time, or a little later, and in the
circumstances he might now have been of much service to
his master, but he had returned to Syria. Long weary of
leading a vagabond life at the heels of an adventurer, he
had determined to seize the first convenient excuse for
cutting himself adrift. Such an opportunity 'Abd-er-
Rahmân had given him. One day, being asleep, Sâlim did
not hear his master's summons, whereupon the latter threw a
bowl of water over him, and Sâlim cried in anger : " Since
thou treatest me as a common slave, I leave thee for ever.
I am under no indebtedness to thee ; thy sister is my rightful patron, and to her I shall return ! "

The other freedman, the faithful Badr, remained. He it
was whom 'Abd-er-Rahmân sent over to Spain, there to
consult with the Omayyad clients, who, to the number of
four or five hundred, formed part of the two " divisions " of
Damascus and Kinnisrîn settled in the territories of Elvira
and Jaen. Badr took with him a letter from his patron,
in which 'Abd-er-Rahmân explained that he had been for
five years a fugitive in Africa from the wrath of Ibn Habîb,
who sought the life of every member of the Omayyad family.
" It is amongst you, the clients of my house," continued the
Prince, " that I fain would dwell, for I am convinced that
ye would prove my faithful friends. But, alas, I dare not
pay a visit to Spain, for the Emir of that country, like the
Emir of Africa, would lie in wait for me ; he would regard
me as an enemy, a pretender. And in truth, have not I,
grandson of the Khalif Hishâm, a right to the Emirate ?
Since, then, I cannot enter Africa as a private individual, as

a claimant only will I come. But I will not embark until
I receive your assurance that I have in your country some
chance of success, that you will aid me to the best of your
power, and that you will look upon my cause as your
own." He ended by promising to confer the most exalted
dignities upon his clients in the event of their supporting
him.

On reaching Spain, Badr sent this letter to 'Obaidallah
and Ibn Khâlid, the leading clients of the Damascus
division. Having read it, these two chiefs fixed a day for
deliberating on the matter with the other clients, and also
invited Yûsuf ibn Bôkht, the chief of the Omayyads in the
Kinnisrîn division, to the conference. On the day appointed
they discussed plans of action with their tribesmen. Difficult though the enterprise appeared, they soon agreed that
it was worth attempting. In coming to this decision the
clients were, indeed, fulfilling a plain duty; for, from the
Arab point of view, clientage implied a sacred and indissoluble bond—an artificial kinship—and the descendants of
a freedman were bound in all circumstances to aid the descendants of him who had manumitted the founder of their
family. But the decision at which they arrived was also
based on self-interest. Under the Arab dynasties, the ruling
family—including the clients as well as the relatives of the
sovereign—held, practically, all the highest dignities in the
State. In espousing 'Abd-er-Rahmân's cause, therefore,
the clients were also promoting their own aggrandisement.
They found a difficulty, however, in deciding upon the
means to be adopted, and resolved to consult Sumayl—then
besieged in Zaragoza—before taking any steps. He was
known to be out of humour with Yûsuf, because the latter
had not come to his aid, and he was credited with a linger-
ing affection for the Omayyads, as former benefactors to his
family. In any case, they believed that he could be implicitly trusted, since he was too magnanimous to betray a
confidence received under a seal of secrecy. It was therefore mainly for the purpose of conferring with him that
some thirty Omayyads, accompanied by Badr, joined the
Kaisites on their way to relieve Sumayl.

We have already seen that the Kaisites' expedition was
crowned with complete success; and we now resume the
thread of our narrative, which was dropped just as the
Omayyad clients were asking Sumayl to accord them a
private interview.

The chief granted their request, and they began by begging him to regard as confidential the important tidings which they had to communicate. He assented, and 'Obaidallah thereupon informed him of Badr's arrival and read him 'Abd-er-Rahmân's letter, adding submissively: "Advise us: we will follow your counsels; we will do what you approve of, and refrain from any course you may take exception to." Sumayl replied thoughtfully: "This is a grave matter; do not ask me for an immediate reply. I will ponder over what you have told me, and later I will acquaint you with the opinion I have formed."

Badr was then introduced; Sumayl made him no promise, but gave him gifts similar to those which he had presented to his supporters. Sumayl then set out for Cordova. On arriving there he found Yûsuf assembling troops in order to punish the rebels in the district of Zaragoza.

In May 755, Yûsuf, on the eve of his departure, sent for the two chiefs of the Omayyad clients—whom he regarded as his own, since their patrons had been deposed—and bade them order the Omayyads to join his force. "It is out of the question, my lord," replied 'Obaidallah; "these unfortunate men have been, by long years of want, rendered unfit to take the field. All those who had any strength left went to Sumayl's assistance, and they are now out-wearied by their long winter march." "Take them a thousand pieces of gold," replied Yûsuf; "let them buy corn; they will soon recover their vigour." "A thousand pieces of gold for a reinforcement of five hundred men? That is a small sum, especially in times of scarcity such as these." "As ye will: I shall offer you no more." "Keep thy money, then; we shall not accompany thee."

Nevertheless, when 'Obaidallah and his companion had retired from the Emir's presence they changed their minds. "After all," they argued, "it might be better to accept the money, since it would be of great use to us. Our tribesmen will of course not join Yûsuf's army, but will remain at home to be prepared for eventualities; we can devise some pretext to account for their absence. Let us accept this sum from Yûsuf. A part of it we can distribute amongst our comrades, who will thus be enabled to buy corn, and the rest we will use in furtherance of our own designs." They accordingly returned to the Emir, and told him that they would accept his offer. As soon as the money was in their

hands they returned to their tribesmen in the district of
Elvira, and gave to each of them ten pieces of silver, on
Yûsuf's behalf, telling them that this small sum was
intended for the purchase of food. But they did not tell
their comrades that Yûsuf had given them much more, that
he wished the clients to join his army, and that the thousand
pieces of gold were intended for their pay.[1]

In the meanwhile Yûsuf set out from Cordova with
some troops, and taking the way to Toledo, encamped in
the district of Jaen, at a place then known as the Ford of
Fath, to the north of Mengibar, where the Guadalquiver
is crossed on the route to the passes of the Sierra Morena,
and where the existing ferry, in consequence of the events
which preceded the battle of Baylen in 1808, has gained a
European celebrity.[2] Yûsuf was waiting there for the
troops which were marching to join him from various
quarters, and was disbursing pay, when the two Omayyad
chiefs, knowing that in his eagerness to confront the rebels
of Zaragoza, he would not remain long at the Ford of Fath,
presented themselves before him. "Why have not our
clients yet arrived?" asked Yûsuf. "Be of good cheer,
Emir, and may God's blessing light on thee," replied
'Obaidallah; "thy clients are not like certain persons well
known to us both. They would not for all the world that
thou shouldst engage the enemy without them. These
were their very words the other day; but they bid me at
the same time ask you to accord them a short delay. The
spring harvest promises, as thou knowest, to be a rich one,
and they would fain reap their crops before joining thee at
Toledo." Having no reason to suspect deceit on the part of
'Obaidallah, Yûsuf believed his words and told the Omayyad
to return to his tribesmen and bid them, at any rate, set
out as soon as they found it practicable. Shortly afterwards, Yûsuf resumed his march. 'Obaidallah and his
companion accompanied him for some distance, and then
bidding him farewell, and promising soon to join him with
the other clients, they returned towards the Ford of
Fath.

On their way they met Sumayl and his guard. Having
spent the night in one of his habitual debauches, the Kaisite
chief had been asleep when Yûsuf set out, and did not start

---

[1] The gold piece was worth twenty silver pieces; it follows, therefore, that the
two chiefs retained about thee-fourths of Yûsuf's remittance.

[2] See Napier, *Hist. of the War in the Peninsula*, Bk. i. chap. 8.

until much later. Seeing the two clients approaching, he
exclaimed in surprise: "Do you return to bring me some
tidings?" "No, my lord," they replied; "Yûsuf permitted
us to leave him, and we are pledged to rejoin him at Toledo
with the other clients; but, if it please you, we will accompany you for a little way." "I shall rejoice greatly in your
company," said Sumayl. After they had for some time
conversed on indifferent matters, 'Obaidallah approached
Sumayl closely and whispered in his ear that he wished to
speak with him privately. Upon a sign from their chief
the guards fell back, and 'Obaidallah continued: "It is of
that matter concerning the son of Mu'âwiya, which we have
already broached to you. His messenger has not yet
departed." "I have by no means forgotten the subject,"
replied Sumayl; "on the contrary, I have meditated deeply
upon it, and according to my promise I have not mentioned
it even to my closest friends. Take now my answer: I con-
.ider that the person in question merits the throne and my
support. Write and tell him this, and if God willeth we
will aid him. As for that old bald-pate"—thus he designated Yûsuf—"he cannot hinder me from doing what I
will. I shall tell him that he must give his daughter, Umm
Mûsâ,[1] in marriage to 'Abd-er-Rahmân, and thereupon
resign the Emirate of Spain. If he doth my bidding we
will thank him; if not, we will cleave his bald head with
our swords, and that will be no more than he deserveth."

Overjoyed to have received so favourable an answer, the
two chiefs kissed Sumayl's hand in token of gratitude, and
having thanked him for the support which he had promised
their patron, they left him, and returned to the Ford of
Fath.

It is clear that Sumayl, who had not slept-off the effects
of his potations, had risen that morning in a very ill-humour
with Yûsuf; yet all that he had said to the clients, far from
being the fruit of meditation, had been spoken on the spur
of the moment. In fact, with habitual indolence, he had
never given serious thought to 'Abd-er-Rahmân's business,
and had wholly forgotten it. It was not until after he had
raised such high hopes in the two clients that he began to
weigh the *pros* and *cons*, and then one consideration swept
aside all others. "What will become of the liberty of the
Arab tribes," he said to himself, "if an Omayyad prince

[1] Widow of Katan, son of that 'Abd al-Malik (the Fihrite) who had been
Governor of Spain.

reigns in Spain? When a monarchy is established, what power will remain with us, the tribal chiefs? Nay, whatever grievances I may have against Yûsuf, things had better remain as they are." Having reached this conclusion, he summoned a slave and ordered him to ride with all speed and bid the two clients wait for him.

The latter had already proceeded a league upon their way, discussing Sumayl's fair promises and convinced that 'Abd-er-Rahmân's success was now assured, when 'Obaid-allah heard his name shouted from behind. He stopped, and a horseman rode up. It was the slave sent by Sumayl, who cried: "Await my master: he is coming, and hath somewhat to say to you." Astonished at this message, and at not being ordered, on the contrary, to return to Sumayl, the two clients for the moment feared that they were about to be arrested and handed over to Yûsuf; however, they turned back and soon saw the General approaching at full gallop, mounted on his white mule "The Star." Seeing him without an escort, the two chiefs took heart, and Sumayl upon coming up with them said: "Since you brought me that letter from the son of Mu'âwiya and made me acquainted with his messenger, I have pondered much over the matter." (In so saying, Sumayl did not speak the truth, or at least his memory was at fault; but it would never have done for him to admit that he had forgotten so important a matter, and he was too thorough an Arab to stickle at a lie.)

"I approved of your design," he continued, "as I told you just now; but since you left me, it has occurred to me, on second thoughts, that your 'Abd-er-Rahmân belongs to a family so powerful that—" and Sumayl made use of a phrase too vigorous to be here reproduced with decorum. "As for the other, he is a good fellow at bottom, and allows himself to be guided by us—with rare exceptions—docilely enough. Besides, we are under deep obligations to him, and it would ill become us to leave him in the lurch. Take heed, therefore, what you do; and if on returning to your homes you persist in your project, it is likely that you will soon see me coming again to meet you—but not in friendship. Mark my words; I make oath that the first sword to leap from its scabbard against your pretender will be mine. And now depart in peace, and may Allah inspire you and your patron with wisdom!"

Dismayed by these words, which, at a blow, shattered all their hopes, and fearing to nettle this man of wrath, the clients answered humbly : " May the blessing of God light upon your lordship ! Never could our opinions differ from yours." " That is well," said Sumayl, softened and touched by these respectful words, " but let me, as a friend, warn you to make no attempt at making political changes in this country. All you can do is to aim at procuring for your patron some honourable post in Spain. Provided that he promises not to aspire to the Emirate, I can venture to assure you that Yûsuf will accord him a kindly welcome, and will give him his daughter in marriage, not without a suitable dowry. Farewell, and may your journey be pleasant !" So saying, he made " The Star " execute a *demi-volte*, and clapping spurs to her flanks rode off at top speed.

Having nothing more to hope for from Sumayl or the Ma'addites in general, who usually followed their chief's advice, there seemed nothing left for the clients of the rival faction but to throw themselves into the arms of the other race, the Yemenites, and incite them to take vengeance upon the Ma'addites. Since they were determined to carry out their design at all costs, they resolved to take this course, and on their way homeward they appealed to all the Yemenite chiefs on whom they thought they could rely, and invited them to take up arms in 'Abd-er-Rahmân's support. Their success exceeded all expectations. The Yemenites, who were eating their hearts in sullen anger, brooding over their defeat at Secunda, and knowing that they were condemned to endure the Ma'addites' yoke, were ready to rise at the first signal, and range themselves under the banner of any pretender, whoever he might be, who would give them an opportunity of slaying their hereditary foes.

Assured of the Yemenites' assistance, and knowing Yûsuf and Sumayl to be occupied in the North, the Omayyad clients judged the moment favourable for their patron's embarkation. They accordingly bought a ship, and entrusted to Tammâm, who had eleven companions, five hundred pieces of gold. Part of this sum he was to give to the Prince ; and the rest was to be used to satisfy the greed of the Berbers, whose character rendered it very unlikely that they would let their guest depart without a ransom. The money was that which Yûsuf had given the clients in order that they might join his forces during the campaign against the rebels of Zaragoza. Little did he imagine when he parted with it, that it would be employed in bringing to Spain a prince who would contend with him for the Emirate.

[AUTHORITIES: *Akhbâr majmû'at*, ff. 69–72, 77–80; Makkarî, Bk. vi.; Ibn Adhârî, i. 49–50; Ibn al-Kûtiyya, f. 9.]

CHAPTER XIV

'ABD-ER-RAHMÂN IN SPAIN

FOR several months 'Abd-er-Rahmân, who had quitted the Nafza for the Maghîla tribe, on the coast of the Mediterranean, despondently dragged out a monotonous existence, awaiting with ever-increasing anxiety the return of Badr, from whom he had received no tidings. His fate trembled in the balance; if his daring scheme miscarried, all his visions of happiness and glory would fade away, and he saw himself resuming the life of an outcast and a vagabond, or seeking a hiding-place in some remote corner of Africa; while if Fortune smiled upon his bold enterprise, Spain would afford him, not merely a safe harbourage, but wealth and power with their attendant joys.

Thus torn asunder betwixt hope and fear, 'Abd-er-Rahmân, who, although by no means devout, punctiliously observed the forms of religion, was one evening engaged in the prescribed prayers, when he saw a vessel approaching land; at that instant one of the men on board leaped into the sea, and struck out for shore. The Prince recognised the swimmer; it was Badr, who, in his impatience to greet his master once again, could not wait until the anchor was dropped. "Good tidings!" he cried, as soon as he caught sight of the Prince. On gaining the beach he briefly related what had passed, and enumerated the chiefs on whom 'Abd-er-Rahmân could rely, as well as the persons on board the ship which was ready to convey him to Spain. "You will not want for money," he added, "for we have brought you five hundred pieces of gold." Overjoyed, 'Abd-er-Rahmân welcomed his partisans. The first who presented himself was Abû Ghâlib Tammâm. 'Abd-er-Rahmân, on learning his name, drew thence a happy augury. There was indeed no name better adapted to inspire hope in one who, like 'Abd-er-Rahmân, believed firmly in omens; for *Tammâm* means "attaining," and *Ghâlib*, "victorious." "We shall attain our object," cried the Prince, "and be victorious!"

The presentations over, an immediate embarkation seemed desirable. The Prince had made his preparations, when a crowd of Berbers came running up and threatened to detain him unless they were given largesse. This difficulty had been foreseen, and Tammâm handed money to each according to his standing in the tribe. Even when the anchor had been weighed, a Berber who had been overlooked in the distribution leaped into the sea, and seizing one of the ship's ropes, demanded his share. Exasperated by such importunity, one of the clients drew his sword and cut off the hand of the Berber, who fell back and was drowned. Once out of reach of the Africans, the vessel was decked with flags in honour of the Prince, and it was not long before they reached the port of Almuñecar.[1] The delight with which 'Abd-er-Rahmân set his foot upon the soil of Spain can be easily imagined, as well as 'Obaidallah's and Ibn Khâlid's joy as they embraced their patron, whose arrival they had awaited at Almuñecar. After passing a few days at al-Fontîn,[2] Ibn Khâlid's country-house—situated near Loja, between Archidona and Elvira—the Prince took up his residence in 'Obaidallah's castle of Torrox, situated a little further to the west, between Isnajar and Loja.[3]

In the meantime Yûsuf, who had reached Toledo, grew uneasy at the prolonged absence of the Omayyad clients. He postponed his departure from day to day in the hope that they would arrive. Sumayl, who suspected the true cause of their non-appearance but who remained faithful to his promise and preserved the secret of their designs, became impatient at this long halt at Toledo. He wished to make an end of the Zaragozan rebels as quickly as possible, and one day when Yûsuf was complaining afresh of the clients' tardiness, his lieutenant remarked disdainfully: "It ill becomes your dignity to wait for such riff-raff. I fear that the chance of finding the enemy inferior to ourselves in number and resources will slip by if we remain here much longer." For the irresolute Yûsuf such words falling from Sumayl were a command. The army accordingly set out. But on confronting the enemy, they found fighting unnecessary, for the rebels, seeing that they were greatly outnumbered, sought terms. Yûsuf offered them an amnesty condition-

[1] September, A.D. 755.
[2] The position of the villa, which at the end of the ninth century still belonged to Ibn Khâlid's descendants, is indicated by Ibn Hayyân (ff. 76, 83).
[3] Its position is clearly indicated by Ibn Hayyân (f. 83): it is, of course, to be distinguished from the modern Torrox, on the coast, 18 m. W. of Almuñecar.

ally on their handing over three Kurashite chiefs—'Âmir, his son Wahb, and Hobâb. The insurgents—for the most part Yemenites—had little compunction in acceding to this condition, believing that Yûsuf would show clemency to men who were almost his fellow-tribesmen. They therefore surrendered their leaders, and Yûsuf summoned a council of his officers to pass judgment upon the prisoners, who were meanwhile loaded with chains.

Sumayl, who had conceived for these Kurashites a personal hatred which would never end save with the lives of its luckless objects, emphatically voted for their decapitation. None of the other Kaisites shared his opinion; they agreed that they had no right to condemn to death men who were Ma'addites like themselves : they feared, too, lest they should incur the vengeance of the powerful Kuraish and their allies. The two chiefs of the family of the Ka'b ibn 'Âmir—Ibn Shihâb and Husain—supported this view with more warmth than any of the other Kaisites. With rage in his heart, and a resolve to speedily avenge himself on those who had dared to thwart him, Sumayl yielded. Yûsuf, thereupon, granted the three Kurashites their lives, but kept them prisoners.

Sumayl soon found an opportunity of ridding himself of the two chiefs who had prevailed against him, and who, not long before, had refused to march to his aid when he was besieged in Zaragoza. The Basques of Pamplona, following the example set them by the Spaniards of Galicia, had thrown off the Arab yoke. Sumayl therefore suggested to Yûsuf that he should send a division of the army against them and entrust its command to Ibn Shihâb and Husain. He made this proposal in order to remove such obstructive opponents, at least for a time, and with a secret hope that they would never return from an expedition through a difficult country beset with rugged mountains.

Yûsuf yielding, according to his wont, to the ascendancy exercised over him by his friend, did as desired, and having appointed his own son, 'Abd-er-Rahmân, Governor of the Frontier, set out for Cordova. As he halted on the banks of the Jarama[1] a courier arrived with the news that the troops sent against the Basques had been utterly routed, that Ibn Shihâb was slain, and that Husain had returned to Zaragoza with a handful of men who had escaped destruction. To Sumayl no tidings could have been more grateful,

[1] " Wâdî-Sharanba " in the *Akhbâr majmú'at*; Ibn al-Abbâr (p. 52) calls it the " Wâdî-ar-ramal "—the sandy river, *i.e.* the Guadarrama.

M

and on the morrow, at daybreak, he said to Yûsuf: "Nothing could be more fortunate! Allah hath rid us of Ibn Shihâb. Now let us make an end of the Kurashites. Let them be brought hither and beheaded!" By dint of reiterating his opinion that this execution was absolutely necessary, Sumayl at length succeeded in convincing the Emir, who accordingly acquiesced in the suggestion.

The heads of the three Kurashites had fallen. The morning meal, at the usual hour of ten o'clock,[1] was served, and Yûsuf and Sumayl sat at table. The Emir was gloomy and dejected: remorse for the triple murder which he had just committed weighed upon him: he reproached himself, too, for having sent Ibn Shihâb and his brave men to certain destruction: he felt that the blood of his victims cried for vengeance, and a dark foreboding whispered that his reign was drawing to a close. Oppressed with anxiety, he scarcely touched a morsel of food. Sumayl, on the other hand, exhibited a brutal gaiety and made a hearty meal, while he did his best to reassure the feeble Emir, whom he had made an instrument for gratifying his own personal animosities and his accomplice in an atrocious crime.

"Banish your gloomy thoughts," he urged: "What wrong have you committed? If Ibn Shihâb has been slain, the fault is not yours: he fell in battle, and in war such may be the lot of any man. If the three Kurashites have been executed, they did but meet with their deserts; they were dangerous rebels, and your exemplary severity will prove a salutary warning to any who may think of imitating them. Spain is henceforth an appanage of your house; you have founded a dynasty which will endure till the coming of Antichrist. Who will be so rash as to dispute your authority?"

But vain was Sumayl's endeavour to dissipate by such arguments as these his friend's brooding melancholy, and, the meal ended, he returned to his tent and sought his *siesta* in the apartment reserved for his two daughters.

Left alone, Yûsuf threw himself upon a couch, rather from habit than because he felt an inclination for repose: sleep seemed banished by his sombre misgivings. Suddenly he heard the soldiers cry: "A courier, a courier from Cordova!" Yûsuf started up: "What is that they say?" he asked the sentinels posted at the door of his tent. He was informed that a slave had arrived, mounted on Umm

---

[1] *Cf.* Burckhardt, *Bedouins*, p. 36.

'Othmân's mule. "Bring him hither instantly!" cried
Yûsuf, who could not conjecture why his wife had thus
sent a messenger in hot haste, but knew that it must be on
grave and pressing business.

The courier entered, and handed the Emir a letter which
ran to this effect: "A grandson of the Khalif Hishâm has
arrived in Spain. He has taken up his abode at Torrox,
in the castle of the infamous 'Obaidallah ibn 'Othmân. The
Omayyad clients have declared for him. Your lieutenant at
Elvira, who marched against him with such troops as he
had at his disposal, has been repulsed: his men were cud-
gelled, but no one was killed. Hasten to take such measures
as you deem expedient."

As soon as Yûsuf had read this letter he sent for Sumayl.
The latter, on the way to his tent, had seen the messenger
arrive, but, with his wonted indifference, had paid little heed
to the matter; not until he was summoned by the Emir at
so unreasonable an hour did he suspect that the courier's
errand was of a serious nature.

"What has happened, Emir," he asked as he entered
Yûsuf's tent, "that you break in upon my siesta? Nothing
troublesome, I trust?" "Yes!" replied Yûsuf, "By Allah,
it is an event of the utmost gravity, and I fear me that God
is about to visit us with retribution for putting those men
to death." "You speak foolishness!" replied Sumayl con-
temptuously; "Take my word for it, those men were too
vile for God to take any heed of them. But what has
happened?" "I have just received a letter from Umm
'Othmân: Khâlid shall read it to you."

Khâlid, the Emir's client and secretary, thereupon read
the letter. Less surprised than Yûsuf, since he had been
forewarned of the event, Sumayl learned with composure
that 'Abd-er-Rahmân had reached Spain. "The business is
indeed a serious one," he said, "and in my opinion we should
march against this pretender instantly, with the troops ready
at hand. Let us give him battle; perhaps we may slay
him; in any case his forces must be so small at present that
we shall easily disperse them, and once having experienced
defeat he will probably lose heart." "I agree," replied
Yûsuf; "Let us set out without delay."

It was soon noised throughout the army that Hishâm's
grandson had landed in Spain, and that they were expected
to march against him. The news caused an extraordinary
commotion in the camp. Already indignant at the base

plot hatched by their chiefs against Ibn Shihâb, which had
cost so many of their tribesmen their lives—indignant also
at the execution of the Kurashites, carried out in defiance
of the judgment of the Kaisite chiefs—the troops were
further wholly disinclined to start upon an expedition for
which they had not been paid. " They wish us to reckon
two campaigns as one," murmured the soldiers; " and we
refuse ! " At nightfall an almost general desertion began ;
the tribesmen communicated with one another, and, re-
uniting in bands, left the camp to return to their homes.
Scarcely ten Yemenites remained : these included the stan-
dard-bearers, who could not quit their posts without forfeit-
ing their honour, and even these did not blame the deserters
and did nothing to hinder them. A few Kaisites particularly
attached to Sumayl, and a contingent from other Ma'addite
tribes, still remained ; but little reliance could be placed
upon these men, for, fatigued by their long marches, they
too yearned to return to their homes, and besought Yûsuf
and Sumayl to lead them back to Cordova. They argued
that to undertake a winter campaign in the Sierra de Regio,
with so small a force, would be to court a greater, in order
to escape a lesser danger ; they further pointed out that the
revolt would doubtless be confined to districts near the coast,
and that any attack on 'Abd-er-Rahmân should be postponed
until the return of the dry season. But once Sumayl had
made up his mind he was immovable, and though there was
much truth in what the soldiers had urged, he persisted
stubbornly in his design. The little force accordingly set
out towards the Sierra de Regio, but before long, Yûsuf,
not uninfluenced by the disaffection of the troops, became
convinced of the impracticability of Sumayl's plan. Winter
had set in ; rains and floods rendered the roads impassable.
In the teeth of Sumayl's opposition, Yûsuf ordered his men
to return to Cordova. He had been confirmed in this resolution by the rumour that 'Abd-er-Rahmân had not
landed in Spain with any designs upon the Emirate, but
merely to find shelter there, and a position suited to his
rank. It was moreover hinted to Yûsuf that if he would
but offer the Prince one of his daughters in marriage, and a
sum of money, 'Abd-er-Rahmân would make no further
claims.

Yûsuf, accordingly, as soon as he reached Cordova,
entered upon negotiations, and despatched three of his
friends to Torrox. These were 'Obaid—a Kaisite chief

whose influence was only inferior to that of Sumayl, and who was a friend of the latter—Khâlid, Yûsuf's secretary, and Îsâ, an Omayyad client and paymaster of the army. The envoys were empowered to present the Prince with rich apparel, two horses, two mules, two slaves, and a thousand gold pieces. They set out with these gifts, but on arriving at Orch (on the frontier of the province of Regio), Îsâ, who although an Omayyad client was sincerely attached to Yûsuf, said to his companions: " I am greatly astonished that such men as Yûsuf, Sumayl, and yourselves can act thus recklessly. Are you so simple-minded as to suppose that if 'Abd-er-Rahmân rejects Yûsuf's proposals, he will let us take these gifts back with us to Cordova ? " Îsâ's warning commended itself to the rest, and they determined to leave him at Orch, with the presents, until 'Abd-er-Rahmân had accepted the proffered conditions.

On arriving at Torrox, the two envoys found the village and the castle crowded with soldiers; for the Omayyad clients, as well as the Yemenites of the Damascus, Jordan, and Kinnisrîn divisions, had flocked thither in great numbers. Having been accorded an audience, they were received by the Prince—surrounded by his little Court, in which 'Obaid-allah occupied the place of honour—and unfolded the object of their mission. They explained that Yûsuf, full of gratitude for the kindness which his illustrious great-great-grandfather, 'Okba ibn Nâfi', had received at the hands of the Omayyads, wished for nothing better than to live on good terms with 'Abd-er-Rahmân, on condition that the Prince laid no claim to the Emirate, but only to the domains formerly possessed by the Khalif Hishâm in Spain: they added that Yûsuf offered the Prince his daughter's hand, with a considerable dowry—that the Emir had sent gifts, which were then at Orch, but would shortly arrive—and that if 'Abd-er-Rahmân would be pleased to visit Cordova he might be sure of a hearty welcome.

These proposals were far from distasteful to the clients. Their first ardour had somewhat cooled, for they recognised that the Yemenites, though ready enough to attack their rivals, were discouragingly lukewarm in the Pretender's cause, and, all things considered, they favoured an understanding with Yûsuf. The following reply was therefore given to the envoys: " Your proposal commends itself to us. Yûsuf may rest assured that our patron has not come to Spain to contest the Emirate, but merely to claim the lands which belong to him by hereditary right."

The Prince himself undoubtedly did not look at the matter in the same light; his ambition could never rest content with the position of a wealthy landed proprietor thus assigned to him; but since he did not yet feel the ground firm beneath his feet, and was wholly dependent on his friends, he assumed a modest and even humble attitude towards them, and not venturing to dispute their decision, prudently kept silent. A superficial observer might have thought that his intellect had not yet emerged from its chrysalis state, or that at least he was under the venerable 'Obaidallah's tutelage.

"I now hand you," said Khâlid, "a letter from the Emir, and you will see that it confirms all that we have just said." The Prince accepted the letter, and handing it to 'Obaidallah bade him read it in a loud voice. This letter, which had been composed by Khâlid in the capacity of Yûsuf's secretary, was written with remarkable elegance of diction, and adorned with exuberant flowers of Arab rhetoric. When 'Obaidallah had read it to the end, the Prince, with his usual sagacity, laid all responsibility upon his friend's shoulders. "Be so good as to answer this letter," he said; "You know my views upon the matter."

There could be no doubt as to the tenour of the reply— 'Obaidallah, on his patron's behalf, would unconditionally accept Yûsuf's proposals—and the Prince had already re-signed himself to this melancholy sacrifice of his ambitious dreams, when an untimely pleasantry of Khâlid's put an end to the negotiations and revived 'Abd-er-Rahmân's hopes.

Khâlid was not an Arab; he was one of the conquered, and a Spaniard. Both his parents had been Christian slaves; but, like a multitude of his compatriots, his father had abjured Christianity. On becoming a Moslem, he had assumed the name of Zayd, and as a reward for his conversion, his master, Yûsuf, had manumitted him. On being received into his patron's palace, the young Khâlid—whom nature had endowed with remarkable intelligence, and a great aptitude for intellectual labour—pursued his studies with much ardour, and at length became so deeply versed in Arabic literature, and wrote the language with so much elegance, that Yûsuf appointed him his secretary. This was a high honour, for the Emirs prided themselves on pos-

sessing as secretaries accomplished scholars who excelled in
a knowledge of Arabic and of the ancient poems. Thanks
to his position, Khâlid soon acquired much influence over
the weak Yûsuf, who with a total lack of self-reliance
always sought guidance from another's will; and in Sumayl's
absence, it was Khâlid who dictated his decisions. Envied
by the Arabs for his influence and ability, and despised by
them for his birth, Khâlid rendered to these rough warriors
scorn for scorn; and when he observed the awkwardness
with which the aged 'Obaidallah—to whom the sword was
more familiar than the pen—proceeded to reply to his
elegant letter, he grew indignant, with all a scholar's vanity,
that the Prince should have entrusted so exalted a task to
one so unpolished and so ignorant of linguistic refinements!
A mocking smile played upon his lips, and he said disdainfully: " Thine armpits will sweat, Abû 'Othmân, ere thou
hast answered such a letter as that! "

Hearing himself so roughly bantered by a despicable
Spanish upstart, 'Obaidallah, whose temper was naturally
violent, flew into a great rage. " Liar! " he cried, " my
armpits will not sweat, for thy letter shall never be
answered! " Uttering these words in a tone of brutal arrogance, he threw the letter in Khâlid's face, and struck him
violently on the head with his fist. " Seize this wretch, and
load him with chains! " he added. The soldiers instantly
obeyed. Then, turning to the Prince, 'Obaidallah said:
" This is our first step towards victory. That man is Yûsuf's
fountain of wisdom; without him he is helpless."

The other emissary, 'Obaid, the Kaisite chief, waited
until 'Obaidallah's wrath had somewhat subsided, and then
said: " Bear in mind, I pray thee, Abû 'Othmân, that
Khâlid is an envoy, and as such is inviolable." " Not so,
my lord," replied 'Obaidallah; " thou art the envoy. Depart in peace! As for that fellow, he was the aggressor, and
his punishment is deserved; he is a renegade [1]—the son of a
base-born wanton! "

In consequence, therefore, of Khâlid's vanity and 'Obaidallah's irascibility the negotiations were broken off: but
'Abd-er-Rahmân, seeing that chance had favoured certain
plans which he dared not avow, was by no means displeased.

When 'Obaid—whom 'Obaidallah respected as the head of
a noble and powerful Arab family—had departed, and Khâlid

---

[1] Ar. *ildje*, a word meaning " renegade " as well as " Christian." *Cf.* Marmol,
Descripcion de Affrica, ii. 17 ; Hoest, *Nachrichten*, p. 147; Charaut, p. 48.

had been thrown into a dungeon, the clients remembered what
had been said about the presents, which had been delayed
at Orch, and resolved to appropriate them : since war had
practically been declared against Yûsuf, they were clearly
legitimate booty.   Some thirty horsemen, therefore, galloped
off at full speed to Orch, but since Îsâ, warned in time, had
hurriedly departed, taking with him all the gifts intended
for the Omayyad prince, the soldiers had to return to Torrox
empty-handed.   For this loss 'Abd-er-Rahmân never quite
forgave his client, although Îsâ endeavoured to convince him
that, as Yûsuf's faithful servant, he had no option save to
act in his master's interest.

When 'Obaid, on his return to Cordova, had reported to
Yûsuf and Sumayl what had taken place at Torrox, the
General exclaimed : " I had foreseen that these negotiations
would break down : I warned you, Emir, that you ought to
attack this pretender during the winter."   This plan, which
though plausible was unfortunately impracticable, had become a fixed idea in Sumayl's mind.

[AUTHORITY : *Akhbâr majmû'at,* ff. 80–83.]

CHAPTER XV

'ABD-ER-RAHMÂN I

THE ensuing Winter was of a severity unusual in Andalusia, and before commencing hostilities, both sides
waited until it was ended. 'Abd-er-Rahmân—or rather
'Obaidallah, who was still at the helm—profited by this
period of forced inaction to invite the Arab and Berber
chieftains to declare against Yûsuf. The Yemenites unanimously replied that at the first signal given by the Prince
they would take up arms in his cause. The Berbers were
divided : some declared for Yûsuf, others for the Pretender.
Of the Kaisite chiefs, only six promised 'Abd-er-Rahmân
their support. Three of these bore a personal grudge
against Sumayl : these were Jâbir, son of that Ibn Shihâb
whom Sumayl had sent to his death among the Basques ;
Husain, Ibn Shihâb's companion, who had narrowly escaped
sharing his fate ; and Abû Bakr ibn Hilâl, the Abdite, who
had a feud with Sumayl, since the latter had once struck his
father. The three others were of the Beni Thakîf, who ever
since the days of the illustrious Thakîfite Hajjâj had been
blindly devoted to the Omayyads.

The antagonists, each reinforced by Berbers, were, in
fact, about to recommence on a larger scale the battle fought
at Secunda ten years before. The opposing forces were less
ill-matched than at first sight appeared. The Omayyads
were numerically superior, but the Pretender could not implicitly rely upon the Yemenites, who felt no deep interest
in his cause, and looked upon the war merely as a means of
avenging themselves upon the Ma'addites. Yûsuf's adherents, on the other hand, formed a body as homogeneous as
Arab tribes, with their mutual jealousies, could ever be
welded into. They all had one object in view—the maintenance of the existing régime.

Yûsuf, good easy old man, who never thwarted their love
of independence—not to say anarchy—was just the Emir for
the Ma'addites ; when his sagacity was at a loss—as was
often the case—Sumayl was at his side to counsel him ; and

Sumayl, though not without enemies even among the Kaisites, enjoyed the esteem of the majority of his tribesmen.

With the advent of Spring, it became known at Torrox that Yûsuf was preparing to take the field, and the leaders therefore decided to march westwards, in order to pick up on their way the Yemenites through whose districts they would pass, and secure the best position for attacking Yûsuf. It was first necessary to pass through Regio, where dwelt the Jordan division. Of this province Archidona was then the capital. The Governor of the district was a Kaisite, Jidâr by name. 'Obaidallah sent to ask him if he would permit the Prince's army to pass through his territory, and Jidâr—whether he owed Sumayl some grudge, or whether he felt the necessity of bowing to the will of a population exclusively Yemenite —sent this reply : " Bring the Prince to the *Mosalla* of Archidona, on the Day of the Breaking of the Fast, and you shall see what I will do." During the afternoon of the day indicated, which in A.D. 756 fell on March 8, the clients and the Prince entered the *Mosalla*—a wide plain outside the town—where a sermon was to be preached, and where all the Moslems of Archidona were expected to be present. When the preacher—or *khatîb*—was about to begin with the usual formula, invoking the blessing of heaven upon the sovereign, Jidâr arose and said : " Pronounce not the name of Yûsuf, but that of 'Abd-er-Rahmân, son of Mu'âwiya, son of Hishâm—for he is our Emir, and the son of our Emir." Then, turning to the crowd, he continued : " People of Regio, what think ye of my words ? " " Be it as thou hast said ! " came back the answering shout. Thereupon the preacher prayed the Eternal to grant his protection to the Emir 'Abd-er-Rahmân, and upon the conclusion of the religious ceremony, the people of Archidona took the oath of fealty and obedience to their new sovereign. And yet, in spite of the alacrity with which the Prince was acknowledged in Regio, the number of chiefs who led their troops to his standard was not large. In compensation, however, four hundred horsemen arrived from the Berber tribe of the Beni al-Khalî—clients of the Khalif Yazîd II, and inhabitants of the district of Ronda (then called Ta-Corona),[1] who, on

---

[1] *Corona* being the Latin word, and *Ta* a Berber prefix. The characteristic name of one of those fortresses built on the summit of a rock, so numerous in the Serrania de Ronda. The abode of the Beni al-Khali is still named Benadalid. It is a small town, with a picturesque castle, S. of Ronda, on the Genil. See Marmol, *Rebelion de los Moriscos*, f. 221 ; Rochfort Scott, *Excursions in Ronda and Granada*, i. 89.

hearing of what had taken place at Archidona, lost no time in joining the army.

Leaving Regio, the Prince passed on to the province of Sidona, inhabited by the Palestine division, and traversed, not without difficulty, the wild and picturesque Serrania de Ronda, by steep tracks which wound along the flanks of precipices.   Arriving at a place inhabited by the Ma'addite tribe of Kinâna—still perpetuated in its modern name of Ximena [1]—he found it deserted by all save the women and children, the men having already departed to join Yûsuf's army.   Deeming it unwise to commence operations by a massacre, the Prince left them unmolested.

Reinforced by the Yemenites of the province of Sidona, who flocked to his banner, 'Abd-er-Rahmân marched towards the province of Seville, where dwelt the Arabs of Emesa. The two most influential Yemenite chieftains of this pro- vince—Abû Sabbâh of the tribe of Yâkib, and Hayât ibn Molâmis of the tribe of Hadramaut—came to welcome the Prince, and about the middle of March 'Abd-er-Rahmân entered Seville, where the oath of allegiance to him was taken.   Soon afterwards, learning that Yûsuf had taken the field and, following the right bank of the Guadalquiver, was threatening Seville, the Prince quitted the city, and marched upon Cordova along the opposite bank of the river.   He hoped thus to surprise the Capital, now almost denuded of troops, and relied upon assistance from the many Omayyad clients and Yemenites among the inhabi- tants.

On entering the district of Tocina,[2] it was observed that while each of the three divisions of the army had its military standard, the Prince had none of his own.   "Merciful Allah!" cried the chiefs; "discord will break out amongst us!"   The Sevillan chieftain Abû Sabbâh thereupon hastily fastened a turban to a spear, and presented the Prince with this banner, which henceforth became the *palladium* of the Omayyads.

While 'Abd-er-Rahmân continued his march towards Cordova, Yûsuf pushed on towards Seville, and before long

---

[1] A small town, with a Roman castle.   See Rochfort Scott, ii. pp. 28 *sq.*   The name "Kinena" is also preserved in Ximena, between Jaen and Jodar, and in Torreximeno, N. of Martos.

[2] According to some authorities, at the town of Colombera; but according to Ibn al-Kûtiyya (f. 11), "Villanova of the Bahrites" (now Brenes).   He adds that the Beni Bahr were a sub-tribe of the Lakhmites.   Brenes is a corruption of the *Ar.* Bahrin.

the two armies found themselves facing one another, divided
by the Guadalquiver, which was then in high flood, and
unfordable.[1] The opposing forces watched each other.
Yûsuf, who had hastened to attack his rival before the
latter received further reinforcements, waited with impatience for the river to fall. For his part, the Pretender wished
to march on Cordova unperceived by the enemy. At sunset
he therefore ordered camp-fires to be lit, that Yûsuf might
believe him to be bivouacking, and then under cover of
darkness he set out in profound silence. Unfortunately for
him, he had forty-five Arab miles to traverse, and he had
scarcely covered one, when Yûsuf was warned of his stealthy
departure. Without losing a moment, the Emir turned
back to save his threatened capital. A veritable race ensued,
but 'Abd-er-Rahmân, seeing that in this contest of speed
Yûsuf would win, tried to deceive him once more by calling a halt. Yûsuf, who watched from the other side of the
river every movement of the enemy, did the like; then,
when 'Abd-er-Rahmân started afresh, so did the Emir,
until he finally halted at Mosâra, close to Cordova, opposite
his rival. The Prince's plan had completely failed, to the
great chagrin of his men, who having had no food but
garbanzos,[2] had trusted to find compensation in the Capital
for their privations.

On Thursday, May 13—the day of the festival of 'Arafa[3]
—the Guadalquiver began to fall, and 'Abd-er-Rahmân,
whose force had been strengthened by many Cordovans, summoned a council of war and thus addressed his captains:
" The time has come for us to arrive at a final decision. You
are acquainted with Yûsuf's proposals. If you consider that
I ought to accept them, I am still ready to do so; but if
your sentence is for war, I am ready for that also. Frankly
tell me your opinion; whatever it may be, it will be mine."
All the Yemenite chiefs having declared for war, their
example was followed by the Omayyad clients, who in their
inmost hearts had not wholly rejected all ideas of a settlement.
War having thus been determined on, the Prince again
addressed the council. " Be it so, my friends," said he; " to-
day we will cross the river, and make ready to join battle
to-morrow. To-morrow is an auspicious day for my house:

[1] In the month of May.
[2] A kind of haricots.
[3] The vigil of the Idn 'l-Azhâ, or Feast of Sacrifice, when the pilgrims proceed
to Mt. 'Arafât. See Hughes, *Dict. of Islam* (1885), p. 21.

it is Friday, and a festival, and it was on just such a day that my great-great-grandfather gained the Khalifate for my family by his victory on the Field of Râhit over a Fihrite, who, like him we are about to fight, had a Kaisite for his Vizier. Then, as now, the Kaisites and the Yemenites were adversaries. Let us hope, my friends, that to-morrow will be, both for Yemenites and Omayyads, a day as glorious as that of Râhit!" The Prince then issued his orders, and appointed the leaders of the different divisions of his army. Meanwhile he had initiated a false and treacherous negotiation with Yûsuf. Wishing to cross the river without fighting, and at the same time to procure rations for his famished troops, he informed the Emir that he was prepared to accept the proposals which had been made at Torrox, and which had been rejected solely in consequence of Khâlid's insolence; he further expressed a hope that Yûsuf would not resist the passage of his army across the river, for when on the same bank they could more readily carry on negotiations—furthermore, since an understanding was on the point of being arrived at, he begged Yûsuf, of his courtesy, to send food for his troops.

Trusting in his opponent's good faith, and hoping that a settlement might be arrived at without bloodshed, Yûsuf entered the snare. He not only offered no opposition to 'Abd-er-Rahmân's passage, but sent him oxen and sheep. It seemed to be the aged Yûsuf's strange destiny always to further unwittingly his youthful rival's designs. Already, the money which he had given the Omayyad clients in order that they might arm themselves on his behalf had served to convey 'Abd-er-Rahmân to Spain; and now the cattle which he sent him served to revive the strength of a famished foe. It was not till the morrow—Friday, May 15, the day of festival—that Yûsuf discovered that he had been duped. He then saw 'Abd-er-Rahmân's army, reinforced by Yemenites from Elvira and Jaen, drawn up in battle array. Compelled to fight, the Emir disposed his forces, although still lacking the reinforcements which his son Abû Zayd was to send him from Zaragoza; his Kaisites, moreover, were dispirited, for they, as well as 'Abd-er-Rahmân, had observed the striking analogy of that Friday to the fatal day of Râhit.

The combat began. The Pretender, surrounded by his clients, and with 'Obaidallah as his standard-bearer, was mounted on a splendid Andalusian charger, which he made

rear and curvet. Few of the mounted men, even of the
chiefs, were, however, provided with horses ; long afterwards,
horses were still so scarce in Andalusia that the light cavalry
usually employed mules.[1]

'Abd-er-Rahmân's high-mettled steed, however, inspired
the Yemenites with fears and suspicions. " Our leader is
very young," they whispered, " and his valour is unproved.
How can we tell whether, stricken with fear, he may not
entrust his safety to that horse, involve his clients in his
flight, and throw our ranks into confusion ? " These
murmurs grew louder, and at length reached the Prince's
ears. He immediately sent for Abû Sabbâh, whose uneasiness was very apparent. The Sevillan chief rode up,
mounted on a venerable mule. " My horse is too mettle-
some," said the Prince, " and he plunges so that I cannot
well take aim. I should prefer a mule, and in all the army
I see none that would suit me so well as yours : he is docile
and almost white through age. He will thus be invaluable,
for I wish my friends to recognise me by my steed. If
things go ill—which God forfend—they will but have to
follow my white mule, and I will show them the path of
honour ; take, therefore, my horse in exchange." " But is
it not meet for our Emir to be seated on a charger ? "
stammered Abû Sabbâh, blushing with shame. " By no
means ! " replied the Prince, lightly leaping to the ground
and speedily bestriding the mule. The Yemenites no sooner
saw him mounted on this aged and sluggish beast than all
their fears vanished.

The issue of the combat was not long doubtful. The
Pretender's cavalry pierced the enemy's right wing and
centre, whereupon both Yûsuf and Sumayl sought safety in
flight, after each had witnessed the death of a son. The
left wing, composed of Kaisites under 'Obaid, held their
ground while the sun rose high, and did not yield until
almost all their leaders, including 'Obaid himself, had been
slain.

The victorious Yemenites had now no thoughts save for
pillage. Some hastened to the abandoned camp of the
enemy, where they found the food prepared for Yûsuf's
soldiers and no inconsiderable booty. Others proceeded to
ransack Yûsuf's palace at Cordova, and two of this party,

---

[1] In the tenth century, Jean de Gorz, Ambassador of the Emperor Otho I at the
Court of 'Abd-er-Rahmân III, saw the light cavalry at Cordova mounted on mules
at a review. *Vit. Johan. Gorz*, c. 132.

belonging to the Yemenite tribe of Tai', crossed the bridge to pillage Sumayl's palace at Secunda. Among other treasures they found there a coffer containing ten thousand gold pieces. Sumayl saw and recognised, from the summit of a hill near the Jaen road, the two men who bore away his coffer: although defeated, and deprived of a beloved son, his pride was undiminished, and he expressed his anger and his thirst for vengeance in a poem of which these verses have come down to us:

"The tribe of Tai' hath received my money on trust; but the day will come when the deposit will be reclaimed. If thou wouldst learn the might of my sword and spear, inquire of the Yemenites; and if they maintain a sad silence, the many battlefields which have witnessed their defeats will answer for them, and proclaim my glory!"

Upon arriving at Yûsuf's palace, 'Abd-er-Rahmân found great difficulty in expelling the pillagers, and he only succeeded by giving them apparel which they complained they were destitute of. Yûsuf's harem also stood in great peril, for, in their hatred of the old Emir, the Yemenites had no intention of respecting it. Yûsuf's wife, Umm 'Othmân, with her two daughters, accordingly implored the Prince's protection. "Cousin," she begged, "be good to us, as God hath been good to thee." "I will," replied 'Abd-er-Rahmân, touched by the misfortune of these ladies, whom he acknowledged as members of a family allied to his own, and he forthwith sent for the Sâhib-as-Salât, or superior of the Mosque. That dignitary was one of Yûsuf's clients, and upon his arrival the Prince bade him conduct the ladies to his house—a sanctuary where they would be safe from the violence of the soldiery: he further restored to them some objects of value which he had rescued from the pillagers. To show her gratitude, one of Yûsuf's daughters gave the Prince a young slave-girl, Holal by name, who afterwards became the mother of Hishâm, the second Omayyad Emir of Spain.

'Abd-er-Rahmân's magnanimous conduct was very distasteful to the Yemenites. He had checked their plundering, although he had promised them rich booty, and he had taken under his protection women they had set their hearts upon; these were encroachments upon their rights as victors. "He shows favour to his own family," exclaimed the malcontents: "We gained the victory for him, and more gratitude is due to us." Even the most sober-minded

Yemenites did not show much disapproval of these murmurs; they acknowledged that the Prince had acted
correctly, but their faces plainly showed that they made
this admission merely to relieve scruples of conscience, and
that at the bottom of their hearts they sympathised with
the malcontents. After all, they had aided 'Abd-er-Rahmân
mainly in order to be avenged on the Ma'addites, and they
had attained their object. At last one of them boldly exclaimed: "We have settled old scores with the Ma'addites.
This man and his clients belong to the same race. Let
us now turn our arms against them, and slay them; thus
in one day we shall gain two victories." This infamous
suggestion was debated in cold blood, as if it were altogether
an open question: some approved it, others did not. Among
the latter were all the Beni Kodâ'a, of whom the Kelbites
were a branch. A decision had not yet been arrived at
when Thalaba, a Judhâmite noble of the Sidona division,
revealed to the Prince the plot which was being hatched
against him. The informer was actuated by a personal
motive. Although of noble birth, he had been ousted by
other candidates when the chiefs of his tribe had been
appointed, and since his successful rivals had voted in
favour of the proposal, he saw an excellent chance of taking
his revenge. In warning 'Abd-er-Rahmân, Thalaba told
him that he could rely upon the Beni Kodâ'a alone, and
that Abû Sabbâh was the prime mover in the conspiracy.
The Prince, thanking him warmly and promising to reward
him later (a promise which he faithfully kept), lost not a
moment in taking the necessary measures. He appointed
the Kelbite 'Abd-er-Rahmân ibn Nu'aym chief of police
in Cordova, and surrounded himself with his clients, who
formed a body-guard. When the Yemenites became aware
that they had been betrayed they thought it well to
abandon their scheme, and permitted 'Abd-er-Rahmân to
betake himself unmolested to the Great Mosque: there,
in his capacity as Imâm, he offered the Friday prayer,
and made an oration to the people, in which he promised
them that he would rule over them as a good sovereign
should.

Though master of the Capital, 'Abd-er-Rahmân was not
yet master of Spain. Yûsuf and Sumayl had suffered a
grievous defeat, but they did not despair of retrieving their
fortunes. In accordance with an agreement they had made
on parting after their flight, Yûsuf sought help at Toledo,

while Sumayl retired to his own division—that of Jaen—
where he called all the Ma'addites to arms. Yûsuf rejoined
him later with the Zaragozan contingent, which he had
fallen in with on the way, as well as with the Toledan troops.
The two chiefs then forced the Governor of the province
of Jaen to withdraw to the fortress of Mentesa, and the
Governor of Elvira to take refuge in the mountains. Meanwhile Yûsuf, learning that 'Abd-er-Rahmân was about to
march against him, ordered his son Abû Zayd to make for
Cordova by a route different from that followed by 'Abd-
er-Rahmân, and to seize the Capital—an operation which
would present no difficulty, since the city contained only a
weak garrison. If this plan succeeded, 'Abd-er-Rahmân
would be obliged to retire in order to recover Cordova, and
Yûsuf would thus gain time in which to procure reinforcements. The plan was successfully carried out. As soon as
'Abd-er-Rahmân had begun his march, Abû Zayd attacked
the Capital without warning, captured it, drove 'Obaidallah,
together with a few soldiers, into the tower of the Great
Mosque, and compelled him to surrender. Not long afterwards, however, learning that 'Abd-er-Rahmân was returning
to attack him, Abû Zayd quitted Cordova, taking with him
'Obaidallah and two slave-girls whom he had found in the
palace. The chiefs who accompanied him openly chided
him for this act. " Your conduct is less magnanimous than
'Abd-er-Rahmân's," they said ; "for when he had your
sisters and your father's wives in his power, he courteously
afforded them protection, while you carry off his damsels."
Abû Zayd felt the justice of this rebuke, and when about
a mile to the north of Cordova he ordered a tent to be
pitched for the two slaves, and left them there, with their
belongings. He then set out to join his father at Elvira.
    As soon as 'Abd-er-Rahmân knew that Abû Zayd had
retired from Cordova, he marched swiftly against Yûsuf;
but matters took an unexpected turn. Feeling themselves
too weak, in the long run, to hold out against the Prince,
Yûsuf and Sumayl sought terms of peace. They declared
themselves ready to recognise 'Abd-er-Rahmân as Emir,
provided that their personal property was left intact and a
general amnesty was proclaimed. The Prince accepted this
proposal, stipulating, however, that Yûsuf should hand over
as hostages two of his sons—Abû Zayd and Abû 'l-Aswad.
These he undertook to treat honourably, imposing on them
no restrictions save that of not quitting the palace, and

N

promising to restore them to their father as soon as peace
was firmly established. In the course of these negotiations
'Abd-er-Rahmân's prisoner, the Spaniard Khâlid, was exchanged for 'Obaidallah : by a freak of fortune, therefore,
the Omayyad client gained his freedom at the price of the
man whom he had imprisoned.

'Abd-er-Rahmân, now universally acknowledged as the
Emir of Spain, rode back to Cordova (July, 756) with Yûsuf
on his right hand and Sumayl on his left. Sumayl showed
himself to be the most polished and well-bred of men, and
'Abd-er-Rahmân in after years was wont to say : " Of a
truth, God giveth sovereignty as he listeth and not according to men's deserts ! All the way from Elvira to Cordova
Sumayl was by my side, yet his knee never touched mine ;
the head of his mule was never in advance of mine ; never
did he ask me an indiscreet question ; never did he commence
a conversation before I addressed him." [1] The chroniclers
add that the Prince had no grounds for similarly eulogizing
Yûsuf.

For some time all went well. The machinations of
Yûsuf's enemies, who wished to impeach him on the pretext
that he had appropriated land to which he had no right,
were unsuccessful : both he and Sumayl were treated with
marked distinction, and 'Abd-er-Rahmân often took counsel
with them in circumstances of difficulty. Sumayl was
entirely resigned to his lot. Yûsuf, incapable of forming
a bold decision on his own initiative, might perhaps also
have grown reconciled to his secondary position ; but he
was surrounded by malcontents—Kurashite nobles, Fihrites
and Hâshimites—who under his reign had occupied posts
of the highest dignity and emolument. These men could
not reconcile themselves to the condition of obscurity to
which they were now reduced, and strove to incite the ex-
Emir against 'Abd-er-Rahmân, misinterpreting the Prince's
simplest words. They succeeded only too well in their
design. Determined once again to have recourse to arms,
Yûsuf sought in vain the assistance of Sumayl and the
Kaisites ; but he met with better success among the Baladîs [2]
—especially those of Lacant,[3] Merida, and Toledo—and one
day 'Abd-er-Rahmân received the news that Yûsuf had

[1] Ziyâd, bastard brother of Mu'âwiya I and Governor of 'Irâk, similarly eulo-
gizes Hâritha. *Cf.* Ibn Khallikân (Slane), i. 325.
[2] *I.e.* the Arabs who entered Spain before the Syrians.
[3] Probably near Fuente de Cantos, N.W. of Seville.

taken flight in the direction of Merida. He instantly
despatched cavalry in pursuit, but it was too late. Sending
for Sumayl, the Prince bitterly reproached him with being
privy to Yûsuf's escape. "I am innocent," replied the
Kaisite : "That is manifest from my not having accompanied
Yûsuf, as I should have done had I been his accomplice."
"It is not possible that Yûsuf has quitted Cordova without
having consulted you," replied the Prince, "and it was your
duty to warn me." Thereupon he threw Sumayl into
prison, as well as Yûsuf's two sons, who were still confined
to the palace as hostages.

At Merida Yûsuf rallied his Arab and Berber adherents,
and with them set out for Lacant, where the townsfolk
favoured his cause : thence he marched on Seville. Almost
all the Baladîs of the province, as well as many Syrians,
flocked to his banner, so that Yûsuf found himself ready to
lay siege to Seville at the head of twenty thousand men.
The governor of the city was a kinsman of 'Abd-er-
Rahmân, 'Abd al-Malik by name, who had landed in Spain
with his two sons in the preceding year. Yûsuf, however,
was of opinion that 'Abd al-Malik, who had at his command
but a small garrison of Syrian Arabs, would not assume the
offensive, and now determined to strike a sudden and heavy
blow by marching straight upon the Capital, before the
Syrian Arabs from the South could reach it. His plan
failed ; for while he was still upon the march the Syrians
arrived at Cordova, and 'Abd-er-Rahmân sallied forth with
them to meet the enemy. Nor had 'Abd al-Malik to wait
long at Seville for reinforcements, for his son 'Abdallah—
believing his father to be besieged—came to his assistance
with troops from the district of Moron, of which he was
governor, and father and son resolved to attack Yûsuf on
his march. Receiving intelligence of the enemy's movements, and fearing lest he should be hemmed in, Yûsuf
faced about in order to crush first the force from Seville and
Moron. Upon his approach, 'Abd al-Malik, wishing to give
'Abd-er-Rahmân time to come up, fell back slowly : Yûsuf,
however, compelled him to halt and give battle. The engagement began, as usual, with a single combat. A Berber,
client of a Fihrite family, advanced from Yûsuf's ranks, and
cried : "Is there any among you who will measure swords
with me ?" As he was a man of colossal stature and prodigious strength, none of 'Abd al-Malik's soldiers durst
accept the challenge. "This is a very disheartening begin-

ning for our men," said 'Abd al-Malik, and turning to his
son 'Abdallah, he continued : " Go thou forth, my son,
against this man—and may God aid thee ! " As 'Abdallah
stepped from the ranks in obedience to his father's orders,
an Abyssinian, a client of his family, inquired his intention.
" I am going to fight yonder Berber," replied 'Abdallah.
" Let that task be mine, my lord," cried the Abyssinian,
darting forth to meet the champion.

Both armies awaited with anxiety the issue of the
combat. The two opponents were well matched in height,
strength, and valour ; for some time the duel proceeded
without either combatant gaining the advantage, but the
ground was sodden with rain, and at last the Berber slipped
and fell. The Abyssinian instantly sprang upon his foe and
cut off both his legs, while 'Abd al-Malik's army, encouraged
by their champion's victory, raised the cry of " God is
great ! " and fell upon Yûsuf's forces with such impetuosity
that they put them to flight. But though a single charge
had thus decided the fortune of the day, 'Abd al-Malik's
men were too few in number to enable him to reap to the
full the fruits of victory. While his soldiers were fleeing in
all directions, Yûsuf, accompanied only by a slave and one
Sâbik, a Persian client of the Temîmites, passed through
the Campo de Calatrava and gained the high-road leading
to Toledo. As he rode at full speed through a village ten
miles from that city, he was recognised, and a man of
Medinese descent, named 'Abdallah ibn 'Amr, cried to his
friends : " To horse ! Let us slay that man—death alone will
give repose to his own soul and to the world ! While he
liveth he will remain a firebrand ! " 'Abdallah's suggestion
was instantly acted upon. His comrades sprang to their
saddles, and since their horses were fresh, while those of the
fugitives were overspent with fatigue, they caught up their
quarry four miles from Toledo, and slew Yûsuf and Sâbik.
The slave alone escaped, and bore to Toledo the sad tidings
of the death of Spain's former Emir.

When 'Abdallah ibn 'Amr presented to 'Abd-er-Rahmân
his ill-fated rival's head, the Prince, who wished to make a
clean sweep of his opponents, ordered Abû Zayd, one of
Yûsuf's two sons, to be executed, and though the life of the
other, Abu 'l-Aswad, was spared in consideration of his
extreme youth, he was condemned to perpetual imprisonment. Sumayl alone now stood in the way. One morning
it was noised abroad that he had succumbed to a fit of

apoplexy while in his cups. The Ma'addite chiefs, admitted to his chamber to satisfy themselves that he had not died by violence, found wine, fruits, and sweetmeats beside the corpse. Nevertheless they suspected that his was not a natural death; and they were right. They were, however, mistaken in supposing that by 'Abd-er-Rahmân's orders Sumayl had been poisoned: he had, in fact, been strangled.

[AUTHORITIES: *Akhbâr majmû'at,* ff. 83–91; Ibn al-Kûtiyya, ff. 10–13; Ibn al-'Abbâr, pp. 42, 50, 54–5; Makkarî, ii. 24.]

CHAPTER XVI

'ABD-ER-RAHMÂN I (*continued*)

'ABD-ER-RAHMÂN had attained the goal he sought. The outcast, who for five years had been buffeted by all the hardships of a vagabond life as he wandered from tribe to tribe across African deserts, had become master of a great country, and his avowed enemies had been swept away.

Yet he did not enjoy in peace the prize won by treachery and murder. His power was not established in the land, the Yemenites were the only party he could rely upon, and he had from the outset never blinked the fact that their support was precarious. Burning to avenge the defeat they had suffered on the fatal field of Secunda, and eager to regain the hegemony of which they had so long been deprived, to them 'Abd-er-Rahmân's cause had never been more than a pretext. In their hearts they would have much preferred to raise one of their own number to the Emirate if their mutual jealousies had rendered this practicable, and it might have been foreseen that they would turn their arms against the Prince as soon as their common foe had been vanquished. And so it fell out. Throughout his reign of thirty-two years 'Abd-er-Rahmân I saw his authority disputed—sometimes by the Yemenites, sometimes by the Berbers, and sometimes by the Fihrites, who, though often routed, arose in renewed vigour after every defeat, like the fabled giant whom Hercules in vain laid low. Fortunately for the Emir, the Arab chiefs seemed incapable of combination; they took up arms either to gratify some personal grudge, or out of mere caprice. They were vaguely aware that to crush the Emir a confederation of all the chieftains was a prime necessity, and yet concerted action was out of the question. Thanks, therefore, to disunion among his foes, to his own indefatigable activity, and to a policy sometimes perfidious and crafty, sometimes violent and cruel, but always shrewd and adaptable, 'Abd-er-Rahmân contrived to maintain his position though he could depend only on his clients, a few allied chiefs, and Berber troops imported from Africa.

Among the most formidable of the many Yemenite insurrections must be reckoned that of 'Alâ ibn Mughîth,[1] which broke out in the year 763. Two years earlier, the Fihrite party, of which Hishâm ibn Ozra, son of a former Governor of Spain, was then leader, had stirred up a revolt at Toledo, and the Emir had not quelled it when 'Alâ— appointed Governor of Spain by Al-Mansûr the 'Abbâsid Khalif—landed in the province of Beja, and hoisted the black[1] flag given him by the Khalif. No standard was more likely to unite the jarring factions, since it did not represent this or that party, but all Islam. The Fihrites of that part of Spain joined the Yemenites, and the position of 'Abd-er-Rahmân, who had been besieged in Carmona for two months, became so critical that he resolved to risk all for all. Learning that a large number of the enemy, wearied with the long siege, had returned to their homes upon various pretexts, he selected seven hundred men, the flower of the garrison, and lighting a great fire near the Seville gate, exclaimed : " Comrades, we must conquer or die ! Let us throw the scabbards of our swords into the flames, and swear to fall like soldiers if the victory cannot be ours ! " Every scabbard was flung into the fire, and 'Abd-er-Rahmân's men, sallying forth, charged with such impetuosity that the besiegers took to flight in utter confusion, with the loss, it is affirmed, of all their leaders and seven thousand men. The victor, in his anger, decapitated the corpses of 'Alâ and his principal associates, and with the object of depriving the 'Abbâsid Khalif of any desire to dispute Spain with him, he caused the heads to be preserved with salt and camphor, and a label having been attached to an ear of each, specifying the name and rank of its owner, they were placed in a sack —together with the black flag, Al-Mansûr's diploma appointing 'Alâ Governor of Spain, and a despatch narrating the defeat of the insurgents. A Cordovan merchant who was bound to Kairwan on business was induced, for a large sum, to take the sack with him thither and deposit it by night in the market-place. The merchant duly executed his commission, and it is said that Al-Mansûr, when apprised of the facts, cried, in an access of terror : " Thanks be to God for having placed the sea between me and such a foe ! "[3]

---

[1] Variously attributed by Arab writers to the tribes of Ya'kûb, Hadramaut, and Judhâm.

[2] The party colour of the 'Abbâsids. See p. 162.

[3] According to some chroniclers the sack was carried by a Cordovan pilgrim to Mecca, where Al-Mansûr then resided.

This victory over the 'Abbâsid party was soon followed by the reduction of Toledo (A.D. 764). Wearied by the long war, the Toledans entered into negotiations with Badr and Tammâm, who commanded the Prince's army, and after surrendering their leaders were accorded an amnesty. As the chiefs were being conveyed to Cordova, they were met by three emissaries from the Prince—a barber, a tailor, and a basket-maker. Following their instructions, the barber shaved the heads and beards of the prisoners, the tailor cut out woollen tunics for them, and the basket-maker provided them with panniers. Some days later the populace of Cordova saw a string of asses entering the town, bearing panniers, whence projected shaven heads, and shoulders ridiculously bedizened with woollen ruffles. Followed by a hooting mob, the luckless Toledans were led through the city and, finally, crucified.

The barbarous punishment inflicted by 'Abd-er-Rahmân on those who had dared to disown his authority was a sufficient proof that he was determined, if need be, to rule by terrorism. Nevertheless, to judge by Matarî's rebellion, which broke out two years after the execution of the Toledan nobles, the Arabs were not easily to be cowed. Matarî was a Yemenite chief of Niebla. One evening, after indulging too freely in potations, the conversation having turned upon the massacre of the Yemenites who had fallen under 'Alâ's banner, Matarî took up his spear, tied a piece of cloth to it, and swore to avenge the death of his tribesmen. On awaking next morning he had entirely forgotten his proceedings on the previous evening, and seeing his spear turned into a standard, asked in astonishment what it meant. He was reminded of his words of the night before. In alarm, he exclaimed : " Tear that kerchief from my spear instantly, lest my folly should be noised abroad ! " But before his order could be executed, he thought better of it. " Nay ! " he cried ; " touch not the banner ! I am not a man to flinch from the consequences of words once uttered, whatever they may have been ! " And he forthwith called his tribesmen to arms. He contrived to hold his own for some time, and when at last he was killed in battle, his comrades fought on so stubbornly, that the Emir was induced to grant them an amnesty.

Abû Sabbâh's turn came. Although 'Abd-er-Rahmân had good grounds for mistrusting this powerful Yemenite— who had counselled his assassination soon after the battle

of Mosâra—he had judged it prudent to avoid a breach
with him, and had made him Governor of Seville : but, in
the year 766, when the Emir had no rebels to contend with,
and thought himself strong enough to defy Abû Sabbâh,
he deprived the latter of his office. The Yemenite, in great
wrath called his tribesmen to arms, and 'Abd-er-Rahmân
soon became painfully aware that the chief possessed much
more influence than he had supposed. He accordingly initiated a treacherous negotiation, offering the Sevillan a personal interview, and sending him by the hand of Ibn Khâlid
a safe-conduct under his sign-manual. Abû Sabbâh accordingly repaired to Cordova, and leaving at the gateway of
the palace the four hundred horsemen who escorted him,
entered into a private conversation with the Emir. It is
said that he exasperated the latter by bitter taunts, that
'Abd-er-Rahmân thereupon tried to stab him, but that the
vigorous resistance offered by the Sevillan chief obliged the
Emir to summon his body-guard, who despatched his
assailant. Perhaps there was more premeditation in this
act of homicide than the Omayyad clients, who have chroni-
cled their patron's deeds, cared to admit.

When Abû Sabbâh was dead, 'Abd-er-Rahmân ordered
a sheet to be thrown over the corpse and all traces of bloodshed to be carefully removed. He then summoned the
Viziers, informed them that Abû Sabbâh was a prisoner in
the palace, and asked them whether he should be put to
death. They all advised that his life should be spared. 'Abû
Sabbâh's removal would be too dangerous," they said ; "for
his troopers stand at the gate, and thy soldiers are at a
distance." One Vizier alone did not share this opinion.
He was a relative of the Emir, and threw his advice into
verse :

"Son of the Khalifs, good is the counsel I give thee! Slay this man
who hateth thee and yearneth to avenge himself upon thee. Let him not
escape, for if he remaineth alive he will cause us dire calamities. Make an
end to him and thou wilt rid thyself of a pestilence. Thrust into his breast
a right Damascus blade ; it is true magnanimity to wipe out such a man by
a violent death ! "

"Be it known to all, then," cried 'Abd-er-Rahmân,
"that I have slain him ! " and heedless of his Viziers' dismay
he withdrew the sheet from the corpse.

The Viziers, who had disapproved of the suggested assassination of Abû Sabbâh merely because they dreaded the

probable effects of such a deed upon his body-guard, soon
discovered that their fears were groundless; for upon a
lackey informing the horsemen that their leader was dead
and that they need wait no longer they rode quietly away.
This astonishing circumstance induces the suspicion that
'Abd-er-Rahmân, with prudent forethought, had previously
bribed the escort.

There was a single Omayyad client, however, whose lofty
character loathed the base treachery of which he had been
unwittingly an instrument; this was Ibn Khâlid, who had
conveyed the Emir's safe-conduct to Abû Sabbâh. He
withdrew to his estate, and thenceforth consistently refused
to assume any office.

Shortly after Abû Sabbâh's murder a serious revolt broke
out among the Berbers, who hitherto had been peaceable.
This was initiated by a schoolmaster, Shakyâ by name—
half fanatic and half impostor—who lived in the east of
Spain. He belonged to the Berber tribe of Miknesa; but,
whether his brain had been turned by overmuch study of
the Koran, traditions of the Prophet, and the early history
of Islam, or whether ambition urged him to pose as a party
leader, he believed—or pretended to believe—that he was a
descendant of 'Alî and Fâtima, Mohammed's daughter. The
credulous Berbers accepted this imposture the more readily,
since the schoolmaster's mother happened herself to bear
the name of Fâtima. At any rate, when Shakyâ, or, rather,
" 'Abdallah, son of Mohammed "—for so he styled himself—
migrated to the district lying between the Guadiana and
the Tagus, the Berbers, who there formed the majority of
the population and were ever ready to take up arms at a
Marabout's bidding, flocked to his standard in such numbers
that they soon found themselves masters of Sontebria,[1]
Merida, Coria, and Medellin.

Defeating the force sent against him by the Governor
of Toledo, Shakyâ won over to his side the Berbers who
served under the command of the Omayyad client 'Obaidallah,
and attacking the other troops of this general, put them to
flight, captured their camp, and withdrawing to the mountains, eluded all 'Abd-er-Rahmân's attempts to bring about
a battle. At length, after six years of desultory warfare,
'Abd-er-Rahmân sought and obtained the assistance of a
Berber who was at the time the most powerful chief in the

---

[1] Now Castro de Santover, on the Guadiela : an important town under the Arabs.
(*De Gayangos*, Notes on Râzî, p. 47.)

east of Spain, and who looked with a jealous eye on the influence and success of the self-styled Fâtimid.

Discord thus arose among the Berbers, and Shakyâ found himself obliged to quit Sontebria and retire northwards; but while 'Abd-er-Rahmân was marching against him and ravaging all the Berber villages which lay in his path, a fresh revolt broke out in the West, where the Yemenites had awaited a favourable opportunity of avenging Abû Sabbâh's murder. Such an opportunity was supplied by the Emir's absence on this expedition, and they marched straight upon the Capital, hoping to seize it by a *coup de main*. Their leaders were the Governors of Niebla and Beja, kinsmen of Abû Sabbâh, and they were reinforced by the Berbers of the West, who had, it appears, for a long time been incited by the Marabout's emissaries.

'Abd-er-Rahmân no sooner received this unwelcome intelligence than he returned with all speed to Cordova, and refusing to rest in his palace for even a single night, advanced against the enemy, whom he found intrenched on the banks of the Bembezar.[1] After a few days spent in unimportant skirmishes, 'Abd-er-Rahmân availed himself of his Berber clients—who included the Beni al-Khalî—to detach the Berbers from their alliance with the Yemenites. Stealing into the enemy's camp after nightfall, the clients easily impressed the Berbers with the idea that if the Emir, who could alone protect them from Arab jealousy and hatred, were deposed, their own expulsion would inevitably follow. "You may be assured of the Prince's gratitude," added the clients, "if you abandon a cause detrimental to yourselves, and espouse his." Their advice prevailed: the Berbers promised to betray the Yemenites during the battle which was to be fought on the morrow. They kept their word. Before the engagement began they said to the Yemenites: "We can only fight on horseback, but you are well skilled in fighting on foot; mount us therefore on all the horses which you have." The Yemenites, having no reason to mistrust them, acceded to their request. When it was too late, they regretted their credulity. The battle had scarcely begun when the mounted Berbers rode off to join the Omayyad cavalry, and while they vigorously charged the Yemenites their brethren fled from the field. The Yemenites were overwhelmed on all sides. A dreadful carnage ensued: in blind frenzy 'Abd-er-Rahmân's soldiers

---

[1] Also, it would seem, known as the Wady-Kais (River of the Kaisites).

laid low indiscriminately all whom they encountered, in spite of their orders to spare the fleeing Berbers. Thirty thousand corpses lay strewn over the field and were buried in a trench which was still pointed out in the tenth century.

In central Spain the Berber revolt was not suppressed until after ten years of warfare—when Shakyâ was assassinated by two of his adherents—and it was still in progress when a formidable confederacy summoned to Spain a foreign conqueror. The members of the confederacy were the Kelbite Al-Arâbî,[1] Governor of Barcelona; the Fihrite, 'Abd-er-Rahmân ibn Habîb, Yûsuf's son-in-law, surnamed " The Slav "—since his tall, slender figure, fair hair, and blue eyes resembled the type of that race of which many representatives were to be found among the slaves in Spain—and Abu 'l-Aswad, Yûsuf's son, whom 'Abd-er-Rahmân had condemned to perpetual imprisonment, but who had evaded the vigilance of his jailers by posing as a blind man. (At first Abu 'l-Aswad's blindness was discredited. He was subjected to the most difficult tests; but his yearning for liberty lent him the ability not to betray himself in the smallest particular, and he played his part with such perseverance and talent for imposture that in the end he was universally believed to be sightless. Having thus lulled his jailers into carelessness, he concerted a plan of escape with one of his clients, who had obtained permission to visit him from time to time. One morning when the prisoners had been led through a subterranean passage to perform their ablutions in the river, the client and some friends posted themselves, with horses, on the opposite bank. At a moment when he was unobserved Abu 'l-Aswad plunged into the stream, swam across, sprang into the saddle, and riding at full gallop to Toledo, reached that city in safety.)

So bitter was the hatred of these three chiefs for 'Abd-er-Rahmân, that they resolved to implore the aid of Charlemagne, although that conqueror—the fame of whose exploits already resounded through the world—was the most implacable enemy of Islam. The confederates accordingly, in 777, journeyed to Paderborn, where Charlemagne was then holding a " May-field,"[2] and proposed an alliance with him against the Emir of Spain. Charlemagne fell in with the

---

[1] Sulaimân ibn Yakdhân al-Arâbî.

[2] An annual assembly of nobles held in the spring or summer, at which royal edicts were promulgated and military expeditions planned.

proposal without hesitation. Just then his hands were free, and he could meditate new conquests. The Saxons had submitted—as he supposed—to his dominion and to Christianity; thousands of them were then at Paderborn awaiting baptism; Wittekind, their most formidable chief, had been banished from his country to seek refuge with a Danish prince. It was decided, therefore, that Charlemagne should cross the Pyrenees with a large force; that Al-Arâbî, and his allies to the north of the Ebro, should reinforce him and acknowledge him as their sovereign, and that "The Slav," after raising levies among the African Berbers, should lead them into the province of Tadmir, where he would co-operate with the northern invaders by raising the standard of the 'Abbâsid Khalif as Charlemagne's ally.[1] This powerful confederacy, whose plan of attack had been formed after mature deliberation, threatened to prove vastly more dangerous for 'Abd-er-Rahmân than any which had preceded it. Fortunately for him the projects of the allies were less ably executed than devised. "The Slav" landed in Tadmir with a Berber army; but he arrived prematurely, for Charlemagne had not crossed the Pyrenees; and when he sought help from Al-Arâbî, the latter replied that according to the plan of campaign agreed upon at Paderborn, it was his duty to remain in the North and support Charlemagne's army. The blood-feud between Fihrites and Yemenites was too deeply rooted for the suspicion of treachery not to arise. Believing himself betrayed by Al-Arâbî, Ibn Habîb marched against him, was defeated, and returning to the province of Tadmir was assassinated by a Berber of Oretum, of whom he had imprudently made a confidant, little suspecting that he was one of the Emir's agents.

When Charlemagne's army drew near the Pyrenees (A.D. 777), one of the three Arab chiefs on whom he relied was already dead. The second, Abu 'l-Aswad, afforded him such feeble assistance that neither Frankish nor Arab chroniclers mention it. There remained, therefore, only Al-Arâbî and his northern allies—such as Abû Thaur, Governor of Huesca, and Galindo, the Christian Count of La Cerdaña.

Al-Arâbî, however, had not been inactive. Aided by the *Helper* Husain ibn Yahyâ—a descendant of Sa'd ibn 'Obâda who had aimed at the Khalifate after the Prophet's death—he had seized Zaragoza, but when Charlemagne's

---

[1] There is no record of the part allotted to Abu 'l-Aswad in the campaign.

army appeared before the gates of the city, he could not
overcome the repugnance felt by the Moslems to the
admission of the Frankish king within their walls; Husain
ibn Yahyâ, especially, could not consent to such a step without renouncing family traditions which were sacred to him.
Seeing that he could not prevail with his fellow-citizens, Al-
Arâbî, unwilling to be suspected of deceit, voluntarily placed
himself in Charlemagne's hands.

But just as the King was making preparations for the
siege of Zaragoza, he received tidings which upset all his
plans. Wittekind had returned to Saxony; at his summons
the Saxons had again taken up arms; profiting by the
absence of the Frankish army, they had swept the land with
fire and sword, and penetrating as far as the Rhine, they
had captured Deutz, opposite to Cologne.

Compelled to quit in hot haste the banks of the Ebro
for those of the Rhine, Charlemagne marched by the valley
of Roncesvalles. Lurking among the crags and forests
which command the northern end of the valley, the Basques,
animated by inveterate hatred of the Franks and eager for
booty, lay in ambush. The Frankish army were compelled
by the narrowness of the valley to march in an extended
file. The Basques let the main body pass through, but
when the rear-guard, encumbered with baggage, reached
the ravine, they fell upon it, and being lightly armed
and advantageously posted, hurled the Franks back into the
valley, where despite a stubborn resistance they slew them to
the last man—among them being Roland,[1] Warden of the
Breton Mark. The Basques then rifled the baggage-train,
and, protected by the rapidly falling shades of night, dispersed in all directions.[2]

Such was the disastrous issue of Charlemagne's expedition, begun though it had been under the most favourable
auspices. All concerned had contributed to its failure, with
the single exception of the Emir of Cordova, against whom
it was aimed. 'Abd-er-Rahmân forthwith hastened to profit
by the advantages conferred upon him at the hands of his
rebellious subjects at Zaragoza, the Christian Basques, and
a Saxon chieftain of whose name he was probably ignorant.

---

[1] The entire authentic history of this hero of romance is recorded as follows :
"In quo prælio Eggihardus . . . Anselmus . . . et Hruodlandus Brittannici
limitis præfectus, cum aliis compluribus interficiuntur." Einhard, Vit. Car. Mag.
(Migne, Patrol. Cur. Compl., Tom. 97, col. 34).
[2] Cf. Pertz, Monum. Germ., i. pp. 16, 81, 156-9, 296, 349, for the Frankish
annals of these events.

He accordingly marched against Zaragoza to compel that
city to obedience. Before he reached Zaragoza, Al-Arâbî,
who had accompanied Charlemagne during his retreat, but
had since returned to Zaragoza, was no more. The *Helper*
Husain, who regarded him as a traitor to the Faith, had
caused him to be stabbed in the Mosque. Husain, on finding himself beleaguered by 'Abd-er-Rahmân, capitulated.
Some time afterwards he again raised the standard of revolt,
but the citizens, on being again besieged, handed over their
leader to the Emir, who caused him to be beaten to death,
but not until his hands and feet had been cut off. Master
of Zaragoza, 'Abd-er-Rahmân next attacked the Basques,
and made the Count of La Cerdaña his tributary. Abu 'l-
Aswad was the last to essay an insurrection, but at the battle
of the Guadalimar he was betrayed by the general commanding his right wing. The carcases of four thousand of
his companions "furnished food for the wolves and vultures."

'Abd-er-Rahmân had therefore emerged a conqueror
from all the wars which he had been compelled to wage
against his subjects. His triumph earned him the praise
even of his enemies. It is, for instance, related that the
'Abbâsid Khalif Al-Mansûr asked his courtiers one day:
"Who, think ye, deserves to be called the Falcon of the
Kuraish?" Thinking that the Khalif coveted the title, the
courtiers replied without hesitation: "Thou thyself, Commander of the Faithful; thou hast vanquished mighty
princes, subdued many a revolt, made an end of civil strife!"
"Nay," said the Khalif, "it is not I!" The courtiers then
suggested Mu'âwiya I or 'Abd al-Malik. "Neither one
nor the other," replied the Khalif; "as for Mu'âwiya, 'Omar
and 'Othmân had smoothed the way for him; and as for
'Abd al-Malik, he was supported by a powerful faction. The
Falcon of the Kuraish is 'Abd-er-Rahmân, son of Mu'âwiya;
the man who after wandering, solitary, through the deserts
of Asia and Africa had the boldness to seek his fortune,
without an army, in lands unknown to him, beyond the sea.
Having naught to rely upon save his own wits and perseverance, he nevertheless humiliated his proud foes, exterminated
rebels, secured his frontiers against the Christians, founded
a great empire, and reunited under his sceptre a realm which
seemed already parcelled out amongst petty chieftains. No
man before him ever did such deeds." 'Abd-er-Rahmân
himself, with just pride, expressed similar reflections in a
metrical form.

And yet this treacherous, cruel, and vindictive tyrant had paid dearly for his success. If no Arab or Berber chief dared defy him openly, none the less did they curse him in their hearts. No honourable man would enter his service. When he consulted his Viziers with regard to the appointment of a suitable Kady for Cordova, his two sons, Sulaimân and Hishâm, agreed—for once in a way—in recommending for the office a pious and virtuous old man, Musʻab by name. ʻAbd-er-Rahmân accordingly sent for him and offered him the dignity of Kady. But Musʻab, convinced that under a prince who put his power above the law he would be a mere minister of tyranny, declined the post, notwithstanding the Emir's repeated solicitations. Irritated by this refusal, ʻAbd-er-Rahmân, who could not brook the slightest contradiction, began to twirl his moustache—with him a token of a rising tempest—and the courtiers expected a sentence of death to fall from his lips. " But God," says an Arab chronicler, " turned aside his evil thought." The venerable old man inspired him with involuntary respect, and mastering his rage, or at any rate disguising it as best he could, the Emir contented himself with saying : " Depart! and may they who brought thee here be accursed of Allah ! "

Little by little ʻAbd-er-Rahmân saw the support of those upon whom he had been able to rely in all emergencies slipping away. Many of his clients deserted him. Some of them, such as Ibn Khâlid, refused to follow the paths of treachery and cruelty which he trod. Others aroused his suspicions—among these was ʻObaidallah. It is said that wishing to prove himself indispensable to the Emir—who, he imagined, wished to be rid of him—ʻObaidallah had countenanced the defection of his own nephew Wajîh, who had joined the party of the Fâtimite pretender. But ʻAbd-er-Rahmân, as soon as he had Wajîh in his power, treated him with the utmost rigour, and had him beheaded, in spite of ʻObaidallah's entreaties. Some time afterwards, ʻObaidallah was accused—rightly or wrongly—of being concerned in a plot hatched by two relatives of the Emir ; but ʻAbd-er-Rahmân did not possess convincing proofs of his complicity, and, unscrupulous as he was, hesitated to condemn to death, on mere suspicion, the old man to whom he owed his throne. He was therefore clement, in his own way : " I will inflict on ʻObaidallah," said he, " a punishment which will be for him worse than death ! " And he henceforth treated him with cruel indifference.

Even the faithful Badr fell into disgrace. 'Abd-er-Rahmân confiscated his property, confined him to his house, and at last banished him to a frontier town : but it is fair to add that Badr had been lacking in the respect due to his master and wearied him with groundless and insolent complaints.

After quarrelling with his most prominent clients, 'Abd-er-Rahmân finally saw his own family conspiring against him. On becoming master of Spain, he had invited to his court the Omayyads who were dispersed in Asia and Africa; he had loaded them with riches and honours, and was often heard to say : " The greatest blessing which God hath granted me, next to sovereignty, is the ability to offer my kinsmen a home and to benefit them. It is, I admit, flattering to my pride when they marvel at the greatness to which I have attained, and which I owe to God alone." Nevertheless these Omayyads, stimulated by ambitions which could not brook the oppressive absolutism of the head of their family, conspired among themselves. The first plot was hatched by two princes of the blood royal and three nobles. They were betrayed, arrested, and beheaded. Some years later another conspiracy was devised by Moghîra, the Emir's nephew, and Hudhail—the murder of whose father Sumayl, strangled in prison, was yet unavenged. They were also betrayed, and similarly punished. After their execution an Omayyad client presented himself before 'Abd-er-Rahmân. He found the Emir sorrowful and downcast, with his eyes fixed on the ground, and as though buried in melancholy thoughts. Divining what was passing through the mind of his master, whose pride as head of his family had been for the second time wounded, and whose most intimate affections were lacerated, the client approached him cautiously and in silence. " Who hath kinsfolk like mine ! " cried 'Abd-er-Rahmân at last. " When, at the risk of my life, I aimed at a throne, I thought as much of them as of myself. When I had gained my end, I invited them hither and shared with them my wealth. And now they would snatch from me the gifts of heaven. Almighty God ! thou hast punished their ingratitude by laying bare to me their machinations : if I have taken their lives it was to preserve my own. And yet, how wretched is my lot ! All the members of my house are suspect to me, while they, for their part, fear that I am compassing their destruction. Confidence, mutual outpourings of our hearts, are at an end ! What intercourse

o

can there be henceforth between me and my brother, the
father of that miserable youth? How can I know peace
when he is near—I, who by condemning his son to death,
have severed the ties that united us? How can my eyes
meet his?" Then, turning to the client, he added: "Go,
seek out my brother instantly: vindicate my conduct as
best you can: give him these five thousand pieces of gold,
and bid him seek a home wheresoever he willeth—in Africa!"

The client obeyed, and found the unfortunate Walîd
half dead with terror. He reassured him, handed him the
sum sent by the Emir, and related what he had heard.
"Alas!" exclaimed Walîd, with a deep sigh, "another's
crime is visited upon me! The rebellious son who hath
met with a merited death involves me in his ruin—and yet
I never asked for aught save to repose in a corner of my
brother's tent! But his command shall be obeyed: it is
our duty to bow with resignation to God's will." Returning
to his master, the client informed him that Walîd was
already preparing to quit Spain, and reported his words.
"My brother speaks the truth," said the Prince, smiling
bitterly; "but he need not hope to deceive me by such
words, or to conceal his thoughts. I know him! Not for
a moment would he hesitate if he could but slake his thirst
for vengeance in my blood!"

Execrated by the Arab and Berber chiefs, embroiled
with his clients, and betrayed by his family, 'Abd-er-Rahmân
found himself more and more isolated. In the early years
of his reign, when he still enjoyed some popularity—at least
in Cordova—he had delighted to walk almost alone through
the streets of the Capital and to mingle with his subjects.
Now, distrustful and irascible, he hardly ever quitted his
palace, and when he did so he was surrounded by a numerous
body-guard. Since the great insurrection of the Yemenites
and Berbers of the West, he saw in the augmentation of
his mercenary troops the sole means of holding his subjects
in awe. He accordingly bought slaves from the nobles and
enrolled them as soldiers, besides importing a vast number
of Berbers from Africa, and thus built up a standing army
of 40,000 men—all blindly devoted to his person, but wholly
indifferent to the welfare of the country.

'Abd-er-Rahmân was wholly absorbed in pondering over
the best means of imposing discipline on the Arabs and
Berbers, and imbuing them with habits of order and peace.
To realize this aim, he employed all the expedients to which

the kings of the fifteenth century afterwards had recourse in their struggle with feudalism. Melancholy was the condition to which Spain found herself reduced by the fatality of events; melancholy was the part which the successors of 'Abd-er-Rahmân had to play: the path traced out for them by the founder of the dynasty led to the despotism of the sword. It is true that a monarch could not govern Arabs and Berbers in any other way: if violence and tyranny lay in one direction, disorder and anarchy lay in the other. The various tribes might have constituted so many republics —confederated, if possible, against their common foe the Christians of the North: this would have been a form of government in harmony with their instincts and traditions; but a monarchy was essentially ill-suited for both Arabs and Berbers.

[AUTHORITIES: *Akhbâr majmû'at,* ff. 91–8; Ibn al-Kûtiyya, ff. 13–14, 18; Ibn Adhârî, ii. 52–62; Ibn al-'Abbâr, pp. 45, 56; Nuwairî, p. 441; Ibn al-Khatîb (MS. P.), f. 214; Khoshanî, pp. 204–5; Makkarî, ii. 25–33.]

BOOK II

CHRISTIANS AND RENEGADES

CHAPTER I

SPAIN UNDER THE VISIGOTHS

HITHERTO the conquerors have exclusively occupied our attention; we must now follow the fortunes of the vanquished.

To set forth the circumstances which facilitated the conquest of Spain by the Moslems; to sketch the progress of that conquest in its salient outlines; to describe the condition to which the victors reduced the Christian inhabitants, and the effects of their domination upon the lot of that numerous and unfortunate class, the slaves and serfs; to narrate in detail the long and obstinate resistance which all ranks of society—townsfolk and mountaineers, rich landowners and manumitted slaves, aided by the holy zeal of monks and the fortitude of devoted women—offered to the conquerors, when a sturdier generation had succeeded the brood of weaklings that held Spain at the dawn of the eighth century; such is the task which now confronts us.

At the epoch when the Peninsula first attracted the covetous eyes of the Moslems, its weakness proclaimed it an easy prey: the whole social fabric was in a deplorable condition.

The evil was of long standing. As a Roman province, Spain under the last Cæsars presented, like other provinces of the Empire, a melancholy spectacle. "Of all that she once possessed naught save her name remains," wrote an author of the fifth century.[1] On the one hand were to be seen a few possessors of immense estates—the *latifundia*; on the other, a multitude of impoverished citizens, serfs, and slaves. The wealthy, the privileged, the chief magistrates—all those, in fact, who had held high office in the Empire, or upon whom the sovereign had merely conferred titular rank—were exempt from payment of the taxes which crushed the middle class. They lived lives of effeminacy and unbridled luxury in splendid mansions, beside some placid river which

---

[1] Salvianus, *De Gubernatione Dei*, iv. p. 60 (Bremae, 1688). For an account of this writer see Hodgkin, *Italy and her Invaders*, i. p. 504.

mirrored the vineyards and olive groves of smiling uplands.
There the days were spent in gambling, bathing, reading,
horsemanship, and feasting. There, in halls rich with the
painted and embroidered hangings of Persia and Assyria,
slaves daily loaded the board with the choicest viands and
the most generous wines, while the guests reclining upon
couches spread with purple improvised verses, or were
entertained by choirs of musicians, and troops of dancing-
girls.[1]

Such ostentation of wealth did but intensify by contrast
the misery of a numerous class. The turbulent rabble of
the towns were not, it is true, much to be pitied; they were
feared, pampered, supplied with gratuitous rations at the
expense of the other citizens, and were debauched by gross
and barbarous spectacles; but the middle classes, including
the *curials*—or burgesses who were charged with the
administration of municipal affairs—were reduced by Roman
fiscality to a condition of the deepest distress. The munici-
palities, intended as a safeguard against tyranny, had become
at once instruments and victims of every kind of oppression.
Constantine had cut off the chief source of revenue for the
cities and towns, by seizing their corporate property, just at
a time when municipal expenditure was growing in consequence of the increase of poverty; and yet the members of
a *curia*—that is to say all citizens who possessed more than
twenty-five acres of land but did not belong to the
privileged classes—were compelled to make up from their
own purses deficiencies due to the insolvency of the tax-
payers.

The curials were unable to cast off this joint liability,
which was traditional and hereditary; they were indeed
to some extent bound to the soil, for they could not alienate
their estates without authorization from the Emperor, who,
regarding himself as the actual owner of all the land in the
Empire, looked upon his subjects as mere beneficiaries.
Sometimes, in despair, the curials deserted their municipality
and entered military service or undertook servile occupations; but the lynx-eyed, iron-handed Government seldom
failed to discover them and replace them by force in the
curia; and in the alternative, their posts were given to men
of ill-repute, bastards, heretics, Jews, and liberated convicts

---

[1] Though we have no direct evidence as to the mode of life of the wealthy
Spaniards of this epoch, there is every reason to suppose that it resembled that of
their neighbours in Southern Gaul. See C. Sollius Apollinaris Sidonius, *Ep.* ix. 13.

—for the curial dignity, once honourable and privileged, had become an instrument of degradation and punishment.[1]

The rest of the population consisted of serfs and slaves. Agricultural slavery was not extinct; but since the dawn of the imperial epoch the institution of serfdom had slowly developed, fostered on the one hand by the impoverishment and profound distress of the free rural population, and on the other, by the amelioration of the condition of agricultural bondsmen. Serfdom was a condition intermediate between freedom and slavery. At first regulated only by custom or contract, it had become, since the days of Diocletian, a matter of public order and State concern—an object, indeed, of constant preoccupation to the Government, who had to supply at any cost cultivators for the deserted fields and soldiers for the army. It had therefore its own organization, police, and laws. In some respects the serfs, who handed to the possessor of the land which they tilled a settled portion of the produce, were better off than the slaves. Unlike the latter, they could legally marry; they could become owners of land, and their patrons might not confiscate their property—which, however, could not be alienated without the patrons' consent. Nor, in the eyes of the law, were they mere slaves. They paid personal taxes to the State and were liable to be commandeered. On the other hand, serfs, as well as slaves, were subject to corporal punishment, and they could look for no enfranchisement. They were, in fact, slaves of the land though not of a person; they were attached to the soil which they tilled, by indissoluble and hereditary links; the landlord could not dispose of his fields without the serfs, nor of his serfs without the fields.[2]

A still more wretched class were the slaves, who were sold or given away like oxen or household goods. Compared with their masters they were immensely numerous. " Once on a time," writes Seneca, " it was proposed in the Senate that slaves should wear a distinctive dress. The motion, however, was not carried, for fear that our slaves might take to counting us." In the reign of Augustus, a freedman, notwithstanding that he had met with heavy losses during the Civil Wars, possessed more than four thousand slaves. During the later Empire their numbers seem to have increased rather than diminished. One Christian in Gaul owned five thousand, and another, eight

[1] See Giraud, *Essai sur l'hist. du droit français*, i. pp. 140 *sq.*
[2] See Giraud, *op. cit.*, i. pp. 147 *sq.*

thousand.¹ They were treated with pitiless severity: a master would condemn a slave to three hundred lashes for having kept him waiting for hot water.² And what these poor wretches had to endure at the hands of their masters was nothing compared to the cruelties inflicted on them by overseers who were slaves like themselves.

To escape the tyranny of their masters, of the land-owners, and of the Government—burghers, serfs, and slaves alike had but one expedient: this was to flee to the forests and become bandits, or *Bagauds* as they were then termed. Living in the woods the life of primitive man, they avenged themselves on their oppressors by pillaging their splendid villas; and if a wealthy man fell into their clutches he met with swift and terrible retribution.³ Sometimes many bands of such robbers united to form a marauding army, and no longer confining themselves to mere brigandage, threatened cities and the very foundations of society. In Gaul, under Diocletian, the *Bagauds* assumed such a men-acing attitude that it became necessary for a Cæsar to lead a large army against them.⁴

A society thus honeycombed with poverty and misery must needs fall at the first shock of invasion. It mattered little to the majority whether it was by the Romans or by another people that they were oppressed and ill-treated. The privileged classes and the rich land-owners alone had any interest in the maintenance of the existing régime, and most of these, utterly corrupt and worn out by debauchery, had lost all energy and initiative. However, when the barbarian hordes burst in upon the Roman provinces, a few stout hearts were stirred to deeds of patriotism—or, at least, of self-defence. The nobles of Tarragona attempted, though without avail, to arrest the progress of the Visigoths;⁵ and when in the reign of Honorius, the Alans, Vandals, and Suevi, crossing the Rhine, carried fire and sword throughout Gaul and threatened Spain, while the inhabitants of the latter country for the most part awaited their fate with seeming indifference and

¹ Laurentii Pignorii . . . *de Servis* . . . *Commentarius* (Pref.); in Giovanni Poleni, *Utriusque Thesauri* . . . *nov. suppl.*, iii. (1737).
² Ammianus Marcellinus, xxviii. iv. 16. "Si aquam callidam tardius attulerit servus, trecentis adfligi verberibus jubeatur."
³ *Querolus*, I. ii. 194–208 (p. 55, ed. Klinkhamer).
⁴ See D. Bouquet, *Script. rer. francic.*, i. 565, 572, 597, 609. We have no direct evidence of the existence of Bagauds in Spain before the barbarian invasion ; but Idatius (fifth century), who first mentions them, does not regard them as a novelty.
⁵ Isidore, *Hist. Goth.*, p. 493.

lethargic calm—making no effort to avert the peril—two wealthy and noble brothers, Didymus and Verinianus, armed their serfs,[1] and entrenching themselves in the defiles of the Pyrenees, checked the inroad of the barbarians—so easy of defence was the Peninsula. But when the two brothers had been made prisoners and beheaded by the anti-Cæsar Constantine, whom they had refused to acknowledge; and when Constantine had entrusted the defence of the Pyrenees to the Honorians[2]—a corps of barbarians which the Romans had raised to oppose other barbarians; and when the Honorians proceeded to ravage the country which it was their duty to protect, and to escape punishment for their wrong-doing opened the defiles to the hordes who were pillaging the Gauls (A.D. 409), not a man in Spain dreamed of resistance. At the irresistible and inevitable advance of the grim barbarians, the nobles sought oblivion of their dangers in revelry, and clouded their brains in the delirium of debauch. While the enemy were entering the gates of the city, the rich, sunk in gluttony and drunkenness, danced and sang; their trembling lips imprinted kisses on the bare shoulders of beautiful slave-girls—while the populace, as though to accustom themselves to the sight of blood or to intoxicate themselves with the odours of carnage, applauded the gladiators who slew one another in the amphitheatre.[3] Not a single town in Spain had the courage to sustain a siege; everywhere the gates flew open, as though automatically, to the barbarians, who entered cities without striking a blow; they plundered, they burned, but they had no need to kill—if they did so, it was but to satiate a lust for bloodshed.

Those were days of horror. Though the men of that generation inspire us with a mortal disgust, in their effeminacy, cowardice, and decadence—we instinctively pity them. Roman despotism, insupportable though it was, was clement in comparison with the brutality of the barbarians. The calculated tyranny of the Cæsars had at least been orderly and measured; but the Teutons in their blind savagery overthrew and destroyed indiscriminately all that they

---

[1] Orosius, vii. 40.

[2] "Cum Barbaris quibusdam, qui quondam in fœdus recepti atque in militiam allecti, Honoriaci [Honoriani, Honoriacti, Honoraciaci] vocabantur." Oros., vii. 40 (Migne, xxxi. 1166).

[3] What Salvianus says of the Gauls on this head may be applied to the Spaniards, for he declares that the corruption of the latter was the worse. Salv., *op. cit.*, vi. pp. 121-3.

encountered in their course. Utter desolation fell upon town and country. In the wake of this havoc followed scourges, if possible, yet more terrible—pestilence and famine : starving mothers slew their children to feed upon their flesh.

The Balearic Islands, Cartagena, and Seville were -pillaged by the Vandals. Happily for Spain the Vandals passed on into Africa, A.D. 429, with a handful of Alans who had escaped the sword of the Visigoths; but the fierce Suevi—to whom carnage and destruction were the breath of life—remained in Galicia, and were for some time masters of Betica and the district of Cartagena. Almost all the provinces of Spain were successively the scene of their ravages; Lusitania, Cartagena, Betica, Tarragona, and Gascony. Terrible disorder reigned in the last two provinces; the Bagauds, augmented by a multitude of serfs and ruined farmers, spread terror far and wide. Sworn foes of Rome, they were by turns enemies and allies of the invaders. In Tarragona, where they were led by the valiant and daring Basil, they surprised a body of barbarians in the Roman service, while assembled in the church of Tirazona, and slew them to the last man, not even sparing the bishop himself. Afterwards Basil joined the Suevi, with them pillaged the environs of Zaragoza, and taking Lerida by surprise took captive all the inhabitants. Five years later the Suevi allied themselves with the Romans in order to exterminate the Bagauds.

Galicia, beyond all other provinces, was laid waste by the Suevi; it was the centre of their domination, in it were their chief haunts; there they pillaged and massacred for more than sixty years. Their patience at last exhausted, the luckless Galicians ultimately adopted the course which they should have taken at the very first ; they armed themselves and remained on the defensive in strong castles. Now and then they succeeded in capturing some of their enemies, in which case negotiations followed and prisoners were exchanged or hostages mutually demanded. But the Suevi soon broke the peace, and again resorted to plundering. The Galicians sought, without much success, the help or mediation of the Roman governors of Gaul, or of that part of Spain which remained under Roman rule. At last other barbarians, the Visigoths, attacked the Suevi, and defeated them in a bloody battle on the banks of the Orvigo, A.D. 456. But this event, far from delivering the Galicians, exposed them to a new danger. The Visigoths pillaged

Braga (without bloodshed), carried into slavery many of the citizens, used the churches as stables, and stripped the clergy of all their property—to the last vestment. Just as the inhabitants of Tarragona became Bagauds, those of Braga and its neighbourhood organized themselves into bands of brigands. At Astorga the Visigoths proved still more ruthless. When they appeared before its gates, the city was in the hands of a faction which aimed at fighting for Rome. The Visigoths, having entered in the guise of friends, perpetrated a horrible massacre, dragged into slavery a multitude of women, children, and ecclesiastics—among whom were two bishops—demolished the altars, set fire to the houses, and devastated the surrounding country. Palencia met with a like fate. The barbarians then beleaguered a castle near Astorga, but despair had at last given strength and courage to the Galicians, and the garrison of the castle made so gallant a defence that they sustained a long siege victoriously.

Upon the return of the Visigoths to Gaul, the Suevi resumed their brigandage and atrocities. At Lugo one of their bands suddenly burst into a hall where the municipal council were deliberating—in the belief that they had nothing to fear, seeing that it was Passion Week. The councillors were all massacred. At Coimbra another band broke a treaty recently made, and enslaved the inhabitants. Little by little the Visigoths, however, ultimately gained possession of the whole of Spain, and the inhabitants, although deprived of two-thirds of the soil, felt the rule of their new masters a relief after the sufferings they had endured at the hands of the terrible Suevi.

In the midst of numberless calamities and of social chaos, there remained a group of men who had never lost courage, who contemplated the ruins of the old world without much regret, and who, to a certain extent, had sided with the invaders against their Roman fellow-countrymen. These were the *élite* of the Catholic clergy, of the school of S. Augustine. From the commencement of the invasions these priests had taken infinite pains to palliate the excesses of the conquerors : they looked forth over the wide sea of misfortune with a kind of barbarous optimism. A disciple of the Bishop of Hippo [1] (to whom he dedicated his historical work), and an eye-witness of the invasions by the

---

[1] S. Augustine.

Alans, Suevi, and Vandals—the Spanish priest Paulus Orosius
maintains that the barbarians, once they had settled in the
Peninsula, and had partitioned the country, treated the
Spaniards as friends and allies, and that at the time when
he wrote (about A.D. 417), Spaniards were already to be
found who preferred freedom and poverty under barbarian
domination, to oppressive taxation under that of the Romans.
Another priest, Salvianus of Marseilles, writing twenty or
thirty years later, goes much farther and makes a still
bolder claim.   That which Orosius describes as the wish of
a feeble minority, becomes under the pen of Salvianus the
unanimous sentiment of the nation.   Nothing would have
been more unnatural than such a trend of public opinion :
but nothing can be falser than the historian's statement.
On the contrary, it must be recorded for the honour of
humanity, that the sentiment of national dignity was not
enfeebled to such a degree among the subjects of Rome,
who, moreover, had endured a bitter experience which was
a more grievous scourge than despotism itself.   Though too
weak or too cowardly to throw off the yoke, they retained
sufficient pride to hate and loathe the invaders in their hearts.
"Thou avoidest wicked barbarians : I avoid even good
ones," writes Sidonius Apollinaris [1] to one of his friends ;
and his words are a far truer expression of national sentiment than those of priests striving to depict the invasion as
a divine blessing.   And yet the priests had excellent excuses
for writing as they did.   In the first place, no generous
sentiment stood in their way : for them patriotism had no
meaning.   Here below no love of country fired them ; their
fatherland was heaven.   Compassion had faded from their
breasts.   Pillage—even massacre—touched them but lightly.
"What does it matter to a Christian who aspires to life
eternal, how or when he quits this world ? " asks Orosius,
after a somewhat grudging admission that the Suevi and
their allies had committed sundry murders.

For the clergy the interests of the Church were all in all ;
they regarded every political event merely in its aspect as an
advantage or a detriment to her.   As champions of Christianity, it was their lot to refute not only pagans, but many
Christians, who, not yet sufficiently established in the faith,
attributed the unheard-of disasters which had befallen the

[1] Bp. of Clermont ; c. 430–483.   "Man of letters, Imperial functionary, country
gentleman and bishop, who, . . . is still the most interesting literary figure of the
fifth century."   Hodgkin, *Italy and her Invaders*, ii. 298.

Empire to neglect of the ancient religion, and declared that
Christianity had wrought injury to the might of Rome, and
that her former gods would have better protected her.   The
priests answered these unbelievers by explaining—as had
their master, the famous author of the *De Civitate Dei*—
that Rome had always been unfortunate, and that existing
ills were not so grievous as was alleged.   Besides, they had
firmly grasped the truth that to implant new ideas, such as
Christian doctrines, fresh soil was needed.

The priesthood, however, had obtained no hold over the
Roman nobles.   The latter were Christians as a matter of
form, since Christianity had become the State religion, but,
too corrupt to submit to the austere morality which that
religion enjoined, and too sceptical to believe in its dogmas,
these patricians lived only for banquets, diversions, spectacles
—and even denied the immortality of the soul.[1]   "They
prefer the circus to the churches of God," exclaims Salvianus
in pious wrath, "they despise altars and honour theatres !
Every creature is loved and esteemed; the Creator alone
seems to them contemptible and vile !   They scoff at all that
pertains to religion."   The morals of the barbarians were no
purer; the priests were obliged to admit that they were as
unjust, avaricious, deceitful, covetous—in a word, as corrupt
—as the Romans themselves; for as has been justly remarked,
there is a singular resemblance between the vices of decadence and those of barbarism.   But if lacking in virtues, the
barbarians at least believed all that their priests taught
them; they were naturally religious.   In danger, they
looked for help from God alone.   Before a battle their kings
prayed in sackcloth, an act at which a Roman general would
have scoffed; and if they were victorious they recognised the
hand of the Eternal in their triumph.   Further, they
honoured the clergy, and not merely their own Arian clergy,
but the Catholic priesthood as well, whom the Romans
despised and derided for claiming catholicity.[2]   It is not to
be wondered at, therefore, that the barbarians won priestly
sympathy.   They were heretics, it is true, they had been
instructed by "bad teachers"; but why need Catholic
priests despair of converting them ?   And when this conversion had once been effected, what a brilliant future
would open before the Church !

There was no province in which the hopes of these far-

---

[1] See Claudianus Ecdicius Mamertus, *De Statu Animæ*, ii. 8.
[2] S. P. Salviani . . . *opera* (Bremae, 1688), L. vii. pp. 140–2.

seeing minds were not fulfilled, and nowhere were they realized more completely than in Spain, when King Reccared and his Visigoths abjured the Arian heresy and became Catholics, A.D. 587.[1] Henceforth the clergy used every means to humanize and enlighten the Visigoths—already half-Romanized, before their arrival in Spain, by a residence of fifty years in Roman provinces, and by no means insensible to the benefits of order and civilization. Strange indeed was the phenomenon presented by the descendants of barbarians who had haunted the forests of Germany, as they sat immersed in study under the tutelage of prelates. There is extant a curious correspondence between King Recceswinth and Braulion, Bishop of Zaragoza: the king thanks the bishop for having kindly corrected a manuscript which he had sent him, and speaks of omissions, blunders, the stupidity of scribes—*putredines ac vitia scribarum, librariorum ineptiæ*—with all the assurance of a Bentley or a Ruhnken. But the bishops did not confine themselves to moulding the hearts and minds of kings; they themselves undertook legislation and administration. They declared in their public records that they had been appointed, by the Lord Jesus Christ, guardians of the nation.

Surrounded by his nobles, the king prostrated himself humbly before them when they were assembled in council at Toledo, and implored them with sighs and tears to intercede to God on his behalf, and to give wise laws to the State.[2] While the bishops inspired the kings with the belief that piety should be the chief of their virtues,[3] the kings, for their part, understood so well that piety meant obedience to bishops, that even the most profligate meekly suffered themselves to endure ecclesiastical guidance in public affairs.[4]

A new power, therefore, had arisen in the State—a power which absorbed all others, and seemed designed to regenerate both morals and institutions. To it the serfs naturally looked for alleviation of their wrongs. The Catholic clergy, while the Arian heresy flourished, had shown a tender and fatherly solicitude for the poor. They

[1] The Third Council of Toledo, by which Arianism was definitely rejected in Spain, was summoned in A.D. 589.

[2] *Concil. Tolet.* iv. (Dec. 5, A.D. 633), *Esp. sagr.*, vi. 162.

[3] *Ibid.*

[4] "Licet flagitiosus, tamen bene monitus," says Isidore of Beja (c. 15) of Recceswinth. *Esp. sagr.*, viii. p. 290. "Tamen bonæ indolis" is another reading (MS. Mariana).

had opened hospitals for them, and Masonius, the pious
Bishop of Merida, had given so much money to the serfs of
his church, that at Easter they escorted him in silk raiment;
on his deathbed this saintly man even manumitted his most
faithful slaves and provided them with suitable means of
subsistence. It was confidently believed that the clergy
were about to abolish slavery, as an institution opposed to
the spirit, if not the letter, of the Gospel. This noble
doctrine, so loudly preached by the Church in the days of
her weakness,[1] would surely be put into practice now that
she had become all-powerful.

Profound error! The clergy when they attained to
power disavowed the principles which they had set forth
when they were destitute, scorned, and persecuted. Henceforth, possessed of vast domains densely peopled with
serfs, of splendid palaces crowded with slaves, the bishops
recognised that they had been premature, that the time for
emancipating the serfs was not yet, and might not arrive for
centuries to come. S. Isidore of Pelusium marvelled, in
the deserts of the Thebaid, that a Christian could keep a
slave; another S. Isidore, the famous Bishop of Seville, who
was long the life and soul of the Councils of Toledo, and
who was dubbed by the Fathers of the eighth of those
Councils "the glory of the Catholic Church," did not quote,
in treating of slavery, the doctrines of his namesake, but of
the "Sages" of old—Aristotle and Cicero. "Nature," the
Greek philosopher had said, "created some to command,
and others to obey;" while the Roman philosopher had
declared that "It is not unjust that those should serve
who cannot rule themselves." Isidore of Seville says the
same thing[2]—but he contradicts himself, for he admits that
all men are equal in the sight of God, and that Adam's sin
—in which he finds the root of slavery—was wiped out by
the Redemption. We have not the slightest intention of
blaming the clergy for not having enfranchised the slaves,
or of combatting the opinion of those who hold that the
slave was not fit for freedom: we confine ourselves to the
statement of a fact which had very important consequences,
namely that the clergy were inconsistent and did not answer

---

[1] See Neander, *Denkwürdigkeiten aus der Gesch. des Christenthums*, ii. 236–40;
and Ozanam, *La civilisation au Vme siècle*, ii. 50–7.

[2] *Sent.*, iii. 47 : "Æquus Deus ideo discrevit hominibus vitam, alios servos con-
stituens, alios dominos, ut licentia male agendi servorum potestate dominantium res-
tringatur." (Migne, vol. 83, col. 718.)

the serfs' expectations.   The lot of these unhappy folk grew
worse instead of better.   The Visigoths, like other Teutonic
races in other Roman provinces, imposed personal service
upon them in the form of statute labour.   By a remarkable
usage, moreover, apparently unknown to the Romans, the
successive generations of a family of slaves often had to render
their masters specific services.   One family would provide
ploughmen, another fishermen, another shepherds, another
blacksmiths, and so forth.[1]   Neither serf nor slave could
marry without his lord's consent, and if he did so, his
marriage was declared void, and he was forcibly separated
from his wife.   When a serf, or slave, was married to a
woman belonging to another lord, the offspring of the
marriage were shared between the two masters.   In this
respect the law of the Visigoths was less humane than that
of the Empire, for Constantine had forbidden the separation
of man and wife, father and son, or brother and sister.[2]   The
hardships endured by the servile classes under the Visigoths
cannot, indeed, be doubted when we take note of the many
and harsh laws against fugitive serfs and slaves; and in the
eighth century all the serfs of the Asturias, whose condition
had remained that of the whole class formerly throughout
Spain, rose in revolt against their masters.

While the bishops failed in ameliorating the lot of the
serfs, they did no more for the middle class.   The burghers
remained, as hitherto, bound to the soil; what is more, no
citizen had the right to sell his property.   The spirit of
fiscality had passed from the Emperors to the Gothic Kings
with other Roman traditions; it seemed likely that the
disciples would soon outstrip their teachers.   The wretched-
ness of the ruined middle classes was unalleviated—as,
indeed, the Councils admitted.[3]

All the evils of the Roman epoch—the concentration of
wealth, slavery, universal serfdom, by which farmers were
tied to the land and property was inalienable—still flourished.
It was not even as if those who claimed the title of pastors
of the people, appointed by Christ, had been content to
leave things, for the most part, as they had found them.
Alas, in their fanaticism, they proceeded to persecute, with
unparalleled cruelty, a race which was then the most numerous in Spain.   This was to be expected.   Michelet has justly

---

[1] See Muñoz, *Fueros*, pp. 123–5.
[2] See Muñoz, *Del estado de las personas en los reinos de Asturias y Leon*.
[3] *Concil. Tolet.*, viii. ; *Esp. sagr.*, vi. p. 189.

observed : " Whenever, during the Middle Ages, men began
to ask how it was that the ideal Paradise of a world under
the sway of the Church was realized here below as a Hell,
the Church, conscious of the objection, hastened to stifle it
by declaring: 'It is the wrath of God ! It is due to the
crime of the Jews ! The murderers of our Lord are still unpunished !' And a persecution of the Jews was set on foot."

The persecutions began in 616, during the reign of
Sisebut.[1] It was decreed that all Jews must be converted
before the end of the year : when that date had expired
all Jews who persisted in their faith were to be banished—
after receiving a hundred lashes—and their property was to
be confiscated. It is said that under the influence of terror
more than ninety thousand Jews were baptized—these, however, constituting the minority. It is scarcely necessary to
add that such conversions were only apparent : the new
converts continued secretly to circumcise their children, and
to perform all other Mosaic rites : an attempt forcibly to
convert so numerous a race was obviously impracticable.
The bishops of the fourth Council of Toledo seem to have
recognised this, but while permitting the Jews to remain
faithful to the religion of their ancestors, they ordained that
their children should be taken from them to be reared as
Christians. Then the clergy, repenting of such tolerance,
once more had recourse to extreme measures, and the sixth
Council of Toledo ordained that henceforth no elected king
should be entitled to ascend the throne without having previously sworn to execute the edicts promulgated against the
abominable race. Nevertheless, despite laws and persecutions,
the Jews lived on in Spain, and even, by a strange anomaly,
held lands of their own.[2] It seems clear that the statutes
aimed at them were seldom applied in all their rigour. The
power of their persecutors did not equal the will.

For eighty years the Jews suffered in silence ; and then,
their patience breaking down, they determined to be avenged
on their oppressors. About A.D. 694, seventeen years before
the conquest of Spain by the Moslems, they planned a
general rising, in concert with their co-religionists on the
other side of the Straits, where many Berber tribes then
professed Judaism, and where the exiled Jews of Spain had
found refuge. The revolt was probably intended to break
out at several places simultaneously, as soon as the African

---

[1] See H. Graetz, *Hist. of the Jews* (1892), iii. p. 50.
[2] Acts of the Eighth Council of Toledo, Art. 10 (*Esp. sagr.*, vi. 192).

Jews had landed in Spain : but before the scheme could be
put into execution it reached the ears of the Government.
The king, Egica, immediately took the necessary precautions, and having summoned a council at Toledo, he unfolded to his spiritual and temporal advisers the criminal
projects of the Jews, and begged them to punish severely
this untoward race. After hearing the evidence of certain
Israelites, which proved that the conspiracy aimed at nothing
less than to make Spain a Jewish State, the bishops, shuddering with indignation, condemned all the Jews to the loss of
their property and their liberty. The king handed them
over as slaves to Christians—even to those who had been
themselves the slaves of Jews and whom the king had freed.
The masters were bound not to allow their new slaves to
practise the ceremonies of their ancient law ; they were also
bound to deprive them of their children at the age of seven
years, to bring them up as Christians, and not to permit
marriage between Jews ; a Jewish slave, of either sex, being
prohibited from marrying anyone except a Christian who
was also a slave.[1]

There is no reason to doubt that these decrees were
executed in all their rigour.[2] This time it was not merely a
question of punishing unbelievers, but very dangerous conspirators. When the Moslems conquered the north-west
of Africa, the Jews of Spain were groaning beneath an
intolerable yoke ; they ceased not to pray for their deliverance ; and the conquerors who set them free and granted
them religious liberty, subject to the payment of a light
tribute, were in their eyes saviours from heaven.

The Jews, the serfs, and the impoverished burghers were
so many implacable enemies which this decaying and
crumbling society nourished in its bosom. And yet the
privileged classes had no forces with which to oppose the
invaders save those composed of Christian or Jewish serfs.
We have seen that in the last years of the Roman domination the serfs had served in the army. The Visigoths had
kept up this custom. As long as they maintained their
warlike spirit it was not necessary to fix the number of serfs
which each landowner should furnish as his contingent ; but
later, when a craving for the attainment of wealth by the
labour of slaves and serfs arose, it became an urgent matter
that recruiting for the army should be provided for by law.

[1] See Acts of the Seventeenth Council of Toledo (*Esp. sagr.*, vi. p. 234).
[2] See H. Bradley, *The Goths*, p. 356.

King Wamba perceived this. He complains, in one of his decrees, that the landowners, intent upon the cultivation of their domains, enrolled scarcely a twentieth part of their serfs when there was a call to arms, and he ordains that henceforth, every proprietor, be he Goth or Roman, should enroll a tenth part of his serfs.[1] Later, the proportion even seems to have been raised to one half. The number of serfs in the army must, therefore, have greatly surpassed that of free men—which is as much as to say that the defence of the State was for the most part entrusted to soldiers who were far more disposed to make common cause with the foe than to fight for their oppressors.

[1] So in the two Latin MSS. of the *Forum Judicum*, and in the Spanish translation of that code.

[AUTHORITIES: Salvianus, *De Gub. Dei.*, iv. 58, 60, 74; v. 86–95; vi. 115–123; vii. 130–150; Sidon. Apol., *Epist.*, vii. 14 (and passages quoted by Fauriel, *Hist. de la Gaule mérid*, i. 387 *sq.*); Orosius, *Dedication*, and vii. 40–1; Idatius, *Chronicon* (passim); *Forum Judicum*, iv. 1; v. 4, 19; L. ix. ii. 9; *Esp. sagr.*, xiii., 359–60, 382; xxx. 374–7.]

CHAPTER II

THE CONQUEST

SPAIN under the Visigoths, as we have seen, was even worse governed than Spain under the Romans. The germs of dissolution had for a long time lurked in the body politic and had reduced it to such an extremity of weakness, that an army of twelve thousand men, aided by treachery, was able to overthrow it at one blow.

The Governor of Africa, Mûsâ ibn Nusayr, had extended the limits of the Arabian dominion to the Atlantic. The town of Ceuta alone held out against him. Ceuta belonged to the Byzantine Empire, which had formerly included the whole northern littoral of Africa, but the Emperor being too distant to afford it effectual aid, it had entered into close relations with Spain. Julian, the Governor of Ceuta, had sent his daughter[1] to the court of Toledo to be educated as became her birth, but she unfortunately found favour in the eyes of the king, Roderic, who dishonoured her. Beside himself with rage, Julian threw open the gates of Ceuta to the Arabs, but not before he had concluded an advantageous treaty with them : then, dilating upon the wealth and fertility of Spain, he urged Mûsâ to attempt its conquest, and assured the Arab general that the necessary ships should be placed at his disposal. Mûsâ sought instructions from the Khalif Walîd. The Khalif thought the undertaking too perilous. "Explore Spain with some light troops," he replied, "but do not, at any rate for the present, expose a large army to the dangers of an expedition beyond the seas." Mûsâ accordingly sent Abû Zora Tarîf, one of his clients, into Spain with four hundred men and a hundred horses. These troops crossed the Straits in four vessels supplied by Julian, pillaged the neighbourhood of Algeciras, and returned to Africa, July, A.D. 710.

Next year, Mûsâ took advantage of the absence of Roderic, who was engaged in quelling a rising of the Basques, to despatch another of his clients, Târik ibn Ziyâd,

---

[1] Florinda, whose mother was daughter of the previous Visigothic king, Witica.

the commander of his vanguard, with seven thousand Moslems. They were conveyed in batches across the Straits in the four ships which Tarîf had previously made use of, for the Moslems possessed no others. Târik assembled his men on the mountain which still bears his name—Jabal Târik, Gibraltar. At the foot of this mountain lay the town of Carteya.[1] Târik sent a division to attack it, commanded by one of the few Arab officers in his army— 'Abd al-Malik of the tribe of Moâfir.[2] Carteya fell into the hands of the Moslems, and Târik had advanced as far as the Laguna de Janda when he heard that King Roderic was marching against him at the head of a large army. Since there were only four vessels available, it would have been difficult for him to withdraw his men to Africa even if he had wished to do so. But Târik never thought of retreat; ambition, cupidity, and fanaticism urged him on, and calling for reinforcements from Mûsâ, who sent him five thousand more Berbers in some ships which he had built since his lieutenant's departure, he found himself in command of a force of twelve thousand men. This was small in comparison with Roderic's host, but treachery came to the aid of the Moslems.

Roderic had usurped the throne. Aided by many nobles, he had deposed and, as it appears, murdered his predecessor Witica. He was consequently antagonized by a very powerful party, headed by the brothers and sons of the late king. Wishing to conciliate the leaders of this party, Roderic invited them to join him when he marched against Târik. They were obliged by law to obey, but they came full of anger, hatred, and defiance. The king tried to appease them and to win their confidence, but with so little success that they schemed to betray him in the presence of the enemy. It is not that they had any intention of handing over their country to the Berbers—indeed, since they aimed at sovereignty, such a course would have been suicidal—but the disaffected nobles believed, not unreasonably, that the Berbers had not landed with the intention of establishing a dominion, but merely of making a foray. " All that these foreigners want is booty," they argued, " and when they have amassed enough, they will return to

---

[1] In Arabic there is no distinction between "Carteya" and "Cartagena." In the seventeenth century a tower in the ruins of Carteya was called "Cartagena," (now Torre del Rocadillo). *Cf.* Caro, *Antig. de Sevilla*, f. 123; *Esp. sagr.*, iv. 24; *Mem. hist. esp.*, ix. 369.

[2] From whom the famous Almanzor was eighth in descent.

Africa." They trusted that Roderic when defeated would lose his prestige as a brave and fortunate leader and thus enable them to urge their claims to the sovereignty with more success than heretofore; while, if he were slain, their chances would be much improved. They yielded themselves, in fact, to the guidance of a short-sighted selfishness; but if in the event they delivered their country to the infidel, they did so neither wittingly nor willingly.

The battle took place on the banks of the Wady Bekka,[1] July 9, 711. The two wings of the Spanish army were led by two sons of Witica, and mainly consisted of the serfs of these princes. The serfs only too readily obeyed their lords' injunctions to turn their backs upon the foe. The centre, commanded by Roderic in person, held its ground for some time, but at last gave way, whereupon the Moslems smote the Christians hip and thigh. It seems that Roderic was slain; at any rate he was seen no more, and the country found itself without a king just when it had most need of one. Târik grasped the situation. Instead of returning to Africa, in obedience to Mûsâ's instructions, he boldly pushed on. This was all that was needed to bring about the collapse of the crumbling edifice. The disaffected and oppressed everywhere facilitated the task of the invaders. The serfs would not raise a hand, lest in saving themselves they should save their masters. The Jews rose in revolt, and placed themselves at the disposal of the Moslems.

After gaining another victory near Ecija, Târik marched on Toledo with the bulk of his forces, sending detachments against Cordova, Archidona, and Elvira. Archidona was occupied without a blow being struck, the inhabitants having sought safety in the mountains. Elvira was taken by storm, and was garrisoned by a mixed force of Jews and Moslems. Cordova was delivered to the Africans by a shepherd, who informed them of a breach by which they could enter the town. At Toledo the Christians were betrayed by the Jews. Everywhere indescribable confusion reigned. The patricians and bishops lost all presence of mind. "God had filled the hearts of the infidels with dread," writes an Arab chronicler; and, in truth, the panic was universal. The nobles of Cordova fled to Toledo: the nobles of Toledo sought refuge in Galicia. The Metropolitan even quitted the Peninsula, and for greater security

---

[1] A stream which enters the sea not far from Cape Trafalgar, between Vejer de la Frontera and Conil. See *Recherches* (1881), i. 305–7.

betook himself to Rome. Those who did not seek safety
in flight thought more of making terms than of self-defence.
In this category were the princes of Witica's house. Relying upon their act of treachery as furnishing a title to the
gratitude of the Moslems, they asked for and obtained
the crown lands, of which the king had only enjoyed the
usufruct,[1] and which included three thousand farms. Oppas,
one of Witica's brothers, was even appointed Governor of
Toledo.

By an unexpected stroke of good fortune a mere raid
had resulted in a conquest. But this was by no means
gratifying to Mûsâ. He had looked forward to Spain being
conquered—but, by himself: he envied Târik the glory and
material advantages of his victory. Happily there was still
scope for Mûsâ's activities in the Peninsula. Târik had not
captured all the towns, nor had he appropriated all the
wealth of the country. Mûsâ therefore determined to
follow his lieutenant, and in June, 712, he crossed the Straits
with eighteen thousand Arabs. He took Medina Sidonia,
and the Spaniards who joined him engaged to deliver
Carmona into his hands. Presenting themselves armed
before the gates of the town, they posed as men who had
taken flight at the approach of the enemy, and, being
suffered to enter, in the darkness of the night they admitted
the Arabs. Seville presented more difficulty. It was the
largest city in the country, and endured a siege of several
months before surrendering. Merida also resisted stoutly,
but at length capitulated (June 1, A.D. 713). Mûsâ then
marched on Toledo. Târik came to greet his superior
officer respectfully, and on seeing him, dismounted; but
Mûsâ, in great wrath, struck him with his whip. "Why
hast thou advanced without my permission?" he cried: "I
ordered thee only to make a foray and immediately to
return to Africa!"

The rest of Spain—with the exception of some northern
provinces—was conquered without difficulty. Resistance
was useless: in the absence of a leader there could be no
organized defence. Self-interest, moreover, suggested to
the Spanish people speedy submission. On this condition
they obtained favourable terms, while if they only yielded
after resistance, their property was confiscated.[2]

---

[1] *Forum Judicum*, Lib. V., i. 2.
[2] The lands conquered by force of arms were called the *Khoms*, and belonged to
the State. See *Recherches* (1881), i. pp. 72 *sq*.

Viewed as a whole, the conquest was not a great calamity. At the outset, it is true, there was a period of anarchy, as in the case of the Teutonic invasion. The Moslems plundered here and there, burnt a few towns, hanged such nobles as had not been able to escape, and even put children to the sword : but the Arab Government soon repressed such disorders and atrocities, and once tranquillity had been restored the spiritless population of those days submitted to their lot without many murmurs. The Arab dominion was, indeed, at least as endurable as that of the Visigoths. The conquerors left the vanquished their own laws and judges ; and gave them Counts, or Governors, of their own race, who were entrusted with the collection of taxes and the settlement of disputes. Territories which the Arabs had won by the sword, as well as those which had belonged to the Church and to the fugitive nobles, were parcelled out among the conquerors ; but the serfs attached to them were not disturbed. This policy was everywhere adopted by the Arabs. The natives alone understood agriculture, and the victors were far too proud to stoop to such an occupation. The serfs were therefore compelled to cultivate the soil as heretofore, handing to the Moslem owners four-fifths of their crops. Those attached to the lands of the State—a numerous body, for these lands comprised a fifth part of the confiscated territory—were called upon for only a third part of their produce. At first this was paid into the Treasury, but after a while, this practice was modified. Some of the State lands were divided into fiefs, which were granted to Arabs who settled in Spain later on—those, for instance, who accompanied Samh, and the Syrians who landed with Balj.[1] The Christian husbandmen, however, found themselves none the worse off; they merely had to yield the third part of the crops to their own lords instead of to the State. The position of the rest of the Christians depended on the terms which they had been able to make, and these in some cases had been far from unfavourable. Those inhabitants of Merida, for instance, who were actually in the city when it capitulated, were deprived of none of their goods : the property and ornaments of the churches were alone confiscated. In the province of which Theodemir was Governor, and which contained, among other towns, Lorca, Mula, Orihuela, and

[1] See above, p. 140.

Alicante, the Christians lost absolutely nothing. They merely undertook to pay a tribute, partly in money and partly in kind.[1] Speaking broadly it may be said that the Christians kept the greater part of their property, and moreover were empowered to alienate it, a right which they had not enjoyed under the Visigoths. They were, however, obliged to pay to the State a poll-tax at the rate of forty-eight dirhems[2] for the rich, twenty-four for the middle class, and twelve for those who lived by manual labour. Payment was made of a twelfth part at the end of each lunar month;[3] but women, children, monks, cripples, the blind, the sick, beggars, and slaves were exempt. Landed proprietors had further to pay the *kharâj*[4]—which was a tax upon crops, varying in different districts with the nature of the soil, but amounting on the average to twenty per cent. The poll-tax was remitted for those who embraced Mohammedanism, but the *kharâj* was unaffected by the conversion of the taxpayer. The condition of the Christians under the Moslems, compared with what it had been formerly, was therefore not one of great hardship. The unbounded tolerance of the Arabs must also be taken into account. In religious matters they put pressure on no man. On the contrary, unless the Government was an exceptionally devout one—which was seldom the case—it had no particular desire to see the Christians converted to Islamism; this involved too great a loss to the treasury.[5] The Christians were not ungrateful. They were under obligations to their conquerors for the tolerance and justice shown them; and preferred their rule to that of, for instance, the Franks.[6] Throughout the eighth century insurrections were accordingly very rare; in fact, the chroniclers have recorded but one—that of the Christians of Beja, who seem to have been the tools of an ambitious Arab chieftain. Even the priests, during the early years, were not greatly discontented, although they had the best reason to be so. Some idea of their point of view may be gathered from a Latin chronicle written at Cordova in 754, and attributed

---

[1] The treaty made by Theodemir with 'Abd al-'Azìz (son of Mûsâ) is given in Casiri, ii. 106.

[2] About £12 in present value.

[3] See *Esp. sagr.*, xi. p. 523.

[4] Or, *Jizya.* See Muir, *Life of Mohammad* (1912), p. 432.

[5] See Bk. i. ch. x.

[6] " Urbs erat interea Francorum inhospita turmis, Maurorum votis adsociata magis," writes Ermoldus Nigellus of Barcelona, i. 67. (Migne, *Patrol. Curs. Compl.*, vol. 105.)

—though erroneously—to one Isidore, Bishop of Beja.[1]
Although a Churchman, this historian is much more
favourably disposed to the Moslems than any other Spanish
writer earlier than the fourteenth century. He is by no
means lacking in patriotism, and bewails the misfortunes of
Spain—the rule of the Arabs being in his eyes a barbarian
domination, *efferum imperium*—but if he hates the conquerors
it is as men alien in race rather than in religion. Deeds
which would have made ecclesiastics of another epoch burn
with indignation do not extort from him a word of blame.
He relates, for instance, that King Roderic's widow married
'Abd al-'Azîz, Mûsâ's son; but he is not scandalized at the
match, which he seems to regard as quite normal.

In some respects the Arab conquest was even a benefit
to Spain; for it brought about an important social revolution, and put an end to many evils under which the country
had groaned for centuries. The power of the privileged
classes, of the clergy and the nobility, was reduced almost
to extinction, and since the confiscated land had been divided
among a very large number of persons, what was practically
peasant proprietorship had been instituted. This proved
highly beneficial, and was one of the causes of the flourishing state of agriculture in Moslem Spain. The conquest
had, moreover, ameliorated the condition of the servile classes.
Islamism was much more favourable to the emancipation of
slaves than was Christianity—as interpreted by the bishops
of the Visigothic dominion. Speaking in God's name,
Mohammed had granted permission to slaves to ransom themselves. The enfranchisement of a slave was a good work,
and many sins could thereby be expiated.[2] Slavery among
the Arabs was therefore neither harsh nor permanent.
After some years of servitude a slave was often declared
free, especially if he had embraced Islamism.[3] The lot of
those serfs who were attached to the lands of Moslems was
also improved. They became, to some extent, farmers who
enjoyed a certain meed of independence, for since their
masters disdained to occupy themselves with agricultural
work, they were at liberty to till the ground after their own
methods. As for the slaves and serfs of Christians, the

---

[1] The unknown author of this very important but corrupt and obscure
Chronicle seems to have been a Cordovan. For the civil wars preceding the
arrival of 'Abd-er-Rahmân I in Spain, and also for details of the conquest, his
testimony is of the highest value. See *Recherches* (1881), i. pp. 2–14.

[2] See D. S. Margoliouth, *Mohammed* (2nd ed.), p. 462.

[3] See Jackson, *Account of Marocco*, p. 248; *Account of Timbuctoo*, p. 219.

conquest provided them with a very easy path to freedom. They had, in fact, merely to escape to some Moslem's domain, and utter these words: "There is but one God, and Mohammed is the Messenger of God," and forthwith they became Moslems, and in the phrase of Mohammed, "Allah's freedmen." Many serfs gained their liberty in this manner, and there is no ground for surprise at the readiness with which they apostatized. In spite of the limitless power enjoyed by the clergy under the Visigoths, Christianity had never been very deeply rooted in the land. Almost wholly pagan when Constantine established Christianity as the State religion, Spain had remained so long faithful to her ancient cults, that at the time of the Arab conquest, Christianity and Paganism still disputed the ground, and the bishops were obliged to fulminate threats and to take energetic measures against the worshippers of false gods.[1] Even among professing Christians religion was rather of the lips than of the heart. The descendants of the Romans were imbued with some of their ancestors' scepticism; while those of the Goths cared so little for religious dogmas, that they transformed themselves from Arians to Catholics as soon as King Reccared had set the example. Distracted by other cares, the wealthy prelates of the Visigothic kingdom, who had to refute heretics, discuss doctrines and mysteries, govern the realm, and persecute the Jews, had no time to lose " in making themselves lowly with the lowly—whispering to them the first words of truth, as a father delights in prattling with his child," to use S. Augustine's words: while compelling folk to accept Christianity, they had not made them love it. It is therefore scarcely strange that the serfs could not resist temptation when the conquerors offered them freedom on condition that they became Moslems. Some of these luckless people were still pagans; the rest knew so little of Christianity, and the religious education which they had received was so elementary, or so futile, that Catholic and Mohammedan mysteries were to them equally impenetrable;[2] but what they knew and understood only too well was that the priests had cruelly disappointed the hopes of

---

[1] *Cf.* Art II. of the Acts of the Sixteenth Council of Toledo (A.D. 693). At the end of the sixth century Masonius, Bp. of Merida, converted many pagans. *Esp. sagr.*, xiii. 358.

[2] The inhabitants of the Alpuxarras in the seventeenth century, though styled "Old Christians," and of pure Spanish blood, were almost wholly ignorant of Christianity. Pedraça, *Hist. ecles. de Granada*, f. 95.

manumission which they had themselves once inspired, and they longed to throw off, at all costs, the yoke under which they groaned. They were not, however, the only class to abandon their former faith. Many nobles did the like, either to escape the poll-tax, or to preserve their property when the Arabs violated treaties—or even because they sincerely believed in the divine origin of Islamism.

Thus far we have described only the benefits conferred upon the social condition of the country by the Arab conquest; but it is just to add that in some relations the invasion had ill effects. Religion, for instance, was free, but the Church was not: she was on the contrary subjected to shameful and grievous servitude. The right of summoning Councils, as well as that of appointing and deposing bishops, passed from the Visigothic kings[1] to the Arab Sultans[2]—just as in the North it had passed to the kings of the Asturias,[3] and this fatal right, entrusted to enemies of Christianity, proved an inexhaustible source of evil, shame, and scandal to the Church. The Sultans supplied the places of absent bishops, at such Councils, with Jews and Moslems. They sold the office of bishop to the highest bidder, so that Christians had to confide their dearest and most sacred interests to heretics—to libertines who even during the solemn festivals of the Church joined in the orgies of Arab courtiers—to sceptics who openly denied a future life, and to scoundrels who, not content with selling themselves, sold their flocks also. Upon one occasion the revenue officers complained that many Christians at Malaga contrived to avoid the poll-tax by concealing themselves. Thereupon Hostegesis, bishop of the diocese, promised to compile a complete list of tax-payers. He kept his word. During his annual circuit he begged all his diocesans to furnish him with their names, as well as those of their kinsfolk and friends; he wished—so he said—to inscribe them on a roll, so that he might be able to pray individually for each member of his flock. The Christians, who trusted their shepherd, fell into the trap. Henceforth not ·one of them eluded the poll-tax; thanks to the bishop's register, the collectors knew them to a man.

The Arabs, moreover, as their hold upon the country grew firmer, became less punctilious in the observance of

[1] Twelfth Council of Toledo, Art. 6.
[2] Pertz, *Mon. Germ. (Scriptores)*, iv. (*Vita Joh. Gorz.*, c. 129).
[3] Marina, *Ensayo*, ii. 5 *sq.*

treaties than they had been when their power was only growing. This change was brought home to the Cordovans. All the churches in that city had been destroyed except the cathedral, dedicated to S. Vincent, but the possession of this fane had been guaranteed to the Christians by treaty. For several years the treaty was observed ;[1] but when the population of Cordova was increased by the arrival of Syrian Arabs, the mosques did not provide sufficient accommodation for the new-comers, and the Syrians considered that it would be well for them to adopt the plan which had been carried out at Damascus, Emesa, and other towns in their own country, of appropriating half of the cathedral and using it as a mosque. The Government having approved of the scheme, the Christians were compelled to hand over half of the edifice. This was clearly an act of spoliation, as well as an infraction of the treaty. Some years later 'Abd-er-Rahmân I requested the Christians to sell him the other half. This they firmly refused to do, pointing out that if they did so they would not possess a single place of worship. 'Abd-er-Rahmân, however, insisted, and a bargain was struck, by which the Christians ceded their cathedral for a hundred thousand dinars,[2] but obtained permission to rebuild the churches which had been destroyed. 'Abd-er-Rahmân on this occasion acted equitably, but such was not always the case, for it was he who broke the treaty which Witica's sons had made with Târik, and which had been ratified by the Khalif. He confiscated the domains of Ardabast, one of these princes, on the bald pretext that they were too extensive for a Christian. Other treaties were modified, or abrogated, quite arbitrarily, so that in the ninth century scarcely any traces of them remained. Further, the Moslem divines taught that the Government ought to manifest its zeal for religion by raising the assessment of the tribute exacted from the Christians, and so many extraordinary imposts were levied upon them that in the ninth century the Christians in many cities, including Cordova, were ruined or impoverished.[3] In other words, that happened in Spain which happened in every other country conquered by the Arabs ; their rule, at first mild and humane, degenerated into intolerable despotism. From

---

[1] The church was in possession of the Christians in A.D. 747.

[2] About £440,000 present value.

[3] On one occasion a special contribution of 100,000 dinars was levied on the Cordovan Christians.

the ninth century onwards, the conquerors of the Peninsula
followed to the letter the Khalif 'Omar's blunt advice:
" We must *devour* the Christians ; and our descendants
must devour theirs, so long as Islam endures." It was not,
however, the Christians who complained most bitterly of
the Arab domination a century after the conquest. The
most discontented class were the Renegades—called by the
Arabs *Muwalladûn*, " the adopted." The Renegades did
not all hold the same views. Some of them were of the
class called " secret Christians " [1]—that is to say, men who
bitterly repented of their apostasy. These were indeed
miserable, for they could never return to the fold. On
this point the law of Islam is inexorable. Once the Renegade pronounced the Moslem profession of faith, he was a
Moslem for ever, however importunate the cries of his
conscience. It mattered not whether the fateful words were
spoken in a moment of anger, of weakness, or of distress—
when money was lacking for the poll-tax, or under fear
of a degrading punishment at the sentence of a Christian
judge—in any case apostasy from Islam was death. The
descendants of Renegades, who wished to return to the pale
of the Church, were in a yet sorrier plight—for they suffered
for the fault of an ancestor. The law declared them Moslems
because they were the children of a Moslem ; and they, too,
would forfeit their lives if they denied Mohammed. Islam
claimed them in their cradles and followed them to their
graves. It was, therefore, quite natural that the repentant
Renegades murmured : but they were in the minority ; the
greater number were sincere Islamites. And yet the latter
had their grievances also. At first blush this seems strange.
Most of the Renegades were freedmen, and were therefore
men whose lot had been ameliorated by the conquest ; how
then did it happen that they were disaffected towards the
Arabs ? The answer is simple. " History abounds with
such instances," says De Tocqueville ; " Revolutions are
not always caused by matters going from bad to worse.
They more frequently break out when a nation which has
endured uncomplainingly the most onerous laws, suddenly
rebels against them when the load is lightened." It must
be added that the social position of the Renegades was
intolerable. The Arabs usually excluded them from lucrative posts and all offices under Government ; they pretended

---

[1] " Christiani occulti." Eulog., *Mem. Sanct.*, lib. ii.

to doubt the sincerity of their conversion; they treated them with unbridled insolence; since the seal of servitude was still imprinted on many of the recently manumitted, they branded converts indiscriminately with the name of slave, or son of a slave,[1] although among them were included some of the noblest and wealthiest landowners in the country. The Renegades did not tamely endure this treatment. They were conscious of their dignity, and of the material force at their back; for they formed the majority of the population. They would not admit that power was the exclusive appanage of an isolated caste; they would accept no longer a position of constraint and social inferiority, nor endure the disdainful insolence and domination of what were, after all, mere bands of foreign soldiers in scattered cantonments. They therefore took up arms and threw themselves boldly into the struggle. The revolt of the Renegades, in which the Christians took part to the best of their ability, assumed a diversity of forms which might have been anticipated at a period characterised by heterogeneity of conditions. Each province, each important city, broke out into insurrection independently, and at different times; and that this fact made the struggle but the fiercer and more obstinate the sequel will make manifest.

---

[1] It is remarkable that the Arabs never applied these epithets to Christians. See *Notices*, pp. 258–9.

[AUTHORITIES: Ibn al-Kûtiyya, ff. 4, 15; Ibn 'Adhârî, ii. pp. 11, 114, 244–5, 273; Makkarî, i. 359, 368; ii. 1, 17; Sams., *Apol.*, ii. 2–5, 8; Alvar., *Ep.*, xiii. 3; Ibn Batûta, i. 198; *Akhbâr majmûʻat*, f. 74; Istakhrî, p. 33; Al-Basrî, p. 124.]

CHAPTER III

THE DAY OF THE FOSSE

IN the Sultan's Capital the Renegades—including the descendants of those strictly so called—were numerous. They consisted for the most part of freedmen, who cultivated land which they had purchased, or worked as day-labourers on the domains of the Arabs. Strong, industrious, and thrifty, they seem to have been fairly well off, since most of them lived in the southern suburb,[1] one of the best quarters of the city; but they succumbed to revolutionary passions, and in the reign of Hakam I they were to be led by ambitious theologians into an insurrection which ended in a terrible catastrophe.

'Abd-er-Rahmân I had been too jealous of his authority to allow the Fakihs[2] to acquire an influence which would thwart his despotic measures; but under the reign of Hishâm, his son and successor, their influence considerably increased. Hishâm was a sincerely religious prince, and a model of virtue. When he came to the throne, his subjects were uncertain whether he would incline to good or to evil if the alternatives were presented to him, for he had shown that while he could be kindly and generous, he could also, upon occasion, be vindictive and cruel. But uncertainty on this head was soon set at rest. An astrologer having predicted the young sovereign's early death, Hishâm abjured all worldly pleasures, and sought his own salvation by works of charity. Clad in the simplest garb, he would wander alone through the streets of the Capital, mingle with the people, visit the sick, enter the hovels of the poor, and with tender solicitude interest himself in every detail of their woes and necessities. Often at dead of the night, in drenching rain, he would steal from his palace with food for some pious sufferer, and watch beside his lonely pallet. Punctual in the performance of his religious duties, he encouraged his subjects

---

[1] Formerly Secunda.

[2] *Fakîh* (theologian) as opposed to *fakîr* (dervish); the former being one of an official hierarchy allied to the Government, while the latter, whose name literally means "poor man," found their chief support among the poor.

to follow his example, and on stormy nights he would distribute money among those who attended the mosques undeterred by foul weather.

Just at this epoch a new school of theologians had arisen in the East. It acknowledged for its head a famous Imâm, Mâlik ibn Anas, of Medina, the founder of one of the four orthodox sects of Islam.[1] For this Imâm Hishâm conceived profound veneration. On the other hand, his rulers, the 'Abbâsids, had incurred Mâlik's mortal hatred, since, on the charge that he had given the support of his renowned name to an 'Alid pretender, he had been bastinadoed and his arm had been dislocated. Mâlik was therefore prejudiced in favour of the Emir of Spain, as the opponent of his torturers, even before he was made aware how eminently that monarch merited his esteem ; but when his disciples sang the praises of Hishâm's piety and virtues, the Imâm's admiration and enthusiasm knew no bounds : in Hishâm he saw the ideal of a Moslem prince, and he proclaimed him alone worthy of sitting on the Khalifs' throne. On their return to Spain the students did not fail to inform their sovereign of the warm esteem evinced for him by Mâlik, and Hishâm, highly flattered, did all he could to spread the Imâm's tenets in Spain. He encouraged theological students to make a journey to Medina in order to study there, and in selecting judges and ecclesiastics he always gave the preference to Mâlik's disciples.

When Hishâm died (A.D. 796), the new school of theology was therefore held in high respect. It could boast of many young, able, and ambitious adherents, among whom was the Berber Yahyâ ibn Yahyâ.[2] Never had Mâlik met with so assiduous and zealous a pupil. Once as the Imâm was lecturing, an elephant passed along the street. The students rushed out of the hall to get a closer view of the strange beast; Yahyâ alone remained in his place, to the great surprise of the venerable lecturer, who was not in the least annoyed at being deserted for the mightiest of quadrupeds. " Why do you not go out with the rest ? " he asked mildly ; " there are no elephants in Spain." " I left my country to see you, and profit by your teachings," replied Yahyâ, " and not to gaze at an elephant ! " So

---

[1] Born A.D. 715. His *Kitâb al-Muwatta'* is the earliest authority on Mohammedan law. Hârûn al-Rashid was Mâlik's pupil. Algeria is Mâlikite to the present day. See C. Huart, *Arabic Literature* (1903), p. 236.

[2] Of the tribe of Masmûda, client of the Arab tribe of Beni 'l-Laith ; his grandfather had accompanied Tàrik.

pleased was Mâlik with this reply that he dubbed Yahyâ the *âkil*[1] of Spain. At Cordova Yahyâ's reputation was of the highest, and he was regarded as the most learned theologian in the country. But to his great knowledge he joined a greater pride, and this extraordinary man added to the zeal of a modern demagogue a mediæval pope's thirst for power.

The new monarch's character was antipathetic to Yahyâ and the other followers of Mâlik. And yet Hakam was not irreligious. Brought up by a pious client of his grandfather, who had made pilgrimage to Mecca, he had early learned to honour religion and its ministers. He took pleasure in conversing with theologians, and he held the Kadies in the greatest respect, even when they pronounced judgment against his relatives, his intimate friends, or himself. But being of a gay and sociable disposition, and well fitted to drink life to the lees, for him the ascetic ideal of the Fakihs had no charm. In spite of their repeated remonstrances, he fostered a passionate love of the chase, a diversion which was by no means to their taste, and, what was worse, he regarded the prohibition of wine as null and void. All these faults they might, however, have pardoned ; but what they could not forgive was that, jealous of his own authority, he refused to grant them in public affairs an influence as commanding as they desired. It seemed that he either could not, or would not, realize, that the Fakihs—united closely by the new bond of Mâlikism— henceforth constituted a power in the State with which the sovereign would be obliged to reckon.

Disappointed in their hopes, and full of that priestly pride which is all the more inflexible when hidden under a cloak of humility, the theologians degenerated into demagogues. Unsparing of calumnious rhetoric, they never referred to their sovereign without horror, and ordered prayers to be offered for his conversion, such as follows: " O profligate, who persistest in thy wickedness, who despisest the commandments of thy Lord, save thyself from the debauchery in which thou art plunged, and arouse thyself from thy sinful apathy ! " Prejudiced as they were, the Renegades of Cordova were readily moulded in accordance with the theologians' wishes. They began by praying for the hardened sinner, and one day as he was walking in

---

[1] Subtle, sagacious man.

the streets of the Capital they threw stones at him; but the monarch and his body-guard cut a way for themselves through the crowd with their swords, and the rising was quelled (A.D. 805).

Yahyâ, Îsâ ibn Dînâr, and other theologians thereupon entered into a plot with a section of the nobility, and offered the throne to Ibn Shammâs, Hakam's first cousin. Ibn Shammâs replied that before agreeing to their proposals he must be informed of the names of those upon whom he could rely. The conspirators promised to draw up a list of their supporters, and fixed a date when they would come by night and deliver it to the prince. Thereupon Ibn Shammâs proceeded secretly to Hakam's palace and revealed the plot.

Having listened to him incredulously, the monarch indignantly exclaimed: "Thou wouldst stir up my wrath against the most respected men in my capital! By Allah, thou shalt prove the truth of thy words, or forfeit thine head!" "Be it so," replied Ibn Shammâs, "but send me a man in whom you trust, on the night I have named." Hakam consented, and at the hour appointed, his secretary, Ibn al-Khadâ, and his favourite page Hyacinth[1]—a Spanish Christian—proceeded to his cousin's house. After concealing the two visitors behind a curtain Ibn Shammâs summoned the conspirators. "And now let us learn," he said, "who those are upon whom you can rely." As the names of the accomplices were announced, Ibn al-Khadâ wrote them down. But the list included men who were ostensibly the most devoted adherents of the sovereign, and the secretary, dreading lest he should hear his own name, thought it prudent to reveal his presence by making his pen scratch the paper. At the sound the conspirators sprang to their feet in consternation, exclaiming to Ibn Shammâs, "Thou hast betrayed us, O enemy of God!" Many of them secured safety by instant flight. Among these was Îsâ ibn Dînâr, as well as Yahyâ, who sought refuge in Toledo, a city which had asserted its independence. Others, however, were less fortunate, and seventy-two conspirators, including six of the most prominent Cordovan nobles, fell into the hands of the Government, and were crucified.

Next year, A.D. 806, during Hakam's absence from the Capital for the purpose of quelling an insurrection at Merida,

---

[1] Ar. *Yazinto*, Sp. *Jacinto*. The Arabs, like the Romans, often named their slaves after precious stones.

the people of Cordova once more revolted. Matters had assumed a very alarming aspect, when the Sultan returned in hot haste, curbed the sedition, and beheaded or crucified the most dangerous demagogues.

If these wholesale executions were not enough to intimidate the Cordovans, the terrible fate which not long afterwards overtook the Toledans, showed them that Hakam—whose naturally mild disposition was becoming more and more embittered by the rebellious spirit of his subjects—recoiled neither from treachery nor massacre if he thought them necessary for the subjugation of rebels.

Toledo, the former capital of the Visigothic Kingdom, remained by virtue of its ancient fame, the learning of its priests, and the influence of its metropolitans, "the royal city" [1] in the eyes of the conquered people. They regarded it, both politically and ecclesiastically, as the most important town in Spain. It contained but few Arabs and Berbers within its walls, for the invaders had settled rather on the estates of the fugitive nobles in the surrounding country, than in the town itself. High-spirited and brave, the citizens were distinguished by so ardent a love of liberty that, in the opinion of an Arab chronicler, "never were the subjects of any monarch so unruly and seditious." The poet Gharbîb, who belonged to a renegade family, enjoyed vast popularity, and kept the sacred fire alive in his poems and discourses. The Sultan himself feared him. During Gharbîb's lifetime Hakam dared not take measures against Toledo; but on the poet's death, the Sultan confided to Amrûs—a Renegade of Huesca—his secret intentions with regard to the turbulent Toledans, adding: "You alone can help me to punish these rebels, since they would refuse to accept an Arab for their Governor, but would welcome you, as a man of their own race." He then unfolded his design; a horrible scheme which Amrûs entirely approved, and promised to carry out. The slave of his ambition, this man regarded neither religion nor morality. Desirous, just then, of the Sultan's support, he was ready to sacrifice his fellow-countrymen; later on, seduced by the idea of founding a principality under Frankish protection, he was to betray the Sultan to the son of Charlemagne.[2]

Hakam appointed Amrûs Governor of Toledo (A.D. 807), and at the same time sent a missive to the citizens: "By an

---

[1] *Urbs regia*, Isidore of Beja, c. 49; *Medina-al-Molûk*, Kazwinî, ii. 366.
[2] See M. Bouquet, *Recueil des Historiens des Gaules, &c.* (1744), v. 58–60.

act of condescension which manifests our extreme solicitude for your interests"—thus it ran—"instead of sending you one of our own clients, we have chosen for your Governor one of your compatriots." Amrûs, for his part, omitted no means of gaining the confidence and esteem of the populace. Feigning a warm attachment to the national cause, he lost no opportunity of avowing his implacable hatred of the Sultan, the Omayyads, and the Arabs in general, and when he felt secure of popular favour, he said to the notables of the city: " I am well aware of the cause of the disastrous disputes which have so frequently arisen between yourselves and your Governors; I know that the soldiers quartered in your homes have often disturbed the peace of your households, and have been a fertile source of brawls. Such quarrels can be averted if you will permit me to build at one end of the city a castle to serve as a barrack for the troops: you will thus be relieved from their vexations."

Trusting implicitly in their fellow-countryman, the Toledans not only fell in with his suggestion, but expressed a wish that the castle should be built in the midst of the city rather than in the outskirts. When the stronghold was complete, Amrûs installed his troops in it, and sent word to Hakam, who lost no time in ordering one of the generals on the frontier to call for reinforcements, on the pretext that the enemy threatened an advance. The general obeyed his instructions, and troops from Cordova and other towns set out under the command of three Viziers and the Crown Prince 'Abd-er-Rahmân, then scarcely fourteen years old. One of the lieutenant-generals was entrusted with a letter —not to be handed to the Viziers until they were received in audience by Amrûs.

Upon reaching the neighbourhood of Toledo the army was informed that the enemy had retired; thereupon Amrûs hinted to the nobles of the city that as an act of courtesy they ought to accompany him and pay their respects to the Crown Prince. This they did; but while the young prince conversed with them, and strove to ingratiate himself by treating them with great cordiality, Amrûs had a private interview with the Viziers, to whom the Sultan's letter had just been handed. In this missive detailed instructions were laid down, of which the sequel will show the tenour, since Hakam's orders were executed with the utmost precision.

On rejoining the nobles of Toledo, Amrûs found them

delighted with 'Abd-er-Rahmân's urbanity. "Of a truth," said one of them, " it would do our city high honour if the Prince would favour us with his presence for a few days. His visit would doubtless tend to strengthen and draw closer the friendly bonds which already unite us." The suggestion met with universal approval. The horizon seemed cloudless; the Sultan had sent a Spaniard to be their Governor; he had granted them the liberty which they had long demanded; and the gracious demeanour of 'Abd-er-Rahmân led them to hope that upon his succession to the throne he would follow in his father's footsteps. The nobles accordingly begged the Prince to honour the city with his presence. 'Abd-er-Rahmân at first demurred, for his father had counselled him not to display too much eagerness; but, at last, feigning to yield to the solicitations of the Toledans, he suffered himself to be conducted within the walls of the castle, and immediately ordered preparations to be made for a banquet on the morrow. Invitations to the feast were forthwith sent to all persons, both in the city and its environs, who were distinguished either by their high birth or their wealth.

Next morning the guests thronged to the fortress. They were not allowed to enter in a body, but were admitted one by one, while their horses were led away to the postern-door to await their masters. Now in the courtyard there was a great trench, whence the clay used in the construction of the castle had been dug. Beside this trench stood executioners, and as each guest entered, the sword fell.[1] For several hours this horrible butchery continued, and it is impossible to ascertain the number of the victims who perished on that fatal day, henceforth known as the " Day of the Fosse"; according to some historians they amounted to seven hundred, and according to others, to more than five thousand.

The sun was high in the heavens when a physician, who had seen none of the visitors quitting the castle by either gate, felt misgivings, and inquired of the throng gathered before the principal entrance what had become of the guests who had arrived so long before. A bystander suggested that they might have departed by the other door. " It is strange," replied the physician; " I have waited patiently at the postern, and no one hath passed out." Then as his

---

[1] In A.D. 611, a Persian king, to avenge himself on the Temimites, adopted a similar plan. See Caussin, ii. pp. 576–8.

glance fell on a haze which hung above the ramparts, he cried: "Woe is me! That reek ascendeth not from the baked meats of the feast, but from the blood of your murdered brethren!"

A blank stupor fell upon Toledo, deprived thus, at a blow, of all her wealthiest and noblest citizens, and no avenger of the Day of the Fosse was found within her walls.

[AUTHORITIES: *Akhbâr majmû'at*, 99–102; Ibn al-Kûtiyya, ff. 15–21; Makkarî, i. 491, 899; ii. 154; Nuwairî, pp. 450–2; Ibn al-Khatîb, (MS. P.), ff. 213–14; 'Abd al-Wâhid, 12–13; Ibn Khallikân, i. 615, 655 (ed. Slane); fasc. x. 19–21 (ed. Wüstenfeld); Isid., cc. 49, 62, 69, 77; Ibn Khaldûn, ff. 6–7; *Kartâs*, p. 23; Ibn Adhârî, ii. 68–80.]

CHAPTER IV

HAKAM I

THE massacre of the Day of the Fosse made so strong an impression on the Renegades of Cordova that they remained tranquil for seven years; but at the end of that time the lesson taught by the tragedy seems to have been forgotten—especially since Toledo had again thrown off the yoke. In the Capital, the Renegades and the Fakihs, who daily formed a closer alliance and mutually encouraged one another, grew restive under their master's whip. The Sultan seemed bent upon convincing them that a revolt was impracticable. He surrounded the city with fortifications which commanded it, and continually increased the number of his mounted body-guard—who went by the name of *Mutes*, since they were negroes or other foreign slaves, who could not speak a word of Arabic. But such measures were rather provocative than coercive. The hatred felt by the malcontents grew more manifest in words and deeds, especially in the southern suburb, which contained no fewer than four thousand theological teachers and students. Woe to the soldiers who ventured singly or in small bodies into its narrow winding streets! They were reviled, beaten, even murdered without pity. The monarch himself was insulted. When the muezzin proclaimed the hour of prayer from the minaret, Hakam—whose duty it was to visit the Mosque and offer the customary supplication—would hear voices in the waiting crowd crying out: "Come to prayer, drunkard! Come to prayer!" Every day these cries were renewed, and the authorities in vain sought for those who uttered them; they were never to be found. Once, in the Mosque, a man of the lower orders went so far as to revile and threaten the Sultan to his face, and the crowd applauded the brawler. Hakam, who was both surprised and enraged that his royal dignity should meet with such gross affronts, caused ten of the ringleaders to be crucified, and reimposed the tithe on commodities which his father had abolished. But nothing could bend the pride

and stubbornness of the Cordovans. Demagogues continued
to inflame their passions; moreover Yahyâ returned to the
Capital, and by his sermons, and the magic of his fame, he
intensified as well as directed the movement. A crisis was
approaching, and an accident unexpectedly precipitated the
outbreak.

It was in the month of Ramadân (May 814),[1] and the
preachers were profiting by the fast to inflame the hatred of
the people against the Sultan, when a mameluke one day
requested an armourer in the southern suburb to polish his
sword. " Prithee, wait awhile," said the armourer, "just
now I am busied."   " I have no time to wait," replied the
soldier; " do this instant what I bid thee."   " Ah! dost
thou assume such airs ? " exclaimed the craftsman disdainfully; "thou shalt bide my leisure nevertheless."   " We
shall see ! " cried the trooper; and with one blow of his
sword he stretched the armourer dead at his feet.

The bystanders, infuriated at the sight, cried out that
the time had come for making an end of these insolent
troopers and the debauched tyrant who hired them. The
revolutionary enthusiasm soon spread to the other suburbs,
and a vast crowd hastily armed themselves with all the
weapons they could lay their hands on and marched towards
the palace loudly execrating the monarch's soldiers, clients,
and slaves, who knowing that they could hope for no quarter
if they fell into the hands of the insurgents, fled before
them to seek refuge within the walls of the Sultan's palace.

When from the battlements Hakam saw the multitude
surging onwards like the waves of an angry sea, roaring
with tempestuous fury, he thought that they might yet be
repulsed by a vigorous onslaught, and immediately ordered
his cavalry to charge; but, to his great disappointment,
the mob, far from giving way as he had hoped, firmly
sustained the shock and forced the troopers to retreat.

The peril was extreme. The palace, though fortified,
was not strong enough to hold out for long against the
attack of the insurgents. The defenders, though valiant,
knowing that they would be ruthlessly massacred if the
assailants effected an entrance, yielded to despair. Hakam

---

[1] The Arab chroniclers are strangely at variance on this important date, some
placing the insurrection in A.H. 198 and others in A.H. 202: those who adopt the
latter date are, however, inconsistent. Ibn al-'Abbâr and Ibn Adhârî, e.g., say that
many rebels sought refuge in Toledo, "then in rebellion against Hakam"; but
this is not true for the later date. A.H. 198 is supported by Nuwairî, Ibn al-Kûtiyya,
and Makrîzî.

alone, though he also had lost hope of successful resistance, remained perfectly cool. Summoning his Christian page, Hyacinth, he ordered him to ask one of the ladies of the harem for a phial of civet. Thinking that he must have misunderstood his master's words, the page stood irresolute. Hakam impatiently repeated the order: "Begone, son of an uncircumcised father," he added, "and do quickly what I bid thee!" When Hyacinth returned with the phial, the Sultan took it and proceeded to anoint his hair and beard as calmly as though he were making ready to pay his addresses to some youthful beauty of his seraglio. Hyacinth could not repress an exclamation of astonishment: "Forgive me, my lord," he said; "but you choose a strange moment for perfuming yourself. See you not the danger which threatens us?" "Silence, rascal!" cried Hakam, once more losing patience; but when he had completed his toilette he added: "How could my head be recognised among the rest by the rebels, if it were not distinguished by the perfume it exhales? And now you may bid Hodair come hither to me."

Hodair was officer of the guard at the prison of the Rotonda, in which lay many Fakihs who had been implicated in previous outbreaks. The lives of these men had thus far been spared, but now—seeing clearly that the Fakihs and the populace aimed at his life as well as his throne—Hakam determined that the prisoners should not survive him. Accordingly, when Hodair entered the gallery, the Sultan said to him: "At nightfall fetch these vile sheiks out of the Rotonda, behead them, and nail them to stakes." Knowing that if the palace were taken by assault he would undoubtedly fall a victim, and must then render an account to God for all his deeds, Hodair shuddered with horror at the idea of the sacrilege contemplated by his sovereign. "My lord," he replied, "I dread lest to-morrow we may both be in the dungeons of hell: in vain, then, will be our woeful cries; in vain shall we seek to succour each other!" Nettled by these words, Hakam repeated his orders more imperiously; but when he saw the officer's scruples were insuperable, he dismissed him, and sent for Ibn Nâdir, Hodair's colleague. Ibn Nâdir, who was less scrupulous—or more subservient—promised to execute faithfully his sovereign's orders. Hakam then descended from the terrace fully armed, and calmly inspected his troops, reviving their drooping courage with glowing words. Then summoning his cousin 'Obaidallah, one of the bravest warriors of the

time, he ordered him to place himself at the head of a band
of picked men, cut his way through the mob, and set fire to
the southern suburb.   He reckoned upon the inhabitants
of that quarter hurrying away to extinguish the flames as
soon as they saw their homes blazing.   While 'Obaidallah
attacked the mob in front, Hakam issuing from the palace
with the rest of his men, would assail them in the rear.
This plan, which seemed to yield fair promise of success,
resembled that to which Moslim's victory at Harra had been
due—a fact which has not escaped Arab chroniclers.

Sallying forth suddenly from the gateway of the palace,
'Obaidallah forced back the mob towards the bridge, charged
across the main street and the Ramla, forded the river, and,
joined by the soldiers of the Campiña—who had watched
Hakam's signals during the progress of the insurrection—
proceeded to set fire to the suburb.   As Hakam had foreseen,
the inhabitants of that quarter, when they saw the rising
flames, abandoned their position before the palace, and
hastened to save their wives and children ; a panic thereupon
seized the miserable crowd, simultaneously assailed in front
and rear, and what followed was merely a massacre.   In
vain did the Cordovans throw down their arms and cry for
quarter : terrible and inexorable, the " Mutes "—foreigners
to whom the prayers of the vanquished were meaningless—
slew them in heaps, sparing only some three hundred persons
of distinction.   These they presented, as an act of homage,
to the sovereign, who ordered the prisoners to be nailed,
head downwards, to stakes upon the river-bank.

Hakam then consulted his Viziers as to whether he
should pardon the insurgents who had escaped death, or
hunt them down and exterminate them to the last man.
Opinions were divided, but Hakam leaned to the views of
the more moderate section, who advised him not to push his
vengeance to extremities.   It was, however, decided that
the southern suburb should be razed to the ground, and that
its inhabitants should be ordered to quit Spain within three
days, on pain of crucifixion if they delayed beyond that
period.

Carrying with them the scant remnants of their property,
these unhappy folk, with their families, left the homes in
which they had been born and which they would never re-
visit.   Journeying in small parties—for they had not been
allowed to depart in a body—many of them were stripped
on the way by bands of soldiers, or brigands lying in wait in

ravines and behind rocks. When they reached the shores
of the Mediterranean they embarked—some for the West of
Africa and some for Egypt. The latter, to the number of
fifteen thousand, exclusive of women and children, landed near
Alexandria without experiencing any opposition from the
Government—for Egypt, in chronic rebellion against the
'Abbâsids, was at that time a prey to anarchy.

The exiles seemed to have no alternative to forming an
alliance with the most powerful Arab tribe in the country.
This they did; but not long afterwards, feeling themselves
strong enough to dispense with the protection of these
Bedawin, they broke with them, and in the war which ensued were victorious in a pitched battle. The exiles then
made themselves masters of Alexandria. In spite of several
attacks they held this city until A.D. 826, when one of the
Khalif Ma'mûn's generals forced them to capitulate. Thereupon they decided to migrate to Crete, a part of which still
belonged to the Byzantine Empire. They conquered the
island, and their leader, Abû Hafs 'Omar al-Ballûti (a
native of Fahs al-Ballût, now Campo de Calatrava), became
founder of a dynasty which endured until A.D. 961, when
Crete was conquered by the Greeks.[1]

The other band of Cordovans, consisting of some eight
thousand families, experienced less difficulty in finding a
new home. At the time of their expulsion, Prince Idrîs[2]
was engaged in building a new capital—to be known as
Fez—and since his subjects, who were for the most part
nomads, showed an invincible repugnance to becoming
citizens, he endeavoured to attract foreigners. The exiles
were therefore readily accorded permission to settle in the
city; but it was at the price of ceaseless conflict. An Arab
colony from Kairwan was already established in Fez. These
Arabs and the descendants of the Celto-Romans conceived
an instinctive hatred of one another, and although settlers
in the same land, the two peoples held themselves so obstinately apart, that as late as the fourteenth century the facial
characteristics of the two races were easily distinguishable.
Their tastes, their occupations, their customs were diametri-
cally opposed, and they seemed destined to maintain permanently their racial antipathies. The Arabs were craftsmen
or traders; the Andalusians were farmers. The latter earned
a bare subsistence, the former gained enough and to spare.

---

[1] *Cf.* Quatremère, *Mem. sur l'Egypte,* i.
[2] Great-grandson of the Khalif 'Ali.

In the eyes of the Arab—who loved good cheer, personal adornment, and general refinement—the Andalusian was an uncouth, niggardly churl. On the other hand, the Andalusian—either because he was really content with the monotonous rusticity to which he had been accustomed, or because he concealed under an affected disdain the envy with which his neighbour's wealth inspired him—looked upon the Arab as a fop who wasted his substance on frivolity. Anticipating that quarrels and disputes might break out between the two colonies, Prince Idrîs kept them apart, and assigned to each a walled quarter with its own mosque, bazaar, and mint; but, notwithstanding this precaution, the Arabs and Spaniards lived for several centuries in a state of sometimes stifled, but usually open hostility, and many a time a plot of neutral ground, beside the river which divided the two quarters, was the scene of their affrays.[1]

While the Cordovans, after having seen their fathers, wives, and children slain, were expiating their act of insurrection in exile, the Fakihs, though much more culpable, were pardoned. The revolt had hardly been quelled before Hakam gave them proofs of his clemency. When the order had gone forth to arrest and execute those suspected of having stirred up the rebellion, even if they had not openly joined in it, the police discovered a Fakih, in hiding, in the harem of a magistrate who was his kinsman. The Fakih was on the point of being slain, when the Kady, attracted by the outcries of his wives, rushed in to rescue him; but in vain did he endeavour to procure his kinsman's release by declaring that he had been illegally arrested; the agents replied brusquely that they had received peremptory orders and were going to carry them out. The Kady then hurried to the palace, and, having been accorded an audience, said : " My lord, the Prophet showed mercy to the Kurashites who fought against him, for he pardoned them and loaded them with kindnesses. Thou who art of his family ought above all men to follow his example." He then related what had taken place, and the monarch, touched by his entreaties, not only released the prisoner in question, but proclaimed an amnesty to the other Fakihs, most of whom had sought refuge in Toledo. Their property was restored to them, and they were permitted to settle any-

---

[1] *Notices et Extraits*, xii. pp. 574-7.

where in Spain—except in, or near, Cordova. Even Yahyâ, who had found shelter among a Berber tribe, was pardoned, and having further been permitted to return to court, was once more received into the monarch's favour. Nevertheless, certain persons were excluded from the amnesty. Among these was Tâlhût, an Arab of the tribe of Moâfir. This disciple of Mâlik, who was conspicuous as one of the boldest of the demagogues, lay concealed in the house of a Jew; but at the end of a year, weary of his voluntary confinement —which the Jew had done his best to make as agreeable as possible—he said to his host: "I purpose quitting your house to-morrow, though I have found within its walls a hospitality which I shall never forget. I shall go to my former pupil, the Vizier Abu 'l-Bassâm, who, I understand, has much influence at court. He is under some obligation to me, and perchance he will intercede for me with *that man.*" "My lord," replied the Jew, "trust not in a courtier, lest peradventure he betray you. But if a fear of becoming a burden to me has led you to think of leaving me, I swear that were you to abide here as long as you live you would not discommode my household." In spite of the Jew's entreaties, Tâlhût persisted in his design, and next day, at dusk, he gained the Vizier's palace without detection.

Abu 'l-Bassâm was greatly astonished at the entrance of the outlaw whom he believed to be a hundred leagues from Cordova. "Welcome!" he exclaimed, as he bade Tâlhût sit by his side; "but whence comest thou, and where hast thou been these many days?" The Fakih described how devotedly the Jew had harboured him, and added: "And now I have come to beg you to intercede for me with *that man.*" "Be well assured," replied the Vizier, "that I will do my best to gain pardon for thee. This will not be a difficult task, for the Sultan repents him of his severity. Lie to-night in my house, and to-morrow I will seek the Prince."

Wholly reassured by these words, Tâlhût that night slept the sleep of the just. Little did he suspect that his host, who had so warmly welcomed him, and had by his confidence taken such a load from his heart, was all the time meditating his betrayal to the Prince. Such, however, was the resolve which this crafty and treacherous man had formed when he reached the palace on the morrow, after having taken the necessary steps to render the escape of the Fakih impossible. "What thinkest thou," he asked the Prince with a malicious smile, "of a fat ram which hath been a whole year in the pen?" Hakam, thinking only of the literal import of the Vizier's words, replied gravely: "Such gross meat is unwholesome; to my taste the flesh of an animal that feedeth at large is lighter and more nourishing." "That is not my meaning," replied the Vizier; "but I have Tâlhût safe in my house." "Of a truth? And how came he to fall into your hands?" "By the aid of a few words of welcome."

Hakam thereupon ordered Tâlhût to be brought to him. The Fakih, as he entered the hall where the monarch sat, trembled with fear. Hakam, however, showed no signs of anger, and said in a tone of mild reproach: "Speak the truth, Tâlhût; if thy father or thy son had occupied my throne would they have granted you higher honours or more favours than I have? When didst thou implore my aid for thyself or for others and I did not strive to give thee satisfaction? How often when thou wert sick did I not visit thee? When thy wife died did I not meet thee at the door of thy house? Did I not follow on foot her funeral? After the ceremony did I not return with thee? And this was my reward! Thou soughtest to besmirch my honour—to profane my majesty—ay, and to shed my blood!"

The Sultan's words reassured Tâlhût, and, convinced that his life was in no danger, his habitual self-confidence and insolence returned. Hakam believed that he had touched his heart; but Tâlhût, quite unmoved, and too proud to confess his guilt and ingratitude, replied with haughty abruptness: "I cannot do better than tell the truth: in hating thee I obeyed God; thereafter all thy good offices were useless."

At these words, which sounded like a challenge, Hakam could not repress a start of anger; but immediately mastering his wrath, he replied calmly: "When I commanded thee to be brought hither, I reviewed in my mind all kinds of torture, in order to choose the most cruel; but now I say to thee: He who bade thee, as thou pretendest, to hate me, commandeth me to pardon thee. Depart—and may God shield thee! So long as I live, I swear by the Almighty that thou shalt be held in honour, as heretofore. Would to God," he added with a sigh, "that the past had never been!"

Was it possible to tell the theologian more delicately and more gently that God never commands men to hate? Tâlhût, however, pretended that he did not understand the

R

lesson administered; perhaps, indeed, pride was so deeply
ingrained in his iron heart that he could not understand it.
No word of gratitude fell from his lips; he replied only to
the prince's last words: "If the past had never been," he
said, "it had been better for thee!" This was to threaten
the monarch with awful punishment in a future life; but
Hakam, who was convinced that right was on his side
rather than on the Fakih's, with an effort preserved his self-
possession, and feigning not to have heard Tâlhût's words,
inquired where Abu 'l-Bassâm arrested him. "He did not
arrest me," replied Tâlhût; "I voluntarily placed myself in
his power. I came to him in the name of the friendship
which formerly united us." "And where hast thou dwelt
for the past year?" "With a Jew, in this city." Then,
turning to Abu 'l-Bassâm, who had been a silent auditor of
this conversation, Hakam exclaimed in profound indignation:
"It was a Jew, then, who honoured piety and learning in a
man of an alien religion! He did not fear, in affording him
shelter, to expose to my anger his own person, his wife, his
children, his fortune! But as for thee, thou desirest to drag
me once more into the excesses which I repent. Begone!
and henceforth never let thy presence pollute my sight!"

The treacherous Vizier was disgraced. Tâlhût, on the
other hand, ceased not until the day of his death to enjoy
the favour of the Sultan, who honoured the Fakih's funeral
by his presence.[1]

Hakam, as we have seen, though as ruthless towards the
artisans of the suburb as towards the citizens of Toledo, was
merciful to the divines. But the Fakihs were Arabs or
Berbers. Hakam, true Arab as he was, used weights and
measures of two kinds. Against the vanquished inhabitants
of the country, whom he utterly despised, he thought limitless severity permissible if they ignored his authority; but
when dealing with rebels of his own race, he willingly
pardoned them. The Arab historians, it is true, have explained otherwise Hakam's clemency towards the Fakihs:
they attribute it to remorse of conscience. It need not be
denied that Hakam—who was cruel and violent at times,
but whose humaner sentiments always returned—may have
regretted as crimes some of the steps which he had taken in
moments of rage; such as his orders for the decapitation of

[1] Ibn al-Kûtiyya is responsible for this circumstantial narrative. The tradition
given in Makkari (i. 900) represents Talhût's character in a much less favourable
light.

the Fakihs imprisoned in the Rotonda: but it seems certain that the Omayyad clients, who in writing the annals of their patrons have made desperate efforts to rehabilitate the memory of a prince banished by the clergy to the depths of hell, have exaggerated his penitence. If we are to believe Hakam's own testimony, as given in the verses which he addressed to his son not long before his death, he was firmly convinced that he had the right to act as he did. With these verses we conclude the narrative of his reign:

"Just as a tailor useth his needle to sew together pieces of cloth, so I have used my sword to reunite my divided provinces; for since I came to years of discretion nothing hath been more hateful to me than a dismembered empire. Ask my frontiers if any place is in the power of the enemy; they will answer 'Nay!' but if they answered 'Yea!' thither would I fly clad in my cuirass, and sword in hand. Ask also the skulls of my rebellious subjects—which, like split gourds, lie upon the plain gleaming in the sunshine—they will tell you that I smote them again and again. Panic-stricken, the rebels fled for their lives, but I, ever at my post, scorned death. If I spared not their wives and children, it was because they threatened my family and myself: he who cannot avenge insults offered to his family is devoid of honour, and despised of all men. What if after the exchange of sword-thrusts I made them drink deadly poison? I did but repay the debt which they had compelled me to contract. Of a truth, if death overtook them, it was because destiny willed it.

"Peaceful then are the provinces which I hand down to thee, O my son! They are a couch on which thou mayst repose undisturbed: I have taken care that no rebellion shall break in upon thy sleep."

[AUTHORITIES: *Akhbár majmú'at*, ff. 103–4; Ibn Adhârî, ii. 73–4, 78–9, 81–2; Nuwairî, pp. 453–4, 456; Ibn Khaldûn, f. 7; iii. f. 44; iv. f. 6; Ibn al-'Abbâr, pp. 40–1; Ibn al-Kûtiyya, ff. 22–4; *Kartás*, pp. 21–3, 25, 70–1; Khoshanî, p. 250; Abd al-Wâhid, p. 14.]

CHAPTER V

'ABD-ER-RAHMÂN II

NEVER had the court of the Sultans of Spain been so brilliant as it became under the rule of 'Abd-er-Rahmân II, the son and successor of Hakam. Emulating the splendid prodigality of the Khalifs of Baghdad, the new Sultan surrounded himself with a numerous retinue, adorned his capital, constructed at great cost bridges, mosques, and palaces, and laid out spacious and beautiful gardens through which canals led the waters of mountain torrents. He was a lover of poetry, and if the verses which passed under his name were not always of his own composition, he at least rewarded handsomely his poetic collaborators. 'Abd-er-Rahmân was of a clement disposition, pliable and good-natured to a fault. Even though his servants robbed him before his eyes he did not punish them. Throughout his reign he suffered himself to be dominated by a theologian, a musician, a woman, and a eunuch. The theologian was the Berber Yahyâ, who, as we have seen, had been the chief instigator of the revolt against Hakam in the suburbs. The ill success of that attempt had convinced Yahyâ that he was pursuing a wrong policy, and he realized that the theologians, if they wished to become powerful, should, instead of showing hostility to the prince, acquire influence by ingratiating themselves with him. Although Yahyâ's haughty and imperious nature stooped with difficulty to the rôle which he deemed it desirable to play, his unceremoniousness, his bitter frankness, and his churlish bluntness did him little harm in the eyes of the easy-going Sultan, who, although a student of philosophy, had pious leanings, and looked upon the angry outbursts of the arrogant Doctor as displays of indignant virtue. 'Abd-er-Rahmân indeed tolerated Yahyâ's hectoring speeches and even his fits of ill-humour, submitted with docility to the disagreeable penances laid upon him by his severe confessor, bowed his head before the power of this religious tribune, and abandoned to him the government of the church, and the direction of the judicature. Respected by the prince, upheld by most of the theologians, by the middle class, who feared him, by the commonalty whose cause was identified with his own since the revolt, and even by certain poets—a class of men whose support was by no means to be disdained —Yahyâ enjoyed immense power. Nevertheless he occupied no definite official position; if he governed all within his sphere, it was by virtue of his reputation. At heart an autocrat, though formerly he had scouted despotism, he exercised it without scruple when circumstances called for it. The judges, if they wished to retain office, were obliged to become his unquestioning tools. The Sultan, who sometimes felt a transient desire to free himself from the ascendancy which Yahyâ had established over him, promised more than he could fulfil in undertaking to uphold the judiciary. Yahyâ crushed all who dared to resist him; and a hint from him usually sufficed to ensure the resignation of a recalcitrant Kady.

The influence of Ziryâb [1] the musician was no less power- ful, but it was exercised in another sphere. He came from Baghdad and was, it appears, of Persian origin. He had been a dependant of the 'Abbâsid Khalifs, and had learned music under the famous singer Ishâk al-Mawsilî. One day Hârûn al-Rashîd asked the latter if he had not some new performer to introduce. "I have a pupil who sings by no means badly," replied Ishâk, "thanks to the lessons which I have given him. I have reason to believe that some day he will do me credit." "Bid him appear before me," said the Khalif. Ziryâb had no sooner entered the presence than he won the regard of the prince by his courtly manners and witty conversation. Questioned by Hârûn as to his musical accomplishments, he replied: "I can sing as others do; but, beyond this, I possess an art unknown to all else. My own peculiar style is intended only for a connoisseur so accom- plished as your highness. If it is your pleasure, I will sing to you what no other ear has ever heard." The Khalif having assented, Ziryâb was handed his master's lute. He declined it, and called for an instrument of his own making. "Why dost thou refuse Ishâk's lute?" inquired the Khalif. "If your highness bids me sing after my master's method," re- plied Ziryâb, "I will accompany myself upon his lute; but to exhibit the method which I have invented, it is necessary

---

[1] Or Zaryâb; the surname of Abu 'l-hasan 'Ali ibn Nâfi.

to use my own."[1] Thereupon he explained the principle on which he had made the instrument, and proceeded to sing a song of his own composition. It was an ode in praise of Hârûn, and the Khalif was so delighted with it that he bitterly reproached Ishâk for not having sooner presented to him this marvellous singer. Ishâk excused himself by pleading, with perfect truth, that Ziryâb had carefully concealed his genius; and as soon as he found himself alone with his pupil he addressed him as follows : " Thou hast shamefully deceived me in thus shrouding thy talents ; I will be plain with thee, and will acknowledge that I am jealous of thee— as indeed artists of equal merit, and who cultivate the same art, always are of one another. Moreover thou hast pleased the Khalif, and I know that in a little while thou wouldst supplant me in his favour. This I could pardon in no man, not even in my own son ; and were it not that I have some affection left for thee as my pupil, I should not scruple to slay thee, come what might. Make choice between these alternatives : either depart, and take up thy abode far away from here, and swear that I shall never hear of thee again —in which case I, for my part, will provide thee with money to satisfy thy needs ; or, on the other hand, remain here in spite of me—but in that case I warn thee that I will risk my life and all that I possess to crush thee. Make choice ! " Ziryâb did not hesitate between the alternatives, but accepted the money Ishâk offered him and quitted Baghdad.

Some time later the Khalif commanded Ishâk again to introduce his pupil. " I regret that I am unable to gratify your highness's desire," replied the musician, "but the young man is possessed ; he confesses that the *jinn* converse with him, and inspire him with the melodies which he composes, while so vain is he of his talent that he believes he has no equal in the world. Since he was neither rewarded nor summoned again by your highness, he supposed that his gifts were not appreciated, and he has departed in a rage. Where he now is I know not ; but render thanks to the Eternal, my prince, that you are quit of this man, for he was subject to paroxysms of frenzy, and at such times he was horrible to look upon." The Khalif, though regretting the loss of the young musician who had inspired him with such great hopes, had to content himself with Ishâk's explanations. There was indeed a spice of truth in the old *maestro's* words : Ziryâb really believed that in his dreams

[1] Ziryâb's improvements consisted in the addition of a fifth string to the lute and the use of eagles' talons instead of wooden plectra.

he heard the songs of the *jinn*. Starting out of sleep, he would spring to the foot of his couch, and calling for Ghazzalan and Hîndah, two young inmates of his harem, he would bid them bring their lutes, and then teach them the air which he had heard during his sleep, while he wrote down the words himself. None knew better than Ishâk that there was no insanity in all this: what true artist, indeed, whether believing in *jinn* or not, has not known moments when he has been under the sway of emotions hard to define, and savouring of the supernatural?

Ziryâb set forth to seek his fortune in the West. Having reached Africa, he wrote to Hakam, the Sultan of Spain, to acquaint him with his desire to reside at his Court. So greatly pleased was the Prince with this letter, that in his reply he urged the musician to betake himself to Cordova with all speed, and promised him a handsome salary. Ziryâb accordingly crossed the Straits of Gibraltar with his wives and children; but scarcely had he landed at Algeciras when he heard of Hakam's death. In deep disappointment at this news, he had made up his mind to return to Africa, when the Jewish musician, Mansûr, whom Hakam had sent to meet him, prevailed upon him to abandon his intention, assuring him that 'Abd-er-Rahmân II loved music no less than did his father, and that he would doubtless recompense performers with equal liberality. The event showed that he was not mistaken. On being informed of Ziryâb's arrival, 'Abd-er-Rahmân wrote to him, inviting him to his Court, and commanded the local governors to treat him with the greatest respect; furthermore he provided him with mules, and sent him gifts by the hand of one of his chief eunuchs. On his arrival at Cordova, Ziryâb was installed in a splendid mansion. The Sultan allowed him three days in which to recover from the fatigues of his journey, and then invited him to the palace. 'Abd-er-Rahmân began the conversation by acquainting the musician with the terms upon which he was prepared to retain him at Cordova. These were magnificent: Ziryâb was to receive a fixed monthly pension of two hundred pieces of gold, as well as four gratuities every year, namely, a thousand pieces upon the occasion of each of the two great Mohammedan festivals,[1] five hundred at Midsummer,

---

[1] The Feast of Sacrifice ('Îdu 'l-Azhâ), or Great Festival, on the tenth day of Zû 'l-Hijjah; and the Festival of the Breaking of the Fast ('Îdu 'l-Fitr) on the first day of Shawwâl, when the fast of Ramadân ends. *Cf.* T. P. Hughes, *Dictionary of Islam*, 1885.

and a like sum on New Year's Day. Further, he was to receive yearly two hundred bushels of barley and one hundred of wheat, and finally he was to have the use of several mansions, with their fields and gardens, the capital value of which amounted to forty thousand pieces of gold. It was not until after he had informed the musician of his good fortune that 'Abd-er-Rahmân requested him to exhibit his art, and when Ziryâb had gratified his wish, the Sultan was so mightily enchanted with his skill that henceforth he would listen to no other singer. From that day the Sultan lived on terms of the closest intimacy with Ziryâb, and loved to converse with him upon history, poetry, and all the arts and sciences—for the mind of this astonishing musician was stored with extensive and varied knowledge. In addition to being an excellent poet, and knowing by heart the words and airs of ten thousand songs, he had studied astronomy and geography, and nothing could be more instructive than his discourses on the different countries of the world and the manners of their inhabitants. But what made an even greater impression than his vast knowledge was his wit, his good taste, and the incomparable distinction of his demeanour. No one was such a master of sparkling conversation, no one had such an instinct for the beautiful, and for many-sided virtuosity; no one was apparelled with such taste and elegance, never was there anyone who could arrange a fête or a banquet as he could. Ziryâb was, indeed, looked upon as a superior being, an ideal arbiter of fashion, and in this respect he became a lawgiver to the Arabs of Spain. The bold innovations which he introduced were innumerable: he revolutionised the customs of the people. Formerly hair was worn long and parted on the forehead: tables were laid with gold and silver vessels and spread with napery. Now, however, hair was trimmed low on the brow; glass goblets became the vogue, and table-coverings of leather,[1] for so Ziryâb decreed. He it was who defined the different garments suitable for the changing seasons,[2] and who first taught the Arabs of Spain that asparagus was an esculent not to be despised. Many of the dishes which he devised were named after him. In short, he was taken as a model in the smallest details of

---

[1] The Eng. transln. of *Makkarî* (ii. 120) gives a slightly different version of Ziryâb's innovations in these matters.

[2] They had been accustomed to wear white summer clothing from Midsummer to the end of Sept. only, and winter attire for the remaining nine months.

fashionable life, and by a fortune perhaps unique in the
annals of the world the name of this epicurean exquisite was
held in respect till the very end of the Mohammedan
dominion in Spain, linked with those of illustrious men of
science, poets, soldiers, ministers and princes.

Nevertheless, although Ziryâb had gained such an
ascendancy over 'Abd-er-Rahmân's mind that people
thought it well to address to the musician petitions which
they wished to reach the Sultan's ear, he never seems to
have meddled with politics to any great extent. He knew
the world too well not to be aware that to discuss affairs of
State, to intrigue, or to negotiate, while revelry was toward,
were all evidences of the worst possible taste. Such matters
he left to the Sultana Tarûb and the eunuch Nasr. Tarûb
was a cold and self-seeking woman, a born intriguer, and
consumed by a thirst for gold. She bartered, not her love
—for to such women that is unknown—but possession,
sometimes for a necklace of fabulous price, sometimes for
bags of money which her husband would place outside her
door when she refused to open it. Ruthless, covetous,
scheming, she was hand in glove with a man of like
character—the treacherous and cruel Nasr. The son of a
Spaniard who could not even speak Arabic, the eunuch
hated the devout Christians as only an apostate can. Such
then was the condition of the court of Cordova at this
period. As for the country, it was far from tranquil. In
the province of Murcia there had been a war, lasting for
seven years, between the Yemenites and the Ma'addites.
Merida was in a state of chronic revolt: the Christians of
this city were corresponding with Louis-le-Debonnaire and
scheming in concert with him.[1] Toledo was in a state of
insurrection, and in the neighbouring districts a veritable
jacquerie had been carried on.

A few years after the Day of the Fosse the Toledans had
recovered their independence and destroyed the castle of
Amrûs. In order to recapture this prize, Hakam had once
more resorted to a stratagem. Setting out from Cordova
under the pretext of making a raid in Catalonia, he pitched
his camp in the district of Murcia; then, learning through
his spies that the Toledans were so far from thinking themselves threatened that they even neglected to shut their
gates at night, he suddenly appeared before the walls, and

[1] For a letter from Louis to the Christians of Merida, see *España sagrada*,
xiii. 416.

finding a portal open, he became master of the city without striking a blow. He proceeded to set fire to all the houses in the upper part of the town. Among these houses there was one belonging to a young Renegade, Hâshim by name. This man made his way to Cordova in a state of utter destitution. To gain a livelihood he worked as a blacksmith; and a little later, burning with the desire of avenging his private wrongs as well as those of his fellow-citizens, he entered into a conspiracy with the artisans of Toledo, and quitted Cordova to return to his native town, where he placed himself at the head of the populace, and drove out the soldiers and adherents of 'Abd-er-Rahmân II (829). Hâshim then began to overrun the country with his band, pillaging and burning villages in which dwelt Arabs or Berbers. The marauders rapidly grew more formidable; artisans, peasants, slaves, adventurers of every kind flocked from all sides to swell their ranks. By 'Abd-er-Rahmân's order, the Governor of the Frontier, Mohammed ibn Wasîm, sent a body of troops against them, but the soldiers were repulsed, and for a whole year the blacksmith carried on his devastations with impunity. At last, the Governor, who had received reinforcements and who had been sternly rebuked by the Sultan for his inactivity, resumed the offensive, this time with greater success. After a conflict which lasted for several days, the band lost its chief, and was dispersed.

Toledo, however, was still unsubdued. In the year 834, the Sultan ordered Prince Omayya to lay siege to the town; but the Toledans repulsed the attack of this general so successfully, that Omayya, after having ravaged the surrounding country, was obliged to raise the siege and return to Cordova. The Toledans, when they saw the enemy's army retiring, resolved to harass it during its retreat; but Omayya had left at Calatrava a body of men under the command of the Renegade Maisara, and this officer, becoming aware of the Toledans' intention, laid an ambush for them. Attacked unawares, they experienced a terrible defeat. According to their custom, Maisara's soldiers presented to their captain the heads of those of the enemy who had fallen in the fight; but love for his countrymen was not extinct in the Renegade's heart. At the sight of the mutilated heads, his patriotic sentiments revived in all their force, and reproaching himself bitterly with his devotion to the oppressors of his country, he died a few days later of shame and grief.

Nevertheless, although the Sultan was able from time to time to inflict loss upon Toledo, he could not subdue it, so long as concord reigned within its walls. Unfortunately this came to an end. We are ignorant of what took place within the city, but later occurrences, in the year 873, lead us to suspect that a dispute arose between Christians and Renegades. A Toledan of rank, who bore the name of Ibn Muhâjir and seems to have been a Renegade, quitted Toledo with his adherents, and offered his services to the commandant of Calatrava (836). They were eagerly accepted. By the advice of the deserters it was determined to invest the town and reduce it by famine, Prince Walîd, brother of the Sultan, being entrusted with the conduct of the siege. The investment had already lasted for a year, and famine had made grievous ravages in the town, when a messenger under a flag of truce, sent by the Arab general, arrived, and counselled the Toledans to surrender—pointing out that before long they must perforce yield, and that it would be better for them to do so whilst hope of obtaining favourable terms yet remained. The Toledans refused. Unfortunately for them, the messenger had been a witness not only of their courage but of their destitution and feebleness. Upon his return he urged the general to make a vigorous assault upon the town. Walîd took this advice, and Toledo was stormed, June 16, 837, after having enjoyed complete independence for about eight years. Annalists have not informed us how the Sultan treated the inhabitants; they merely relate that 'Abd-er-Rahmân demanded hostages, and caused the castle of Amrûs to be rebuilt.

During the closing years of 'Abd-er-Rahmân's reign the Christians of Cordova attempted an insurrection of an altogether exceptional kind. It is to this that we must next turn our attention.

Latin chroniclers of the middle of the ninth century furnish us with much information, not merely concerning this revolt, but also with regard to the mode of life, the sentiments and beliefs of the Christians of Cordova, and we shall now endeavour to reproduce faithfully the deeply interesting details which may be gleaned from their pages.

[AUTHORITIES: Ibn Adhârî, ii. 76, 83, 85–7, 93–5; Makkarî, i. 223–5; ii. 83 *sq.*; Eulog., *Mem. Sanct.*, ii. c. 1; Khoshanî, pp. 207, 257, 265–266, 277; Ibn Khallikân, fasc. x. (ed. Wüst.), p. 20; Nuwairî, pp. 458–9; Ibn Khaldûn, ff. 7–8.]

CHAPTER VI

EULOGIUS AND FLORA

OF the Christians of Cordova, many—and those the most enlightened—were far from bewailing their lot; they suffered no persecution, they were allowed the free exercise of their religion, and they were content. Many of them served in the army, others held lucrative posts at Court or in the palaces of wealthy Arab nobles. They followed their masters' example only too faithfully—some set up harems; others became addicted to a hateful Eastern vice.

Captivated by the glamour of Arabian literature, men of taste despised Latin authors, and wrote only in the language of their conquerors. A contemporary writer,[1] more patriotic than the majority of his fellow-citizens, bitterly deplores this fact. " My fellow-Christians," he says, " delight in the poems and romances of the Arabs; they study the works of Mohammedan theologians and philosophers, not in order to refute them, but to acquire a correct and elegant Arabic style. Where to-day can a layman be found who reads the Latin Commentaries on Holy Scriptures? Who is there that studies the Gospels, the Prophets, the Apostles? Alas! the young Christians who are most conspicuous for their talents have no knowledge of any literature or language save the Arabic; they read and study with avidity Arabian books; they amass whole libraries of them at a vast cost, and they everywhere sing the praises of Arabian lore. On the other hand, at the mention of Christian books they disdainfully protest that such works are unworthy of their notice. The pity of it! Christians have forgotten their own tongue, and scarce one in a thousand can be found able to compose in fair Latin a letter to a friend! But when it comes to writing Arabic, how many there are who can express themselves in that language with the greatest elegance, and even compose verses which surpass in formal correctness those of the Arabs themselves!"[2]   Predilection

---

[1] Alvaro.

[2] Christianity, however, had its revenge when Card. Ximenes caused 80,000 Arabic volumes to be publicly burned at Granada, and Arabic was anathematized as " the rude language of an heretical and despised race."

for Arabic literature, and almost universal neglect of Latin were, after all, not surprising. The works of the great poets of antiquity were not extant in Cordova;[1] theological treatises had little attraction for men of the world, and contemporary literature exhibited every sign of extreme decadence. Latin poetry was, it is true, still written, but the rules of quantity having been forgotten, it assumed the form of rhymed verses,[2] in which accent alone was observed, and which moreover were composed in a style as slipshod as it was pretentious.

More than half orientalized, the Christians of Cordova, as a whole, therefore adapted themselves readily to foreign domination. But there were exceptions. National pride and self-respect were not extinct in every breast. A few finer spirits, who disdained to curry favour with the great, and to instal themselves by impudence or cunning in their palaces, shuddered with indignation when they saw their native city—which still prided itself on its ancient title of " Patrician "—become the residence of a Sultan ; they envied the good fortune of those petty States in the north of Spain, which, although involved in endless warfare, were free from the Arab yoke, and were at least governed by Christian princes. Very real grievances occasionally intensified these patriotic regrets. The Sultans now and again issued edicts which deeply wounded the pride and religious scruples of earnest Christians. For instance, circumcision was declared to be obligatory for them as well as for Musulmans. The priests, above all, chafed bitterly. They instinctively hated the Mohammedans—and the more, because they held entirely false views with regard to Mohammed and his teaching. Living as they did amongst Arabs, nothing would have been easier for them than to learn the truth upon these matters, but stubbornly refusing to seek it from the fountain-head so close at hand, they preferred to give credence to, and disseminate, every ridiculous fable, whatever its source, concerning the Prophet of Mecca. It was not to Arab writers that Eulogius, one of the most learned priests of the day, turned for information respecting the life of Mohammed. On the contrary, though doubtless sufficiently familiar with Arabic to read easily

---

[1] The Æneid, and the Satires of Horace and Juvenal, were new to the Cordovans when Eulogius brought them from Navarre in 848.

[2] S. Turner, *Hist. of the Anglo-Saxons*, iii. 655. Marmontel makes some interesting remarks on this subject : *Œuvres* (1787), vol. x. p. 461.

historical works in that language, he relied upon a Latin manuscript which chance had thrown in his way in a Monastery at Pamplona.   From this he learnt, among other things, that Mohammed, when he felt his end approaching, foretold that on the third day after his death angels would come and resuscitate him.   Accordingly, after his soul had " descended into hell," his disciples kept watch diligently beside the body.   At the end of the third day, however, since no angels had appeared, the disciples, thinking that their presence near the corpse—which already exhaled the odour of corruption—perhaps kept heavenly visitants at a distance, withdrew.   Thereupon instead of angels, dogs came,[1] and began to devour the Prophet's body. All that remained was buried by the Moslems, who, to be revenged upon the dogs, decreed the annual slaughter of a large number of these animals.   " And such," cries Eulogius, " are the miracles of the prophet of Islam ! "

Nor were Mohammed's doctrines better understood. Nothing was more natural than that the priests, nurtured upon ascetic ideas, and whose hearts were forbidden to vibrate in sympathy with woman's love, should be scandalized at the polygamy permitted by Mohammed, and yet more at his conception of a celestial paradise peopled with beautiful houris—but it is nevertheless remarkable that they supposed the teaching of Mohammed to have been in every respect the precise opposite of Christ's.   " This enemy of our Saviour," writes Alvaro, " has consecrated to feasting and debauchery the sixth day of the week, which, in memory of our Lord's passion, should be a day of mourning and fasting. Christ preached chastity to his disciples ; Mohammed, to his, preached gross pleasures, impure delights, even incest. Christ preached marriage ; Mohammed, divorce.   Christ enjoined soberness and fasting ; Mohammed, revelry and gluttony."   " Christ," continues Alvaro—though it would be difficult to find in the New Testament the words which he here attributes to his Master—" Christ has ordained that on fast-days a man should hold himself aloof from his lawful wife ; Mohammed has dedicated such days, above all, to carnal pleasures."   Yet Alvaro, though he had but little knowledge of affairs at Court, was doubtless aware that Yahyâ had imposed a severe penance on 'Abd-er-Rahmân II for breaking Mohammed's injunction to observe strict continence during the month of fasting.

[1] " Vice angelica canes ingressi."

The priests had, in fact, imbibed wholly false notions regarding the Mohammedan religion.   Those of their fellow-Christians who were better informed, in vain assured them that Mohammed had preached a pure morality ; it was lost labour, for the ecclesiastics persisted in ranking Islamism with Roman paganism, and regarding it as devil-begotten idolatry.

Nevertheless, the main root of their aversion is to be sought, not in the Musulman religion, but in the Arab character.   The Arabs, who combined a refined sensuality with vivacity and good-humour, could not fail to inspire with invincible repugnance, priests whose hearts were fixed on estrangement from the world, on abject self-denial and galling penances.   Moreover, the ecclesiastics were undoubtedly subject to frequent molestation.   Though Mohammedans of the upper class were too enlightened and too well-bred to insult Christians on religious grounds, the vulgar were intolerant—as they are everywhere.   When a priest showed himself in the street he would be greeted with a cry of " There goes the fool ! " or with a ditty having for its burden a mocking eulogy of the cross,[1] or he would even be assailed with brick-bats at the hands of mischievous urchins.   During funerals the priests would hear from passers-by the imprecation : " May God show them no pity ! " while filth and stones would be showered on the procession.   When the church bells rang at the canonical hours the Moslems would wag their heads and say : " Poor fools ! thus to be deceived by their priests !   How great is their folly to believe the lies they are told !   May God's curse fall upon their deceivers ! "

In the eyes of some Musulmans, indeed, Christians, or at all events priests, were objects of positive aversion; if they had occasion to address them, they stood at a distance, so as not to brush against their garments.   And yet the hapless men who inspired such loathing, who were regarded as unclean, so that contact with them was avoided as with a leper, and who saw realized the words which Jesus spake to his disciples when he said " Ye shall be hated of all men for my name's sake "—well remembered that in the days when the Christian religion was dominant in the land, and fair churches arose on every side, their order was the mightiest power in the State !

---

[1] " No Moslem believes that Isa [Jesus] was crucified, and a favourite fancy is that Judas, changed to the likeness of Jesus, thus paid for his treason (*Evangel. Barnabæ*)."   Burton, *Arabian Nights* (1887), ii. p. 220 *n*.

Wounded in their pride, exasperated by the insults to which they were subjected, and impelled by a feverish desire for action, the priests, the monks, and a few laymen who shared their feelings, did not resign themselves to suffering in silence, to making empty vows, and to eating their hearts in impotent wrath.   In towns sufficiently far from the centre of Moslem domination to admit of the standard of revolt being raised with some hope of success, these fiery enthusiasts would have become soldiers; in the mountains, the life of free-lances or banditti would have been theirs; but whether as soldiers in Toledo, or guerillas in the Sierra de Malaga, they would have waged war to the death against the Mohammedans.   In the Sultan's capital, where recourse to arms was impossible, they became martyrs.

To screen themselves from the insults of the populace, the priests did not quit their abodes save in cases of absolute necessity.   They often feigned sickness, and lay all day upon their beds, in order to escape payment of the monthly poll-tax exacted by the public treasury.[1]   Thus self-condemned to long periods of seclusion, to a solitary and contemplative life, always introspective, they laid up in silence, and with a kind of voluptuous enjoyment, the treasures of their hatred; they felt delight in the daily growth of their rancour and in storing their memories with fresh grievances. After sunset they would arise, and read in the solemn and mysterious silence of the night, by the feeble light of a flickering lamp, certain portions of the Bible—especially the tenth chapter of St. Matthew's Gospel—or the Works of the Fathers and Lives of the Saints; these were, indeed, almost the only books with which they were acquainted. They read how Christ had said: "Go ye, and teach all nations.   That which I tell you in darkness, that tell ye in the light: that which I tell you in the ear, that preach ye upon the housetops.   I send you forth as sheep in the midst of wolves.   Ye shall be brought before governors and before kings for my sake, to testify to them concerning me.   Fear not those who can slay the body, but who cannot slay the soul: fear Him, rather, who can destroy both body and soul, casting them into hell."   They read too in the pages of the Fathers that those, above all, would enter into the beatitude of the elect, who, when concealment would be blameless,

---

[1] "Inquisitio, vel census, vel vectigalis, quod omni lunari mense pro Christi nomine solvere cogimur." Leovigildi, *Presb. Cordub. liber de habitu Clericorum* (in *Esp. sagr.*, xi. p. 523).

voluntarily offered themselves as martyrs, and what chiefly inflamed the morbid imaginations of the priests was the example of those holy men who had suffered persecution at the hands of pagans, and who, instead of flinching from martyrdom, had yearned for that glorious death. Their souls thrilled with a quenchless longing to imitate these heroes of the faith, objects of their tireless adoration. They grudged that they themselves were not subjected to persecution, and in all their prayers they implored the opportunity of performing some great act of faith, such as had been granted to so many other faithful servants of God in the early days of the Church.

This hysterical and fanatical party was under the sway of two remarkable men—Eulogius, a priest, and Alvaro, a layman. Eulogius belonged to an old Cordovan family equally distinguished for its devotion to Christianity and its hatred of Islam. The grandfather of Eulogius, bearing the same name, when he heard the muezzins announcing from their minarets the hours of prayer, used to cross himself and chant the words of the Psalmist: " Keep not thou silence, O God: hold not thy peace! For, lo, thine enemies make a tumult: and they that hate thee have lifted up the head."[1] Great, however, as was the aversion of the family to Musulmans, Joseph, the youngest of the three brothers of Eulogius, held an official post under the Government, while the other two followed commercial pursuits; a sister named Anulo, however, took the veil, and Eulogius himself had been destined for the tonsure from his youth. Becoming a pupil of the priests of the church of S. Zoilus,[2] he studied night and day with such assiduity that he soon outstripped not only his fellow-pupils, but also his teachers. Then, eager to learn more than the priests could teach him, but fearing to offend them by divulging his secret ambitions, the young scholar without their knowledge attended the lectures of the most famous doctors of Cordova, especially those of the eloquent Abbot Spera-in-Deo, author of a refutation of Islamism[3] and of an account of the death of two martyrs who were beheaded at the beginning of the reign of 'Abd-er-Rahmân II.

---

[1] Psalm lxxxiii.

[2] S. Zoilus was martyred at Cordova (perhaps under Diocletian). The church was built by Bp. Agapius and the body of the saint was deposited there. There is a hymn in the Saint's honour in the oldest Mozarabic Breviary. (See *Acta Sanctorum*, vol. xxvii. (June 27), pp. 226 *et seq.*) Eulogius himself was buried there.

[3] Eulogius quotes a fragment in his *Mem. Sanctorum.*

This zealous divine acquired a commanding influence over the young Eulogius, and it was the Abbot who instilled into his mind that life-long and implacable hatred of Islam which characterised his pupil.

In Spera-in-Deo's lecture-room Eulogius became acquainted with Alvaro, a wealthy young Cordovan of high birth, who, although not destined for the priesthood, was assiduous in his attendance at the discourses of the famous Abbot and shared his convictions. Eulogius and Alvaro were well fitted for mutual sympathy and affection; a warm friendship soon sprang up between them, and Alvaro, at an advanced age, when writing his friend's biography, dwells with delight upon the days when he and his fellow-student vowed eternal brotherhood, when they hung upon the lips of the great scholar of whom Betica was justly proud, and when it was their chief delight to indite whole volumes of letters and verses—volumes which they destroyed later on, despite the precious memories linked with them, lest posterity should appraise the writers by such trivial fruits of youthful enthusiasm.

Becoming, in due course, first deacon and then priest of the church of S. Zoilus, Eulogius won by his virtues the esteem of all who knew him. It was his delight to frequent the monasteries, and he soon acquired a powerful influence over their inmates: rapt in pious exaltation to excesses of devotion, he mortified the flesh by watchings and fastings, and besought of God, as a special grace, to be delivered from a burdensome existence and transported to the blessed mansions of the elect.

And yet this life of austerity and gloom was illumined by one tender ray of human love: a passion chaste and spotless in its saintly simplicity, which without being directly referred to by Eulogius, he nevertheless all unwittingly confesses with delightful candour.

There was then living in Cordova a young and lovely maiden named Flora, between whom and Eulogius there grew up a strange spiritual affinity. The child of a mixed marriage, she passed as a Mohammedan; her father, however, having died during her early infancy, she had been instructed by her mother in the Christian faith. A keen aspiration after holy things had sprung up in the heart of the devout girl, but her brother, a zealous Musulman, dogged her steps so that she could attend Mass but rarely. This constraint weighed upon Flora's mind: she began to scruple whether

she did not sin in permitting herself to be looked upon as
an Islamite: was it not written in her cherished Bible:
" Whoso shall confess Me before men, him will I also
confess before My Father which is in heaven; but whoso
shall deny Me before men, him will I also deny before My
Father which is in heaven"? Courageous, high-spirited,
and daring, she was moulded for indomitable resistance: her
whole character was energetic, venturesome, and set upon
extreme courses. Her mind was soon made up. Without
her brother's knowledge she left her home, accompanied by
her sister Baldegotho, whose sentiments were in sympathy
with her own. The two girls found a hiding-place among
the Christians. Their brother's search for them in the
convents proved fruitless, but upon his procuring the imprisonment of some priests whom he suspected of harbouring
the fugitives, Flora, unwilling that Christians should be
persecuted on her account, returned voluntarily to her home,
and presented herself before her brother: "Thou hast been
seeking for me," she said; "thou hast persecuted God's
people on my account. Therefore I am here. And I tell
thee to thy face, and that with pride, that thy suspicions
were well founded. I am a Christian. Try if thou darest
to wrench me from Christ by torments: I will endure them
all!" " Unhappy girl!" exclaimed her brother, "knowest
thou not that by our law the penalty of apostasy is capital?"[1]
" I know it well," replied Flora, "and upon the scaffold I
will cry with no less firmness, 'Jesus, my Lord and my God,
overflowing with love for thee, I find happiness in death!'"
Enraged at such contumacy, the Musulman ruthlessly beat
his sister; but Flora was possessed of one of those exceptionally perfect organisations upon which physical pain seems
to produce no effect, and her brother, seeing that his violence
was fruitless, endeavoured next to influence her by gentle
persuasion. This proving equally ineffective, he thereupon
dragged her before the Kady. " Kady," said he, "this is
my sister: she always honoured our sacred religion and
practised its rites with me, until the Christians perverted
her, and inspired her with contempt for our Prophet and
with the belief that Jesus is God." " Doth thy brother
speak truly?" demanded the Kady of Flora. " Callest thou
that impious man my brother?" she replied. " He is not:

[1] The punishment of death for apostasy was carried out, in the case of a Greek
who was a Turkish subject, as late as 1844. *Cf.* D. S. Margoliouth, *Mohammedanism*
(1911), p. 104.

I disown him! What he saith is a lie. I have never been
an Islamite. He whom I have known and adored from
my earliest infancy is Christ. He is my God, and He alone
shall be my spouse!"

The Kady could have forthwith sentenced Flora to death,
but, touched perhaps by her youth and beauty, and doubtless believing that bodily chastisement would suffice to bring
back this straying sheep into the fold, he ordered two officers
to hold the girl's arms outstretched, while the scourge was
administered on her neck. Then restoring her, more dead
than alive, to her brother, the Kady said: "Instruct her
in our law: and if she does not become of another mind,
bring her back to me."

Returning to his house, the Musulman handed over his
sister to the care of the women of his harem. To prevent
her escaping a second time he gave orders that all the doors
should be kept locked, and as his residence was entirely
surrounded by a high wall, he deemed it unnecessary to
take further precautions. But a woman so courageous as
Flora was not thus to be baffled. In a few days, before her
wounds were fully healed, she felt strong enough to attempt
her escape. Under cover of night she clambered to the roof
of a building within the courtyard: thence she nimbly
scaled the wall, and, slipping to the ground, reached the
street without accident. Hurrying blindly through the
darkness, she had the good fortune to reach the house of a
Christian of her acquaintance. There she remained in concealment for a considerable period, and it was there that
Eulogius saw her for the first time. Flora's beauty, the
irresistible charm of her speech and manner, her romantic
adventures, her unflinching fortitude under sufferings, her
tender piety and mystic exaltation, all combined to inflame
the imagination of the young priest, accustomed though he
was to self-mistrust and self-restraint. He conceived for
Flora an exalted affection, a love purely intellectual, a
love such as may be conceived in the habitations of angels,
where incorporeal souls are swayed by sacred desires.

Six years later Eulogius recalled the most trivial details
of this their first meeting; far from fading, remembrance
seems to have grown more vivid with years, as these passionate words of a letter to Flora testify: "Holy sister,
time was when thou didst vouchsafe to show me thy neck,
all torn with the lash, bereft of the lovely and abundant
tresses which once veiled it. It was because thou didst

look upon me as thy spiritual father, and deem me pure
and chaste as thyself. Tenderly I laid my hand upon thy
wounds; fain would I have sought their healing with a kiss,
but I dared not. . . . When I departed from thee I was as
one that walketh in a dream, and my sighs ceased not."

Fearing discovery in Cordova, the devoted girl, accompanied by her sister Baldegotho, sought concealment elsewhere. The circumstances in which Eulogius and Flora
once again beheld each other will appear in the sequel.

[AUTHORITIES : Eulog., *Mem. Sanct.* ; *Apol. Mart.* ; *Ep. ad Wili.* ; Alvar.,
    Indic. lumin. ; *Vita. Eulog.* ; Sams., *Apol.*, ii. c. 2, 4, 6 ; Ibn Khallikân,
    fasc. x. (ed. Wüst.), p. 20.]

CHAPTER VII

THE MARTYRS OF CORDOVA

WHILE the Christian Zealots of Cordova gave way to morbid dreams and aspirations, fostered in gloom and embittered by inaction, an event took place to redouble, if it were possible, their hatred and their fanaticism.

A priest of the church of S. Acisclus, Perfectus by name, when out marketing one day, entered into conversation with some Moslems—for he spoke Arabic fluently. After a while religious topics were touched upon, and the Moslems asked Perfectus his opinions with regard to Mohammed and Jesus Christ. "Christ," he replied, "is my God; but, as for your Prophet, I hardly dare to tell you what we Christians think of him; for, were I to do so, you might take offence, and hand me over to the Kady, who would condemn me to death. However, if you will assure me that I need have no fear, I will impart to you, in strict confidence, what is written in the Gospel concerning him, and you shall judge in what repute he is held among Christians."

"You may rely on us," replied the Moslems; "have no fear, but tell us what men of your faith think of our Prophet, and we will swear not to betray you."

"Know then," said Perfectus, "that it is written in the Gospel, 'False prophets shall arise, and shall show signs and wonders, to seduce, if it were possible, even the elect.' [1] The greatest of these false prophets is Mohammed."

Warming to his theme, Perfectus then went further than he had intended, and proceeded to launch a torrent of abuse against Mohammed, as being "the servant of Satan." The Moslems suffered him to depart in peace; nevertheless they bore him a grudge, and some time later, on seeing Perfectus approaching, they deemed themselves no longer bound by their oath, but shouted to the bystanders: "Behold this insolent fellow! In our presence he vented such horrible blasphemies against our Prophet that the most patient of you, had you heard them, would have been goaded to fury."

[1] Mark xiii. 22.

278

Forthwith Perfectus, "as though," to use the words of
Eulogius, "he had overset a hive of bees," found himself
surrounded by an infuriated crowd who flung themselves
upon him and dragged him before the Kady with such
precipitancy that his feet scarcely touched the ground.
"This priest," cried the Moslems to the magistrate, "hath
blasphemed our Prophet. You will know, better than we,
what punishment such a crime deserveth."

Having examined witnesses, the Kady asked Perfectus
what he had to say for himself in reply. The poor priest,
who was far from being of the number of those who were
eager for martyrdom, and who trembled in every limb,
could think of no better defence than a bare denial of the
words attributed to him. This was of no avail: his guilt
was fully established, and the Kady in accordance with the
law of Islam condemned him to death as a blasphemer.
Loaded with chains, Perfectus was thrown into prison, there
to await execution on a day to be fixed by the Chamberlain
Nasr. All hope was therefore lost for the luckless priest,
a victim of Moslem treachery, and imprudent reliance on
a Moslem oath. But the certainty of approaching death
nerved him with the courage which had failed him in the
Kady's presence. Indignant at the breach of faith which
would cost him his life, and convinced that nothing could
either save him or aggravate his offence, he avowed boldly
that he had reviled Mohammed; he gloried in his crime;
he ceased not to curse comprehensively the false prophet,
his doctrines, and his disciples, and prepared himself for
martyrdom. He prayed, he fasted, and rarely were his
eyelids closed in sleep. Month after month passed by. It
seemed as though Nasr had either forgotten the priest, or
was deliberately protracting his agony. The Chamberlain
had, in fact, with a refinement of cruelty, determined to
postpone the execution of Perfectus until the festival—held
on the first of Shawwal—with which the Musulmans celebrate the termination of Ramadân, the month of fasting.
That year (A.D. 850) the festival fell in the Spring, on the
18th of April. From early dawn Cordova, which while the
forty days of the fast lasted had been in the morning silent
and deserted, presented an animated and somewhat grotesque
spectacle. The streets could scarcely contain the crowds
which streamed towards the mosques. The richer folk were
apparelled in new and magnificent attire; the slaves were
decked out in garments bestowed on them by their masters;

children strutted along in their fathers' sweeping robes. Every quadruped that could be ridden was requisitioned, and bore on its back as many persons as it could carry. Every face was a picture of happiness; friends as they met congratulated and embraced each other. As soon as the religious ceremony was at an end the interchange of visits began. Everywhere the daintiest viands and the choicest wines awaited the guests, and the doors of the wealthy were besieged by the poor, who, like a flock of hungry crows, pounced upon the fragments of the feast. Even for the women, confined during the rest of the year behind triply bolted doors, this day was one of liberty and merry-making. While their fathers and husbands were waxing glorious over their cups, they paraded the streets—with palm-branches in their hands and scattering cakes among the poor—on their way to the cemeteries, where, under the pretext of bewailing the dead, they devised many an intrigue.[1]

In the afternoon, when the Guadalquiver was covered with innumerable craft, filled with more or less inebriated Mohammedans, and when crowds of the Cordovans had assembled in a spacious plain on the farther bank—ostensibly to hear a sermon, but actually to indulge in additional junketing—Perfectus was informed that, by the orders of the Chamberlain, his death penalty was forthwith to be paid. Perfectus knew that executions took place on the very plain where the joyous crowds were assembled at that moment. He was prepared for the scaffold, but the idea of mounting it amidst a scene of universal merriment, the thought that his punishment would serve as a mere diversion for the mob —a novel pastime—filled him with rage and anguish. "I prophesy," he cried, inflamed with righteous anger, "that this Nasr, this arrogant man before whom the heads of the noblest and oldest families bow down, this man who holds sovran power over Spain—I prophesy that he will not live to see the anniversary of this festival amidst which his cruelty hath decreed my death!" Perfectus showed no sign of weakness. On his way to the scaffold he cried, "Yea, I did curse your prophet, and I curse him now! I curse him as an impostor, an adulterer, a child of Hell! Your religion is of Satan! The pains of Gehenna await you all!" Repeating again and again these objurgations, with a firm step he mounted the scaffold, around which thronged

---

[1] Lane, *Mod. Egyptians,* ii. 266–9; *Mission historial de Marruecos,* p. 46; Lyon, *Travels in N. Africa,* pp. 108–9.

an eager and fanatical crowd gloating over the decapitation
of a Christian who had blasphemed Mohammed.

In the eyes of the Christians Perfectus had become a
saint. With the Bishop of Cordova at their head, they
lowered his coffin, with great pomp, into the grave where
lay the bones of S. Acisclus.[1] Moreover they openly
declared that God would exact retribution for the death of
his servant. In the evening, after the execution, a boat
capsized, and two of the eight Musulmans which it contained were drowned. Thereupon Eulogius cried, "God
hath avenged his soldier. Our cruel persecutors have translated Perfectus to heaven, and the waves have engulphed
two of them, to yield them into the jaws of hell!"

A further satisfaction awaited the Christians. The
prediction of Perfectus was accomplished: before a year
elapsed Nasr met with a sudden and dreadful death. This
powerful eunuch fell a victim to his own treachery. The
Sultana Tarûb was desirous of securing for her own son
'Abdallah the succession to the throne—to the prejudice of
Mohammed, who, though the eldest of 'Abd-er-Rahmân's
forty-five sons, had been born to him by another wife, Bohair
by name. Notwithstanding her great influence over her
husband, Tarûb had nevertheless not succeeded in winning
him over to her design. She thereupon turned to Nasr,
whose hatred of Mohammed she well knew, and begged
him to relieve her both of her husband and of Bohair's son.
The eunuch promised to carry out her wishes, and thinking
it expedient to begin with the father, he had recourse to the
physician Harrânî, who had come to Cordova from the
East and had speedily gained a great reputation and a
considerable fortune by the sale of a secret specific against
intestinal troubles, for each phial of which he demanded
the exorbitant price of fifty pieces of gold. Nasr asked the
physician whether he thought it worth his while to do him
a favour, and on the latter assuring him that such was his
chief desire, the eunuch handed him a thousand pieces of
gold, and bade him prepare a very deadly poison known as
bassûn-al-molûk.

Harrânî penetrated Nasr's design. Divided between
the fear of poisoning the monarch, and that of incurring
the wrath of the powerful Chamberlain, the physician accordingly prepared the poison and sent it to Nasr, but at the

---

[1] A martyr under Diocletian's persecution.

same time privately advised the Sultan, through an inmate of the harem, not to drink any potion offered him by the eunuch. Nasr presented himself in due course before his master, and hearing the Sultan complain of his ill health, he recommended a sovran remedy which he had learnt from a famous leech. "I will bring it to you to-morrow morning," said he, "for it must be taken fasting."

The next day, when the eunuch brought the poison, the monarch examining the phial, remarked: "Mayhap this remedy is harmful; make trial of it first yourself." Thunderstruck, but not daring to disobey, lest he should reveal his criminal intent—hoping, moreover, that Harrâni might provide an antidote for the poison—Nasr swallowed it. As soon as it was possible for him to do so without arousing suspicion, the chamberlain fled from the palace, sought out Harrâni, briefly told him what had happened, and implored him for an antidote. The physician prescribed goats' milk. But it was too late. The poison was already burning his entrails; in the paroxysms of a violent flux Nasr expired.

The Christian priests were ignorant of what had passed at the palace. They knew, however, that Nasr had died suddenly, and it was even whispered that he had been poisoned, but they knew no more. It would appear that the Court tried to hush up this baffled plot, in which several persons of high rank were implicated, and a record of it has only come down to us through the curious revelations of a client of the Omayyads who wrote at a period when it might be freely spoken of, since all the conspirators were dead. The priests, however, learned enough of the matter for their own purposes: the cardinal fact was that the prediction of Perfectus—known to a great number of Christians and Moslems who had been his fellow-prisoners—had been signally fulfilled.

Not long after these events, the harsh and unjust treatment of a Christian merchant by certain Moslems still more exasperated the Zealots.

The merchant in question, John by name, was an entirely inoffensive man, and the thought had never crossed his mind that it might be his fate to suffer in the cause of Christ. Devoted to his business, he grew prosperous, and as he knew that the name of Christian was no recommendation in the eyes of Moslem purchasers, he had fallen into the habit of invoking Mohammed when crying up his wares. " By Mohammed! this is of superfine quality. By the Prophet, (to whom may God be gracious), you will not find better goods, seek where you will!" Phrases such as these grew habitual to him, and for a long time he had no reason to regret the fact. His rivals, however, who were less favoured by customers, begrudged John's steadily increasing prosperity; they were therefore ever on the watch for an opportunity of doing him an injury. One day, hearing him as usual invoking Mohammed, they said to him : "Thou hast our Prophet's name forever on thy tongue, in order that they who know thee not may take thee for a believer. It is insufferable to hear thee swearing by Mohammed every time thou tellest a lie!"

John began to protest that if he used Mohammed's name it was with no intention of offending Moslems, but at last, as the dispute waxed hot, he cried, " I will never again utter your Prophet's name, and cursed be every man who pronounces it!" Scarcely had these words fallen from him when he was seized and borne off to the Kady amidst cries that he was a blasphemer. When questioned by the magistrate, John maintained that he had had no intention of insulting any one, and that the accusation was due to trade jealousy. The Kady—whose duty it was either to acquit him, if he believed him innocent, or to condemn him to death if he believed him guilty—did neither. He adopted a middle course, and sentenced John to four hundred lashes, to the great disappointment of the populace, who protested that the merchant was worthy of death. The wretched man underwent his punishment, and then, seated on an ass with his face to the tail, he was led through the streets of the city while a crier walked before him proclaiming " Such is the punishment of him who dares to mock the Prophet!" John was then loaded with chains and thrown into prison. When Eulogius visited him several months later, the scars caused by the scourge were still visible on his flesh. Not many days later the Zealots, who had long reproached themselves for their inaction, entered the lists. The goal of their longings was death at the hands of the infidel. To achieve that end they had merely to revile Mohammed. This they did. The monk Isaac set the example. A native of Cordova, the son of noble and wealthy parents, Isaac had received a careful education. He was a thorough master of Arabic, and while still a youth had been appointed *kâtib* [1] by 'Abder-Rahmân II. At the age of twenty-four, however, being

---

[1] Secretary : see Nicholson, *Lit. Hist. of the Arabs* (1907), p. 257 *n*.

suddenly smitten by conscientious scruples, he turned his back upon the Court and the brilliant career which seemed opening before him and buried himself in the Convent of Tabanos, which his uncle Jeremias had built at his own cost to the north of Cordova.   Surrounded by high mountains and dense forests, this convent, where a far stricter discipline was maintained that was usual elsewhere, was justly regarded as a hotbed of fanaticism.   In this retreat Isaac found his uncle, his aunt Elizabeth, and several others of his kinsfolk, all of whom had delivered themselves wholly to the gloomy spirit of asceticism.   The force of example, seclusion amidst wild and dreary scenery, fastings, watchings, prayers, macerations, long poring over the Lives of the Saints—all these influences combined to arouse in the young monk's soul an access of fanaticism which bordered on frenzy, and he believed himself called upon by Christ to immolate himself in His cause.   He accordingly set out for Cordova, and presenting himself before the Kady, said : " I am desirous of embracing thy faith, if thou wilt deign to instruct me therein."   " Very willingly," replied the Kady, who rejoiced in the opportunity of making a convert and proceeded to expound the tenets of Mohammedanism ; but in the midst of his discourse Isaac exclaimed : " Your Prophet hath lied, he hath deceived you ; may he be accursed, wretch that he is, who hath dragged so many wretches with him down to hell !   Why dost not thou, as a man of sense, abjure these pestilent doctrines ? Is it possible that thou believest in the impostures of Mohammed ?   Embrace Christianity—therein lies salvation ! "   Beside himself at the unheard-of audacity of the young monk, the Kady opened his lips without being able to utter a word, and shedding tears of rage, smote Isaac on the cheek.

" What ! " cried the monk, " darest thou to smite God's own image ?   For this thou shalt one day render account."

" Calm thyself, Kady," said the assembled counsellors, " be mindful of thy dignity, and remember that our law forbiddeth us to insult even him who hath been condemned to death."

" Unhappy man," said the Kady at length, addressing the monk, " perchance thou art drunk, or hast lost thy reason, and knowest not what thou sayest.   Canst thou be ignorant that the immutable law of him thou so recklessly revilest, condemns to death those who dare to speak of him as thou hast spoken ? "

"Kady," replied the monk quietly, "I am in my right mind, and I have never tasted wine. Burning with the love of truth, I have dared to speak out to thee and the others here present. Condemn me to death: far from dreading the sentence, I yearn for it; hath not the Lord said: 'Blessed are they which are persecuted for the truth's sake, for theirs is the kingdom of heaven'?"

The Kady began to feel sorry for the fanatical monk. Having dismissed him to prison, he sought permission from the Khalif to mitigate the penalty in the case of a man who was evidently insane. But 'Abd-er-Rahmân, exasperated at the posthumous honours paid to Perfectus, ordered the law to be carried out in all its rigour, and to prevent the Christians from ceremoniously interring Isaac's body, he further ordained that the corpse should be for several days hanged head downwards on a gibbet, that it should then be burned, and that the ashes should be cast into the river. These orders were duly executed (June 3, 851); but although the monarch thus deprived the monks of precious relics, they made amends by enrolling Isaac among the saints, and by relating the miracles which he had worked not only during his childhood but even before he was born.[1]

The lists were now open. Two days after Isaac's execution, a Frank, named Sancho—one of the Sultan's guards and a pupil of Eulogius—blasphemed Mohammed and was beheaded. On the following Sunday (June 7), six monks, amongst whom were Jeremias—Isaac's uncle—and one Habentius, who had lived in perpetual seclusion in his cell, appeared before the Kady and cried, "We also echo the words of our holy brothers, Isaac and Sancho!" Thereupon they duly blasphemed Mohammed, and added, "Now avenge your accursed Prophet! Inflict on us your sharpest tortures!" Their heads fell. Then Sisenand, a priest of the church of S. Acisclus, and a friend of the two monks, in a vision beheld them descend from heaven and point him to a martyr's death. He, too, was decapitated. Before mounting the scaffold he exhorted Paul the deacon to follow his example. Paul's head fell four days later (July 20). A young monk of Carmona, Theodemir by name, was the next to court successfully the same fate.

---

[1] "Tribus namque vicibus une die, paulo antequam nasceretur, visus est loqui: cujus rei novitate perterrita mulier, pene mortua, vim verborum nequaquam potuit intelligere." *Acta Sanctorum* (June 3), p. 318.

Eleven martyrdoms in less than two months constituted a triumph of which the Zealots were truly proud ; but the other Christians, who desired nothing else than to live in peace, were naturally perturbed by this strange outbreak, which was not unlikely to arouse mistrust of all Christians among the Moslems and to bring about a persecution. " The Sultan," they said to the Zealots, " allows us to exercise our own religion and does not oppress us ; to what purpose, then, is this fanatical zeal ? Those whom you dub martyrs are nothing of the kind ; they are suicides, incited by pride—the source of all sins. Had they read the Gospel they would have found written therein : ' Love your enemies, do good to them that hate you.' Instead of reviling Mohammed they ought to have borne in mind the saying of the Apostle, ' Slanderers shall not enter the Kingdom of God.' The Moslems say to us : ' If God had intended to prove that Mohammed was a false prophet, and had inspired these fanatics with the resolution they have taken, he would have worked miracles to convert us to your faith. But, far from this, God has permitted the bodies of these so-called martyrs to be burned and their ashes to be cast into the river. Your sect profits nothing by these executions, and ours is not harmed thereby. What folly these acts of suicide are ! ' How can we reply to these objections, which appear to us only too well founded ? "

Such were the arguments used not only by laymen but by the majority of the priests.[1] Eulogius undertook to reply to them : and began the composition of his *Memorial of the Saints*—the first book of this work consisting of a bitter and violent diatribe against those who " with sacrilegious lips dare to revile and blaspheme the Martyrs." In refutation of those who dwelt upon the tolerance of the unbelievers, Eulogius painted in darkest colours the annoyances to which the Christians, and especially the priests, had been exposed. " Alas ! " cries he, " if the Church revealeth herself in Spain like a lily amongst briars, if she shineth like a torch in the midst of a corrupt and perverse nation, let not this blessing be imputed to the impious people before whom, in punishment for our sins, we are abased, but to God alone—to Him who said to His disciples, ' Behold I am with you always, even to the end of the world ! ' " The

---

[1] " Plerique fidelium et (heu proh dolor !) etiam sacerdotum." Eul., *Mem. Sanct.*, p. 245.

writer then proceeds to accumulate quotations from the
Bible and legends of the Saints to prove that not only is
it permissible to seek martyrdom spontaneously, but that
it is a work of piety, meritorious and approved by God.
" Know ye," he says to his opponents, " miscreants that ye
are, who dare to belittle the glory of the Saints, know ye
that at the Last Day ye shall be confronted with them and
answer for your blasphemies before God ! "

The Arab Government was, for its part, justly alarmed
at this strange form of revolt; for the fanaticism of the
Zealots was only one aspect of their character—they were
also imbued with warlike ardour and an almost savage desire
of political vengeance.[1] The pressing problem, however, was
how to prevent these maniacs from committing suicide upon
the scaffold.   If they blasphemed Mohammed, they must
needs be condemned to death ; on that point the law was
inexorable.   Only one device seemed likely to prove effica-
cious, and that was to assemble an ecclesiastical council, and
induce it to promulgate a decree forbidding Christians to
court so-called martyrdom.   'Abd-er-Rahmân adopted this
course : he assembled the bishops, and being precluded
from personal attendance at their meeting, he appointed
as his representative a Government official who was a
Christian.

Eulogius and Alvaro speak with the utmost horror of
" this *kâtib*, this *exceptor*, this wicked, arrogant, and cruel
man, whose vices were only equalled in abundance by his
wealth—a Christian only in name, who from the first has
been the detractor and inveterate enemy of the martyrs."
They carried, indeed, their hatred and execration of the
man to such a pitch that they studiously avoid mention of
his name.

We learn, however, from Arab writers that he was one
Gomez, son of Antonian, son of Julian.

Endowed with an active and penetrating mind, Gomez,
who by the unanimous testimony of Christians and Moslems
spoke and wrote Arabic with remarkable purity and elegance,
had gained the favour, both of his immediate chief 'Abdallah
ibn Omayya, and of the Sultan himself.   His influence at
Court, at the period with which we are dealing, was very
great.   Absolutely indifferent in matters of religion, he had
a supreme contempt for fanaticism, but he would probably

---

[1] Eulogius and Alvaro frequently speak of the martyrs as " Soldiers of God,
fighting against an impious foe."

have contented himself with launching epigrams and sarcasms at the poor fools who insisted on losing their heads without rhyme or reason, had he not feared that their folly might entail upon himself very unpleasant consequences. He thought he could already detect in the demeanour of Moslems towards Christians a growing coldness which bordered on mistrust, and he asked himself, with some anxiety, whether they might not end by confusing reasonable with fanatical Christians, and whether in that case he himself and other Christian officials might not lose their lucrative posts, and perhaps also their savings. At the council, therefore, Gomez was not merely the interpreter of the Sultan's wishes : self-interest was at stake, and urged him to stem effectually the flood that threatened to overwhelm him.

[AUTHORITIES : Eulog., *Mem. Sanct.*, pp. 237–49, 269; ii. c. 1–6, 15; iii. c. 2 ; Alvar., *Indic. lum.*, pp. 225–44; Harrânî (art. on Ibn abî-Osaibia); Ibn al-Kûtiyya, ff. 31–4; Khoshanî, pp. 291–2; Ibn al-Abbâr, p. 94.]

CHAPTER VIII

ACCESSION OF MOHAMMED

THE sessions of the Council opened under the presidency of Reccafred, Metropolitan of Seville. Gomez explained the situation and depicted the fatal consequences which might flow from the untimely zeal of the revilers of Mohammed, who deserved to be anathematized rather than canonized, since they exposed all their fellow-Christians to the dangers of persecution. He accordingly invited the bishops to promulgate a decree censuring the conduct of the self-styled martyrs, and forbidding the faithful to follow their example. It seemed likely, however, that this step might in itself prove inefficacious, since the chief Zealots—among whom Eulogius was conspicuous—might have the audacity to censure the acts of the Council, and, despite the decree, induce other simple and credulous persons to blaspheme the Prophet before the Kady. This was to be prevented at all costs, so Gomez further invited the bishops to imprison those persons whom they deemed dangerous.

Saul, Bishop of Cordova, thereupon opened the defence of the martyrs. He had sided with the Zealots, less from conviction, than in order to divert attention from his own antecedents, which were far from irreproachable. Elected Bishop by the clergy of Cordova, but unable to obtain the Sultan's confirmation of their choice, Saul had promised four hundred pieces of gold to the eunuchs of the palace if they would obtain the sovereign's approval. The eunuchs demanded a guarantee, and Saul executed a deed, drawn up in Arabic, whereby he undertook to charge the stipulated sum upon the revenues of the diocesan estates—to the detriment of the priests, who had the sole right to this income. The eunuchs succeeded in overcoming their master's reluctance to ratify the choice of the clergy; and Saul, to rehabilitate himself with the rigid and austere Christians who had not ceased to cast his infamous bargain in his teeth, warmly embraced the doctrines of the Zealots. At the splendid obsequies of Perfectus, which had given so much

offence to the Government, the bishop had ventured to head
the procession of the clergy, and now he undertook to put
forward arguments furnished by the Bible and the Lives of
the Saints in justification of the fanatics' opinions. His
reasoning did not, however, commend itself to the other
bishops; on the contrary, they were strongly inclined to
issue a decree in the sense indicated by Gomez. Nevertheless they found themselves in an embarrassing position;
since the Church of old had smiled upon the suicide and
canonized him, they could not disapprove the conduct of
the self-styled martyrs without condemning in the same
breath the saints of the primitive Church. Not daring,
therefore, to reprehend on general principles this excuse for
self-destruction, nor to censure those who had sought
martyrdom in later days, they resolved merely to forbid
Christians henceforth to aspire to this holy death. Gomez,
who appreciated their scruples, was content with this decision—the more so since the Metropolitan promised him to
take severe measures against the fanatical party.

The decree of the Council was no sooner promulgated
than Eulogius and his friends used it as an instrument
against its authors. "This decree," they said, "does not
condemn the martyrs of the present year: indeed, it con-
templates an increase in their numbers. And what means
the prohibition against aspiring to the crown of martyrdom?
Its inconsistency with the rest of the decree argues that it
was dictated by fear. The Council's approval of martyrdom
is as manifest as is its dread of openly avowing it."

These passionate and turbulent souls thus arrogantly defied the authority of the prelates. But they either had not
foreseen all the consequences of their own audacity, or overrated their courage ; for when the Metropolitan Reccafred,
faithful to his promise, and supported by the Government,
ordered the imprisonment of the chiefs of the faction, including the Bishop of Cordova, consternation ensued. It
was vain for Eulogius to declare that if he and his friends
hid themselves, perpetually changed their residence, or took
to flight under various disguises, it was because they did not
yet feel themselves worthy of martyrdom ; the truth was
that they clung to life more eagerly than it was convenient
for them to admit. Such timidity was only too potent even
among the leaders—" A falling leaf made us tremble with
fear," wrote Eulogius—but among the disciples it was over-
powering. Laymen and priests, who a little while before

had lavished panegyrics upon the martyrs, changed their views with astonishing rapidity ; there were many who even abjured Christianity and embraced Islamism. In spite of their precautions, the Bishop of Cordova and many priests of his party were discovered and arrested. The same fate befell Eulogius. He was at work upon his *Memorial of the Saints*, when the officers broke into his house, arrested him in the midst of his terrified family, and haled him to prison. There he met Flora once more. How she came to be a prisoner has now to be related.

In a convent near Cordova there was a young nun, Mary by name. She was sister of one of the six monks who had simultaneously reviled Mohammed before the Kady and had been decapitated. After the death of her beloved brother, she fell into a profound melancholy, but one day a fellow-inmate of the convent announced that the martyr had appeared to her and had spoken these words : " Tell Mary my sister no longer to bewail my loss, for soon she will join me in heaven." From that moment Mary wept no more ; her mind was made up ; she would die the death of her brother. On her way to Cordova she entered the church of S. Acisclus to pray, and knelt beside a maiden who was addressing fervent orisons to the saints. It was Flora, who, in her ardour, had quitted her refuge and was also preparing for martyrdom. Mary joyfully confided her resolve to her companion. The girls embraced, and vowed never to part, but to die together. " I go to rejoin my brother ! " cried the one : " And I," said the other, " shall find happiness in Jesus ! " Full of enthusiasm, they proceeded on their way, and presented themselves before the Kady. " I, the child of a pagan father," said Flora, " was a long while ago cruelly treated by thee because I refused to deny Christ. Afterwards, in my weakness I hid myself ; but to-day, full of faith in my God, I fear not to confront thee. I avow, as steadfastly as before, that Christ is God ; and I brand thy so-called prophet as an adulterer, an impostor, and a villain ! " " As for me, Judge," exclaimed Mary in her turn, " I am sister of one of those six heroes who perished on the scaffold because they derided your false prophet ; and I no less plainly declare that Christ is God, and that your religion is the invention of the Devil ! "

Although both deserved death, the Kady, touched perhaps by their youth and beauty, had compassion on them. He endeavoured to make them retract their words, and even

when he found his efforts vain, he contented himself with
imprisoning them.

In prison they were at first unflinching and stout-hearted :
they prayed, fasted, sang the hymns of the Church, and indulged in ascetic meditations ; but at last their fortitude was
sapped by the tedium of their long captivity, by the entreaties of those who would save them, and, above all, by the
menace of the judge, who knowing that they dreaded dishonour more than death, had warned them that if they did
not retract, they would be devoted to prostitution. Eulogius
was only just in time to support them. Agonising was the
trial he had to face. To encourage her for whom his heart
yearned with unspoken love to mount the scaffold—from
such a task the sternest bigot might well recoil ! And yet,
far from trying to dissuade Flora, or damping her enthusiasm
and turning her from her project, he employed all his rhetoric
to strengthen the girl's wavering courage. We may blame,
or lament, his blind fanaticism, but we must not hastily
brand him as cold and callous. In spite of the apparent
calm under which he concealed its torments, his heart was
wrung with bitter anguish.[1] The impetuous aspirations of
an ardent and impressionable soul were again aroused : love
—if so we may name the spiritual bond which united him to
Flora—love wrestled with conscience. Nevertheless, capable
of sacrificing all in the cause which he championed, he tried
to check the tumult of his heart ; and not wishing to avow
his weakness, he sought to benumb his grief by spurring
himself to a feverish activity. Night and day he read and
wrote. He composed a treatise to persuade Flora and her
companion that nothing is more meritorious than martyrdom.[2] He finished his *Memorial of the Saints*,[3] and sent it
to Alvaro with the request that he would revise it. He
wrote a long letter to his friend Wiliesind, Bishop of Pamplona. He even found enough calmness and detachment of
mind to compose a tractate on Prosody. In this his object
was to arouse the dormant patriotism of his fellow-citizens
and inspire them with a taste for that ancient literature
which, in a city which had given birth to Seneca and Lucan,
ought to have been cherished as a national heritage. The
priesthood under the Visigoths thought that no flowers
should be plucked or admired which had not been bedewed

---

[1] " Luctum non amitto quotidianum," he writes to Alvaro.
[2] The *Documentum martyriale*.
[3] Book i., and chaps. i.–vi. of Bk. ii.

with the water of baptism,[1] but Eulogius believed that in
the literature of the Romans he had found a weighty
counterpoise to that of the Arabs, with which the Cordovans
were infatuated. It had already been his good fortune to
rescue for them Latin manuscripts comprising works of
Virgil, Horace, and Juvenal, which he had found in Navarre;
and struck with the contempt evinced by all men of taste
for rhythmical verse, he wished to instil into his fellow-
citizens the scientific rules of Latin prosody, so that they
might imitate the models of the Augustan age.

Meanwhile his eloquence bore fruit. Under its glamour,
Flora and Mary displayed a firmness and enthusiasm which
amazed even Eulogius himself, accustomed as he was to
mystic exaltation. He was prone to deify the objects of
his admiration, and Flora in his eyes became a saint surrounded by a divine aureole. The Kady sent for the girl at
her brother's request, and made one last endeavour to save
her, but in vain. On her return to the prison, Eulogius
visited her. "Methought I looked upon an angel," he said;
"a celestial light shone round about her; her countenance
was radiant with joy; already she seemed to taste the bliss
of heaven; and with a triumphant smile she related to me
the Kady's questions and her replies. As I heard the words
fall from those lips sweeter than honey, I strove to confirm
her in her resolve by pointing to the crown which was laid
up for her. In adoration I prostrated myself before that
seraph form; I commended myself to her prayers, and reanimated by her discourse, I returned with a lighter heart
to my gloomy cell." The day which saw Flora and her
companion perish on the scaffold (Nov. 24, 851), was for
Eulogius a day of triumph. "My brother," he writes to
Alvaro, "the Lord hath been very gracious to us, and hath
visited us with great joy. Our virgins, instructed by us,
amidst bitter tears, in the living word, have won the palm
of martyrdom. Having vanquished the Prince of Darkness
and trodden under foot all earthly affections, they have gone
joyously to meet the bridegroom who reigneth in the
heavens. Invited to the marriage-feast by Christ, they have
entered the abode of the blessed, singing a new song and
saying: 'To thee, O Lord, our God, be honour and glory!
For thou hast snatched us from the powers of hell; thou hast
made us worthy of the joyful heritage of the saints; thou

---

[1] See Isidore of Seville, *Sentent.*, iii. 3.

hast called us to thine everlasting kingdom!' The whole
Church rejoiceth in their victory; but I, above all, have
the right to glory therein, for I strengthened them in their
intent when their hearts began to fail them."

Five days later, Eulogius, Saul, and the other priests
were set at liberty. Eulogius did not hesitate to attribute
his deliverance to the intercessions of the two saints, who
before leaving the prison to mount the scaffold had promised
that when they came into the presence of Christ they would
beseech Him to set the captives free. Saul henceforth was
submissive to Reccafred's commands; Eulogius, on the
contrary, redoubled his endeavours to multiply martyrs,
and succeeded only too well. Incited by him, priests,
monks, "secret Christians," women—all reviled Mohammed,
and were executed. To such a pitch did the audacity of
these fanatics reach, that two of them, an old monk and a
youth, entered the Great Mosque, and cried aloud: "The
kingdom of heaven is at hand for the faithful, but for you
infidels hell yawns, and it will shortly open and swallow you
up!" The infuriated congregation almost tore them to
pieces, but the Kady interposed his authority, and imprisoned
the blasphemers. After their hands and feet had been cut
off,[1] they were decapitated (Sept. 16, 852).

Six days later, 'Abd-er-Rahmân died suddenly. According to the account of Eulogius, the aged monarch was seated
on the terrace of the palace, when his glance falling upon
the gibbets to which were fastened the mutilated bodies of
the latest martyrs, he commanded the remains to be burned.
Scarcely had the order been given before he was struck with
apoplexy, and that night he breathed his last.

Since 'Abd-er-Rahmân had not decided which of his two
sons, Mohammed and 'Abdallah, was to succeed him, and
both aspirants to the throne were ignorant of their father's
death, all depended on the choice made by the eunuchs of
the palace. Those who had attended 'Abd-er-Rahmân
during his last moments promptly locked the gates of the
castle, in order to prevent any rumour of the Sultan's death
escaping, and summoned their colleagues. One of the most
influential eunuchs addressed the assembly. "Comrades,"
he said, "an event of the deepest importance to us all
has happened. Our master is no more." Thereupon the
eunuchs began to weep and lament. "This is no time for

---

[1] A punishment sanctioned by the Koran (*Sura*, v. 37).

tears," he continued; " our lamentations can be postponed.
The moments are precious. Let us first guard our own
interests and those of our fellow-Moslems. To whom do ye
award the throne?" "To our lord, the son of our bene-
factress the Sultana!" they cried with one voice.

Tarûb's intrigues seemed, therefore, to have borne fruit;
by dint of bribery and promises she had won over the
eunuchs, and thanks to them, her son 'Abdallah would
ascend the throne. But would the nation approve the
choice of the eunuchs? It was doubtful, for 'Abdallah was
chiefly distinguished for the laxity of his morals; his orthodoxy was more than suspect, and the people detested him.
The eunuch Abu 'l-Mofrih, a pious Moslem who had made
pilgrimage to Mecca, was conscious of these drawbacks.
" Is the opinion just given that of you all?" he asked.
" It is!" was the unanimous reply. " In that case, it is
mine also," he went on: " I have a better reason than any of
you to show my gratitude towards the Sultana, for she has
lavished more favours upon me than on others. Nevertheless this is a matter which calls for our mature consideration;
for if we elect 'Abdallah, our power in Spain is at an end.
Henceforth, when we walk in the streets we shall be reviled.
' Accursed be these eunuchs, who, when they might have
conferred the throne upon the best of princes, chose the
worst!' Such is the accusation which will assail our ears.
Ye know 'Abdallah, and ye know his associates. If he
ascends the throne what dangerous innovations must not
Moslems look for! Religion will be imperilled! Remember that ye will be called to account for your choice,
not only by men, but by God Himself!"

These words, which were indisputably true, made a profound impression upon the assembly. Already half convinced, they asked Abu 'l-Mofrih to nominate his candidate.
" I propose Mohammed," he said; " a devout man of
irreproachable morality." " That may be," replied the
eunuchs; " but he is niggardly and austere." " You call
him niggardly," said Abu 'l-Mofrih, " but how can he who
hath naught to give show his liberality? When he reigns,
and is master of the public treasury, he will show you his
gratitude; be well assured of that!"

Abu 'l-Mofrih's counsel having prevailed, all present
swore upon the Koran to acknowledge Mohammed; and the
two eunuchs Sadûn and Kâsim, who to curry favour with
Tarûb had been hitherto the most ardent supporters of

'Abdallah's candidature, henceforth thought of nothing except how to make peace with his rival. Kâsim begged his
colleagues to intercede for him, and this they promised to
do; while Sadûn was given the privilege of announcing to
Mohammed his accession to the throne.

As it was yet night, and the city gates were shut, Sadûn
took with him the keys of the Bridge Gate—Mohammed's
palace being situated on the opposite bank of the river.
To reach the bridge it was necessary to pass through
'Abdallah's palace, where all were awake and indulging in
the usual revelry: however, since no suspicions had been
aroused, Sadûn found no difficulty in gaining admission,
after which he crossed the bridge and reached Mohammed's
dwelling. The Prince had already risen, and was at the
bath, when he was informed that Sadûn desired to speak
with him. Quitting the bath, he dressed and ordered the
eunuch to be introduced. " What brings you here so early,
Sadûn?" he asked. " I come," replied Sadûn, " to announce
that we, the eunuchs of the palace, have elected you as your
father's successor. He is dead; may his soul rest with God!
Behold his ring!"

Mohammed could not credit Sadûn's words. He suspected that his brother was already on the throne, and had
sent the eunuch to assassinate him. Intent only on saving
his life, he cried: " Sadûn, spare me, as you fear God! I
know that you are my enemy; but will you shed my blood?
If needs be, I will quit Spain: the world is wide: I will
seek some place afar off, where I may live without giving
umbrage to my brother." Sadûn found great difficulty in
reassuring the Prince and persuading him that he had spoken
the simple truth. At length his solemn protestations prevailed, and he added: " You are astonished that I have been
chosen to bring you these tidings; but I entreated my
comrades to make me their messenger, in the hope that you
would pardon my past conduct." " May God pardon thee
as I do!" cried Mohammed: " and now I will summon my
chamberlain, Mohammed ibn Mûsâ, and we will concert
measures together."

In existing circumstances the most important step for
Mohammed to take was to gain possession of the Sultan's
palace: this achieved, his brother would not dare to dispute
his right to the throne, and he himself would be universally
acknowledged. But how could he pass through 'Abdallah's
dwelling without raising suspicions? There lay the diffi-

culty. If the guards saw Mohammed enter at such an
early hour, they might guess the truth, and bar his progress.
The chamberlain, on being consulted by his master, suggested
calling in the assistance of the prefect Yûsuf ibn Basîl, who
had three hundred men at his command. His advice was
taken, but Yûsuf, on learning how matters stood, deemed it
prudent to be neutral, and declined to place his agents at
Mohammed's disposal. " I will not intervene," he said, " in
a contest for the throne : but we clients will obey him who
becomes master of the palace."

Returning to the Prince, the chamberlain reported Yûsuf's
answer, and added : " To win all, somewhat must be risked !
I have a suggestion to make. You know, my lord, that
your father often sent for your daughter, and I used to
conduct her to his palace. Assume, therefore, a woman's
attire ; we will pass you off as your own daughter, and by
God's help, all will go well." The scheme was adopted : all
three were mounted on horseback—Sadûn riding first, and
Mohammed and the chamberlain following, the former clad
as a woman and heavily veiled. On reaching 'Abdallah's
palace they heard within singers and instruments of music,
and Mohammed whispered this verse from an ancient poet :
" Happy be we in our quest, as ye in your heart's desire ! "

The guards were carousing in a chamber above the gateway when they heard the cavalcade approach. One of them
descended to open the doors and challenged Sadûn with :
" Who goes there ? " " Silence, thou prying rascal ! " replied Sadûn, " and show more respect for a lady ! " The
soldier had no suspicions, and admitted the party. Shutting
the doors, he returned to his comrades and told them that
Mohammed's daughter had just passed through, with Sadûn
and her father's chamberlain.

Believing the main difficulty to have been overcome,
Mohammed said to his chamberlain : " Remain here : I will
soon send you assistance ; and then take heed that no one
leaves this palace." He then proceeded with Sadûn only.
The eunuch knocked at the gate of the palace where the
old monarch lay dead. The porter opened it. " Is this
lady Mohammed's daughter ? " he asked incredulously.
" Assuredly," replied Sadûn. " That is strange," replied the
porter : " I have often seen her arrive at this gate, and she
always seemed much smaller than this person. Thou art
deceiving me, Sadûn ; and I swear that nobody who is
unknown to me shall enter this door. Let the woman lift

her veil, or take herself off!" "What!" cried Sadûn, "darest thou insult a princess?" "Whether she be one I know not: but I repeat that if she showeth not her face she shall not enter." Seeing that the porter was obdurate, Mohammed raised his veil. "It is I," he said: "and I am here because my father is dead." "In that case," replied the porter, "the matter is a graver one than I supposed. But thou shalt not enter this doorway, my lord, until I ascertain whether thy father be alive or dead." "Follow me," said Sadûn, "and thou shalt be convinced." The porter closed the door, and leaving Mohammed outside, he accompanied Sadûn to the death-chamber, where beholding the Sultan's corpse, he shed tears, and turning to Sadûn said: "Thou hast spoken truth, and I am at thine orders." Then opening the gate he kissed Mohammed's hand and cried: "Enter, my prince! May God grant to thee good fortune, and through thee to all Moslems!"

Mohammed immediately caused the oath of allegiance to be administered to all the high officers of the State, and took the necessary steps to make any resistance on his brother's part useless; and as the first rays of dawn silvered the peaks of the Sierra Morena, Cordova learned that she had a new master.

[AUTHORITIES: Eulog., *Mem. Sanct.; Doc. mart.; Epp.;* Alvar., *Epp., Vit. Eulog.;* Ibn al-Kûtiyya, ff. 32–3.]

CHAPTER IX

EMIRATE OF MOHAMMED

THE new monarch was narrow-minded, and of a cold and selfish disposition. He evinced, as we have seen, no grief at his father's death ; indeed, he rejoiced at it, and took no pains to conceal his sentiments on the subject. One evening, after spending the day in revelry at Rosâfa,[1] a delightful country house of his near Cordova, Mohammed rode back to the Capital with his favourite Hâshim. Heated with wine, they were chatting discursively, when a gloomy thought passed through Hâshim's mind: " O descendant of the Khalifs," he cried, " how fair this world would be if death were not ! " " What an inept observation ! " replied Mohammed ; " If death were not, I should not be reigning. Death is an excellent thing : my predecessor is dead, and I am on the throne ! "

The eunuchs, when they demurred to electing Mohammed on the ground that he was miserly, had not misjudged his character. He began by reducing the salaries of officials and the pay of the soldiers. He next dismissed his father's veteran ministers and gave their posts to young and inexperienced men, on the understanding that part of their emoluments should find its way into the Sultan's privy purse. He dealt with all financial matters personally, and with minute and pedantic exactitude. In auditing an account amounting to a hundred thousand pieces of gold, he would wrangle with the treasury clerks over a dirhem. He was universally despised, or hated, for his parsimony ; the Fakihs alone, still exasperated at the audacity of the martyrs who had dared to blaspheme the Prophet in the Great Mosque, supported him because they believed him to be devout and an enemy of the Christians. Mohammed in this respect fully answered their expectations. On the day of his accession he dismissed all the Christian officials and soldiers—except Gomez, whose religious indifference he knew, and whose talents he appreciated. The Sultan's tolerant predecessors had shut their

---

[1] The name, also, of a palace near Damascus.

eyes when the Christians enlarged their old churches or
built new ones; but Mohammed, who determined to apply
the Moslem law in all its rigour, ordered all that had been
built since the conquest to be pulled down.   To please their
master, and ingratiate themselves with him, the zealous
ministers exceeded their instructions, and not only caused
churches which had stood for three centuries to be demolished, but set on foot a cruel persecution of the Christians.
In consequence of this, many Christians—indeed, the majority
if we are to believe Eulogius and Alvaro—abjured their
faith.   Gomez had set them an example.   He had for
several years been virtual head of the Chancellery during
the long illness of the Chancellor 'Abdallah ibn Omayya.
Upon the death of the latter, having heard that the Sultan
had remarked: "If Gomez were of our religion I would
gladly appoint him Chancellor," Gomez declared himself a
Moslem, and obtained the coveted dignity.   While a Christian he had scarcely ever attended divine service; but as a
Moslem he observed all religious practices so punctiliously
that the Fakihs pointed him out as a model of piety, and
dubbed him " the turtle-dove of the Mosque." [1]

In Toledo the effects of the Sultan's intolerance were
widely different.   Three or four years before, Eulogius,
returning from a journey in Navarre, had spent several days
in that city, where he was hospitably received by the pious
Metropolitan, Wistremir. There was good reason to believe
that he took the opportunity of exciting the hatred of the
Toledans against the Arab Government by painting in sombre
colours the wretched condition of the Christians in Cordova;
at any rate the Toledans held Eulogius in high respect, and
were keenly interested in the martyrs of the Capital.   As
soon, therefore, as they learnt that Mohammed had begun
to persecute their fellow-Christians, they took up arms,
entrusted the command to a citizen named Sindola,[2] and,
fearing for the safety of their hostages at Cordova, secured
the person of their Arab Governor, informing Mohammed
that if he valued his Governor's life it would be well for him
immediately to send the hostages back to Toledo.   The
Sultan did so, and the citizens duly released their Governor:
but war was declared, and so great was the fear inspired by

[1] Gomez seems to have retained his Christian name, but his son, who also held
a post in the chancellery and died in 911, bore that of 'Omar.
[2] Probably equivalent to the Visigothic "Swintila" or "Chintila." Cf. *Esp.
sagr.*, xxxvii. p. 316.

the Toledans that the garrison of Calatrava hastily evacuated that fortress, feeling themselves insecure. The Toledans
dismantled this stronghold; but not long afterwards the
Sultan sent troops thither and rebuilt the ramparts (A.D. 853).
He then despatched two generals against Toledo: but the
Christians advanced through the defiles of the Sierra Morena
to meet the enemy, whom they surprised near Andujar and
routed, capturing their camp.

The Toledans then pushed on to Andujar, and threatened the Capital itself. Mohammed, who felt that in order
to avert this danger he must take energetic measures,
assembled all the troops at his disposal and led them in
person against Toledo (June, A.D. 854). Sindola, for his
part, deeming his own forces insufficient, sought allies. He
appealed to the King of Leon, Ordoño I, who immediately
despatched a large army, under Gaton, Count of Bierzo,[1] to
aid him.

So strongly was the city now garrisoned that Mohammed
seems to have abandoned all hope of subduing it: but he
succeeded in inflicting a heavy loss upon the enemy.
Placing the bulk of his troops in ambush behind the rocks
through which the Guadacelete flows, he marched against
the town at the head of a small force and marshalled his
artillery against the walls. Seeing so feeble a body about
to make an assault, the Toledans, amazed at the enemy's
rashness, urged Count Gaton to make a vigorous sortie.
Gaton eagerly seized such an opportunity of distinguishing
himself. At the head, therefore, of his own men and the
Toledans he attacked Mohammed's troops, but the latter
immediately took to flight and enticed their foe into the
ambuscade. As the Toledans and Leonese were in hot
pursuit they suddenly found themselves surrounded and
attacked by a swarm of the enemy. Scarcely a man escaped.
"The son of Julius,"[2] writes a court poet, "exclaimed to
Mûsâ who marched before him: 'Lo, I see death on all
sides! In front of me, behind me, below me!' . . . The
rocks of the Guadacelete mourn with re-echoed wailings this
multitude of slaves and uncircumcised."

The barbarous victors decapitated eight thousand corpses,
and making a mound of the heads, leaped upon it, while the
air rang with their yells. Later Mohammed had these heads

[1] According to Ibn Adhâri, brother of Ordoño I. Ibn Khaldûn asserts that the
King of Navarre also furnished a contingent.
[2] The name of some Christian leader, as Mûsâ is of a Renegade.

fastened to the walls of Cordova and other towns, and even sent some of them to African princes.

Satisfied with the victory he had gained, and certain that the Toledans—who admitted a loss of twenty thousand men—would not now molest him, Mohammed returned to his Capital, having made provision that the Toledans should be harassed by the Governor of Calatrava and Talavera and by his son Mundhir, in turn. Meanwhile he continued to oppress the Christians of Cordova. He caused the monastery of Tabanos to be demolished, not unjustly regarding it as a hotbed of fanaticism. He farmed out the taxes payable by the Christians, with the result that the imposts were greatly increased. Nevertheless the zeal of the fanatics showed no diminution, and while the "martyrs" continued voluntarily to present their heads to the executioner, Alvaro and Eulogius did not cease to defend their action. The former wrote with this object his *Indiculus luminosus*, and the latter his *Apologia Martyrum*. At Cordova such apologies were necessary; for the Christians of that city were submissive and patient, and attributed their sufferings to the senseless conduct of the Zealots, rather than to the Sultan's intolerance. In Toledo and the neighbouring towns, on the other hand, the Christians sympathised so keenly with the Zealots, and especially with Eulogius, that the bishops of the province, having to nominate a Metropolitan upon Wistremir's death, unanimously elected Eulogius himself. The Sultan refused to let him enter Toledo, but the bishops persisted in their resolution, and trusting that sooner or later the veto might be removed, they forbade the election of another Metropolitan while Eulogius lived.

To the disparaging criticisms of their fellow-citizens the Zealots could therefore oppose the tokens of goodwill and esteem shown them by the Toledans. Ere long they could also claim the authority of two French monks, who showed clearly that they ranked the martyrs of that day with those of the primitive Church.

These two monks, named Usuard and Odilard, belonged to the Abbey of S. Germain-des-Prés, and arrived at Cordova in the year 858. Their abbot, Hilduin, had sent them to Valencia to fetch the body of S. Vincent, but learning on the way that the martyr's bones had been translated to Benevento,[1] they began to fear that they would be

---

[1] Or, according to another account, they had been carried by a monk named Auldaldus to Zaragoza, where they were venerated as those of S. Marinus. See F. Meyrick, *The Church in Spain* (1892), p. 288.

obliged to return home empty-handed, when they heard at
Barcelona of the recent martyrdoms at Cordova. "The
journey thither will be arduous," they were told; "but
if you accomplish it, sacred relics will surely be your
reward."

A journey through Spain was, indeed, in those days
always perilous and sometimes impracticable. Since the
routes were infested with brigands, travellers were obliged
to combine and form caravans; but such occasions rarely
presented themselves, and when the two monks—who were
resolved to brave all dangers if by any means they could
acquire relics—reached Zaragoza, eight years had elapsed
since a caravan had left that city for Cordova. It was their
good fortune, however, to find such an expedition on the
point of starting. They joined it. The Christians of the
town, convinced that the whole party would be massacred
in some mountain gorge, wept as they bade them farewell.
Their fears, however, were not realized; the two monks were
rewarded for the fatigues of their journey, and reached in
safety the capital of the Moslem dominion, where they were
hospitably entertained by a deacon of the church of S.
Cyprian. Their endeavours to obtain relics were for a long
time fruitless. An influential personage who took a deep
interest in their mission—Leovigild, surnamed Abadsolomes
—tried to obtain the remains of Saints Aurelius and George,
which lay in the Monastery of Pinna-Mellaria; [1] but to these
the monks attached so much value that in spite of the
formal commands of Bishop Saul, they refused to deliver
them to the French. The bishop thereupon came in person
and compelled them to yield, though the monks still
maintained that he had no right to deprive them of their
precious possessions.

After spending nearly two months at Cordova, Usuard
and Odilard set out on their homeward journey, taking with
them a huge bundle. This bore the bishop's seal, and was
addressed to King Charles the Bald, that the Moslems
might be induced to believe that the bale, which actually
enclosed the bodies of Aurelius and George,[2] merely contained presents for the French King. This time their
journey was less difficult and perilous. The Sultan was

---

[1] "The rock of honey"; many bee-hives were kept on the hill on which it
stood. The saints had been buried only six years before.

[2] The head of Aurelius, however, which was missing, was supplied by that of
his wife Natalia. *Acta Sanctorum,* Jul. Tom. vi. p. 462.

about to lead an army against Toledo, and since all the regiments, except those forming the garrison of the Capital, were under orders to march, the monks found no difficulty in attaching themselves to one of the companies. In the camp they found Leovigild, who escorted them to Toledo. From that city to Alcala de Henares the route was safe, for at the approach of the army, the barons—half brigands, half guerillas—who usually stripped travellers, had all abandoned their castles to seek refuge within the walls of Toledo.   On their return to France, the two monks deposited the relics—which had worked a multitude of miracles on the way [1]—in the church at Esmant, a village belonging to the Abbey of S. Germain, where most of the monks were then gathered together, since their monastery had been burned by the Normans.   The relics were afterwards transferred to S. Germain, and exposed to the veneration of the faithful of Paris.   So much interest did they arouse in Charles the Bald that he sent one Mancio to Cordova, to collect precise information concerning Aurelius and George.[2]

The expedition against Toledo, which had given the French monks an opportunity of returning to their country, turned out in accordance with the Sultan's hopes.   He once more had recourse to stratagem.   Occupying the bridge with his troops, he instructed his engineers to undermine the piers, unperceived by the Toledans, and when the work had nearly been accomplished, he withdrew his men and lured the enemy to pursue them.   The structure suddenly gave way, and the Toledan soldiers perished in the waters of the Tagus.

The grief felt by the Toledans at this disaster was only equalled by the joy felt at the Sultan's court, where every success, however indecisive, was exaggerated.   "The Eternal," said a poet,[3] "could not permit a bridge built to carry squadrons of unbelievers, to stand.   Bereft of her citizens, Toledo is sad and deserted as a tomb."

Not long afterwards Mohammed grasped an opportunity of ridding himself of his mortal foe in Cordova.

There was then in the Capital a young girl named Leocritia.   Born of Moslem parents, but secretly instructed in the mysteries of Christianity by a relative who was a nun,

---

[1] *Acta Sanctorum*, Jul. Tom. vi. p. 462.
[2] *Esp. sagr.*, x. pp. 534–65.
[3] Abbâs ibn-Firnâs (Makkarî, i. 101).

she at last confessed to her father and mother that she had been baptized. Her indignant parents, after vainly trying to entice their daughter back into the fold of Islam, had recourse to corporal punishment. Beaten night and day, and fearing to be publicly accused of apostasy, Leocritia appealed to Eulogius and his sister Anulo for shelter. Eulogius, who perhaps felt memories of Flora, whom Leocritia resembled in many respects, rising in his breast, assured her that he would keep her in hiding as soon as she succeeded in making her escape from home. This Leocritia effected by an artifice. She feigned to have abjured Christianity, and to have overcome her dislike for worldly pleasures ; and when she saw that her parents were reassured, she left her home one day in her gayest apparel, declaring that she was going to a wedding. But she sought out Eulogius and Anulo, who informed her where one of their friends dwelt who would receive her.

Although her parents, assisted by the police, sought for her everywhere, Leocritia at first eluded their search ; but on one occasion, after she had spent the day with Anulo,. whom she dearly loved, it unfortunately happened that the servant whose duty it was to conduct her to her lodging by night, did not arrive until daybreak, and fearing lest she might be recognised, Leocritia resolved to remain with Anulo till the next night. This delay proved her undoing. That day the Kady was informed by a spy, or a traitor, that the girl whom he sought was then with Eulogius' sister. By the magistrate's orders the house was surrounded by soldiers, and Leocritia and Eulogius himself—who happened to be within—were arrested. On being asked by the Kady why he had harboured the girl, Eulogius replied : " We are commanded to preach and to expound our religion to those who seek us. This damsel wished to be instructed by me in our faith ; I acceded to her wishes as well as I could, and I would do the like for you, Kady, if you made the same request."

Since proselytism, to which Eulogius thus pleaded guilty, was not a capital offence, the Kady merely condemned him to be beaten. Eulogius instantly made up his mind. Perhaps his resolution was due rather to pride than to courage, but he decided that it was a hundred times better for such a man as himself to seal with his blood his life-long principles than to submit to an ignominious punishment. " Whet thy sword ! " he cried to the Kady : " restore my

U

soul to its creator; but think not that I will permit my
body to be torn with the lash!"

Thereupon he poured forth a torrent of imprecations
against the Prophet. He expected to be instantly condemned to death; but the Kady, who respected him as the
primate elect of Spain, did not venture to assume so great
a responsibility, and sent him to the palace in order that the
Viziers might decide his fate.

When Eulogius entered the council-chamber, one of the
officers of state, who knew him well and wished to save his
life, addressed him thus: "I am not surprised, Eulogius,
when madmen and imbeciles offer their heads without cause
to the executioner; but how cometh it that a learned man
like thyself, and one that enjoyeth general esteem, followeth
their example? What frenzy impelleth thee? Why hast
thou thus plotted against thine own life? I pray thee heed
my words: bow to necessity; utter but a single word
retracting what thou hast said before the Kady—and in
that case, I will answer for my colleagues and myself that
thou shalt have nothing to fear."

In these words the speaker expressed the feelings of all
enlightened Moslems; they pitied the fanatics much more
than they hated them, and regretted that in obedience to
the law they were obliged to put to death poor wretches
whom they regarded as lunatics. Perhaps Eulogius, who
hitherto had not experienced a thirst for that martyrdom
which he had encouraged so many others to seek, and who
was after all the head of an ambitious rather than a fanatical
party, felt at that moment that the Moslems were less
barbarous than he had supposed; but he knew at the same
time that he could not recant without exposing himself to
the just contempt of his associates. He therefore replied
as the other martyrs, his disciples, had replied in similar
circumstances, and the Viziers were reluctantly obliged to
condemn him to death. Eulogius was immediately led to
execution. He showed great resignation. A eunuch
struck him on the cheek, and the priest, in literal obedience
to the precept of the Gospel, turned to him the other,
saying: "Smite that also!" The eunuch took him at his
word. Eulogius then mounted the scaffold with firmness
and courage, fell upon his knees, raised his hands heaven-
wards, made the sign of the cross, uttered a short prayer in
a low voice, and laying his head upon the block received the

fatal blow (March 11, 859). Four days later, Leocritia, convicted of apostasy, met a similar fate.[1]

The execution of the primate elect caused profound emotion, not only at Cordova—where numerous miracles wrought by the saint's relics were soon reported—but throughout Spain. Many chronicles of the north of the Peninsula, which make scarcely any reference to events in Cordova, record with great precision the date of the martyrdom, and twenty-four years later, Alfonso, King of Leon, in making a treaty of peace with the Sultan Mohammed, inserted a clause by which the bones of the Saints Eulogius and Leocritia were to be delivered to him.

Though deprived of their leader, the Zealots continued to blaspheme Mohammed in order to die on the scaffold; but the corroding tooth of time wrought its inevitable effect, and this strange fanaticism, which had flourished in Cordova for so many years, slowly yielded to the universal law—and after a while only the memory of it survived.

A new epoch opens. The Renegades and Christians of the mountains of Regio rose in rebellion. This revolt, formidable enough in itself, was accompanied or followed by an almost universal insurrection in the Peninsula, and furnished the Christians of Cordova with an opportunity of showing in another way their detestation of the name of Mohammed.

[1] See *Acta Sanctorum*, March 15. It is said that S. Leocritia (Lucretia) was beheaded and thrown into the river "to be eaten by fishes," but was ultimately buried in the church of S. Genet. See A. B. C. Dunbar, *Dict. of Saintly Women* (1904), i. p. 468.

[AUTHORITIES: Ibn Adhârî, ii. 96–9, 109, 114–15; Eulog., *Mem. Sanct.*, ii. 16; iii. 1–3, 5, 10–11, &c.; *Epist.*, p. 330; Ibn al-Kûtiyya, f. 29; Alvar., *Vit. Eulog.*, c. 10–16; Sams., ii. c. 9; Khoshanî, p. 293; Arîb, ii. 153; Nuwairî, p. 463; Ibn Khaldûn, f. 9.]

CHAPTER X

THE MOUNTAINEERS OF REGIO

THE traveller from Cordova to Malaga, who prefers enduring stoically the fatigues and privations of a romantic excursion through a wild but beautiful country to being jolted in a carriage along monotonous and wearisome roads, at first traverses an undulating and well-cultivated district, as far as the Genil, and then a level plain which extends to Campillos. There he enters the Serrania of Ronda and Malaga, the most picturesque part of Andalusia. Here and there this mountain range attains true sublimity, with its majestic forests of oaks, cork-trees, and chestnuts, its deep and gloomy ravines, its torrents thundering over precipices, its ruined castles and villages clinging to the sides of mighty crags whose summits are bare of vegetation and whose flanks seem blackened and calcined by the lightning; elsewhere the landscape smiles with vineyards and meadows, with groves of almond, cherry, citron and pomegranate, or with thickets of oleanders yielding more flowers than leaves; here, shallow streams wind capriciously by orchards whose pears and apples supply all southern Spain : there, lie fields of flax, hemp, and, above all, of corn, whence is made a bread which is held to be the whitest and most delicious in the world.

The inhabitants of the Serrania are vivacious, comely, light-hearted, and witty : they love song and laughter; they delight in dancing to the click of the castanets, and the music of the guitar or mandoline. Nevertheless, these people are vain and quarrelsome, boastful yet courageous, and of a temper so passionate that the mortal blow often follows quick upon the angry glance : a festival frequently involves the stabbing of two or three holiday-makers. The women, though of singular beauty, have masculine traits; tall and robust, they do not shirk the most laborious tasks; they bear heavy burdens with ease, and sometimes indulge in wrestling matches with one another.

In times of peace these mountaineers are chiefly employed

in smuggling[1] English goods from Gibraltar into the interior, and they have acquired wonderful skill in evading the swarm of custom-house officers. Sometimes in considerable force, under a trusted chief, they descend into the plains to sell their goods, and have been known to offer a stout resistance to troops sent against them. In troublous times, when civil discord runs high, many of them take to brigandage, either as *ladrones* or *rateros*. Though not professional brigands, the latter—who are recruited among the shepherds, unemployed villagers, lazy artisans, wandering harvesters, innkeepers who lack customers, or even small farmers—rifle, in an amateurish way, travellers who are not provided with a proper escort; but if the latter are well-armed, the *ratero* hides his carbine, takes up his spade, and feigns to be engaged in agriculture.[2] To be found everywhere, these robbers of the lowest rank are always ready to lend their aid, upon occasion, either to the true brigands or to the police, and, like prudent allies, they always join the winning side. The true brigands, who observe military discipline, and ride in companies, are much more dignified. The *rateros*, to escape accusation, often assassinate those whom they have robbed; but the *ladrones* only kill those who show fight; well-bred and courteous, especially towards ladies, they strip travellers with the utmost civility. Far from being despised, they stand high in popular esteem. They defy the law, are in revolt against society, terrorize the districts they exploit, yet they enjoy a certain prestige. Their daring, their adventurous life, their urbanity—all appeal to women, even when terrified. When at last they fall into the hands of justice and are hanged, their fate excites sympathy and compassion. In modern times José Maria became famous as a bandit chief, and his name will long survive in the memory of the Andalusians as a model brigand.[3] Mere chance impelled him to adopt his career. Having committed homicide in a moment of passion, he fled to the mountains to avoid arrest; and there, having no means of subsistence save his carbine, he organized a band of followers, supplied them with horses, and systematically robbed travellers. Brave, active, intelligent, and having a perfect knowledge of the country, he succeeded in all his

---

[1] See C. Rochfort Scott, *Excursions*, i. pp. 110 *sq.*

[2] There is even a lower grade—the *raterillo*, a mere footpad. See Ford, *Gatherings from Spain* (1846), p. 199.

[3] See Ford, *ut supra*, ch. xvi., and S. S. Cook, *Sketches in Spain*, ch. xv.

enterprises, and evaded every attempt to arrest him.
Throughout the country he had confederates bound to him
by oath, and when he needed a man to complete his band,
he could make choice among at least forty eligible candidates—so highly valued was the honour of serving under
him. He had relations even with the magistrates themselves: in a proclamation of the Captain-general of the
province the authorities of four districts were named as his
accomplices. So great was his power that he was master of
all the southern routes, and the post-office authorities, for
the right of free passage, paid him a yearly fee of eighty
francs for each vehicle. He ruled his bandits more despoti-
cally than any autocrat ever ruled his subjects, and a fierce
spirit of justice governed all his decisions.

In time of war, smugglers and brigands, such as these,
accustomed as they are to grappling with untamed nature,
prove extremely formidable adversaries. It is true that they
fail in attacks which require a certain degree of combination;
and it is also true that in the open they cannot stand against
the scientific manœuvres of regular troops ; but amidst the
rugged, winding, and narrow paths of the mountains, their
agility and knowledge of the ground give them an immense
advantage over ordinary soldiers. The French learnt this
lesson when the phantom king, placed by Napoleon on the
throne of Spain, tried to subject these intrepid mountaineers
to his hated authority. Whenever the French hussars could
attack them in the open, they sabred them by hundreds ;
but in the zigzag tracks on the brink of dizzy precipices,
where their horses were only an additional source of danger,
the same hussars fell into ambushes at every turn. At
moments when they least expected it, they found themselves
exposed to flank attacks from clouds of sharpshooters, who,
without ceasing fire, quickly regained rocky heights where
they could not be pursued, and even as they retreated wiped
out whole parties of the defenceless French. Amidst the
horrors of war, the mountaineers could not refrain from
occasionally displaying their innate love of practical joking.
At Olbera, where the French hussars had demanded a steer,
the inhabitants brought them an ass cut in quarters. The
hussars found their veal rather mawkish, and in subsequent
skirmishes the mountaineers as they fired would cry out:
" Who dined off a jackass at Olbera ? " This was, in their
opinion, the deadliest insult which could be offered to a
Christian.

In the ninth century, this province, then called Reiya, or rather Regio,[1] of which Archidona was the capital, contained an almost exclusively Spanish population, resembling in every respect its present inhabitants—having the same traits and habits, the same vices and virtues. Some of these mountaineers were Christians, but the majority were Moslems; all were Spaniards who nursed an implacable hatred for their country's oppressors. Passionate lovers of liberty, they resolved that foreign tyranny should not enrich itself much longer at their expense, and they watched for the opportunity of throwing off the yoke. The moment so impatiently awaited could not be far off. The victories daily won by their compatriots in other provinces showed the mountaineers that with courage and daring it would not be impossible to attain their ends. Toledo was already independent. For twenty years the Sultan had in vain endeavoured to subject it to his authority. The Christians, who had maintained their preponderance in the city, had placed themselves under the protection of the King of Leon, and although betrayed by the Renegades, they had compelled the Sultan, in 873, to enter into a treaty with them, by which the maintenance of their republican form of government was assured; and they enjoyed an almost independent political existence, being merely subject to yearly tribute. Another independent State had been founded in Aragon— the Northern Marches of the Arabs—by the Beni Kasî, an old Visigothic family which had embraced Islamism. Towards the middle of the ninth century this house had grown so powerful, thanks to the talents of Mûsâ II, that it ranked on an equality with reigning dynasties. At the time of Mohammed's accession, Mûsâ II was master of Zaragoza, Tudela, Huesca, and all Aragon. Toledo was in alliance with him, and his son Lope was commandant in that city. A valiant and tireless soldier, Mûsâ turned his arms now against the Count of Barcelona, or of Alva, and now against the Count of Castile, or the Franks. On reaching the height of his fame and power, respected and courted by all his neighbours—even by the French King, Charles the Bald, who sent him splendid gifts—Mûsâ posed as a monarch without anyone daring to say him nay, and finally, wishing to be in

---

[1] Regio Malacitana, according to Spruner. Ibn Khaldûn, and others, make Reiya a town, and confuse it with Malaga. Malaga was the capital of the province under the Visigoths, and again after the reign of 'Abd-er-Rahmân III. Cf. *Recherches* (1881), i. 317-20.

name what he was in fact, he boldly assumed the title of
"the third King in Spain." After the death of this remarkable man (A.D. 862),[1] the Sultan, it is true, once more
assumed authority over Toledo and Zaragoza; but his
resulting complacency was short-lived. Ten years later,
Mûsâ's sons, aided by the people of the province, who had
been accustomed to no rule save that of the Beni Kasî, expelled the Sultan's troops. Mohammed tried to subdue
them, but the Beni Kasî, supported by the King of Leon,
Alphonso III (who was so close an ally that he had entrusted them with the education of his son Ordoño), resisted
the Sultan's attacks.

The North was therefore free, and leagued against the
Sultan. At the same time a daring Renegade of Merida,
Ibn Merwân,[2] had founded an independent principality in
the West. Falling into the Sultan's hands—upon the
surrender of Merida, where he had been a leader in the
insurrection—he became captain in the body-guard; but in
875, the Prime Minister, Hâshim, who bore him some
grudge, said to him in the presence of the Viziers: "A dog
is of more worth than thou!" and to crown the insult,
smote him in the face. Vowing in his rage to risk all
rather than again endure such treatment, Ibn Merwân called
his friends together, and fleeing with them, seized the castle
of Alanje, to the south of Merida, where he stood on the
defensive. Besieged in this stronghold by the royal troops,
and running short of provisions, so that he and his men were
forced to live on the flesh of their horses, Ibn Merwân did
not capitulate until, at the end of three months, the supply
of water failed: considering, however, the desperate straits
to which he was reduced, the terms he obtained were not
disadvantageous, for he was permitted to withdraw to
Badajoz, which was not in those days a walled town. Once
safe out of the Sultan's clutches, Ibn Merwân, however,
became his dangerous and implacable foe. Uniting his
band to another, also composed of Renegades, under the
leadership of one Sadûn, he called to arms the Renegades of
Merida and other places, and preached a new religion to
his compatriots, in which Christianity and Islamism were
blended. Forming an alliance with Alfonso III, King of
Leon [3]—the natural ally of all rebels against the Govern-

---

[1] He was killed by his son-in-law Izrâk, Governor of Guadalaxara, in a fit of
jealousy. *Recherches* (1881), i. 215.

[2] 'Abd-er-Rahmân ibn Merwân ibn Yûnos.

[3] Ibn Merwân was hence known as "the Galician."

ment—Ibn Merwân spread terror far and wide : he wreaked
his vengeance, however, solely on the Arabs and Berbers, as
his country's enemies, but on these he took bitter revenge
for his personal injuries and those of his nation.   With a
view to suppressing these acts of brigandage, Mohammed
despatched an army under the command of his son Mundhir
and his minister Hâshim.   Ibn Merwân advanced to meet
the enemy, and sending Sadûn to seek aid from the King
of Leon, he threw himself into Caracuel.[1]   Hâshim encamped near this fortress, of which extensive remains still
exist, while one of his lieutenants occupied that of Monte-
Salud.   Soon afterwards, the lieutenant reported that Sadûn
was nearing Monte-Salud with the Leonese auxiliaries, but
that his force was numerically weak and could be easily
surprised.   The officer was mistaken ; Sadûn commanded a
considerable army, but wishing to lure his enemy into a
trap, that wily general had spread a false report concerning
its strength.   His device was entirely successful.   Deceived
by his lieutenant's report, Hâshim advanced with a few
squadrons against Sadûn.   The latter, fully informed by his
spies, retreated to the mountains.   There he lay in ambush
in a defile; his men, concealed behind the surrounding
rocks, fell upon the enemy at a moment when they expected
no attack, and inflicted heavy losses.   Hâshim himself,
covered with wounds, was made prisoner, after he had seen
fifty of his officers fall beside him.   He was taken to Ibn
Merwân, and found himself at the mercy of the man whom
he had so cruelly insulted.   Ibn Merwân, however, in his
generosity, did not even reproach him, but treating him with
the respect due to his rank, sent him to his ally the King of
Leon.
    The Sultan, on learning what had happened, became
furious.   He was doubtless distressed that his favourite was
a captive, but he was much more distressed at the thought
that he could not honourably refuse to ransom him from the
King of Leon : and Alfonso demanded a hundred thousand
ducats ! This severely tried the generosity of the miserly
Mohammed.   He found endless excuses for not paying this
vast sum.   " If Hâshim is a prisoner," he argued, " it is his
own fault.   Why is he so foolhardy ?   He is a hare-brained
fellow who acts without consideration and who never listens
to good advice ! " However, when his minister had languished

---

[1] Between Ciudad-Real and Almodovar del Campo.

in prison for two years, the Sultan agreed to pay part of the ransom. Hâshim himself promised to pay the King of Leon the rest later, and leaving his brothers, his sons, and his nephews as hostages, returned to Cordova intent upon revenging himself on Ibn Merwân. Meanwhile that chieftain had laid waste the districts of Seville and Niebla, and the Sultan, who could make no headway against him, had asked him to name the conditions on which he would cease from the forays which were ruining the country. Ibn Merwân's reply was arrogant and menacing. " I will cease from my forays," he said, " and I will order the Sultan's name to be mentioned in the public prayers, provided that he cedes me Badajoz, allows me to fortify it, and dispenses me from payment of tribute and from obedience to him in any respect ; otherwise, I defy him." Humiliating though these conditions were, the Sultan had accepted them. Hâshim now tried to persuade his master that in the altered circumstances it would be by no means impossible to subdue this overweening rebel. " Formerly," he urged, " Ibn Merwân, having no fixed abode, could always, with his horsemen, evade our pursuit, but now that he is tied to a town, he is in our power. We can lay siege to it and force him to surrender." Hâshim succeeded in winning over the monarch to his views, and having been authorized to set out with an army, he had reached Niebla, when Ibn Merwân sent Mohammed a message couched in these terms : " I am informed that Hâshim is marching westwards. I am well aware that he trusts to besiege me, and thus to take his revenge ; but I swear that if he advances further than Niebla, I will burn Badajoz to the ground, and resume my depredations." The Sultan was so cowed by this threat, that he immediately recalled the Minister and his army to Cordova, and henceforth evinced not the least desire to subdue his too formidable foe.

While the insurgents, therefore, had shown themselves brave and resourceful, the Government had proved itself both weak and cowardly. Every concession granted to the rebels, every treaty made with them, had tended to diminish the prestige so necessary for inspiring respect in an unsubdued and disaffected population much more numerous than their conquerors. The mountaineers of Regio, emboldened by the tidings which reached them from the North and West, grew restless in their turn. In the year 879, tumults and insurrections broke out in many parts of the province.

The Government, by no means blind to the dangers which threatened from this quarter, were greatly alarmed at the news which they received.   Stringent measures were hurriedly adopted.   The chief of an important band was seized and brought to Cordova.   Fortresses were hastily erected on the heights which it was most important to guard.   All such measures resulted in arousing the mountaineers rather than cowing them.   They still possessed, however, but little power of combination.   What they lacked was a leader of commanding character, able to direct towards a definite goal the organized enthusiasm of a patriotic people. If such a man were forthcoming, he would but have to give the signal, and all the dwellers in the mountains would arise and follow him.

[Authorities: Sebast., c. 26; Nuwairî (a.h. 259); Ibn Adhârî, ii. 102–6; Ibn Khaldûn, f. 10; Ibn al-Kûtiyya, f. 37; Ibn Hayyân, f. 11; *Chron. Alb.*, c. 62.]

CHAPTER XI

'OMAR IBN HAFSÛN

AT the epoch when the Andalusian mountaineers began to grow restless, there lived in a village near Hisn-Aute (now Yznate), to the North-east of Malaga, a landowner named Hafs. He came of a good family, being fifth in descent from a Visigoth, Alfonso, who had borne the title of Count ;[1] but at a time of political and religious changes, the grandfather of Hafs—who during the reign of Hakam I had quitted Ronda and settled near Hisn-Aute—was induced, through stoicism or apathy, to become a Moslem. His descendants were ostensibly Islamites, but at the bottom of their hearts they fostered a pious regard for the religion of their ancestors. Thanks to his thrift and industry Hafs had amassed a considerable fortune. His less wealthy neighbours held him in respect, and indeed honoured him by calling him, not Hafs, but Hafsûn—the termination being equivalent to a title of nobility. Nothing, probably, would have disturbed the even tenour of his peaceful life if the misconduct of his son 'Omar, over whom he failed to exert paternal control, had not caused him ceaseless disquietude. Vain, arrogant, and of a quarrelsome disposition, this young man showed the worst side of the Andalusian character. An imagined affront threw him into a paroxysm of rage ; a word, a gesture, a glance, sufficed—and many a time had he been carried back to the homestead covered with wounds and bruises. With such a temperament it was inevitable that he would sooner or later commit homicide or himself be killed. One day, during an unnecessary quarrel, he laid one of his neighbours dead at his feet. To save his son from the gallows, the distracted father fled with him from the farm, where his family had dwelt for three-quarters of a century, and sought refuge in the Serrania de Ronda, at the foot of Mount Bobastro. In that wild spot the young 'Omar, who loved to lose himself in dense forests and gloomy

---

[1] The father of Hafs was named 'Omar, and his grandfather, Ja'far al-Islâmi (the Renegade).

316

gorges, ended by becoming a bandit, or *ratero*, as he would now be called. Falling into the hands of justice, he was bastinadoed by order of the Governor of the Province. On seeking to cross once more his father's threshold, the old man drove him forth as an incorrigible scoundrel. Thereupon 'Omar, unable to gain a livelihood in Spain, made his way to the coast, and embarked in a vessel bound for Africa. After leading a vagabond life for some time, he at last reached Tahort, where he became apprenticed to a tailor who was a native of Regio and a former acquaintance. One day as 'Omar was working with his master, an old man entered the shop and producing a piece of cloth, requested the tailor to make him a garment. The tailor, offering his visitor a seat, entered into a conversation in which the apprentice joined. The old man inquired who the youth was. "A neighbour of mine at Regio," replied the tailor, "and he hath come hither to learn my trade." "When didst thou leave Regio?" asked the customer. "Some forty days ago," replied 'Omar. "Knowest thou Mount Bobastro?" "My home is at the foot of that mountain." "Indeed! Hath an insurrection broken out there?" "Assuredly not." "Yet a little while!" murmured the old man, who after a pause continued, "Knowest thou in the neighbourhood of that mountain one 'Omar, son of Hafsûn?" At the mention of his name, 'Omar grew pale, and lowering his brow was silent. His interrogator looked at him attentively, and noticed that he had lost an eye-tooth. The old man was a Spaniard who firmly believed in the renascence of his race, and while he had often heard of 'Omar's escapades, he believed the youth to be one of those lofty natures destined to be potent for either good or ill, and thought he saw in this unruly son, this ruffler and mountain robber, the making of a great leader. 'Omar's silence, his pallor, his confusion, the missing tooth—for the old man had heard that 'Omar had lost one in a fray—all confirmed him in the belief that he was addressing Ibn Hafsûn himself, and wishing to give a noble aim to the fiery youth's ambition, he exclaimed, "Thinkest thou to escape from thy poverty by wielding a needle? Return to thy own country, and wield the sword instead! Thou shalt be a terror to the Omayyads, and rule a great nation!" Later on these prophetic words doubtless proved a stimulus to 'Omar's ambition, but for the moment they had a quite contrary effect. Fearing lest he should be recognised by persons less well-disposed towards

him, and handed over to the Spanish Government by the
Prince of Tahort, who was subservient to the Sultan of
Cordova, he fled in haste from the town, his baggage consisting
of two loaves which he hid in the sleeves of his cloak.
Returning to Spain, he did not venture to visit his home,
but sought refuge with an uncle, to whom he related the
old man's words. This uncle, who was credulous as well as
enterprising, had faith in the prediction. He advised his
nephew to yield to his destiny and head an insurrection,
promising to afford him all the aid in his power. 'Omar
was easily persuaded, and his uncle, having assembled some
forty peasants, suggested that they should form a company
under the command of his nephew. 'Omar organized this
willing band, and encamped with them on Mount Bobastro
(A.D. 880-1), where stood the ruins of a Roman fortress,
now called El Castillon.[1] The repair of these ruins presented
no difficulty, and a better place could not have been selected
as a stronghold for either robbers or rebels. The fortress
stood on a lofty and precipitous rock; inaccessible on the
east and south, it was almost impregnable. It had the
advantage of lying near the great plain which extends from
Campillos to Cordova. Into this plain 'Omar's band could
conveniently make incursions to carry away cattle, or levy
unauthorized taxes on isolated farmers. To such expeditions
'Omar at first confined himself, but he soon regarded mere
highway robbery as beneath him, and when his band—
augmented by the accession of those who had any inducement to withdraw from society and ensconce themselves in
safety behind strong walls—sufficed to hold in awe the
feeble military forces of the district, he began boldly to push
on to the very gates of towns and to signalize himself by
audacious and brilliant feats of arms. Justly alarmed, the
Governor of Regio decided at length to attack the marauders with all his available troops, but he was repulsed, and
in his precipitous flight abandoned even his pavilion to the
insurgents. The Sultan, attributing this disaster to the
Governor's incapacity, superseded him. But the new
Governor was no more successful, and was indeed so deeply
impressed by the strength of Bobastro that he made a truce
with 'Omar. The truce did not last long, and 'Omar, though
frequently attacked, held out in his mountain stronghold
for two or three years: at length, forced to surrender by

---

[1] But identified by M. Simonet with the ruins of Las Mesas de Villaverde. See
Recherches (1881), i. pp. 321-6.

Hâshim the Prime Minister, he was brought to Cordova with all his men. The Sultan, who saw an excellent officer in 'Omar, and trusty soldiers in his followers, received him graciously, and offered to enroll his entire force in the army. Recognising that for the time being they could do no better, 'Omar accepted this proposal.

Not long afterwards, in 883, when Hâshim led an expedition against Mohammed son of Lope—then chief of the Beni Kasî—and Alfonso, King of Leon, 'Omar, who accompanied him, found opportunities of distinguishing himself on several occasions, notably in the affair of Pancorvo. Calm and cool when necessary, but prompt and fiery in action, he speedily won the esteem of the commander-in-chief; but on his return to Cordova it was not long before he had reason to complain of Ibn Ghânim,[1] the Prefect of the city, who, out of spite against Hâshim, delighted in harassing officers such as 'Omar, who enjoyed that minister's favour. The Prefect incessantly made 'Omar change his quarters, and supplied him with corn of the worst quality. 'Omar, who was of a far from patient disposition, could not conceal his resentment, and one day showing Ibn Ghânim a crust of hard, black bread, he exclaimed, "As you hope for God's mercy, can such bread be eaten?" "Who art thou, thou scurvy rascal," replied the Prefect, "who darest to address me so insolently?" Returning to his quarters in deep indignation, 'Omar met Hâshim proceeding to his palace, and told him all. "They do not recognise your worth," said the Minister as he passed on, "but it rests with you to make it evident."

Disgusted with the Sultan's service, 'Omar proposed to his men that they should once more withdraw to the mountains and resume the free and adventurous life which they had so long led together. They wished for nothing better, and by sunset they had all quitted the Capital and were on their way to Bobastro (A.D. 884).

'Omar's first care was to regain possession of the castle. The task was difficult, for Hâshim, who well understood the importance of this fortress, had garrisoned it with a considerable force, and having further strengthened it with bastions and towers, deemed it impregnable. But 'Omar, confident in his good fortune, was not discouraged. With his uncle's help he reinforced his band with some resolute men, and then,

---

[1] Mohammed ibn Walid ibn Ghânim.

without giving the garrison time to organize resistance, vigorously attacked the castle and expelled the defenders so precipitately that they left behind them a youthful inamorata of the commander's, who proved so pleasing to 'Omar that he made her his wife, or mistress.

From this moment 'Omar, the José Maria of the ninth century, but to whom fortune was kinder than to that would-be hero, was no longer a robber chief, but the leader of the Spaniards of the South. He appealed to all his compatriots, whether Moslems or Christians. " Already too long," so ran his manifesto, " have ye endured the yoke of this Sultan who robs you and grinds you with taxes. Will ye let yourselves be down-trodden by Arabs who look on you as slaves? Think not that personal ambition prompts me to speak thus : my only ambition is to avenge your wrongs and deliver you from servitude." " Whenever 'Omar spake thus," writes an Arab historian, " those who heard him rendered him thanks and promised to obey him." According to the testimony even of his enemies—from whom alone we learn his history—'Omar's former faults entirely disappeared. Instead of being arrogant and quarrel-some, he became affable and courteous to the least of his soldiers : those who served under him displayed an affection for him amounting to idolatry, and obeyed him with a dis-ciplined obedience which was almost fanatical. Whatever the danger that threatened they would march at his first signal—into the fire if need were. Ever in the front rank and in the thick of the fight, 'Omar fought as a common soldier, wielding lance and sword with the best of them. He always selected the most redoubtable champions, and never withdrew from a combat until it was won. No man exposed himself more cheerfully to danger, or set a more brilliant example. He generously rewarded all services rendered to him ; an ample share of booty always fell to those who had notably distinguished themselves ; he honoured bravery even in an enemy, often setting at liberty those who had yielded only after a stout resistance. On the other hand, he severely punished evil-doers. His rough and ready judgments were not based upon the formal testimony of witnesses : his personal conviction that the accusation was well founded sufficed. Hence, although brigandage was in the blood of these people, the mountain-region soon enjoyed, thanks to 'Omar's prompt justice, complete security. The Arabs assure us that in those days a woman laden with money might traverse the district from end to end without fear. Nearly two years elapsed before the Sultan took any serious steps against this formidable champion of a long oppressed nationality; but at the beginning of June, 886, Mundhir, heir-presumptive to the throne, set out to attack the lord of Alhama, an ally of 'Omar's and like him a Renegade. 'Omar hastened to his friend's assistance, and threw himself into Alhama. After a siege of two months, the Renegades, whose provisions began to run short, resolved to cut their way through the enemy. Their sortie, however, was unsuccessful: 'Omar received several wounds, his hand was mutilated, and after losing many of his men, he was obliged to retire within the fortress. Fortunately for the Renegades, Mundhir, not long afterwards, received news which compelled him to raise the siege and return to Cordova: his father had died (August 4, 886). 'Omar took advantage of this event to extend his dominion. He approached the castellans of a number of strongholds and invited them to make common cause with himself. They all recognised him as their sovereign, and henceforth he was virtually king of Southern Spain. He found, however, in the Sultan who now ascended the throne a foeman worthy of his steel. The prince was energetic, prudent, and brave, and the Omayyad clients believed that if he had been spared to reign for another year he would have compelled all the rebels in the South to lay down their arms. At any rate he vigorously withstood them: the districts of Cabra, Elvira, and Jaen became the theatre of a fierce struggle wherein each party met with varying fortune. In the Spring of 888, Mundhir took the field in person against the insurgents, captured several fortresses on his march, devastated the country round Bobastro, and laid siege to Archidona. The Renegade Aishûn, who was in command of the garrison, was not exempt from the boastfulness which is still imputed to the Andalusians. Insisting upon his personal courage, which no one disputed, he exclaimed again and again: " If the Sultan can catch me, let him crucify me between a dog and a swine ! " He forgot that the Sultan had a surer means of securing him than by force of arms. Certain inhabitants of the town were amenable to bribery, and one day as Aishûn entered unarmed the house of one of these traitors, he was suddenly seized, and after being loaded with fetters, was handed over to the Sultan, who crucified him in the manner indicated by the prisoner

X

himself.   Archidona soon afterwards surrendered.   The
Sultan then made prisoners of the three Beni Matrûh who
held castles in the Sierra de Priego, and having crucified
them with nineteen of their officers, he proceeded to lay
siege to Bobastro.   Confident in the impregnability of his
rock, Ibn Hafsûn was so little perturbed by the siege that
he thought of nothing save how to play a trick upon the
Sultan.   A practical joke was very dear to him.   He accordingly made peace proposals to Mundhir.   " I will come and
dwell in Cordova," he said: " I will be a general in your
army, and my sons shall become your clients."   Mundhir
fell into the trap.   Summoning the Kady and principal
divines of Cordova, he commanded them to draw up a
treaty of peace on the lines proposed by Ibn Hafsûn.   The
latter then presented himself before the Sultan—who had
established his head-quarters in a neighbouring castle—and
begged him to send graciously a hundred mules to Bobastro
to carry away his goods and chattels.   The Sultan consented, and as the army quitted the neighbourhood of
Bobastro, the mules were sent to the fortress under the
escort of ten centurions and a hundred and fifty troopers.
Carelessly guarded, since it was believed that he could be
trusted, Ibn Hafsûn escaped by night, returned with all
haste to Bobastro, ordered a party of his men to follow him,
attacked the escort, captured the mules, and drove them
into safe custody behind the massive walls of the castle.

Enraged at having allowed himself to be tricked, Mundhir
swore in his wrath that he would recommence the siege of
Bobastro and never raise it until the perfidious Renegade
surrendered.   Death dispensed him from his vow.   His
brother, 'Abdallah, who was precisely of his own age, coveted
the throne, but had no hope of ascending it if his brother
died leaving a son old enough to succeed him.   He therefore
contrived to bribe Mundhir's surgeon, and this man in bleeding the Sultan used a poisonous lancet, with the result that
Mundhir expired after a reign of barely two years (June 29,
888).   Warned by the eunuchs, 'Abdallah, who was then at
Cordova, repaired to the camp with all haste, informed the
Viziers of his brother's death, and caused the oath of allegiance to be administered first to them, and then successively
to the Kurashites, the Omayyad clients, the government
officials, and the generals.   Since the soldiers were grumbling
at Mundhir's resolve—for they were convinced that Bobastro
was impregnable—it was easy to foresee that they would

desert when they learned that the Sultan was no more. An officer called 'Abdallah's attention to their disaffection, and advised him to conceal the fact of his brother's death and to bury him somewhere in the neighbourhood. 'Abdallah rejected this advice with well-dissembled indignation. ".What!" he exclaimed, "shall I abandon my brother's corpse to the tender mercies of a people who ring bells and worship crosses! Never! Though I should perish in its defence, I will convey it to Cordova!" Mundhir's death was then announced to the soldiers, who could not have received more welcome intelligence. Without waiting for orders from the new Sultan, they forthwith made preparations for returning to their homes, and as 'Abdallah marched towards Cordova, his army steadily melted away.

Ibn Hafsûn, who did not hear of Mundhir's death until the homeward march had begun, hastened to profit by the disorder which marked this precipitate retreat. He had captured many stragglers and much booty, when 'Abdallah sent his page Fortunio to beg the Spanish chieftain not to attack what was practically a funeral procession—adding the assurance that he wished for nothing better than to live at peace with him. Whether from generosity or policy Ibn Hafsûn immediately refrained from further pursuit.

'Abdallah reached Cordova with scarcely forty horsemen: all his other soldiers had abandoned him.

[AUTHORITIES: Ibn Khaldûn, ff. 9, 10, 91; *Hist. des Berb.* (Slane), i. xxxvii; Ibn Adhârî, *Introd.*, 44–6; ii. 48 *n.*, 106–9, 111, 117–21, 123; Ibn al-Khatîb, MS. E. (Art. on 'Omar ibn Hafsûn); Ibn al-Kûtiyya, ff. 37–9; Nuwairî, pp. 464–5; Ibn Hayyân, ff. 2–4.]

CHAPTER XII

SAUWÂR

'ABDALLAH ascended the throne under sinister auspices. The fabric of the State, long sapped by racial antipathies, seemed about to crumble into ruin. Ibn Hafsûn and his mountaineers might, in themselves, have proved no insuperable obstacle; but the Arab nobles, taking advantage of the general disorder, had also begun to lift their heads and aim at independence. This movement was more formidable for the monarchy than the revolt of the Spaniards—such at least was 'Abdallah's opinion. Since, therefore, if he were not to be wholly isolated, it was necessary for him to come to an understanding either with the Spanish people or with the nobles, he resolved to make advances to the former. He had already shown marks of favour to some of them, and had been on terms of close intimacy with Ibn Merwân, "the Galician," when they were comrades in the Sultan Mohammed's body-guard. He now offered the government of Regio to Ibn Hafsûn, conditionally on the recognition by that chieftain of the royal supremacy. At first this new policy seemed justified by its success. Ibn Hafsûn did homage, and showed his confidence in the Sultan by sending his son and some of his captains to the Court. The Sultan, for his part, did all he could to cement the alliance; he treated his guests with the utmost friendliness, and loaded them with gifts. After several months had elapsed, however, Ibn Hafsûn made no further attempt to restrain his soldiers, who pillaged hamlets and villages up to the very gates of Ossuna, Ecija, and even Cordova itself; and when the royal troops sent against these marauders were routed, he openly broke with the Sultan and expelled his agents.

'Abdallah, after all, had not succeeded in winning over the Spaniards, and in trying to do so he drifted into a grave conflict with his own race. It was scarcely to be expected that in the provinces, where the royal authority had become almost imperceptible, the Arabs would yield obedience to a monarch who was hand in glove with their enemies.

Events taking place in the province of Elvira first claim our attention. If pious memories have any influence over men's hearts, no province ought to have been more devoted to the Christian religion than that of Elvira. It had been the cradle of Spanish Christianity; in it had been heard the preaching of the Seven Missionaries [1]—who, according to ancient tradition, had been the disciples of the Apostles at Rome—when all the rest of the Peninsula was plunged in pagan darkness. Later, about A.D. 300, the capital of the province [2] had been the scene of a memorable Council. The Spaniards of Elvira, indeed, long remained faithful to the religion of their ancestors. In the Capital the foundations of a great mosque had been laid, soon after the conquest, by Hanash Sanânî, one of Mûsâ's most pious followers, but so few were the Moslem inhabitants of the town, that a century and a half later this mosque remained as Hanash had left it. The churches, on the other hand, were numerous and wealthy: even at Granada, although a great part of that city was in the hands of the Jews, there were at least four, and one of them—outside the Elvira gate—which had been built at the beginning of the seventh century by Gudila, a Gothic noble, was of incomparable magnificence. [3]

But during the reigns of 'Abd-er-Rahmân II and Mohammed, apostasy spread and became general. In the province of Elvira people were no more deaf to the voice of self-interest than elsewhere, while the shameless debaucheries and notorious impiety of the maternal uncle of Hostegesis —Samuel, Bishop of Elvira—had naturally inspired many Christians with an aversion for a religion whose ministers were so unworthy. Persecution did the rest. This the infamous Samuel himself directed. Deposed at length for his scandalous conduct, he hastened to Cordova and declared himself a Moslem. Henceforth he behaved with the utmost

---

[1] Thus commemorated in a hymn in the Mozarabic liturgies:

> " Hi sunt perspicui luminis indices,
> Torquatus, Tesifons, atque Hesicius;
> His Indaletius sive Secundus
> Juncti Euphrasio Cæcilioque sunt."

Cf. *Esp. sagr.*, iii. 361-77, 380-4.

[2] N.E. of Granada, near the modern Pinos Puente.

[3] It was because Granada was partly an episcopal and partly a Jewish town that it was not made the capital of the province by the Arabs. Cf. *Recherches* (1881), i. 339-40.

cruelty towards his former flock, whom the Government had handed over to his indiscriminating ferocity, and many of them found in apostasy the only means of saving their lives and property. In the end, so numerous did the Renegades become in Cordova, that the Government deemed it necessary to provide them with a spacious mosque. This edifice was completed in 864, during the reign of Mohammed.

The Arabs of the province were, for the most part, descendants of the soldiers of Damascus, who, disliking the narrow confines of a town, had settled in the open country. These rural Arabs, relatively to the Spaniards, formed an extremely proud and exclusive aristocracy. They had but few dealings with the inhabitants of the Capital; a sojourn in Elvira—a gloomy city, situated amidst dreary hills of volcanic origin, barren and rocky, whereon the summer flower was as rare as the winter snowflake—had no attraction for them; but on Fridays, when they entered the town, ostensibly to attend public worship but actually to display their richly caparisoned chargers, they never failed to treat the Spaniards with elaborate disdain. Aristocratic haughtiness is never more frankly offensive than when displayed by men whose mutual relations are characterised by polished courtesy. In the eyes of the Arabs, the Spaniards, whether Christians or Moslems, were " the vile rabble "—such was the established phrase. They thus invited an inexpiable grievance against themselves, and open collisions between the two races became frequent: already, some thirty years before the epoch with which we are about to deal, the Spaniards had besieged the Arabs in the Alhambra, where they had sought refuge.[1]

At the commencement of 'Abdallah's reign, we find the Spaniards engaged in deadly strife with the Arab nobles. The latter, who had entirely broken with the Sultan, had chosen for their leader a brave soldier of the tribe of Kais, Yahyâ ibn Sokâla by name. Driven out of their villages by their opponents, they had occupied a fortified position in a castle to the north-east of Granada, near Guardahortuna. They infested the district around this castle, the Spanish name of which was formerly Monte Sacro, afterwards corrupted, by Arab pronunciation, to Montexicar. The Renegades and Christians, commanded by Nâbil, accordingly

---

[1] No details of this war are known : it is referred to by the Spanish poet Abli : see p. 330, *infra*.

laid siege to this stronghold, slew a number of its defenders,
and at length captured it. Yahyâ ibn Sokâla saved himself by flight, but so few of his adherents were left that
he was obliged to lay down his arms and come to terms
with the Spanish. Henceforth he often visited the Capital.
He probably became involved in a conspiracy; at any rate,
in the Spring of 889 the Spaniards fell upon him, without
warning, and slew him, together with his companions; they
then threw the bodies into a well and began to hunt down
the Arabs like deer.

The joy of the Spaniards was great. "The spears of
our foes are broken!" sang their poet Ablî:[1] "We have
lowered their pride! 'The vile rabble' have laid the axe
at the root of their power. Long will their dead, whom we
cast into the well, await in vain an avenger!"

The plight of the Arabs was the more perilous since
they were at variance among themselves. The anarchy
into which they had fallen had revived the fatal rivalry of
Ma'addites and Yemenites; in many districts, such as that of
Sidona, the two races were in active hostility. In the province of Elvira, when a successor to Yahyâ had to be chosen,
the Yemenites, who seem to have been in a majority,
struggled with the Ma'addites for the hegemony. To be
divided against themselves at such a critical period was to
invite utter ruin. The Yemenites fortunately realized this
in time; they gave way, and by agreement with their rivals
conferred the leadership on Sauwâr.[2] This intrepid chieftain became the saviour of his people, and in after years it
was said: "If Allah had not given Sauwâr to the Arabs,
they would have been exterminated."

A Kaisite, like Yahyâ, Sauwâr would naturally desire
to avenge the death of his fellow-tribesman, but he had
another motive for seeking retribution, since at the storming
of Monte Sacro he had seen his eldest son slain by the
Spaniards. From that moment he had been consumed by
a thirst for vengeance. According to his own testimony
he was already advanced in years: "Women no longer
value my love," he says in one of his poems, "since my
locks have grown hoary;" and, indeed, he brought to the

---

[1] 'Abd-er-Rahmân ibn Ahmad; surnamed Ablî from his native place Abla, near
Guadix.
[2] Fourth in descent from Honaida, chief of the Beni Kais, who settled at
Maracena, in the district of Albolote, N. of Grenada, where his descendants still
dwell.

sanguinary task which he was about to accomplish a stubborn ferocity almost inconceivable in a young man, but explicable in a veteran who, dominated by one final passion, shuts his soul against all pity and all human sentiment. It would almost seem that he believed himself a destroying angel, and that all his gentler instincts—if such existed—were stifled by the self-conviction of his divine mission.

After summoning as many Arabs as he could to his standard, Sauwâr's first object was to regain possession of Monte Sacro. He had a twofold motive for this; he wished to hold a fortress which might serve as a base in further operations—and to slake his revenge in the blood of the slayers of his son. Although Monte Sacro was fully manned the Arabs took it by assault. Sauwâr exacted a terrible vengeance; he put to the sword all the soldiers of the garrison, to the number of six thousand. He then stormed other castles. Every victory was followed by frightful carnage; never did this terrible man spare a Spaniard's life; whole families were annihilated and for numberless estates no heirs were found.

In their distress, the Spaniards of Elvira besought Jad, Governor of the Province, to aid them, promising henceforth to submit to him. Jad consented, and at the head of his own troops and the Spaniards, he attacked Sauwâr.

The Arab chieftain awaited his adversaries without flinching. The battle was hotly contested, but the Arabs gained the day, pursued the foe to the gates of Elvira, and slew seven thousand of them. Jad himself fell into the hands of the victors. This successful encounter, known as the Battle of Jad, filled the Arabs with indescribable joy. Hitherto they had confined themselves to making attacks on castles, but now, for the first time, they had beaten their enemy in the open field, and had offered a multitude of victims to the *manes* of Yahyâ. Thus does Sa'îd ibn Jûdî, one of their bravest warriors and best poets, express their emotions:

"O ye apostates and infidels, who to your dying hour declare the true faith to be false,[1] we slew you to avenge our Yahyâ. We slew you. It was God's will! Ye sons of slaves, recklessly did ye stir the wrath of brave men who have never neglected to avenge their slain comrades. Prepare to feel their anger, to receive in your loins their flashing swords. At the head of the warriors who brook no insult, and are courageous as lions, an illustrious chieftain marches against you. An illustrious chieftain! His renown surpasses that of all others; he inherits the nobility of his

---

[1] Words addressed by Mohammed to Jews and Christians, in the Koran.

RISING IN ELVIRA

incomparable ancestors. He is a lion; he is sprung from the purest blood of Nizâr; he is the stay of his tribe as none else is. He cometh to avenge his tribesmen; those mighty men who trusted in his vows. He hath avenged them! He hath put to the sword the sons of the pale ones, and those who still live groan in their fetters. We have slain you in thousands; but the death of a myriad slaves does not atone for that of one noble.

" Alas! in their madness they murdered our Yahyâ when he was their guest! They butchered him, these vile and despicable slaves! Base are all their deeds; but this crime was madness! Their miserable fate convinceth them of their folly. Traitors, villains! Ye assassinated him in spite of all your oaths and treaties!"

After his brilliant victory, Sauwâr concluded treaties with the Arabs of Regio, Jaen, and even Calatrava, and recommenced his depredations and massacres. The Spaniards, utterly disheartened, could devise no other means of safety than to throw themselves into the arms of the Sultan. They therefore implored his protection. The Sultan would gladly have granted it, had it been in his power; as it was, he could but promise his friendly intervention. Sauwâr was accordingly informed that he might be entrusted with a large share in the Government of the province, provided that he submitted to the Sultan's authority, and promised to leave the Spaniards in peace. Sauwâr accepted these conditions. He and the Spaniards solemnly swore mutual amity, and material order was re-established throughout the province. Unfortunately the resulting calm was deceitful; unrest and passion still rankled in all hearts. Having no enemies to exterminate in his immediate neighbourhood, Sauwâr attacked the allies and vassals of Ibn Hafsûn. His cruel exploits and the piteous appeals of their fellow-countrymen suddenly revived the sentiment of nationality among the people of Elvira. With a common impulse they flew to arms, the whole province followed their example; the war-cry was raised in every family, and the Arabs—attacked and beaten on all sides—hastened to take shelter in the Alhambra.[1]

Captured by the Spaniards, re-captured by the Arabs, the Alhambra was little more than a majestic but almost defenceless ruin. It was, however, the only place of refuge left for the Arabs, and if they suffered it to be taken they would certainly be slaughtered to the last man. They therefore resolved to defend it to the uttermost. As long as the sun was in the heavens they vigorously repelled the

[1] For an account of the first Alhambra see J. F. Simonet, *Descripcion del Reino de Granada* (1861), pp. 30 *sq.*

incessant assaults of the Spaniards, who, with fury in their
hearts, reckoned on making an end once for all of their
ruthless oppressors. At nightfall, by the light of torches,
the defenders repaired the walls and bastions of the fortress;
but fatigue, watchings, the prospect of instant death if they
slackened their efforts for a moment, threw them into a state
of feverish excitement which made them an easy prey to
superstitious terrors which they would have blushed for in
other circumstances. One night, while they were at work
on the fortifications, a stone flew over the ramparts and fell
at their feet. An Arab picked it up, and found attached
to it a scrap of paper; this when unrolled displayed three
verses, which he read in a loud voice amidst the profound
silence of his comrades:

> "Their villages are desolate, their fields lie fallow, over them the whirl-
> wind raises the sand. Shut up in the Alhambra they plan new crimes;
> but there also they will have to submit to continual defeats, as did their
> fathers when exposed to our spears and swords."

As he read these lines, by the uncertain light of torches
whose flames fitfully illumined the darkness, the Arabs, who
had already begun to despair of victory, fell a prey to the
gloomiest presentiments. "These verses," said one of them
later on, "seemed to us a warning from heaven; as we
listened to them, we were seized with a terror which could
not have been increased if we had been beleaguered by all
the armies of the earth." Some of them, less impressionable
than the rest, tried to reassure their comrades by telling
them that the pebble had not fallen from heaven, as they
seemed disposed to believe, but had been thrown among
them by the hand of an enemy, and that the verses were
probably the composition of the Spanish poet Ablî. By
degrees this idea prevailed, and they called upon their own
poet Asadî to compose a defiance of the enemy, in the same
metre and with the same rhyme. Such a task was no
novelty for Asadî; he had often engaged in poetical duels
of the kind with Ablî; but he was of a nervous temperament, his imagination was easily affected, and now—more
moved and troubled than any of the rest—he racked his
brains before he could produce even two verses, and they
showed clearly that inspiration was lacking:

> "Our villages are not desolate neither do our fields lie fallow. Our
> castle protects us against all attacks; here we find glory; here we plan
> triumphs for ourselves and defeat for you."

To complete the reply, a third verse was needed; Asadî, overwhelmed by his own emotions, could not hit upon one. Blushing with shame, and with downcast eyes, he stood confused and speechless, as though he had never composed a verse in his life.

This unlooked-for difficulty was not likely to revive the downcast courage of the Arabs. Partly reassured, they had already been inclined to see nothing supernatural in what had happened; but when they found that, quite unexpectedly, inspiration had failed their poet, their superstitious fears were redoubled. Overcome with shame, Asadî retired to his apartment, where suddenly he heard a voice saying: "Of a truth when we sally forth, ye shall experience a defeat so terrible that in one moment the hair of your wives and children shall grow white!" It was the third verse, which he had racked his brains for in vain. He looked around, but saw no one. Firmly convinced that the words had been uttered by an unseen spirit, he ran to the chief Adhâ, his intimate friend, and related to him what had happened. "Let us rejoice!" cried Adhâ. "Truly, I am of thy opinion; this verse was the work of a spirit, and we may rest assured that the prediction will be accomplished. It must be so: this vile race must perish, for God hath said: 'Whoever in making exact reprisal for injury done him, shall again be wronged, God will assuredly aid him.'" [1]

Convinced that the Eternal had taken them under his protection, the Arabs wrapped the paper containing their poet's verses round a pebble and cast it amidst the enemy.

A week later they saw the Spanish army, twenty thousand strong, preparing to attack them on the eastern side, and placing their engines on a hill. Instead of allowing his brave men to be massacred within a ruined fortress, Sauwâr preferred to lead them out against the enemy. As soon as the battle was joined, he abruptly quitted the field, with a body of picked men. Making a detour, unobserved by the foe, he flung himself against the division posted on the hill with such impetuosity that he put them to rout. The sight of what was happening above them threw the Spaniards upon the plain into a panic, for they thought that the Arabs had received reinforcements. A frightful carnage ensued; pursuing their routed foes to the gates of Elvira, the Arabs slew twelve thousand, or, according to some accounts, seventeen thousand men.

[1] *Koran:* xxii. 59.

This is how Sa'îd ibn Jûdî sang of this second engagement, known as the Battle of the City:

"They had boasted, these sons of the pale ones, 'When our army encounters you, it will fall on you like a tempest. Ye will not resist it, ye will tremble with fear, the strongest castle will not shelter you!' Yet we drove back that army when we met it, as one driveth away the flies that flutter over one's broth, or as one driveth forth camels from a stable. Of a truth the tempest was terrible; the rain fell in great drops, the thunder roared, and the lightnings split the clouds—but not on us did the storm burst. Your ranks fell beneath our trusty swords, as corn beneath the reaper's sickle.

"When they beheld our onslaught, our swords struck such terror into their hearts that they turned their backs and fled: then fell we upon them and pierced them with our spears. Some we took captive and loaded with fetters; others, a prey to mortal anguish, ran for their lives and found the earth too strait. Ye have found in us a chosen band who can right well brand the heads of their enemies when that rain of which ye spake falls in great drops. We are of the sons of 'Adnân, who excel in making forays, and the sons of Kahtân who swoop like vultures on their prey. Our chief, a mighty warrior, a true lion, everywhere renowned, is of the right stock of Kais; for many a year the noblest and bravest have acknowledged his pre-eminence in valour and magnanimity. Honourable is he! Sprung from a family of valiant knights whose blood hath never mingled with an alien race, he falleth upon his foes as becometh an Arab and a Kaisite—a bulwark of faith is he against the infidel!

"Of a truth Sauwâr brandished that day a right good sword which severed heads as only a blade of fine temper can! It was by his arm that Allah slew the unbelievers banded against us. When the fatal moment had arrived for the sons of the pale ones, our chief was at the head of his brave warriors, steadfast as a mountain; their number was so great that the earth seemed too narrow to bear them. All the mighty men charged at full speed on their neighing chargers.

"Ye desired war; to you it was fatal, and on you did God bring sudden destruction!"

So critical was the position in which the Spaniards found themselves after this disastrous battle, that they had no alternative to imploring the aid and acknowledging the authority of the chief man of their race, 'Omar ibn Hafsûn. They adopted this course, and before long Ibn Hafsûn, who was not far off, entered Elvira with his army, reorganized the city militia, gathered beneath his standard a force made up from the garrisons of the neighbouring castles, and sallied forth against Sauwâr. That leader had profited by the interval to obtain reinforcements from the Arabs of Jaen and Regio, and his army was now so numerous that he ventured to hope for success when he met 'Omar. Nor was his hope frustrated. After losing many of his best troops, and not sparing his own blood, Ibn Hafsûn was obliged to fall back. Accustomed to victory, this reverse enraged him.

He put the blame on the inhabitants of Elvira, reproached them for misconduct during the fray, and in his anger levied huge contributions on the citizens, declaring that they must themselves pay for a war waged entirely in their own interests. He then returned to Bobastro with the bulk of his army, leaving the defence of Elvira to his lieutenant, Hafs ibn el-Moro.

Among the prisoners whom he took with him was the gallant Sa'îd ibn Jûdî. During his captivity this excellent poet composed these verses :

" Have courage, and hope, my friends! Be sure that joy will succeed sorrow, and that you will depart hence exchanging misfortune for happiness. Others who have spent years in this prison, to-day traverse the fields in the bright sunshine. Alas! if we are captives, it is not because we surrendered, but because we allowed ourselves to be surprised. Had a foreboding warned me, the point of my spear would have protected me, for the horsemen know my bravery and boldness in the hour of danger.

" And thou, traveller, take greetings to my noble father and my tender mother, who will hear with transport that thou hast seen me. Salute also my beloved wife and report to her these words : 'I always shall think of thee, even to the Day of Judgment : I shall present myself before my Creator, my heart filled with thy image. Of a truth the grief which thou now feelest afflicts me more bitterly than durance, or the prospect of the grave.'

" Perchance I shall be put to death here, and buried : yet a brave man, such as I, preferreth to fall gloriously on the battlefield and become the food of vultures! "

After Ibn Hafsûn's departure, Sauwâr fell into an ambuscade, and was slain by the inhabitants of Elvira. When his corpse was borne into the town the air rang with shouts of joy. Drunk with vengeance, the women glared like beasts of prey at the body of him who had bereft them of brothers, husbands, and children, and then with yells of rage cut it into morsels—and devoured it![1]

The Arabs chose as their new leader Sa'îd ibn Jûdî, whom Ibn Hafsûn had lately set at liberty (A.D. 890). Although Sa'id had been Sauwâr's friend and had sung praises of his gallant deeds, he resembled him in no respect. Of noble birth—his grandfather had been successively Kady of Elvira and Prefect of Cordova under Hakam I—he was moreover an ideal Arab cavalier, and his contemporaries attribute to him the ten qualities of a perfect gentleman. These were, liberality, courage, skill in horsemanship, personal beauty,

---

[1] Worthy of such ancestors were the Andalusian women, who, in the days of Napoleon I, threw themselves with horrible yells on the wounded French, and vied with one another to inflict tortures upon them, thrusting knives and scissors in their eyes. See M. de Rocca, *Memoirs* (1815), p. 255.

poetic talent, eloquence, strength, the arts of wielding the spear, of fencing, and of bending the bow. He was the only Arab whom Ibn Hafsûn dreaded to encounter in the field. When, before a battle, Sa'îd challenged Ibn Hafsûn to single combat, the latter, brave though he was, did not dare to cross swords with him. On one occasion, in a mêlée, Sa'îd suddenly found himself face to face with Ibn Hafsûn. The latter tried to elude him, but Sa'îd seized him round the body, threw him to the ground, and would have slain him, had not Ibn Hafsûn's soldiers interposed and forced him to release his hold.

This bravest of knights was also the most susceptible to the softer passions. None yielded more readily to the allurement of a gentle voice or beautiful tresses, none felt more keenly the seductive power of a lily hand. One day, during the reign of Mohammed, as he passed by Prince 'Abdallah's palace in Cordova, a melody sung in a woman's voice fell upon his ear. The song proceeded from a room on the first floor, the window of which gave upon the street, and the singer was the beautiful Jehâne. She was with the prince, her master, now pouring out wine for him, and now singing. Attracted by an indefinable fascination, Sa'îd placed himself in a corner, where he could listen at his ease, unobserved by passers-by. With his eyes fixed upon the window, he listened, lost in ecstasy, and burning with desire to see the fair songstress. After waiting for a long time, he at last caught a glimpse of a small white hand, as it extended a cup to the prince. That was all; but the incomparable elegance of the hand, and the soft and expressive voice, made the heart of the poet throb, and set fire to his brain. Alas! an insuperable barrier divided him from the object of his love. In despair he tried to divert his passion into other channels. He purchased at an immense price the most beautiful slave whom he could find, and he called her Jehâne. But in spite of the girl's efforts to please her comely lord, she did not succeed in making him forget her namesake; thus he lamented:

"The sweet song which I heard, ravished my soul, and replaced it by a sorrow which slowly consumes me. It is to Jehâne, whom I shall eternally remember, that I have given my heart, though our eyes have never met. O Jehâne, object of all my desires, cherish that truant soul of mine which hath fluttered to thy keeping! With tears I invoke thy beloved name, with the fervour and devotion of a monk who invokes his saint as he prostrates himself before his image!"

Notwithstanding such ardent verses, breathing the spirit of a Provençal troubadour, Sa'îd did not long retain memories of the fair Jehâne. Fickle as the wind, wandering ceaselessly from desire to desire—enduring passions and platonic reveries were not for him; witness these verses of his composition which Arab writers never quote without piously adding, " May God forgive him ! "

" The sweetest moment in life is when the wine-cup circles; when after a quarrel one is reconciled to one's lover; or, yet again, when we mutually embrace and are once more at peace.

" I traverse the circle of pleasures as a frenzied war-horse that taketh the bit between his teeth ; I leave no desire ungratified !

" Steadfast when the angel of death hovers over my head in the day of battle, a pair of bright eyes can sway me as they will."

He had, therefore, already forgotten Jehâne, when a new beauty was brought to him from Cordova. When she presented herself before him modesty induced her to lower her eyes, whereupon Sa'îd improvised these verses :

" Why, fair one, dost thou turn thy glance from me to fix it on the ground ?   Can it be that I am unpleasing in thy sight ?   By Allah, that is not usually the sentiment I inspire, and I dare assure you that I am better worth thy regard than is the pavement ! "

Sa'îd was undoubtedly a most brilliant representative of the nobility; but he had not Sauwâr's sterling qualities. The death of that great chief was therefore a loss for which Sa'îd could not compensate.   Thanks to Sauwâr's care, who had rebuilt many half-ruined Roman fortresses—such as Mentesa and Basti (Baza)—the Arabs were able to hold their own under his successor; but although they had no quarrel with the Sultan, who had recognised Sa'îd, they gained no further victories over the Spaniards.   The Moslem chroniclers, who are very reticent with regard to Sa'îd's expeditions—a sufficient proof that they were not usually successful—only inform us that at least on one occasion Elvira submitted to his authority.   When he made his entry into the town, Ablî, the Spanish poet, presented himself and recited a set of verses composed in his praise.   Sa'îd rewarded him liberally; but when the poet had departed, an Arab exclaimed : " Didst thou give money, Emir, to that man ?   Hast thou forgotten that not long ago he was the vilest firebrand of them all ?   Did he not dare to say : ' Long will the dead whom we threw into the well, wait in vain for an avenger ! ' "

Sa'îd seemed to feel a scarcely healed wound re-opened; his eyes blazed with wrath, and he cried to a kinsman of Yahyâ ibn Sokâla, "Follow that man, slay him, and let his own corpse be thrown into a well!" The command was promptly obeyed.

[Authorities: Ibn Hayyân, ff. 22–3, 37–49, 92–4; Ibn al-Kûtiyya, f. 37; Sams., *Apol.*, ii. 4; Ibn al-Abbâr, pp. 80–7; Ibn al-Khatib, MS. (G.), 5; Arts. on Sauwâr, MS. (E.), and on Sa'îd ibn Jûdî (*Notices*, p. 258).]

CHAPTER XIII

THE RENEGADES OF SEVILLE

DURING the progress of the struggle between the Spaniards of Elvira and the Arab nobility, events of much gravity were taking place at Seville.

Nowhere was the national party so strong. From the days of the Visigoths, Seville had been the chief seat of learning and Roman civilization, and the residence of the noblest and wealthiest families.[1] The conquest had scarcely affected the social order. Of the Arabs, who preferred the surrounding country, but few dwelt in the city. Descendants of Romans and Goths therefore formed the majority of the inhabitants. Agriculture and commerce had made them wealthy: many ships from over the sea came to Seville—then accounted one of the best harbours of Spain—to embark cargoes of cotton, olives, and figs, which the land produced in abundance. Most of the Sevillans had early abjured Christianity, for we find that in the reign of 'Abd-er-Rahmân II a large mosque had been built for their use; but their manners and customs, their leanings, even their family names—such as Beni Angelino, and Beni Sabarico[2]—betrayed their Spanish origin.

These Renegades were for the most part peaceable, and far from hostile to the Sultan, whom they looked upon, indeed, as the natural guardian of public order; but they feared the Arabs—not so much those of the city, who appreciated the benefits of civilization, and did not concern themselves with tribal or racial animosities, as those of the rural districts. The latter had preserved their bluntness, their inveterate national prejudices, their aversion to every race except their own, their warlike spirit, and their attachment to ancient families whom they had obeyed for immemorial generations. Filled with envy and hatred of the wealthy

---

[1] " Jure mihi post has memorabere nomen Hiberum
    Hispalis, æquoreus quam præterlabitur amnis,
    Submittit cui tota suos Hispania fasces."—*Ausonius.*

(The variant reading *Emerita* seems ruled out by the fact that the Guadiana at Merida is not a tidal river.)

[2] Found in charters of the N. of Spain : cf. *Esp. sagr.*, xxxiv. 469.

Spaniards, they were ready to plunder and even massacre them at the first opportunity, or their leaders' invitation. The Arabs of the Axarafe were especially formidable, and the Spaniards—amongst whom there was current an old prediction that their city would be consumed by fire from the Axarafe—had concerted measures against being taken unawares by the sons of the Desert brigands, who were organized in twelve corps, each with its own leader, banner, and armoury, and who had formed alliances with the Ma'addite Arabs of the province of Seville and the Botr-Berbers of Moron.

Among the influential Arab families of the province two were pre-eminent—the Beni Hajjâj and the Beni Khaldûn. The former, though wholly Arab in their ideas, were nevertheless descended in the female line from Witica, the last Gothic King save one. His grand-daughter, Sara, had been married, as a widow, to one 'Omair of the Yemenite tribe of Lakhm, and four children were the issue of this marriage—a stock whence as many great families sprang, the Beni Hajjâj being the wealthiest. It was to Sara that the Beni Hajjâj owed their extensive domains in the Sened,[1] for an Arab historian—himself a descendant of Witica through Sara—remarks that 'Omair had children by other wives, but that none of their descendants could rival hers. The other family, that of the Beni Khaldûn, were also of Yemenite origin; they belonged to the tribe of Hadramaut and their property lay in the Axarafe. The members of these two great houses were not only farmers and soldiers, but merchants and shipowners. They usually resided in their country castles, or *borj*,[2] but from time to time visited their mansions in the city.

At the beginning of 'Abdallah's reign, Koraib was chief of the Beni Khaldûn. He was treacherous and deceitful, but possessed all the qualifications of a party leader. Faithful to the traditions of his race, he detested the monarchy: it was his desire that the caste to which he belonged should grasp once more the domination which the Omayyads had filched from it. First he tried to stir up a revolt in the town itself. With this object he appealed to the Arab inhabitants, and endeavoured to revive their love of liberty.

---

[1] The district between Seville and Niebla.

[2] In charters of the thirteenth century frequent mention is made of the " Borg Aben-Haldon," or the "Torre Aben-Haldon." *Cf.* Espinosa, *Hist. de Sevilla*, ii. 4, 16, 17.

He was not successful. These Arabs were for the most part Kurashites, or clients of the reigning family, and were royalists—or, at any rate, belonged to what might now be called the party of law and order. All they asked was to live in peace, undisturbed in their business and pleasures. They therefore felt no sympathy with Koraib's designs; his adventurous temper and unbridled ambition inspired them with aversion and alarm. When he spoke to them of liberty, they told him that they hated anarchy, that they would not be the tool of any man's ambition, and that they could dispense with his sinister counsels.

Realizing that he was wasting time in the city, Koraib returned to the Axarafe, where he speedily aroused the enthusiasm of his fellow-tribesmen, who promised, almost to a man, to take up arms when he gave the signal. He thereupon formed a league—comprising the Hajjâj, the two Yemenite chiefs of Niebla and Sidona, and the chief of the Bornos Berbers of Carmona—with the object of detaching Seville from the Sultan's dominions and plundering the Spaniards. The patricians of Seville, who had lost sight of Koraib, were ignorant of this plot; from time to time vague rumours reached their ears, but they had no precise information and no suspicion of a dangerous conspiracy.

Desiring to take vengeance, first of all, upon those who had refused to listen to him, and at the same time to show them that their sovereign could not defend them, Koraib secretly informed the Berbers of Merida and Medellin that the province of Seville was almost denuded of troops, and that if they had any hankering after rich booty it lay ready to their hands. Always ready for rapine, these semi-barbarians took the field, seized and pillaged Talyâta,[1] slaying the men and enslaving the women and children. The Governor of Seville made a levy of all those able to bear arms and marched against the Berbers. Learning that they were already masters of Talyâta, the Governor pitched his camp on a height known as the Hill of Olives. This was only three miles distant from the enemy, and both sides prepared for battle on the morrow. Koraib, who, like the other nobles, had furnished his contingent to the Spanish force, informed the Berbers, during the night, that he would facilitate their victory by deserting with his men

---

[1] There were at least four places so named. This seems to have been about half a league from Seville, to the S. of the bridge over the Guadaira. See *Recherches* (1881), i. 308–11.

during the battle. He kept his word, and in his flight drew the whole army with him. Pursued by the Berbers, the Governor did not halt until he reached the village of Huebar—five leagues from Seville—where he entrenched himself. The Berbers made no attempt to dislodge him, but returned to Talyâta, where they encamped for three days, ravaging the neighbouring district. They then returned to their homes laden with booty.

This terrible foray had already ruined many land-owners, when a new calamity fell upon the Sevillans. This time the treacherous Koraib had nothing to reproach himself with: his projects were spontaneously furthered by a chief of the hostile race—the Renegade, Ibn Merwân. Seeing his neighbours of Merida return laden with rich spoils, the lord of Badajoz came to the conclusion that he had merely to assume the offensive, to do the like. Nor was he mistaken. Advancing to within ten miles of Seville, he pillaged the district for many days, and when he returned to Badajoz he had little reason to envy the Berbers of Merida.

The conduct of their Governor, who had remained inactive while savage hordes were devastating their territories, exasperated the Sevillans against him and his sovereign. In deference to their complaints, the Sultan, it is true, deposed this inefficient Governor; but his successor, though of blameless reputation, was equally incompetent to maintain order in the province, and repress the daring marauders, who multiplied alarmingly.

The most formidable of these brigands was Tamâshekka, a Bornos Berber of Carmona, who robbed travellers on the highway between Seville and Cordova. The Governor of Seville dared not, or could not, take any steps against him, but at length a brave Renegade of Ecija—Mohammed ibn Ghâlib—promised the Sultan to stamp out this horde of brigands if he might be permitted to build a fortress near the village of Siete Torres, on the frontier of Seville and Ecija. The Sultan accepted his offer, the fortress was built, Ibn Ghâlib occupied it with a large force of Renegades, Omayyad clients, and Botr-Berbers, and the brigands were soon made aware that they had to deal with quite another adversary than the Governor of Seville.

Security was being re-established, when one morning at sunrise the news spread through Seville that during the night an encounter had taken place between the garrison of

Ibn Ghâlib's castle and the united tribes of Khaldûn and Hajjâj, that one of the Beni Hajjâj had been slain, and that his comrades had brought his corpse to the city. It was further rumoured that the Beni Hajjâj had appealed to the Governor for justice, but that he had declined to take the responsibility in such a case, and had referred them to the Sultan.

While Seville was astir over this news the complainants were already on their way to Cordova, followed by some Sevillan Renegades, who, having learnt from Ibn Ghâlib what had happened, undertook to plead his cause. At their head was one of the most influential citizens, Mohammed ibn 'Omar ibn Khattâb ibn Angelino, whose grandfather had been the first of the family to embrace Islamism, while the name of Beni Angelino had been adopted by the house from that of his great-grandfather.

The complainants having been ushered into the Sultan's presence, their spokesman addressed him thus: " We were passing peaceably along the highway, Emir, when Ibn Ghâlib suddenly fell upon us. We sought to defend our- selves, and in the struggle one of our number was slain. We are ready to make oath that we speak the truth, and we ask you to punish this traitor, Ibn Ghâlib. We venture to add, Emir, that those who advised you to put your trust in this Renegade, counselled you ill. Make inquiry con- cerning the men under his command; you will find that they are criminals, and the dregs of the populace. Be assured that this man is a traitor; for the moment he may seem faithful to you, but we have good reason to believe that he has a secret understanding with Ibn Hafsûn, and that some day he will betray the province to him." Mohammed ibn Angelino was then introduced in his turn. " Learn the truth of the matter, Emir," said the patrician : " The Khaldûn and Hajjâj planned to surprise the castle during the night; but Ibn Ghâlib was on his guard, and seeing his castle attacked, opposed force with force. If one of his assailants was slain, the fault is not Ibn Ghâlib's; he acted within his rights, in self-defence. Heed not, we pray thee, the lies of these turbulent Arabs. Ibn Ghâlib deserveth well of thee; he is one of thy most devoted servants, and in freeing the country of brigands he rendereth thee an important service."

The Sultan perhaps thought the case doubtful, or feared to offend one party by siding with the other ; at any rate he declared that, wishing for fuller information, he would send his son Mohammed to Seville to inquire into the matter.

The young prince, heir-presumptive to the throne, soon reached Seville. He summoned Ibn Ghâlib and the Hajjâj before him, and examined them successively; but since they persisted in recriminations, Mohammed, in default of impartial witnesses, knew not how to arrive at a decision. While he still hesitated, passions grew higher, and the excitement felt by the patricians extended to the populace. At last the prince declared that he would postpone his decision, but that meanwhile Ibn Ghâlib might return to his castle. The Renegades claimed the victory. They declared that the prince was manifestly on their side, and that if he did not formally pronounce judgment, it was from a wish not to enrage the Arabs. The Beni Khaldûn and Beni Hajjâj were of the same opinion, and were deeply offended. Resolved to avenge themselves and raise the standard of revolt, they quitted the town, and whilst Koraib called the Hadhramites of the Axarafe to arms, 'Abdallah, chief of the Hajjâj, assembled the Lakhmites of the Sened under his banner. The two chiefs then agreed upon a plan of campaign. It was decided that they should both strike a blow simultaneously. 'Abdallah would seize Carmona, and on the same day Koraib would surprise the fortress of Coria— on the eastern frontier of the Axarafe—having previously driven off the herds, belonging to the Sultan's uncle, which found pasturage on one of the two islands at the mouth of the Guadalquiver. Koraib, who was too dignified to con-descend to cattle-lifting, entrusted this part of the enterprise to his cousin Mahdî—a libertine, whose debaucheries scan-dalized Seville. Mahdî first proceeded to the fortress of Lebrija, opposite to the island. He was received by Sulaimân, an ally of Koraib's, who held the castle. He then crossed over to the island itself, where two hundred oxen and about a hundred horses were feeding in charge of one man. The Arabs slew the unfortunate herdsman, and driving the cattle to Coria, seized the fortress and secured their booty within it. 'Abdallah ibn Hajjâj, meanwhile, aided by the Bornos Berber Jonaid, captured Carmona by surprise, the Governor making his escape to Seville.

The boldness and celerity displayed by the Arabs spread alarm throughout the city. Prince Mohammed sent a message in all haste to his father begging for instructions and reinforcements.

The Sultan on receiving his son's letter, summoned his council. Opinion was divided. One of the Viziers, on being accorded a private interview with the Sultan, advised him to become reconciled with the Arabs, after putting Ibn Ghâlib to death. "When that Renegade," he said, "is no more, the Arabs will be satisfied; they will surrender Carmona and Coria, return your uncle's property, and make submission to you."

To sacrifice a loyal subject to the Arabs and thus embroil himself with the Renegades, without being sure of conciliating their opponents, would be not only a treacherous but a foolish stroke of policy for the Sultan. Nevertheless he determined to take the Vizier's advice, and ordered his client Jad—who had just been set at liberty by Sauwâr —to march with some troops to Carmona. "Declare yourself on the side of the accusers of Ibn Ghâlib," he said, "and put him to death; then do all you can to entice the Arabs to submit to my authority, and do not use force against them until you have exhausted all your powers of persuasion."

Jad set out, but although the object of his expedition was not avowed, a rumour was spread that it was not directed against the Beni Khaldûn but against Ibn Ghâlib. The Renegade was accordingly on his guard, and he had claimed Ibn Hafsûn's protection, when he received a letter from Jad.

"Fear nothing," wrote the General; "the object of my march is not what you seem to suppose. It is my duty to punish the Arabs for their violence, and since you are at variance with them, I look for your assistance." Ibn Ghâlib was deceived by this perfidious message, and when Jad approached the castle joined him with a small force. Jad then ostensibly prepared to besiege Carmona; but on arriving before the town he sent another letter to the leader of the Hajjâj to the effect that he would sacrifice Ibn Ghâlib provided that the clan would make submission to the Sultan. The bargain was struck; Jad beheaded Ibn Ghâlib, and the Hajjâj evacuated Carmona.

When the Renegades of Seville heard of the foul treachery to which their ally had fallen a victim, all their wrath was directed against the Sultan. They took counsel together, and it was proposed that they should avenge themselves for Ibn Ghâlib's murder upon Omayya, Jad's brother —a renowned soldier who was then Governor of Seville.

The suggestion was adopted, but since nothing could be done until they were masters of the city, Ibn Angelino undertook to persuade the prince to entrust its defence to the Renegades. The patricians then resolved to send urgent messages to their allies, the Ma'addite Arabs of the province of Seville and the Botr-Berbers of Moron, begging for their immediate assistance.

While the messengers were on their way, Ibn Angelino, accompanied by some of his friends, presented himself before Prince Mohammed. " Prince," said they, " it may be that we have been calumniated at court and accused of some crime of which we are innocent ; or that a deadly plot has been hatched against us in the Sultan's council; or perhaps, indeed, Jad, that infamous traitor, is on his way to attack us with so vast an army that we cannot resist him. If thou wouldst therefore save us, and unite us to thee by bonds of gratitude, entrust us with the keys of the city and the responsibility of watching over its safety, until these matters are cleared up. It is not that we distrust thee, but thou art well aware that once the troops have entered the city thy protection will be unavailing." Mohammed, already at variance with the Arabs, and with but a weak garrison at his disposal, had no choice except to yield to the Renegades' request.

The Renegades, now masters of the town, awaited the Ma'addites and the Botr-Berbers, who arrived on the morning of Tuesday, Sept. 9, 889. A dense mob immediately attacked Omayya's palace. The rising was so sudden that the Governor had not even time to put on his boots. He sprang on his horse, and galloped at full speed to the prince's palace. The disappointed rebels pillaged Omayya's dwelling, and then rushed with fierce shouts to that of the prince, and surrounded it. The crowd was continually augmented by tradesmen, artisans, and labourers. The bewildered prince hastily sent messengers to Ibn Angelino, Ibn Sabarico, and other patricians imploring them to come to him and concert some means of quelling the tumult.

These patricians, who had hitherto held aloof, were at a loss what to do. They were, indeed, in a difficult position. On the one hand they dreaded lest they might fall into a snare if they visited the prince, but on the other hand it was clear that if they refused, they would be accused of connivance in the revolt, and this they dreaded still more. After due consideration they resolved to visit Mohammed—but

they took precautions; they donned coats of mail beneath
their apparel, and before entering the palace they posted
well-armed Sevillans and soldiers from Moron at the doors.
"If we have not returned when the Muezzin summons
the faithful to noon-tide prayer," they said, "burst into the
palace and come to our rescue."

Having given these instructions, they sought the prince's
presence. He received them very graciously; but, while they
were still conversing, the guards lost patience, became suspicious, and forced open the gate. They first rushed to the
stables and seized the horses and mules; they then ran to
the gate of the outer wall,[1] situated at the other end of the
court opposite to the main entrance. Here they were confronted by an unexpected obstacle—Omayya himself.

This brave soldier, on hearing the cries of the insurgents
in the stables, forthwith arrested Ibn Angelino and his
colleagues; he then posted his own servants and those of
the prince on the portico of the *fasil* gate, and had a quantity
of projectiles heaped up there, so that when the Renegades
and their allies approached it they were assailed by a
hail of arrows, stones, and even furniture. Although the
assailants were numerically superior, the defenders were
more advantageously placed. Encouraged by Omayya—
who though bleeding from many wounds in the head and
breast, incited them by gestures and example—the little
garrison of the palace resolved to sell their lives dearly, and
despair gave them almost superhuman strength.

The fight lasted from noon to sunset. During the night
the assailants bivouacked in the courtyard, and next morning
the attack was renewed.

But the royalists, and the friends of law and order, who
should have flocked to the rescue of the Governor—what
meanwhile were they doing?

Faithful to their motto, "Each for himself," and submitting to the inevitable ascendancy which vigorous resolution exercises over feebleness, they had barricaded themselves
in their houses and left it to the Governor to extricate himself from his difficulties as best he could. Doubtless they
wished him well, but their devotion did not extend to risking
their lives to save him.

They had not, however, been entirely inactive. When
the tumult began they sent a courier to Jad to warn him of

---

[1] The *fasil* or "avant-mure."

the danger threatening his brother and the prince. Having accomplished this not very arduous duty, they contented themselves with wondering whether the general would arrive in time to quell the insurrection. Jad no sooner learnt what was taking place in Seville than he set out with as many horsemen as could hastily be mustered. On the morning of September 9, just as the struggle in the courtyard recommenced, he arrived on the south side. A picket of Renegades tried to bar his passage, but he cut them down and forced his way into the suburb where dwelt the Kurashite 'Abdallah ibn Ash'ath. This royalist told him briefly how matters stood. " Lose not a moment! Charge!" cried the general. Sword in hand he galloped against the mob. The Sevillans held their ground. Jad's charger was killed under him ; his troopers fell back. He tried to stimulate them to another effort ; he called them by name, he conjured them to be firm. The bravest rallied, renewed the charge, and attacked the leaders of the people by preference. Jad flung himself upon one of the Sevillan leaders and slew him. The jostling crowd fell into inextricable confusion. The horsemen attacked it with redoubled energy, and the Sevillans were soon fleeing in all directions.

Overjoyed, Jad rushed into the palace, folded his brother to his heart, and respectfully kissed the prince's hand. " God be praised," he cried, "I have saved you!" " Opportunely," replied his brother ; " half-an-hour later, and we should have been past help." " Of a truth," added the prince, " we were prepared for death. But now let thoughts of vengeance fill our hearts! Let us punish these rebels by sacking their houses; let Ibn Angelino and his accomplices be dragged from prison to the executioner, and let their property be confiscated!"

Whilst these unfortunate men were being led to death, Seville presented a dreadful spectacle. Greedy for blood and booty, Jad's horsemen massacred the fugitives and pillaged their dwellings. Luckily for the Renegades, a kind of neighbourly alliance existed between them and the Omayyad clients in Seville. In virtue of this friendliness the clients obtained clemency for their fellow-citizens, and ere long the Sultan granted a general amnesty. But this was merely a respite; the Renegades were on the brink of destruction.

After Prince Mohammed had returned to Cordova with Jad and his troops, messengers from Ibn Hafsûn—then at peace with the Sultan—arrived to demand Jad's head, since that general had put Ibn Ghâlib, their master's ally, to death.

Ibn Hafsûn's power, and the fear with which he inspired the Sultan, were so great, that Jad, though he had merely carried out his sovereign's orders, felt a not unreasonable fear lest he should be sacrificed to the Renegade chief. Flight seemed to offer him the only chance of escaping this danger, so he quitted the Capital secretly by night to seek refuge with his brother the Governor of Seville. He was accompanied by his two brothers, Hâshim and 'Abd al-Ghâfir, a few friends—including two Kurashites—his pages, and slaves. Following the right bank of the Guadalquiver, the fugitives reached at daybreak the castle of Siete Filla. Here they were granted permission to make a short halt. Unfortunately, however, the robber band of the Berber Tamâshekka was then hovering in the neighbourhood, and Ibn Ghâlib's brothers, who were members of it, had observed the arrival of the horsemen. They recognised Jad, and, eager to avenge their brother's death, they pointed out to their chief how easy it would be to carry off the horses, which had been left outside the castle walls. Tamâshekka and his brigands accordingly swooped upon their prey, and had their hands upon the horses' bridles, when Jad and his friends, attracted by the outcry of their slaves, fell upon them sword in hand. The brigands defended themselves vigorously, and being superior in numbers, slew Jad, his two brothers, and a Kurashite.

This affray had fatal consequences for the Spaniards in Seville. It was upon them that Omayya, impotent to punish the real culprits, wreaked his vengeance for the death of his three brothers. He delivered them into the hands of the Beni Khaldûn and the Beni Hajjâj, whom he summoned to the city, giving them full authority to exterminate all Spaniards—Moslems or Christians—wherever they were to be found, at Seville, at Carmona, or in the country. A frightful massacre ensued. In their blind fury the Yemenites cut the throats of the Spaniards in thousands. The streets ran blood. Those who flung themselves into the Guadalquiver, to escape the sword, almost all perished in its waters. The few Spaniards who survived this terrible catastrophe were reduced from opulence to the most abject poverty.

The Yemenites long preserved the memory of this bloody day; their malice outlived the ruin of their enemies.

In the manor houses and villages of the Axarafe and the Sened, the minstrels in the long evenings often took the grim drama as the theme of their songs, and the Yemenites, their eyes gleaming with fierce hatred, were never weary of listening to verses such as these :

" Sabre in hand we exterminated that brood of slaves ! Twenty thousand of their corpses lay strewn upon the ground ; the waves of the river bore the rest away. Vast was their number of yore—how thin have we made their ranks.

" We, the children of Kahtân, are scions of the princes who reigned of old in Yemen—they, slaves themselves, are sprung from slaves.

" Vile dogs ! In their foolhardiness they dared to beard the lions in their lair ! We have battened upon their spoils ; we have hurled them down to join the Thamûdites,[1] in the eternal flames of hell ! "

---

[1] *Koran, Sura*, vii. 71–9 : they scorned the prophet Sâlih, and hamstrung the camel that, for a sign, proceeded miraculously from a rock. Mohammed mistook the hewn tombs of N. Arabia for the dwellings of the Thamûdites. See Nicholson, *Lit. Hist. of the Arabs* (1907), p. 3.

[AUTHORITIES: Ibn Hayyân, ff. 49–56, 59, 63–5 ; *Akhbâr majmú'at*, f. 56 ; Makkarî, i. 89 ; Râzî, p. 56 ; Ibn al Kûtiyya, ff. 3, 26.]

CHAPTER XIV

'ABDALLAH

IT was the Arab nobles rather than the Sultan who profited by the ruin of the Renegades of Seville. Henceforth the Khaldûn and the Hajjâj were masters of the province; the royalists were too weak and too cowardly to dispute their authority, and made no attempt to do so: Omayya alone endeavoured to cope with them. He did his best to sow discord between the Berber Jonaid and 'Abdallah ibn Hajjâj, who had shared authority at Carmona; he tried to bring about a breach between Koraib and his party and to win the latter over by the most dazzling promises; he even took steps to rid himself at a blow of all these turbulent Yemenites. But his efforts were fruitless. It is true that he induced Jonaid to assassinate 'Abdallah; but the deed did Omayya more harm than good, for the Beni Hajjâj elected, as 'Abdallah's successor, his brother Ibrâhîm, a gifted man, much more to be feared than 'Abdallah had ever been. Koraib, although he feigned to lend an ear to the proposals made to him, was too crafty to be deceived by them, and Omayya's great project for exterminating the Yemenites completely failed. He had ordered, with this object in view, a wall to be built round that quarter of the town which contained the palace and the Great Mosque, announcing that this enclosure would be reserved exclusively for the garrison. The Arabs, suspecting that some day as they entered or quitted the Mosque they would be massacred by the Governor's creatures, remonstrated, but ineffectually. The populace then forcibly prevented the masons from continuing their work. Omayya arrested the more seditious citizens and took hostages from them to answer with their lives for their kinsmen's submission. This did not mend matters. The Yemenites knew that the fear of bringing about a terrible vendetta against himself and his family would prevent Omayya from harming the hostages, and one day, when most of the garrison were abroad, seeking provisions, they attacked the palace. The Governor thereupon ascended to the roof with his remaining soldiers, hurled missiles at the assailants, and placing the hostages in a conspicuous position threatened to behead them. The rioters jeered him. They declared that since all the provinces had thrown off the Sultan's yoke they, naturally, had no wish to be behindhand. "We are very tractable," they added with bitter irony; "and we will engage to become model subjects as soon as a single revolted province surrenders." For Omayya himself, they added, there was only one course open—to depart: if he did so, they would not harm him. The Governor, proud and stubborn though he was, perforce bent before the storm. He promised to quit the city on condition that his life was spared. Thereupon Koraib, Ibrâhîm, and three other leaders ascended the terrace before the eastern door of the mosque and solemnly made oath five times that they would do him no hurt, and would escort him to a place of safety. Omayya, who from his coign of vantage could see and hear them, then released the hostages. But he himself was in no hurry to depart; ashamed of his weakness, and believing that the danger had passed, he made another effort to gain the upper hand. The Arabs immediately recommenced hostilities. Resolved not to yield a second time, Omayya formed a desperate resolution. He slew his wives, hamstringed his horses, burned everything of value that he possessed, and then, emerging from the palace, threw himself on his enemies and fought until he fell dead.

Henceforth all-powerful, but judging that the moment for declaring their complete independence had not yet arrived, the Yemenites wrote to inform the Sultan that they had put Omayya to death because he was hatching a rebellion. The Sultan, unable to punish them, accepted their singular explanation and sent them another Governor. The poor man was a puppet the strings of which were held by Koraib and Ibrâhîm. But though he suffered himself to be as wax in the hands of his tyrants, they harassed him without cessation. They grudged him the most trifling expenses, and even cut down his scanty rations. The Sultan, thinking that he might possibly mend matters, replaced this Governor by another, and sent his uncle Hishâm with him to Seville. But no army accompanied them, and the power of the Yemenites remained undiminished. The Governor and Hishâm discovered this only too quickly. The latter

had a son, named Motarrif.   This young libertine indulged
an intrigue with one of Mahdî's mistresses.   Discovering
this, Mahdî lay in wait for his rival one night and stabbed
him.   When Hishâm heard of the tragedy, he waited till
sunrise before visiting the spot where his son's body lay—
fearing lest he himself should be stabbed if he left his palace
while it was still dark.   Punishment of the assassin was out
of the question.   Not long afterwards the Khaldûn intercepted
a letter from the Governor, urging the Sultan to avenge
Motarrif's murder and put an end to anarchy.   Showing the
Governor this missive, they loaded him with threats and
reproaches, and to complete his ignominy put him under
arrest for several days.

Such was the situation at Seville in the year 891, the
fourth of 'Abdallah's reign.   At that date nearly all the rest
of Moslem Spain had thrown off its allegiance; every Arab
lord, African or Spanish, had appropriated his share of the
Omayyad heritage.   The Arabs' share had, however, been
the smaller.   At Seville alone were they powerful; everywhere else they held their ground with difficulty against the
other two races.   Many of them, such as Ibn Attâf, lord of
Mentesa—Ibn Salîm, lord of Medina-Beni-Salîm, in the
district of Sidona—Ibn-Waddhâh, lord of Lorca—and Al-
Ancar, Governor of Zaragoza, carried out the Sultan's orders
only when it suited them to do so; but they had not openly
broken with him—conscious of their weakness, they fostered
the possibility of reconciliation.

The Berbers, who had reverted to Government by tribal
chiefs, were more powerful and less tractable.   Mallâhî, a
private soldier, had seized the citadel of Jaen.   Two brothers,
Khalîl and Saʿîd, of a very ancient family, owned two castles
in the district of Elvira.   The provinces now known as
Estremadura and Alentejo were almost entirely in the
Berbers' power.   The Beni Ferânik ruled the tribe of Nafza,
in the environs of Truxillo.   Another Berber, Ibn Tâkît, of
the tribe of Masmûda, who had taken up arms in Estremadura, in Mohammed's reign, and made himself master of
Merida—whence he had expelled the Arabs and Berbers of
the tribe of Ketâma—was unceasingly at war with Ibn
Merwân, lord of Badajoz, whom he had not forgiven for
aiding the Sultan's troops when they besieged Merida.[1]
But the most powerful family among the Berbers was that

---

[1] Ibn Khaldûn, f. 10.

of the Beni Dhu 'n-Nûn. Their chief was Mûsâ, an abominable robber and scoundrel. Always active, he carried fire
and sword through the land. His three sons resembled him
in brutality and physical strength. They were Yahyâ, the
most treacherous and cruel of his race—Fath, lord of Uclés—
and Motarrif, lord of Huete, who was perhaps less wicked
than his brothers. Each of them led a robber band which
pillaged and slew far and wide.

The Renegades, though more powerful than the Berbers,
were less barbarous; many of their chieftains were friendly to
civilization—that is to say, Arab civilization: in the strife
against the conquerors their intellectual superiority was recognised. In the province of Oksonoba—now Algarve, the
most southerly province of Portugal—ruled Bakr, great-
grandson of Zadulphus, a Christian. His father, Yahyâ, declared himself independent towards the end of Mohammed's
reign. First seizing Santa Maria, he eventually became
master of the whole province. Bakr himself resided at
Silves, in royal state. He had his council, his chancellery,
and a well-armed and disciplined army. The scientific fortifications of Santa Maria were renowned, as well as its splendid
iron gates and its noble church,[1] second in reputation only
to that known as the Church of the Raven, a famous place
of pilgrimage.[2] Instead of looking on travellers and merchants as his prey, Bakr commanded his subjects to show
them protection and hospitality, with the result that in
Oksonoba, it was said, the traveller found himself among
friends and kinsfolk. Strong by virtue of his alliances
with Ibn Hafsûn, Ibn Merwân of Badajoz, and other chiefs
of his race, Bakr was nevertheless peaceable. The Sultan
having offered him the Governorship of the province,
he had accepted it, since it committed him to nothing.
His neighbour and ally on the north was 'Abd al-Malik ibn
Abî 'l-Jawâd, whose chief towns were Beja and Mertola.
Farther to the east, in the mountains of Priego, the valiant
Ibn Mastana held sway, Ibn Hafsûn's most active ally.
His numerous castles—one of which was Carcabûlia, now
Carabuey—were deemed impregnable. The lords of the
province of Jaen were all allies or vassals of Ibn Hafsûn.
These were Khair ibn Shâkir, lord of Jodar, who a little

---

[1] See Kazwînî, ii. 364.
[2] On Cape St. Vincent. "Sur la faîte de l'édifice sont dix corbeaux, personne
ne sait pourquoi ils y existent, personne ne jamais pu constater leur absence ; les
prêtres desservant l'église disent que ces oiseaux ont quelque chose de merveilleux."
Idrîsî, ii. 22. Cf. Esp. sagr., viii. pp. 187 sq.

before the period of which we are speaking had fought
against Sauwâr, chief of the Arabs of Elvira, and seized
a great many of his castles—Saʿîd Ibn Hodhail, lord of
Monteleon—the Beni Hâbil, four brothers who held several
fortresses, including Margarita and San Estevan—and Ibn
Shâlia, who possessed, among other castles, Ibn ʿOmar's and
Cazlona. The last-named baron was possessed of immense
wealth, remunerated poets lavishly, and lived in great luxury.

"Our prince's palaces," wrote the poet Obaidîs, his
secretary—who had deserted the Sultan's court for Ibn
Shâlia's—"are like those of Paradise, and in them all pleasures
are to be found. Within are halls which rest not upon pillars
—halls of marble bordered with gold." Another chieftain,
Daisam ibn Ishâk, lord of Murcia, Lorca, and almost the
whole of Tadmir, was also a lover of poetry, and had at his
disposal an army in which were five thousand horsemen.[1]
His generosity and urbanity earned him, moreover, the
affection of all his subjects.

But the Sultan's most formidable antagonist continued to
be Ibn Hafsûn, who in the last two years had gained great
advantages. ʿAbdallah, it is true, had marched against
Bobastro in the spring of 889. On his way he captured a few
hamlets and ravaged some cornfields ; but this military promenade of forty days had no practical result, and the Sultan
had scarcely returned to Cordova before Ibn Hafsûn seized
Estepa and Ossuna, while the inhabitants of Ecija hastened
to acknowledge him as their sovereign and begged him
to occupy the town with his troops. "Ecija is a sink of
iniquity," said the Cordovans, "deserted by the virtuous,
the wicked alone abide therein."

Alarmed at his antagonist's rapid success, ʿAbdallah had
set out once more against him with such troops as he could
muster, when Ibn Hafsûn, content with his successes, felt
inclined to temporise, and suggested terms. He offered the
Sultan peace on condition that he was confirmed in the
government of the territories he already held. Only too
glad to get off so cheaply, ʿAbdallah consented.

But Ibn Hafsûn interpreted peace in his own fashion.
It was not long before he attacked the Bornos Berber Abû
Harb, one of the Sultan's most faithful adherents, in his
fortress in Algeciras. Abû Harb being killed, his soldiers
surrendered the stronghold to the Renegade.

---

[1] Ibn al-Kûtiyya, f. 45.

z

The Sultan, therefore, found but little satisfaction in the pacific intentions proclaimed by Ibn Hafsûn; but, on the other hand, some of the more impetuous followers of the latter complained of what they considered the weakness and inaction of their leader. Such policy was detrimental to them; forays and booty were their sole means of subsistence. One of them, Ibn Mastana, rather than remain idle, preferred to join the neighbouring Arabs—who had lately fortified themselves in Kala-Yahcib (Alcala la Real) —in their forays against loyal and peaceable country-folk. The latter appealed for help to the Sultan. Greatly embarrassed—for he could not abandon his faithful subjects to their fate, and yet had no soldiers to spare—'Abdallah resolved to write to Ibn Hafsûn, urging him to combine in an expedition against Ibn Mastana and his Arab allies. Ibn Hafsûn, who had designs of his own, and who disapproved of the alliance between Ibn Mastana and the enemies of his race, acceded to the Sultan's proposal much more readily than the latter had ventured to hope. But after he had joined the troops under the command of the Omayyad general, Ibrâhîm ibn Khamîr, Ibn Hafsûn secretly sent Ibn Mastana a letter reproaching him for his alliance with the Arabs: " Nevertheless," he added, " I count upon you as a faithful champion of the national cause. For the moment, you have no choice except to continue in revolt. But fear nothing; this army will do you no hurt." Ibn Hafsûn by no means exaggerated his influence over the troops. So completely had he eclipsed the Omayyad general that he treated the Sultan's soldiers as he thought fit; on any pretext he put them under arrest; he took away their horses and gave them to his own men; and when Ibrâhîm ibn Khamîr raised objections, he always had ready a plausible reply. His march through the enemies' country was therefore a mere military promenade, as he had promised Ibn Mastana; but he took the opportunity of coming to an understanding with the Spaniards on the way and of assisting the inhabitants of Elvira, who had just been beaten by Sauwâr at the Battle of the City. He did not, as we have seen, meet with his usual success in the latter expedition, but he was not discouraged by so slight a check. Strengthened by his recent alliances, and realizing, perhaps, that his adherents were growing weary of his temporising and ambiguous policy, he believed that the moment had come for casting off the mask. He accordingly threw

Ibrâhîm ibn Khamîr and many other Omayyad officers into prison, and declared war against the Sultan.

He soon found useful allies in the Christians of Cordova. The days had gone by when martyrdom was their only means of showing religious zeal and hatred of their conquerors. Amidst the general confusion they determined to assist by force of arms in their own liberation. Even those who had lately been the instruments of the Omayyads became their bitterest foes. Among these was the Count Servando. Son of a serf of the Church, he had shrunk from no baseness to win the monarch's favour. Knowing that the best way of doing this was to replenish the treasury, he had overwhelmed his fellow-Christians with taxes, and thus forced them to abjure their faith. "Not content with slaying the living," says a contemporary, "he did not even respect the dead"; for to inflame the hatred of the Moslems against the Christians, he exhumed the bodies of martyrs from beneath altars, and displayed them to the Sultan's ministers, inveighing against the audacity of the fanatics who had accorded such honourable sepulture to the victims of Moslem justice. No man was more detested by the Christians. The priests exhausted their vocabulary to find terms of abuse for him. He was "crazy, shameless, arrogant, greedy, cruel, mulish, presumptuous"; they declared that in his audacity he opposed the will of the Eternal, and was the child of the Devil. They had further excellent reasons for thus hating him. Servando laid such a heavy tax on the churches of the Capital that they could not pay their own priests, and had to put up with the cringing sycophants, paid by the State, whom Servando was pleased to appoint. Moreover, he had been the mortal enemy of their martyrs and of their patrons, for whom he laid traps with truly devilish cunning. On one occasion he accused the Abbot Samson and Valentius, Bishop of Cordova, of having incited one of their flock to blaspheme the Prophet, and thus addressed the Sultan: "Let your highness send for Samson and Valentius, and let them be asked whether they think this blasphemer has spoken the truth. If they answer affirmatively, let them be punished as blasphemers; but if on the other hand fear induces them to repudiate the accused, let them be given daggers and ordered to slay him. The refusal to do so will prove that the man is their tool. Then, in my turn, let me be given a sword, and I will slay them all three."[1] But twenty

[1] Sams., *Apol.*, cc. 5 9.

years had elapsed since he had spoken thus; times had changed, and men of Servando's stamp had changed with them. With considerable foresight, he suddenly conceived a strong antipathy for the Sultan, who was tottering on his throne, and a keen sympathy for the leader of the national party, who seemed likely to succeed him. He accordingly began to smile upon his fellow-Christians whom he had formerly persecuted, entered into a conspiracy with them, and strove to raise an insurrection. The Court discovered some of his designs, and arrested his brother ; but Servando, warned in time, managed to escape with his accomplices. Once outside the Capital he was safe, for the Sultan's power did not extend beyond the walls. Having now nothing to fear, he resolved to occupy the important stronghold of Polei,[1] one day's journey to the south of Cordova. Since this was no better guarded than the Sultan's other fortresses, he succeeded in his attempt. Once installed in Polei, Servando proposed an alliance with Ibn Hafsûn. The latter gladly accepted the offer, sent him some troops, and advised him to make continual forays in the vicinity of Cordova. No better organizer of such raids than Servando could be found. He knew every inch of the country, and was—we are assured by the Arab chroniclers—a daring horseman. He would leave his castle at nightfall, and return at daybreak—leaving devastated crops, burnt villages, and corpses strewn upon the ground to mark his track. He was at last himself killed in a foray, but his companions carried on the bloody work which he had initiated.

Ibn Hafsûn, who had recently captured Baena, was now master of all the main fortresses to the south of the Guadalquiver. Almost all Andalusia acknowledged him, and the Sultan was so well aware of the fact that he no longer bestowed on anyone the empty title of Governor of Elvira, or of Jaen. Proud of his power, the chief of the Renegades next planned to ensure its permanence. He was convinced that Cordova would soon fall into his hands, making him master of Spain ; but he knew that if he remained merely the leader of the Spaniards, the Arabs would certainly not submit to his authority. To be formally named Governor of Spain by the Khalif of Baghdad, was a necessary step

---

[1] Placed by Idrîsî five leagues from Cordova, and near to Santaella. Now called Aguilar (de la Frontera). In a charter (1258) cited by Lopez de Cardenas, *Memorias de la ciudad de Lucena* (Ecija, 1777, p. 165), we find " Aguilar, formerly Polei." *Recherches*, i. 307.

towards the attainment of his ambition.   His prestige would suffer no diminution; the authority exercised by the Khalifs over provinces so far removed from the centre of the Empire was merely nominal, and if the Khalif would consent to appoint him Governor, he had a right to hope that the Arabs would not refuse obedience, for he would then no longer be a mere Spaniard, but the representative of the dynasty which they held in the highest respect.

Having determined on this course, Ibn Hafsûn opened negotiations with Ibn Aghlab, who governed Africa on behalf of the 'Abbâsid Khalif, and to conciliate him, sent him sumptuous gifts.   Ibn Aghlab received his overtures amicably, sent him gifts in return, and encouraged him in his project, promising to induce the Khalif to confer the coveted diploma.

While awaiting the moment when he could hoist the 'Abbâsid standard, Ibn Hafsûn approached Cordova and established his headquarters at Ecija.   Thence he visited Polei from time to time, to hasten the construction of fortifications which would make his position there impregnable, to raise reinforcements for the garrison, and, if needs be, to encourage them.   In a few months—perhaps a few days—he would enter the Capital as a conqueror.

Cordova was plunged in profound gloom.   Without being actually beleaguered, it endured all the hardships of a siege.   As the Arab historians observed, the city was in the condition of a frontier town momentarily exposed to attacks of the enemy.   Many a time the citizens were awakened at night by the cries of miserable peasants who were being massacred on the other side of the river by the troopers from Polei.   On one occasion one of these horsemen had the audacity to cross the bridge and hurl his spear at the statue above the gate.   "The State is threatened with utter destruction," wrote a contemporary: "calamities follow one another without cessation; pillage and theft are rife; our wives and children are led away into slavery."   The inactivity of the weak and cowardly Sultan was denounced on all sides.   The soldiers grumbled because they were not paid.   The provinces having cut off their contributions, the treasury was wholly exhausted.   The Sultan had borrowed certain sums, but he employed the little money thus raised to pay those Arabs in the provinces who still clung to him.   The empty market-places testified to the collapse of trade.   The price of bread was exorbitant.   None dared to think of the future; despondency weighed on every heart. " Ere long," wrote the contemporary already quoted, " the churl will rule, and the noble will grovel in the dust! " It was remembered with alarm that the Omayyads had lost their palladium, the banner of 'Abd-er-Rahmân I. The Fakihs, who regarded every calamity as a divine punishment, and who called Ibn Hafsûn the scourge of God's wrath, appalled the citizens with terrifying predictions. " Woe unto thee, Cordova! " they cried: " Woe unto thee, vile courtesan, sink of uncleanness and corruption, abode of calamity and tribulation, for thou hast neither friends, nor allies ! When the captain with the great nose and ill-boding countenance, whose vanguard is of Moslems and rear-guard of idolaters,[1] standeth at thy gates, know then that thy desolation draweth nigh. Then will thy inhabitants flee to Carmona, but an accursed place of refuge will it be ! " The preachers fulminated from their pulpits against the " House of Iniquity," as they called the palace, and they announced with precision the exact time when Cordova would fall into the hands of the infidels. " Abominable Cordova," cried a preacher: " thou hast incurred the hatred of Allah since thou gatheredst to thy-bosom strangers, and criminals, and harlots; against thee shall the wrath divine be made manifest. . . . Ye see how civil strife rageth throughout Andalusia; think, therefore, no longer of earthly things. The deadly stroke will come from that quarter where stand the two mountains, the black and the brown. . . . The beginning will be in the month Ramadân—then a month, and yet another, will pass by, and then there will be a terrible catastrophe in the great square before the House of Iniquity. Keep watch then over your wives and children, O citizens of Cordova! Take heed that none dear to you goeth near the House of Iniquity or the Great Mosque, for on that day neither woman nor child will be spared. On a Friday will the tribulation begin, between noon and four o'clock, and will endure till sunset. A place of safety will be the hill of Abû Abda, where formerly stood the church."[2]

None fell into deeper dejection than the Sultan himself. That throne which he had so eagerly coveted, and which he had won at the price of fratricide, had become for him

[1] Lit. "polytheists"; i.e. Christians.
[2] Implying that Ibn Hafsûn's Christians would respect the sacred site and not stain it with blood.

a bed of thorns. He had come to the end of his resources.
He had pursued what he had believed to be a sound policy,
and it had failed. It was out of the question for him to
adopt his late brother's vigorous policy, for lack of men and
money. Moreover 'Abdallah always detested war. He
was a pious and domesticated prince, who made but a sorry
figure in the camp or on the battlefield. He was therefore
obliged to persevere in a peaceful policy, at the risk of being
once more tricked by the crafty Renegade who had already
so often deceived him. But Ibn Hafsûn, sure of victory,
was in no mood for compromise. 'Abdallah in vain offered
him peace on the most favourable terms; Ibn Hafsûn
rejected it with disdain. Every time he met with a rebuff,
the Sultan, despairing of mortal help, turned to God, shut
himself up in his closet with a hermit,[1] and composed such
melancholy verses as these:

"All worldly things are transitory; nothing is enduring here below.
Hasten, therefore, O sinner, to say farewell to all earthly vanities and be
converted. In a little while thou wilt be in the tomb and the cold earth
will lie on thy once comely face. Apply thyself only to thy religious duties,
give thyself to devotion, and seek the compassion of the Lord of heaven."

A day came, however, when 'Abdallah summoned up
courage; it was towards the end of the year 890, when a
messenger came to offer him, on behalf of Ibn Hafsûn, the
head of Khair ibn Shâkir, the lord of Jodar. The Sultan
saw a ray of hope, he imagined that his terrible adversary
was about to accord the peace which he had so long
solicited; he looked upon Khair ibn Shâkir's head as a
pledge of coming reconciliation. Ibn Hafsûn—so he
thought—would show his gratitude for the advice he had
given him; for it was 'Abdallah who had warned him that
Khair was playing a double game and acknowledged a rival
chief in Daisam, Prince of Tadmir. Extremely jealous of
his authority, Ibn Hafsûn had thereupon executed swift
and terrible justice. Khair having asked for a reinforcement, he sent it him, but at the same time gave his
lieutenant, El Royol,[2] secret orders to cut off the traitor's
head.

But Ibn Hafsûn soon disillusioned the Sultan; instead
of entering into negotiations, he besieged the fortresses in
the province of Cabra which still sided with 'Abdallah.

[1] See Khoshani, p. 322, with regard to 'Abdallah's respect for hermits.
[2] Ar. Al-Ohaimir, "the ruddy."

The situation could scarcely be worse. 'Abdallah at last realized that he must risk all to gain all. He informed the Viziers that he was determined to attack the enemy. The astounded Viziers pointed out the danger to which he would be exposed. " Ibn Hafsûn's troops," they said, " are more numerous than ours, and we shall be dealing with foes who give no quarter." Nevertheless he persisted in his project; and, indeed, though he set little store by his birth and dignity, the Sultan preferred an honourable death upon the battlefield to his existing ignominy.

[AUTHORITIES: Ibn Hayyân, ff. 7–23, 33, 39–40, 56–9, 68–71, 77–8, 99–100; *Tarîkh ibn Habîb*, pp. 157–60; *Akhbar majmû'at*, f. 111.]

CHAPTER XV

THE BATTLE OF POLEI

IBN HAFSÛN greeted the Sultan's bold resolve with mingled delight and astonishment. " The whole herd is ours!" he exclaimed in Spanish to Ibn Mastana: " Oh that 'Abdallah's heart may not fail him. Five hundred ducats to the man who announces that he has set out!" Soon Ibn Hafsûn received news at Ecija, that the Sultan's pavilion had been set up in the plain of Secunda. He immediately determined to burn it: if he succeeded, 'Abdallah would be covered with ridicule. Ibn Hafsûn reached the plain at nightfall with a small body of cavalry, and made a sudden attack on the slaves and archers who guarded the great tent; but though few in number, they made a stout resistance, and, attracted by their shouts, the soldiers poured out of the city to their aid. As he had merely designed to play a trick upon the Sultan, Ibn Hafsûn no sooner saw that his scheme had miscarried than he ordered his men to retire at full gallop to Polei. The Sultan's horse pursued and cut down a few of them.

Though really unimportant, this nocturnal affray assumed gigantic proportions in the eyes of the Cordovans. At daybreak all the citizens came forth to meet the Sultan's cavalry as they returned with some captured horses and a few severed heads. The populace could not sufficiently admire these trophies, and told one another with joy and pride that Ibn Hafsûn, straying from the highway in his flight, had reached Polei with but a single horseman.

Soon, however, a more serious conflict had to be faced, and so great was the numerical disparity of the two forces that the outlook was not encouraging. The Sultan's army consisted of fourteen thousand men, of whom only four thousand were disciplined troops; while Ibn Hafsûn's force was thirty thousand strong. 'Abdallah, however, gave the order to march, and advanced towards Polei.

On Thursday, April 15, 891, the army reached the stream which flows about half a league from the Castle, and it was well understood on both sides that the battle would take place next day—Good Friday.[1]

On the morrow the Sultan's forces stood to arms betimes, while Ibn Hafsûn drew up his men at the foot of the hill on which the Castle stood. The latter, confident of victory, were full of enthusiasm and eager for the fray. Far different were 'Abdallah's emotions. His army was his last resource; on it rested the fate of the Omayyads; if disaster overwhelmed it, all would be lost. By a crowning misfortune it was ill-led, and the commander-in-chief, 'Abd al-Malik ibn Omayya, came near to playing into the enemy's hands by a bungling manœuvre. He had actually begun to advance when he became dissatisfied with his position, and ordered a retrograde movement to a hill lying to the north of the fortress. This was being carried out, when the general of the vanguard—a gallant Omayyad client, 'Obaid-allah of the family of the Beni Abî Abda—galloped to the Sultan and exclaimed: " May God have mercy on us ! Whither dost thou lead us, Emir? Shall we turn our backs upon the foe ? They will deem us panic-stricken and will cut us to pieces ! " He was right : Ibn Hafsûn perceived his adversary's mistake and made ready to profit by it. The Sultan did not dispute the justice of 'Obaidallah's criticism, and asked his advice. " Set on ! and leave the issue in God's hands ! " was the General's reply. " Be it so," said the Sultan.

Without a moment's delay, 'Obaidallah rode back to his division and ordered it to attack. The troops obeyed, but almost despaired of success. " What thinkest thou of the issue of this battle ? " asked an officer of the theologian Abû Merwân—son of the famous Yahyâ ibn Yahyâ, and like him renowned for his learning and piety, so that he was called " The Sheik of the Moslems." " I can give you no other answer, cousin," replied the doctor, " than these words of the Almighty : ' If God help you, none shall overcome you ; but if He abandon you, who is he that shall help you ? ' "[2] The rest of the army was in no better heart than the vanguard. The soldiers had received orders to lay

---

[1] By the rule laid down by the Nicene Council, Easter-day A.D. 891 would fall on April 4 ; but since the Arab historians place the battle of Polei in A.H. 278 (beginning April 15, A.D. 891), it is probable that the Andalusians kept Easter by the rule of their compatriot Migetius, condemned by Adrian I in a letter addressed to Bishop Egila. Cf. *Esp. sagr.*, v. p. 532. See also F. Meyrick, *The Church in Spain* (1892), p. 231.

[2] *Koran, Sura III.*, v. 154.

down their baggage, pitch the tents, and form in battle array; but just as they were busied in stretching a canopy for the Sultan, one of the poles broke and the canopy came to the ground. "An evil omen!" muttered all who saw it. "Take courage!" exclaimed a superior officer; "that is no ill omen; the same accident formerly occurred on the eve of battle, and yet we won a brilliant victory." So saying, he propped the canopy with a pole which he had found among the baggage.

In the first line, which was already in action, the officers and divines found it necessary to explain away presages of evil. They cited from a vivid memory, or perhaps from a fertile imagination, an auspicious precedent whenever it was called for. In the front rank, clad in helmet and cuirass, fought Rahîsî, a veteran warrior and distinguished poet. At every stroke with sword or spear he improvised a verse. Suddenly he fell mortally wounded. "An evil omen!" cried the soldiers in consternation; "we are the first to lose a man." "Nay," replied the divines, "it is, on the contrary, a right happy omen, for at the battle of the Guadacelete, where we routed the Toledans, the like happened."

The engagement soon became general. The uproar was deafening; the blare of trumpets mingled with the vociferations of Moslem doctors and Christian priests as they respectively chanted passages from the Koran and the Bible. Quite unexpectedly 'Abdallah's left wing obtained an ever-increasing advantage over Ibn Hafsûn's right. Forcing back the enemy, the rank and file vied with one another in decapitating the fallen, for the Sultan had promised a reward to every soldier who brought him a head. 'Abdallah himself, however, took no part in the fight. Seated beneath his canopy, he watched others fighting for him, and with his usual hypocrisy, recited such verses as these: "Let others put their trust in multitudes of soldiers, in engines of war, in their own courage: as for me, I trust only in the one God, the Eternal!"

The right wing of the Andalusians, having been completely routed, the Sultan's army threw itself as a whole against the enemy's left. Ibn Hafsûn there commanded in person, but in spite of all his efforts, and although he displayed his customary valour, his troops gave way. Impetuous rather than steady, and as easily disheartened as excited, they despaired of the issue all too soon, and turning their backs on the enemy, took to flight. Some fled towards Ecija, followed by the enemy's horse, who cut them down by the hundred; others—Ibn Hafsûn himself among them—sought refuge in the Castle, but since the gateway was blocked by fugitives from the right wing, the new-comers tried in vain to force a way for themselves, and to save their chief, the soldiers on the walls hoisted him from his saddle and dragged him over the ramparts.

While the throng pressed at the gate of the Castle, the Sultan's troops pillaged their enemies' camp. Intoxicated by a triumph which was the greater because unexpected, they diverted themselves by jeering the foe—who were all Christians in their eyes—for having experienced so crushing a defeat two days before Easter. " How merry was the sport," cried a soldier; " How joyous the festival! Pity it is that the greater part of them will not see Easter-day !" "A glorious festival, of a truth," replied another, " with many victims : every religious festival should thus be graced !" " Behold what a remedy lieth in a good sword-cut !" added a third ; " They drank like fishes at their Communion, and if we had not sobered them they would be drunk still!" " Have you observed," asked a fourth, who had a smattering of history, "how closely this battle resembles that of the Field of Râhit ? That was fought on a Friday, which was a festival, and our victory is no less brilliant than that which the Omayyads then won. Behold these swine that lie dismembered at the foot of the hill ! Of a truth I pity the earth condemned to bear their corpses; if it had a voice it would protest!" Later, the Court poet, Ibn 'Abdi Rabbihi,[1] reproduced these coarse and brutal jests, these guard-room witticisms, in a long poem, mainly characterised by bad puns and worse taste, but at least possessing the merit of vividly reproducing the hatred and contempt felt by the royalists for the Andalusians.

The Sultan's troops had further cause for rejoicing. Ibn Hafsûn wished to cling to his castle and endure a siege : but the contingent from Ecija pleaded that duty recalled them to their own town, which would probably be besieged by 'Abdallah. Ibn Hafsûn vigorously opposed their departure, and would have forcibly detained them in the Castle, but they made a breach in the northern wall and escaped. Thus left to themselves, the remaining soldiers declared

---

[1] 860–940 : descended from a freedman of Hishâm ibn 'Abd-er-Rahmân ; author of an Anthology, "The Unique Necklace." See C. Huart, *Arabic Literature* (1903), p. 215.

that they were too few to defend the fortress, and that it must be evacuated. At length Ibn Hafsûn yielded to their clamours. In the dead of night they sallied forth from the fortress, and the retreat soon became a headlong flight. Amidst terrible confusion, Ibn Hafsûn sought in the darkness for a horse, and at length found a miserable jade, belonging to a Christian trooper; bestriding this, he endeavoured to spur into a gallop the wretched steed, which for years had never even broken into a trot. But there was need of haste. Their flight had been observed, and the royalists were in hot pursuit. Ibn Mastana, who rode beside Ibn Hafsûn, preserved, in spite of the danger which threatened, all the gaiety and indifference of a true Andalusian. " Well," he exclaimed to his companion, " you promised five hundred ducats to the man who brought you news that the Sultan had taken the field. It seems to me that God hath repaid you with usury. But it is no light task to beat the Omayyads; what think you ? " " I think," replied Ibn Hafsûn, who, with rage in his heart, was in no mood for pleasantries, " I think that our misfortunes are due to the cowardice of men like thyself—if, indeed, ye be men ! " At daybreak Ibn Hafsûn, with four others, reached the town of Archidona ; halting there but for a moment, he ordered the inhabitants to follow him to Bobastro as soon as possible, and proceeded on his way to that fortress.

'Abdallah, for his part, having occupied the Castle of Polei—where he found a large sum of money, and abundance of provisions and engines of war—called for the register in which were inscribed the names of all his Moslem subjects. The prisoners were then brought before him, and he announced that the lives of all those who were enrolled as Moslems would be spared, provided that they made oath that they were Moslems still; as for the Christians, they would be beheaded, unless they embraced Islamism. All the Christians, to the number of about a thousand, elected rather to die than to abjure their faith. One only, whose heart failed him as the executioner raised the sword, saved his life by apostasy. The rest met their death with heroism, and perhaps these obscure soldiers have a better claim to the title of martyr than the fanatics of Cordova who had been honoured with it forty years before.

Leaving a sufficient garrison in Polei, the Sultan next laid siege to Ecija. Since this town had a large garrison, thanks to the number of fugitives who had sought refuge there, it made a stout resistance. Unfortunately it was scantily provisioned. After some weeks scarcity began to be felt, and as it daily increased, capitulation had to be contemplated. The Andalusians accordingly tried to make terms : but the Sultan demanded unconditional surrender. This was refused, although the ravages of famine in the town were such that the citizens, in despair, exhibited their starving wives and children on the ramparts and implored mercy. At last the Sultan yielded. He granted a general amnesty to the besieged ; and then having taken hostages and appointed a Governor for the town, he set out for Bobastro, and encamped near that fortress.

But at Bobastro, in a district of which he knew every hillock, valley, and defile, Ibn Hafsûn was really invincible. The Cordovan troops knew this too well. They soon began to murmur. They declared that the campaign had already lasted long enough, that they did not wish to exhaust their little remaining strength in operations that could have no result, and that their adversaries would stand to gain rather than lose from a conflict in which their superiority when acting on the defensive would be once more exhibited. Constrained to yield to these views, the Sultan gave the order to fall back on Archidona. On their way the Cordovans had to traverse a narrow defile, where they were attacked by Ibn Hafsûn; but thanks to 'Obaidallah's skill and courage they emerged with credit from the encounter. Proceeding to Elvira, where he took hostages, the Sultan then led his army back to Cordova.

[AUTHORITY : Ibn Hayyân, ff. 71–80.]

CHAPTER XVI

'ABDALLAH (*continued*)

THE Sultan's victory at Polei had saved him at a moment when all seemed lost. Polei, Ecija, and Archidona—the advanced posts of the national party—were taken; Elvira submitted; Jaen, whence Ibn Hafsûn had withdrawn his troops, followed the example of Elvira. These were indeed notable successes, and made the greater impression on public opinion inasmuch as they were entirely unexpected. Ibn Hafsûn had, as he was only too well aware, lost much of his prestige. His ambassadors to Ibn Aghlab, instead of being warmly welcomed, as heretofore, were now coldly received. They were informed that the Governor was too much occupied with troubles in Africa to meddle with Spanish affairs. He naturally had no wish to support a pretender who allowed himself to be beaten, and there was no longer any chance of Ibn Hafsûn being nominated Governor of Spain by the Khalif. The Sultan, on the other hand, was rehabilitated in the eyes of the populace. Peaceable citizens, weary of anarchy, saw in the re-establishment of royal authority the sole means of security, and took up a more decided attitude. And yet, though the advantage gained by the Sultan could not be ignored, it might easily be exaggerated. Ibn Hafsûn had undoubtedly met with a serious rebuff, but his power was far from being exhausted. He did not despair of recovering it : but for the moment he needed peace, and sued for it. The Sultan expressed his willingness to grant it on the condition that he received as a hostage one of Ibn Hafsûn's sons. Ibn Hafsûn consented, but since he meant to renew hostilities as soon as it suited him, he substituted the son of one of his treasurers, whom he had adopted. The fraud was at first undetected ; but suspicions were afterwards aroused, and on the truth being known, the Sultan reproached Ibn Hafsûn for his breach of faith, and demanded one of his actual sons as a hostage : the demand was refused, and the war recommenced. The Andalusian chieftain recovered with surprising rapidity the territory which he had lost. Knowing that he could rely

368 SPANISH ISLAM [II. 16

on the populace of Archidona, he sent emissaries thither who induced them to revolt. The two agents to whom the Sultan had entrusted the government of the town were arrested by night, and handed over to Ibn Hafsûn as he entered the gates with his troops (A.D. 892). Soon afterwards deputies from Elvira came to tell him that their town had also shaken off the yoke and relied on his support. He accorded it, and garrisoned the citadel. But the royalist party, which was numerous at Elvira, did not admit its defeat. Aided by the Governor of Ubeda, they took up arms, expelled Ibn Hafsûn's soldiers, elected a municipal council, and admitted into the town the Governor appointed by 'Abdallah. The partisans of independence, intimidated by the proximity of the Sultan's army—then besieging Carabuey, one of Ibn Mastana's fortresses—made no resistance to this revolution. But as soon as the army had returned to Cordova they once more raised their heads, and communicating secretly with Ibn Hafsûn, introduced some of his soldiers into the citadel during the night. Soon afterwards, Ibn Hafsûn, informed of the success of the scheme by beacon-fires which his partisans had lit, entered with the main body of his troops, while the royalists, suddenly awakened by their adversaries' shouts of triumph, were so completely taken aback that they attempted no resistance. They were punished by the confiscation of all their property, and the Sultan's Governor was beheaded.

Master of Elvira, Ibn Hafsûn next turned his arms against Ibn Jûdî and the Arabs of Granada. Knowing that the encounter which was imminent would be a decisive one, Ibn Jûdî summoned all his allies to his support. Nevertheless he experienced a severe defeat, and since he had had the imprudence to cut himself off from his base at Granada, his troops, who had to traverse all the Vega before they could gain the shelter of their fortress, were cut down in great numbers. The inhabitants of Elvira regarded this victory as ample compensation for all their previous losses, and believed the Arabs to have been irretrievably defeated.

Elated by this success, Ibn Hafsûn marched against Jaen. There he met with similar good fortune. He gained possession of the town, entrusted it to a Governor, and left a garrison in it. He then returned to Bobastro.

The year 892 had therefore restored to Ibn Hafsûn all that he had lost in the preceding year, save Polei and Ecija. For the next five years his power remained undiminished, except by the loss of Elvira. He had taken the royalists of that town by surprise, but had exasperated rather than vanquished them. They accordingly seized the first opportunity of rising. In 893, the Sultan's army, after making a raid in the vicinity of Bobastro, appeared before the gates of Elvira. Prince Motarrif, in command of the army, offered the citizens a general amnesty, if they would give up Ibn Hafsûn's lieutenant and his troops. The royalists induced the citizens to consent, and henceforth Elvira remained submissive. Patriotism and love of liberty grew cold. Moreover, the inhabitants of Elvira had fought against the Arabs of Granada rather than against the Sultan; it was against the Arabs that they had sought Ibn Hafsûn's aid; and since the battle of Granada the Arabs had ceased to be formidable. Enfeebled by defeat, they were still more weakened by intestine feuds. They had split into two factions, one attached to Sa'îd ibn Jûdî and the other to Mohammed ibn Adhâ—the powerful lord of Alhama—against whom Sa'îd harboured so violent a hatred that he had set a price on his head. Sa'îd's imprudent and even reckless conduct made matters worse. By his foolish pride and numerous gallantries, he had incurred the hatred of many chiefs, and at last Abû 'Omar 'Othmân, whose domestic happiness he had ruined, determined to wash away his shame in the blood of the seducer. Warned that his wife had made an assignation with the Emir in the house of a Jew, he concealed himself there with one of his friends, and slew Sa'îd as he entered (December, 897).

This homicide brought the feud to a climax. The murderer and his friends had time to escape to the fortress of Noalexo, to the north of Granada, where they proclaimed Ibn Adhâ Emir. Not wishing to fall out with the Sultan, they begged him to ratify their choice, and at the same time eudeavoured to persuade him that they had killed Sa'îd for the good of the State, alleging that he had planned an insurrection, and had composed such verses as these:

"Go, my messenger, and tell 'Abdallah that swift flight alone can save him; for a mighty warrior hath raised the standard of revolt beside the River of Reeds. Son of Merwân, yield us the sovereignty; it is to us, the sons of the Bedawin, that it belongs of right! Hasten, and bring my bay charger, with his gold-embroidered trappings, for my star is in the ascendant."

Perhaps these verses were really Sa'îd's; they were not unworthy of him. Be this as it may, the Sultan, who was

gratified at the condescension of the Arabs in thus justifying
their conduct, sanctioned their proceedings.   But the former
friends of Sa'îd did not acknowledge Ibn Adhâ.   They were
full of indignation at the murder of their chief.   Inconsolable at his loss, they forgot his frailties, and their grievances
against him—remembering only his virtues.   Mikdam ibn
Moâfâ, whom Sa'îd had unjustly condemned to the lash,
composed these verses to his memory :

> " Who will feed and clothe the poor, now that he who was generosity
> itself lies in the grave?   Ah, let the meadows be bare of verdure, let the
> trees be leafless, let the sun himself rise no more, now that Ibn Jûdî is dead,
> the like of whom neither men nor jinn shall ever look upon again ! "

"What!" cried an Arab when he heard these verses
recited by their author, "dost thou sing the praises of him
who had thee beaten?"   "By Allah!" replied Mikdam,
"even his unjust sentence benefited me, for the memory of
that punishment has turned me aside from many sins to
which I was formerly addicted.   Do I owe him no gratitude
for that?   Moreover, after I was beaten, I was ever unjust
to him; thinkest thou that my injustice could abide after
his death?"

Others, who had been Sa'îd's intimate friends, thirsted
for revenge.   "The wine which the cup-bearer hands me,"
says Asadî in a long poem, "will never recover its zest, until
I obtain my heart's desire, and see the horsemen charging to
avenge him who but yesterday was their joy and pride!"

But though Sa'îd was avenged, the Arabs persisted in
their blood-feud.   The Sultan and the Andalusians meanwhile remained passive and suffered their foes to cut one
another's throats.

The submission of Elvira was a great gain to the
Sultan, nor was it his only success.   Convinced that there
was little use in making war upon Ibn Hafsûn, he turned
his arms against less doughty rebels.   It was not his policy
to crush them ; he made no attempt to seize their towns or
castles; he was content with exacting tribute.   With this
object he sent his army on two expeditions each year.   It
ravaged cornfields, burnt villages, and besieged fortresses,
but as soon as a rebellious chief had consented to pay tribute
and had given hostages, he was left in peace, and another
was attacked.   Expeditions of this kind could not yield
decisive and brilliant results, but they were, nevertheless,
extremely useful.   The treasury was empty, and the

Government was well aware that to carry on operations on a large scale the sinews of war were needed. Now these raids were lucrative, especially that of 895, directed against Seville. The state of affairs in that city remained unaltered: its Governor was appointed by the Sultan; 'Abdallah's uncle Hishâm resided there—and it was ruled by the Khaldûn and Hajjâj. The chiefs of these clans were quite content with their position, which yielded them all the sweets of independence and none of its dangers; they did as they pleased, they paid no tribute, and yet they were not in revolt against their sovereign. Their own interests could scarcely be better served than by the maintenance of this state of things, and when in 895, an agent of the Sultan's arrived to "convoke the ban," Ibrâhîm ibn Hajjâj and Khâlid ibn Khaldûn—Koraib's brother—hastened to respond to the summons, and proceeded with their contingents to Cordova. Their ally Sulaimân, of Sidona, and his brother Maslama followed their example.

It was generally supposed that an expedition was contemplated against the Renegades of Tadmir. Koraib's surprise and alarm may therefore be imagined when he learned that instead of marching eastward, the army was approaching Seville; and that, though Sulaimân had managed to escape, all the other officers and men from Seville and Sidona had been arrested by Motarrif.

Prompt and decisive measures were necessary, and Koraib took them. Posting guards at every gate of the palace, he burst into the hall where Prince Hishâm sat. " Good news! " he cried, his eyes blazing with wrath. " I have learnt that Motarrif has arrested my brother and all my kinsmen in his army! Now, I swear by all that is most sacred, that if the prince attempts the life of one of them, thy head falls. We will see how far he will venture. Meanwhile, thou and thine are my prisoners. No servant of thine shall leave the palace on any pretext, even to buy food. That there is no store of provisions within concerns me not. Wouldst thou see the fatal sword hanging over thy head? Is the prospect of dying of hunger pleasing to thee? To save thy life there is but one way: write to the prince, tell him that thy head will answer to me for the lives of my kinsfolk, and bid him release the prisoners! "

Knowing that Koraib was not a man to stop at threats, Hishâm forthwith obeyed him; but the letter which he wrote to Motarrif did not have the expected result; for the prince, instead of liberating his prisoners, continued to advance on Seville, and summoned Koraib to open the gates. Fearing for his kinsmen's lives, and being unwilling to resort to force until auxiliary troops from Niebla and Sidona had arrived, Koraib deemed it prudent to show moderation. He accordingly allowed the Sultan's troops to enter the city in small bodies to purchase food ; he further promised to pay tribute, and released Hishâm, whose one wish was to find himself in safety outside the walls of Seville.

Next turning his arms against the Ma'addite Tâlib ibn Maulûd,[1] Motarrif attacked his two fortresses, Montefique (on the Guadaira) and Monteagudo.[2] After a vigorous defence Tâlib promised to pay tribute, and gave hostages. At Medina-ibn-as-Salîm and Vejer his example was followed. Lebrija was taken by assault, and Motarrif placed a garrison in it ; but Sulaimân, to whom the fortress belonged, and who was then at Arcos, attacked the Sultan's army before it reached Mairena, and inflicted on it heavy losses. In revenge for this check, Motarrif beheaded three kinsmen of Sulaimân, who were among his prisoners.

Towards the end of August the army again appeared before Seville. Motarrif believed that Koraib would prove as amenable as before. He was mistaken. Koraib had profited by his respite, and had put the city into a state of defence. His allies had joined him, and he resolved to hold out. Motarrif found the gates shut. He thereupon put Khâlid ibn Khaldûn, Ibrâhîm ibn Hajjâj, and other prisoners in chains. This step was futile. Far from being intimidated, Koraib sallied forth and attacked the advance-guard. For a moment the result hung in the balance ; but Motarrif's officers rallied their men, and the Sevillans were repulsed. Motarrif then put Khâlid and Ibrâhîm to the torture, and attacked Seville on three consecutive days. His assaults were fruitless ; but wishing to avenge himself as far as possible on the Khaldûn and the Hajjâj, he seized a castle on the Guadalquiver belonging to Ibrâhîm, and after burning the ships which lay in the basin, he ordered the walls to be razed to the ground : Ibrâhîm, though hampered by his fetters, was compelled to ply an axe in the demolition of his own fortress. After destroying another castle, belonging to Koraib, Motarrif then turned his face towards Cordova.

[1] An ally of the Renegades of Seville.
[2] Near Xeres : cf. Maldonado, *Illustraciones de la Casa de Niebla*, p. 96 (Memorial historico, ix.).

When the army had returned to the Capital, and the tribute from Seville had been paid, a Vizier counselled his master—who had tried to win over Ibn Hafsûn, but had made no attempt at reconciliation with the Arab aristocracy —to set his prisoners at liberty, after binding them by oath henceforth to obey him. "By keeping these nobles in prison," he argued, "you are but serving the interests of Ibn Hafsûn, who will not fail to seize their castles. Try rather to attach them to you by ties of gratitude; they will then aid you against the chief of the Renegades."

The Sultan took this advice. He offered liberty to the prisoners, conditionally on their giving hostages, and swearing fealty to him fifty times in the Great Mosque. They took the required oaths and gave hostages—among them being Ibrâhîm's eldest son, 'Abd-er-Rahmân; but scarcely had they returned to Seville before they broke their oaths, refused tribute, and openly revolted. Ibrâhîm and Koraib divided the province equally between them.

Matters remained on this footing until 899, but the very equality of the power possessed by the two chiefs was an inevitable source of discord between them. They quarrelled, and the Sultan did his best to stir the fire. Koraib was informed of the slighting terms in which Ibrâhîm had spoken of him, and Ibrâhîm learnt Koraib's ill-opinion. One day 'Abdallah received a letter from Khâlid expressing keen hostility against Ibrâhîm, and writing his reply at the foot, he gave it, with other missives, to a servant for delivery. The servant inadvertently dropped it. A eunuch picked it up, read it, and hoping for a reward, handed it to one of Ibrâhîm's envoys, charging him to deliver it to his master.

A glance at the letter confirmed Ibrâhîm in the belief that the Khaldûn were plotting against his authority, his liberty, and perhaps his life. He deemed it advisable, however, to compass his revenge by stratagem, and, expressing great friendliness, invited them to dine with him. They accepted his invitation. During the meal Ibrâhîm produced Khâlid's letter and bitterly reproached his guests. Khâlid sprang up and drawing a dagger from his sleeve struck Ibrâhîm with it on the head. Ibrâhîm's head-dress was slashed, and he received a wound in the face, but his soldiers, in answer to his summons, rushed in and put the two Khaldûn to death. Ibrâhîm threw their heads into the courtyard, and then attacking the guards who were posted there, slew some and put the rest to flight.

Henceforth Ibrâhîm was sole master of the province; but thinking it advisable to justify his conduct to the Sultan, who still had his son in keeping, he sent him a letter assuring him that he could not have acted otherwise; that the Khaldûn had never ceased urging him to rebel; that at the bottom of his heart he had never sympathised with their projects, and that if appointed Governor of the province, he would undertake to defray all expenses required by the public service, and, in addition, pay the Sultan seven thousand ducats annually. 'Abdallah accepted his proposal, but at the same time sent one Kâsim to Seville to govern the province jointly with Ibrâhîm. The latter had no wish for a colleague, and after the lapse of a few months informed Kâsim that he could cheerfully dispense with his services.

Having thus cavalierly rid himself of Kâsim, Ibrâhîm set his mind on getting his son restored to him. But in answer to his frequent requests, the Sultan firmly refused to give up his hostage. Hoping to intimidate the monarch, Ibrâhîm thereupon refused to pay tribute, and offered his alliance to Ibn Hafsûn (A.D. 900).

This offer was very gratifying to the Andalusian chieftain, who three years before had regained possession of Ecija. In the previous year, after much hesitation, he had taken a decisive step: with all his family, he had embraced Christianity. In his inmost heart he had long been a Christian; the fear of losing his Moslem allies had been the only obstacle which hindered him from following the example of his father, who had returned to the fold of the Church several years before. The event showed that his fears were well founded. Yahyâ, son of Anatole, one of his most distinguished officers, deserted him: he had been proud to serve under the Moslem 'Omar ibn Hafsûn, but his conscience forbade him to serve under the Christian Samuel— such being 'Omar's new baptismal name.[1] Ibn al-Khalî, the Berber lord of Cañete, hitherto his ally, now declared war against him, and made overtures to the Sultan. Ibn Hafsûn's apostasy everywhere produced a profound sensation. The Moslems related with horror that in the dominions of " the accursed one " all the highest offices were held by Christians, while the faithful had nothing to hope for and were treated with marked distrust. With the aid of the Fakihs the Court made skilful use of these more or less well-founded rumours,

[1] *Vita Beatæ Virginis Argenteæ*, c. 2.

and tried to persuade the faithful that their eternal salvation would be imperilled if they did not rise like one man and wipe out "the abomination."[1]

In such circumstances nothing could have been more gratifying to Ibn Hafsûn than the proposals made to him by the lord of Seville. He was seeking allies on all sides; he had begun negotiations with Ibrâhîm ibn Kâsim, lord of Acîla (in Africa), with the Beni Kasî, and with the King of Leon, but an alliance with Ibn Hajjâj would be best of all, for he trusted that it would reinstate him in the good opinions of the Moslems. He therefore hastened to conclude the treaty, and when Ibrâhîm had sent him money and cavalry his power became as great as it had ever been.

Ill-luck dogged the Sultan. His policy always recoiled upon himself. His attempt to conciliate the most powerful Arab chieftain had failed as completely as his previous attempts to win over the chief of the Spanish party. His situation was desperate. To offer effectual resistance to the league now formed against him it would be necessary to put all his forces in the field, and this would involve the abandonment of the annual expeditions by which alone tribute could be extracted from the rebels; he therefore ran the risk of succumbing for lack of money. One course only was open to him—to humble himself before Ibn Hafsûn and offer terms of peace so advantageous that they could scarcely be refused. We do not know what these terms were; we are only informed that the negotiations were lengthy, that peace was concluded in 901, and that Ibn Hafsûn sent four hostages to Cordova—among whom were Khalaf, one of his paymasters, and Ibn Mastana.[2]

This peace, however, was of short duration. Whether Ibn Hafsûn found it disadvantageous, or whether the Sultan did not fulfil his part of the treaty, we do not know; at any rate war broke out afresh in 902. In that year Ibn Hafsûn had an interview with Ibn Hajjâj at Carmona. "Send me," he said, "the pick of your horse under *the noble Arab* (meaning Fajîl ibn Abî Moslim, commander of the Sevillan cavalry), for I intend to cross swords with Ibn Abî Abda on the frontier. I trust to defeat him, and in that case we will pillage Cordova on the next day." Fajîl, who was present at this conversation, and who, true Arab that he was, felt far

---

[1] Ar. *Khabîth.*

[2] Ibn Hayyân asserts that Ibn Hafsûn made the first advances: this seems highly improbable in the circumstances.

more sympathy for the Sultan's cause than for the Spaniards',
was offended by the light and disdainful tone in which Ibn
Hafsûn had spoken. "Abû Hafs," he said, "despise not
the army of Ibn Abî Abda. Though small, it is yet great;
and though all Spain were united against it, yet would it not
turn its back." "My lord," replied Ibn Hafsûn, "your
words are vain. What can this Ibn Abî Abda do? How
many soldiers hath he? As for me, I have six thousand
horsemen; add to these five hundred under Ibn Mastana,
and, say, an equal number of your own men. When all
these troops are united we can eat up the army of Cordova."
"On the other hand, we may be defeated," said Fajîl; "but
you must not take it amiss if I do not encourage your design, for you know Ibn Abî Abda's soldiers as well as I."

In spite of Fajîl's opposition, Ibn Hajjâj approved of
his ally's scheme, and ordered his general to join forces
with him.

Informed by spies that the Omayyad general had moved
from the Genil, and had pitched his camp in the district of
Estepa, Ibn Hafsûn advanced to attack him. Although
accompanied only by his cavalry, he gained a brilliant
victory, and inflicted a loss upon the enemy of more than
five hundred men. Towards evening, the infantry, fifteen
thousand strong, arrived upon the field. Without giving
them time to rest, Ibn Hafsûn ordered an immediate advance. Then, entering Fajîl's tent, he exclaimed: "Now,
my lord, let us take the field!" "Against whom?" asked
Fajîl. "Against Ibn Abî Abda." "O Abû Hafs, to desire
two victories in one day is to tempt the Eternal! It is to
show him ingratitude! You have put the enemy to shame;
you have inflicted upon him so heavy a loss that it will be
long ere he recovers from it. Ten years must elapse before
he can take his revenge. Refrain at present from driving
him to despair."

"We will overwhelm him with forces so superior that
he will thank heaven if he finds time to throw himself into
his saddle and seek safety in flight!"

Fajîl arose, but as he buckled on his breastplate, he
exclaimed, "God is my witness that I had no part in this
rash project!"

While the allies, in the hope of surprising the enemy,
marched on in profound silence, Ibn Abî Abda, still sore at
his defeat, sat at table with his generals. Suddenly a cloud
of dust in the distance attracted their attention. One of

the principal officers, 'Abd al-Wâhid Rûtî, left the tent to observe it more carefully. On returning, he said, "My friends, the darkness prevents me from seeing clearly, but it seems to me that Ibn Hafsûn, with his cavalry and infantry, hopes to surprise us." Instantly the officers seized their arms, rushed to their horses, leaped into their saddles, and led forth their men against the foe. As they drew near them several officers cried out, "Cast away your spears, and use your swords!" This order was instantly obeyed, and the royalists thereupon attacked their opponents with such fury that they slew fifteen hundred of them, and compelled the rest to seek refuge in their camp.

Next morning tidings reached the Sultan that his army, after meeting with a reverse, had gained a victory. In his anger against the confederates he ordered the hostages to be put to death. Three of Ibn Hafsûn's hostages were beheaded; the fourth, Ibn Mastana, saved himself by swearing fealty to the Sultan. Next came the turn of 'Abd-er-Rahmân, son of Ibn Hajjâj; but his father had spared neither gold nor promises to procure him friends at court, and he had persistently declared that as soon as the Sultan restored his son to him, he would return to his allegiance. Among his friends was the Slav Badr; and Badr made bold to appeal to 'Abdallah just as 'Abd-er-Rahmân's head was about to fall. "Sire," he said, "forgive my presumption, yet deign to listen to my words: Ibn Hafsûn's hostages are no more, and if you also put to death the son of Ibn Hajjâj, you will unite those two men in life-long enmity against you. It is impossible to conciliate Ibn Hafsûn, for he is a Spaniard; but it is not impossible to win over Ibn Hajjâj, for he is an Arab."

The Sultan summoned his Viziers and consulted them.[1] They unanimously approved of Badr's advice. On their departure, Badr once more addressed the Sultan and assured him that if he set the son of Ibn Hajjâj at liberty, he might in future count upon the fidelity of the Sevillan chief. Seeing that the monarch still hesitated, he begged one of his most influential friends, the treasurer Tojîbî, to draw up a memorial advising the Sultan to follow Badr's advice. A perusal of this document removed 'Abdallah's hesitation, and he bade Tojîbî restore 'Abd-er-Rahmân to his father.[2]

We need not dwell upon the joy felt by Ibn Hajjâj as

---

[1] No other Sultan appointed so many Viziers: he sometimes had thirty.
[2] Ibn Hayyân erroneously gives the date as A.H. 287, for A.H. 289.

he embraced his well-beloved son, whom for six long years
he had fruitlessly entreated to be restored to him. Nor
did he now shrink from showing his gratitude. When he
declared, in the letter which he addressed to the Sultan
after the death of the Khaldûn, that the latter had always
incited him to rebellion, he seems to have spoken the truth.
Koraib had been his evil genius, and now that treacherous
and ambitious man was no more, a great change came over
Ibn Hajjâj. Without actually breaking with Ibn Hafsûn
—to whom he continued to send presents—he ceased to be
his ally, and instead of showing hostility to the Sultan, he
paid his tribute and sent his contingent of troops with
regularity. His position relatively to the sovereign was
henceforth that of a tributary prince ; but in his own
domains his power was limitless. He had an army in his
pay ; he appointed every official in Seville from the Kady
and the Prefect of Police to the merest bailiff. Nor were
symbols of his sovereignty lacking—a privy council, a
body-guard of five hundred knights, and a brocaded robe on
which his name and titles were embroidered in gold. He
exercised his power with princely magnanimity. Rigorous
in his justice, he showed no pity to evil-doers, and maintained order with a strong hand. Prince and merchant, a
man of letters and a patron of the arts, his ships brought
him gifts from foreign potentates, rich fabrics from the
looms of Egypt, scholars from Arabia, and singing-girls
from Baghdad. The beautiful Kamar,[1] whose talents he
had heard so highly praised that he bought her for an
immense sum, and the Bedawy Abû Mohammed Odhrî—a
grammarian of Hijâz—were among the brightest ornaments
of his court. The latter, who whenever he heard an in-
correct phrase or inapt word, was wont to exclaim, " Ah,
citizens, why do you maltreat your language ? " was an
oracle in all that concerned purity of speech and correctness
of style. The witty Kamar added to her musical talent
natural eloquence, poetic genius, and exalted pride. One
day when some empty-headed nobles had been disparaging,
in foolish pride of birth, her origin and past life, she composed these verses :

" They said : ' When Kamar arrived here she was in rags ; heretofore
it was hers to conquer hearts by her languishing looks ; she walked in the

---

[1] " The Moon."

mud of the roads, she wandered from town to town; she is of low extraction; her place is not among nobles, and her sole merit is her ability to write letters and verses.' Ah! if they were not clowns they would speak otherwise of the stranger! By Allah! what men are these, who despise the only true nobility—that which talent confers? Who will deliver me from the unlettered and doltish? The most shameful thing in the world is ignorance, and if ignorance were a woman's passport to Paradise, I would far rather that the Creator sent me to hell!'"

She appears, indeed, to have conceived no high opinion of the Arabs in Spain. Accustomed to the polished courtesy of Baghdad, she found herself out of place in a country which contained many traces of primitive boorishness. The Prince alone found favour in her eyes, and it was in his praise that she composed these verses:

"In all the West there is but one man who is truly noble—and he is Ibrâhîm, who is nobility incarnate. To dwell with him is the greatest of delights, and when one has experienced it, to dwell in another country would be misery." [1]

Kamar was not exaggerating when she thus praised Ibrâhîm's liberality. All shared her opinion; and the poets of Cordova, whom the miserly Sultan had almost suffered to die of hunger, flocked to his court—the poet-laureate, Ibn 'Abdi Rabbihi, at their head. Ibrâhîm scarcely ever failed to reward them with princely munificence. On one occasion only he withheld his bounty; this was when Kalfât, a venomous satirist, recited to him a poem full of biting sarcasms against the ministers and courtiers of Cordova. Although Ibn Hajjâj owed a grudge to more than one of these personages, he showed no sign of approval, and when the poet had made an end, he remarked coldly: "You err in thinking that I am a man to take pleasure in listening to vulgar scurrilities." Kalfât returned empty-handed to Cordova. Disappointed and furious he poured forth his gall:

"Blame me not, my wife, if I do naught but shed tears since my last journey. That journey hath caused me inconsolable grief. I hoped to have found a generous man yonder, and I found only a brainless gowk!"

Ibn Hajjâj was not a man to tolerate such gibes. When he heard how the poet had revenged himself, he sent him this message:
"If thou refrainest not from thy mockery, I swear by all

---

[1] Sâlimî (in Makkarî, ii. 97) cites some verses attributed to Kamar, implying that she was homesick : but they are clearly the composition of a man.

that is holy that I will have thee beheaded as thou liest on thy bed at Cordova!"

Henceforth Kalfât wrote no more Satires against the lord of Seville.

[AUTHORITIES: Ibn Hayyân, ff. 5, 8–11, 22, 47–8, 59–63, 77, 80–87, 90–8, 102; Nuwairî, p. 466; Ibn Khaldûn, 11; Makkarî, ii. pp. 97, 361; Ibn al-Khatîb (*Notices,* p. 259); Ibn Adhârî, i. 241; ii. 128–32, 143; Ibn al-Kûtiyya, ff. 45–7.]

CHAPTER XVII

'ABD-ER-RAHMÂN III

THE Sultan's reconciliation with Ibn Hajjâj proved the commencement of a new era which saw the restoration of the royal power. Seville had been the nursery of rebellion in the West, and now that it had succumbed, all the other districts, from Algeciras to Niebla, perforce submitted. During the last nine years of 'Abdallah's reign tribute was paid with such punctuality that it was no longer necessary to send troops to collect it. The Sultan was therefore enabled to concentrate his forces against the South. This fortunate result was due to Badr's wise counsels, and the Sultan, who was under deep obligations to him, gave striking proofs of his gratitude. He conferred on him the title of Vizier, admitted him to intimacy, and reposed such complete confidence in him that Badr, though not Prime Minister in name, virtually held that office.

In the South the Sultan's arms henceforth met with almost uninterrupted success. In 903 his army captured Jaen; in 905 it won the battle of Guadalbollon against Ibn Hafsûn and Ibn Mastana; in 906 it took Cañete from the Beni al-Khalî; in 907 it compelled Archidona to pay tribute; in 909 it deprived Ibn Mastana of Luque; in 910 it captured Baeza, while in the following year the inhabitants of Iznajar revolted against their lord, Fadl ibn Salama, Ibn Mastana's son-in-law, and slaying him, sent his head to the Sultan. Even in the North a great improvement was manifest. At a critical moment—in the year 898—there had been a fear lest the two most powerful Spaniards in the North and South respectively might enter into alliance. Mohammed ibn Lope, of the family of the Beni Kasî, had promised to visit the province of Jaen, there to confer with Ibn Hafsûn. Being, however, prevented from coming in person by a war in which he was engaged with al-Ankar, Governor of Zaragoza, he sent his son Lope in his place. Lope had reached Jaen, and was awaiting Ibn Hafsûn's arrival, when he received news of the death of his father, who had been killed

at the siege of Zaragoza: he accordingly hurried home
without meeting Ibn Hafsûn. Nothing more was heard of
the projected alliance, which had caused so much alarm at
the royal court, and Lope, far from showing hostility to
'Abdallah, sought his favour, whereupon the Sultan appointed him Governor of Tudela and Tirazona. Lope
employed his troops in ceaseless wars with his neighbours—
including the lord of Huesca, the King of Leon, the Count
of Barcelona, the Count of Pallars, and the King of Navarre
—until he was killed in an encounter with the last, in 907.
His brother 'Abdallah, who succeeded him, also fought, not
against the Sultan, but against the King of Navarre. The
Beni Kasî had ceased to be a source of danger to the
Omayyads.

The political horizon was everywhere clear. At Cordova
the future was contemplated with confidence. The poets
chanted pæans such as had not been heard for many years.
Nevertheless the royal power had as yet made slow progress,
and nothing decisive had been accomplished, when 'Abdallah
died, on October 15, 912, in the sixty-eighth year of his
age and the twenty-fourth of his reign.

The heir-presumptive to the throne was 'Abd-er-Rahmân,
the son of 'Abdallah's eldest son—the unfortunate
Mohammed, who had been assassinated by his brother
Motarrif at his father's instigation.[1] An orphan from his
tenderest years, 'Abd-er-Rahmân had been brought up by
his grandfather, who, a prey to ceaseless remorse, seems to
have concentrated on the child all the affection of which he
was capable, and long before his death named him his
successor. But 'Abd-er-Rahmân was not yet twenty-two,
and it was to be feared that his uncles or great-uncles might
dispute the throne with him; for there was no settled law
of succession: when the throne fell vacant, it was usually
occupied by the eldest, or the most capable, of the royal
family. Against all expectation, however, there was no
opposition to 'Abd-er-Rahmân's accession; on the contrary,
princes and courtiers hailed the event with joy, and seemed
to see in it a pledge of future prosperity and glory. · The
fact was that the young prince had already learnt how to
win affection, and had inspired all who knew him with a
high opinion of his talents.

'Abd-er-Rahmân III, in carrying on the work begun by

---

[1] See Dozy, *Introd. à la Chron. d'Ibn-Adhârí*, pp. 47–50.

his grandfather, adopted totally different methods. For 'Abdallah's timid and tortuous procedure he substituted a policy which was frank, resolute, and daring. Disdaining to mince matters, he told the Spanish insurgents plainly that what he required of them was not tribute, but their castles and their towns. To those who submitted he promised full pardon, to the rest exemplary punishment. At first sight, such claims seemed likely to unite all Spain against him. But it was not so. His masterful determination quelled, instead of arousing, ill-will, and his policy, far from being rash, was dictated by the intellectual and political tendencies of the day.

A gradual but universal change had come over the country. The Arab aristocracy was no longer what it had been when 'Abdallah came to the throne. It had lost its most illustrious chiefs; Sa'îd ibn Jûdî and Koraib ibn Khaldûn were no more; Ibrâhîm ibn Hajjâj, too, had lately died,[1] and there were none possessed of sufficient talent or consequence to fill the blank left by the death of these eminent men. The Spaniards, it is true, still had their leaders, and their power seemed but little weakened. But these leaders had grown old, and the rank and file were not of the mettle of thirty years before, when, full of enthusiasm, they rose like one man at the summons of Ibn Hafsûn to rid themselves of foreign domination. That early fervour had grown cold. The sanguine and vigorous generation of 884 had been supplanted by another without the grievances and at the same time lacking the pride, energy, and passion of its predecessor: not having suffered from royal oppression, it had no reason to detest it. Folk murmured, it is true, but the ills they deplored did not arise from despotism but from anarchy and civil war. Every day they had seen the royal troops, or the insurgents, ravaging fields which promised a fair harvest, felling olives in full bloom and orange-trees laden with fruit, or burning villages to the ground; but what they had not seen, and waited for in vain, was the triumph of the national cause. The Sultan's throne sometimes seemed to totter, but a moment afterwards it was firm as a rock. This was discouraging. It was instinctively felt, if not openly confessed, that a great national uprising, if it did not attain its object during the first flush of enthusiasm, would never attain it. And if such

---

[1] In A.D. 910 or 911.

was the general impression at a time when success alternated between the two parties, it deepened when the insurgents met with an unbroken series of reverses, and instead of making headway, drifted backwards. It began to be asked what was the use of all this havoc, involving the death of so many brave men, and whether it were not a punishment for pillaging and slaying in a cause not pleasing to heaven. The inhabitants of the larger towns, who especially hankered after repose and well-being, were the first to ask themselves such questions, and finding no satisfactory answers, they decided that, all things considered, peace at any price—if accompanied by a revival of manufactures, and consequent prosperity—was better than a patriotic war, with confusion and anarchy. Elvira submitted spontaneously; Jaen was taken without resistance, and Archidona consented to pay tribute. In the Serrania—the cradle of the rebellion—enthusiasm did not subside so quickly, but even there signs of weariness and discouragement began to show themselves. The mountaineers no longer flocked to enrol themselves under the national flag, and Ibn Hafsûn was obliged to follow the Sultan's example and enlist mercenaries from Tangier. From that time the character of the war was changed. Mere havoc increased—for each side aimed at depriving the enemy of the means of hiring African troops—but the conflict lacked the fierce energy of earlier days, and was much less sanguinary. The Berbers of Tangier, always ready to change sides for an increase of pay,[1] looked upon the war merely as a lucrative pastime : they spared adversaries who fought by their side yesterday and might be their comrades again to-morrow. In many a fight not more than two or three men were killed : sometimes there were no fatalities. When a few men had been wounded and a few horses hamstrung, it was considered that enough had been done. To aim at winning, with such soldiers as these, the independence which the enthusiastic uprising of an infuriated population had failed to secure was clearly a chimerical project. Ibn Hafsûn himself seems to have realized this, for in the year 909, he acknowledged as

---

[1] In 896, during the siege of Velez, many of the Sultan's troops, both horse and foot, went over to the enemy in the hope of higher pay ; the same thing occurred at Lorca. In 897 twelve soldiers from Tangier, serving under Ibn Hafsûn, offered their services to the Sultan. In the last year of 'Abdallah's reign his Berber regiments deserted *en masse* and joined Ibn Hafsûn's forces. Soon, however, they quarrelled with their new comrades, most of them were massacred, and the survivors returned to the Sultan, who pardoned them. (Ibn Hayyân, ff. 88-9, 91, 107 ; Arib, ii. p. 152.)

sovereign 'Obaidallah the Shî'ite, who was heading an insurrection in the North of Africa against the Aghlabites. Nothing came of this strange alliance, but it proved that Ibn Hafsûn could no longer reckon upon his own country-men.

To these causes of the general enfeeblement of courage and enthusiasm must be added the profound demoralisation of the Castellans, especially in the provinces of Jaen and Elvira. These "barons" had entirely forgotten that they took up arms for a patriotic motive. In their cloud-capped strongholds they had become mere brigands, heedless of law and religion, who from their embattled fastnesses watched for travellers, and swooped upon them like birds of prey, making no distinction between friend and foe. Every hamlet and town cursed these tyrants, and whosoever would demolish their massive towers, and level the hateful walls of their castles, might count on the gratitude of the neighbouring population. But the Sultan alone could do this, and the hopes of the oppressed naturally turned to him.

It must further be remarked, that the conflict was no longer national and universal, but had assumed a religious character. Ibn Hafsûn at first had made no distinction between Moslems and Christians; so long as a man was a Spaniard, willing to fight in the good cause, and could wield a weapon, his religion was not inquired into. But after he himself and his most powerful ally, Ibn Mastana, had openly embraced Christianity, and, with a view to restoring to that religion its former magnificence, had built splendid churches in every district, the conditions were wholly changed. Henceforth Ibn Hafsûn, or Samuel as he now called himself, showed confidence in none but Christians; lucrative posts and high dignities were for them alone. Bobastro became the focus of a fanaticism as austere and gloomy as that which sixty years before had animated the monks of Cordova. Ibn Hafsûn's own daughter, the zealous and intrepid Argentea, set an example. Despite the entreaties of her father, who, upon the death of his wife Colomba, wished his daughter to preside over his household, Argentea had established a kind of convent within the fortress itself, and, despairing like many others of the triumph of the Spaniards, she fostered a yearning for martyrdom—a monk having predicted that she was destined to die for Christ.[1] Now this zeal for Christianity with con-

---

[1] *Vita Beat. Virg. Argenteæ*, c. 2, 3 (*Esp. sagr.*, x.).

tempt for Islamism was a stumbling-block to many who had hitherto fought for national independence. Notwithstanding their hatred of the Arabs, they were deeply attached to the religion which they had imbibed from them, and it must not be forgotten that a Spaniard is almost always a fervent believer, whatever religion he may have adopted. Former serfs, and descendants of serfs, desired at all costs to prevent Christianity once more becoming the dominant religion, in the fear that if it did so, old claims would inevitably be revived, of which they would be the victims. Religion itself therefore became a firebrand. Everywhere Spanish Christians and Spanish Moslems regarded one another with jealousy and suspicion; and in some districts sanguinary conflicts ensued between them. In the province of Jaen the Renegade Ibn as-Shâlia, on re-capturing Cazlona, a fortress which the Christians had taken from him, put the whole garrison to the sword (A.D. 898).

The national party, therefore, were much less powerful than they seemed. Among them that sacred fire by which alone great and heroic deeds can be accomplished, burned low; they were disunited, and had grown weary of conflict; among them were many who had no aversion to reconciliation with the Sultan, the natural defender of orthodoxy—if only that Sultan was not 'Abdallah. Reconciliation with the misanthropic and hypocritical tyrant who had poisoned two of his brothers, executed a third, and put to death two of his sons, on mere suspicion and without trial,[1] had been unthinkable. But he was dead, and his successor in no way resembled him. 'Abd-er-Rahmân was endowed with every quality necessary to win the sympathy and confidence of a people—to please, to dazzle, and to rule. He had the winning presence with which wielders of sovereign power are not endowed in vain—his were the grace that fascinates and the brilliancy which commands. All who approached him lauded his talents, his clemency, and his moderation; of the last he had already given proof by a reduction of taxes. Impressionable minds, too, were influenced by the sad fate of his father, assassinated in the prime of life, and by recalling that the luckless prince had once sought refuge at Bobastro under the national flag.

The young monarch therefore ascended the throne under very favourable auspices. The great towns were eager to

---

[1] See Dozy, *Introd. à la Chron. d'Ibn Adhârí*, pp. 44–62.

open their gates to him. Ecija set the example. On
December 31, 912, two months and a half after 'Abdallah's
death, it surrendered to its besieger Badr, who had lately
received the title of *hájib* (prime minister). But 'Abd-er-
Rahmân wished to gather bays for himself upon the battlefield. On the return of Spring (April, 913), he took
command of the army, and resolved to bring the Castellans
of Jaen to submission. For several years the troops had
not seen a Sultan at their head—for since the campaign of
Carabuey, in 892, 'Abdallah had not shown himself in camp
—and the absence of the sovereign doubtless had a bad
effect on the *morale* of the soldiers. They greeted, however,
with enthusiasm the brilliant young monarch who was
ready to share not only their glory, but their hardships and
dangers.

On entering the province of Jaen, 'Abd-er-Rahmân
learned that Ibn Hafsûn was in league with the revolutionary party at Archidona, and hoped to gain possession
of that town. He therefore detached a brigade, and ordered
the general in command to throw himself into Archidona
with all speed. This was done, and Ibn Hafsûn's hopes
were dashed. The Sultan himself proceeded to lay siege
to Monteleon. The lord of that castle, Sa'îd ibn Hodhail,
one of Ibn Hafsûn's earliest allies, preferred negotiating to
fighting. His fortress was invested on a Sunday and it
surrendered on the following Tuesday.

Ibn as-Shâlia, Ishâk ibn Ibrâhîm, the lord of Mentesa,
and seven other Castellans scarcely waited for the Sultan
to arrive before their gates, to make submission and beg for
the *aman*. This 'Abd-er-Rahmân granted, and sent them
to Cordova with their wives and children, placing lieutenants
in the abandoned fortresses. In the province of Elvira the
like happened, and the Sultan met with no opposition until
he reached Fiñana. There Ibn Hafsûn's partisans were in
the ascendant, and persuaded the other inhabitants that the
town was impregnable. But it made no long resistance.
The town stood on the summit of a hill, and after seeing
the houses on the slopes beneath them burnt, the lukewarm
among its citizens asked for terms, and consented to surrender the irreconcilables, as demanded by the Sultan.
'Abd-er-Rahmân next ventured amongst the almost inaccessible tracks of the Sierra Nevada. There also the Castellans
surrendered without exception. Then hearing that Ibn
Hafsûn was threatening Elvira, the Sultan without a

moment's delay sent troops to the assistance of that town.
Upon the arrival of the reinforcements the militia of Elvira,
who prided themselves on their zeal, marched against the
enemy, and defeated them near Granada, taking prisoner
a grandson of Ibn Hafsûn.

In the meantime 'Abd-er-Rahmân besieged Juviles,
where Christians from other castles had taken refuge. The
siege lasted for a fortnight, at the end of which time the
Andalusian Moslems craved the Sultan's clemency and pro-
mised to deliver up to him the Christians among them.
They kept their word, and the Christians were beheaded.
Then, passing Salobreña, and marching in the direction of
Elvira, 'Abd-er-Rahmân captured San Estevan and Peña
Forata, two eagles' nests which had been the terror of the
inhabitants of Elvira and Granada. A campaign of three
months had sufficed to pacify the provinces of Elvira and
Jaen and to rid them of brigands.

The turn of the Sevillan aristocracy had now come.
Upon the death of Ibrâhîm ibn Hajjâj, his eldest son, 'Abd-
er-Rahmân, had succeeded him at Seville, and his second
son, Mohammed, at Carmona; and when this 'Abd-er-
Rahmân died in 913, Mohammed—the idol of the poets,
for, like his father, he showered gifts upon them—aimed at
proclaiming himself also lord of Seville. He failed, however, in his design. He had shown an inclination to arbitrary rule, and Seville wished to be independent; he was
moreover accused, perhaps falsely, of having poisoned his
brother. His cousin, Ahmad ibn Maslama, a brave soldier,
was accordingly chosen instead of him. Mohammed was
deeply mortified, and since the Sultan, who had not seen
fit to recognise the new lord, had despatched an army
against Seville, he came to Court to offer his services, which
the Sultan accepted.

The siege was so vigorously carried on that Ahmad ibn
Maslama found himself obliged to seek an ally, and approached Ibn Hafsûn. The latter once more came to the
rescue of the threatened Arab aristocracy. But Fortune
had turned her back upon him. Sallying forth from
Seville, with his allies, to attack the royal troops, who
had set up their head-quarters on the right bank of the
Guadalquiver, he met with so severe a defeat, that leaving
the Sevillans to their own devices, he retreated with all
speed to Bobastro.

Ahmad ibn Maslama and the other Sevillan nobles now

knew that further resistance was useless. They therefore opened negotiations with Badr, who had lately joined the camp, and having obtained a promise from him that their usages and customs should remain as they were under the Hajjâj, they opened the gates of the city (December 20, 913).

Mohammed ibn Hajjâj, who believed that the capture of Seville would redound to his advantage, and from whom the negotiations had been carefully concealed, was greatly surprised to receive a letter from Badr announcing that the city had surrendered, and that therefore he might withdraw from Cordova. He retired, but with a heart swelling with wrath, and vowing vengeance. On his way to Carmona he seized a herd of cattle belonging to certain Cordovans, and then shut himself up in his fortress and bid defiance to the Sultan. 'Abd-er-Rahmân took the matter quietly; he sent an official to Mohammed to point out to him firmly yet urbanely that the days were over when nobles could with impunity appropriate other folks' goods, and that he must consequently restore the lifted herd. Mohammed gave up the cattle, but, with all his intelligence, he failed to realize that times had changed. Hearing that the Government had pulled down the walls of Seville, he resolved to seize the city by a *coup de main*, and attacked it without warning. His rash enterprise failed, but the Sultan was so long-suffering as again to send him an emissary to warn him that his ideas were old-fashioned. The prefect of police, Kâsim ibn Walîd, the Kelbite, was entrusted with the mission. It could not have been put in better hands; Kâsim during 'Abdallah's reign had been for some months a colleague of Ibrâhîm ibn Hajjâj; he was an intimate friend of Mohammed, and recently during the siege of Seville they had been much thrown together. The Sultan's expectations were not disappointed; Kâsim acquitted himself with so much tact and intelligence, and argued so persuasively, that Mohammed at last promised to present himself at Court, provided that he might leave his lieutenant at Carmona. The Sultan consented to this arrangement, and Mohammed arrived at Cordova, in April, 914, with a numerous retinue. The sovereign showed him the utmost courtesy, and presented valuable gifts to him and his men-at-arms; he also granted Mohammed the title of Vizier and invited him to take part in a new campaign which was on foot.

'Abd-er-Rahmân was, in fact, determined to attack the

insurrection at its very heart—the Serrania de Regio.　He did not, of course, expect to gain there rapid and brilliant successes like those of the previous year in Jaen and Elvira. In the Serrania, whence Islamism had been almost entirely banished, he would have Christians to deal with, and the Sultan had learnt that Spanish Christians usually defended themselves much more stubbornly than Spanish Moslems. He believed, moreover, that even among the Christians some would be found who, persuaded that he was as just as he was resolute, would submit spontaneously.　It must, indeed, be said to the honour of the Government, that Christians who capitulated were treated with the greatest leniency.　For example, the mistress of a Christian noble who had surrendered during the previous year and had since resided in Cordova, appealed to the Kady, and pointing out that she was a Moslem and a free-woman, desired to be released from her position of subjection, since it was not lawful for a Christian to possess a Moslem concubine.　The prime minister, Badr, no sooner heard of the lady's proceedings than he sent the Kady this message: " The Christian in question is here in virtue of an act of capitulation which must not be violated.　You know better than anybody that treaties should be scrupulously observed.　Do not venture therefore to take this slave away from her master ! " The Kady was somewhat surprised at this message; the Minister seemed to be encroaching upon his province.　After making sure that the message was really from the *hâjib*, he said to the messenger : " Inform your master that it is my duty to respect the sanctity of oaths, and that I can make no exception in my own case.　I intend to deal, if not prevented, with the demand of this lady, who is, be it remembered, a Moslem and free."　On receiving this reply Badr had no doubt of the Kady's bias.　He sent him, however, another message : " I have no desire to interfere with the course of justice, and I have no right to require of you an unjust decision.　I only ask you to take into consideration the rights which this Christian noble has acquired by virtue of the treaty which he made with us.　You are well aware that it is your duty to treat Christians with equity and great circumspection.　But you must decide for yourself."

We are not told whether the Kady was convinced, or whether he held that the law was above treaties ; but Badr's conduct in the circumstances was at any rate a proof of the sincerity of the Government, and the conciliatory spirit which animated it. It was a wise and generous policy, and it accorded with 'Abd-er-Rahmân's character. So little bigoted was the monarch that on one occasion he wished to confer one of the highest magisterial posts—that of the Kady of Cordova—on a Renegade whose parents were still Christians, and the Fakihs found much difficulty in dissuading him.

'Abd-er-Rahmân's expectations with regard to the Christian Castellans of the Serrania were not disappointed. Many of them asked for and were granted an amnesty; but Tolox, where Ibn Hafsûn animated the garrison by his presence, held out so stubbornly that the Sultan could not capture it. On one occasion when the garrison made a sortie, a sanguinary combat ensued. Another castle also made so stout a resistance that 'Abd-er-Rahmân swore in his anger that he would taste no wine and participate in no feast until it had fallen. He was soon released from his vow, capturing this castle as well as another. At about the same time the royal fleet rendered good service by intercepting vessels laden with provisions for Ibn Hafsûn— that chief being now reduced to such straits that he was obliged to turn to Africa for supplies.

On his way back to his capital, the Sultan passed Algeciras, and then marched through the provinces of Sidona and Moron. It was Carmona that he especially wished to visit, and on June 28, 914, he arrived before its gates.

Habîb, Mohammed's lieutenant, had there raised the standard of revolt. It was doubtful whether he had done this of his own accord; some declared that it was at his master's instigation. 'Abd-er-Rahmân thought the suspicion well founded, and threw Mohammed into prison, after depriving him of his viziership. The siege of Carmona then commenced. Habîb defended it for twenty days, and then asked for and obtained the *aman*. Mohammed ibn Hajjâj, now that he was powerless for harm, was soon set at liberty; but he did not long enjoy his freedom, for he died in April, 915, and was the last of the Hajjâj to play a part in history.

In the same year a terrible famine, caused by a long drought, rendered a campaign impossible. The populace of Cordova died by thousands, and there were scarcely men left to bury the dead. The Sultan and his Minister did all they could to alleviate the distress, but they found it difficult to check the insurgents, who, pressed by hunger, issued forth from the mountains to snatch the scanty food remaining in the plains. Next year Orihuela and Niebla were subdued, and the Sultan had so thoroughly established his authority that he was able to order raids to be made against the Christians in the North, when death delivered him from his most formidable enemy: in the year 917, Ibn Hafsûn breathed his last. This event caused great rejoicing at Cordova, where confidence was felt that the insurrection would now soon be extinguished.

The heroic Spaniard, who for more than thirty years had defied the invaders of his country, and who had often made the Omayyads tremble on their throne, had reason to thank Providence that he was permitted to die when he did, and was thus spared the melancholy spectacle of his party's ruin. He died unvanquished; and in the existing circumstances, that was all that he could have hoped for. It was not his lot to liberate his fatherland, or to found a dynasty; none the less he stands forth a truly heroic form, the like of whom Spain had not produced since the days when Viriathus swore to deliver his country from the Roman yoke.

[AUTHORITIES: Ibn al-Kûtiyya, f. 47; Ibn Hayyân, ff. 4–13, 81–95, 102–7; Ibn Adhârî, ii. pp. 143, 161–2, 133–5; Arîb, ii. pp. 145–178; Khoshanî, ff. 133–6; Ibn Khaldûn, ff. 11–12; Ibn al-'Abbâr, p. 97; *Akhbár majmú'at,* f. 116.]

CHAPTER XVIII

'ABD-ER-RAHMÂN SUPREME

THE war in the Serrania lasted ten years longer. 'Omar ibn Hafsûn had left four sons—Ja'far, Sulaimân, 'Abd-er-Rahmân, and Hafs—who, with one exception, inherited the courage, if not the talents, of their father. In March, 918, Sulaimân was forced to enrol himself in the Sultan's army, and to take part in the campaign against the king of Leon and Navarre. 'Abd-er-Rahmân, who was in command of Tolox, and whose tastes were literary rather than military, also surrendered, and was taken to Cordova, where he spent the rest of his life in copying manuscripts. Ja'far's power was, however, still formidable—at least the Sultan seems to have thought so, for when he besieged Bobastro in 919, he did not disdain to parley with him, and on Ja'far's offering hostages and an annual tribute, he accepted the proposal. Soon afterwards, however, Ja'far committed what proved a fatal error. In his opinion his father had erred in declaring himself and his family Christians; and, in a certain sense, this view was correct, for Ibn Hafsûn had undoubtedly alienated the Andalusian Moslems by his change of religion; but, the step once taken, neither Ibn Hafsûn nor his sons could draw back; henceforth they must rely solely on the Christians and stand or fall with them. Among the Christians alone was effective enthusiasm to be found—the Moslems everywhere played the traitor. What had happened not long before at Balda illustrated this fact. When this fortress was besieged by the Sultan, the Moslem portion of the garrison went over bodily to the enemy, while the Christians suffered themselves to be slain to the last man rather than surrender. Ja'far, however, who never fully understood his position, still believed in the possibility of being reconciled with the Andalusian Moslems, and to win them over, hinted his intention of returning to Islamism. This step proved his ruin. Shuddering at the thought of serving under an infidel, his Christian soldiers entered into a conspiracy, and, with the connivance of his brother Sulaimân, assassinated him (A.D. 920): Sulaimân, who was at hand, was immediately declared chief.

His reign was calamitous. Bobastro was a prey to the bitterest discords. An insurrection broke out; Sulaimân was expelled, the prisoners were set at liberty, and the palace was sacked; but shortly afterwards his partisans crept into the town; he himself followed in disguise, and bribing the inhabitants by prospects of pillage, he called them to arms. Once more master, and implacable in his vengeance, he beheaded most of his opponents. "Allah," writes a Cordovan historian, "allowed the infidels to cut each other's throats, that their race might be rooted out."

Sulaimân did not long survive his restoration. Unhorsed in a skirmish, February 6, 927, he was slain by the royalists, who avenged themselves on his corpse, cutting off the head, hands, and feet. His brother Hafs succeeded him, but the fatal hour had sounded. In June 927, the Sultan beleaguered Bobastro, determined not to raise the siege before it capitulated. Throwing up earthworks on every side, and rebuilding a half-ruined Roman tower in the vicinity, he completely surrounded the town and cut it off from supplies. For six months Hafs held out. But he surrendered on Friday, January 21, 928, and Bobastro was occupied by the Sultan's troops. Hafs was deported to Cordova with the rest of the inhabitants, and later on served in 'Abd-er-Rahmân's army. His sister Argentea retired to a convent, where she would probably have been allowed to remain in peace, had she been content to live in obscurity; but she was a fanatic who had long yearned for the martyr's palm, and she provoked the authorities by boasting that she was a Christian—though in the eyes of the law she was a Moslem, as was her father when she was born. She was thereupon condemned to death as an apostate, and met her fate with heroic courage, showing herself a worthy daughter of the indomitable 'Omar ibn Hafsûn (A.D. 931).

Two months after the surrender of Bobastro, the Sultan entered that town in person, wishing to view with his own eyes the proud stronghold which for half a century had defied the incessant attacks of four Sultans. When from its ramparts he gazed upon the embattled bastions and the mighty towers; when his eyes fell upon the scarped mountain on which it stood, and the profound precipices around it, he exclaimed that it had not its equal in the world; and filled with gratitude to the Eternal, who had delivered it into his hands, he fell upon his knees and poured forth his heart in thankfulness. It is recorded that throughout his sojourn at Bobastro he observed a strict fast. Unhappily for his fame, he allowed a concession to be wrung from him which should have been refused. Wishing to see the formidable town which had been the bulwark of the religion which they held in detestation, certain Fakihs' had followed in the Sultan's train, and once at Bobastro they gave him no rest until he allowed them to open the tombs of 'Omar ibn Hafsûn and his son Ja'far. Then, as the bigots beheld them lying interred in the Christian manner, they were not ashamed to break in upon the repose of the warriors who slept their eternal sleep, and dragging the corpses from the tomb, they sent them to Cordova, there to be nailed to stakes. "Their bodies," exclaims a contemporary chronicler, in savage glee, "thus became a salutary warning to the ill-disposed, and a grateful spectacle for the eyes of true believers."

Strongholds still in the hands of the Christians now hastened to make submission. The Sultan levelled them all—with the exception of a few which he deemed it prudent to spare, in order to over-awe the country—and the most influential and dangerous inhabitants were conveyed to Cordova.

By the time that the pacification of the Serrania was complete, the Sultan had also quelled the rebellion in several other quarters. In the mountains of Priego the sons of Ibn Mastana had been forced to yield up their castles; in the province of Elvira, the Berbers of the Beni Muhallab had laid down their arms. Monte Rubio, on the frontier of Jaen and Elvira, had been captured. Situated on a lofty and precipitous mountain, this fortress had long caused the Government serious annoyance. A band of Christians had their eyry there, whence they swooped down to pillage hamlets, or to rob and massacre wayfarers. In 922 their lair was unsuccessfully besieged by the Sultan for a full month; it was not captured until four years later. In 924 many rebels of the province of Valencia surrendered. In the same year the Sultan withdrew from the northern frontier all the Beni Kasî—who were enfeebled by warfare among themselves and against the King of Navarre—and enrolled them in his own army. Two years later the general Abd al-Hamîd fought a successful campaign against the Beni Dhu 'n-Nûn.

Having no longer anything to fear from the South, the Sultan was able to concentrate his arms against rebels in other provinces. His victories were swift and decisive. In 928 he despatched an expedition against the sheik Aslamî, lord of Alicante and Callosa, in the province of Tadmir. This Arab, who was a free-booter and scoundrel of the very worst kind, had always professed zeal for religion. Growing old, he had abdicated in favour of his son 'Ab-der-Rahmân, wishing—so he said—to devote his remaining days to his own salvation. He attended, indeed, with the utmost regularity all sermons and public prayers, but this show of piety did not prevent him from occasionally marauding in his neighbours' lands, and when his son was killed in a fight with the royalists, he once more assumed power. He did not, however, long enjoy it; the general Ahmad ibn Ishâk captured his fortresses one after another, and Aslamî, compelled to surrender, was conveyed to Cordova with all his family. At about the same time Merida and Santarem capitulated to the troops sent against them by the Sultan, without drawing a sword. Next year Beja submitted after a fortnight's brave resistance. 'Abd-er-Rahmân then threatened Khalaf ibn Bakr, prince of Oksonoba; but that Renegade expressed his willingness to pay tribute, pleading the remoteness of his province as an excuse for not having paid it before. He was beloved by his subjects, as his predecessors had been, and the Sultan feared that if he were deposed the inhabitants of Algarve might be driven to desperation. Contrary to his wont, therefore, he made a bargain with the prince, consenting that Khalaf ibn Bakr should become, not a subject, but a vassal—stipulating, however, that he should pay an annual tribute, and harbour no rebels. The reduction of Badajoz, where a descendant of Ibn Merwân, "the Galician," still reigned, proved a more difficult matter. This town did not capitulate until after a siege which lasted for a whole year (A.D. 930).

To be master of the heritage of his ancestors, 'Abd-er-Rahmân had now only to reduce Toledo. His first step was to send thither a deputation of Fakihs, to point out to the inhabitants that since the whole country had now submitted it was foolish of them to pose as republicans. This attempt proved futile. Ardently loving the liberty which they had enjoyed for eighty years, both under the protection of the Beni Kasî and under that of the kings of Leon, the Toledans sent an evasive, if not arrogant, reply.

Seeing that extreme measures were imperative, the
Sultan laid his plans with his habitual promptness and
decision. In May, 930, before the main army, which he
intended to send against the rebels, had assembled, he sent
one of his generals, the Vizier Sa'îd ibn Mundhir, to besiege
Toledo. In June the Sultan himself marched against the
town with the bulk of his forces, and pitching his camp on
the banks of the Algodor, near the castle of Mora, he
summoned the commander of that fortress to surrender.
The summons sufficed ; the Renegade saw that resistance
to the Sultan's troops would be futile. 'Abd-er-Rahmân,
placing a garrison in Mora, then moved his camp nearer
Toledo, pitching it on a mountain then known as Jarancas.
Looking out over the gardens and vineyards, he came to the
conclusion that the burial-place near the gateway would
be best suited for his head-quarters. He transferred his
troops, therefore, to this cemetery, and causing the crops
and fruit-trees near the city to be levelled and the villages
to be burned, he attacked Toledo with great vigour. Nevertheless the siege lasted for more than two years. The Sultan,
whom nothing discouraged, built a town upon the mountain
of Jarancas, and Al-Fath (Victory), erected in a few days,
was a pledge to the Toledans that the siege would never be
raised. The beleaguered city still counted on the King of
Leon, but his army was routed by the royalists.[1] Famine
at length compelled the Toledans to open their gates.
'Abd-er-Rahmân's joy at gaining possession of the city was
as great as that which he displayed when he became master
of Bobastro, and fervent were the thanksgivings which he
offered to the Almighty.

Arabs, Spaniards, Berbers—all had now been vanquished
and had been forced to bow the knee before the kingly
power. The principle of absolute monarchy was proclaimed
more emphatically than ever, amidst universal silence.
But the losses sustained by the opposing parties in this
long strife were unequal. The Arab nobles, who were the
representatives of personal liberty—as the Teutons had
been in France and Italy—were undoubtedly the chief
sufferers. Obliged to submit to a form of government
more nearly absolute, and much more effective, than that
which they had tried to overturn—a government intrinsically hostile to them, and aiming systematically at depriving

---

[1] An account of this expedition of Ramiro II is given in Book iii.

them of all influence on the course of events—the Arab
nobles were condemned slowly to drift during each successive reign further from their former dominant position. And
this fact proved a consolation to the Spaniards, for in it they
saw a partial victory. Having taken up arms in hatred less
of the Sultan than of the Arab aristocracy, they could flatter
themselves that they had, to a certain extent, been victorious,
since, if they had no other satisfaction, they were at least
henceforth sheltered from the contempt, the insults, and the
oppression of the nobles. They no longer constituted a
people apart, a race of pariahs. The object aimed at by
'Abd-er-Rahmân, and which in course of time he practically
attained, was the fusion of all the races of the Peninsula
into a veritable nation. The old national dividing lines had
been obliterated—or, at any rate, greatly blurred—to be
succeeded by distinctions of ranks and conditions. The
resulting equality of races was, it is true, an equality under
subjection, but in the eyes of the Spaniards it was an
immense gain, and for the moment they asked for nothing
more. At bottom, their ideas of liberty were still very
vague; they had no prejudice against absolute monarchy
and administrative despotism; on the contrary, such a form
of government was traditional with them; they had known
none other under Visigothic kings or Roman emperors;
and in this connection it is noteworthy that even when
fighting for independence, they had made but feeble efforts
to establish liberty.

[AUTHORITIES: Arîb, ii. 104, 175–224; Ibn Khaldûn, ff. 11, 13; *Vit.
Beat. Virg. Argent.*, c. 4 (*ad fin.*); Ibn al-Kûtiyya, f. 47: Ibn
Hayyân, ff. 16–17.]

BOOK III

THE KHALIFATE

CHAPTER I

THE FÂTIMIDS

IN order not to interrupt the history of the Andalusian rebellion, we have already reached, in our narrative, the year 932, which saw its termination. A foreign war now claims our attention, and it is necessary to revert to the commencement of the reign of 'Abd-er-Rahmân III.

The insurrection of the Spaniards and of the Arab nobles was not the only peril which menaced the existence of the State: two neighbouring powers, one ancient, and the other of recent origin, were also sources of danger: these were the kingdom of Leon and the African Khalifate, recently founded by a Shî'ite sect, the Ismâ'ilis.

The Shî'ites, or upholders of Divine Right, agreed in believing that the Imâmate—that is the temporal and spiritual headship of all Islam—lay with the descendants of 'Alî, and that the Imâm was impeccable. But though in agreement on fundamentals, the Shî'ites were nevertheless split into several sects, which held different views as to which of the descendants of the sixth Imâm, Ja'far the Veracious, had the right to the Imâmate. Ja'far had several sons, of whom the eldest was Ismâ'îl and the second Mûsâ, and since Ismâ'îl had predeceased his father, in the year 762, the majority of the Shî'ites had recognised Mûsâ as Imâm after Ja'far's death. But the minority would not submit to him. Declaring that God himself by the mouth of Ja'far had named Ismâ'îl as the next Imâm, and that the Supreme Being could not change his intention, the Ismâ'ilis, as they were called, refused to acknowledge the authority of any except the descendants of Ismâ'îl. But the latter were devoid of ambition. Discouraged by the failure of the Shî'ites in all their enterprises, and not desirous of sharing the lot of their ancestors—most of whom had met with premature deaths by violence or poison—they shunned the dangerous and compromising homage of their partisans, and sought seclusion in Khorasan and Candahar.[1]

---

[1] Al-Juwainî, *Journ. asiat.*, Vᵉ série, t. viii. pp. 363–4.

401

2 C

Thus abandoned by their natural leaders, the Ismâ'îlis seemed doomed to extinction, when the daring and ability of a Persian inspired them with new vigour.

In Persia the progress of Islamism had been closely parallel to that which it had made in Spain. It had received into its fold a large number of proselytes, but it had not stifled other religions, for the ancient cult of Magianism flourished side by side with it. If the Moslems had rigorously carried out the Law of Mohammed they would have offered the Ghebers the alternative of conversion or the sword. Having no Sacred Book revealed by a prophet whom Moslems could recognise as such, the Fire-worshippers had no claim to toleration. But in existing circumstances the Law of Mohammed was not applicable. The Ghebers were very numerous; they were devoted heart and soul to their religion; and they stubbornly rejected every other faith. The immolation of all these brave men merely because they chose to seek salvation in their own way was unthinkable. Such an act would not only have been barbarous in the extreme but very dangerous, for it might have provoked a universal insurrection. Partly actuated by humanity and partly by policy, the Moslems accordingly ignored the law, and, having admitted the principle of toleration, they allowed the Ghebers to practise their religious rites publicly, and every town or village had its altar. The Government even protected the Ghebers against the Moslem clergy, and bastinadoed imâms and muezzins who had attempted to turn fire-temples into mosques.[1]

But if the Government was tolerant towards the avowed adherents of the ancient religion, who as peaceable citizens caused no disorder in the State, it did not and could not spare the sham Moslems, who after their so-called conversion were still pagans at heart and endeavoured secretly to transform Islamism by engrafting thereon their own doctrines. In Persia as in Spain apparent conversions due to worldly interests had been numerous, and the insincere Moslems were for the most part restless and ambitious men. Rebuffed by the Arab aristocracy, everywhere very exclusive, they dreamed of a revived Persian nationality and empire.[2] Against such agitators as these the Government took measures of the utmost rigour; to restrain and punish them the Khalif Mahdî even set up an inquisitorial tribunal which

---

[1] Chwolsohn, *Die Ssabier und der Ssabismus*, i. 283–91.
[2] *Ibid.*, p. 289.

continued to exist up to the end of the reign of Hârûn al-Rashîd.[1] As usual, persecution led to rebellion. Bâbak, chief of the Khurramites—or libertines, as their opponents called them—revolted in Azerbâijân. For twenty years, 817–837, this Ibn Hafsûn of Persia held in check the armies of the Khalifs, and the latter lost two hundred and fifty thousand men before they succeeded in capturing him.[2] But a task of even greater difficulty than that of forcibly repressing armed revolts, was that of detecting and extirpating the secret societies generated by persecution. These stealthily disseminated either the ancient Persian doctrines, or philosophical ideas yet more dangerous, for in the East the conflict of many religions had given rise to a numerous class of thinkers who repudiated and despised them all. "All these alleged religious duties," they said, "are at best only useful for the vulgar, and are in no way binding on cultured folk. The prophets were so many impostors who aimed at gaining supremacy over their fellow men."[3]

From the bosom of these secret societies there emerged, at the beginning of the ninth century, the second founder of the sect of the Ismâ'îlis. His name was 'Abdallah ibn Maymûn, and he sprang from a Persian family which had professed the doctrines of the followers of Bardesanes, who recognised two deities, one of whom created light and the other darkness. 'Abdallah's father was a free-thinking oculist,[4] who, to escape the clutches of the inquisition—to which seventy of his friends had fallen victims—sought refuge in Jerusalem, where he secretly taught the occult sciences while professing piety and great zeal for the Shî'ite party. Under his father's tutelage 'Abdallah became not merely a skilful juggler and a learned oculist, but an erudite student of theological and philosophical systems. He at first attempted, by the aid of pretended miracles, to pose as a prophet, but the attempt proving unsuccessful, he gradually conceived a much vaster project.[5]

To link together into one body the vanquished and the conquerors; to unite in the form of a vast secret society with many degrees of initiation, free-thinkers—who regarded religion only as a curb for the people—and bigots of all

[1] Weil, ii. 107.
[2] See E. G. Browne, *Lit. Hist. of Persia*, i. ch. ix.
[3] Al-Makrîzi, *Journ. asiat.*, IIIᵉ série, t. ii. p. 134.
[4] Nicholson, *Lit. Hist. of the Arabs* (1907), p. 271.
[5] E. G. Browne, *Lit. Hist. of Persia*, i. 405 *sq.*

sects; to make tools of believers in order to give power to
sceptics; to induce conquerors to overturn the empire they
had founded; to build up a party, numerous, compact, and
disciplined, which in due time would give the throne, if not
to himself, at least to his descendants, such was 'Abdallah
ibn Maymûn's general aim—an extraordinary conception
which he worked out with marvellous tact, incomparable
skill, and a profound knowledge of the human heart.

The means which he adopted were devised with diabolical
cunning.   Outwardly he was an Ismâ'îlite.   This sect
seemed doomed to extinction for lack of a leader: he
breathed new life into it by promising one.   "The world,"
such was his doctrine, "has never been without an Imâm.
The line of Imâms has descended from father to son from
the days of Adam, and will persist to the end of time.   The
Imâm never dies until a son has been born to him to be his
successor.   But the Imâm is not always visible.   Sometimes
he is manifested, and at other times he is hidden, just as
night and day succeed one another.   When the Imâm is
visible his doctrine is veiled.   But when the Imâm is hidden
his teachings are revealed, and his messengers appear among
men." [1]   In support of this doctrine 'Abdallah cited passages
from the Koran.   It served his turn to keep awake the
hopes of the Ismâ'îlites, who accepted the idea of the
"Hidden Imâm," but believed that he would ultimately
appear and with him the reign of peace and justice on the
earth.   In his inmost heart, however, 'Abdallah despised
this sect, and his professed attachment for the family of 'Alî
was assumed to further his projects.   A Persian at heart,
he included 'Alî, his descendants, and the Arabs, in one
comprehensive anathema.   He rightly believed that if an
'Alid had succeeded in founding an empire in Persia, as the
Persians had wished, it would not have been to their benefit,
and he counselled his confidential friends to slay ruthlessly
all the descendants of 'Alî who fell into their power. [2]   It
was, therefore, not among the Shî'ites that he sought his
true supporters, but among the Ghebers, the Manicheans,
the pagans of Harran, and the students of Greek philosophy; [3]
on the last alone could he rely, to them alone could he
gradually unfold the final mystery, and reveal that Imâms,

[1] Al-Juwaini, *Journ. asiat.*, Vᵉ série, t. viii. pp. 364-5.
[2] Silvestre de Sacy, *Exposé de la religion des Druzes*, Introd. p. clxiv, Paris, 1838.
[3] De Sacy, *op. cit.*, pp. cxlix-cliii.

religions, and morality, were nothing but an imposture and
an absurdity. The rest of mankind—the "asses," as 'Abdallah called them—were incapable of understanding such
doctrines. But to gain his end he by no means disdained
their aid; on the contrary he solicited it, but he took care
to initiate devout and lowly souls only in the first grades of
the sect. His missionaries, who were inculcated with the
idea that their first duty was to conceal their true sentiments
and adapt themselves to the views of their auditors, appeared
in many guises, and spoke, as it were, in a different language
to each class. They won over the ignorant vulgar by feats
of legerdemain which passed for miracles, or excited their
curiosity by enigmatical discourses. In the presence of the
devout they assumed the mask of virtue and piety. With
mystics they were mystical, and unfolded the inner meaning
of phenomena, or explained allegories and the figurative
sense of the allegories themselves. Turning to advantage
the calamities of the epoch and the vague hopes of a happier
future fostered by all the sects, they promised to Moslems
the early advent of the Mahdî announced by Mohammed,
to the Jews that of the Messiah, and to the Christians that
of the Paraclete. They even appealed to the orthodox
Arabs, or Sunnîs, who were the most difficult to win over
because theirs was the dominant religion, but whose countenance was desirable as a shelter from suspicion and govern-
mental interference, and whose wealth they needed for the
furtherance of their designs. They flattered the national
pride of the Arabs by assuring them that all the riches of
earth belonged to their race, while the Persians were slaves
by birth, and they sought to gain their confidence by displaying a contempt for riches and a deep piety; once that
confidence was gained they harassed the Arab by their im-
portunities and prayers until he became *perinde ac cadaver*,
and then easily persuaded him that it was his duty to
support the sect by pecuniary gifts and to bequeath all his
property to it.[1]

By means such as these the extraordinary result was
brought about that a multitude of men of diverse beliefs
were all working together for an object known only to a
few of them. The progress of the work, however, was
slow. 'Abdallah knew that he himself would not see its
accomplishment;[2] but he charged his son Ahmad, who

[1] De Sacy, *op. cit.*, pp. cxii, cliii–clvi.   [2] *Ibid.*, p. clxii.

succeeded him as "Grand Master," to carry it on. Under
Ahmad and his successors the sect made rapid progress, the
more so because a large number of the other branch of the
Shî'ites joined it. This branch, as we have seen, acknowledged as Imâms the descendants of Mûsâ, the second son
of Ja'far the Veracious; but since the twelfth, Mohammed,
had disappeared, at the age of twelve, in a cavern which
he had entered with his mother (A.D. 879), and his followers
—the Duodecimans as they were called—had become weary
of awaiting his reappearance, they were easily induced to
enrol themselves among the Ismâ'îlites, who had the
advantage of possessing a living chief ready to make himself
known as soon as circumstances allowed.

In 884, an Ismâ'îlite, Ibn Haushab, who had formerly
been a Duodeciman, began to preach openly in Yemen.
He took possession of Sa'nâ, and despatched thence missionaries to almost every province of the empire. Two of them
went to "plough"—such was the Shî'ite phrase—the land
of the Ketamians in the province of Constantine, and when
they were dead Ibn Haushab replaced them by one of his
disciples, named Abû 'Abdallah.

Active, daring, eloquent, as well as shrewd and tactful,
Abû 'Abdallah knew how to adapt himself to the narrow-
minded Berbers, and was well fitted for his task, although
he seems to have been initiated only into the lower grades
of the order—for even the missionaries were sometimes
ignorant of its final object.[1] He began by teaching the
children of the Ketamians and strove to gain the confidence
of his hosts; then, when he felt sure of success, he threw off
the mask, declared himself the precursor of the Mahdî, and
promised the Ketamians the pleasures of this world and
the next if they would take up arms in the holy cause.
Influenced by the mystic discourses of the missionary, and
perhaps by the allurement of pillage, the Ketamians were
easily persuaded; and since their tribe was then the most
numerous and powerful of all, and had preserved much of
its old independence and warlike spirit, their success was
extremely rapid. After capturing all the towns belonging
to the last Aghlabite prince—whose dynasty had reigned for
more than a century—they compelled him to flee from his
residence with such haste that he had not even time to take
his mistress with him. Abû 'Abdallah then placed the

---

[1] De Sacy, *op. cit.*, p. cxix.

Mahdî on the throne, A.D. 909. This was Sa'îd, Grand Master of the sect, a descendant of 'Abdallah al-Kaddah,[1] who posed as a descendant of 'Alî, and assumed the name of 'Obaidallah. As Khalif, the founder of the Fâtimid dynasty carefully concealed his true doctrines. Perhaps he would have shown more candour if another country—Persia for instance—had been the scene of his triumph; but since he owed his throne to a semi-barbarous horde, ignorant of philosophical speculations, he was obliged not only to dissimulate personally, but to restrain the advanced members of the sect from untimely audacities of expression. The true character of the sect was not openly manifested until the beginning of the eleventh century, when the power of the Fâtimids was so firmly established that they had nothing to fear, and when, thanks to their powerful armies and vast wealth, they attached little importance to their alleged hereditary right.[1] But at first the Ismâ'îlites resembled some other Moslem sects in their intolerance and cruelty. Devout and learned Fakihs were bastinadoed, mutilated, or crucified for having spoken with respect of the first three Khalifs,[2] or forgotten a Shî'ite formula, or pronounced a *fetwa* according to Mâlik's code. Absolute submission was required in the converted. To avoid having his throat cut as an unbeliever, a husband was compelled to witness the violation of his wife, after which he was beaten and spat upon. 'Obaidallah, it is fair to say, tried to check the brutality of his soldiers, but with little success. His subjects, who declared that they had no need of an invisible God, willingly deified the Khalif—conformably to the ideas of the Persians, who taught the incarnation of the Deity in the person of the monarch—but only on condition that he allowed them to do all that they wished. The atrocities committed by these barbarians in the towns they captured were unparalleled. At Barca, their general had some of the citizens cut to pieces and roasted; then after compelling the rest to eat of this flesh, he cast them into the flames. Plunged in silent stupor, the miserable Africans could only direct their hopes beyond

---

[1] "The oculist," see p. 403.

[2] The Khalif Mu'izz, when asked for proofs of his descent from the Prophet's son-in-law, replied boldly, as he drew half his sword from the scabbard, "Behold my genealogy!" and then bestowing handfuls of gold upon the bystanders, he added, "Behold my proofs!" All declared the evidence irrefragable. *Journ. asiat.*, IIIe série, t. iii. p. 167.

[3] 'Obaidallah ordered all the Companions of Mohammed, except 'Ali and four others, to be cursed in the public prayers.

the grave. "Since God permitteth such deeds," writes a contemporary, "it is manifest that this present world is beneath His notice. But the Last Day will come, and then He will judge!"

Their claims to universal monarchy rendered the Fâtimids dangerous to all the Moslem States, but they were especially a peril to Spain. They early hankered after that rich and beautiful country. 'Obaidallah had scarcely taken possession of the territory of the Aghlabites before he entered into negotiations with Ibn Hafsûn, and the latter acknowledged him as his sovereign. This singular alliance led to no result; but the Fâtimids were not discouraged. Their spies traversed all parts of the Peninsula in the guise of merchants, and an idea of the nature of the reports which they brought to their masters can be gathered from the account of his travels given by one of them, Ibn Hawkal. At the very beginning of his description of Spain he writes thus:[1] "That which chiefly astonishes foreigners when they set foot in this Peninsula, is the fact that it still belongs to the sovereign who reigns there; for the inhabitants are spiritless and servile, they are cowards, they are wretched horsemen and are wholly incapable of defending themselves against disciplined troops: and yet our masters—on whom be the blessing of God—well know the true worth of this country, how great is the revenue it yields, and what are its beauties and delights."

If the Fâtimids had succeeded in gaining a foothold in Andalusia they would undoubtedly have found followers. The idea of the advent of the Mahdî was common to Spain with the rest of the Moslem world. In 901, as will appear hereafter, an Omayyad prince claimed to be the looked-for Mahdî; and in a book written some twenty years before the foundation of the Fâtimid Khalifate[2] there occurs a prophecy by the famous theologian 'Abd al-Malik ibn Habîb (853), according to which a descendant of Fâtima would reign in Spain, would conquer Constantinople—still regarded as the metropolis of Christianity—would slay all the males in Cordova and the neighbouring provinces, and would sell their wives and children, "so that a boy could be bought for a whip, and a girl for a spur." As usual, it was chiefly the lower classes who believed in prophecies of this kind, but even among the well-educated, and especially among freethinkers, the Fâtimids would perhaps have found adherents.

[1] Leyden MS., p. 39.   [2] *Taríkh ibn Habîb*, p. 160.

Philosophy had penetrated Spain under Mohammed, the fifth Omayyad Sultan; but philosophy was held there in disrepute, and intolerance was much more rife there than in Asia. The Andalusian theologians, indeed, who had journeyed to the East, spoke with devout horror of the tolerance of the 'Abbâsids, and especially of those meetings of the learned of all religions and sects, where metaphysical questions were discussed without regard to revelation, and where even Moslems sometimes turned the Koran into ridicule.[1] The common people, however, detested the philosophers, whom they regarded as impious and were ever ready to burn or stone. Freethinkers were therefore obliged to conceal their views, and naturally found the constraint irksome. Would they not therefore be ready to support a dynasty whose principles accorded with their own? It seemed probable; and the Fâtimids, it would appear, were of this opinion—it even appears to us that they tried to found a lodge in Spain, and that they sent thither with that object the philosopher Ibn Masarra (883–931). This Ibn Masarra was a pantheist of Cordova, who had made an especial study of translations of certain Greek books attributed by the Arabs to Empedocles. Accused of impiety, and compelled to leave the country, he travelled in the East, where he familiarized himself with the doctrines of various sects, and seems to have joined the secret society of the Ismâ'îlites. We are led to believe this by his conduct after his return to Spain, for instead of flaunting his opinions, as he had done in his youth, he concealed them, and made great parade of piety and austerity. The heads of the secret society, we may suppose, had taught him that he must make a stalking-horse of orthodoxy. Thanks to this mask and to his winning eloquence, he deceived the vulgar and at the same time attracted many pupils to his lectures, leading them step by step from faith to doubt, and from doubt to disbelief. He did not, however, succeed in duping the clergy, who, in just alarm, burned, not the philosopher himself—for this 'Abder-Rahmân III would not allow—but his books.[2] Though there is no direct evidence that Ibn Masarra was an Isma'îlite missionary, it is at any rate certain that the Fâtimids made endeavours to found a party in Spain and to some extent succeeded.[3] Their domination would doubtless have pleased

---

[1] *Journ. asiat.*, Vᵉ série, t. ii. p. 93; Chwolsohn, ii. 622.
[2] Amari, *Biblioteca Arabo-Sicula*, pp. 614–15 (*Tarîkh al-hôkamâ*). Abû Bakr al-Zubaidî wrote a treatise to refute Ibn Masarra.
[3] See below, p. 427.

the freethinkers, but it would have been a terrible scourge for the masses, and especially for the Christians. A coldly barbarous remark of the traveller Ibn Hawkal shows what the latter would have had to expect at the hands of the fanatical Ketamians. After having observed that the Christians, who numbered many thousands in the villages, often caused the Government much trouble by their revolts, Ibn Hawkal suggests a ready means of rendering them innocuous in future—namely their total extirpation. The only objection to this otherwise excellent scheme appeared to him to be its tediousness. It was however merely a question of time! It is clear that the Ketamians would have fulfilled to the letter the prediction of 'Abd-al-Malik ibn Habîb.

While the Arabs of Spain were thus threatened from the South, the peril to which they were exposed from the North, where the kingdom of Leon was rapidly increasing in power, was still greater.

Nothing could have been humbler than the origin of the kingdom of Leon. In the eighth century, when their native province had surrendered to the Moslems, three hundred men under the gallant Pelagius found refuge in the lofty mountains to the east of the Asturias. A large cavern served them as a dwelling—the Cave of Covadonga. The entrance of this cave is situated at a considerable height above the ground; it is hollowed out of an immense rock at the foot of a winding valley, deeply excavated by a torrent and so narrowly confined between two precipitous walls of rock that a mounted man can scarcely penetrate it.[1] A handful of resolute men could easily hold the position even against a greatly superior force. And this is what the Asturians did. They were, however, in a wretched plight, and some of his companions having surrendered and others having died of hunger, Pelagius eventually saw his followers reduced to some thirty men and ten women—their only food being the honey stored by bees in the chinks of the rocks. The Moslems thereupon let them alone, thinking that there could be nothing to fear from a band of thirty men, and that it would be lost labour to pursue them into this dangerous valley where so many brave men had already met with an inglorious death. Thanks to this respite, Pelagius was able to reinforce his band, and when many

---

[1] Moralès, *Corónica General*, iii. 3, 4.

fugitives had joined him, he assumed the offensive and made raids on Moslem settlements. Determined to check these depredations, the Berber Monûsa, who was then Governor of the Asturias, despatched an officer named 'Alkama against him. But 'Alkama's expedition was a most disastrous one; his men were utterly routed and he himself was killed. Pelagius' success encouraged the other Asturians; they rose, and Monûsa, whose force was not strong enough to repress the rebellion, and who feared lest his retreat should be cut off, abandoned Gijon, his head-quarters, and took the road towards Leon; but he had scarcely gone seven leagues before he was suddenly attacked and suffered considerable loss, with the result that on reaching Leon his troops, completely discouraged, refused to return to those rugged mountains which had been the scene of their losses.[1]

Having thus thrown off the yoke of foreign domination, the Asturians soon afterwards gained a notable accession of strength. On the eastern side their province bordered upon the duchy of Cantabria, which had never submitted to the Moslems, and when its ruler Alfonso, who had married the daughter of Pelagius, ascended the throne of the Asturias, the Christian forces were almost doubled. Thereupon they naturally determined to drive their conquerors still farther south. Circumstances favoured them. The Berbers, who in almost all the northern districts formed the bulk of the Moslem population, embraced the doctrines of the Nonconformists, rose against the Arabs, and expelled them; but, marching south, they were beaten in their turn, and hunted down like deer. Decimated by the sword, they were still more reduced by the dreadful famine which, beginning in A.D. 750, ravaged Spain for five consecutive years. The majority thereupon resolved to leave the Peninsula and rejoin their tribesmen in Africa. Taking advantage of this emigration, the Galicians rose against their oppressors in 751, and acknowledged Alfonso as their king. With his aid they slew a great number of the enemy and forced the rest to withdraw towards Astorga. In 753-4 the Berbers were pushed still farther south. They evacuated Braga, Porto, and Viseu, so that all that coast as far as the mouth of the Douro was free from the enemy. Still retreating, they abandoned Astorga, Leon, Zamora, Ledesma, Salamanca, and fell back on Coria, or even on Merida. On the

---

[1] Monûsa survived his defeat many years, and died in La Cerdaña; the Spanish chroniclers assert that he was slain while retreating.

eastern side they evacuated Saldaña, Simancas, Segovia, Avila, Oca, Osma, Miranda on the Ebro, Cenicero, and Alesanco (the last two in Rioja). The principal frontier towns in Moslem territory were therefore, from west to east, Coimbra on the Mondego, Talavera and Toledo on the Tagus, Guadalaxara, Tudela, and Pamplona.

Civil war and the great famine had therefore combined to free a great part of Spain from the Moslem domination, which had lasted for scarcely more than forty years. Alfonso, however, reaped little profit from his successes. He traversed the deserted country and slew the few remaining Moslems whom he found there, but lacking serfs to cultivate such an extensive territory, and money to rebuild the fortresses which the Moslems had dismantled or razed on their departure, he could not effectually occupy the country, and took the natives with him when he returned to his own kingdom. He could only occupy the districts bordering on his former domains. These were the Liebana (the south-eastern part of the province of Santander), Old Castile (then known as Bardulia), the coast of Galicia, and perhaps the town of Leon. The rest of the country was for a long time a desert which formed a natural barrier between the Christians of the North and the Moslems of the South.[1]

But Alfonso's successors carried out the work which he had been unable to accomplish. In almost ceaseless warfare against the Arabs, they made Leon their capital, and gradually rebuilt the most important towns and fortresses. In the second half of the ninth century, when almost all the South was in insurrection against the Sultan, the Christians pushed their frontier as far as the Douro, where they built four strongholds—Zamora, Simancas, San Estevan de Gormaz, and Osma—which formed an almost impregnable barrier against the Moslems, whilst the vast, but dismal and barren tract which extended from the Douro to the Guadiana was occupied by neither the Leonese nor the Arabs, but was still in dispute. On the west, the Leonese were in closer contact with their natural enemies, for their frontier there extended beyond the Mondego. But these frontiers were often crossed. Taking advantage of the Sultan's weakness, they extended their bold forays as far as the Tagus and the Guadiana, and the tribes—for the most part Berbers—which

---

[1] Even considerable towns, such as Astorga and Tuy, remained uninhabited until after A.D. 850. *Recherches* (1881), i. 123.

dwelt between these two rivers were the less able to resist them since they were usually at war among themselves. They were therefore reduced to paying blackmail to the Christians.

But at length the Moslems' hour of revenge seemed to have come. In the year 901, an Omayyad prince, Ahmad ibn Mu'âwiya, who was an adept in the occult sciences as well as desirous of a throne, announced himself to the Berbers as the Mahdî, and summoned them to his standard in order to march against Zamora. This town had been rebuilt in 893, under Alfonso III, by his allies the Christians of Toledo, and had henceforth been the terror of the Berbers, since the Leonese made it a base for their forays and placed their booty in safety within sevenfold walls and trenches. Ahmad's call to arms met with great success. Ignorant, credulous, and thirsting for revenge, the Berbers flocked to a prince who worked elaborate miracles, and assured them that the walls of cities would fall down at their approach. In a few months the impostor had collected an army of sixty thousand men. He led them towards the Douro, and on reaching Zamora, he sent a defiant letter to King Alfonso III, who was in the town, threatening him with destruction if he and his subjects did not instantly embrace Islamism. On reading the letter Alfonso and his chief men trembled with indignation, and with the intention of forthwith punishing its writer, they mounted their horses and rode out to attack him. The Berber cavalry came to meet them, and since the Douro was low (it was the month of June), the combat took place in the bed of the river. Fortune did not favour the Leonese. The Berbers put them to rout, and preventing them from re-entering the town, drove them into the interior of the country.

The first fight, however, proved no true presage of the result of the expedition. The self-styled Mahdî had acquired an immense influence over his soldiers; believing that it was beneath his dignity to give his orders orally, he gave them by signs, and his slightest gesture was obeyed; but the more he gained the respect of the rank and file the more he aroused the jealousy of the leaders, who foresaw that if the expedition succeeded, they would be supplanted by the "prophet," in whose mission they had no great faith. They had already, without success, sought an opportunity to assassinate him, and during the pursuit of the enemy, the most powerful chief, Zalal ibn Ya'ish, of the

tribe of Nefza, declared to his friends that in defeating the
Leonese, they had committed a grievous error which must
be corrected as soon as possible. He easily won them over,
and they decided to upset the Mahdî's plans. They therefore sounded the retreat, and on reaching their advanced-
posts on the right bank of the Douro, they collected their
baggage, and declared that they had been beaten and that
the enemy was at their heels. They were the more readily
believed, since they were accompanied by only a part of the
troops, the rest either having not obeyed or not heard the
order. Panic seized the Berbers. Seeking safety in flight,
a great number of the soldiers rushed towards the Douro,
and the garrison of Zamora, seeing this, made a sortie and
cut down many of the fugitives as they tried to cross the
river. The Leonese, nevertheless, were held in check by the
main Moslem army, which was still on the left bank, and
were not in a condition that day, nor the next, to make
their victory decisive. But desertion, which soon became
general among the Mahdî's troops, came to their aid. The
Mahdî declared in vain that God had promised him the
victory; faith in him had been lost, and when, on the third
day, he saw himself deserted by almost all his men, he
abandoned hope. Resolved not to survive his shame, he
spurred his horse into the midst of the enemy, and found
the death he sought. His head was nailed to one of the
gates of Zamora.

The issue of this campaign naturally increased the
audacity of the Leonese. Counting on the assistance of
the Toledans, and yet more on the co-operation of Sancho
the Great, King of Navarre, who had recently earned for
his country an importance which it could not previously
boast of, they came to look upon Moslem Spain as a prey
which could not escape them. Their eyes were turned
towards the South. Still so poor that, for lack of a coinage,
they bartered commodities,[1] and taught by their priests—to
whom they were blindly devoted and whom they loaded
with gifts—that war against the infidel was the surest
means of gaining heaven, they would fain seek in wealthy
Andalusia the blessings of this world and of the next.
Could Andalusia escape their domination? If she succumbed, terrible would be the fate of the Moslems. Cruel
and fanatical, the Leonese rarely gave quarter; when they

---

[1] *Esp. sagr.*, xix. p. 383.

captured a town they usually put all the inhabitants to the sword. Tolerance such as that accorded by the Moslems to Christians could not be expected of them. What would become of that brilliant and progressive Arab civilization, at the hands of barbarians who could not read; who had to call in "Saracens" when they wished to measure their fields;[1] and who, when they mentioned a "library," meant thereby the Holy Scriptures? It is manifest, therefore, that the task which lay before 'Abd-er-Rahmân III at the beginning of his reign was a great and noble one—he had to save not only his country but civilization itself: the difficulties that confronted him were moreover of the most formidable nature. The prince had to subdue his own subjects, as well as to repel, on the one side the northern barbarians, whose insolence increased as the Moslem empire grew weaker—and on the other side the barbarians of the South, who had suddenly seized a vast territory and believed that the Andalusians were at their mercy. But 'Abd-er-Rahmân did not quail before his mission. We have already seen how he subdued and pacified his own realm; we have now to relate how he prepared to encounter his external foes.

[1] Berganza, i. 197.

[AUTHORITIES: 'Arîb, i. 190; Ibn Adhârî, i. 295; ii. 27; Sa'îd of Toledo, f. 246; Homaidî, ff. 27, 47; Abû 'l-Mahâsin, i. pp. 420–1; Makkarî, i. 136; ii. 9, 10, 121, 376, 671–2; Ibn Khallikân, fasc. vii. 61; Isid., c. 58; Mon. Sil., c. 42; Chron. Conimb., ii.; Chron. Albeld., c. 64; Ibn Hayyân, ff. 83, 98–102; Samp., c. 14.]

CHAPTER II

SUPREMACY OF 'ABD-ER-RAHMÂN III

EARLY in his reign, 'Abd-er-Rahmân III was forced into a quarrel with the Leonese which was not of his seeking. In the year 914, Ordoño II, the undaunted King of Leon, commenced hostilities by devastating the territory of Merida. Seizing the fortress of Alanje, he put all its defenders to the sword, and made slaves of the women and children. Such was the terror felt by the people of Badajoz that, to escape the fate of their neighbours, they collected a quantity of precious merchandise, and, with their prince at their head, humbly begged the Christian King to accept it. Ordoño graciously consented, and then as a victor, and laden with booty, recrossed the Tagus and Douro. On his return to Leon, he dedicated a Church to the Virgin in token of gratitude.

Since the people of the districts raided by Ordoño had not yet submitted to the Sultan, 'Abd-er-Rahmân might excusably have shut his eyes to the incursion. Such, however, was not his policy. Well aware that he must conquer the hearts of his rebellious subjects by proving himself able to defend them, he determined to chastise the King of Leon. He accordingly, in July, 916, despatched against him an army under Ibn Abî Abda, his grandfather's veteran general. This expedition, which was the first since the so-called Mahdî's attempt, fifteen years before, was little more than a raid—though a profitable one for the Moslems. Next year, 'Abd-er-Rahmân, at the earnest solicitation of the people of the frontiers, who complained that the Leonese had burned the suburbs of Talavera (on the Tagus), ordered Ibn Abî Abda to take the field once more, with a large army, including mercenaries from Tangier, and besiege the important fortress of San Estevan de Gormaz—or Castro Moros. The campaign opened favourably: closely beleaguered, the defenders of San Estevan were soon reduced to extremities, and were on the point of surrendering. But Ordoño came to the rescue. He attacked Ibn

Abî Abda, whose army comprised, unfortunately for himself, not only the African troops but a number of borderers upon whose fidelity and valour it was impossible to rely. Half Berbers, half Spaniards, these men, when pillaged by the Leonese, piteously implored the Sultan's protection—but they had no idea of self-defence or of allegiance to their sovereign. They allowed themselves to be defeated, and in their headlong retreat threw the whole army into terrible confusion. Seeing the battle lost, the gallant Ibn Abî Abda chose to die at his post rather than seek safety in flight : many of his soldiers rallied to his side, and shared their general's fate under the swords of the Christians. According to Arab historians, the rest of the army succeeded in reaching Moslem territory in good order; but Christian chroniclers, on the other hand, relate that the rout of the Moslems was so complete that the hills, the forests, and the plains, from the Douro to Atienza, were strewn with their corpses.

'Abd-er-Rahmân, refusing to be discouraged, immediately took steps to repair this disaster, but while he was making preparations for a new campaign in the following year, his attention was turned to affairs in Africa.

Although he was not actually at war with the Fâtimids —and the latter, intent on the conquest of Mauritania, had given him no grounds for complaint—'Abd-er-Rahmân foresaw that as soon as they had accomplished their task they would turn their arms against Spain. He thought himself bound, therefore, to assist Mauritania to the best of his ability, and to maintain that country as a bulwark between Spain and the Fâtimids. Nevertheless, it would be unwise to declare war prematurely, for while he still had to quell an insurrection at home and to bring the Christians of the North to their knees, it would be imprudent to risk a landing of the Fâtimids on the coast of Andalusia. He could but secretly aid and encourage such princes as were desirous of defending themselves against the invaders of their territories.

An opportunity of giving effect to this policy occurred in 917, when the prince of Nakûr [1] was attacked by the Fâtimids. This prince was of Arabian origin, and his family had ruled over the district of Nakûr from the time of the conquest; they had always been distinguished for their

---

[1] A town of Riff (Morocco), about 40 l. W.S.W. of Cape Tres Forcas; later called Mezemma. *Recherches* (1881), ii. 279.

attachment to the faith, and ever since two princesses of the family had been ransomed by the Sultan Mohammed from the Norman pirates,[1] their relations with Spain had been most cordial. A cadet of this house—a devout Fakih who had four times made pilgrimage to Mecca—crossed over to Spain, during 'Abdallah's reign, to take part in the Holy War. Attacked by Ibn Hafsûn on landing, he reached the Sultan's camp alone, all his escort having been slain, and he himself afterwards fell in an encounter with Daisam, chief of the province of Tadmir.

Saʿîd II was the reigning prince of Nakûr when the Fâtimids invaded Mauritania. Summoned to surrender, he refused, and had the imprudence, with the aid of his poet laureate—a Spaniard—to add an insult to the refusal. The Khalif had appended to his summons certain verses, their gist being that if the people of Nakûr would not surrender, he would exterminate them, but that if they submitted justice should reign in their land. But the poet laureate, Ahmas of Toledo, replied thus :

" By the temple at Mecca I swear that thou liest ! Thou knowest not what justice is, and the Eternal hath never heard a sincere or pious word from thy lips. Thou art a hypocrite and an infidel ; whilst thou preachest to churls, thou breakest the Law which should be the rule of all our actions. Our desires are set upon great and exalted things, amongst which the religion of Mohammed is supreme ; thy thoughts are fixed upon all that is base and vile ! " [2]

The Khalif, 'Obaidallah,[3] in great wrath, immediately ordered Messâla, Governor of Tahort, to attack Nakûr. Having no citadel into which to retire, the aged Saʿîd II marched to meet the enemy, held them in check for three days, and then, betrayed by one of his captains, perished on the field with nearly all his soldiers (A.D. 917). Messâla thereupon entered Nakûr, putting the men to death and making slaves of their wives and children.

Warned by their father, three of Saʿîd's sons had time to set sail for Malaga. On their arrival at that port, 'Abd-er-Rahmân ordered that they should be hospitably received, and he informed them that if they would visit Cordova he would gladly welcome them, but that should they prefer to remain at Malaga, he would not thwart their wishes. The

---

[1] The Normans took Nakûr in A.D. 858. The princesses were Ama-ar-Rahmân and Khanùla, daughters of Wâkif ibn Motasim ibn Sâlih. *Recherches* (1881), ii. 281.

[2] See *Goettingische gelehrte Anzeigen* (1858), pp. 1091–2.

[3] See above, Bk. ii. ch. xvii.

princes replied that they thought it expedient to remain as
near as possible to the theatre of events, since they hoped
soon to return to their country. Their hopes were justified.
On setting out for Tahort, after spending six months at
Nakûr, Messâla entrusted the command of the latter town to
Dhalûl, a Ketamian officer. Dhalûl was left with a slender
garrison, and the princes, who had been kept informed by
their friends of recent happenings, equipped some ships and
sailed for Nakûr, agreeing that the crown should belong to
him who arrived there first. Sâlih, the youngest brother,
won the race. The Berbers of the littoral received him with
enthusiasm, and proclaiming him Emir, marched against
Nakûr and slew Dhalûl and his garrison. Master of the
country, the prince, now Sâlih III, immediately sent a letter
to 'Abd-er-Rahmân, to thank him for his hospitality and
announce his victory. At the same time he proclaimed
the Sultan sovereign over all his States, and in return 'Abd-
er-Rahmân sent him tents, banners, and arms.

Even if affairs at Nakûr could have made 'Abd-er-
Rahmân forget that he had yet to avenge the rout of his
army and the death of the brave Ibn Abî Abda—whose
head Ordoño had nailed to the walls of San Estevan besides
that of a wild boar—the Christians would have recalled him
to his duty. In the spring of 918, Ordoño, with his ally
Sancho of Navarre, ravaged the vicinity of Najera and
Tudela, and Sancho afterwards captured the suburbs of
Valtierra and burnt the great mosque of that fortress.
'Abd-er-Rahmân thereupon entrusted the command of his
army to the *hâjib* Badr, and ordered the borderers to rejoin
his standard and wipe out the disgrace they had incurred
the previous year. The expedition set out from Cordova on
July 7, and, reaching Leonese territory, vigorously attacked
the enemy's army entrenched in the mountains. Two
actions were fought, on August 13 and 15 respectively, near
a place called Mutonia, and on each occasion the Moslems
gained a signal victory: even their own chroniclers admit
that the Leonese were fain to console themselves with
David's comments on the uncertainty of arms. 'Abd-er-
Rahmân had thus atoned for his defeat, but thinking the
Leonese were not yet sufficiently humiliated, and eager to
share personally the laurels gained by his generals in the
war against the infidels, in June, 920, he took personal command of the army. Osma he captured by a stratagem.
The commander of that place made the Sultan the most

brilliant promises, subject to the condition that he would leave him in peace. 'Abd-er-Rahmân took advantage of the man's cowardice. Feigning to accede to his overtures, he turned aside towards the Ebro by the route to Medinaceli, but abruptly wheeling to the left and directing his course towards the Douro, he sent a body of cavalry in advance, with orders to ravage the outskirts of Osma. Taken by surprise, the garrison fled to the forests and mountains, and the Moslems entered the fortress without striking a blow. Having burned it, they proceeded to attack San Estevan de Gormaz. This fortress also they found deserted. They razed it to the ground, as well as the neighbouring castle of Alcubilla. The Moslems then marched on Clunia, a very ancient town, then important, but of which only ruins now remain. It seemed that the Leonese had agreed that resistance should nowhere be offered, for Clunia was found to be entirely abandoned. The Moslems destroyed most of the houses, as well as the churches.

Yielding to the entreaties of the Moslems of Tudela, 'Abd-er-Rahmân then resolved to turn his arms against Sancho of Navarre. Marching by easy stages, so as not to fatigue his troops, he took five days on his march from Clunia to Tudela; then, placing a body of cavalry under the orders of the Governor of the latter town, Mohammed ibn Lope, the Sultan ordered him to attack the fortress of Carcar which Sancho had built to overawe the people of Tudela. This also the Moslems found deserted, as was Calahorra—whence Sancho himself had fled in haste, to throw himself into Arnedo. However, when the Moslems had crossed the Ebro, Sancho attacked their advance-guard. In the combat which ensued, the Sultan's troops showed that they could do somewhat besides capturing and burning undefended fortresses; for they put the enemy to total rout and drove them to the mountains. The advance-guard achieved this victory unaided, and 'Abd-er-Rahmân, who was with the centre, did not even know that his troops had been in touch with the enemy until apprized of the fact by the severed heads which were presented to him.

Beaten, and unable to stand alone against the Moslems, Sancho secured Ordoño's co-operation. The two kings resolved to attack either the advance-guard or the rear-guard of the enemy, as circumstances dictated. In the meanwhile the Christians, who had not quitted the mountains, hung upon the flanks of the Moslem columns as they passed through the valleys and defiles. To terrify their opponents they now and again raised loud shouts, and taking advantage of the ground, succeeded in inflicting some losses. The Moslem army found itself, indeed, in a perilous situation; it had to deal with agile and intrepid mountaineers who bore in mind the disaster which their ancestors had inflicted on Charlemagne's host in the valley of Roncesvalles, and who awaited an opportunity of treating 'Abd-er-Rahmân's in like manner. The Sultan was well aware of the danger which threatened him, and on reaching a valley, named, from the reeds which covered it, the Val de Junqueras,[1] he halted and pitched his tents. The Christians thereupon committed a fatal blunder; instead of clinging to the hills, they descended into the plain and rashly accepted the battle offered them by the Moslems. A terrible defeat was the price of their temerity. The Moslems pursued them till the sun went down, capturing many leaders, including two bishops—Hermogius of Tuy, and Dulcidius of Salamanca—who, after the custom of those days, had donned armour. More than a thousand Christians had sought refuge in the fortress of Muez. 'Abd-er-Rahmân surrounded it, captured it, and put all its defenders to the sword.

The victorious Moslems overran Navarre, demolishing fortresses without encountering any resistance, and were able to boast that they had burned everything in a space of ten square miles. Their booty, especially in the form of provisions, was immense; in their camp corn was sold for next to nothing, and they were obliged to burn much of their stores from sheer inability to carry them all away.

Victorious and covered with glory, 'Abd-er-Rahmân, on September 8, gave the order to retire. On reaching Atienza he took leave of the frontier troops—who had behaved well at the battle of the Val de Junqueras—and rewarded them with gifts. On September 24, he reached Cordova, after an absence of three months.[2]

'Abd-er-Rahmân was entitled to hope that after this triumphant campaign the Christians would have but little inclination for further raids on Moslem territory; but he had to deal with enemies not easily discouraged. In 921 Ordoño made another foray,[3] and if a Christian chronicler, who perhaps somewhat exaggerated his compatriots' success,

[1] Between Muez and Salinas de Oro.
[2] Raguel, *Vita S. Pelagii* (Schot, iv. 348).
[3] *Esp. sagr.*, xxxvii. p. 269.

MS-O*

is to be believed, the King of Leon penetrated to within
a day's journey of Cordova. Two years later, Ordoño captured Najera, while his ally Sancho of Navarre gained possession of Viguera, of which exploit he was so proud that
he exclaimed with the prophet: " I have dispersed them,
I have compelled them to seek refuge in distant and unknown
realms." [1]

The capture of Viguera produced consternation in
Moslem Spain, for it was reported that all the defenders
of the town, including members of the most illustrious
families, had been massacred.[2] Even if 'Abd-er-Rahmân
had been unwilling to take vengeance for this disaster,
public opinion would have compelled him to do so. But
he needed no instigation. He would not, in his wrath, even
wait for the return of the season in which campaigns usually
began, and in April, 924, he led his army out of Cordova,
" to vindicate God and the faith against the vile race of
infidels," as an Arab historian phrases it. On July 10 the
Sultan reached Navarrese territory, but so great was the
terror his name inspired that the enemy abandoned all their
strongholds as he approached. He passed by Carcar, Peralta,
Falces and Carcastillo—pillaging and burning on his way—
and then, making for the Capital, advanced into the interior.
Sancho tried to check his progress through the defiles, but
he was on every occasion repulsed with loss, and 'Abd-er-
Rahmân reached Pamplona without hindrance, to find the
city deserted. The Moslems destroyed many of the houses,
as well as the cathedral, a famous resort of pilgrims. The
Sultan then ordered the demolition of another church held
in great veneration, which Sancho had built, at great cost,
on a neighbouring hill. Sancho made strenuous efforts to
save it, but in vain. Further attempts at resistance were
no more successful. Having received reinforcements from
Castile Sancho twice attacked the Moslem army on its
march, but was repulsed with loss. The Moslems' casualties,
on the other hand, in the glorious " Campaign of Pamplona,"
were insignificant. The haughty King of Navarre was at
last humbled, and for a long time reduced to impotence.

Neither had 'Abd-er-Rahmân anything to fear from
Leon. The brave Ordoño had died before the Campaign of
Pamplona. His brother, Fruela II, who succeeded him,
reigned for only a year, during which time his sole contribu-

---

[1] *Esp. sagr.*, xxxiii. p. 466.   [2] A few nobles escaped.

tion to the war was the despatch of some reinforcements to the King of Navarre. Upon his death Sancho and Alfonso, sons of Ordoño II, contended for the crown. Aided by Sancho of Navarre, whose daughter he had married, Alfonso —fourth of the name—proved successful. But Sancho was not discouraged. Assembling an army, he was crowned at Santiago de Compostela. He then, after capturing Leon by siege, wrested the throne from his brother. Two years later, however, in 928, Alfonso recaptured Leon with the help of the Navarrese, but Sancho retained possession of Galicia.[1]

'Abd-er-Rahmân did not concern himself with this long civil war. The internecine struggle among the Christians gave him time to stamp out the embers of revolt in his own dominions, and now that he neared the aim of his ambition he resolved to affect a new dignity. The Omayyads of Spain had hitherto been content with titles such as Sultan, Emir, or "Son of the Khalifs." Tacitly acknowledging that the name of Khalif belonged exclusively to the monarch who held sway over the Holy Cities, Mecca and Medina,[2] they resigned it to their inveterate foes, the 'Abbâsids. But now that the 'Abbâsid Khalifs were puppets in the hands of the "Mayor of the Palace,"[3] and their authority extended no further than over the territory of Baghdad—the local Governors having become practically independent—there was nothing to prevent the Omayyads from assuming a title which their subjects, and especially the African tribes, would respect. 'Abd-er-Rahmân therefore ordained, in 929, that from Friday, January 16, he was to be designated, in all public prayers and official documents, as Khalif, Commander of the Faithful, and Defender of the Faith (al-Nâsir li-dîni 'llâh).

Meanwhile Africa claimed all his attention. He negotiated an alliance with Mohammed ibn Khazer, chief of the Berber tribe of Maghrâwa, who had routed the Fâtimid troops, and slain their commander Messâla with his own hand. Ibn Khazer immediately expelled the Fâtimids from Central Maghrib—almost conterminous with Algiers and Oran—and compelled that district to acknowledge the sovereignty of the Spanish monarch. 'Abd-er-Rahmân also

---

[1] In a charter of 929, Sancho is quaintly termed "Serenissimus Rex Dñs. Sancius, universe urbe Gallecie princeps"; Recherches (1881), i. 149.

[2] Ibn Khordâdbeh, Oxford MS., p. 90.

[3] Or Generalissimo, Amîru 'l-Umará: see Nicholson, Lit. Hist. of the Arabs (1907), p. 264.

succeeded in detaching from the Fâtimid cause the gallant chief of the Miknesa, Ibn Abî 'l-Afia, who had hitherto been their mainstay; and, since the possession of a fortress on the African Coast was desirable, the Khalif also demanded and obtained the cession of Ceuta (931).

It seemed as though the Christians of the North were bent on allowing the Khalif uninterrupted leisure to devote himself to African affairs. Their first civil war came to an end upon Sancho's death in 929. A new conflict broke out in 931. In that year, Alfonso IV, in deep affliction at the death of his wife,[1] abdicated in favour of his brother Ramiro —second of the name—and entered the monastery of Sahagun. Before long, however, finding the monotony of a monastic life distasteful, he quitted the cloister to be proclaimed King at Simancas. In the eyes of the priests this was a scandalous proceeding, and they threatened Alfonso with hell-fire if he did not return to the monastery. He yielded; but being of a weak and vacillating character, he soon repented and threw off his frock; moreover, taking advantage of the absence of Ramiro II, who had gone to assist the Toledans—then besieged by the Khalif's troops— he occupied Leon. Ramiro returned with all speed, and in his turn besieged Leon and captured it; then, to prevent his brother from ever again claiming the crown he put out his eyes—as well as those of his three cousins, the sons of Fruela II, who had taken part in the revolt.[2]

'Abd-er-Rahmân soon recognised the change which had taken place. The time had passed when he could ignore the Kingdom of Leon. Warlike and valiant, Ramiro fostered a fierce and implacable hatred against the Moslems. It was his first care to aid Toledo—that proud Republic, which, alone in Moslem Spain, still defied the armies of the Khalif, and which had hitherto been the faithful ally and protector of the Kingdom of Leon. He accordingly took the field, and, on his march, captured Madrid. He did not, however, succeed in saving Toledo. A division of the besieging army advanced against him, and compelled him to retreat and leave the city to its fate. Toledo, as we have already seen, then surrendered in despair.[3] In the following year, 933, Ramiro was more fortunate. Learning from Fernan Gonzalez, Count of Castile, that the Moslems were

---

[1] *Esp. sagr.*, xxxiv. p. 241.
[2] To render them ineligible for the throne.
[3] See above, p. 397.

threatening Osma, he marched against them and defeated them. 'Abd-er-Rahmân took his revenge in 934. It was his wish that the plains around Osma, which had witnessed a Moslem defeat, should be the scene of a Moslem victory; but he vainly tried to lure Ramiro from his stronghold, the King of Leon deeming it prudent to refuse battle. Leaving an investing force before Osma, the Khalif continued his progress northwards. On his march many atrocities were committed, especially by the African troops, who in an enemy's country knew no pity. Near Burgos they massacred all the monks of San Pedro de Cardeña, to the number of two hundred. Burgos itself, the capital of Castile, was demolished. Many fortresses met with the same fate.

Not long afterwards, however, matters assumed a very threatening aspect in the North. A powerful league was formed against the Khalif, of which Mohammed ibn Hâshim, the Todjîbite, was the chief promoter.

The Beni Hâshim, who since the conquest had settled in Aragon, had rendered good service to the Sultan Mohammed when the Beni Kasî were still supreme in that province,[1] and for more than forty years the dignity of Governor, or Viceroy, of the Northern Marches had been hereditary in their family. They were almost the only clan left in a position of dignity by 'Abd-er-Rahmân III, who had deprived the Arab nobles of all influence. Mohammed ibn Hâshim, however, was not well-disposed to the Khalif, and—whether it were that he yearned to avenge the slights offered to his order, or that he believed 'Abd-er-Rahmân's apparent goodwill to be dictated by fear, or that he dreamed of a throne for himself and his children—he made overtures to the King of Leon, promising to acknowledge him as suzerain in return for his aid against the Khalif. Ramiro lent a ready ear to these suggestions, and during the campaign of 934, Mohammed openly showed himself a rebel by refusing to join the Moslem army. Three years later he acknowledged Ramiro's suzerainty. Some of his generals refused to follow him in the path of treason, and broke with him; but Ramiro led his troops into the province, stormed the fortresses which still held out for the Khalif, and handed them over to Mohammed. Ramiro and Mohammed then concluded an alliance with Navarre, where the youthful Garcia reigned, under the

---

[1] The Beni Kasî were an ancient Visigothic family, who abjured Christianity at the time of the Arab conquest. For an account of their warfare with the Todjîbites see *Recherches* (1881), i. 211 *sq*.

guardianship of his mother Theuda, widow of Sancho the Great.

All the North was, therefore, leagued against the Khalif. The danger which seemed to have been dispelled again threatened. The Khalif faced it with his customary vigour.

In 937, placing himself at the head of an army, he marched against Calatayud—then under the command of Motarrif, a kinsman of Ibn Hâshim's, and including in its garrison a number of Christians from Alava sent by Ramiro. Motarrif himself fell in the first skirmish. His brother Hakam succeeded to the command; but after having been driven from the town into the citadel, he sued for terms, and stipulating for an amnesty for himself and his Moslem troops, surrendered to the Khalif. The men of Alava, who were not included in the capitulation, were put to the sword.

'Abd-er-Rahmân followed up this first victory by the capture of some thirty castles, and then turned his arms successively against Navarre and Zaragoza. He entrusted the siege of Zaragoza to a prince of the blood, Ahmad ibn Ishâk, commander of the cavalry, whom he had lately made Governor of the Northern Marches; but this officer soon gave serious cause for complaint.

Although the Beni Ishâk had for many years lived a life of obscurity and poverty at Seville, and had not avoided mis-alliances, 'Abd-er-Rahmân had not disdained to acknowledge their connection with his family—remote though it was—and had conferred many favours upon them. Nevertheless they were discontented with their position. Their ambition was boundless; Ahmad, then head of the family, claimed nothing less than to be nominated heir-presumptive to the throne, and whilst he was conducting the siege of Zaragoza with a feebleness and dilatoriness which aroused the anger of the Khalif, he had the audacity to send the latter a formal demand to this effect in writing. 'Abd-er-Rahmân, exasperated by such insolence, sent him an answer couched in these terms:

" Having it in our heart to please thee, we have hitherto extended our favour to thee; but we now know that it is impossible to change thy character. Poverty suiteth thee best, for unaccustomed riches have filled thee with insufferable pride. Was not thy father a common trooper under Ibn Hajjâj? Wast not thou thyself a seller of asses at

Seville? We took thy family under our protection at their entreaty; we succoured it and made it rich and powerful, we conferred upon thy late father the title of Vizier,[1] and made thee general of all our cavalry and governor of the chief of our frontier provinces. And now thou despisest our orders, neglectest our interests, and fillest up the measure by demanding to be made our heir! What merits, what titles of nobility canst thou allege? Aptly may the well-known lines be applied to thee and to thy family : ' Ye are low-born, and linen sorteth not with silk ! If ye are Kurashites, as ye boast, take to yourselves wives of that illustrious tribe ; but if ye are mere Copts, thy pretensions are ridiculous in the extreme !' Was not thy mother the hag Hamdûna ? Was not thy father a common soldier ? Was not thy grandfather door-keeper in the house of Hauthara ibn Abbâs ? Did he not make ropes and mats in the porch of that lord's house ? Be thou accursed of God, thou and all those who laid a snare for us in counselling us to take thee into our service ! Wretch, leper, son of a dog, come and abase thyself at our feet !"

Thus infamously dismissed, Ahmad, aided by his brother Omayya, initiated a plot. The Khalif discovered their intrigues and exiled them. Omayya then seized Santarem, raised the standard of revolt, and entered into communication with the King of Leon; to the latter he rendered useful service by indicating the most vulnerable parts of the Moslem empire ; but one day when he was absent from the town, one of his officers re-established in it the Khalif's authority. Omayya then betook himself to Ramiro. His brother continued to intrigue with untiring ardour. He formed a design of betraying Spain to the Fâtimids, with whom he communicated. 'Abd-er-Rahmân foiled his plot. Ahmad was arrested, condemned as a Shî'ite, and executed.[2]

In the meantime, the Khalif had triumphed in the North. Besieged in Zaragoza, Mohammed capitulated, and since he was the most powerful and distinguished man in the kingdom, next to the sovereign, 'Abd-er-Rahmân deemed it prudent to pardon him and confirm him in his office. Queen Theuda, on her part, after suffering an unbroken series of reverses, besought the Khalif's clemency, and acknowledged

---

[1] A.D. 915 or 916. [2] See above, p. 409.

him as suzerain of Navarre. Over the whole of Spain, therefore, with the exception of the kingdom of Leon and a part of Catalonia, 'Abd-er-Rahmân now reigned supreme.

[AUTHORITIES: Mon. Sil., c. 44–7; Ibn Khaldûn, ff. 13–15; 'Arîb, ii. 175–81, 183–9, 195–201, 211–12, 220–2; Samp., c. 17–19, 22; Al-Basrî, pp. 94–7 (ed. Slane); Ibn Hayyân, f. 15; Ibn Adhârî, i. pp. 178–83; ii. 162; Ibn Khaldûn, *Hist. des Berb.*, i. pp. 282–5 (text); *Akhbâr majmû'at*, f. 114.]

CHAPTER III

FERNAN GONZALEZ

DURING the first twenty-seven years of his reign 'Abd-er-Rahmân III had experienced an unbroken series of successes, but fortune is fickle, and a day of adversity at last dawned.

A great change had come over the realm. The nobles, who formerly had been supreme, were now set at naught, and crushed beneath the sovereign's authority. 'Abd-er-Rahmân detested them : he did not realize that a monarch might safely entrust well-defined influence and authority to the aristocracy. "Your king is, I grant, a wise and able monarch," said the Khalif one day to an envoy from Otto I,[1] "but one feature of his statesmanship does not commend itself to me : instead of retaining the government entirely in his own hands, he admits his vassals to a share of it. He even places them in possession of his provinces, thinking thereby to attach them to himself. This is a grave error. Condescension to the nobility has no other effect than that of nourishing their pride and their propensity to rebel." [2] The Khalif assuredly did not fall into the error with which he reproached the German monarch, but he fell into another not less serious—he made no attempt to soothe the susceptibilities of the nobles. Ruling as an autocrat (after 932 he even dispensed with a *hâjib* or Prime Minister), he conferred most of the highest offices upon men of low extraction— freedmen, foreigners, slaves, men in short who were wholly dependent on his good pleasure, and were pliant and docile instruments in his hands. But those who especially enjoyed his confidence were the body known as *Slavs :* it is from 'Abd-er-Rahmân's reign that their influence dates, and since this body was destined to play an important part in Mohammedan Spain, it is here desirable to enter into some details concerning them.

---

[1] "Otto the Great" (936-973); crowned King of the Germans on the death of his father the Emperor Henry I.

[2] *Vita Johannis Abbatis Gorziensis,* c. 136 : in Pertz, *Mon. Germ. Hist. (Scriptores),* tom. iv.

Originally the name of *Slavs* (Ar. *Saqâliba*) was applied to prisoners captured by Germanic nations in their wars against Slavonic tribes, and sold by them to the Saracens of Spain; but in course of time, a multitude of men belonging to other races began to be classed as Slavs, and the name was applied to all foreigners who served in the harem, or in the army, whatever their origin.[1] An Arab traveller of the tenth century explicitly states that the Slavs who were the retainers of the Khalif of Spain, comprised Galicians, Franks (French and German), Lombards, Calabrians, and natives of the northern coasts of the Black Sea. Some of them had been captured by Andalusian pirates; others had been purchased in Italian ports—for the Jews, trading upon the distress of the people, trafficked in children of both sexes and brought them to the sea-ports, whence they were carried in Greek or Venetian vessels to their Saracen purchasers. Another class, namely the eunuchs destined to be attendants in the harems, were imported from France, where large establishments for the supply of these creatures existed, under the direction of Jews: that of Verdun was far-famed,[2] and there were others in the South.[3]

Since most of the captives were of tender years when they reached Spain, they readily adopted the religion, language, and customs of their masters. Some of them were highly educated, and later on we hear of their forming libraries and composing verses. Such lettered Slavs became, indeed, so numerous that one of them, a certain Habîb, devoted an entire work to an account of their verses and their adventures.

The Slavs had always been numerous at the Court or in the army of the Emirs of Cordova, but never more so than under 'Abd-er-Rahmân III. They numbered 3750 according to some accounts, and 6087, or even 13,750, according to others. Perhaps these statistics refer to different periods of 'Abd-er-Rahmân's reign, for it is certain that he never ceased adding to the number of his Slavs. Though themselves bondsmen, they had slaves of their own, and held large estates. 'Abd-er-Rahmân entrusted to them the most important military and civil functions, and in his hatred of the aristocracy he compelled men of noble lineage—descendants of the heroes of the Desert—to abase themselves

[1] The Cordovan chroniclers call Otto I " King of the Slavs."
[2] Liudprand, *Antapodosis*, vi. 6.
[3] *Cf.* Reinaud, *Invasions des Sarrasins en France*, pp. 233 *sq.*

before these upstarts whom they utterly despised. While
the nobles were thus at daggers drawn with the Khalif, the
latter formed the design of undertaking a more important
expedition against the King of Leon than any which he had
previously made. With this object he laid out vast sums
of money, summoned a hundred thousand men to his
standard, and, assured of a brilliant and decisive victory, he
prospectively dubbed the forthcoming expedition the Campaign of the Invincible Host. Unfortunately, however, he
appointed a Slav, Najda, as Commander-in-Chief. This
choice brought to a climax the disaffection of the Arab
officers. They vowed in their wrath that the Khalif should
expiate his contemptuous treatment of the old nobility by a
disgraceful defeat.

In 939 the army set out for Simancas. Ramiro II and
his ally Theuda,[1] the queen regent of Navarre, took the
field against it, and on the 5th of August a general action
took place. The Arab officers accepted defeat, and retreated ;
but they had probably not foreseen the consequences. The
Leonese followed in pursuit. On reaching the town of
Alhandega, to the south of Salamanca, on the banks of the
Tormes, the Moslems rallied, and faced the enemy ; but
they were utterly defeated, and the Khalif himself narrowly
escaped the swords of the Christians. After Alhandega the
retreat became a rout ; all order and discipline were lost ;
the ranks were broken, and a cry of *sauve qui peut!* was
raised. Horse and foot fled pell-mell together ; the road was
strewn with the bodies of men and officers ; whole regiments
were wiped out. Tidings of Ramiro's complete and signal
victory were borne far and wide. They penetrated to the
further ends of Germany as well as to the most distant
regions of the East, arousing, however, very diverse emotions,
of joy and dismay. Christians saw in the victory a certain
augury of the triumph of their faith—Moslems, a cause
for grave alarm. Even 'Abd-er-Râhmân himself was crest-
fallen. His general Najda had been slain,[2] and the viceroy
of Zaragoza, Mohammed ibn Hâshim, who had been taken
prisoner in the first battle—that of Simancas—was bewailing
his fate in a dungeon at Leon.[3] The Khalif's army was in
fact annihilated ; he himself had escaped captivity or death

---

[1] Otherwise Tota or Tutah.
[2] Perhaps during flight : at any rate he is heard of no more.
[3] The Khalif made every endeavour to procure his release, but Mohammed did
not regain his liberty for two years.

by a miracle, and only a little band of forty-nine had accompanied him in his flight. These disasters made such an impression on his mind that never afterwards did he take the field with his army.[1]

Fortunately for the Khalif, the outbreak of a civil war among the Christians prevented Ramiro from fully reaping the fruits of his victory.

Castile aimed at separation from the Kingdom of Leon: even in the reign of Ordoño II, Ramiro's father, it had broken into open rebellion. The king announced that in order to settle the dispute amicably he would hold a council of Tejiare, or Teliare—on the banks of the Carrion, a stream dividing Leon from Castile—at which he invited the four Counts of Castile to be present. Upon their arrival, how-ever, the king caused them to be arrested and beheaded. The Leonese, while candidly admitting that this judicial procedure was somewhat irregular, admired their king's astuteness; but the Castilians were of a different mind. Deprived of their leaders, they were for the moment helpless, but they ceased not to pray for the hour when they should see at their head a man capable of wreaking vengeance on the treacherous Leonese. At last the hour, so impatiently waited for, struck. Castile found her avenger in the person of Count Fernan Gonzalez, who became one of the favourite heroes of medieval ballads, and who is still mentioned by Castilians with profound respect. Whilst the redoubtable forces of 'Abd-er-Rahmân III were engaged in burning his monasteries, his fortresses, and even his capital, it was useless for Fernan—the Great Count as he was called [2]—to think of throwing off the Leonese yoke; but believing that, for the present at any rate, there was nothing to be feared at the hands of the Arabs, and deeming that the time had come for his destined enterprise, he declared war upon the king. The Khalif on his part seized the opportunity of reorganising his army, and by November, 940, it was ready to ravage the frontiers of Leon, under Ahmad ibn Yila, governor of Badajoz. At the same time fortune seemed inclined to make amends in Africa for the disaster which had overtaken 'Abd-er-Rahmân in Spain.

Hitherto the Khalif had, it is true, achieved many successes in Africa—but there was another side to the shield.

---

[1] For further details of the battle of Alhandega, see *Recherches* (1881), pp. 156–70.
[2] " Egregius comes "; cf. Berganza, *Antiguedades de España* (1719), i. 215.

Now and then his vassals had contrived to be worsted; his endeavours to induce them to act in concert had not always been effectual; sometimes, indeed, he had been unable to induce them to keep the peace among themselves; but he had at any rate succeeded in keeping the Fâtimids in Africa occupied, and had incapacitated them from making a descent on the coast of Spain, which after all was his main object. He now seemed to be on the point of gaining a further advantage.

An enemy more formidable to the Fâtimids than all the rest combined had raised the standard of revolt. This was Abû Yazîd, of the Berber tribe of Iforen. The son of a merchant, he had consorted in his youth with the doctors of the sect of the Khârejites, who still claimed an immense number of adherents in Africa. Later, having been reduced to poverty by the death of his father, he had earned his bread by teaching children to read. At first a schoolmaster and then a missionary, like the founder of the Fâtimid Empire, he urged the Berbers to revolt in the name of the true religion and of liberty, promising them a Republican form of government, so soon as they had taken the capital, Kairwan.

Abû Yazîd's victories were as miraculous as those of his enemies a few years before. The Fâtimid armies melted away, like snow in the springtime, before this ill-favoured dwarfish man clad in sackcloth and mounted on a grey ass. The Sunnîs,[1] wounded to the heart by the blasphemies and intolerance of the Fâtimids, flocked to his standard; the very monks and hermits took up arms in the cause of the Nonconformist leader. He seemed to make it his business to justify the hope which they reposed on his toleration. When, in 944, he made his entry into the Capital he invoked the blessing of heaven on the first two Khalifs, who were held accursed by the Fâtimids, and he urged the townsfolk to conform to the rite of Mâlik, which the Fâtimids had prohibited. The Sunnîs breathed once more. They could again walk in procession, with banners and drums, a pleasure of which they had been deprived for many years, and Abû Yazîd, who on these solemn occasions led them himself, gave them yet another proof of his tolerance: he concluded an alliance with the Khalif of Spain, and sending him an embassy recognised him, if not as the temporal, at least as

---

[1] The orthodox Moslems, followers of the *Sunna*, or precedent. See D. S. Margoliouth, *Mohammedanism*, p. 160.

the spiritual chief of the vast dominions he had conquered.[1]
The fortunes of the Fâtimids seemed to be at their lowest
ebb. Whilst their Khalif Kâyim, son and successor of
'Obaidallah, was closely besieged in Mahdia by the formidable Abû Yazîd, the Khalif of Spain seized through his
African vassals almost all the North-West, and stirred up
Kâyim's foes against him in every quarter. 'Abd-er-Rahmân
further entered into alliance with the King of Italy, Hugues
of Provence (who had a disaster to avenge, namely the
sacking of Genoa by a Fâtimid admiral),[2] and he made a
similar treaty with the Byzantine Emperor, who longed to
wrest Sicily from Kâyim.[3]

In the twinkling of an eye all was changed ! Intoxicated
with his successes, Abû Yazîd grew puffed up with pride.
Not content with the reality of power, and forgetful of the
means by which he had attained to it, he thirsted for display
and empty pomp; he changed his sackcloth cloak for a
silken robe and his grey ass for a splendid charger. Such
folly proved his destruction ; the majority of his adherents
were levellers and republicans, and these, wounded in their
convictions, abandoned him ; some returned to their homes,
others went over to the enemy. Warned by this experience,
Abû Yazîd renounced the habits of luxury which he had
contracted, and assumed once more, with his sackcloth cloak,
his former frugal and austere life. But it was too late.
The glamour of his prestige had vanished. He might, perhaps, have still counted on the Sunnîs, had he not—in a
moment of fanatic rage—opened their eyes to the insincerity
of his tolerance. On the eve of a battle he ordered his men
to abandon their brothers in arms, the soldiers of Kairwan,
to the fury of the Fâtimid troops. This treacherous order
was only too well obeyed. From that day the Sunnîs held
Abû Yazîd in detestation : weighing tyrant against tyrant,
and heresiarch against heresiarch, they preferred the Fâtimid
Khalif, and this the more since Al-Mansûr, who had lately
succeeded his father, was more capable than his predecessors.
Obliged to raise the siege of Mahdia, Abû Yazîd returned
to Kairwan, where he narrowly escaped a plot which the
inhabitants had hatched against him. After being for long

---

[1] Several chroniclers give wholly erroneous accounts of Abû Yazîd's first sojourn
at Kairwan. Ibn Sadûn (in Ibn Adhârî, i. 224-6) is here followed : he was almost a
contemporary, and his circumstantial narrative has an air of truth wanting in the
others.

[2] A.D. 936.

[3] Cf. Histoire de l'Afrique de Mohammed-Ben-Abi-el-Raïni-el-K'aïrouani,
tradnite de l'arabe, par E. Pellissier et Rémusat, Paris, 1845, p. 104.

the quarry of the Fâtimid soldiers, he at last fell into their hands, covered with wounds. He was confined in an iron cage, and after his death (947), his skin, stuffed with straw, was borne through the streets of Kairwan, and nailed to the ramparts of Mahdia, where it hung until dispersed in tatters by the winds. The fall of the Sectaries was almost as grave a blow to 'Abd-er-Rahmân as his defeat at Simancas, or at Alhandega; for in the West the Fâtimids speedily recovered their lost territories and compelled 'Abd-er-Rahmân's vassals to seek safety at the Court of Cordova.

In the North, on the other hand, all went as the Khalif wished—in other words, the country was a prey to ceaseless conflict. War, as we have seen, had broken out between Ramiro II and Fernan Gonzalez. Fortune favoured Ramiro. Capturing his adversary by surprise, he threw him into a dungeon at Leon, and conferred the lordship of Castile, first upon a Leonese—Assur Fernandez, Count of Monzon—and later upon his own son Sancho. The king proceeded further to confiscate Fernan's allodial lands. These he did not, however, keep wholly as his own. With a view to popularity, he granted some to the most influential knights and ecclesiastics of the province.[1] But he failed in his design. While profiting by Ramiro's liberality, the Castilians remained devoted, heart and soul, to their deposed lord. The king's gifts were regarded as those of an interloper. In deeds of sale, and the like, in which, after the date, it was customary to insert the names of the reigning King and the Count, the name of the Count imposed upon them by Ramiro was sometimes given—but only when it was unavoidable, that is to say when written under official supervision—usually the name of Fernan Gonzalez appeared. The Castilians further manifested their devotion to their Count in another way. Having caused a statue of him to be made, they rendered homage to his sculptured image.[2] Then, beginning to lose patience at Fernan's long captivity, they took a bold resolution best described in the phrases of an old and beautiful romance:[3]

"All have made oath together that they will not return to Castile without their lord, the Count.

"His statue they have placed in a chariot and they are resolved not to return unless he returns with them.

---

[1] The Count's orchard, for example, was given to the Monastery of Cardeña. For details see Berganza, *op. cit.*, ii. Escr. 32–4.

[2] *Crónica rimada*, p. 2 (*Wiener Jahrbücher, Anzeige-Blatt*, vol. cxvi.).

[3] "Juramento llevan hecho."

" Having done homage, they place the Count's banner by the side of the
statue, and all, both young and old, kiss the hand of the image.

" Burgos and its environs are deserted : none remain there save women
and little children."

Alarmed at the approach of the Castilians, the King at
length submitted. Fernan was set at liberty, but only upon
severe and humiliating conditions : he was obliged to swear
fealty and submission, to renounce all his possessions,
and to promise his daughter in marriage to Ordoño, the
King's eldest son. Such was the price of the Count's freedom, and it was but natural that he should be determined
never again to lend his aid to a monarch who had compelled
him to sign such a compact. The Castilians, who had not
succeeded in reinstating in authority him who they still
called their lord, were as disaffected as ever. Ramiro II
had therefore lost the aid of his most valiant captain, and
the co-operation of his bravest subjects. Hence his helplessness. He allowed the Musulmans to make a foray
in 944, and two more in 947 ; he could not prevent them
from rebuilding and fortifying the town of Medinaceli, which
henceforward became the bulwark of the Moorish Empire
against Castile. The victor of Simancas and Alhandega
could at most stand on the defensive. It was not until the
year 950 that he once more invaded Moslem territories, and
on this occasion he gained a victory near Talavera : but this
was his last success : by January in the following year his
life was at an end.[1]

After Ramiro's death a war of succession broke out.
The King had been twice married. His first wife, a
Galician, had borne him a son, Ordoño ; and his second wife
—Urraca, sister of Garcia of Navarre—another son, Sancho.
By right of primogeniture Ordoño naturally claimed the
throne ; but Sancho, who had good reason to rely upon the
support of the Navarrese, also laid claim to it, and endeavoured to win over Fernan Gonzalez and the Castilians to
his side. In the circumstances, it was not difficult for
Fernan to make choice between the rivals. It was impossible for him to sympathise keenly with Ordoño, who was,
it is true, his son-in-law, but had become so by hateful compulsion. On the other hand, ties of blood as well as self-
interest attracted him to Sancho. The latter was his nephew,[2]

---

[1] The date has been disputed, but Dozy (*Recherches* (1881), pp. 170–3) has produced overwhelming evidence in favour of 951.

[2] Sancho's mother and Fernan's wife were sisters.

and could reckon on the support of Theuda of Navarre, Fernan's mother-in-law. If the Count had still hesitated Sancho's dazzling offers must have overcome his indecision, for the prince promised to restore to him his confiscated possessions and the lordship of Castile. Fernan accordingly declared for Sancho, summoned his men to arms, and accompanied by Sancho and a Navarrese army marched against the city of Leon to wrest the crown from Ordoño III.

"The Eternal," remarks an Arab chronicler, "stirred up this civil strife that victories might fall to the lot of the Musulmans!" And indeed while the Christians were cutting each others' throats beneath the walls of Leon, 'Abd-er-Rahmân's generals were victorious at all points on the frontier. Every message that arrived at Cordova from the North bore tidings of some profitable raid or brilliant victory. The Khalif was enabled to exhibit to the populace bells, crosses, and decapitated heads in heaps: on one occasion, in 955, no less than five thousand heads were shown, and it was said that as many more Castilians—for it was they who had suffered defeat—had fallen in the engagement. Fernan Gonzalez had, it was true, gained a victory near San Estevan de Gormaz; [1] it was also true, that Ordoño III, having at length repulsed his brother and compelled the Galicians, who had also revolted, to recognise him, had made reprisals by pillaging Lisbon; but this was but trifling compensation for the destruction which the Musulmans had wrought upon the Christians, and Ordoño, who dreaded further revolts, ardently desired peace. In 955 he sent an ambassador to Cordova to sue for it. 'Abd-er-Rahmân, who also desired a cessation of hostilities, because he wished to turn his arms in another direction, lent a not unwilling ear to Ordoño's overtures, and in the following year he sent as ambassadors to Leon, Mohammed ibn Husain and the learned Jew Chasdaï ibn Shaprût, [2] Inspector-General of Customs. The negotiations did not last long. Ordoño announced that he was ready to make concessions—probably offering to relinquish or raze certain fortresses—the bases of a treaty were agreed upon, and the envoys returned to Cordova to obtain its ratification by the Khalif. Although the compact was an honourable one and undoubtedly advantageous, 'Abd-er-Rahmân considered that it might have

---

[1] *Esp. sagr.*, xxiii. p. 378.

[2] "Abu-Yussuf Chasdaï ben Isaac Ibn-Shaprut" (915–970); Graetz, *Hist. of the Jews* (1892), iii. 220–235.

been made still more favourable, but as, at the age of nearly
seventy, he could no longer reckon on the morrow, he came
to the conclusion that the matter concerned his son rather
than himself. He accordingly consulted him and asked for
his decision. Hakam, who was pacifically disposed, advised
the ratification of the treaty, which the Khalif thereupon
signed. Not long afterwards he made a compact with
Fernan Gonzalez, the upshot being that the Navarrese were
the Musulmans' only remaining enemies in Spain.

If 'Abd-er-Rahmân had on this occasion proved more
tractable than was his wont, it was because he wished to
direct his arms against the Fâtimids. The power of these
princes was daily increasing. Burning with desire to take
vengeance on the rulers of Europe, who were already rejoicing over what seemed their impending ruin, the Fâtimids
first impressed the Byzantine Emperor with the weight of
their wrath by laying waste Calabria.[1] Then 'Abd-er-
Rahmân's turn came. In 955, when every indication
seemed to point to a meditated descent upon Spain by
Mu'izz, the fourth Fâtimid Khalif, it happened that a large
vessel, despatched by 'Abd-er-Rahmân with merchandise to
Alexandria, met at sea a ship coming from Sicily on board
of which there was a messenger sent by the Governor of
that island to his sovereign Mu'izz. This fact seems to
have come to the knowledge of the Captain of the Spanish
vessel. It is indeed possible that 'Abd-er-Rahmân had
suspected that the despatches conveyed by the messenger
contained a plan of attack upon Spain, and that he had
ordered the Captain to intercept them. Be this as it may,
the Captain attacked the Sicilian ship, captured it, pillaged
it, and took possession of the despatches.

Mu'izz soon made reprisals. By his orders the Governor
of Sicily set sail with a fleet against Almeria, and captured
or burned all the vessels in that port. He even captured
the very ship which had furnished him with such a specious
excuse for this expedition, and which had just returned
from Alexandria with singing-girls for the Khalif and costly
merchandise. The Sicilian Governor then landed troops,
and after pillaging the environs of Almeria, once more set
sail.[2]

'Abd-er-Rahmân responded vigorously to this attack.
His first act was to order curses to be invoked upon the

[1] Cf. Amari, Storia dei Musulmani de Sicilia, ii. pp. 242–8.
[2] Cf. Amari, op. cit., ii. 249–50, and works there cited.

Fâtimids daily at public prayer; his second, to order his Admiral Ghâlib to pillage the coast of Ifrikia.[1] This expedition, however, proved less successful than the Khalif had hoped. The Andalusians at first gained some successes, but they were ultimately repulsed by the troops who guarded the province, and compelled to re-embark.

'Abd-er-Rahmân had reached this point in his conflict with the Fâtimids, when he entered into the negotiations with the King of Leon. Wishing to employ all the troops and resources of the Empire against Africa, he naturally desired peace with the Christians of the North, and it was for this reason that he did not show himself too exigent in the conditions he laid down.

As soon as peace had been ensured he turned all his attention to Africa. A vast expedition was made ready. The shipwrights in the dockyards had not a moment of rest, everywhere troops were marching towards the seaports, and thousands of sailors were being enrolled, when by the death of Ordoño III, in the spring of 957, the Khalif's plans were suddenly checked. We have already seen that Ordoño had only obtained peace on certain conditions, and among these the cession or demolition of certain fortresses was undoubtedly of prime importance. But Sancho—his brother's former rival, who had succeeded him without opposition—refused to execute this clause of the treaty. 'Abd-er-Rahmân, therefore, was compelled to employ the forces which he had wished to send to Africa against the Kingdom of Leon, and he gave orders in this sense to the gallant Ahmad ibn Yila, Governor of Toledo.[2] That general took the field, and in July gained a great victory over the King of Leon. This triumph doubtless afforded some consolation to the Khalif, who had not desired this new war and who willingly would have avoided it, had honour allowed. He was soon to experience satisfaction yet sweeter, in seeing his enemy at his feet.

[1] Mod. Ar. *Ifriqiyah* (Tunisia); Berb. *Ifriqa*.
[2] 'Abd-er-Rahmân had appointed him in 954.

[AUTHORITIES: Ibn al-'Abbâr, pp. 24, 140 ; Makkarî, i. 92, 235, 372-3 ; ii. 57 ; Ibn Hawkal (Leyd. MS.), p. 39 ; Ibn Adhârî, ii. 224-7, 229-30, 233-8 ; Samp., c. 19, 23-5 ; Ibn Khaldûn, f. 15.]

CHAPTER IV

SANCHO THE FAT

"KING Sancho," says an Arab writer, "was arrogant and vain-glorious."[1] This phrase was doubtless borrowed from some contemporary Leonese chronicler, and both authors imply thereby that Sancho aimed at breaking the power of the nobility and regaining the absolute authority possessed by his ancestors. The nobles consequently hated him; and with their hatred was mingled contempt. Sancho had indeed lost the qualities which had at first endeared him to his subjects. The luckless prince had grown so immensely corpulent that he could no longer mount his horse, and was obliged to lean for support on an attendant while walking.[2] He had consequently become an object of derision, and after a while the deposition of such an absurd travesty of a monarch began to be mooted.

Fernan Gonzalez, who aspired to become a king-maker, and who had already made one unsuccessful essay in that capacity, fomented and directed the disaffection of the Leonese.[3] A plot was hatched in the army, and one fine day, in the spring of 958, Sancho was driven from his kingdom.

While the dethroned monarch was sorrowfully making his way to Pamplona, the residence of his uncle Garcia, Fernan Gonzalez and the other notables met to elect another king. Their choice fell upon Ordoño, fourth of that name. He was son of Alfonso IV, and consequently Sancho's cousin, but he had nothing save his parentage to commend him to the suffrages of the electors. His deformed figure (he was hunch-backed) was matched by a cringing, mean, and vicious disposition,[4] so that in later days he was always distinguished as Ordoño the Wicked;[5] nevertheless, since

---

[1] The chronicler adds, "and warlike." *Recherches* (1881), i. p. 97. Sampiro uses almost the same words of Ramiro III.

[2] *Cf.* the poem of Dunash, str. iv., in Luzzatto, *Notice sur Abou-Iousouf Hasdaï ibn-Schaprout*, p. 24.

[3] *Recherches* (1881), i. p. 97.

[4] See below, pp. 449 *sq.*

[5] "El Malo," *Arab. Al-khabíth.*

there was no other adult member of the royal family living, his election was practically unavoidable. The Count of Castile gave to him in marriage his daughter Urraca, widow of Ordoño III, who thus became Queen of Leon for the second time.

While the election of his successor was taking place, Sancho was relating at Pamplona the misfortunes which had overtaken him. His grandmother, the aged and ambitious Theuda, who still ruled Navarre in her son's name, though he had long attained an age which entitled him to govern for himself, warmly espoused Sancho's cause, and vowed to reinstate him at all costs. This was, however, by no means an easy undertaking, for, while Sancho possessed not one powerful friend in his late kingdom, Navarre on the other hand was too weak to attack Leon and Castile single-handed. It was therefore incumbent upon Theuda to seek an ally—and that a strong one. Moreover, in order that Sancho should retain his throne after it had been restored to him, it was absolutely necessary that he should cease to be a laughing-stock by reason of his unfortunate obesity. This corpulence was not constitutional; it was the result of some distemper which an able physician could doubtless banish—and it was at Cordova alone, that focus of all intellectual brilliancy, that such a physician could be found. It was at Cordova, too, that Theuda believed she saw the ally she needed. She determined, in short, to seek at the Khalif's hands a leech to cure her grandson, and an army to replace him on his throne.

It would, of course, be mortifying to her pride to take such a step; it was bitterly distasteful to crave the assistance of an infidel with whom she had been at war for more than thirty years, and who had scarcely let a twelvemonth pass without devastating her valleys and burning her villages; yet Theuda's love for her grandson, her ardent wish to see him once more on the throne, and her indignation at his shameful ill-treatment, all conspired to overcome her natural repugnance, and she accordingly despatched an embassy to Cordova.

When the envoys had acquainted the Khalif with the objects of their mission, he replied that he would gladly send a physician to Sancho, and also that—on certain conditions to be unfolded by one of his ministers who would proceed to Pamplona—he would furnish armed assistance to the dethroned king.

Upon the departure of the Navarrese envoys, 'Abd-er-
Rahmân sent for Chasdaï the Jew, and having given him
instructions bade him betake himself to the Court of
Navarre. The Khalif could not have made a better choice.
Chasdaï united in his own person all the qualities necessary
for such a mission : he spoke the language of the Christians
fluently, and he was at once a physician and a statesman :
praises of his judgment, his talents, his erudition, and his vast
ability were in all men's mouths : not long before, an ambassador from the further end of Germany had declared that he
had never met with such a master of diplomatic subtlety.[1]

Upon his arrival at Pamplona, the Jew soon gained
Sancho's confidence by personally undertaking his treatment
and promising him a speedy cure. He then informed him
that the Khalif, in return for the service he was prepared to
render him, demanded the cession of ten fortresses. Sancho
promised to make them over so soon as he had regained his
throne. But this was not all : Chasdaï had also been
instructed to extort Theuda's consent to visit Cordova,
accompanied by her son and grandson.

The Khalif, desirous of gratifying his own self-esteem,
while at the same time regaling his people with the un-
exampled spectacle of a Christian queen and two kings
humbly prostrating themselves at his feet and craving his
assistance, had strongly insisted on this condition : but it
had been foreseen that the proud Theuda would set her
face against the demand. To make a journey to Cordova
would be, indeed, a greater humiliation for the Queen than
that to which she had already subjected herself in entering
into friendly relations with her inveterate foe. This was
accordingly the most delicate and thorny part of Chasdaï's
mission : even to make such a proposal, still more to induce
Theuda to agree to it, required extraordinary tact and ability.
But the Jew justified his reputation of being the adroitest of
men. The haughty Queen of Navarre was subjugated " by
the charm of his words, the ripeness of his wisdom, the
power of his cunning and his manifold wiles "—to use the
words of a contemporary Jewish poet—and believing that
her grandson's reinstatement could be obtained at no less a
price, she consented, after a powerful exercise of self-control,
to undertake the proposed journey.

---

[1] " Judeum quendam, cui nomen Hasdeu, quo neminem umquam prudentiorem
se vidisse aut audisse nostri testati sunt."   *Vita Johannis Abbatis Gorziensis:* in
Pertz, *Mon. Germ. Hist. (Scriptores)*, tom. iv. p. 371.

Spain then saw a strange sight. Followed by a long train of nobles and priests, the Queen of Navarre journeyed by easy stages to Cordova, accompanied by Garcia and the luckless Sancho, whose health was not yet much improved, and who walked supported by Chasdaï. Grateful as the spectacle was to the national pride of the Moslems, it was yet sweeter to the self-esteem of the Jews, seeing that it had been wholly brought about by a man of their own faith. Their poets vied with one another in celebrating Chasdaï's return:

"Bow down, O ye mountains, to Judah's chief!" sings one of them: "Let laughter fall from all men's lips! Let the waste places and the forests burst into song! Let the desert rejoice, let it blossom and yield fruits, for he cometh, the Chief of the Academy, he cometh with singing and with joy! While he was not therein, the famous city with its fair walls was sorrowful and in darkness: the poor, who saw no longer his countenance shining as the stars, were in affliction: the proud held dominion over us: we were bought and sold into slavery: they thrust out their tongues to swallow up our possessions: they roared upon us like lions' whelps, and we were sore dismayed, for he, our defender, was afar off!—God hath given him to us as our chief: he standeth at the right hand of the king, who calleth him prince, and hath exalted him above the mighty. When he passeth by, no man dareth to open his lips. Without sword or arrows, by the words of his mouth alone, he hath taken by storm the fenced cities of the devourers of accursed flesh!" [1]

Upon the arrival of the Queen and the two Kings at Cordova, the Khalif granted them one of those stately audiences which made so deep an impression on foreigners, and which were eminently fitted to give a lofty idea of his power and wealth. It was undoubtedly a moment of keen gratification to 'Abd-er-Rahmân when he saw at his feet the son of his formidable enemy Ramiro III, as well as the son of the victor of Simancas and Alhandega, and that proud and valiant queen who in memorable battles had in person led her troops to victory: but, whatever were his inmost feelings, he repressed all his external evidence of them, and received his guests with exquisite courtesy.

Sancho renewed the promise, which he had already given to Chasdaï, of ceding to the Khalif ten specified fortresses, and it was resolved that whilst the Moorish army attacked the Kingdom of Leon, the Navarrese should invade Castile, so as to lure the forces of Fernan Gonzalez away from that quarter.[2]

---

[1] See Graetz, *Hist. of the Jews* (1892), iii. 232.
[2] *Recherches* (1881), i. 98.

Meanwhile 'Abd-er-Rahmân had not lost sight of Africa. On the contrary, he had vigorously pushed forward warlike preparations, and the year which saw the Queen of Navarre's arrival at Cordova saw also the embarkation in seventy ships of a large army under the command of Ahmad ibn Yila. The expedition was successful, for the Andalusians burned Mersâ al-Kharez, and laid waste the environs of Susa and Tabarca.

A little later a Moslem army marched against the Kingdom of Leon. Sancho accompanied it. Thanks to Chasdaï's remedies, he had lost his excessive corpulence, and had become as lithe and active as in former days. Zamora was the first town to be taken,[1] and by April, 959, Sancho's authority was restored over a great part of the Kingdom. The Capital, however, still adhered to Ordoño IV ; but when in the autumn of 960, the latter took to flight and sought refuge in the Asturias, it surrendered to Sancho. Having thus recovered his kingdom, Sancho sent an envoy to the Khalif to thank him for his aid, and at the same time proclaimed to the neighbouring powers his resumption of sovereignty. In the letters which he despatched to this effect, he denounced in vigorous terms the disloyalty of the Count of Castile.[2] Perhaps he still feared opposition from Fernan: if so, his fears were soon dispelled. In accordance with the original plan of campaign, the Navarrese had invaded Castile, and in the same year, 960, they gave battle to the Count and were fortunate enough to take him prisoner. Henceforth Ordoño's cause was lost. An object of universal hatred and contempt, he had only been propped upon the throne by Fernan, whose creature he was. The Asturians before long expelled him from their province and made submission to Sancho. Ordoño thereupon sought refuge at Burgos, but will be heard of again.

While these events were taking place in the North, the Khalif, who had imprudently exposed himself to the biting winds of March, had fallen sick, and there were even fears for his life. The physicians, however, succeeded in warding off the imminent danger, and in the early days of July 'Abd-er-Rahmân had so far recovered as to be able to give audience to his great officers of state. But his cure was only apparent : he experienced a relapse, and expired,

---

[1] *Recherches* (1881), i. 98.   [2] *Ibid.*

October 16, 961, in the seventieth year of his age, and the forty-ninth of his reign.

Of all the Omayyad princes who reigned in Spain, 'Abd-er-Rahmân III was unquestionably the greatest. His achievements approached the miraculous. He had found the country a prey to anarchy and civil war, rent by faction, parcelled out amongst a hundred petty chiefs of diverse races, exposed to incessant raids by the Christians of the North, and on the point of being absorbed either by the Leonese or the Fâtimids of Africa. Despite innumerable obstacles he had saved Andalusia from herself, as well as from foreign domination. He had raised her to a nobler and mightier position than she had ever before attained. He had won for her peace and prosperity at home, and consideration and respect abroad. He found the public treasury in a lamentable state of depletion, he left it overflowing. A third of the national revenue, which amounted in all to 6,245,000 pieces of gold, sufficed for normal expenditure; a third was placed in reserve, and 'Abd-er-Rahmân laid out the rest upon public works. It has been computed that in the year 951 the royal coffers contained the immense sum of twenty million gold pieces, and a traveller, not unversed in finance, assures us that 'Abd-er-Rahmân and the Hamdânid then reigning in Mesopotamia, were the two richest princes of that epoch.[1] The state of the country harmonised with the prosperity of the public treasury. Agriculture, manufactures, commerce, the arts and sciences, all flourished. The traveller's eyes were gladdened on all sides by well-cultivated fields, irrigated upon scientific principles, so that what seemed the most sterile soil was rendered fertile. He was struck, too, by the perfect order which, thanks to a vigilant police, reigned in even the least accessible districts. He marvelled at the cheapness of commodities (the most delicious fruit could be bought for next to nothing), at the prevalent spruceness of attire, and especially at a universal standard of well-being which permitted everyone, with scarcely an exception, to ride a mule instead of journeying on foot. Many different manufactures enriched Cordova, Almeria, and other towns. Commerce was so highly developed that, according to the Report of the Inspector-General of Customs, the import and export duties provided the larger part of the national

---

[1] The Hamdânid dynasty reigned at Aleppo, A.D. 923–1003. See Nicholson, *Lit. Hist. of the Arabs* (1907), pp. 269–71.

revenue.[1] Cordova, with its half-million inhabitants, its
three thousand mosques, its splendid palaces, its hundred
and thirteen thousand houses, its three hundred public
baths, and its twenty-eight suburbs, yielded in size and
magnificence only to Baghdad, a city, indeed, to which the
inhabitants loved to compare it.[2] The fame of Cordova
penetrated even distant Germany : the Saxon nun Hroswitha, famous in the last half of the tenth century for her
Latin poems and dramas, called it the Jewel of the
World.[3] The rival city which 'Abd-er-Rahmân built was
no less admirable. One of his concubines having bequeathed
him a large fortune, the monarch wished to devote the
money to ransoming prisoners of war, but his agents having
ransacked the Kingdoms of Leon and Navarre without finding a single prisoner, his favourite wife Zahrâ said to him :
" Devote this money to founding a city, and call it after
my name." The idea took the Khalif's fancy. Like most
great princes, he had a passion for building, and in
November, A.D. 936, he laid, at about a league to the north
of Cordova, the foundations of a town destined to perpetuate
the name of Zahrâ. Nothing was spared to make it as
magnificent as possible. For twenty-five years ten thousand
workmen, provided with fifteen hundred beasts of burden,
laboured at its construction, yet it was unfinished at its
founder's death. A bounty of four hundred dirhems
granted by the Khalif to everyone who took up his abode
there, attracted throngs of inhabitants. The royal palace,
within which all the marvels of the East and the West
vied with one another, was of immense size—as, indeed, is
evidenced by the fact that the female inmates of the harem
numbered six thousand.[4]

'Abd-er-Rahmân's power became truly formidable. A
splendid navy enabled him to dispute the mastery of the
Mediterranean with the Fâtimids, and secured him in the
possession of Ceuta, the key of Mauritania. A numerous

[1] Letter from Chasdaï to the King of the Khozars, in Carmoly, *Des Khozars au Xe siècle*, p. 37.
[2] "Do not talk of the court of Baghdad and its glittering magnificence ; do not praise Persia and China and their manifold advantages ; for there is no spot on earth like Cordova," sings an Arab poet, q. by *Makkarí*, i. 202 (transl.).
[3] Hroswitha : *Pass. S. Pelagii.*
[4] For an account of the excavations in progress upon the site of Al-Zahrâ, see *The Times*, Dec. 28, 1910, "An Arabic Pompeii." For illustrations of some of the objects discovered, and a discussion of the style of art displayed, see "Hispano-Arabic Art at Medina Az-Zahra," by B. and E. M. Whishaw, *Burlington Magazine*, Aug. 1911.

and well-disciplined army—perhaps the finest in the world in those days [1]—gave him a marked preponderance over the Christians of the North. The proudest monarchs sought his alliance. The Byzantine Emperor, the rulers of Germany, Italy, and France, sent embassies to his Court.

Such achievements as these were unquestionably great, but what strikes the student of this brilliant reign with astonishment and admiration is not so much the edifice as the architect—the force of that comprehensive intellect which nothing eluded and which showed itself a no less admirable master of the minutest details than of the most exalted conceptions. This subtle and sagacious man, who unifies the nation and consolidates its resources, who by his alliances virtually establishes a balance of power, and who in his wide tolerance calls to his councils men of another religion, is a pattern ruler of modern times, rather than a medieval Khalif.

---

[1] Cf. *Vita Joh. Gorz.* (ut supra), c. 135.

[AUTHORITIES: Ibn Hawkal, pp. 38, 40–2; Samp., c. 26; Makkarî, i. 252–3, 344–6, 370 *sq.*; Ibn Adhârî, ii. 161, 201, 237–9, 246–8; Ibn Khaldûn, f. 15; *Hist. des Berb.*, ii. 542 (transl.); *Esp. sagr.*, xxxiv. 267–70.]

CHAPTER V

HAKAM II

THE Courts of Leon and Pamplona, notwithstanding the important services 'Abd-er-Rahmân III had rendered them, did not lament his death; on the contrary, they saw in it a means of evading their treaty obligations, and of escaping from Moslem tutelage, which had grown irksome since it was no longer needed. The opportunity seemed a good one of breaking pledges which had been extorted from them. 'Abd-er-Rahmân's successor, Hakam II, was reputed pacific; he would not, perhaps, insist on the rigorous fulfilment of a treaty concluded with his predecessor—in any case it was advisable to wait and see whether his success in the field equalled his father's.

Hakam soon had an opportunity of gauging his neighbours' intentions. Sancho, on being summoned to surrender the fortresses specified in the treaty, found many excuses for delay. Garcia, on being requested to hand over his prisoner, Fernan Gonzalez, flatly refused to do so.[1] Further, he set Fernan at liberty, stipulating, however, that he should break with his son-in-law, Ordoño IV. Fernan made the required promise, and by his orders, Ordoño, then at Burgos, was torn from his wife and two daughters, and conveyed under a strong escort to Moslem territory. Then Fernan—who, unlike the kings of Navarre and Leon, was bound by no treaty—recommenced hostilities against the Arabs, with the result that in February, 962, Hakam was obliged to warn his generals and governors to mobilise their troops.

In the meantime Ordoño the Wicked, with the twenty lords who remained faithful to him, had reached Medinaceli. There his hopes were raised by the sight of preparations for an expedition. His cousin had recovered his throne with the help of 'Abd-er-Rahmân, and he might recover his own by the help of Hakam. He accordingly signified to Ghâlib, Governor of Medinaceli, his desire to proceed to Cordova and seek the monarch's protection.

[1] *Recherches* (1881), p. 98.

Ghâlib inquired Hakam's wishes on the matter. Hakam, who was not sorry to have a pretender in his power, but who would not commit himself definitely, replied that Ordoño might be conducted to Cordova, but that he would make him no promise. Ghâlib, accordingly, started for Cordova early in April, accompanied by Ordoño and his escort. On their way they were met by a detachment of Hakam's cavalry, sent to conduct his guests to the environs of the Capital, where they were joined by a still larger body. Ordoño spared no pains to ingratiate himself with the officers of the escort. He lavished flatteries upon them, and upon entering Cordova, asked to be shown the tomb of 'Abd-er-Rahmân III. On its being pointed out to him he bared his head, and falling on his knees, turned towards the tomb, and prayed for the soul of him by whom a little while before he had been driven from the throne. He was animated by the one hope of regaining his crown; to effect that object he shrank from no humiliation.

After spending two days in a richly furnished palace, assigned to him for a residence, Ordoño was informed that the Khalif would give him audience at Al-Zahrâ. He donned a robe and mantle of white silk—probably as an act of homage to the Omayyads, whose family badge was white—and wore a head-dress adorned with precious stones. The principal citizens of Andalusia—amongst them Walîd ibn Khaizorân, judge of the Christians at Cordova, and 'Obaid-allah ibn Kâsim, the Metropolitan of Toledo—came to conduct him to Al-Zahrâ, and to instruct him in details of etiquette, with regard to which the Court was very punctilious.

As they passed the serried ranks of soldiers which lined the approaches to Al-Zahrâ, Ordoño and his Leonese companions feigned to be amazed, and even terrified, by this military display. They lowered their eyes and crossed themselves. On arriving at the outer gateway of the palace, they all dismounted, except Ordoño and his Leonese. At the gate called as-sodda the Leonese quitted their saddles; but Ordoño, and the general Ibn Tomlos, whose duty it was to introduce him to the Khalif, rode on until they arrived at a porch where seats had been placed for Ordoño and his companions—the spot where Sancho had also waited to be introduced to the monarch when he came to implore his aid. After some delay, the Leonese were permitted to enter the audience-chamber. At the door Ordoño bared his head,

2 F

and removed his cloak in token of respect: he was then
requested to approach, and on finding himself before the
throne, on which sat Hakam—surrounded by his brothers
and nephews, the Viziers, the Kady, and the Fakihs—he
advanced slowly towards the Khalif, halting to bow the
knee at every few steps. Hakam extended his hand to be
kissed, and Ordoño retired—being careful not to turn his
back upon the throne—and seated himself on a sofa covered
with brocade, which had been placed for him fifteen feet
away. The Leonese nobles then approached the Khalif,
observing the same ceremonial, and after kissing his hand,
ranged themselves behind their master, near whom stood
Walîd ibn Khairzorân, who was to act as interpreter in the
ensuing conversation.

The Khalif remained silent for a few moments—to give
the ex-king time to recover from the emotion with which
the sight of such an august assembly could not fail to affect
him—and then addressed him in these words: "Rejoice
that thou hast come hither, and hope great things from our
bounty, for we shall vouchsafe thee greater favours than
thou darest to expect."

When these gracious words had been interpreted to
Ordoño, his face grew radiant with joy. He arose, and
kissing the carpet which covered the steps of the throne,
exclaimed: "I am the slave of the Commander of the
Faithful! I rely on his magnanimity; his lofty virtues
shall be my stay; to him I yield full power over myself and
my subjects. Whithersoever he commandeth me to go,
thither will I go; I will serve him with a sincere and loyal
heart!" "We believe thee worthy of our favour," replied
the Khalif; "thou wilt be overjoyed when thou findest that
we highly honour you above all Christians; thou wilt exult
at having conceived the idea of coming hither to seek protection in the shadow of our throne." When the Khalif
had thus spoken, Ordoño knelt once more, and, invoking
the blessing of heaven on the monarch, made petition in
these words: "Not long ago my cousin Sancho sought the
aid of the late Khalif against myself. His request was
granted; he obtained succour such as none but the greatest
of sovereigns can bestow. I, in my turn, plead for help;
but on widely different grounds. My cousin came hither
constrained by necessity; his subjects censured his conduct
and hated him; they chose me in his place, though I sought
not the honour—God is my witness! I dethroned him and

drove him from the realm. By dint of entreaties he procured from the late Khalif an army which reinstated him.
But he showed no gratitude for these benefits; he has fulfilled his obligations neither to his benefactor nor to thee, O
Commander of the Faithful and my lord. But as for me,
of my own free will I have quitted my kingdom, and I am
here to place at the disposal of the Commander of the
Faithful, my person, my soldiers, and my fortresses. Am I
not justified, therefore, in claiming that there is a wide
difference between my cousin and myself? I dare to add
that I have given proof that I excel him in confidence and
generosity." "We have heard thy statement," said the
Khalif, "and enter into thy feelings. Soon thou shalt see
how we requite thy goodwill. Thou shalt receive from us
bounties as great as those which thy rival received from our
father of happy memory, and although thine adversary was
the first to implore our protection, that is no reason why we
should esteem thee the less, or refuse thee that which we
previously granted him. We will send thee back to thy
country rejoicing; we will establish the foundations of thy
sovereignty, we will make thee ruler over those who acknowledge thee as their king; and we will give into thy keeping
a treaty, in which we will fix the respective bounds of thy
realm and that of thy cousin. Further, we will debar him
from raiding the territory which he must needs concede to
thee. In a word, the favours which thou wilt receive from
us will transcend thy highest hopes. God knoweth that we
speak from the heart!" When Hakam had made an end,
Ordoño once more fell upon his knees, with profuse thanks,
and on rising retired from the presence-chamber, walking
backwards. On reaching another hall, he told the eunuchs
who accompanied him that he had been dazzled to stupe-
faction by the majesty of the spectacle which he had beheld,
and observing a chair used by the Khalif, he once more
knelt before that piece of furniture. He was then conducted
to the *hâjib*, Ja'far. On seeing that dignitary he made him
a profound obeisance, and would have kissed his hand, had
Ja'far permitted it; but the Prime Minister, embracing him
and inviting him to sit by his side, assured him that he
might implicitly rely upon the Khalif's promises. He then
invested Ordoño with a robe of honour on the Khalif's
behalf. The king's companions were similarly complimented,
each according to his rank, and then, after saluting Ja'far
with the profoundest respect, they all returned to the porch,

where Ordoño found awaiting him a superb charger, richly caparisoned, from the Khalif's stables. The king threw himself into the saddle, and with a heart overflowing with hope, returned with his Leonese and the general Ibn Tomlos to the palace allotted to him. Not long afterwards he was handed a treaty to sign, by which he bound himself to live at peace with the Khalif, to surrender his son Garcia as a hostage, and not to form an alliance with Fernan Gonzalez. As soon as Ordoño had signed the document, Hakam put at his disposal an army under the command of Ghâlib; and, further, gave him as counsellors, Walîd[1]—judge of the Christians at Cordova, Asbagh ibn 'Abdallah ibn Nabîl— bishop[2] of that City, and 'Obaidallah[3] ibn Kâsim—Metropolitan of Toledo. To the care of these Garcia was to be entrusted, and they were enjoined to do their utmost to reconcile the Leonese to Ordoño as their sovereign.

All these preparations were sedulously noised abroad, with a view to intimidate Sancho. This end was attained. Sancho felt his position to be extremely precarious. Galicia stubbornly refused to acknowledge him, and it seemed clear that Ordoño, if he returned with a Moslem force, might reckon on support from that quarter. Even the other provinces, which had submitted to Sancho but did not love him, seemed likely to expel him for the second time rather than expose themselves to invasion. Sancho's mind was soon made up. In May he sent certain counts and bishops to Cordova to inform the Khalif, on his behalf, that he was prepared to carry out all the clauses of the treaty. Henceforth, Hakam, who had obtained all he wanted, never dreamed of fulfilling the promises he had made to Ordoño, with the result that that luckless pretender's grovelling acts of homage were all wasted. He does not seem to have long survived the destruction of his hopes; all that history further records of him is that he died at Cordova, and there is reason to believe that the event took place before the end of 962.

Ordoño's death dissipated all Sancho's fears. Reckoning on the support of his allies—the Count of Castile, the King of Navarre, and the Catalan Counts Borrel and Miron —he once more assumed an independent attitude, and disregarded his treaty obligations as heretofore.

---

[1] W. *ibn Moghith* (Ibn Khaldûn), or W. *ibn Khaizorân* (Makkarî).

[2] "The Catholico" (Ibn Khaldûn) : this title seems to have been given to the Bishop of Cordova, as it was to the Bishop of the Nestorians.

[3] Or, *'Abdallah* (Ibn Khaldûn).

Hakam therefore found himself reluctantly compelled to declare war against the Christians. He first turned his arms against Castile, taking San Estevan de Gormaz (A.D. 963), and forcing Fernan Gonzalez to sue for peace— a peace scarcely concluded before it was broken. Ghâlib then won the battle of Atienza. Yahyâ ibn Mohammed Todjîbî, Governor of Zaragoza, defeated Garcia, and that king further lost the important town of Calahorra, which Hakam surrounded with new fortifications—at the same time rebuilding the ruined fortress of Gormaz in Castile. In fact, although the Khalif was no lover of war, and waged it unwillingly, he nevertheless waged it so effectually that he forced his opponents to sue for peace. Sancho of Leon sought terms in 966. The Counts Borrel and Miron, who had suffered many reverses, followed his example, and undertook to dismantle such of their fortresses as were nearest to the Moslem frontiers. Garcia of Navarre also sent certain counts and bishops to Cordova, and a powerful Galician noble, Count Rodrigo Velasquez, sent his mother as an envoy, whom Hakam received with high honour and on whom he conferred costly gifts.

The peace which the Khalif had now made with nearly all his neighbours proved a lasting one. Hakam himself was a lover of peace, and the Christians were soon afterwards plunged into such hopeless anarchy that it was useless for them to dream of war against the Moslem. Whilst still engaged in negotiations with Hakam, Sancho had attacked Galicia, which had never submitted to him; and he had succeeded in subjugating the district to the north of the Douro, when Count Gonsalvo, who had massed a large force against him to the south of that river, asked for an interview with him. This took place, but the treacherous Gonsalvo caused poisonous fruit to be given to the king, who had no sooner tasted it than he felt his life ebbing. But though the poison acted upon his heart, it had not an immediately fatal effect. By gestures and broken words Sancho expressed a wish to be carried to Leon; but on the third day of his journey he died.[1]

His son Ramiro, third of the name, then only five years old, succeeded him, under the guardianship of his aunt Elvira, a nun of the convent of San Salvador of Leon; but the nobles would not submit to a woman and a child, and

---

[1] At the end of A.D. 966. Risco, *Hist. de Leon*, i. p. 212.

hastened to declare themselves independent. The state was accordingly parcelled out among a number of petty princes, and reduced to complete impotence. An army of eight thousand Danes who had served under Richard I of Normandy and whom that Duke had sent into Spain when he had no further need of them, ravaged Galicia with impunity for three years.[1] The Queen Regent Elvira dared not, therefore, contemplate a renewal of warfare with the Arabs.

Raids against Castile continued for some time, but in 970 the death of Fernan Gonzalez procured the Khalif peace from that quarter. Henceforth Hakam was able to indulge his literary tastes and develop the prosperity of his country.

Never had so learned a prince reigned in Spain, and although all his predecessors had been men of culture, who loved to enrich their libraries, none of them had sought so eagerly for rare and precious books. At Cairo, Baghdad, Damascus and Alexandria, Hakam had agents who copied, or bought for him—grudging no cost—ancient and modern manuscripts. With these treasures his palace overflowed; on all sides, too, were to be seen copyists, binders, and illuminators.

The catalogue of the Khalif's library occupied forty-four volumes, of which each comprised twenty sheets—or fifty according to some chroniclers—though they contained only the titles of the works. Some writers assert that the number of volumes amounted to four hundred thousand. All of these volumes Hakam had read, and most of them he had annotated. At the beginning or end of each book he wrote the name, surname, and patronymic of its author, his family and tribe, with the year of his birth and that of his death, and anecdotes relating to him. These notices were precious: no one was more learned in literary history than Hakam, and his annotations were always held authoritative by Andalusian scholars. Books composed in Persia and Syria were often known to him before they had been read by scholars in the East. Learning that an historian of ʿIrâk, Abu 'l-Faraj al-Isfahânî, was engaged on a history of Arab poets and minstrels,[2] he sent him a thousand dînârs,

---

[1] For an account of this invasion see *Recherches* (1881), pp. 294 *sq.*

[2] *Kitâb al-Aghânî*, "The Book of Songs" (this has been published). See C. Huart, *Arabic Literature* (1903), p. 184.

with a request that he would transmit to him a copy of his
work when completed.   Abu 'l-Faraj, full of gratitude,
hastened to comply with his wish.   Before publishing his
splendid anthology, still the admiration of the learned, he
sent the Khalif of Spain a careful copy, together with a
poem in his honour, and a work on the genealogy of the
Omayyads.   He was rewarded by another gift.   Hakam's
liberality to the learned, whether Spaniards or foreigners,
was indeed boundless, and they accordingly flocked to his
Court.   The monarch encouraged and protected them all—
even philosophers, who were at last enabled to devote
themselves to their studies without the fear of being
massacred by bigots.

All branches of learning flourished under so enlightened
a prince.   The primary schools were good and numerous.
In Andalusia nearly every one could read and write, while
in Christian Europe persons in most exalted positions—
unless they belonged to the clergy—remained illiterate.
Grammar and rhetoric were also taught in the schools.
Hakam, however, believed that instruction was not yet as
widely diffused as it ought to be, and in his tender solicitude for the poorer classes, he founded in the Capital
twenty-seven seminaries, in which children of poor parents
were educated gratuitously, the teachers being paid out of
the Khalif's privy purse.   The University of Cordova was
then one of the most renowned in the world.   In the
principal Mosque—for it was there that lectures were
delivered—Abû Bakr ibn Mu'âwiya the Kurashite treated
of the traditions relating to the Prophet.   Abû 'Alî al-Kâlî,
of Baghdad, there dictated a large and admirable compilation, containing an immense amount of curious information concerning the ancient Arabs, their proverbs,
their language, and their poetry.   This miscellany he afterwards published under the title of *Amâlî*, or " Dictations."
Grammar was taught by Ibn al-Kûtiyya, who in al-Kâlî's
opinion was the most erudite grammarian of Spain.   The
representatives of other sciences were no less renowned.
The students attending the lectures were accordingly to
be reckoned by thousands.   The majority of them were
students of what was known as *Fikh*—namely theology and
law—for that science was then the gateway to the most
lucrative posts.

In the bosom of this University was nurtured a man

whose fame was destined to fill not only Spain but the whole world, and whose marvellous career must now occupy our attention.

[AUTHORITIES: Makkarî, i. 136, 252–6; Samp., c. 26–8; Ibn Khaldûn, ff. 16–17, and *Prolégomènes;* Ibn Adhârî, ii. 250–7, 274, 396; *Meyá,* 15; *Chron. Iri.,* c. 10; Mon. Sil., c. 70; Ibn al-ʿAbbâr, 101–3; Saʿîd de Toledo, f. 246; Ibn Khallikân (transl.), i. 210–12.]

CHAPTER VI

IBN ABÎ ʿÂMIR

ONE day, early in the reign of Hakam II, five students supped together beneath the trees of a garden in the outskirts of Cordova. After the meal the boon-companions waxed merry over their dessert—all, that is, save one, who sat in silent thought. This young man was tall and well-favoured; his countenance revealed nobility, pride—perhaps arrogance; and his mien was that of a man born to command. At last, awaking from his reverie, he cried abruptly—" Mark my words; some day I shall be ruler of this country!" His comrades burst into laughter at this exclamation, but the speaker was not disconcerted: "Now, let each of you," continued he, "name the office he desires, and I will confer it upon him when I attain to power."

"Good!" cried one of the students, "these fritters are excellent; if it is all one to you, make me Inspector of Markets—and then I shall enjoy to my heart's content cates that cost me nothing!"

"As for me," said another, "I doat upon these figs from my native province. Appoint me Kady of Malaga."

Then quoth the third, "These delicious gardens are a great delight to me; I crave to be made Prefect of the city."

The fourth student, however, held his peace, taking umbrage at the overweening airs of his comrade. But the latter, with insistence, demanded of him his wish. The student thus urged sprang up, and twitching him by the beard, replied, "When thou governest Spain, sorry braggart that thou art, thou mayest order me to be smeared with honey, to attract bees and gad-flies, and then, seated on a jackass, with my face to the tail, to be led through the streets of Cordova!"

His fellow-student glanced fiercely at the speaker, but mastering his wrath with an effort, replied: "So be it! Each of you shall have his wish. The day will come when I shall call to mind all that each has said."

The repast ended, the company dispersed, and the student

who had indulged in such whimsical and grandiose conceits
betook himself to the house of one of his maternal relatives,
where he lodged. His host accompanied him to his little
chamber on the upper floor and tried to draw him into conversation ; but the young man, absorbed in thought, replied
only in monosyllables. Seeing that he could extract nothing
from him, his host bade him " good-night " and left the room.
Next morning, since the student did not appear at breakfast,
his kinsman mounted to the garret to arouse him, and observing with surprise that the couch had not been laid upon,
and that the youth was sitting upon a bench, his head sunk
upon his breast, exclaimed, " It would appear that you have
passed a sleepless night ! " " True ! " replied the student ;
" I have been kept awake by perplexing thoughts." " And
their subject ? " " I have been bethinking myself whom I
shall nominate as Kady when I govern Spain, and when the
present Kady is dead. I have mentally passed the whole
realm under review, and I have only found one man worthy
of the office." " And he, perchance, is Mohammed ibn as-
Sâlim ? " [1] " Marvellous ! that is the very man ! How
strangely we accord ! " It is clear that the student was
obsessed by a fixed idea—an idea which was his dream by
day, but at night deprived him of sleep.

Let us inquire into the lineage of this youth, who though
lost in the crowd that thronged the Capital, indulged in such
high hopes, and who, though without a friend at Court, was
convinced that one day he would become the chief Minister
of State.

His name was Abû 'Âmîr Mohammed. His family,
that of the Beni Abî 'Âmir, belonging to the Yemenite tribe
of Moafir, was noble, but not illustrious. His ancestor
'Abd al-Malik,[2] one of the few Arabs found in the Berber
army with which Târik invaded Spain, distinguished himself
in command of the division which captured Carteya, the first
Spanish town to fall into the hands of the Moslems.[3] As a
reward for his services the Castle of Torrox, situated on the
river Guadiaro in the province of Algeciras, was conferred
upon him, with its demesne. 'Abd al-Malik's descendants,
however, only resided on the estate at rare intervals. They

[1] Mohammed ibn-Ishâk ibn-as-Sâlim.
[2] From whom he was eighth in descent, as follows : 'Abd al-Malik—Yazid—
Al Walid—Abû 'Âmir Mohammed—'Âmir—'Abdallah—Mohammed (and the
daughter of the Vizier Yahyâ)—Abû Hafs 'Abdallah (and Boraiha)—Abû 'Âmir
Mohammed.
[3] See p. 231 above.

usually spent their youthful years in Cordova with a view
to obtaining a footing at Court, or a magisterial post.   Such,
for instance, was the course pursued by both Abû 'Âmir Mohammed ibn al-Walîd (great-grandson of 'Abd al-Malik),
and his son 'Âmîr.   The last named had held many posts,
and had been the favourite of the Sultan Mohammed, who
went so far as to inscribe his name on coins and standards.
Mohammed, our young student's grandfather, had been for
eight years Kady of Seville, and 'Abdallah, his father, was
a distinguished and very pious theologian and jurisconsult,
who had made pilgrimage to Mecca.   The family had
always aspired to honourable alliances, and not without
success : Abu 'Âmir's grandfather had married the daughter
of the renegade Yahyâ, son of Isaac the Christian, who, after
having been Court physician to 'Abd-er-Rahmân III, had
been appointed Vizier and Governor of Badajoz.   The
mother of Abû 'Âmir was Boraiha, daughter of the magistrate
Ibn Bartâl, of the tribe of Temîm.   Nevertheless, though
ancient and respectable, this family of the Beni Abî 'Âmir
did not rank among the higher aristocracy ; they belonged
to the nobility of the gown, if the phrase is permissible, and
not of the sword.   No 'Âmirid—'Abd al-Malik the follower
of Târik excepted—had followed the career of arms, then
that of the highest dignity : all had been either magistrates
or court officials.   Mohammed himself had been destined
for the judicature, and the day arrived when he bade farewell to the crumbling turrets of his ancestral home to
become a student in the Capital, where he attended the
lectures of the celebrated scholars, already mentioned,
who then graced the University.   He was a young man
of mettle and keen intelligence, by nature enthusiastic, endowed with a soaring imagination and a fiery temper, the
slave withal of a single passion, irresistible in its strength.
The books of his choice were the ancient chronicles of his
nation, and what chiefly fascinated him in their musty pages
were the adventures of men who, though starting from a
much lower station than his own, had reached step by step
the highest dignities of the State.   Such men he took for his
models, and as he by no means kept his ambitious thoughts
to himself, his comrades were sometimes inclined to look
upon him as something of a crackbrain.   But he was far
otherwise.   It is true that one idea seemed to absorb all his
faculties : but this was due to no mental aberration, but to
the prescience of genius.   Endowed with brilliant talents

—resourceful, resolute, and daring if need be, but pliant, cautious, and crafty when circumstances demanded—far from scrupulous, moreover, as to the means to be employed in the attainment of his high ambition—he could, without presumption, aspire to all. He possessed to an unequalled degree, energy, and the power of an unswerving pursuit of a fixed idea: the goal once marked, his will became alert, inflexible, and directed to that single object. He made but a humble start in life. When he had completed his studies, he was driven to support himself by opening an office hard by the palace gateway, where he put into writing the requests of those who desired to make petition to the Khalif. Later on he obtained a subordinate post in the tribunal of Cordova, but he was unable to find his way into the good graces of his chief, the Kady. The holder of that office was then the very Ibn as-Sâlim whom Mohammed esteemed so highly—not, indeed, without reason, for he was a learned and upright man, and one of the best Kadies that Cordova had ever had : [1] he was, however, of a cold and matter-of-fact temperament, and had an innate antipathy to persons of a character unlike his own. His young subordinate's unconventional ideas, and habitual absent-mindedness, displeased the Kady greatly; he wished for nothing better than to be quit of him, and by a singular chance it was the magistrate's aversion which procured for Mohammed that which he longed for most—a place at Court. The Kady complained of his assistant to the Vizier Mus-hafy, and asked him to procure for the young man some other employment. Mus-hafy replied that he would bear the matter in mind, and not long afterwards, when Hakam II was casting about for a steward competent to manage the property of his eldest son 'Abd-er-Rahmân, then five years old, Mohammed ibn Abî 'Âmir was recommended for the post by the Vizier. The appointment to the stewardship did not, however, rest solely with the Khalif; it rested, indeed, mainly with his favourite Sultana, Aurora,[2] a Basque by birth, who had an immense influence over her lord. Several candidates were presented to her, among them Ibn Abî 'Âmir, who charmed her by his distinguished appearance and polished courtesy. He was preferred to his rivals, and on Saturday, February 23, 967, he was appointed steward of 'Abd-er-Rahmân's property,

---

[1] He was appointed Kady of Cordova in Dec. 966, in succession to Mundhir ibn-Sa'îd Bollûtî, decd. (*Khoshanî*, p. 352).

[2] In Arabic, less euphoniously, *Sobh* (the dawn).

with a monthly salary of fifteen pieces of gold. He was then twenty-six years of age. Mohammed spared no pains to ingratiate himself still further with Aurora, and so well did he succeed that she appointed him steward of her personal property, and seven months after gaining a footing at Court he was made Master of the Mint.[1] Thanks to this last office considerable sums of money were always at his command, and he profited by the fact to make friends for himself among the great. Whenever one of the nobles found himself at the end of his resources—a condition to which their style of living often reduced them—he found Mohammed ready to come to the rescue. The story runs, for instance, that Mohammed ibn Aflah, a client of the Khalif's and a court functionary, when deeply in debt by reason of his lavish expenditure on the occasion of his daughter's marriage, brought a bridle adorned with jewels to the Mint, and asked Ibn Abî 'Âmir to advance him some money on the security of this article: it was, he added, the only valuable possession left to him. Scarcely had Ibn Aflah finished speaking before the Master of the Mint ordered an assistant to weigh the piece of harness and to give him its weight in silver pieces. Astounded by such generosity—for the leather and iron-work of the bridle were very heavy—Ibn Aflah could hardly believe his ears, but he was convinced that they had not deceived him when, a few moments later, he was desired to hold up his cloak to catch a very torrent of silver pieces, sufficient not only to pay his debts, but to leave him a considerable balance. After this he was wont to say: " I love Ibn Abî 'Âmir with all my soul, and if he were to bid me rebel against my sovereign, I should not hesitate to obey him."

By such means as these Ibn Abî 'Âmir built up a party devoted to his interests, but he deemed it his first duty to satisfy every caprice of the Sultana and to load her with gifts such as she had never before received. His devices were often highly ingenious. Once, for example, he had the silver model of a palace made, at a great cost, and when the splendid toy was completed, he caused it to be borne by slaves to the Khalif's palace—to the great marvel of the towns-folk, who had never before seen such a magnificent piece of silversmith's work. Aurora was never weary of admiring this costly gift, and henceforth lost no opportunity

[1] His name appears on coins of the period.

of singing the praises of her protégé and advancing his fortunes. The intimacy between them grew, indeed, so close that it provided food for scandal. Ibn Abî 'Âmir, however, did not neglect the other inmates of the harem. They were enraptured by his liberality, the suavity of his speech, and his incomparable distinction of manner. The old Khalif could not understand the situation : " I cannot conceive," he said one day to an intimate friend, "how this young man contrives to gain the hearts of the ladies of my harem. I lavish on them everything they can desire, and yet no gift that does not come from him is to their liking. I scarcely know whether to regard him as an extremely clever servant, or as a potent magician. But I am never quite easy in my mind about the public money which passes through his hands."

Certainly the young Master of the Mint ran great risks in the direction hinted of by Hakam. He had been very generous to his friends, but it was at the expense of the Treasury, and since his rapid rise had naturally aroused envy, his enemies at length accused him before the Khalif of malversation. He was summoned to appear at the palace without delay in order to render his accounts and deposit the money for which he was answerable. He promised to come, but hastening to his friend the Vizier Ibn Hodair, and frankly explaining to him his awkward and indeed dangerous plight, he begged him to advance the money necessary to make up the deficit. Ibn Hodair instantly handed him the sum required. Forthwith Ibn Abî 'Âmir betook himself to the Khalif, and producing his accounts as well as the money for which they proved him responsible, put his accusers to confusion. In their eagerness to disgrace him, they had, in fact, paved the way to his complete triumph. The Khalif treated them as calumniators, and lavished praises on his able and upright Master of the Mint. The latter was loaded with new dignities. Early in December, 968, Hakam conferred on him the post of trustee of vacant estates, and eleven months later that of Kady of Seville and Niebla. Upon the death of the young 'Abd-er-Rahmân, he was appointed steward to Hishâm, who became heir-presumptive to the throne (July, 970). Nor was this all : in February, 972, Ibn Abî 'Âmir was made commander of the second regiment of the body-guard, whose duty it was to act as the city police. At the age of thirty-one, therefore, he found himself installed in five or six important and lucrative posts.

He henceforth lived in an appropriate style of almost princely luxury. The palace which he built at Rosâfa was of un-exampled splendour. There he kept open house : an army of secretaries and assistants selected from the highest ranks of society thronged its halls: the doorway was ever besieged with suitors. Ibn Abî 'Âmir, moreover, missed no opportunity of courting popularity, and with complete success. Praises of his kindness, his courtesy, his liberality, his noble char-acter, were on all men's lips ; there were not two opinions on the subject.

But although the student of Torrox had attained to high estate, he would fain mount yet higher, and with this end in view, he held it above all things necessary to make friends among the generals. Affairs in Mauritania gave him the desired opportunity.

The war in this country between the partisans of the Omayyads and those of the Fâtimids had never ceased, but its character had changed. 'Abd-er-Rahmân III had warred with the Fâtimids in order to preserve his country from foreign invasion. But at the epoch of which we now speak that danger no longer threatened. The Fâtimids had turned their arms against Egypt. In 969 they had conquered that country, and three years later their Khalif Mu'izz had quitted Mansûria, the capital of the empire, to take up his residence on the banks of the Nile, after having appointed the Kinhe-jite prince, Abu 'l-Futûh Yûsuf ibn Zîrî, Viceroy of Ifrikia and Mauritania.

Henceforth Spain had nothing to fear from the claimants of descent from 'Alî, and since his African possessions cost him much more than they yielded, Hakam would perhaps have done well to abandon them. The Khalif deemed, how-ever, that such a course would be a stain upon his honour, and instead of relinquishing these domains, he on the contrary tried to extend their borders, and with this object entered upon a war of conquest against the Edrisid princes, who held the country on behalf of the Fâtimids.

Hasan ibn Kennûn, who reigned over Tangier, Arzilla, and other places on the coast, was one of their number. He alternately declared himself on the side of the Omayyads and of the Fâtimids as one or other gained the upper hand ; but he had a leaning towards the latter, who seemed to him less dangerous than the Omayyads, whose possessions marched with his own. He was the first to declare for Abu 'l-Futûh when that viceroy entered Mauritania as a conqueror. Hakam owed Ibn Kennûn a grudge for this defection, and after Abu 'l-Futûh's departure, he ordered his general Ibn Tomlos[1] to undertake a punitive expedition against him and bring him to his knees. At the beginning of August, 972, Ibn Tomlos embarked with a large force, and having been joined by a great part of the garrison of Ceuta he marched against Tangier. Ibn Kennûn, who commanded there, sallied forth to meet him, but suffered so complete a defeat that he could not even withdraw into the city. Left to itself, Tangier was soon obliged to surrender to the Omayyad admiral, who blockaded the port, while the land forces seized Delûl and Arzilla.

Thus far the Omayyad forces had been victorious, but their good fortune was not persistent. Summoning fresh levies to his standard, Ibn Kennûn resumed the offensive and marched against Tangier. Ibn Tomlos, who came to meet him, was defeated and found death upon the battle-field. Thereupon all the Edrisid princes raised the standard of revolt, and Hakam's officers, who had retreated to Tangier, sent him word that if reinforcements were not despatched without delay, the Omayyad dominion in Mauritania would be at an end. Realizing the gravity of the danger, Hakam immediately determined to send the flower of his army to Africa, under his best general, the gallant Ghâlib. Summoning him to Cordova, he ordered him to set out forthwith, and added, "Take heed that thou returnest as a victor; know that thou canst only atone for a defeat by dying on the battlefield. Spare no money; scatter it lavishly among the adherents of the rebels; dethrone all the Edrisids, and send them prisoners to Spain."

Ghâlib crossed the Straits with a force of picked Spanish troops. He landed at Kasr-Masmûda, between Ceuta and Tangier, and immediately advanced. Ibn Kennûn tried to check him: no pitched battle, however, took place, but a series of skirmishes which lasted for several days, during which Ghâlib took measures to bribe the leaders of the enemy's army. He succeeded. Seduced by the gold offered to them, and by the splendid garments and swords set with jewels which dazzled their eyes, almost all Ibn Kennûn's officers deserted to the Omayyad standard. The Edrisids had no alternative to throwing themselves into a fortress situated on a mountain ridge not far from Ceuta, bearing

---

[1] Mohammed ibn Kâsim ibn Tomlos.

the appropriate name of " The Eagles' Rock." [1]　The Khalif
received with joy the tidings of this first success ; but when
he learnt how much money Ghâlib had expended in bribing
the Berber chiefs he realized that the general had taken
somewhat too literally the advice he had given him.　In
fact, whether the treasure of the State had been squandered
in Mauritania, or stolen, the expenses with which the Khalif
was saddled passed all measure.　With a view to putting
an end to this prodigality, or peculation, Hakam determined
to send into Africa, as Comptroller-General of Finance,
some man of tried integrity.　His choice fell upon Ibn
Abî 'Âmir, whom he appointed Chief Justice [2] of Mauritania,
with instructions to keep a watch over the doings of all
the generals, and especially over their financial operations.
At the same time he sent orders to his officers, both civil
and military, to undertake no measures without previously
consulting Ibn Abî 'Âmir and ascertaining that he approved
of their plans.

For the first time in his life, Ibn Abî 'Âmir found himself in touch with the army and its leaders ; but he would
doubtless have preferred this to have taken place in
different circumstances and under other conditions.　The
task which confronted him was one of extreme difficulty.
Self-interest urged him to ingratiate himself with the
generals, and yet he found himself sent into the field to
exercise over them a control which could not fail to be more
or less unwelcome.　Thanks, however, to the marvellous
tact of which he alone knew the secret, he was able so
to conduct matters as to reconcile his interests and his
duty.

He executed his mission to the entire satisfaction of the
Khalif, and at the same time controlled the officers with
such discretion that far from bearing him a grudge as might
have been feared, they never wearied of singing his praises.
Neither did he neglect to cultivate friendships with the
African princes and the chiefs of the Berber tribes, friendships which afterwards proved of great value to him.　He
initiated himself in camp life, and gained the affection of the
rank and file : a secret instinct perhaps told them that in
this Kady there was the making of a soldier.

Ghâlib, having brought all the other Edrisids into
subjection, next proceeded to besiege Ibn Kennûn in his

---

[1] Ar. *hadjar an-nasr.*　　　　　　　　[2] Ar. *Qâdî'l-Qudât.*

2 G

eyry, and since this fortress was, if not impregnable, at all
events very difficult to storm, the Khalif sent fresh troops
into Mauritania, drawn from the garrisons which protected
the northern frontiers of his empire and commanded by
the Vizier Yahyâ ibn Mohammed Todjîbî, Viceroy of the
Northern Marches. These reinforcements arrived in October,
973, and the siege was thereupon carried on so vigorously
that Ibn Kennûn was forced to capitulate (towards the end
of February, 974). The terms he asked for and obtained
were that the lives of his soldiers, his family, and himself
should be spared, and that they should not be deprived of
their property; but he had to surrender his fortress and
betake himself to Cordova.

Mauritania having been thus pacified, Ghâlib once more
crossed the Straits, accompanied by all the Edrisid princes.
The Khalif and the notables of Cordova came out to meet
the victor, and Ghâlib's triumphal entry was one of the
most splendid that the capital of the Omayyads had ever
witnessed (September 21, 974). The Khalif showed great
generosity towards the vanquished, and especially towards
Ibn Kennûn. He loaded him with gifts of every kind, and
since his men, seven hundred in number, were renowned for
their valour, he took them into his service, and enrolled
them in the ranks of his army.

Ghâlib's entry into Cordova marked the last red-letter
day in Hakam's life. Not long afterwards, towards
December, he experienced a serious attack of apoplexy.
Feeling that his end was at hand, he gave himself up to
good works. He enfranchised a hundred of his slaves,
reduced by one-sixth the royal taxes throughout the Spanish
provinces of the empire, and ordained that the rents of the
saddlers' shops in Cordova, which belonged to him personally, should be devoted, in perpetuity, to the payment of
teachers entrusted with the instruction of poor children.
Affairs of State, with which he could but rarely concern
himself, he left to the management of the Vizier Mus-hafy,
and it soon became manifest that another hand was at the
helm. More thrifty than his master, Mus-hafy came to the
conclusion that the administration of the African provinces
and the maintenance of the Edrisid princes cost the State
too much. Accordingly, having made the princes enter
into an engagement not to return to Mauritania, he sent
them to Tunis, whence they proceeded to Alexandria;
then, recalling from Africa the Vizier Yahyâ ibn Mohammed

Todjîbî, who since Ghâlib's departure had been viceroy of
the African possessions, he entrusted the latter to two
native princes, Ja'far and Yahyâ, sons of 'Alî ibn Hamdûn.
This last measure was dictated to Mus-hafy not merely by
a wise economy, but by the fear with which the Christians
of the North had inspired him.　Emboldened by the
Khalif's illness, and by the absence of his best troops, the
Christians had recommenced hostilities in the Spring of 975,
and, with the aid of Abu 'l-Ahwas Man, of the family of
the Todjîbites of Zaragoza,[1] they had besieged several
Musulman fortresses.　Mus-hafy justly considered that in
these circumstances his first care should be the defence
of the country, and as soon as the gallant Yahyâ ibn
Mohammed had returned, he sent him to resume his post
as Viceroy of the Northern Marches.

The Khalif during the remaining months of his life
devoted his thoughts exclusively to the best means of securing the throne to his son, who was yet an infant.　Before
his accession to the throne Hakam had not seen his fondest
wish realized—that of being a father—and at a somewhat
advanced age he had despaired of the event, when in the
year 962 Aurora had presented him with a son who received
the name of 'Abd-er-Rahmân.　Three years later another son,
Hishâm, was born.　The Khalif was overjoyed at the birth
of these two children, and from this period dates the almost
limitless influence which Aurora exercised over her husband.
But the parents' joy was soon dashed ; at an early age the
elder son, the hope of their declining years, died.　Hishâm
alone survived, and the Khalif anxiously debated within
himself whether his subjects, instead of recognising the
child as their sovereign, would not be more likely to confer
the crown upon one of his uncles.　This uncertainty was
quite natural.　Hitherto no monarch had occupied the
throne of Cordova during his minority, and a regency was
extremely repugnant to Arab notions.　Hakam, however,
would not for the world have yielded the succession to any
other than his son ; moreover, had not an early prophecy
predicted that the sceptre would depart from the Omayyad
dynasty if ever the succession should diverge from the
direct line ?

To secure the throne to his son, the Khalif considered
that the most effectual means would be to cause allegiance

---

[1] See *Recherches* (1881), pp. 211 *sq.*

to him to be sworn as soon as possible. For this purpose
he convoked a solemn session of the notables of the realm.
On the day appointed[1] he announced his intentions to the
assembly, and invited all the members to sign an instrument
declaring Hishâm heir to the crown. None dared to withhold his signature, and the Khalif further ordered Ibn Abî
'Âmir, and Maisûr, the Secretary of State (one of Aurora's
freedmen),[2] to cause a number of copies of the document
to be made and distributed throughout the Spanish and
African provinces, with an invitation not only to the
notables but to the people at large to append their signatures
thereto. This order was immediately complied with, and
since awe of the Khalif precluded disobedience, signatures
were everywhere forthcoming. Henceforth Hishâm's name
was inserted in the public prayers, and Hakam died (October
1, 976),[3] in the firm conviction that his son would succeed
him, and that if need be, Mus-hafy, with Ibn Abî 'Âmir
whom he had appointed Chamberlain, would know how to
make the Andalusians keep the oath which they had taken.

[1] Feb. 5, 976.
[2] Ibn Adhârî calls him *al-Ja'fari*. Ja'far was a nickname given by Hakam to
Aurora; hence her freedmen bore the name of Ja'fari. (The Khalifs were fond
of designating the ladies of the harem by masculine names.)
[3] Ibn Adhârî (ii. 269) has *Ramadân* in error for *Safar*.

[AUTHORITIES: Ibn Adhârî, ii. pp. 249, 251–3, 260–70, 273–6; Ibn al-
    Khatîb (MS. G.), f. 117; 'Abd al-Wâhid, pp. 17–19, 26; Makkarî,
    i. 252, 259, 904; ii. 59, 61; Ibn Abî Usaibi'a; Ibn al-'Abbâr, pp.
    148, 152; *Kartâs*, pp. 56–8; Ibn Khaldûn, *Hist. des Berbers*, ii. 149–
    152; iii. 215–16 (transl.); Ibn 'Abd al-Malik Marrakushi (Paris MS.),
    682 suppl. ar., f. 1017.]

CHAPTER VII

ACCESSION OF HISHÂM II

HAKAM breathed his last in the arms of his two chief eunuchs, Fâyik and Jaudhar. They alone knew that the end had come, and they resolved not to announce his death until they had determined on the line of action most advantageous to themselves.

Although slaves, these two eunuchs—one of whom held the office of Keeper of the Wardrobe and the other that of Grand Falconer—were exalted personages, and possessed no trifling power. They had in their pay, and at their beck and call, a large number of armed attendants who were neither eunuchs nor slaves. Besides these, they had under their orders a body of a thousand Slav eunuchs, who, though slaves of the Khalif, were men of substance, owning mansions and broad domains. The members of this corps, which was looked upon as the chief ornament of the Court, enjoyed unbounded privileges. They victimised and maltreated the Cordovans in a thousand ways, and the Khalif, despite his love of justice, had always shut his eyes to their misdoings and even to their crimes. To any who drew his attention to the acts of violence committed by the Slavs he had one unvarying reply : " These men are the guardians of my harem ; they possess my full confidence, and I cannot be for ever reprimanding them ; but I feel convinced that if my subjects will treat them with the courtesy and respect which is their right, they will find no cause for complaint." Thus unduly pampered, these Slavs grew vain and arrogant. They came to regard themselves as the most influential body in the State, and their leaders, Fâyik and Jaudhar, really imagined that the choice of a new Khalif rested with themselves alone. Neither of them had relished the idea of Hishâm's succession. If he ascended the throne during his minority, the minister Mus-hafy, between whom and themselves no love was lost, would be the actual ruler, and their influence would decline. The nation had, it is true, already sworn allegiance to Hishâm ; but the two eunuchs appraised a political oath at its real value, and were well aware that the majority of those who had taken it had done so reluctantly: they were equally well aware that public opinion was averse to a regency, and that the people would ill brook a temporal and spiritual ruler who had not yet attained his twelfth year. On the other hand, they hoped easily to repair their gravely damaged popularity, if, in response to a general demand, they conferred the crown on a prince of maturer age. To these considerations there was to be added another, namely, that such a prince would be under deep obligations to those to whom he owed his accession, and that therefore they might look forward to governing in his name. The eunuchs therefore speedily resolved to set Hishâm aside, and further agreed to offer the throne to his uncle Mughîra, then twenty-seven years old, on the condition, however, that he would nominate his nephew as his successor—for they were unwilling to appear ready to disregard wholly their late master's wishes.

"And now that our plan of action is resolved upon," said Jaudhar, "let us straightway summon Mus-hafy to our presence, behead him, and then proceed to carry out our project." But Fâyik, who was less far-sighted, but more humane, than his colleague, shuddered at the idea of murder. "Wouldst thou, my brother, slay our master's Minister," he cried, "though he hath done nothing worthy of death? Let us not begin by shedding innocent blood! In my opinion Mus-hafy is not to be feared, and will not hinder our designs." Jaudhar did not share this belief, but since Fâyik was his official superior, he was constrained to yield the point. The two eunuchs thereupon decided to win over Mus-hafy by soft words, and summoned him to the palace. On his arrival they informed him of the Khalif's death, and having unfolded their scheme, requested his co-operation. The eunuchs' design was altogether hateful to the Minister, but knowing the men, and what they were capable of, he feigned approval. "Your project," said he, "is certainly the wisest possible. Proceed with it, and my friends and I will help you to the extent of our power. You will do well, however, to secure the assent of the chief men of the realm: this will be the best means of preventing a revolt. As for me, my duty is plain: I will guard the gateway of the palace, and await your orders."

Having thus succeeded in inspiring the eunuchs with a false sense of security, Mus-hafy called some of his friends

together, including his nephew Hishâm, Ibn Abî 'Âmir,
Ziyâd ibn Aflah (a client of Hakam II), Kâsim ibn
Mohammed (son of the general Ibn Tomlos who had been
slain in Africa while fighting against Ibn Kennûn), and
other persons of influence. He summoned also the captains
of the Spanish troops, and the officers of the African regiment on which he felt most reliance—that of the Beni
Birzel. Having mustered all his partisans, he informed them
of the Khalif's death and of the eunuchs' scheme, and then
went on to say: "If Hishâm ascends the throne we shall
have naught to fear and we can act as we will; but if
Mughîra supplants him we shall lose our offices, and perhaps
our lives, for that prince hates us."

The whole assembly were of his mind, and further resolved to frustrate the eunuchs' project by putting Mughîra
to death before he learned his brother's decease. Mus-hafy
acquiesced in this design; but when he proceeded to inquire
who was prepared to carry it out, he met with no response.
No one seemed willing to dishonour himself by such a deed.

Ibn Abî 'Âmir thereupon addressed the assemblage:
"Failure in our policy," said he, "is not to be thought of.
We are determined to support our leader: his orders must
be obeyed; and since none of you appears willing to carry
the matter through, I myself will undertake it, with our
chief's permission. Have no fear, but put your trust in me."
These words excited general surprise. It was not expected
that a civilian official would take upon himself an assassination which warriors familiar with bloodshed shrank from.
His offer was, however, eagerly accepted; it was moreover
agreed on all hands that Ibn Abî 'Âmir was the very man
to give effect to the policy determined on! Had he not
the honour of being admitted to the intimacy of the Khalif
Hishâm and of enjoying the esteem of many other members
of the royal family? Who, then, could be better fitted for
carrying out so delicate a task?

Ibn Abî 'Âmir forthwith mounted his horse, and,
accompanied by the General Bedr,[1] a body-guard of a
hundred men, and some Spanish squadrons, he proceeded to
Mughîra's palace. Upon reaching it he posted the body-
guard at the gateway, formed a cordon round the palace
with the other troops, and entering unattended the apartments of the prince, informed him that the Khalif was no

---

[1] A client of 'Abd-er-Rahmân III.

more and that Hishâm had succeeded him. "Nevertheless," he added, "the Viziers fear that the latter circumstance may not meet with your approval, and they have
sent me to inquire your feelings on the matter."

The prince turned pale at these words. He knew their
import only too well, and seeing the sword hanging over
his head, he replied in a trembling voice: "Words fail me
to tell thee how much my brother's death grieveth me, but
I rejoice to hear that my nephew hath succeeded him.
May his reign be long and prosperous! Be so good as to
inform those who sent thee that I will obey them in all
things, and that I shall keep the oath of allegiance to
Hishâm which I have already taken. Exact from me what
pledges thou wilt; but, if thou hast come for another
purpose, I entreat thee to have pity on me. Ah! I conjure
thee by the Eternal to weigh well thy intentions and to
spare my life!"

Ibn Abî 'Âmir was stirred with compassion for the
young prince, and, won over by his candour, believed in
the sincerity of his protestations. He had not blenched at
the idea of murder when he deemed it essential for the
welfare of the State and his own self-interest, but he had no
desire to imbrue his hands in the blood of a man from whom
he believed nothing was to be feared. He accordingly
despatched a note to Mus-hafy to the effect that the prince
was unfeignedly well-disposed, and need cause no misgivings, and on these grounds he asked to be authorized to
spare Mughîra's life. The soldier whom he sent with this
missive to Mus-hafy soon brought the reply. It ended
with these words: "Your scruples will ruin all, and I
begin to suspect you are playing us false. Do your duty,
or we put another in your place."

Ibn Abî 'Âmir showed this letter to the prince, whose
sentence of death it was; then, unwilling to be witness of
the dreadful deed about to be done, he quitted the room
and bade the soldiers enter it. They knew full well what
was expected of them. Having strangled their victim they
hung his body in an adjoining chamber, and informed the
domestics that Mughîra had hanged himself upon their
insisting on his rendering homage to his nephew. Soon
afterwards they received orders from Ibn Abî 'Âmir to
bury the corpse in the hall and to wall up the doorways.

His task accomplished, Ibn Abî 'Âmir returned to the
Minister and informed him that his orders had been carried

out. Mus-hafy thanked him warmly, and in evidence of his
gratitude bade him sit by his side.

Fâyik and Jaudhar speedily discovered that Mus-hafy had
over-reached them and had baffled their scheme. Both of
them were enraged, but especially Jaudhar. "Now you
will admit," cried he to his colleague, "that I was right
when I urged that the removal of Mus-hafy should have
been our first step—but you would not heed me." They
were, however, constrained to put a good face on the matter,
and, seeking an audience with the Minister, made their
excuses, admitting that their hasty proposal was injudicious,
and that his own policy was far preferable. Mus-hafy,
although he hated the eunuchs with a hatred which was
fully reciprocated, did not see his way to punishing them at
the moment; he therefore ostensibly accepted their apology
and, to all appearance, peace was restored.

On the following morning,[1] the inhabitants of Cordova
were summoned by proclamation to present themselves at
the palace. Upon their arrival they found the young prince
already in the throne-room. Near him stood Mus-hafy,
with Fâyik and Jaudhar on either hand. The other
dignitaries were also in attendance. The Kady Ibn as-
Sâlim administered the oath, first to the uncles and cousins
of the monarch, and then to the Viziers, the court officials,
the chief Kurashites and the notables of the city. When
this had been done Ibn Abî 'Âmir was intrusted with the
administration of the oath to the rest of the assembly.
This was no easy task, for some present were recalcitrant.
Thanks, however, to his eloquence and persuasive power,
Ibn Abî 'Âmir met with such success that not more than
two or three persons persisted in their refusal. Everyone
had a word of praise for the tact and ability displayed on
this occasion by the Master of the Mint.

Thus far all had gone smoothly for Mus-hafy and his
adherents, and the horizon seemed cloudless. The populace,
to judge by their calm and submissive attitude, had become
reconciled to the idea of a regency, though lately it had
inspired them with aversion and dismay. But appearances
were deceitful; fires yet smouldered beneath the ashen
crust. In privacy curses were invoked on the greedy and
ambitious magnates who had seized the supremacy and had
inaugurated their reign by the murder of the luckless

---

[1] Monday, Oct. 2.

Mughîra. The eunuchs took care to foment disaffection
among the inhabitants of Cordova, and before long the
spirit of discontent became so strong that at any moment
it might flame into revolt. Ibn Abî 'Âmir, who was under
no illusion with regard to popular sentiment, advised Mus-
hafy to over-awe the crowd by a display of military force,
to arouse their deep-seated loyalty by showing them their
youthful Khalif, and to conciliate them by the abolition of
some impost. The Minister approved of these measures,
and it was decided that the young Khalif should be presented
to the people on Saturday, October 7. On the morning of
that day, Mus-hafy, who hitherto had borne only the title
of Vizier, was promoted—or rather, promoted himself—to
the office of *Hâjib*, or Prime Minister, while Ibn Abî 'Âmir,
by the expressed wish of Aurora, was advanced to the
dignity of Vizier, and entrusted with the government of the
State jointly with Mus-hafy. Hishâm II then rode on
horseback through the streets of the Capital, escorted by a
large body of troops and accompanied by Ibn Abî 'Âmir.
At the same time a decree was promulgated abolishing the
duty on oil, one of the most odious of the taxes, because
pressing most heavily on the lower classes. These measures,
especially the last, produced the predicted effect, and since
Ibn Abî 'Âmir had been careful to noise it abroad, through
his friends, that it was he who had suggested the abolition
of the oil-tax, the humbler townsfolk, amongst whom riots
generally originated, acclaimed him the true friend of the
poor.

The eunuchs nevertheless continued to hatch conspiracies,
and Mus-hafy was informed by his spies that persons strongly
suspected of acting as intermediaries between the eunuchs
and their friends outside the palace were forever passing
and repassing through the Iron Gate. To facilitate vigilance the Prime Minister caused this portal to be walled up,
so that the only entrance to the palace was by way of the
Sodda Gate. He further adjured Ibn Abî 'Âmir to use his
best endeavours to entice from their allegiance to Fâyik and
Jaudhar those of their armed attendants who were neither
eunuchs nor slaves. This Ibn Abî 'Âmir undertook to do,
and thanks to bribes and promises he succeeded so well that
five hundred men quitted the service of the two eunuchs for
his own. Since he could in addition reckon on the support
of the African regiment of the Beni Birzel, his forces were
now far superior to those of his opponents. Jaudhar was

well aware of this, and in high dudgeon at the turn matters
had taken, he tendered his resignation as Grand Falconer
and sought permission to quit the Khalif's palace. This
step was, however, merely a ruse. In the belief that his
services were indispensable, he felt sure that his request
would be refused, and that he would then have the opportunity of dictating to his adversaries the terms on which he
would retain his office. But his hopes were dashed: his
resignation was accepted. Jaudhar's adherents were greatly
exasperated, and launched out into threats and invectives
against Mus-hafy and Ibn Abî 'Âmir. One of their chief
men, Dorrî, the sub-chamberlain, made himself conspicuous
by the violence of his language. Mus-hafy accordingly
urged Ibn Abî 'Âmir to find some means of getting rid of
this man. The means lay ready at hand. Dorrî was lord
of Baeza, and the inhabitants of that district had suffered
much through the tyranny and greed of their master's
agents. Ibn Abî 'Âmir seized his opportunity. He
privately assured the people of Baeza that if they wished to
lodge a complaint against their lord and his deputies they
might feel confident that the Government would decide in
their favour. They took the hint, and Dorrî was summoned,
under an order from the Khalif, to appear at the Vizier's
palace in order to be brought to account before his subjects.
He obeyed, but on reaching the palace and finding himself
confronted by a strong military force, he feared for his life,
and would fain have retraced his steps. Ibn Abî 'Âmir,
thereupon, seizing him by the throat, detained him. In the
scuffle which ensued Dorrî clutched his adversary by the
beard. Ibn Abî 'Âmir instantly called the soldiers to his
assistance. The Spanish troops did not stir: they held the
lord of Baeza too much in awe to lay hands upon him. But
the Beni Birzel had no such scruples: they rushed forward,
seized Dorrî, and began to maltreat him. A blow from the
flat of a sword laid him senseless on the ground. He was
carried to his residence, where during the night he was
despatched.

Conscious that by this murder they had declared war
against the Slavs, the two ministers instantly took decisive
measures. Fâyik and his friends received an order from
the Khalif to quit the palace without delay: they were
then indicted upon a charge of malversation, and mulcted
in heavy penalties, which by impoverishing them effectually
prevented them from henceforth injuring the ministers.

Fâyik, who was deemed the most dangerous man among them, was treated with still greater rigour, being banished to one of the Balearic islands, where he eventually died. The eunuchs who were less deeply implicated were retained in their posts, and one of them, Sokr, was appointed Chamberlain and Captain of the Body-guard. These measures, although suggested to the duumvirs by self-interest, nevertheless made for their popularity. The hatred felt by the Cordovans towards the Slavs, at whose hands they had suffered so much, was intense; not less their joy at the ruin of their persecutors.

On the other hand the Government caused grave disquietude by their inaction against the Christians of the North. The latter, who, as we have seen, renewed hostilities as soon as Hakam II fell sick, grew bolder and bolder, and pushed their daring forays to the very gates of Cordova. Mus-hafy lacked neither money nor men wherewith to repel them, but he was wholly ignorant of war and took no efficient steps to defend the country. The Sultana Aurora naturally felt alarm at the advance of the Christians and the consequent disquietude of the Andalusians. She confided her fears to Ibn Abî 'Âmir, who had long been indignant at the feebleness and incapacity of his colleague, and he reassured the Sultana by declaring that if he were granted adequate supplies and given the command of the army he would guarantee the defeat of the enemy.

The upshot of this conference was that Ibn Abî 'Âmir candidly pointed out to his colleague that if he persisted in inaction power would soon slip from his grasp, and that it was not only his duty but his interest to take energetic steps without delay. Mus-hafy, recognising the force of this advice, assembled his Viziers and proposed the despatch of an expedition against the Christians. This proposal was approved, though not unanimously; the assembly, indeed, showed itself mainly concerned about the command of the army; for the responsibility seemed to them so great that not one of the Viziers was desirous of taking it upon himself. " I will undertake to lead the troops," said Ibn Abî 'Âmir at last, " on condition that I may select them myself, and that I am accorded a subsidy of a hundred thousand pieces of gold." The sum mentioned seemed exorbitant to one of the Viziers, and he said so. " Very good," retorted Ibn Abî 'Âmir, " take two hundred thousand and command the army yourself—if you dare ! " But the Vizier did not dare, and it was resolved to entrust Ibn Abî 'Âmir with the command, and to supply him with the sum stipulated.

With a force of picked troops, selected from all parts of the empire, Ibn Abî 'Âmir set out, towards the end of February, 977. Crossing the frontier, he laid siege to the fortress of Los Baños,[1] one of those rebuilt by Ramiro II after his notable victory at Simancas. Making himself master of the suburbs he secured much booty, and about the middle of April he returned to Cordova with a large number of prisoners. The result of this campaign, although of little practical importance, caused, as was natural in the circumstances, great delight in the Capital. For the first time since the war began the Musulman army had taken the offensive, and had indeed taught the enemy a lesson which they took to heart so effectually that henceforth they no longer disturbed the slumbers of the Cordovans. This was, of course, no small boon to the townsfolk, and for the moment they asked for nothing more; but if they exaggerated the success achieved, it is impossible to overrate the importance of the campaign to Ibn Abî 'Âmir himself. Desirous of winning the affection of the army—still perhaps somewhat mistrustful of the ex-Kady who had become a general—he lavished upon it the money which he had received as a subsidy, and throughout the campaign all were welcome to his table. This policy was crowned with success. Officers and men were enraptured by the Vizier's affability—not to speak of his munificence, and the skill of his cooks. Henceforward, he could rely upon their devotion: so long as he continued thus bountifully to reward their services they were his, body and soul.

[1] Arab chroniclers call it Alhama, a literal translation of Balneos, the name applied by Sampiro to the modern Los Baños.

[AUTHORITIES: Ibn Adhârî, ii. pp. 270, 276–82; Makkarî, ii. pp. 59–61 : Ibn al-'Abbâr, pp. 141, 148.]

CHAPTER VIII

THE FALL OF MUS-HAFY

AS Ibn Abî ʿÂmir's power increased Mus-hafy's influence proportionately waned. The latter was a man of mediocre abilities. He sprang from a humble stock, but his father, a Berber of the district of Valencia, had been Hakam's tutor, and the son had early shared the affection and esteem which that prince had felt for the father. Mus-hafy, moreover, was not lacking in those accomplishments which Hakam chiefly appreciated: he was a man of letters and a poet. His good fortune had been surprising. At first Hakam's private secretary, he had become successively commander of the second division of the city guard, Governor of Majorca, and first Secretary of State. But he had never succeeded in forming friendships. He had all an upstart's arrogance: and his insufferable vanity galled the nobles, who despised him for his mean extraction. Upon becoming Prime Minister he seemed at first desirous of correcting this fault, but he soon resumed his overweening airs. His integrity was gravely suspected. It is true that but few high functionaries were then free from a like reproach, and his open peculations might have been condoned if he had shared the spoils with others—but, quite unpardonably, he kept them for himself. He lay open, moreover, to a charge of nepotism; almost all posts of importance were occupied by his sons and nephews. Of the talents requisite for a statesman, Mus-hafy possessed none. In matters lying outside mere routine he could neither come to a decision nor take action: it consequently became the duty of others to decide and to act for him, and it was to Ibn Abî ʿÂmir that he usually turned. Would the latter for long remain contented with the rôle of confidant and adviser which Mus-hafy wished him to play? Far-sighted observers doubted it, and believed that the time was not far distant when Ibn Abî ʿÂmir would be actual instead of virtual Prime Minister. And they were right. Ibn Abî ʿÂmir had already determined to compass Mus-hafy's downfall: to that end he worked assiduously but secretly. His demeanour towards his colleague remained unchanged; he continued to treat him with undiminished outward respect; but behind the scenes he thwarted him at all points, and never let slip an opportunity of calling Aurora's attention to his blundering incapacity. Mus-hafy suspected nothing of this; Ibn Abî 'Âmir, far from inspiring him with fears, was regarded by him as his best friend: the man Mus-hafy dreaded was Ghâlib, Governor of the Frontier, whose influence over the army was unbounded. Ghâlib, for his part, hated and despised Mus-hafy, and was at no pains to conceal the fact. Justly proud of the laurels he had won on countless battlefields, he was indignant that a mere nonentity, a man who had never drawn sword, should become Prime Minister. He boldly declared that the high office was his own of right. Theoretically, he was under Mus-hafy's orders; but he showed clearly enough by his conduct that the Government could not reckon on his support. Since Hakam's death, he had waged war against the Christians with a supineness which sorted but ill with the notorious vigour of his character. Thus far he had committed no act of treachery or of overt rebellion, nor had he sought the aid of the Christians; but his conduct hinted that before long he might do all these things, and in that case the downfall of the Minister was inevitable. It would be impossible for Mus-hafy to stand against the ablest general and the best troops in the empire, with the Leonese and Castilians as their allies. Moreover, at the very first check he experienced his numerous enemies would seize their opportunity, and deprive him of his office, his wealth, and perhaps his life.

Mus-hafy was not so obtuse as to be blind to the dangers which threatened him, and in his anxiety he sought counsel from his Viziers, and especially from Ibn Abî 'Âmir. He was urged by them to purchase Ghâlib's friendship at all costs. Mus-hafy assented, and Ibn Abî 'Âmir tendered his offices as mediator. The coming campaign, he observed, would give him an opportunity of conferring with the General, and he would do his utmost to bring about the desired reconciliation.

But Ibn Abî 'Âmir's intentions belied his words. To attain the pinnacle of glory pointed out by his soaring ambition he did not disdain to follow the most tortuous methods, and instead of trying to reconcile the rivals, he determined

to set them more bitterly at variance.   He took steps accordingly.   Whilst he assured Mus-hafy of his whole-hearted
devotion to his interests, he expatiated to Aurora on Ghâlib's
brilliant abilities : he ceased not to urge that the services
of that general could not be dispensed with, and that they
must be secured by granting him a higher title than that
which he already enjoyed.   Nor was his perfidious advice
fruitless.   By Aurora's influence Ghâlib was promoted to the
dignity of *Dhu 'l-Wizâratain*[1] (chief civil and military administrator) and Generalissimo of the Army of the Frontier.
Mus-hafy, for his part, far from opposing this promotion,
approved it, for Ibn Abî 'Âmir had assured him that it was
the first step towards a reconciliation.

On May 23rd, only a month after his return to Cordova,
Ibn Abî 'Âmir, who had just been appointed Commander-
in-Chief of the Army of the Capital, set forth on his second
expedition.   At Madrid he had an interview with Ghâlib, to
whom he showed the greatest deference, and whose heart he
won by declaring that he considered Mus-hafy quite unworthy of his high office.   A firm alliance soon sprang up
between the two generals, who agreed to work together to
overthrow the Prime Minister.   Then, crossing the frontier,
they stormed the fortress of Mola,[2] where they captured
much booty and many prisoners.   The campaign at an end,
the two generals took leave of one another, but at parting
Ghâlib said to his new friend : " The expedition has been
crowned with success : it will redound greatly to your fame,
and the Court in the midst of its rejoicings will not trouble
itself about your ulterior motives.   Profit by this: do not
leave the palace till you have been appointed Prefect of the
Capital in the place of Mus-hafy's son."   Ibn Abî 'Âmir,
promising to bear this counsel in mind, retraced his steps to
Cordova, while Ghâlib returned to his Government.

The honours of the campaign really rested with Ghâlib :
by him it had been planned and carried out in every detail,
and Ibn Abî 'Âmir, who had scarcely served his apprentice-
ship in the field, had been most careful not to oppose in any
particular an experienced general who had grown old in the
profession of arms.   But Ghâlib, wishing to advance his
young ally, presented the facts in quite a different light.   He
made haste to inform the Khalif that his colleague in the field
had done wonders—that to him alone credit for the successes

[1] *Lit.* "holder of two vizierships."   See Ibn Khallikân (Slane's transl.), iii. 130.
[2] Site unknown.

obtained was due—and that he deserved a splendid reward.
This despatch reached Cordova before Ibn Abî 'Âmir's
return, and greatly disposed the Court in his favour.   He
accordingly found no difficulty in superseding Mus-hafy's son
as Prefect of the Capital.   What, indeed, could be refused
to a general who for the second time returned as a victor,
and whose abilities and valour were extolled by the greatest
soldier of the day ?   Moreover, Mus-hafy's son was held in
low esteem ; he had owed his promotion solely to his father's
influence, and, far from justifying it by his own conduct, he
had proved quite unworthy of his office.   So inordinate was
his greed, that a trifling bribe would induce him to shut his
eyes even to the most abominable crimes.   It was declared,
and justly, that law and order were at an end in Cordova :
that brigands of high and low degree ran riot in her midst,
that honest folk feared to sleep at night lest they should be
robbed or murdered in their own homes—in short, that the
inhabitants of a frontier town ran less risk than those of the
Khalif's Capital.

Armed with his commission as Prefect, and clad in the
robe of honour which had been conferred upon him, Ibn Abî
'Âmir presented himself forthwith at the palace of the
Prefecture.   There, finding Mohammed Mus-hafy seated
amidst all the pomp pertaining to his rank, his successor
showed him the Khalif's mandate and informed him that he
might withdraw.   With a sigh he obeyed.

The new Prefect was scarcely installed in his post before
he took the most drastic measures to restore security to
the Capital.   He informed the agents of police that it was
his determination to proceed against wrong-doers without
respect of persons, and he threatened them with condign
punishment if they suffered themselves to be bribed.   Cowed
by his firmness and knowing that the eye of their master was
ever upon them, the agents henceforth did their duty.   The
result was immediately manifest in Cordova.   Robberies and
murders became more and more infrequent.   Order and
security once more reigned : honest folk could sleep in peace
while the law kept watch and ward.   The Prefect moreover
gave signal proof that he was sincere in his declaration that
he would spare no man.   His own son having transgressed,
and fallen into the hands of the police, he caused the young
man to be beaten with so many stripes that he died soon
afterwards.

Mus-hafy's eyes were at last opened.   The dismissal

2 H

of Mohammed—effected in his absence and without his knowledge—left him no room to doubt Ibn Abî 'Âmir's duplicity. But what could the Prime Minister do? His rival's power already exceeded his own. Ibn Abî 'Âmir could rely upon the Sultana—whose lover he was said to be—as well as upon the nobility, who, bound to the Omayyads by ties of clientage, claimed hereditary tenure of court offices, and greatly preferred to see at the head of affairs a man of ancient lineage, than an upstart who offended them by an absurd display of unjustifiable arrogance. The new Prefect could moreover rely upon the army, which had become more and more attached to him, as well as upon the inhabitants of the Capital, who were deeply beholden to him for his restoration of security. Mus-hafy could oppose to all these advantages nothing save the support of a few isolated individuals who owed their prosperity to him, but on whose gratitude he could not reckon with confidence.

In this strife between mediocrity and genius the forces were wholly unequal. Mus-hafy was well aware of this; he felt that he had but one hope of safety left, and he resolved to secure the goodwill of Ghâlib at any cost. He accordingly wrote to the General, making him dazzling promises of a kind most likely to appeal to him, and finally, to cement their alliance, he asked the hand of Ghâlib's daughter Asmâ for his own son 'Othmân. The General suffered himself to be cajoled. Laying aside his hatred, he replied that he accepted the Minister's offers and consented to the proposed marriage. Mus-hafy hastened to take him at his word, and the marriage contract had been drawn up and signed before Ibn Abî 'Âmir got wind of these schemes, so detrimental to his own projects. Without a moment's delay, he set in motion every influence at his command to thwart his colleague's plans. At his request the most powerful personages of the Court sent letters to Ghâlib, and he himself wrote, warning the General that Mus-hafy was laying a snare, reminding him of all his grievances against the Minister, and adjuring him to abide by the promises which he had made during the late campaign. As for the projected marriage, he added that if Ghâlib desired an honourable alliance for his daughter, it would be well for him to give her, not to the son of an upstart, but to the writer himself.

Ghâlib became convinced that he had made a mistake.

He informed Mus-hafy that the proposed marriage could not take place, and in August or September a new contract was drawn up and signed, in virtue of which Asmâ and Ibn Abî 'Âmir became betrothed. A little later, on Sept. 18th, the latter once more took the field. Proceeding by way of Toledo and joining his forces to those of his future father-in-law, he captured from the Christians two castles, as well as the suburbs of Salamanca. On returning home the title of *Dhu 'l-Wizâratain* was conferred upon him, together with a monthly salary of eighty pieces of gold. The *hâjib* himself received no more.

The date fixed for the wedding was now at hand, and the Khalif, or rather his mother—who, if she was indeed Ibn Abî 'Âmir's mistress, evinced no signs of jealousy—invited Ghâlib to accompany his daughter to Cordova. The General upon his arrival was loaded with honours. The title of *hâjib* was conferred upon him, and as he already held that of *Dhu 'l-Wizâratain*, which Mus-hafy could not boast of, he became henceforth the highest dignitary in the State. Ghâlib accordingly occupied the place of honour on ceremonial occasions, with Mus-hafy on his right hand and Ibn Abî 'Âmir on his left. The marriage of the latter with Asmâ was celebrated on New Year's Day—a Christian festival in which, however, Moslems participated. The Khalif took upon himself the entire expense, the banquets were of incomparable magnificence, and never in the memory of the Cordovans had been seen a retinue so splendid as that which surrounded Asmâ as she quitted the Khalif's palace to proceed to that of her betrothed. The marriage, it may be added, though prompted by policy, turned out a happy one. In Asmâ were united a cultured intellect and fascinating beauty ; she gained dominion over her husband's heart, and he always gave her the preference over his other wives.

Mus-hafy, from the moment when Ghâlib rejected the alliance, felt himself lost. He found himself in solitude. His own creatures deserted him to offer incense to his rival. Time was, when if he repaired to the palace they contended for the honour of accompanying him ; now he went alone. His power had sunk to zero. Measures of the highest importance were enacted behind his back. The unfortunate old man saw that the storm was about to burst, and awaited it with apathetic resignation.

The dreaded blow fell even sooner than he had expected.

On Monday, March 26, 978, Mus-hafy, his sons and his
nephews, were deprived of all their offices and dignities.
They were then put under arrest, and all their property was
declared sequestrated until they should be adjudged guiltless
of the crime of malversation laid to their charge.

Although this event could have caused him little surprise, Mus-hafy showed deep emotion. His conscience was
ill at ease. Remembrance of the many acts of injustice
which he had committed during his long career weighed
upon his soul. When he bade farewell to his family he
exclaimed, " Ye will never see me again, alive ; the dread
prayer has been answered ; I have awaited this moment for
forty years." When asked the meaning of these strange
words, he replied : " While 'Abd-er-Rahmân was still upon
the throne, it fell to my lot to prosecute and pass judgment upon a prisoner. I found that he was innocent, but
for reasons of my own I declared him guilty : he suffered an
ignominious punishment, his goods were forfeited, and he
was thrown into prison. He had long lain there, when one
night during my sleep I heard a voice saying : ' Set that
man free ! I have heard his prayer, and one day his lot shall
be thine ! ' I started from sleep in great terror. I sent for
the prisoner and besought his pardon. He refused it. Then
I adjured him at least to tell me whether he had addressed
a prayer to the Eternal concerning me. ' Yea,' he answered,
' I prayed God that thou mightest die in a dungeon as strait
as that in which I so long have languished.' I repented me
of my injustice, I released its victim—but my remorse had
come too late ! "

The accused were conducted to the state prison at
Al-Zahrâ. The general Hishâm Mus-hafy, nephew of the
Minister, who had incurred Ibn Abî 'Âmir's displeasure by
claiming the honour of certain successes gained during the
last campaign, was the first victim of his wrath. On reaching the prison he was forthwith executed. Mus-hafy's trial
took place before the Council of State, and was of long
duration. There was ample evidence that during his tenure
of office he had been guilty of malversation : a part of his
property was accordingly confiscated, and his splendid
palace in the Rosâfa quarter was sold by auction. Fresh
accusations, however, came pouring in, and the Viziers,
seeking thereby to please Ibn Abî 'Âmir, eagerly welcomed
them. Mus-hafy, found guilty under many different counts,
and subjected to as many forfeitures, was gradually deprived

of the whole of his property, but the Viziers, believing that a scantling yet remained, continued to harass him.   The last time that he was summoned to appear before his judge, Mus-hafy was so enfeebled by age, captivity, and grief, that he could scarcely drag his feet along the weary way from Al-Zahrâ to the court.   His pitiless warder nevertheless gruffly urged him to hasten and not to keep the Council waiting. " Have patience, good fellow," said the old man : " You long for my death, and your wish will be granted.   Would that I could purchase death, but God puts too high a price upon it ! "   Then he improvised these verses :

" Trust not in Fortune, for she is fickle !   But lately lions were in fear of me, and now I tremble at a fox !   Ah ! how shameful is it that a man of worth should be driven to sue for pity to a varlet ! "

On reaching the court, Mus-hafy seated himself in a corner of the hall without making obeisance to any of his judges. The Vizier Ibn Jâbir, a parasite of Ibn Abî 'Âmir, observing this, exclaimed : " Art thou then so ill-bred as to be ignorant of the simplest rules of courtesy ? "   Mus-hafy remained silent, but after fresh insults from Ibn Jâbir, he at last replied : " Thou thyself failest in due deference ; thou repayest my favours with ingratitude, and darest thou tell me that I fail in courtesy ? "   Somewhat nonplussed by these words, but soon recovering himself, Ibn Jâbir cried : " Thou liest ! What good offices hast thou rendered me ? "   And he proceeded to enumerate his grievances against the prisoner. When he ceased Mus-hafy replied : " I seek not your gratitude for such acts as those : yet it is true, that when you embezzled money entrusted to you, and when the late Khalif—May his soul rest with God !—would have had thy right hand cut off, I procured pardon for thee ! "   Ibn Jâbir vowed that this accusation was a vile calumny.   " I adjure all those who know aught of the matter," cried the old man indignantly, " to declare whether I have spoken the truth or not."   " Yea," replied the Vizier Ibn Iyâsh, " there is some truth in what you say ; but in the circumstances it were wiser for you not to rake up these bygones."   " You are perhaps right," replied Mus-hafy, " but I lost patience with this man, and was constrained to speak my mind."

Another Vizier, Ibn Jahwar, had listened to this dispute with rising repugnance.   Although he had little love for Mus-hafy, and had assented to his ruin, he knew that respect was due even to a foe, and especially a fallen foe.   Addressing Ibn Jâbir in a tone of authority justified by length of service and a name as ancient and almost as illustrious as that of the Khalif himself, he said : " Knowest thou not, Ibn Jâbir, that those who have fallen under the monarch's displeasure are not entitled to salute the great officers of the State ? The reason is clear ; for if the dignitaries returned the salute, they would fail in their duty to the Sultan, and if they did not return it, they would fail in their duty to the Eternal. A man disgraced must not make obeisance, as Mus-hafy well knows."

Abashed by the lesson thus administered, Ibn Jâbir kept silence, while a faint twinkle of joy illuminated the old man's lack-lustre eyes.

The examination of the prisoner began. As fresh charges were brought against Mus-hafy in order to mulct him in further penalties, he cried : " I swear by all that is most sacred that I am penniless. Were I to be cut to pieces, I could not pay a single dirhem ! " He was believed, and dismissed to prison.

Henceforward, he was alternately free and a captive— but always miserable. Ibn Abî 'Âmir seemed to take a barbarous pleasure in tormenting him. It is difficult to account for the implacable hatred he showed towards this commonplace and now harmless man. It can only be conjectured that he never forgave the useless crime which Mus-hafy had forced him to commit in the murder of Mughîra.

Be this as it may, Ibn Abî 'Âmir took Mus-hafy with him wherever he went, without even supplying his barest necessities. One of the Minister's secretaries relates that during a campaign he saw Mus-hafy lying beside his master's tent devouring a wretched mess of meal and water—the best repast his son 'Othmân could procure for him. Grief and gnawing despair wasted him, and he breathed forth his woes in tuneful and affecting verses. But although he had told his warder that he longed for death, he clung to life with singular tenacity, and as foresight and energy had failed him when he held power, dignity failed him in adversity. To propitiate " the Fox " he stooped to the most humiliating petitions. Once he begged Ibn Abî 'Âmir to entrust him with the education of his children. But the Minister, who did not imagine that Mus-hafy's self-respect had sunk so low, suspected a trap : " He wishes to damage my reputation, and hints that I am a simpleton. In days gone by I have been seen by many at the door of his palace, and to remind them, he wishes to be seen to-day in the courtyard of mine."

For five years Mus-hafy dragged out his existence in sorrow and suffering. Then, since he seemed bent on clinging to life, despite his years and the misfortunes they had brought in their train, he was put to death—either by strangulation or poison, but on this point the Arab chroniclers are not agreed.

Ibn Abî ʿÂmir, on learning that his former rival was no more, ordered two of his officers to superintend his burial. One of them, the secretary Mohammed ibn Ismâʿîl, has described the scene as an eye-witness : " The corpse presented no signs of violence. It lay covered with the cast-off cloak of one of the turnkeys. A man sent for by my colleague Mohammed ibn Maslama washed the body (I relate the simple truth) on an old door that had fallen from its hinges. We carried the bier to the grave, followed only by the Imâm of the mosque, whom we had requested to recite the prayers for the dead. No passer-by dared to glance at the corpse. This was a lesson which sank deep into my soul. One day, in the plenitude of Mus-hafy's power, I had desired to present a petition to him in person. I took my stand on the route which he would follow, but his retinue was so numerous, and the streets were so thronged with folk eager to see and salute the Minister, that I found it impossible, do what I would, to approach him, and I was obliged to hand my petition to one of the secretaries who rode beside the cavalcade to receive such documents. On my return from the grave I compared this scene with that which I had just beheld, and, as I mused on Fortune's mutability, my heart sank and a profound melancholy oppressed my bosom."

[AUTHORITIES: Ibn al-ʿAbbâr, 141–2 ; Ibn Adhârî, ii. 268, 271, 282–291 ; Nuwairî, p. 470 ; Makkarî, i. 395–6, 275–6 ; ii. 60–2.]

CHAPTER IX

ALMANZOR

THE day which witnessed the deposition and arrest of Mus-hafy saw also the promotion of Ibn Abî 'Âmir to the rank of *hâjib*. Henceforth he shared the supreme authority with his father-in-law, and so great was his power that it might well have seemed madness to oppose it. Nevertheless it was opposed. The party which had wished to place the crown on another brow than that of the little son of Hakam II, and of which Jaudhar was the moving spirit, still existed, as the satirical verses sung in the streets of Cordova, in defiance of the police, but too plainly proved. Ibn 'Abî 'Âmir would not tolerate the slightest allusion to the perhaps too close intimacy which existed between the Sultana and himself; he actually put to death a singing-girl whose master, in the hope of selling her to the Minister, had taught her an amorous ditty with Aurora for its subject; nevertheless ribald verses such as these were hummed in the streets :

"The end of the world draweth nigh! Destruction impendeth, for abominations are rife! The Khalif is a stripling, and a brace of lovers share his teeming dam!"[1]

Those who confined themselves to lampooning the Court ran no great risk ; but Jaudhar ventured much further. In league with 'Abd al-Malik ibn Mundhir, President of the Court of Appeal, he hatched a conspiracy, the object of which was to assassinate the youthful Khalif, and to put on the throne another grandson of 'Abd-er-Rahmân III, namely 'Abd-er-Rahmân ibn 'Obaidallah. A number of Kadies, divines, and men of letters—among whom was included the talented poet Ramâdî—were implicated in the plot. To Ibn Abî 'Âmir Ramâdî bore a mortal grudge, for he had been Mus-hafy's friend, and was one of the little band who had remained faithful to the Minister even when

---

[1] (Following Ibn Adhârî, ii. 300, rather than Makkarî, i. 396.) In the popular opinion, the Sultana's other lover was the Kady, Ibn as-Sâlim.

Fortune had turned her back upon him. A longing for vengeance consumed the poet, and he launched many a biting lampoon against the *hájib*.

The conspirators were the more confident of the success of their scheme since the Vizier Ziyâd ibn Aflah, then Prefect of the Capital, connived at it. With him they took counsel as to the day and hour for carrying out their design. Jaudhar—who though no longer a courtier, still had, by virtue of his office, ready access to the monarch—was charged with his assassination: this achieved, the accomplices would immediately proclaim 'Abd-er-Rahmân IV.

On the day appointed, as soon as the Prefect had quitted the palace for his abode in a distant quarter of the city, accompanied by his retinue, Jaudhar craved, and was accorded, an audience. The eunuch, entering the presence-chamber, forthwith attempted to stab the Khalif, but one Ibn Arûs, who happened to be at hand, threw himself upon the assassin before he could accomplish his object. A struggle ensued, in which Jaudhar's garments were torn to pieces, but Ibn Arûs called the guard to his assistance, and the eunuch was arrested. Soon afterwards Ziyâd ibn Aflah, learning that the plot had failed, arrived at the palace in all haste. Ibn Arûs reproached him for his carelessness, and gave him clearly to understand that he believed him an accessory in Jaudhar's attempted crime. The Prefect excused himself as well as he could, protested his loyalty, and with a view to lull suspicion by a display of zeal, he caused all the suspected persons to be immediately arrested and conveyed, with Jaudhar, to the prison at Al-Zahrâ.

The conspirators were brought to trial without delay, and swift judgment was passed upon them. The President of the Court of Appeal was found guilty of high treason, but the judges, instead of precisely specifying his punishment, merely held that his case was covered by the following verse of the Koran:

"Behold the recompense of those who war against God and His Messenger, and go about to commit disorders on the earth, shall be that they shall be slain or crucified, or have their alternate hands and feet cut off, or be banished the land." [1]

It will be observed that the specification of punishments in this verse is very vague, and the tribunal left to the

[1] *Koran, Sura V. 38.*

Khalif the selection of the most appropriate. In existing circumstances the decision rested with the Council of State, and Ziyâd ibn Aflah, who was a member of this body and was above all things desirous of regaining Ibn Abî 'Âmir's favour, was the first to propose the infliction of the severest penalty. His advice prevailed, and 'Abd al-Malik ibn Mundhir suffered crucifixion. The pretender, 'Abd-er-Rahmân, was also put to death. We are not informed of the decision in Jaudhar's case, but there can be little doubt that he too was crucified. Ramâdî's fate, though not to be envied, was more endurable. Ibn Abî 'Âmir, who wished to exile him, yielded to the entreaties of the poet's friends and permitted him to remain in Cordova, but under a cruel restriction: he caused it to be proclaimed by heralds that any one who spoke to Ramâdî would be severely punished. Thus condemned to perpetual silence, the poor poet henceforth wandered—to use an Arab author's expression—"like a dead man" through the crowded streets of the Capital.[1]

This conspiracy showed the Minister that his most inveterate foes were to be found amongst the ranks of those by whose side he had studied literature, theology, and law. This was, doubtless, in part the effect of envy. But yesterday their equal and fellow-student, Ibn Abî 'Âmir had risen too high not to be envied by the ecclesiastics and lawyers. But this was not the sole, nor even the chief cause of the aversion he inspired in them: they detested him yet more for the religious indifference which they attributed to him. A few philosophers and free-thinking poets excepted, the students brought up at the feet of the Cordovan professors were sincere Islamites. Now Ibn Abî 'Âmir, rightly or wrongly, passed as a very lukewarm Moslem. It would not have been prudent to reproach him openly with lax views in the matter of faith, but it was whispered that he loved philosophy and was secretly a keen student of that science. In those days this was a very grave accusation. Ibn Abî 'Âmir was aware of this. Philosopher or not, he was primarily a Statesman, and in order to deprive his enemies of the formidable weapon they might wield against him, he resolved to show by a signal act of orthodoxy, what a sound Musulman he was.

Summoning the most distinguished divines, such as Acîlî, Ibn Dhakwân, and Zubaidî, he conducted them to the great

[1] Ramâdî seems, however, to have been pardoned, for he was one of the poets who accompanied Ibn Abî 'Âmir upon his expedition against Barcelona in 986.

library of Hakam II, and telling them that he had determined to destroy all the treatises on Philosophy, Astronomy,
and other sciences forbidden by religion, he bade them weed
out the obnoxious volumes. The divines at once set to work,
and when their task was accomplished the Minister ordered
the condemned books to be burned, and to show his zeal for
the faith committed some to the flames with his own hands.
That this was an act of vandalism few knew better than the
enlightened Ibn Abî 'Âmir himself, but none the less it produced an excellent effect amongst the Fakihs and the lower
orders—the more so because the Minister henceforth posed as
the enemy of philosophy [1] and the mainstay of religion. He
treated preachers with the utmost respect, loaded them with
favours, and listened to their pious harangues, however
lengthy, with a patient attention which was wholly edifying.
Further, he transcribed the Koran with his own hand, and
henceforth on his journeys always took the copy with him.

Having thus established a reputation for orthodoxy, and
one so well grounded that none thenceforth dared to dispute
it, Ibn Abî 'Âmir turned his attention to the Khalif, who
as he grew older was the more to be feared.

According to his tutor Zubaidî, Hishâm II, as a child,
showed much promise; he acquired knowledge with remarkable facility, and was endued with a soundness of judgment
rare in children of his age. But when, while yet a mere
boy, he ascended the throne, his mother and Ibn Abî 'Âmir
set to work systematically to stifle his faculties. We are
not justified in asserting that they introduced him prematurely to the pleasures of the harem—for although the
fact that Hishâm died childless lends some colour to the
suggestion, it rests on no positive evidence—but it is at
least certain that they did their best to bemuse his intellect
by over-insistence on religious observances, and endeavoured
to impress on him the belief that the cares inseparable from
the personal exercise of sovereignty would distract his mind
from the contemplation of divine things, and imperil his
salvation.

They had been partially successful : Hishâm was given
to good works, he read the Koran assiduously, he prayed
and fasted ; but his understanding was not yet so dulled as
to render Ibn Abî 'Âmir quite easy about him, for the Minister
feared lest sooner or later some one else might gain an

---

[1] See Michele Amari, *Biblioteca Arabo-Sicula*, p. 674.

ascendancy over the youthful monarch and open his eyes to
his real situation.

So long as affairs of State were transacted in the Khalif's
palace, this danger would be present. Numerous generals
and officials were for ever coming and going, and the merest
chance might throw the Khalif into the arms of one of them,
who, if at all an able and ambitious man, could ruin the
Minister in the twinkling of an eye. It was necessary to
remove this danger. Ibn Abî 'Âmir therefore resolved that
the business of government should be carried on elsewhere,
and to this end caused a new town to be built, to the east
of Cordova, on the Guadalquiver, containing a large palace
for himself, and other palaces for the chief officials. This
town, which received the name of Zâhira, was built in two
years, and the government offices were forthwith transferred
thither. Zâhira soon welcomed a large population within
its walls. The upper classes migrated from Cordova and
Al-Zahrâ to be nearer the source of all favours; the tradesmen followed them, and Zâhira before long grew till its
suburbs joined those of Cordova.

It was henceforth easy to keep watch over the Khalif
and to prevent him from meddling with State affairs. The
Minister, however, adopted further means of isolating him
as completely as possible. Besides surrounding him with
guards and spies, he had a wall and moat constructed round
the palace, and any person approaching them was severely
punished. Hishâm was, in truth, a prisoner; he could not
quit the palace, his every word and act were immediately
reported to the Minister, and he gathered nothing concerning
public business except what the latter vouchsafed to him.

While caution was still advisable, Ibn Abî 'Âmir gave
out that the young monarch had handed him the reins of
government the better to devote himself to spiritual concerns;
but later, when assured of success, he wholly ignored Hishâm
and even forbade mention of his name.

Meanwhile the Prime Minister was meditating another,
and no less important stroke of policy. He determined to
reorganize the army.

He was actuated by two motives—one patriotic, the
other personal; while desiring to see Spain take rank among
the leading States of Europe, he wished to rid himself of
his colleague Ghâlib. Now the existing army, composed,
as it was, mainly of Spanish Arabs, was not fitted for either
purpose. The military organization was undoubtedly de-

fective. Too much power lay in the hands of the chiefs of
the *Jund*[1] and too few soldiers were at the disposal of the
crown. It is true that the sovereign could summon not
only the troops drawn from the *Jund*, but also those of the
frontier—who seem to have been the best ; yet custom decreed that the latter should not be mustered save in the
case of necessity, and they formed no part of the standing
army, which was by no means a large one. It could boast
of only five thousand horse, although the cavalry then constituted the most important arm, and decided the fate of
battles. Moreover the quality of these troops left much to
be desired. The traveller Ibn Hawkal remarks that the
Andalusian horsemen, their legs dangling heedless of the
stirrups, presented a far from smart appearance, and he adds
that the commander of the Spanish army owed his victories
to craft rather than to courage. This writer's testimony
must not, however, be implicitly trusted. Since he wished
his lord, the Fâtimid Khalif, to attempt the subjugation of
the Peninsula, he has perhaps unduly disparaged the Spanish
troops ; there is, however, undoubtedly truth in his criticisms,
and it is undeniable that the Arabs of Spain, enervated by
luxury and the effects of climate, had gradually lost much of
their martial spirit. Ibn Abî 'Âmir could not hope to achieve
brilliant conquests with such an army. Moreover, he could
not rely upon it in the event of his attacking Ghâlib, and
he foresaw that a struggle with his colleague was inevitable.
Ghâlib, it is true, did him good service when he was scheming Mus-hafy's overthrow—but he had now no further use
for the General, who clearly stood in his path. Ghâlib
indeed by no means approved of some of the Minister's
measures, and was strongly opposed to the immurement of
the Khalif. As a client of 'Abd-er-Rahmân III and an
ardent royalist, he felt grief and indignation at seeing his
patron's grandson kept in custody like a malefactor. Ibn
Abî 'Âmir, who chafed at opposition, resolved, therefore, to
rid himself of his father-in-law, and only hesitated as to the
means. Ghâlib was not a man like Mus-hafy, to be overthrown by a mere Court intrigue; he was an illustrious
soldier, who, if he made up his mind to rescue his Sovereign
from the Minister's toils, could count upon nearly the whole
army, whose idol he was. Ibn Abî 'Âmir was under no
delusions on this point, and he saw clearly that to gain his

[1] See *Recherches* (1881), i. pp. 80–3.

ends, other troops, attached to himself alone, were needed. Foreign soldiers, in fact, must be procured. Mauritania and Christian Spain would provide him with them.

Hitherto Ibn Abî 'Âmir had paid little attention to Mauritania. His sojourn there as Chief Justice had convinced him that regions so distant and barren were rather a burden than an advantage to Spain, and agreeably with Mus-hafy's policy, he had contented himself with maintaining at its full complement the garrison of Ceuta. He had entrusted the administration of the rest of the country to native princes, taking care to attach them to himself by bounties of every kind. This policy was sound enough from the Spanish point of view, but for Mauritania its results were disastrous. Seeing the country abandoned to its own defence, Bologguin, viceroy of Ifrikia, invaded it in the year 979. He gained victory after victory, and driving before him the princes who recognised the suzerainty of the Omayyad Khalif, he compelled them to seek refuge within the walls of Ceuta. But the victories of Bologguin, far from thwarting Ibn Abî 'Âmir's plans, favoured them. The Berbers, penned up in Ceuta, found themselves in grievous straits, and since their conqueror had deprived them of all they possessed, they knew not whither to turn for bare subsistence. An excellent opportunity thus presented itself to the Spanish minister of acquiring at a stroke a large body of serviceable cavalry, and he promptly seized it. He intimated to the Berbers that if they would take service in Spain they should want for nothing, and receive high pay. They responded to his appeal in large numbers. Ja'far, Prince of Zâb, renowned for his valorous exploits, was enticed by the glowing promises of the Minister, and landed in Spain with six hundred horsemen. The Berbers had every reason to congratulate themselves on the step they had taken. Ibn Abî 'Âmir's liberality to them was unparalleled. "When these Africans reached Spain," writes an Arab chronicler, "their garments hung in tatters, and each bestrode a sorry jade, but in a little while they were to be seen, clad in the richest attire, caracoling through the streets on high-mettled chargers: never could they have beheld, even in dreams, such splendid mansions as those in which they were lodged!" They grew rapacious; but if they were never weary of soliciting, neither was Ibn Abî 'Âmir ever weary of giving, and he appeared deeply touched by their gratitude. He protected them from slights and insults, and

even forbade ridicule of their occasional attempts to speak
Arabic; for they habitually spoke their mother tongue, of
which the Arabs understood not one word.　One day when
the Minister was inspecting his soldiers, a Berber officer,
Wânzemâr by name, came up to him, and stammered out
in atrocious Arabic: "My lord, I pray thee, grant me
a roof over my head, for I am obliged to sleep in the
open air!"　"How so, Wânzemâr?" asked his master,
"have you disposed of the dwelling I gave you?"　"You
have driven me out of it, my lord," was the reply,
"by the excess of your bounty.　So broad are the acres
which you have conferred on me, that my chambers are filled
with corn, and there is no room for myself.　Perhaps you
will advise me, since my corn discommodes me, to throw it
out of the windows: but be pleased to remember, my lord,
that I am a Berber—a man who a little while ago was
destitute and often on the verge of starvation.　Such an one,
you can easily understand, would think twice before casting
away his corn!"　"I cannot call you a brilliant orator," replied the Minister, smiling, "but your words seem to me
more eloquent and affecting than the most highly polished
discourses of our learned academicians."　Then, turning to
the Andalusians who stood around, and who were stifling
their laughter at the Berber's oration, he added: "Learn the
right way of showing gratitude, and of gaining fresh favours!
This man whom ye deride throws you into the shade, despite all your fine phrases: he doth not forget benefits received; he doth not grumble querulously as is your wont."
Thereupon he conferred upon Wânzemâr a splendid mansion.

　　The Christians of Spain also provided Ibn Abî 'Âmir
with excellent troops.　Poor, greedy, and unpatriotic, the
men of Leon, Castile, and Navarre were readily attracted by
the Arab's offer of high pay, and once they had enlisted
under his banner, his kindness, his liberality, and the spirit
of equity which seemed to animate all his dealings, endeared
him to them—the more readily since justice was a scarce
commodity in their own country.　Ibn Abî 'Âmir was ever
solicitous for his Christian troops.　Sunday was made a day
of rest for all the soldiers, irrespectively of their religion, and
in the event of a dispute between a Christian and a Moslem,
the former was always favoured.　It is not surprising, therefore, that the Christians became as warmly attached to him
as the Berbers.　They were all, literally, his own men.
They had renounced and forgotten their fatherland, and

Andalusia did not supply its place; they scarcely understood its language. Their true home was the camp, and
although paid out of the public exchequer they were not
servants of the State, but of Ibn Abî ʿÂmir himself. They
owed their good fortune to him, they were his dependants,
and they were his to employ as he listed.

While thus giving foreigners a preponderance in the
army, the wily Minister changed the organization of the
Spanish troops, which had hitherto been incompatible with
State control. From time immemorial, regiments, companies, and squadrons had coincided with tribes and their
subdivisions. Ibn Abî ʿÂmir abolished this usage, and
drafted the Arabs into different regiments without regard
to the tribes to which they belonged. A century earlier,
when the Arabs were still imbued with the spirit of clanship,
such a measure—involving, as it did, a radical change in
the law of recruiting and depriving the nobles of their last
shreds of power—would doubtless have evoked vehement
protests, and perhaps a general insurrection : but so greatly
had times changed that the revolution was effected without
opposition. The tribal system had become a legend.
Multitudes of Arabs knew not to what tribe they belonged,
and the confusion hence arising was the despair of genealo-
gists. Hakam II, who revered the past, and was skilled in
its history, had attempted, it is true, to revive the memories
of a bygone time; he ordered learned men to investigate
genealogies, and wished every man to be enrolled in his
tribe; but his efforts were both impolitic and at variance
with the spirit of the age, which almost everywhere showed
a tendency to unification and fusion of races. In giving the
finishing stroke to the tribal system, Ibn Abî ʿÂmir was
therefore merely completing the work of assimilation begun
by ʿAbd-er-Rahmân III and approved by the nation.

While thus preparing for a struggle, Ibn Abî ʿÂmir still
lived outwardly on good terms with his father-in-law. But
the latter was too sagacious to be deceived as to the objects
of the great changes which his son-in-law had worked in
the army, and determined to break with him. One day,
while they stood together on the tower of a frontier castle,
Ghâlib loaded the Minister with reproaches. Ibn Abî ʿÂmir
retorted with no less vivacity, and the dispute grew so hot
that Ghâlib, in his rage, cried: " Dog that thou art !
Thou claimest supreme authority and schemest the overthrow of the dynasty ! " Then, foaming with rage, he drew

his sword and rushed upon the Minister. Some officers
tried to intercept him, but only partly succeeded: Ghâlib
wounded Ibn Abî ʿÂmir, and then, terror-stricken, threw
himself from the tower. Fortunately for him, he clutched
a projection while falling, and thus saved his life.

After such an encounter war was inevitable; nor was it
long delayed. Ghâlib declared himself champion of the
Khalif's rights; a body of troops joined his standard and he
obtained further help from Leon. Many combats ensued,
in which some of the most prominent courtiers were slain.
At the final engagement, Ibn Abî ʿÂmir's men were on the
point of being routed, when Ghâlib, charging at the head
of his cavalry, had the misfortune to strike his head against
his saddle-bow. Seriously injured, he fell from his horse,
upon which his soldiers and their Christian allies took to
flight, and the Prime Minister won a decisive victory.
Ghâlib's body was found among the slain (A.D. 981).

Ibn Abî ʿÂmir was, however, not content with inflicting
this defeat, crushing though it was. He determined to
punish the Leonese for aiding his rival, and at the same
time to show his fellow-countrymen that in creating a
splendid army he had been instigated by patriotism as well
as by self-interest. He accordingly invaded the kingdom
of Leon and inflicted on it condign punishment. His advanced guard, commanded by a prince of the blood named
ʿAbdallah—better known by his nickname of " Flint-heart " [1]
—entered and sacked Zamora (July, 981). It is true that the
Moslems did not succeed in capturing the citadel, but they
took revenge by laying waste the environs with fire and
sword. Four thousand Christians were put to death,[2] and
in one district alone a thousand villages, or hamlets, almost
all of which were populous and contained monasteries and
churches, were destroyed. Ramiro III, then not twenty
years old, promptly entered into alliance with Garcia
Fernandez, Count of Castile, and with the King of Navarre.
The three princes marched against Ibn Abî ʿÂmir and gave
him battle at Rueda, south-west of Simancas: they were defeated, and the important fortress of Simancas fell into the
hands of the Moslems. Few prisoners were taken: soldiers
and citizens alike were put to the sword. Although the
season was far advanced, Ibn Abî Âmir next marched against

---

[1] In allusion, it seems, to his avarice.
[2] An equal number being made prisoners: for further details of the campaign
see *Recherches* (1881), pp. 173–6.

the city of Leon.   Ramiro sallied forth to check his advance.
Fortune seemed to smile on the King's audacity : he repulsed the foe, and drove them back to their camp.   In the
camp Ibn Abî 'Âmir occupied a kind of platform to watch
and direct the combat.   Seeing the flight of his troops, he
trembled with rage and vexation, and leaping down from
his throne, he doffed his golden helmet and crouched in the
dust.   Right well his men knew the meaning of this posture.   Their general was accustomed to signify thereby his
displeasure when they failed of their duty in the field.   The
sight of his uncovered head produced a magical effect ;
ashamed of their rebuff, the soldiers exclaimed that they
would atone for it at all costs, and with fierce cries they
hurled themselves upon the foe with such impetuosity that
they put them to flight ; then, in hot pursuit, they chased
them to the gates of Leon and would have captured the
city if a violent storm of snow and hail, suddenly breaking,
had not obliged them to stay their hands.

When Ibn Abî 'Âmir, compelled by the approach of
winter to retire, had returned to Cordova, he formally
assumed a surname—a practice which hitherto had been confined to the Khalif alone—and this surname, by which we
shall henceforth designate him, was that of Almanzor.[1]
He insisted, moreover, upon being accorded all the honours
which were the right of royalty alone.   Upon entering his
presence everyone—even the viziers and princes of the blood
—was required to kiss his hand.   So great indeed was the
desire of gaining his favour, that kisses were respectfully
imprinted even on the hands of those of his children who
were scarcely out of their cradles.

Almanzor's power now seemed irresistible, and it might
have been thought that he had no rival.   The great
Minister, however, was not of that opinion.   He believed
that there was still a man who, if not at the moment
dangerous, might become so—namely, Ja'far, Prince of Zâb.

Ja'far had rendered him valuable assistance in his
struggle with Ghâlib ; but, distinguished as he was by high
birth and military renown, he had excited the jealousy of
both Minister and nobles.   Almanzor therefore resolved
upon a deed which has left an indelible blot upon his fame.
Having given secret instructions to two Todjíbites, Abu
'l-Ahwas Man and 'Abd-er-Rahmân ibn Motarrif, he invited

---

[1] *Al-mansûr billâh,* " Victorious by the help of God."

Ja'far to a banquet. The invitation was accepted. The feast was a lavish one, the guest had already been made merry by the generous wines, when the cup-bearer presented a brimming goblet to the Minister: "Offer it," said the latter, "to him whom I honour most." The embarrassed cup-bearer hesitated, not knowing which of the noble guests his master intended. "Beshrew thee for a fool!" cried Almanzor, "Offer it to the vizier Ja'far!" Flattered by such a token of esteem, Ja'far arose, took the cup, and drained it at a draught. Soon, heedless of decorum, he fell to dancing. His corybantic gaiety proved infectious, and the other guests followed his example. The carousal was prolonged far into the night, and when it broke up, Ja'far was deeply intoxicated. As he reeled homewards, accompanied only by a few pages, he was suddenly assailed by the soldiers of the two Todjîbites and, before he could defend himself, was slain (Jan. 22, 983).

Ja'far's head and right hand were secretly conveyed to Almanzor, who professed to be ignorant of the instigators of the assassination, and displayed the deepest sorrow at the crime.

[AUTHORITIES: Ibn Hazm (*On Love*), ff. 32, 38, 59, 101; Ibn al-'Abbâr, 103, 151–5; Ibn Adhârî, i. 240; ii. 258–316; Makkarî, i. 136, 186, 260–286, 396; ii. 51, 64, 442; Ibn Khaldûn, *Hist. des Berbers*, ii. 553 *sq.*; iii. 237; 'Abd al-Wâhid, p. 17; Ibn al-Khatîb (MS. G.), f. 181; Sa'îd of Toledo, f. 246; Ibn Hawkal, p. 40; Mon. Sil., c. 70; Nuwairî, p. 470.]

CHAPTER X

ALMANZOR (*continued*)

ALMANZOR'S complicity in the murder of Ja'far may or may not have been suspected; the crime was at any rate soon forgotten in the popular enthusiasm aroused by fresh victories. For Almanzor the internal affairs of Leon had taken a very favourable turn. The disasters which had overtaken Ramiro III in the campaign of 981 had proved that monarch's ruin. The Leonese nobles were fain to be rid of a prince who seemed dogged by misfortune and yet wounded their pride by claiming autocratic power. An insurrection broke out in Galicia, where the nobles resolved to place Bermudo, Ramiro's cousin, upon the throne, and, on Oct. 15, 982, crowned him in the church of Santiago de Compostela. Ramiro immediately marched against the usurper, and at Portilla de Arenas, on the frontier of Leon and Galicia, a desperate but indecisive battle was fought. After this, fortune favoured Bermudo's arms more and more, and, about March, 984, he wrested the city of Leon from his rival. Ramiro, who had taken refuge in the vicinity of Astorga, found himself driven, in order to avoid total defeat, to crave assistance from Almanzor, and to acknowledge him as over-lord; soon after this, however, the king died (June 26, 984). His mother then tried to govern with Moslem aid, but she soon found that support withdrawn. Bermudo foresaw that unless he stooped to follow Ramiro's example, he would have great difficulty in bringing the recalcitrant nobles to their knees. He therefore appealed to Almanzor, and seems to have made more tempting promises than the queen-mother, for the Minister espoused his cause and placed a considerable Moorish force at his disposal. Thus aided, Bermudo succeeded in bringing the whole realm into subjection; but henceforth he was merely Almanzor's lieutenant, and a large body of Moslem troops remained in his kingdom, to watch as well as protect him. Almanzor, having thus made Leon a tributary province, resolved next to turn his arms against Catalonia. Since this country was a fief of the Kings of France, the

Khalifs had hitherto treated it with respect, lest by attacking
it they should embroil themselves with the French.   Almanzor, however, had no such misgivings: he knew that
France was a prey to feudal anarchy, and that from her the
Catalan counts could not hope for assistance.   Having
assembled a large force, he set out from Cordova on May 5,
985, taking with him forty salaried poets to hymn his
victories.[1]   Passing Elvira, Baeza and Lorca, he entered
Murcia, where he became the guest of Ibn Khattâb—a
private land-owner, holding no official rank but possessing
wide domains whence he derived immense revenues.   A
client of the Omayyads, he probably came of Vizigothic
stock and was perhaps a descendant of that Theodemir
who, at the time of the conquest, had made such advantageous terms with the Moslems that he and his son
Athanagild reigned as almost independent princes over the
province of Murcia.[2]   Be this as it may, Ibn Khattâb was
as open-handed as he was wealthy.   For thirteen days, not
only Almanzor and his suite, but the whole army, from
vizier to trooper, were his guests.   He took care that the
Minister's board should be sumptuously served; never did
the same dainties nor the same table equipage appear twice
upon it—while one day he pushed prodigality to the extent
of offering his guest a bath of rose-water.   Accustomed as
he was to luxury, Almanzor was amazed at his host's pro-
fusion: he praised it without stint, and in token of his
approbation, released him from payment of a portion of the
land-tax.   The Minister further enjoined the magistrates
who administered the province to show Ibn Khattâb the
utmost deference, and to consult his wishes as far as possible.

Quitting Murcia, Almanzor continued his march to
Catalonia, and after defeating Count Borrel, arrived before
Barcelona on Wednesday, July 1.   On the following Monday
he took it by storm.   Most of the soldiers and the citizens
were put to the sword and the rest were enslaved.   The
town was then pillaged and burned.[3]

Almanzor, always indefatigable, had scarcely returned
from this, his twenty-third campaign,[4] when, eager for new

[1] A list of these poets is given by Ibn al-Khatîb.
[2] In the thirteenth century the Beni Khattâb called themselves Arabs, but
their ancestors in the tenth century never claimed such an origin.
[3] Prospero de Bofarull y Mascaró, *Los Condes de Barcelona vindicados*, i. 163–4
(1836).
[4] Almanzor had made numerous campaigns against the Count of Castile and
the King of Navarre, of which no details are extant.

conquests, he turned his attention to Mauritania. For several years this country had been subject to Bologguin, Viceroy of Ifrikia, but towards the end of that prince's reign, and still more after his death (May, 984), the Omayyad faction had shown signs of revival. Several towns, such as Fez and Sijilmesa, had already shaken off the Fâtimid yoke, when an almost forgotten African prince reappeared upon the scene. This was the Edrisid, Ibn Kennûn. In the days of Hakam II, Ibn Kennûn, as we have related, had surrendered to Ghâlib, and having been brought to Cordova had remained there until Mus-hafy allowed him to reside in Tunis, subject to an undertaking that he would not return to Mauritania. This promise, however, Ibn Kennûn never intended to keep. Repairing to the court of the Fâtimid Khalif, he importuned that prince, during ten years, to reinstate him. Supplied, at length, with troops and money, he returned to his native country, and having purchased the support of many Berber chiefs, he seemed in a fair way to attain his object. This Almanzor could not permit, and he took the necessary steps to check the Edrisid, despatching a large force to Mauritania under his cousin Askeleja. The war did not last long ; too feeble to offer effectual resistance, Ibn Kennûn surrendered, after obtaining from Askeleja a promise that his life should be spared and that he should be permitted to reside at Cordova as before.

Such a promise, made to a man who was as ambitious as he was treacherous, was undoubtedly an imprudent one, and it may well be doubted whether Askeleja had been authorized to give it. The Arab chroniclers throw little light upon the matter, but Almanzor's conduct leads us to suspect that Askeleja exceeded his powers. The Minister declared the compact null and void, and Ibn Kennûn was brought to Spain, and was beheaded at night, on the road from Algeciras to Cordova, in September or October, 985.

Although Ibn Kennûn had been a cruel tyrant, who took a savage delight in hurling his prisoners from his "Eagles' Rock," the circumstances of his death seem everywhere to have excited commiseration. He was, it must be remembered, a *sharíf*, or descendant of 'Alî, the Prophet's son-in-law. To compass the death of such an one was sacrilege, in the eyes of the ignorant and superstitious masses. Even the rough troopers who, in obedience to orders, had carried out the execution, felt scruples, and a whirlwind which suddenly arose and flung them to the

ground they regarded as a miraculous retribution from
heaven.   Some inveighed against the impiety of Almanzor's
deed, others against his perfidy, declaring that he should
have kept the pledge given by his lieutenant as though it
had been his own.   These charges were made openly,
despite the dread inspired by the Minister, and the growing
disaffection became so manifest, that Almanzor could not
shut his eyes to the state of public opinion and began to
feel grave disquietude.   Judge then of his wrath when he
learnt that Askeleja was more indignant than any one, and
that in the hearing of his men he had dared to speak of his
kinsman's act as treachery.   Such effrontery called for
exemplary punishment.   Almanzor forthwith ordered his
cousin to return immediately to Spain, impeached him of
malversation and high treason, and his execution duly followed, in October or November, 985.   The popular clamour
was redoubled.   Pity for Askeleja was added to that for
the luckless *sharif*, and it was asked whether Almanzor had
not given fresh proof of his ruthlessness and of his contempt
for even the ties of blood in compassing his cousin's death.
Ibn Kennûn's kinsfolk, disappointed in the hopes which
they had formed when that prince seemed likely to make
himself master of Mauritania, did their utmost to stir up
discontent.   On their designs reaching Almanzor's ears, he
decreed their banishment.   They were accordingly expelled
from both Spain and Mauritania, but before they departed,
one of them, named Ibrâhîm ibn Edris, discharged a last
shaft against the Minister in the shape of a lengthy poem
which enjoyed much popularity, and of which the following
verses are a specimen :

"Miserable exile that I am!   Endless is my sad lot!   Misfortune dogs
me; he is my creditor, who the moment the bill falls due presents it to
me. . . . Events have stupefied me : grievous is our calamity and irremedi-
able.   I can scarcely believe my eyes, which seem to deceive me.   Can
the Omayyads still exist, and permit a hunch-back[1] to rule their vast
empire?   Lo! Soldiers march beside a litter wherein is a red baboon!
. . . Sons of Omayya, ye who of old shone like the stars at midnight, how is
your glory departed!   Once ye were like lions, but ye are such no longer.
Therefore The Fox hath seized the sovereignty!"

"The Fox"—for we see that the nickname bestowed in
Mus-hafy's verses still clung to Almanzor—had become convinced that he must take speedy steps to regain his popularity.

[1] Sheer slander : from impartial testimony we know that Almanzor was a
well-made man.

He accordingly determined to enlarge the Mosque, which had become too small to accommodate the Cordovans as well as the multitude of African troops. He began by expropriating the owners of the houses situated on the land required. This measure was one which needed very delicate handling to be rendered acceptable; but Almanzor was extraordinarily tactful in such matters. Summoning each householder alone into his presence—in itself a high honour —he would say to him: "My friend, it is my intention to enlarge the Mosque, that sacred edifice whence we address our prayers to heaven, and I wish to purchase your house for the good of the Moslem community and at the expense of the Treasury, which overflows with riches—thanks to the booty which I have wrested from the unbelievers. Tell me, therefore, the value you set upon your property; be not diffident; boldly name your price!" Upon the owner naming what he doubtless considered an exorbitant sum, the Minister would cry, "That is far too little! Your modesty is excessive. Come now, I will give you twice as much!" Whereupon, the happy owner was not only paid in ready money, but was provided with another house. Nevertheless a lady was found who for a long time refused to give up her home. In her garden there stood a beautiful palm-tree to which she was greatly attached, and when at last she consented to part with her property it was only on condition that another house should be bought for her, having in its garden just such another tree. This was hard to find: but the Minister, on hearing the lady's stipulation, exclaimed: "What she asks for must be obtained, if we have to empty the exchequer!" After great difficulty a house to the lady's liking was discovered, and bought for her at an exorbitant price.

Such liberality bore fruit. The Minister might be open to grave reproach, but it could not be denied that he was capable of generous and princely dealing, whilst the devout were obliged to admit that the enlargement of the Mosque was a highly meritorious design.

And, when once the work had been begun, what a sight met the Cordovans' eyes! A multitude of Christian captives, with irons on their ankles, were employed to clear the ground. Never before, it was said, had Islam's star shone with such glory; never had the unbelievers been so deeply humiliated! And then, Almanzor himself—the all-powerful ruler, the greatest Captain of the day—might have been seen plying the pickaxe, the trowel, or the saw, like a simple labourer—and all to the glory of God! In view of such a spectacle, detraction's voice was silenced.

While the enlargement of the Mosque was still in progress, war against Leon was renewed. The Moslem troops quartered in that kingdom treated it as a conquered country, and when Bermudo II complained of their conduct to Almanzor, the latter replied disdainfully. At last the king lost patience, and, mustering his courage, expelled the Moslems.

Almanzor felt it necessary to teach Bermudo another lesson, and, at the bottom of his heart, by no means regretted this renewal of war; for battles, victories, and conquests would provide the citizens with more desirable subjects of conversation than other matters, which, in his opinion, in no wise concerned them. Warlike topics were soon abundantly provided. Capturing Coimbra in June, 987, Almanzor so far wrecked the town that it remained desolate for seven years. Next year, crossing the Douro, the Moslem army burst into Leon like a torrent, bringing death and destruction in its train. Towns, castles, convents, churches, hamlets —none were spared. Bermudo had thrown himself into Zamora, doubtless in the belief that this town would be the first to be attacked, but Almanzor passed it by, and marched straight on Leon. He had on a previous occasion nearly succeeded in capturing the city, but its strong citadel, massive towers, gateways of solid marble, and Roman walls more than twenty feet thick, enabled it to hold out for a long time against all the efforts of the enemy. At length a breach was made near the Western Gate, at a moment when the Commander of the garrison, Gonsalvo Gonzalez,[1] a Galician Count, was struck down by grievous sickness. But so pressing was the danger, that the Count, ill though he was, forthwith donned his armour and was borne on a litter to the breach. By his exhortations and his mere presence he revived the flagging courage of the soldiers, and for three days they succeeded in keeping the enemy at bay, but on the fourth, the Moslems burst into the town through the Southern Gate. A dreadful carnage ensued. The Count himself, whose heroism should have inspired respect, was slain in his litter. The massacre over, the work of destruction began. Scarcely one stone of Leon was left upon another. The

---

[1] Lucas of Tuy, the sole authority on the point, calls him "Guillaume Gonzalez" —an impossible name—probably misinterpreting the abbreviation "G. Gonzalez." See *Recherches* (1881), i. 181–2.

gateways, towers and walls, the citadel, the dwelling-houses, were utterly demolished. A single tower, standing near the Northern Gate, and of about the same height as the others, was left standing, by Almanzor's command, in order to show future generations the former strength of the city which he had swept off the face of the earth.

The Moslems then withdrew in the direction of Zamora, and having burned on their way the splendid monasteries of San Pedro d'Eslonsa and Sahagun,[1] they laid siege to that city. Bermudo displayed less courage than his lieutenant at Leon, and secretly took to flight. The inhabitants thereupon surrendered the town to Almanzor, who gave it up to pillage. Nearly all the Counts now acknowledged Almanzor as their sovereign, and the districts bordering on the sea were all that were left to Bermudo.

On his return to Zâhira after this glorious campaign, Almanzor was obliged to turn his attention to urgent matters of grave importance, for he discovered that many persons of influence were plotting against him, and that his son 'Abdallah, a youth of twenty-two, was of their number.

Though a brave and dashing cavalier, 'Abdallah was not beloved of his father. The fact was that the latter had reason to doubt his paternity; though of this the young man was unaware. 'Abdallah, at any rate, saw that his brother 'Abd al-Malik, who was his junior by more than six years—and greatly his inferior, he considered, in talents and courage—was always preferred by Almanzor, and he had conceived bitter resentment against his father even before arriving at Zaragoza, where resided the Viceroy of the north-eastern frontier, the Todjîbite 'Abd-er-Rahmân ibn Motarrif. The atmosphere of this Court proved poison to 'Abdallah. His host was the head of an illustrious family in which the viceroyship of the province had been hereditary for a century, and since Almanzor had successively laid low the most powerful men in the empire, the Viceroy naturally feared that, as the last remaining noble, it would soon be his turn to fall victim to the Minister's ambition. He had resolved not to await passively this event, but to revolt at the first favourable opportunity. He thought this had now arrived; and 'Abdallah seemed a very suitable instrument. He fomented the young man's animosity against his father,

---

[1] See Risco, *Hist. de Leon*, i. 228, and *Esp. sagr.*, xxxiv. 308.

and began to hint of rebellion. At last they determined to
take up arms as soon as circumstances permitted, and agreed
that in the event of their being victorious they would parti-
tion Spain between them, 'Abdallah ruling in the South,
and 'Abd-er-Rahmân in the North. Many highly-placed
functionaries, both in the army and the civil service, joined
in the plot, among them being 'Abdallah " Flint-heart,"
then Governor of Toledo. The conspiracy was a formidable
one, but its ramifications were too wide-spread to remain
long hidden from the vigilant Minister. Vague rumours,
gradually acquiring precision, came to Almanzor's ears, and
he immediately took effectual measures to baffle his enemies'
designs. Recalling 'Abdallah, he inspired him with false
confidence by loading him with tokens of approbation and
affection. He next sent for 'Abdallah " Flint-heart," and
relieved him of the government of Toledo, but so courteously,
and on such a plausible pretext, that the prince's suspicions
were not aroused. A little later, however, Almanzor deprived
him of his viziership, and forbade him to quit his dwelling.

Having thus rendered harmless two of the chief conspirators, the Minister prepared to take the field against
Castile, and ordered the generals of the frontier to join him.
'Abd-er-Rahmân obeyed with the rest. Almanzor thereupon secretly instigated the soldiers of Zaragoza to lodge
complaints against the Viceroy. This they did, and upon
'Abd-er-Rahmân being accused of appropriating part of their
pay, Almanzor deposed him (June 8, 989). Not wishing,
however, to become embroiled with the whole clan of the
Beni Hâshim, he appointed 'Abd-er-Rahmân's son, Yahyâ
Simeja, Viceroy of the northern frontier in his father's stead.
A few days later 'Abd-er-Rahmân was arrested, but without
receiving any hint that the plot had been discovered: it was
merely announced that an inquiry would be held as to the
way in which the ex-viceroy had employed the sums entrusted to him for the payment of his troops.

Not long after this, the young 'Abdallah, in obedience
to orders, rejoined the army. Almanzor endeavoured to
regain his affection by acts of kindness, but in vain. 'Abdallah was determined definitely to break with his father,
and during the siege of San Estevan de Gormaz, he stole
away from the camp, accompanied only by six pages, to
seek refuge with Garcia Fernandez, Count of Castile.
The Count promised him his protection, and in spite of
Almanzor's threats kept his word for a year. But during

this period he suffered reverse after reverse: he was not only defeated in the open field; but in August, 989, he lost Osma—which Almanzor garrisoned with Moslems—and in October Alcoba was wrested from him: finally he was forced to sue for peace and to surrender 'Abdallah.

A Castilian escort conducted the young rebel towards Almanzor's camp. He set out seated on a splendidly caparisoned mule, a gift from the Count, and being convinced that his father would pardon him, he felt no uneasiness. On the way he met a Musulman detachment under the command of Sa'd. This officer having kissed 'Abdallah's hand, assured him that he had nothing to fear, for his father looked upon what he had done as a mere act of folly, which in so young a man might be pardoned. Such were his assurances while the Castilians were present; but when they had retired, and the cavalcade reached the Douro, Sa'd fell back to the rear, and the soldiers bade 'Abdallah dismount and prepare for death. At these words, unexpected though they were, the valiant 'Âmirid showed no emotion. He leaped lightly from his mule, and with a tranquil mien, yielded his neck, without a tremor, to the fatal stroke (Sept. 9, 990). His accomplice 'Abd-er-Rahmân had already paid the penalty. Found guilty of malversation, he had been beheaded at Zâhira. 'Abdallah " Flint-heart " had, however, succeeded in escaping and had found protection with Bermudo.

Almanzor was by no means content with having trampled out the conspiracy. He had not forgiven the Count of Castile for harbouring 'Abdallah, and by way of reprisal, he instigated Sancho, the Count's son, to rebel, in turn, against his father. Supported by most of the influential Castilians, Sancho took up arms in 994, and Almanzor, who immediately declared for him, seized the fortresses of San Estevan and Clunia. Almanzor, however, wished to bring the war to a speedy close. His courtiers, accustomed to agree with him, at any rate ostensibly, shared his impatience, and there was no better mode of pleasing the Minister than to assure him that Garcia seemed likely soon to yield. Now the poet Sâ'id one day presented him with a deer, which he led by a cord, and recited a not very brilliant poem, in which the following verses occurred:

" I, your slave, whom you rescued from poverty and loaded with bounties, bring you this deer. I have named him 'Garcia,' and I bring him with his neck in a noose, in the hope that my prognostic may come true."

By a strange chance the prediction was fulfilled : Garcia had been made prisoner, between Alcocer and Langa, on the banks of the Douro, on that very day (Monday, May 25, 995). Five days later the Count died from the effect of his wounds,[1] and Sancho's authority was henceforth undisputed : he was, however, obliged to pay yearly tribute to the Moslems.

In the autumn of the same year Almanzor took the offensive against Bermudo, to punish him for having harboured another conspirator. The king was in pitiable case. He possessed scarcely the shadow of authority. The nobles had laid their hands on his territories, his serfs, and his flocks ; these they had shared by lot among themselves, and when he expostulated they laughed him to scorn. Even land-owners, to whom he had entrusted the defence of a castle here and there, broke into revolt. Every now and then a rumour of Bermudo's death was spread—but whether it were true or not mattered little. It was indeed sheer foolhardiness in him to brave Almanzor. What hope could he have of resisting that all-conquering warrior ? Absolutely none ; and he soon repented of his imprudence. Having lost Astorga—which after the destruction of Leon he had made his Capital, but which on the approach of the foe he had prudently abandoned—he adopted the wisest course, and sued for peace. This he obtained on condition that he surrendered 'Abdallah " Flint-heart," and paid a yearly tribute.

Having taken their Capital from the Counts Gomez of Carrion — who, it appears, had slighted his authority— Almanzor marched homewards, bringing with him the unfortunate 'Abdallah, who had been delivered up to him in November. As might have been foreseen, a bitter punishment was inflicted on this prince. Loaded with chains, and mounted on a camel, he was led ignominiously through the streets of the Capital, preceded by a herald who proclaimed : " Behold 'Abdallah, son of 'Abd al-'Azíz, who forsook Islam to make common cause with the enemies of the faith !" When he heard these words for the first time, the prince in his indignation cried out, " Thou liest ! Say rather, ' Behold a man who fled through fear : he aimed at sovereignty, but he is neither a polytheist nor an apostate !' "

'Abdallah, however, had no force of character : he did

---

[1] Some chronicles give " viii. ka!. *Ianuarii*," in error for *Junii*.

not remember that a conspirator needs, above all things, to arm himself with courage. When lying in prison, in daily dread of the scaffold, he showed cowardice unworthy of his high birth and strongly contrasted with the fortitude displayed by his fellow-conspirator, the son of Almanzor. In verses which he sent to the Minister he pleaded that his flight was an ill-advised act, and he sought to appease Almanzor's wrath by flattery, calling him the noblest of men : " Never," he wrote, " hath the unfortunate besought thy pity in vain : thy bounties and mercies are as the rain from heaven." Such cringing availed him a little. Almanzor spared his life because he despised him : but 'Abdallah remained in prison and did not regain his liberty till after the Minister's death.

[AUTHORITIES : Ibn Khaldûn, " History of the Christian Kings of Spain " (transl.), in Dozy's Recherches (1881), i. 89–116 ; Hist. des Berbers, iii. 219, 237 ; Samp., c. 29 ; Chron. Iri., c. 12 ; Ibn al-'Abbâr, 113–19, 154, 251–3 ; Ibn al-Khatîb (MS. G.), 180–1 ; Ibn Adhârî, i. 248 ; ii. 301 sq. ; Kartás, 58–9 ; Makkarî, i. 359–60, 389 ; ii. 57 ; Abd al-Wâhid, 24–5 ; Abu 'l-Fidâ, ii. 534 ; Chron. Burg., p. 309 ; Ann. Compl., p. 313 ; Ann. Compo., p. 320 ; Ann. Tol., i. p. 384 ; Esp. sagr., xix. pp. 382 sq. ; xxxvi. iv.]

CHAPTER XI

SANTIAGO DE COMPOSTELA

ALMANZOR, who had been sovereign *de facto* for twenty years, had set his heart on reigning *de jure*. Blind indeed were those who did not foresee that this was the goal towards which he had been advancing—slowly, warily, with calculated steps, but with a pertinacity not to be mistaken.

In 991 he resigned his title of *hájib*, or Prime Minister, in favour of his son 'Abd al-Malik, then scarcely eighteen years old, announcing at the same time that henceforth he desired to be referred to as Almanzor, simply.

In 992 he decreed that to documents issuing from the chancellery his own seal, instead of the Khalif's, should be affixed; and he assumed the surname of Muwaiyad, which the Khalif also bore.

In 996 he commanded that the designation of *sayid* (lord) should be applied to himself alone, and at the same time he assumed the title of *malik karím* (noble king).

King, therefore, he had become—but, as yet, not Khalif. If any obstacle stood in the way of his attainment of the supreme dignity, it was assuredly not Hishâm II. He was not to be dreaded. Although the Prince was now in the prime of life, he had never shown the least initiative, nor evinced the slightest desire to shake off the yoke which lay upon him. There was nothing, moreover, to be feared from the princes of the blood. Almanzor had put to death the most formidable, exiled others, and reduced the rest almost to poverty. He was far from having any cause to think the army likely to thwart his ambitions. Composed as it was, for the most part, of Berbers, Christians of the North, Slavs, and soldiers who had been prisoners of war in their infancy—in fact, of adventurers of every kind—the army was his own: do what he would, he could rely on their blind obedience. What then need Almanzor fear?

He feared the nation. Hishâm II was a stranger to his people: few, even in his Capital, had seen his face, for upon the rare occasions on which he quitted his gilded prison

to visit one of his country palaces, he was surrounded by
the ladies of the harem; like them he was, moreover,
wrapped in a large hooded cloak, so that he could not be
distinguished among the women, while the streets through
which he passed were lined with troops by the Minister's
express orders. Yet, in spite of his seclusion, Hishâm was
beloved of his people. Was he not son of the just and
virtuous Hakam II, and grandson of the illustrious 'Abd-
er-Rahmân III ? Was he not, above all, the legitimate
monarch ?

Reverence for the principle of legitimacy was firmly
rooted in every heart, but it flourished in even greater
vigour among the commonalty than among the nobles.
The latter, for the most part of Arab origin, could perhaps
convince themselves that a change of dynasty from time
to time might be useful, or even necessary: but no such
ideas entered the minds of the people, who were of Spanish
stock. Side by side with religious sentiments, love for the
dynasty was ingrained in their hearts. Although Almanzor
had brought the country glory and prosperity hitherto
undreamed of, the people could not forgive him for making
the Khalif, to all intents, a State prisoner, and they were
ready to break out into general insurrection if the Minister
dared to make any attempt to place himself upon the
throne.

Almanzor was well aware of this fact—hence his prudence
and hesitation—but he trusted to a gradual change in public
opinion: he flattered himself with the hope that in the end
the Khalif would be wholly forgotten, and that all thoughts
would centre on himself alone: in that case the change of
dynasty would cause no convulsion.

It was well for Almanzor that he had postponed his
crowning project. He was soon to be convinced that after
all his power hung by a thread. Despite his conquests and
his renown, he came near to being overthrown by a woman.
That woman was Aurora. She had once loved him, but
the age of tender sentiments had passed for both of them;
they quarrelled, and, as often happens, love was replaced in
their hearts, not by indifference but by hatred. Aurora did
nothing by halves: devoted as a lover, in resentment she
was implacable. She resolved upon Almanzor's ruin, and
to this end she stirred up something like indignation even
in the tranquil harem. She expostulated with her son and
told him that honour demanded that he should play the

man and at last break the yoke which a tyrannical minister
had laid upon him.   She worked a miracle : she aroused in
the feeblest of mortals a faint flicker of determination and
energy. This Almanzor soon discovered. The Khalif began
by treating him coldly ; then, taking courage, he hazarded
some reproaches. Wishing to lay the tempest, the Minister
removed from the seraglio certain persons whom he deemed
dangerous, but as he could not rid himself of her who was
the soul of the conspiracy, this measure merely served to
inflame the enemy's rage. The Navarrese woman was
tireless : possessor of an iron will, she proved an opponent
worthy of her former lover's steel. Her agents everywhere
spread a report that the Khalif judged that the time had
come for him to exercise personal and untrammelled
sovereignty, and that he counted upon his people's loyalty
to deliver him from his gaoler. The Sultana's emissaries
even crossed the Straits, and, simultaneously with riotous
outbreaks in Cordova, the standard of revolt was raised
by Zîrî ibn Atîa, Viceroy of Mauritania, who declared that
he would no longer permit his rightful sovereign to be kept
in durance by a domineering minister.

Zîrî was the only man whom Almanzor still feared : the
only man, rather, whom he had ever feared, for as a rule he
despised his enemies too much to stand in dread of them.
This semi-barbarian chieftain had preserved in the African
deserts an energy, resolution, and pride of race which seemed
to belong to an earlier age, and already, though sorely against
the grain, Almanzor had submitted to the ascendancy of
his swift, penetrating, and caustic intellect. Some years
before, he had received a visit from Zîrî, and upon that
occasion had loaded him with tokens of esteem ; he had conferred upon him the title of Vizier with the emoluments
attached to that dignity and inscribed all the members of
his retinue upon the military pay-sheet, and, finally, Zîrî
had not been suffered to depart until he had been amply
repaid for the expenses of his journey and his presents. But
by this generosity the Viceroy was quite untouched. When
he landed once more in Africa, he raised his hand to his
head and said, " For the present, thou still belongest to
me ! "   Later, upon one of his servants addressing him as
" My lord Vizier," " Lord Vizier ? " he exclaimed : " To
the devil with thy ' lord Vizier ' !   I am an Emir, and son of
an Emir. Ibn Abî 'Âmir—niggard that he is—instead of
paying me good hard cash, bedizens me with a degrading

title ! By the living God ! he would not be what he is if
Spain contained any besides fools and cowards ! Thanks to
heaven, I am at home again, and that proverb lieth not
which saith, ' Better hear tell of the devil than see him.' "
These words, which would have cost any other speaker his
head, reached the ears of Almanzor, who however appeared
to disregard them, and not long afterwards even appointed
Zîrî viceroy of all Mauritania. Almanzor, although he
feared, and perhaps hated, him, believed Zîrî to be sincere
and loyal. The event showed that he was mistaken. Beneath a mask of blunt frankness Zîrî concealed not a little
craft and ambition. He allowed himself to be easily tempted
by Aurora's promised bribe, and by the chivalrous part she
suggested his playing. He would lift Almanzor's yoke from
the Khalif's neck—and replace it by his own.

Aurora was fully aware that payment in advance was
necessary, and with a woman's wit, had hit upon a plan for
procuring the money and conveying it to her ally. The
treasury, situated within the palace of the Khalifate, contained about six million pieces of gold ; taking thence eighty
thousand pieces, Aurora placed them in a hundred jars
which she filled up with honey, cordials and household
condiments. These jars, appropriately labelled, she entrusted to certain Slavs who conveyed them outside the
city to a spot which she indicated. The artifice was successful. The Prefect's suspicions were not aroused, and the
Slavs were allowed to pass with their burdens. The money
was already on its way to Mauritania, when Almanzor by
some means discovered the stratagem. He was seriously
alarmed. Perhaps he would have been less perturbed if
he had known that Aurora had merely made free with the
monarch's store, but all the circumstances seemed to point
to her having acted by the Khalif's authority, and if that
was the case the situation was indeed critical. Something,
however, must be done. Almanzor accordingly assembled
the viziers, magistrates, divines, and other personages of
importance in the court and the city.

Having informed the assembly that the Khalif, entirely
devoted as he was to religious exercises, had made no
attempt to prevent the ladies of the harem pilfering from
the treasury, he demanded formal permission to remove
the exchequer to a safer place. The authorization was
granted, but without practical result, for when the officials
presented themselves at the palace to remove the money,

Aurora refused to admit them, alleging that the Khalif forbade the coffers to be touched.

Almanzor was confronted by a dilemma. To employ force would be to offer violence to the Khalif himself, and if Almanzor were to venture upon such a step insurrection would instantly follow: the city was ripe for revolt, and awaited but the signal. Perilous though the situation was, it would nevertheless not become hopeless until Zîrî landed with an army in Spain and the Khalif proved himself a man of steadfast determination. But Zîrî was still in Africa, and the Khalif was infirm of purpose; Almanzor therefore did not yet lose heart. Playing a desperate game, he contrived, unknown to Aurora, to gain audience of the monarch. Such was the ascendancy of a masterful spirit over vacillating timidity, that after a few minutes' converse the Minister found himself once more king. The Khalif confessed that he was incapable of personal rule, and he further authorized the removal of the treasure. But this did not satisfy Almanzor. In order to cut the ground from beneath the feet of the ill-disposed, he insisted on a solemn declaration, in writing. The Khalif promised to sign whatever was placed before him, and Almanzor forthwith drew up a document by virtue of which Hishâm resigned to him the administration of the realm as heretofore. This instrument was signed by the Khalif in the presence of many notables who affixed their signatures as witnesses (February or March, 997), and Almanzor took care to give it all possible publicity.

Thenceforth all fear of a revolt in the Capital was at an end. Who would attempt to set free a captive who shrank from liberty?

Almanzor, however, thought it well to put the populace in good humour. They were for ever clamouring for a sight of their monarch. It should be granted to them. Hishâm, accordingly, made a progress on horseback through the streets sceptre in hand, and wearing on his head the lofty headdress which the Khalifs alone were entitled to assume. He was accompanied by Almanzor and the entire court. Dense crowds thronged the route, but perfect order was maintained, and not a single seditious cry was raised.

Aurora bowed to the inevitable. Humiliated, weary, heart-broken, she sought in religion forgetfulness of the past, and compensation for her lost hopes.[1] There remained

---

[1] See the concluding verses of the elegy on the death of Aurora by Ibn-Darrâdj Castallî : Tha'âlibî, Yetîma, Bodl. MS. (Seld. A. 19, and Marsh. 99).

Zîrî. He had become much less formidable now that he could no longer reckon upon moral support from the Khalif nor funds from Aurora. Almanzor felt that the time for negotiation had passed. He accordingly declared Zîrî an outlaw, and ordered his freedman Wâdhih to take the field against him at the head of a well-equipped force.

It might have been thought unlikely that Almanzor would undertake another war before this Mauritanian campaign had been concluded. But he had no hesitation in doing so. The Minister had in fact already planned, in concert with the Counts of Leon, a vigorous expedition against Bermudo, who, with too much reliance on the diversion in his favour which he thought Zîrî's revolt would cause, had ventured to refuse payment of tribute. Although circumstances had changed, Almanzor adhered to this design : perhaps he wished to show Zîrî, Bermudo, and all his enemies, actual and potential, that he was well able to wage two wars simultaneously. However this may be, he had not over-estimated his ability, for the campaign he was about to enter upon—afterwards known as that of Santiago de Compostela—was destined to be the most famous of all those waged during the conqueror's long career.

With the exception of the Eternal City, there was no place in Europe more renowned for its sanctity than Compostela in Galicia. Its fame, however, was not of very long standing. It was in the days of Charlemagne, so ran the legend, that certain folk told Theodemir, Bishop of Iria (now El Padron), that they had seen during the night strange lights in a thicket, whence also proceeded ravishing strains of unearthly music. Suspecting a miracle, the bishop prepared himself for the proof by three days of prayer and fasting : then, entering the thicket, he discovered a marble tomb. By divine inspiration he was enabled to announce that this was none other than the sepulchre of the Apostle S. James, son of Zebedee—who, according to tradition, had preached the Gospel in Spain—and the bishop was further able to relate that after the Apostle had been beheaded at Jerusalem by order of Herod, the disciples bore the body to Galicia, and buried it there. In another age these assertions would, perhaps, have been disputed, but in those days of simple faith none had the hardihood to raise irreverent doubts when the Church spoke, and even if some had been disposed to be incredulous, the solemn declaration of Pope Leo III that the tomb in question was truly that of S.

James, cut short all criticism.[1] Theodemir's opinion was
therefore regarded as a revelation, and the Galicians rejoiced
that in their land rested the bones of an Apostle. It was the
wish of Alfonso II that the Bishop of Iria should henceforth reside near the spot where the Apostle lay, and over
the tomb he built a church. At a later period Alfonso
erected a larger and more beautiful edifice, and, in consequence of the many miracles worked within its walls, this
soon acquired great renown. By the end of the tenth
century the famous shrine of Santiago de Compostela had
become the resort of pilgrims from France, Italy, and
Germany, and even from the remotest regions of the
East.[2]

In Andalusia, therefore, everybody had heard of Compostela and its splendid Cathedral, which—to use the phrase
of an Arab chronicler—was to Christians what the Ka'ba
at Mecca was to Musulmans. Nevertheless, to the Andalusians the holy place was known only by hearsay : to see it,
it was necessary to be taken captive by the Galicians, for no
Arab prince had yet dreamed of penetrating, with an army,
this rugged and distant region.

But what none had even attempted, Almanzor resolved
to accomplish : he wished to show that what was impossible
for others was feasible for himself, and he conceived the
ambition of destroying the most hallowed sanctuary of
Islam's foes, the shrine of that Apostle who, the Leonese
believed, had often fought in their ranks.

On Saturday, July 3, 997, Almanzor set out from
Cordova at the head of his cavalry. He proceeded, by way
of Coria, to Viseu, where he was joined by a number of
Counts who acknowledged his authority ; thence he pushed
on to Oporto, where he found his fleet which had sailed from
Kasr-Abî-Dânis (now Alcacer do Sal, in Portugal). The
fleet had conveyed the infantry—who had thus been spared
a long march—as well as ample stores of arms and provisions.
The vessels, moored stem to stern, formed, moreover, a
bridge by which the army crossed the Douro. Since the
district between the Douro and the Minho belonged to
friendly Counts, the Moslems traversed it without encountering any difficulties save those due to the physical features of
the region, the most formidable of which was a lofty and

---

[1] According to another account it was the Pope who first gave the information
attributed above to the Bishop. See F. Meyrick, *The Church in Spain* (1892), p. 237.
[2] *Esp. sagr.*, iii. xix.

precipitous mountain-range over which Almanzor's sappers constructed a road.

Crossing the Minho, the army entered the enemy's country. Henceforth vigilance was needed—the more so since the Leonese contingent seemed none too well disposed. Their consciences, so long torpid, suddenly awoke at the thought that they were about to commit the foulest sacrilege,. and they might have frustrated the expedition, had not Almanzor, who had got wind of their designs, checkmated them before it was too late. The narrative of the chroniclers is, in effect, as follows: The night was chill and rainy when Almanzor summoned a Moslem trooper on whom he could rely. "Ride with all haste," he said, "to the defile of Taliares:[1] there act as sentinel, and bring me the first man who approaches the pass." The horseman instantly rode off, reached the defile, and watched throughout the night, execrating the bad weather, but without seeing a living being. Just as the first streaks of dawn appeared, how- ever, there was to be seen approaching, from the direction of the camp, an old man seated on an ass. He was apparently a wood-cutter, and carried with him the tools of his calling. The sentinel challenged him, and asked him whither he was going. "To fell trees in the forest," replied the peasant. The soldier was embarrassed. Could this be the man whom the General desired to be brought to him? It seemed highly improbable that he would care to see this beggarly old man. Accordingly he allowed the wood-cutter to pass on. A few moments later, however, he remembered that Almanzor's orders had been precise, and that it was perilous to disobey them. Putting spurs to his horse, he caught up the old man. "I must conduct you," he said, " to my master Almanzor." " What can Almanzor have to say to such an one as I?" asked the wood-cutter: " Suffer me, I pray thee, to go on my way and earn my bread." " Nay," replied the trooper, " willy-nilly thou must come with me." The old man perforce obeyed, and they returned together to the camp.

The Minister, who had not gone to bed, showed no surprise at seeing the wood-cutter, and turning to his Slav attendants, said, " Search this man!" The order was obeyed, but nothing incriminating was found upon him. " Search

[1] Near the Minho; as appears from a charter of Bermudo II (*Esp. sagr.*, xix. 381).

the trappings of his ass," then added Almanzor. This time his suspicions were justified; concealed in the saddle-cloth a letter was discovered, addressed by some Leonese in the Moslem army to their compatriots, informing them that on one side the camp was ill-protected and might be attacked with success. Having learnt from this letter who the traitors were, Almanzor immediately had them beheaded, as well as the pretended wood-cutter who had acted as intermediary. Such an energetic measure proved effectual. Intimidated by the General's prompt severity the other Leonese made no further attempts to communicate with the enemy.

The army resumed its march, and before long poured like a torrent into the plains. The monastery of SS. Cosmas and Damian[1] was pillaged, and the fortress of San Payo was stormed. A large number of the inhabitants of the district sought refuge on the larger of two islands, or rather low rocks, in the Bay of Vigo, but the Moslems, hitting upon a ford, crossed over to the island and stripped the fugitives of everything they had carried thither. Next, crossing the Ulla, they pillaged and destroyed Iria (El Padron), itself a famous place of pilgrimage, and on August 11 they reached Compostela. They found the town deserted, for all the inhabitants had fled at the approach of the foe. A solitary monk knelt before the tomb of the Apostle. "What doest thou here?" demanded Almanzor. "I am praying to S. James," replied the old man. "Pray on!" said the Minister, and he forbade the soldiers to molest the monk.

Almanzor set a guard over the tomb to protect it from injury, but the rest of the town was handed over to destruction: not only were the ramparts and the houses demolished but the church itself, which, says an Arab writer, "was razed so effectually that on the morrow no one would have supposed that it had ever existed." The neighbouring territory was then laid waste by flying squadrons that pushed on as far as San Cosmo de Mayanca, near Coruña.

After remaining for a week at Compostela, Almanzor ordered a withdrawal in the direction of Lamego.[2] Arriving at that town he took leave of his allies, the Counts, not

---

[1] In the mountains between Bayona and Tuy; afterwards known as that of San Colmado. See Sandoval, *Antiguedades de Tuy*, 120.

[2] Or, according to Ibn Adhârî, "Malego."

without conferring on them rich gifts consisting for the most part of costly fabrics. From Lamego he despatched to the Court a detailed account of the campaign, and of this Arab writers have preserved not only the substance, but perhaps the very words. In due time Almanzor made his entry into Cordova accompanied by a multitude of Christian captives bearing on their shoulders the gates of Santiago and the bells of the church. The doors were placed in the roof of the unfinished mosque,[1] and the bells were suspended in the same edifice to serve as lamps. Who could have foreseen that the day would come when a Christian king would re-store those bells to Galicia, borne on the backs of captive Moslems?

The campaign in Mauritania had gone less favourably for Almanzor. Wâdhih, it is true, had at the outset met with some success: he had seized Arzilla and Nekûr, and had surprised Zîrî's camp by night, inflicting heavy losses, but soon after this, his good fortune deserted him; and de-feated in his turn, he was obliged to take refuge in Tangier. Thence he despatched a message to the Minister, asking for reinforcements. These were speedily forthcoming. As soon as he received his lieutenant's letter, Almanzor ordered a large force to Algeciras, and to expedite their embarkation he proceeded to that port himself. His son 'Abd al-Malik Muzaffar, to whom he entrusted the command of the expedi-tion, crossed the Straits with a well-equipped army. He landed at Ceuta, and the news of his arrival produced an excellent effect, for most of the Berber princes who had hitherto sided with Zîrî flocked to his standard. Having effected a junction with Wâdhih's troops, he took the field, and soon came in touch with Zîrî's army, which was advancing to oppose him. A pitched battle was fought in October, 998. The desperate conflict raged from dawn to sunset. A crisis at last came when Muzaffar's soldiers seemed on the verge of defeat, but at that moment Zîrî received three wounds at the hand of one of his own negroes, whose brother he had put to death. The assailant instantly rode off at full speed to tell the news to Muzaffar. Since Zîrî's standard was not lowered the prince at first discredited the deserter's story, but on being convinced of its truth, he charged and utterly routed the enemy. Zîrî's power was finally broken: the regions under his influence

---

[1] See *Recherches* (1881), i. p. 101.

were restored to the Cordovan Khalifate, and about three years later, in 1001, he died in consequence of the re-opening of the wounds inflicted on him by his negro assailant.

[AUTHORITIES: Ibn Adhârî, i. 262; ii. 315–18; *Kartâs*, 65–7, 73; Makkarî, i. 389, 393; ii. 64, 146, 318–19; Nuwairî, p. 471; Ibn-Khaldûn, *Hist. des Berbers*, ii. 41; iii. 243–8.]

CHAPTER XII

DEATH OF ALMANZOR

ALMANZOR'S career was drawing to a close. In the spring of 1002 he set out on his last campaign. He had always craved to die in the field, and so firmly was he convinced that his prayer to this effect would be granted that he invariably carried his shroud in his baggage. This had been stitched by his daughters, and the linen of which it was made was purchased with money accruing from lands around his ancestral home at Torrox; for his winding-sheet must be spotless and unpolluted, and he deemed that his revenues from other sources could not be thus characterised. As he grew old he became more devout, and since the Koran declares that God will save from the fires of Hell him whose feet are covered with the dust of His highway [1]— gathered, that is, in holy wars—it was Almanzor's wont, whenever he reached a halting-place, to shake off carefully the dust from his clothes and to preserve it in a casket made for the purpose. With this dust, such were his injunctions, he was to be sprinkled when he had breathed his last and was laid in the tomb, for he was persuaded that the toils which he had endured in religious warfare would prove his best justification before the Judgment Throne.

Almanzor's final campaign, which was directed against Castile, was as successful as all its predecessors. He penetrated as far as Canales,[2] and destroyed the monastery of S. Emilian, patron saint of Castile, just as he had destroyed, five years before, the church of the patron saint of Galicia.

Upon his homeward march Almanzor felt aggravation in the symptoms of a malady from which he suffered. Distrusting the physicians, who were agreed neither as to the nature of his disorder nor its treatment, he stubbornly refused medical aid, and became convinced that he would not recover. No longer able to mount his horse, he was borne in a litter. He endured torments. " Of the twenty

---

[1] *Koran, Sura,* ii. 149.   [2] In Rioja, 20 m. S. of Najera.

thousand soldiers in my army," he exclaimed, "not one
suffers anguish like mine!"

After being thus carried by his men for a fortnight, he
at last reached Medinaceli. A single thought possessed his
mind. His authority had never been undisputed, and it
had at times hung in the balance in spite of his many
victories and great renown; he feared therefore that after
his death a revolt would ensue and that all power would be
wrested from his family. Ceaselessly tormented by this
apprehension, which embittered his last days, he summoned
his eldest son 'Abd al-Malik to his bedside, and in giving
him his last instructions urged him to hasten to the Capital
—after entrusting the command of the army to his brother
'Abd-er-Rahmân—and upon arriving there to seize the reins
and hold himself in readiness to quell instantly the slightest
symptom of rebellion. 'Abd al-Malik promised to obey his
injunctions, but such were Almanzor's misgivings, that as
often as his son, believing the interview at an end, prepared
to withdraw, he called him back: the dying man was oppressed by the fear that he had forgotten some essential
detail, and on each occasion he found some fresh counsel for
his son. The young man burst into tears, but his father
chided him for his weakness in displaying grief. When
'Abd al-Malik had at last been allowed to depart, Almanzor
rallied a little and sent for his officers. They scarcely recognised their General: so pale and emaciated had be become that he looked like a spectre, and he had almost lost
the power of speech. Partly by signs, partly in broken
words, he bade them farewell, and shortly afterwards, during
the night of Monday, August 10, he breathed his last. He
was buried at Medinaceli, and on his tomb was engraved
this inscription:

His history is written upon the earth if thou hast eyes to read it. By
Allah! the years will never produce his like, nor such another defender of
our coasts.

The epitaph composed by a Christian monk and preserved in his chronicle is, however, not less illuminating.
"Almanzor," he writes, "died in 1002: he was buried in
Hell."[1] These simple words, wrung from the hatred of a
fallen foe, are more eloquent than the most pompous
panegyric.

[1] *Chron. Burg.*, p. 309.

Never, indeed, did the Christians of northern Spain have another such adversary to contend with. Almanzor conducted more than fifty campaigns against them—his usual habit being to undertake two every year, in the Spring and Autumn respectively—and in none of these had he failed to enchance his fame. Not to speak of a multitude of towns—amongst which the three Capitals, Leon, Pamplona[1] and Barcelona would be included—he had laid waste the sanctuaries of the patron saints of Galicia and Castile. "In those days," writes a Christian chronicler,[2] "divine worship was extinguished in Spain: the glory of Christ's servants was brought low: the treasures of the Church amassed in the course of centuries were all pillaged." The Christians, therefore, shuddered at Almanzor's name. The terror which he inspired more than once rescued him from perils into which his audacity led him: even when his enemies actually had him in their power, they dared not seize their opportunity. Once, for instance, he penetrated a hostile region through a narrow defile between two lofty mountains; and although his troops ravaged and pillaged in all directions the Christians did not venture to resist them. Upon retracing his steps, however, Almanzor found the pass occupied by the enemy. As it was impossible for the Moslems to force it, their position was hazardous; but their General instantly conceived a bold design. After selecting a place suitable for his project, he caused sheds and huts to be erected, and ordered a number of prisoners to be decapitated and a rampart to be constructed with their bodies. Then, after his cavalry had scoured the country without finding provender, he collected implements of husbandry and set the soldiers to work at tilling the ground. Greatly perturbed at operations which seemed to imply that the Moslems had no intention of quitting the country, the Christians proposed peace on condition that the enemy would abandon their booty. But Almanzor rejected the proposal: "My soldiers," he replied, "prefer to remain where they are: they recognise that it is scarcely worth their while to return home, for the next campaign will begin almost immediately." After further negotiations the Christians ultimately agreed to allow Almanzor to depart with his booty, and their dread of him was such that they even undertook to provide him with

[1] See a charter of 1027, in Llorente, *Noticias de las tres Provincias Vascongadas*, Madrid, 1806, iii. 355.
[2] *Monachi Silensis Chronicon* (*Esp. sagr.*, xvii.), c. 72.

beasts of burden to carry it, to supply him with provisions as far as the frontier, and to remove the corpses which obstructed the route of his army.[1]

Upon another occasion a standard-bearer, during a retrograde movement, forgot his standard, and left it planted in the ground on the summit of a hill overlooking a Christian town. There the flag flew for many days, during which the Christians did not venture to ascertain whether the Moslems held the position or not.

It is related that an envoy from Almanzor to the Court of Garcia of Navarre—where he was loaded with honours—while visiting a church chanced upon an aged Moslem woman, who told him that she had been made prisoner as a child, and had ever since lived as a slave within the sacred precincts. She begged the envoy to draw Almanzor's attention to her case: he promised to do so, and shortly afterwards returned home and rendered an account of his mission to the Minister. When he had made an end of his report, Almanzor asked him whether he had seen anything in Navarre which displeased him. Thereupon the envoy mentioned the Moslem slave. "By Allah!" cried Almanzor, "that is what thou shouldst have begun with!" Forthwith taking the field, he advanced to the frontier of Navarre. In great alarm Garcia wrote to him asking what fault he had committed, seeing that he was not conscious of having done aught to offend him. "What!" exclaimed the Minister to the messengers who brought the letter, "Did he not swear to me that there remained not in his country a single Moslem prisoner of either sex? He lied! It hath come to my knowledge that there is a Moslem woman in one of your churches, and I do not quit Navarre until she hath been placed in my hands." Upon receiving this answer, Garcia lost not a moment in sending to Almanzor the woman he demanded, together with two others whom search had brought to light. At the same time the King made oath that he had neither seen nor heard of these women, adding that he had ordered the destruction of the church which Almanzor had alluded to.

While Almanzor was the terror of his foes, he was the idol of his soldiers. They looked upon him as a father, always solicitous about their every need. In matters of military discipline, however, he was relentless. One day

[1] *Cf.* Rodrigo de Toledo, *Hist. Arabum*, c. 31.

when he was inspecting his troops, he noticed in the ranks the glitter of a sword which should have been sheathed. He instantly ordered the offending soldier to be brought before him. "Darest thou," exclaimed Almanzor flushing with rage, "darest thou draw thy sword before the word of command is given?" "I did but wish to show it to a comrade," stammered the culprit; "I meant not to draw it from its scabbard: it slipped forth by chance." "Vain excuse!" cried Almanzor, who turned to his staff and added: "Let this man's head be struck off with his own sword, and let his body be borne along the ranks as a lesson in discipline!" Such an example inspired the troops with salutary dread. When they filed past him in review they preserved a solemn silence. "The very horses," writes an Arab author, "seemed to know their duty; a neigh was rarely heard."

Thanks to the army, which he had created and disciplined, Almanzor won for Mohammedan Spain power and prosperity which she had never before enjoyed, even in the days of 'Abd-er-Rahmân III. But this was not his sole merit: not only his country, but civilization itself was under other obligations to him. He admired and fostered intellectual culture, and although obliged on political grounds to give no encouragement to philosophers, he delighted in affording them protection when he could do so without running counter to ecclesiastical prejudices. It happened, for instance, that a certain Ibn as-Sonbosî[1] was arrested and imprisoned on suspicion of infidelity. Many witnesses bore testimony against him, and the Fakihs adjudged him deserving of death. The sentence was on the point of being executed when a very influential Fakih, Ibn al-Makwâ, who had declined to sit upon the tribunal, hurriedly entered. By dint of amazing sophisms, which did more honour to his kindness of heart than to his logic, he succeeded in getting the sentence revoked, despite the violent opposition of the presiding Kady.[2] The latter straightway fell under Almanzor's displeasure. Delighted at finding an opportunity of curbing the fierce fanaticism of the bigots, the Minister exclaimed: "We must support religion, and all true believers are entitled to our protection. The tribunal has declared

---

[1] Kâsim ibn Mohammed Sonbosî: several other men of letters were arrested at the same time, and were placed every Friday before the door of the Mosque, while a herald cried, "Let all who can bear witness against these men, do so!" *Recherches* (1881), ii. 237.

[2] Ibn as-Sari, *ibid.*

that Ibn as-Sonbosî is of their number; nevertheless, the President made unheard-of efforts to procure his condemnation: the Kady is therefore a bloodthirsty man, and, as such, cannot be permitted to live." This was intended merely as a warning. The Kady was thrown into prison for a few days, and it may be presumed that henceforth he showed less rigour towards unfortunate sceptics who ventured to disregard received dogmas.

Men of letters found a hearty welcome at Almanzor's Court; there, too, a bevy of poets were lodged, who drew stipends, and sometimes accompanied their patron on his campaigns. Among these, Sâ'id of Baghdad, though not the most illustrious, was the most conspicuous and the most entertaining. Though the Andalusians, ever jealous of strangers, would have been delighted to do so—they could not deny that he was a talented writer of verses and romances, and a clever improvisator; but at the same time he was regardless of truth, and the most impudent hoaxer imaginable. Once started, there was no checking him, and he would pour forth a flood of wondrous mystifications. If asked to interpret a non-existent word, he always had an explanation ready, and a confirmatory passage from an ancient writer. If he were to be credited, there was no book which he had not read. One day, wishing to unmask him, some scholars shewed him, in Almanzor's presence, a book consisting wholly of blank leaves, except the first, on which they had inscribed, " The Garland of Subtle Conceits : by Abu 'l-Ghauth Sanânî." Neither work nor author had ever existed, but Sâ'id after a glance at the title-page cried, " Ah! I have read that book!" and kissing it reverently, mentioned the town in which he had studied it, and the professor who had expounded it. " In that case," said the Minister, snatching the book from his hands lest he should open it, "you know the nature of its contents." "Assuredly," replied Sâ'id: "It is true that it is long since I read the work, and I do not know it by rote, but I remember well that it consists solely of grammatical disquisitions, and contains neither poetry nor history." The bystanders thereupon burst into laughter. On another occasion Almanzor had received from a provincial Governor, named Mabramân ibn-Yazîd, a letter dealing with *kalb* and *tazbîl*, *i.e.* husbandry and manure. Addressing Sâ'id, he asked: " Hast thou seen a book by Mabramân ibn-Yazîd, bearing the title of '*Al-kawâlib wa-'z-zawâlib*'?" " By Allah, yes!" replied Sâ'id, "I read, in Baghdad, a copy of that book made by the celebrated Ibn Doraid, and in the margin there were marks like the feet of an emmet." "Thou impostor!" cried the Minister, "the name I mentioned is not that of an author, but of one of my Governors, who has sent me a letter touching tillage and the like." "That may be," replied Sâ'id, "but do not suppose that I am indulging in fabrication: I never invent. I pledge my honour that the book and the author you have just mentioned actually exist, and if your Governor bears the same name as the writer, I can only say that it is a strange coincidence!" Another time Almanzor showed him the Anthology compiled by the celebrated Al-Kâlî.[1] "If it be your pleasure," Sâ'id immediately exclaimed, "I will dictate to your Secretaries a far finer book than that, containing naught but relations omitted by Al-Kâlî." "Be it so!" replied Almanzor, who asked for nothing better than to see dedicated to himself a book even more remarkable than that which Al-Kâlî had dedicated to the late Khalif: in fact, he had invited Sâ'id to Spain in the confident hope that he would eclipse the glory of Al-Kâlî, who had conferred distinction on the reigns of 'Abd-er-Rahmân III and Hakam II. Sâ'id immediately set to work, and in the mosque at Zâhira dictated his "Bezels." When the book was finished it was eagerly examined by the scholars of the day. To their great surprise—but secret satisfaction—they found that it was the merest moonshine from beginning to end. The philological comments, the anecdotes, verses, proverbs—all had sprung from the author's fertile imagination. At any rate so said the scholars, and Almanzor believed them. This time he was really indignant with Sâ'id; but although he ordered the book to be thrown into the river, he did not withdraw his favour from its writer. Ever since the day when Sâ'id had predicted that Garcia, Count of Castile, would be made prisoner—a prophecy which, as we have seen, was fulfilled [2] —the Minister had conceived for him not merely a high regard, but a superstitious respect. The poet, for his part, testified his gratitude in a thousand ways, and of this Almanzor was keenly sensible. Once, for instance, it occurred to Sâ'id to collect all the purses which the Minister had given him full of money, and to make with them a

---

[1] The *Kitâb al-Amâlî* (Book of Dictations), a vast collection of literary and linguistic notes and anecdotes. See *supra*, p. 455.

[2] See p. 508.

cloak for his black slave Kâfûr; he then repaired to the palace, and having succeeded in putting Almanzor in a good humour, he said, " My lord, I have a boon to ask of thee."—" And its nature?"—" Merely that my slave Kâfûr may appear before thee."—" A strange petition!"—" Yet grant it!"—" Be it so, then!" Kâfûr, a man " tall as a palm-tree," accordingly entered the chamber, clad in a robe of many colours, resembling a mendicant's patchwork cloak. " Poor fellow!" cried the Minister, " What a wretched garb! Why dost thou clothe him in rags?" " My lord, the riddle is easily read: thou must know, then, that thou hast already given me gold in such plenty, that the purses which held it suffice to clothe even a man of Kâfûr's stature!" A smile of satisfaction stole to Almanzor's lips: " Thou knowest how to render thanks with a good grace," he said, " and it is well-pleasing to me." Forthwith he sent new gifts to the poet, including a handsome mantle for Kâfûr.

It must, after all, be admitted that if such men as Sâ'id basked in the Minister's smile, it was because the latter did not possess the taste and discrimination in literary matters possessed by most of the Omayyads. Almanzor deemed it his duty to subsidize poets, but he looked upon them more or less as luxuries in keeping with his lofty station, and he was not endowed with the nice discernment which would have enabled him to distinguish true brilliants from paste.

If, however, his genius did not include literature within its scope, it was on the other hand eminently practical. The material interests of the country found in him an enlightened upholder. Improvement in means of communication never ceased to occupy his mind. He constructed numberless roads. At Ecija he threw a bridge across the Genil: at Cordova he built another over the Guadalquiver which cost forty thousand gold pieces.

All his undertakings, small and great, showed the stamp of his genius. When he contemplated a measure of high importance he usually asked the advice of his council—but he very rarely followed it. The Councillors were indeed men who never wandered from the beaten track: slaves of routine, they knew what 'Abd-er-Rahmân III or Hakam II had done in such and such circumstances, and they never dreamed that there might be an alternative course. When they saw Almanzor persisting in his own designs, they would exclaim that all was lost—until the event confuted their forebodings.

2 I.

In estimating Almanzor's character we cannot forget that both in the attainment and retention of power he had stooped to actions which morality condemns, and had even committed crimes which we have not attempted to palliate : but justice compels us to add that so long as his ambitions were not at stake, he was loyal, generous and just. Tenacity of purpose, as we have already indicated, was the cardinal feature of his character. Once he had formed a resolution, he never wavered. By an effort of will he would endure physical pain as impassively as mental anguish. One day, when suffering from some affection in his foot, he had it cauterised during a session of the Council. Meanwhile he continued placidly to discuss public affairs, and the Councillors would have known nothing of the matter if the odour of burnt flesh had not revealed the truth. His every action spoke of extraordinary determination and perseverance : he was as steadfast in friendship as in hatred ; he never forgot a service nor forgave an injury. These characteristics were brought home to the fellow-students to whom, in early days, Almanzor had offered choice of the posts which they would desire to occupy in the event of his becoming Prime Minister.[1] The three students who upon that occasion had feigned to take his words seriously, duly obtained the offices which they had coveted, but the fourth, who had replied with contumely, expiated his imprudence by the loss of his property.

On the other hand when Almanzor was conscious of having done an injustice he sometimes succeeded in breaking down his own obstinacy. One day when it was proposed to pardon certain prisoners, as Almanzor glanced at the list his eye fell upon the name of one of his servants, against whom he had conceived a strong animosity and who for a long time had lain in unmerited durance. "This man," wrote the Minister on the margin of the list, "shall remain where he is till Hell claims him." But that night he sought repose in vain : his conscience tormented him, and between sleeping and waking he thought he saw a being of hideous aspect and superhuman strength, who said to him: "Set that man at liberty, or pay the penalty of thine injustice!" He tried to banish this grim vision from his mind, but without success, and at last ordering writing-materials to be brought to his bed-side, he made out an order for the

[1] See p. 457 supra.

prisoner's release, appending these words: "To Allah alone
this man oweth his liberty; Almanzor grudgeth it."

On another occasion he sat drinking with the Vizier
Abu 'l-Moghîra ibn Hazm in one of the superb gardens of
Zâhira—for in spite of the respect in which he held the Faith,
he never refrained from wine, except during the last two
years of his life: it was evening—one of those delicious
evenings known only in favoured southern climes. A
beautiful singing girl, beloved by Almanzor, but herself
enamoured of the Minister's guest, chanted these verses:

"The day departs, and already the moon shews half her disc. The
setting sun glows like a rosy cheek, and the growing dusk is the down that
covers it; the crystal of the goblets is like the icicle, and the wine within
is liquid fire. My eyes have made me commit unforgivable sins. Alas!
my kinsfolk, I love a youth who avoids my affection though he is near me.
Ah! that I could throw myself into his arms and clasp him to my heart!"

Abu 'l-Moghîra knew only too well the import of these
verses, and he had the imprudence to sing as follows in reply:

"How, alas, can I approach loveliness that is hedged about with swords
and spears! Ah! If I were sure in my heart that thy love were sincere,
gladly would I risk my life to possess thee! No perils daunt a man of
noble heart when he determines to reach the goal."

Almanzor could no longer restrain himself. With a
roar of fury, he drew his sword, and turning to the songstress cried in a voice of thunder, "Tell the truth! Is it to
the Vizier that thou addressest thy verses?" "A falsehood
might save me," replied the brave girl, "and yet I will not
lie. Yes—his glance hath pierced my heart; love made me
speak and proclaim what I would fain have kept hidden.
I am in thy power, my lord, but thou art gracious, and
lovest to pardon a fault confessed." So saying, she wept.
Almanzor had already half forgiven her, but turning his
wrath against Abu 'l-Moghîra he assailed him with a torrent
of reproaches. The Vizier endured them in silence, but when
Almanzor had made an end, he replied: "My lord, I acknowledge that I have committed a grievous fault; but what
could I do? Every man is the slave of his destiny; no man
can choose his own fate, but must submit; mine has decreed
that I should love where I ought not." Almanzor kept
silence for a little while. At last he said, "I pardon you
both. Abu 'l-Moghîra, she whom thou lovest is thine; I
myself give her to thee."

The Minister's love of equity became proverbial. It

was his will that justice should be done without respect to persons, and the favour he extended to certain individuals by no means placed them above the law. A man of the common people presented himself one day before him : " Guardian of justice," he said, " I have a complaint to make against one who standeth behind thee," and he pointed to a Slav who held the office of shield-bearer, and whom Almanzor held in high esteem. " I have summoned him before the judge," continued the man, " but he refuseth to appear." " What !" cried Almanzor, " he hath refused to appear, and the judge hath not compelled him ? I credited 'Abd-er-Rahmân ibn Fotais (such was the judge's name) with more energy. But unfold to me, my friend, thy grievance." The man thereupon explained that the Slav had broken a contract made with him. Having heard him to the end, Almanzor exclaimed : " What trouble these servants of ours cause us !" Then, addressing the Slav, who trembled with fear, he added, " Hand the shield to him who standeth next to thee, and go in all humility to the court to answer the charge made against thee, that justice may be done." " Do thou," he continued, turning to the prefect of police, " conduct these two men to the judge, and tell him that if this Slav of mine hath broken his contract, I desire him to receive the severest punishment, whether by imprisonment or otherwise." The judge having decided in favour of the complainant, the latter returned to Almanzor to thank him. " Spare me thy thanks," said the Minister ; " thou hast gained thy case ! It is well, thou canst rest content ; this I cannot yet do, for I still have to punish, on my own account, the rascal who did not blush to do a base action although he was in my service." So saying, he dismissed the suitor.

Another time his major-domo was involved in a lawsuit with an African merchant. He was called upon by the judge to give evidence on oath, but thinking that he was shielded from legal proceedings by his exalted office, he refused to do so. One day, however, as Almanzor was proceeding to the Mosque, accompanied by his major-domo, the merchant accosted him and related what had happened. The Minister instantly placed the major-domo under arrest, ordered him to be taken before the judge, and afterwards, on learning that he had lost his case, deprived him of office.

To sum up : if we find ourselves obliged to condemn the means which Almanzor employed in the pursuit of sovereignty, we are also compelled to admit that he made noble use of his power once he had achieved it. If destiny had willed him to be cradled on the steps of a throne the world might perhaps have found little with which to reproach him; in such circumstances, he might, indeed, have figured as one of the greatest princes whose memory history enshrines; but seeing the light, as he did, in a mere provincial manor-house, he was impelled, in order to attain the goal of his ambition, to hew a way for himself through a thousand obstacles, and we cannot but regret that in his efforts to overcome them, he seldom concerned himself about the legitimacy of his methods. He was in many respects a great man, and yet, even without judging him too strictly by the immutable canons of morality, we find it impossible to love, and difficult even to admire him.

[AUTHORITIES: Ibn Adhârî, ii. 309–11, 320–1; Makkarî, i. 259, 273–4, 387, 392, 406–7; ii. 52 sq., 65; Ibn al-'Abbâr, p. 151; Ibn al-Khatîb (MS. G.), ff. 118, 181; Homaidî, ff. 100–3; 'Abd al-Wâhid, pp. 19–25; Ibn Khallikân (Slane), i. p. 322.]

CHAPTER XIII

SANCHOL

UPON Muzaffar's return to Cordova after his father's death, a popular tumult broke out. The people with loud clamours called upon their rightful sovereign to come forth and personally rule them. Hishâm II in vain pleaded that he still desired to live a life free from cares: the mob persisted in their demands, and Muzaffar was obliged to disperse them by armed force. After this, however, tranquillity once more reigned. It is true that a grandson of 'Abd-er-Rahmân III, also named Hishâm, conspired against Muzaffar, but the latter received timely warning, and frustrated the plot by putting the chief conspirator to death (December, 1006).

Muzaffar, as ruler, followed in his father's footsteps. He gained many victories over the Christians, and while he remained in power the prosperity of the country grew. The men of later days even spoke of this epoch as a golden age.[1] Nevertheless a great change had slowly taken place. The old Arab society, with all its virtues and its defects, had disappeared. 'Abd-er-Rahmân III and Almanzor had both aimed at bringing about national unification, and this had been at last effected. The ancient Arab nobility had gone under in the conflict which they had waged against the kingly power: they were not only vanquished and broken, but impoverished and ruined: every day some ancient and once honoured name became extinct. The nobles of the court, attached as they were to the Omayyads by bonds of clientage, had fared better: the wealthy families of Abû Abda, Shohaid, Jahwar, and Fotais, still occupied enviable positions. But at that time the most powerful men in the State were the Berber generals and the Slavs,[2] who owed their fortune to Almanzor. Nevertheless, as upstarts and foreigners, they inspired but little respect: they were looked upon, moreover, as barbarians, and many

---

[1] Records of this period are lacking.
[2] Including Christians from the N. of Spain serving in the Moslem army.

were the complaints of their acts of oppression. The middle-classes, on the other hand, had become enriched by manufactures and commerce. Even during the troublous reign of the Sultan 'Abdallah, merchants and manufacturers, as we have seen, quickly amassed large fortunes, with no other capital than money lent them by their friends, and now that the country enjoyed perfect tranquillity, it was not surprising that such fortunes were frequently and easily made. Nevertheless, the State, outwardly so flourishing, bore within it the germs of its own dissolution. Racial strife had ceased, only to reappear, in another form, as a war of classes. The workman hated his employer, the middle-class envied the nobility, and all concurred in execrating the generals—especially the Berber generals. At the heart of universal inexperience there stirred vague longings after the untried and the unknown. Religion was subjected to fierce attacks. The measures taken by Almanzor against the philosophers had not borne the fruit hoped for by the clergy. Free-thinkers multiplied, and scepticism, always deep-seated in the Arab character, gradually assumed a more scientific shape. The disciples of Ibn Masarra—the Massaría, as they were called—had become a numerous sect. Other schismatics propagated the most subversive doctrines. One of the sects seems to have originated among the divines themselves. Its members had, at all events, studied the traditions relating to the Prophet, but their researches must have been, in the eyes of an orthodox theologian, very superficial, and were by preference confined to apocryphal works composed by materialists who wished to sap the foundations of Islamism. Hence their fantastic conception of the universe. The earth, they said, rests upon a fish; the fish is balanced on a bull's horn; the bull stands on a rock, which in turn is supported on the neck of an angel. Below the angel darkness is spread out, and under the darkness there extends an illimitable ocean.[1] Beneath these obscure and grotesque tenets, which were probably purely symbolical, the theologians detected a grave heresy—the sect believed in the infinity of the universe! These Schismatics moreover taught that while religion may be spread by force or fraud, it cannot be proved by arguments which appeal to the reason. Nevertheless, they regarded with hostility the teachings of the Greek philosophers,

---

[1] *Cf.* Gobineau, *Trois ans en Asie*, p. 347, and Ibn Khaldûn, *Prolégomènes* (transl. Slane), i. pp. 2–3, *n.* 3.

upon which, however, another persuasion based their principles.

The doctrines of the last-named sect were purely natural-
istic. The study of mathematics had led them on to that
of astronomy. Belief in religion, they contended, must rest
upon mathematical proofs of its truth: as these were not
forthcoming, they declared it absurd. They held in contempt all the commandments: prayer, fasting, alms-giving,
pilgrimages, were in their eyes mere folly. The ecclesiastics
did not fail to apply to them the reproaches with which in
all ages theologians have been eager to assail those whose
opinions differ from the received doctrines: they accused
them of devoting their lives to filthy lucre, in order to wallow
in sensuality without restraint, heedless of the laws of morality.

After all, the sects which openly attacked Islamism were
not those most to be feared: others, which wished to remain
at peace with it, and which reckoned among their adherents
not merely Musulmans, but Christians and Jews, were more
dangerous. Under the name of " Universal Religion "[1] they
preached indifferentism; and when a religion perishes, it is
not—as the Moslem theologians were aware—through external attacks, but always through internal apathy. Those
who held these lax doctrines differed among themselves on
certain points: some went further than others; but all agreed
in a sovereign contempt for dialectics. " The world," they
said, " teems with religions, heresies, schools of philosophy,
all bitterly at variance with one another. Take the case of
the Christians: The Melchite[2] cannot endure the Nestorian;[3]
the Nestorian loathes the Jacobite,[4] and they all damn one
another. Among the Moslems, the Mu'tazilite[5] brands as
infidels all who do not see eye to eye with him; the Nonconformist thinks it his duty to slay members of any other
sect, and the Sonnite has nothing in common with either
of them. Among the Jews we see like dissensions. The
philosophers are less quarrelsome, but quite as divergent.
If we inquire which of these innumerable theological and
philosophical systems enshrines the truth, we find there is
nothing to choose between them. Their respective champions

[1] Ar. Al-milla al-kullíya.
[2] Orthodox Eastern Christians.
[3] The Monophysites, who denied the union of two natures in one person in Christ.
[4] The Monophysites of Syria, so named from Jacobus Baradœus. A small number still exist.
[5] See Nicholson, *Lit. Hist. of the Arabs* (1907), pp. 222 *sq.*

employ arguments which are equally valid—or equally fal-
lacious : they merely differ in the dexterity with which they
chop logic.   To convince ourselves of this we have but to
listen to a debate between men of different views.   What do
we find ?   The victor of to-day is the vanquished of to-
morrow, and in these assemblies of the learned the weapons
used are as untrustworthy as those of war.   The fact is that
each disputant prates of things of which he neither has, nor
ever can have, any knowledge."

Some of the sceptics, however, accepted certain conclusions.   There were those who believed in the existence of a
God, the Creator of all things, and in Mohammed's mission :
" Other doctrines," they said, " may or may not be true ; we
neither affirm or deny them, we simply cannot tell ; but
our consciences do not allow us to accept doctrines the truth
of which has not been demonstrated."   Such formed 'the
moderate party.   Others acknowledged a Creator only, and
the most advanced were without positive religious belief.
They declared that neither the existence of God, nor the
creation of the world, had been proved, but that at the same
time there was no evidence that God did not exist, or that
the world had never had a beginning.

Some held that it is expedient to profess, at least outwardly, the religion into which we are born ; others maintained " Universal Religion " to be the one thing needful,
and they included under that name the moral principles
common to all religions and approved by reason.

Innovators in matters of religion had a great advantage
over innovators in matters of Government : they knew what
they wanted.   In the political world, on the other hand, no
one had definite views.   Discontent with the existing order
was prevalent, and it seemed that by pressure of circumstances society was being impelled towards a revolution.
Such a revolution Almanzor had foreseen.   One day, as he
gazed upon his splendid palace at Zâhira, standing in the
midst of its magnificent gardens, he suddenly burst into
tears, and exclaimed, " Unfortunate Zâhira ! would that I
knew who it is that in a little while will destroy thee ! "
Upon his companion expressing surprise at this exclamation,
Almanzor went on : " Thou thyself wilt witness the catastrophe.   I see this fair palace sacked and in ruins, and I see
the fire of civil war devouring my country ! "   Yet if this
revolution took place, what would be its object and its
methods ?   No man could tell : but on one point all were

agreed -–the family of Almanzor must be driven from power.
In this there was nothing surprising. Monarchical nations
begrudge the exercise of authority by any save the monarch
himself. All ministers who have, as it were, stood in the
Sovereign's place, have become the objects of bitter and implacable hatred, however great their talents and deserts. This
consideration in itself suffices to explain the aversion which
the 'Âmirids inspired ; but it should not be forgotten that
they had also wounded the sentiments and affections of
loyalists. Though they had so far been content with ruling
in the name of the hereditary Khalif, they had made it clear
that they aimed higher—at the throne itself: this ambition
had embittered against them, not only the princes of the
blood, who were numerous, but the ecclesiastics—who were
strongly attached to the principle of legitimacy—and the
people at large, who were, or believed themselves to be, devoted to the dynasty. The nobles of the court, moreover,
desired the fall of the 'Âmirids, since they hence anticipated
an increase of their influence, while the lower orders applauded in advance any revolution, as enabling them at once
to gratify their hatred of the wealthy, and to rob them.
This last fact, it might be supposed, would have made the
well-to-do classes more prudent. Cordova had become a
manufacturing town, containing thousands of artisans, and
a trifling outbreak might suddenly assume a very grave
character, and precipitate a terrible conflict between rich and
poor. But such was the general inexperience that the imminence of this danger seems to have occurred to no one.
The well-to-do classes looked upon the working men as their
allies, and believed that all would go well once the 'Âmirids
were got rid of.

The fall of the 'Âmirids was therefore a consummation
almost universally longed for when Muzaffar died in his
prime (October, 1008). His brother 'Abd-er-Rahmân succeeded him. This young man was an object of antipathy
to the priests. In their eyes there was an ineffaceable stain
upon his birth, for his mother was the daughter of a certain
Sancho—either the Count of Castile, or the king of Navarre.
Since 'Abd-er-Rahmân was always called Sanchol,[1] i.e.
Sancho the Little, it is by this nickname that he is known in
history. His conduct was not calculated to earn condonation of his parentage. A shameless free-liver, he never

[1] Now, usually, *Sanchuelo:* on Sancho, Count of Castile, see *Recherches* (1881),
i. pp. 203–10.

scrupled to drink wine in public, and it was related, with deep indignation, that on hearing one day the muezzin cry from a minaret, "Hasten to prayer!" he had exclaimed, "Why not hasten to carousal? That would be much better!" He was further accused of having poisoned Muzaffar: the story ran that having divided an apple with a knife one side of which was poisoned, he ate one half himself and gave the other to his brother.[1] These accusations were perhaps more or less guess-work, but it is at least certain that Sanchol did not possess the tact and ability of either Almanzor or Muzaffar. And yet he rushed in where they had feared to tread.

While virtually reigning, they had left the Omayyad monarch his title; they did not pose as Khalifs, much though they might have desired it. But Sanchol conceived the rash design of getting himself declared heir-presumptive to the throne. He discussed the matter with certain men of influence—among whom the Kady, Ibn Dhakwân, and Ibn Bord, Secretary of State, were the chief—and having secured their support, presented his demand to Hishâm II. The Khalif, puppet though he was, seems to have recoiled for a moment from such a serious step—which was the graver since it was generally believed that Mohammed had declared that the dominion must never pass from the Ma'adite line. He consulted certain theologians, but these happened to be under Ibn Dhakwân's influence. They accordingly advised the Khalif to yield to Sanchol's request, and to allay his scruples they quoted the Prophet's words when he said: "The Last Day shall not arrive before the sceptre passes into the hands of a man of the race of Kahtân." The Khalif yielded, and Sanchol, a month after his brother's death, was declared heir to the throne in virtue of a decree drawn up by Ibn Bord. This decree raised the passions of the Cordovans to boiling point. A lampoon of the day was on everybody's tongue:

"Ibn Dhakwân and Ibn Bord have found a new way of insulting religion. They are rebels against the God of Truth, for they have declared Sancho's grandson heir to the throne."

It was, moreover, gleefully related that a holy man as he passed by the palace of Zâhira exclaimed: "Oh thou palace, which art enriched with the pillage of many houses, God

---

[1] Cf. *Esp. sagr.*, xxiii. p. 403. Another instance of this mode of poisoning is given by Al-Bakri (p. 121, ed. Slane).

grant that ere long every house may be enriched with spoil
of thee ! "

Hatred and ill-will were, in short, universally manifested.
There was, however, as yet no recourse to arms : the populace were still intimidated and restrained by the presence of
the army. But actual revolt was at hand. Deceived by the
tranquillity that apparently reigned in the city, Sanchol
announced his intention of making an expedition against
Leon, and on Friday, Jan. 14, 1009, he set out from the
Capital at the head of his troops. He must needs gratify a
whim by wearing a turban—a head-dress which in Spain
was only worn by lawyers and theologians—and he ordered
his soldiers to follow his example. In this caprice the
Cordovans saw a fresh outrage against religion and its
ministers.

Having crossed the frontier, Sanchol in vain attempted
to drive Alfonso V from his mountain fastnesses. Snow-
storms soon rendered the roads impassable, and he was
obliged to retire ; [1] scarcely had he reached Toledo when
he heard that an insurrection had broken out in the
Capital.

An Omayyad prince, Mohammed by name, had put
himself at the head of the movement. Son of that Hishâm
whom Muzaffar had beheaded, he was consequently great-
grandson of 'Abd-er-Rahmân III. He had been kept in
hiding at Cordova to escape his father's fate, and had by
this time become known to many of the commonalty.
Thanks to his wealth, of which he made no niggard use ;
thanks also to the support afforded him by a fanatical Fakih
named Hasan ibn Yahyâ, and to the co-operation of many
of the Omayyads, Mohammed had soon collected a band of
four hundred bold and resolute men. Rumours of a plot
reached the ears of the 'Âmirid Ibn Askeleja, to whom
Sanchol had entrusted the administration of Cordova in his
absence, but they were so vague that the Governor, although he had several suspected houses searched, discovered
nothing.

Mohammed having fixed upon Thursday, Feb. 25, for
the execution of his design, selected thirty of the most daring
of his men, and ordered them to repair in the evening to the
terrace beside the Khalif's palace, with arms concealed under
their cloaks. " I will join you there," he added, " an hour

---

[1] This expedition has been termed " The Campaign of the Mire."

before sunset; but take heed that you do nothing until I give the signal."

The thirty mustered at the appointed place, where they aroused no suspicions, since the terrace of the palace, which afforded a view of the highway and the river, was a much frequented promenade. Meanwhile Mohammed supplied the rest of his men with arms, and bade them hold themselves in readiness. Then proceeding to the terrace, mounted on a mule, he gave the signal, and the thirty threw themselves upon the guard at the palace gate. Thus unexpectedly attacked, the soldiers were quickly disarmed, while Mohammed rushed to Ibn Askeleja's apartment, where he was chatting and drinking with two girls of his harem. Before he had time to defend himself he was a dead man.

The other conspirators, informed of the deed, immediately started running through the streets, with cries of " To arms! To arms!" Their success exceeded their hopes. The townsfolk, who only awaited a signal to rise in revolt, followed them with shouts of exultation, and the rustics of the environs, hearing the tumult, soon joined the crowd. Rushing to Hishâm's gilded prison, they made two separate breaches in the walls. The unhappy monarch still hoped that a force would come to his rescue. The chief officers of the State were at Zâhira, where they had some Slav regiments and other troops at their disposal. Upon first hearing of the revolt, however, they had trusted that Ibn Askeleja would speedily quell it, and later, when they learnt that the outbreak was of a much graver nature than they had supposed, they were paralysed with fear. The officers were all at their wit's end, and no attempt was made to rescue the Khalif. Hishâm himself, fearing to see at any moment the palace invaded by the mob, at last took the step of sending a messenger to Mohammed, to tell him that if he would spare his life, he would abdicate in his favour. " What!" replied Mohammed to the messenger, " Thinketh the Khalif I have taken up arms to slay him? Nay! rather, because I have seen, with sorrow, that he hath been willing to let the sovereignty be wrested from our family. Let him do what pleaseth him, but if he, of his own freewill, resigns the crown to me, I will gratefully accept it, and in that case I will grant him all that he may ask of me." Then, summoning the theologians and certain notables, he bade them draw up an instrument of abdication, and this having been signed by Hishâm, Mohammed spent the rest of the night within the palace. Next morning, he appointed one of his kinsmen Prime Minister, entrusted to another Omayyad the government of the Capital, and bade them enrol in the army all who willed. So keen and wide-spread was the enthusiasm, that recruits poured in from every class: common folk, rich merchants, farmers from the suburbs, imâms from the mosque, pious hermits, each tried to outstrip the rest—all were ready to shed their blood in defence of the legitimate dynasty against the libertine who had attempted to usurp the throne. Mohammed ordered his Prime Minister to betake himself to Zâhira: the officials there congregated did not even think of defending themselves, but made haste to submit to the new Khalif, and ask his pardon: this he granted, but not before he had bitterly reproached them for their connivance at Sanchol's ambitious designs.

Thus then, in the space of less than twenty-four hours, the 'Âmirid dominion had crumbled to dust. None had looked for so immediate a success. The joy in Cordova was universal, but it was especially marked among the humbler ranks of society. The lower orders, ever precipitate in their joy as in their resentment, saw a vista of prosperity opening before them; but if the middle class had had forebodings of the far-reaching and disastrous consequences of this revolution, they would have thought twice before joining in it, and would have considered that the enlightened despotism of the 'Âmirids—which had conferred on the country enviable prosperity, as well as military glory—was more highly to be valued than anarchy, or the military despotism soon to be imposed upon them.

Even at this juncture the excesses which always accompany popular risings were not wanting. Mohammed, though he could instigate plunder, was not yet strong enough to check it. With commendable foresight he had given orders for the treasures and works of art at Zâhira to be removed to Cordova: but the pillagers were already at work. They stripped the palace of its very doors and wainscoting, and many mansions belonging to dependants of Almanzor and his family shared the same fate. For four days Mohammed could not, or dared not, check the pillagers. At last he succeeded in curbing their audacity, and so vast were the riches of Zâhira that even after the people had done their work a million and a half pieces of gold, and two millions one hundred thousand pieces of silver yet remained.

A little later further hiding-places were unearthed, in which lay two hundred thousand pieces of gold. When the palace was completely gutted, it was set on fire, and in a short time the splendid building was a heap of ruins.

In the meanwhile two official proclamations had been read, after public worship, to the people assembled in the Mosque (Feb. 18). The first enumerated Sanchol's crimes, and enjoined that curses should be invoked upon him in the public prayers; the second announced the remission of several recently imposed taxes. A week later Mohammed publicly proclaimed his assumption of the surname by which we shall henceforth designate him—that of Al-Mahdî,[1] and when he had descended from the throne, a general call to arms against Sanchol was read. The effect of this last proclamation was prodigious. Enthusiasm spread from the Capital to the provinces, and in a very short time Mahdî found himself at the head of a large army: but the revolution had been the work of the people, and they would not fight under the generals, who all had formerly belonged to the court party; the officers were therefore exclusively drawn from the middle and lower classes, and comprised apothecaries, weavers, butchers and saddlers. Moslem Spain was, for the first time, democratised; and power had slipped from the hands not only of the 'Âmirids, but of the aristocracy as a whole.

Sanchol on receiving, at Toledo, news of the outbreak in Cordova, set out for Calatrava. He was determined to quell the revolt by force of arms, but on the march many soldiers deserted, and when he expressed a wish that those who remained should swear fealty to him, they refused, saying that they had already taken the oath and had no wish to renew it. Such was even the reply of the Berbers, whom the 'Âmirids had surfeited with gold, and on whom at least Sanchol thought he could rely. He did not realize that gratitude and loyalty were not among their virtues. Believing the cause of their benefactors a lost one, they thought of nothing but keeping their riches by prompt submission to the new Khalif. Neither did they attempt to conceal their intention, for when Sanchol asked one of the generals, Mohammed ibn Yilâ, his opinion with regard to the feeling of the soldiers towards him, Mohammed replied: " I will not deceive thee as to my own sentiments or those of the

---

[1] Ar. *Al-Mahdî billâh*, "guided by God."

troops. I tell thee plainly, there is not a man who will fight on thy behalf."

"Not a man?" exclaimed Sanchol, who although disabused as to the fidelity of a part of his army, had never expected such an avowal: "How can I convince myself that thy opinion is well founded?"

"Bid thy personal attendants to set out for Toledo, and announce thy intention of following them: thou wilt then see whether a single soldier will accompany thee."

"Mayhap thou speakest truly," said Sanchol sorrowfully; but he did not risk the experiment suggested by the Berber. Forsaken by his army, there was yet left to Sanchol one staunch and trusty friend: this was the Count of Carrion, one of his Leonese allies and a scion of the house of Gomez.[1] "Come with me," said this nobleman; "my castle offers thee a refuge, and if needs be, I will shed the last drop of my blood in thy defence." "I thank thee for thy offer, my excellent friend," replied Sanchol, "but I cannot take advantage of it. I must push on to Cordova, where my friends await me, and where they will rise like one man on my behalf as soon as they hear of my approach. Moreover, I hope—nay, I am well assured—that when I enter the city many of those who at present seem to favour Mohammed, will desert him for me."

"Prince," urged the Count, "abandon these vain and groundless hopes. Believe me, all is lost! Just as the army hath declared against thee, so thou wilt find that not a soul in Cordova will come to thine aid." "That remains to be proved," replied the 'Âmirid; "but my mind is made up, and to Cordova I will go!" "I cannot approve thy design," said the Count, "and I am persuaded that thou art deceived by a fatal delusion; but come what may, I will not quit thy side."

Continuing their march towards the Capital, Sanchol with his remaining troops reached a halting place called Manzil-Hânî. There they bivouacked; but during the night the Berbers, profiting by the darkness, all deserted, and next morning Sanchol found himself left with none but his household servants and the Count's soldiers. The Count once more implored him to accept his offer; but his entreaties were of no avail—the young man rushed recklessly to his doom! "I have sent the Kady to Cordova," he said; "he will ask and obtain clemency for me."

---

[1] *Cf.* Sandoval, *Cinco Reyes*, ff. 62 *sq.*

On the evening of Thursday, March 4, he reached the monastery of Chauch.   On the morrow, the horsemen whom Mahdî had sent to meet him also arrived.   " What wouldst thou of me ? " asked Sanchol : " I pray thee, leave me in peace, for I have submitted to the new Government." " If that be so," replied the officer in command, " follow me to Cordova."

Sanchol had no alternative save to obey this unwelcome order, and not long after setting out they met, during the afternoon, Mahdî's Prime Minister, with a considerable force.   A halt was called, and the seventy women who composed Sanchol's harem having been sent on to Cordova, he himself was brought before the Minister.   Sanchol kissed the ground before the Omayyad several times, and then there was a cry of, " Kiss the hoof of his horse ! "   He obeyed, whilst the Count of Carrion watched in silence the abject self-abasement of the man before whom but lately a mighty empire had trembled.   Sanchol was then mounted on a horse not his own, and after his turban had been torn off, by the Minister's orders, the cavalcade proceeded on its way.

At sunset, upon reaching a halting-place, the troopers were ordered to bind Sanchol hand and foot.   They performed their task somewhat roughly, and Sanchol cried out, " You hurt me ; I pray you slacken the bonds for a moment, and release my hand ! "   His request had scarcely been granted, when he suddenly drew a dagger from his boot, but before he had time to turn it upon himself the soldiers forced it from him.

" I will save thee that trouble ! " exclaimed the Minister, who, hurling him to the ground, slew him as he lay, and then ordered the body to be decapitated.   The Count was also put to death.

The troopers reached Cordova the next day, and laid Sanchol's remains before the Khalif.   Mahdî, having caused the corpse to be embalmed, trampled it under his horse's hoofs.   It was then nailed to a cross, clad in a tunic and drawers, and exposed near a gate of the palace, with the head beside it on a spear.   Near these ghastly remains there stood a man who cried without ceasing, " Behold Sanchol the Blessed ! [1]   May God's curse light upon him, and upon

---

[1] A surname adopted by Sanchol.

2 M

myself!" This was the Captain of Sanchol's body-guard, who had been pardoned on the sole condition that he would thus expiate his proved fidelity to his master.

[AUTHORITIES: Nuwairî, pp. 472–9; Ibn al-'Abbâr, pp. 149–50, 159; Ibn Hayyân (*ap.* Ibn Bassâm, i. ff. 30–1); Ibn Adhârî, ii. 290; Khoshanî, p. 327; Ibn Hazm (*On Religions*), i. 127–8, 228–30; ii. 80, 146; Makkarî, i. 277–8, 379, 387–8; Ibn al-Athîr (A.H. 366); Ibn Bassâm, i. f. 24.]

CHAPTER XIV

MAHDÎ

AT first Mahdî's path seemed smooth. The people of Cordova had placed him on the throne, the Berbers had acknowledged him, and less than five days after the 'Âmirid's death he received a letter from Wâdhih, the most influential of the Slavs and Governor of the Northern Marches, assuring him of his fealty and of his joy at the usurper's execution. Since Wâdhih owed his position to Almanzor, Mahdî had not expected so prompt a submission, and hastened to testify his gratitude—sending the Governor a large sum of money, a robe of honour, and a richly caparisoned charger, besides appointing him administrator of the entire Frontier.

At first sight all parties appeared to have rallied spontaneously in support of the Government; but their unanimity was less complete than it seemed. The revolution had been brought about under a fevered impulse in which common sense found no place; yet cool reflection led to the conviction that the fall of the 'Âmirids had not ended every grievance, redressed every wrong, compensated for every loss —but that under the new régime grave reasons for murmurs and dissatisfaction yet remained. Mahdî had neither talents nor virtues. He was dissolute, cruel, bloodthirsty, and so tactless that he alienated each party in turn. He began by disbanding seven thousand workmen who had enlisted. Since Cordova could not be handed over to the mercies of the lower classes, this was, doubtless, a necessary measure, but it displeased the populace, whose pride at having brought about a revolution did not render them unwilling to draw high pay for doing nothing. Mahdî's next step was to exile from the Capital a great number of 'Âmirid Slavs, and to deprive of their posts those employed in the palace, thus throwing them into the arms of the opposition, though with a little tact he might have won them over. At the same time he alienated the devout. Never leaving the palace, he gave himself up to dissipation, and pious Moslems

related with horror that at his banquets a hundred lutes and
as many pipes made music. " He is as bad as Sanchol," it
was said. He was dubbed "the Wine-bibber"; he was
accused of troubling the peace of many a household; he
was lampooned like his late rival. His sheer barbarism
contributed to the ruin of his popularity. Wâdhih having
sent him the heads of certain inhabitants of the Marches.
who had refused to acknowledge the new Khalif, Mahdî
ordered them to be used as flower-pots and placed on the
banks of the river opposite to his palace. He delighted to
gaze on this grim " garden," and he employed poets—among
whom was Sâ'id, who, after flattering the 'Âmirids, now
pandered to their foes—to compose verses on the subject.

Already at variance with the lower orders, the Slavs, the
pious, and decent folk in general, Mahdî took no steps to
attach the Berbers to him, though they were his natural
allies. It is true that these rough troopers were detested
in the Capital. The populace had not forgiven them for
having been the instruments of 'Âmirid despotism, and if
Mahdî had openly patronised them, he would have lost his
little remaining popularity. Since, however, he could not
send the Berbers back to Africa, he ought at least to have
propitiated them. But he did not. He lost no opportunity
of showing them his contempt and hatred ; he forbade them
to mount a horse, to bear arms, or to enter the palace. In
this his imprudence was amazing. Accustomed to be respected and made much of by the Court, the Berbers had a
keen consciousness of their own worth and power. They
were by no means resigned to being reduced to nonentity,
and one day after many of their houses had been pillaged by
a mob, without interference on the part of the police, Zâwî
and two other chiefs proceeded to the palace and imperiously
demanded the punishment of the culprits. Cowed by their
resolute attitude, Mahdî made excuses, and to appease the
sheiks had the ringleaders of the rioters beheaded. But on
recovering from his fright, he again began to harass the
Berbers.

With all his recklessness, however, Mahdî was not wholly
blind to his insecurity, and what he chiefly feared was lest
the name of Hishâm II might become a rallying cry for all
the disaffected. He determined, therefore, without slaying
his august prisoner, to prove that he was dead. A Christian
who much resembled Hishâm died in April, 1009. Mahdî
thereupon had the corpse secretly conveyed to the palace,

where it was shown to persons who had known Hishâm.
Either the resemblance was really striking, or the witnesses
had been bribed—at any rate they vouched for the corpse
being that of the late Khalif.   Mahdî then summoned representative ministers of religion, notables and citizens, and
after prayers for the dead had been recited, the Christian
was buried in the Moslem Cemetery with all the honours
due to royalty.   The real Hishâm was meanwhile closely
imprisoned in the palace of one of the Viziers.

Reassured on this point, the Khalif once more grew
reckless.   In May he cast into prison Sulaimân, son of 'Abd-
er-Rahmân III, who had, not long before, been named heir
to the throne.   He then let a report be spread that he intended to put ten Berber chiefs to death.   This was more
than enough to incite the Africans to rebellion, and Hishâm,
Sulaimân's son, did his best to inflame their minds.   He
found little difficulty: the seven thousand workmen disbanded by Mahdî formed an army ready to his hand.   On
June 2, they assembled before young Hishâm's mansion, and
acclaimed him Khalif.   Hishâm led them to a plain outside
the city, where they were joined by the Berbers, and the
united forces marched towards Mahdî's palace.

Rudely aroused from his pleasures, the Khalif inquired
the cause of the tumult.   "Thou hast thrown my father
into prison," exclaimed Hishâm, "and we know not what
hath become of him."   Mahdî straightway set Sulaimân at
liberty, but if he thought thus to rid himself of the mob, he
was mistaken, for Hishâm further demanded nothing less
than the throne for himself.   To gain time, Mahdî feigned
to parley with him, but the negotiation was lengthy, and
the labourers and Berbers, growing weary of inaction, began
to plunder and burn the shops in the saddlers' market.   The
Cordovans thereupon flew to arms—not in Mahdî's support,
but to protect their own property—and the troops whom the
Khalif had gained time to summon came to their assistance.
The struggle lasted for a day and a night, but on the morning of Friday, June 3, the Berbers were driven back in
great disorder.   A body of Cordovans pursued them to
the banks of the Guadalmellato; others pillaged their
houses and carried off their wives, and a reward was offered
to everyone who brought in a Berber's head.   The would-be
Khalif, Hishâm, who had been made prisoner as well as
his father, was executed.   When the Berbers rallied they
swore to take a signal revenge, but had not the skill to

form a plan of action. Fortunately Zâwî was of their
number.

Descended from the Kinhejite dynasty, which reigned
over that part of Africa of which Kairwan was capital, Zâwî
was more civilized and more intelligent than most of his
brothers in arms, and it occurred to him that it was essential
to set up a rival to Mahdî. There was an Omayyad ready
to his hand—Sulaimân, Hishâm's nephew, who after taking
part in his uncle's abortive rebellion, had fled with the
Berbers. He it was whom Zâwî proposed to his comrades
as Khalif. Some of the Berbers demurred on the ground
that, though Sulaimân was otherwise unobjectionable, he
lacked the energy needed in the leader of a party, as well
as experience in warfare. Others would not accept an Arab
as their chief. To induce the Berbers to adopt his views,
Zâwî resorted to a time-honoured illustration, doubtless new
to the Berbers. He tied five spears into a bundle, and
giving them to one of the strongest soldiers bade him break
them. The man tried in vain. "Loosen the cord, and
break them one by one," he added. It was quickly done.
"Let this serve as a warning to you," said Zâwî; "united,
you are invincible; disunited, you perish, for you are surrounded by implacable foes. Have regard to your danger,
and tell me quickly what you resolve." "We will follow
your wise counsel," was the unanimous reply; "and if
we fail, the fault will not lie with us." "Swear then,
allegiance to this Kurashite," said Zâwî, leading Sulaimân
forward. "None can then accuse you of aiming at the
subjugation of the country; and since he is an Arab, many
of his race will declare for him, and for you."

When they had taken the oath to Sulaimân, and that
prince had announced that he assumed the surname of
Musta'în, Zâwî again addressed the Berbers. "We are in
a perilous position," he said; "let no man endeavour to
gratify his personal ambition by claiming undue authority.
Let each tribe elect a leader, who shall answer with his life
for the fidelity of his regiment to the Khalif." This was
done, and Zâwî was, of course, elected by his own tribe,
that of the Kinheja. Sulaimân, consequently, had no real
authority over the Berbers, who had independently elected
their chiefs: he was a mere figure-head, and such he remained.
The Berbers first marched against Guadalaxara, and after
capturing this town, they appealed to Wâdhih to make
common cause with them and open the gates of Medinaceli.

But Wâdhih rejected their overtures, and aided by reinforcements from Mahdî, attacked them.   He was defeated, but
the Berbers had little reason to congratulate themselves on
their victory, for Wâdhih intercepted their supplies, and for
a fortnight they had to content themselves with a diet of
herbs.   To relieve their distress they sent envoys to Sancho,
Count of Castile, beseeching the Count's good offices and
suggesting an alliance, if Mahdî and Wâdhih did not desire
peace.

On reaching the Count's residence the Africans found
an embassy from Mahdî already there, who had offered
Sancho horses, mules, money, robes, precious stones and
other gifts, and had promised him many towns and fortresses,
if he would come to the Khalif's aid.   A few months had
wrought a profound change.   No longer did Moslems dictate
terms to Christian princes; a Count of Castile was to
decide the fate of Arab Spain.

Thoroughly informed upon the state of his neighbours'
affairs, and knowing that Mahdî's power hung by a thread,
Sancho promised the Berbers to declare for them if they
would surrender to him the fortresses offered by Mahdî's
envoys.   They consented.   Sancho thereupon dismissed the
other ambassadors, and sent to the Berber camp a thousand
oxen, five thousand sheep, and a thousand waggons laden
with victuals.   The Berbers were thus enabled to take the
field without delay, and, accompanied by the Count and
his contingent, marched on Medinaceli.

On reaching the town they renewed their endeavours to
win over Wâdhih to their cause.   But they were again
unsuccessful, and rightly judging that there was no time
to be lost, they marched on Cordova (July, 1009).   Wâdhih
pursued them with his cavalry, but was driven off with
heavy loss, and reached Cordova with only four hundred
horsemen ; there he was soon joined by one of his lieutenants
with two hundred other troopers who had escaped with
their lives.

On learning that the Berbers were threatening the
Capital, Mahdî, after providing with arms all who were able
to bear them, entrenched himself on a plain to the east of
Cordova.   But instead of awaiting the onset of the enemy
he rashly sallied forth to meet them.   The two armies encountered one another at Cantich (November 5, 1009), and
a squadron of thirty Berbers sufficed to throw into disorder
the undisciplined ranks of their opponents.   In precipitate

flight, citizens, artisans and Fakihs trampled one another under foot. The Berbers and Castilians sabred them by hundreds, and many perished in the waters of the Guadalquiver. It has been estimated that ten thousand men fell on that fatal day.[1]

Wâdhih had early seen that all was lost, and, accompanied by his six hundred horsemen, galloped northwards. Mahdî, for his part, took refuge in his palace, where he was soon besieged by the Berbers. He sought to save himself by abdicating in favour of Hishâm II. The latter was fetched from his prison, and placed where the Berbers could see him: the Kady Ibn Dhakwân was then sent to tell them that Hishâm still lived, and that Mahdî was merely his Prime Minister. The Berbers scoffed at the message. "Yesterday Hishâm was dead," they replied to the Kady, "and you and your Emir recited the burial service over his corpse. How then can he be alive to-day? Nevertheless, if you speak the truth, though we thank God that Hishâm yet liveth, we have no need of him, for Sulaimân is our Khalif." The Kady tried in vain to exculpate his master, but while he was speaking, the Cordovans, overawed by Sulaimân's forces, came forth to greet the prince, and acknowledged him as their sovereign.

Whilst Sulaimân was making his entry into the Capital —where the Berbers and Castilians committed excesses of every kind—Mahdî hid himself in the house of one Mohammed, of Toledo, who supplied him with means to reach that town; for all the frontier, from Tortosa to Lisbon, still owned Mahdi's authority. When Sancho reminded Sulaimân of his promise, the latter had to confess that he could not, at the moment, fulfil it, since the towns in question were not yet in his possession: however, he renewed his engagement to cede them as soon as he could, and Sancho quitted Cordova with his troops—who had not failed to enrich themselves at the expense of the citizens (November 14, 1009). Hishâm's lot remained unchanged. Sulaimân, after compelling him to abdicate in his favour, imprisoned him once more: Sanchol's corpse, at the request of the 'Âmirids' former servants, he allowed to be buried with the usual ceremonies.

Meanwhile Mahdî had reached Toledo, where he was warmly welcomed by the populace. Sulaimân set out to

---

[1] So writes the earliest and most trustworthy chronicler, Ibn Hayyân: others give 20,000 or even 36,000.

attack him, and sent ministers of religion to menace the
Toledans with his displeasure if they remained contumacious.
His threats, however, had no effect, and since he was not
anxious to besiege so strong a place as Toledo, and hoped
it would submit when the rest of the country had set the
example, he turned aside against Medinaceli. Many Slavs
joined his army by the way, and he entered Medinaceli without striking a blow, for Wâdhih had evacuated the town
and withdrawn to Tortosa, whence he wrote to Sulaimân,
offering to acknowledge him if he might be permitted to
remain where he was. His real object was to gain time;
and his ruse succeeded, for Sulaimân fell into the trap, and
left Wâdhih in possession of the frontier.

Wâdhih's hands were henceforth free, and he lost no
time in concluding an alliance with two Catalan Counts,
Raymond of Barcelona and Ermenegild of Urgel—to whom
he promised all they asked—and then marched to Toledo,
with a Catalan army as well as his own, and effected a
junction with Mahdi's troops. Sulaimân called the Cordovans to arms, but since they were unwilling to serve
under Africans, they excused themselves on the plea that
they were unfit for warfare. That this was only too true
they had shown at Cantich, and the Berbers, who preferred
to dispense with soldiers of such a stamp, begged Sulaimân
to confer on them the privilege of gaining the victory for
him. He consented, and on reaching Akaba al-bakar [1]—
about four leagues from Cordova—he encountered the
opposing army, which consisted of thirty thousand Moslems
and nine thousand Christians. Sulaimân was placed by his
generals amidst the rear-guard, with injunctions not to quit
his post, even though the enemy should trample him under
their feet. The Africans then attacked the Catalans, but
in accordance with Oriental tactics, they soon showed their
backs to the enemy, in order to return to the charge with
greater impetuosity. Unfortunately, Sulaimân, though
under his officers' orders, did not comprehend their tactics.
Seeing the advance-guard retreating, he made sure that it
was beaten, and, in the belief that all was lost, he fled at
full gallop—the horsemen around him following his
example. The Berbers, however, returned to the attack,
and charged the enemy with such fury that they slew sixty
Catalan chiefs, amongst whom was Count Ermenegild : but

[1] *Cf.* Idrîsi, ii. 64–5 : now Castillo del Bacar.

when they saw that Sulaimân had quitted his post, they
retired on Al-Zahrâ, leaving the Catalans masters of the
field. Sulaimân, therefore, by his personal ignorance and
cowardice, had lost the battle of Akaba al-bakar, from which
he would probably have emerged victorious if he had com-
prehended his captains' tactics, or obeyed their orders. The
victory, such as it was, rested with the Catalans alone, for
the troops of Mahdî and Wâdhih seem to have taken no
active part in the engagement.

Mahdî returned to Cordova, and that ill-fated city,
pillaged six months before by the Castilians and Berbers,
was pillaged afresh by the Catalans. Mahdî then pursued
the Berbers, who were marching towards Algeciras—slaying
all whom they met and plundering villages—but who halted
and retraced their steps when they heard that they were
the object of pursuit.

On June 21,[1] the armies met near the confluence of the
Guadaira and the Guadalquiver. The Africans took a bitter
revenge for their rebuff at Akaba al-bakar. Mahdî's army
was routed ; many Slav officers and more than three thousand
Catalans were left upon the field, and the Guadalquiver[2] once
more claimed many victims. Two days later the vanquished
troops re-entered Cordova, and the Catalans avenged their
defeat by detestable cruelties. Their victims were chiefly
those who in any way resembled Berbers ; but when Mahdî
urged his men to march once more against the foe, they refused, on the ground that their losses had been too heavy.
They quitted Cordova on July 8, and the citizens, in spite
of all that they had endured at their hands, regretted their
departure ; for the Berber hordes, against whom the Catalans
might have defended them, inspired them with still greater
terror. " After the departure of the Catalans," writes an
Arab chronicler, " the people of Cordova when they met in
the streets condoled with one another, like men who have
lost kinsfolk or property."

Mahdî, after levying an additional tax upon the city for
the payment of his men, once more took the field. But since
the departure of the Catalans his army had lost heart, and
they had scarcely marched seven leagues before they became
panic-stricken at the mere idea of again meeting the terrible
Berbers, and returned to Cordova. Mahdî thereupon awaited

---

[1] Cf. *Esp. sagr.*, xliii. p. 156.
[2] " The waves of the sea," says Nuwairî : but the Guadalquiver is there a
tidal river.

the enemy's attack within the Capital, which he surrounded
with a wall and ditch; but Destiny decreed that Slavs, and
not Berbers, should be the instruments of the Khalif's overthrow. Some of the former, chief of whom was Wâdhih,
served under his flag; but others, such as Khairân and Anbar,
were numbered among his opponents. They now felt, that
to achieve the object of their ambition—namely power—
union was necessary, and they resolved to replace Hishâm II
on the throne. With this object, Wâdhih took steps to
foster discontent among the citizens. He caused exaggerated
rumours to be spread abroad concerning the dissolute life of
"the Wine-bibber," and while publicly lamenting the dis-
orderly conduct of the soldiers he secretly encouraged it.
When by these devices the Khalif's little remaining popularity had been undermined, Khairân, Anbar, and the other
Slav generals in Sulaimân's army offered their services to
Mahdî; the latter eagerly accepted them, but as soon as
these so-called auxiliaries had entered Cordova he realized
that they schemed his ruin, and being powerless to resist
them, he planned once more to seek refuge in Toledo. But
the Slavs prevented him. On Sunday, July 23, 1010, they
rode through the streets shouting "Long live Hishâm II!"
and releasing that prince from his prison they set him upon
the throne clad in royal robes.

Mahdî was at the bath, but learning what was taking
place, he rushed to the presence-chamber, and would have
seated himself by Hishâm's side, had not Anbar seized him
roughly by the arm, dragged him from the throne, and made
him sit facing it. Hishâm thereupon bitterly reproached
him for the ills he had suffered at his hands. Anbar then
once more grasped Mahdî by the arm, and dragging him to
the dais drew his sword to sever his head. Mahdî seized him
round the body, but instantly the weapons of the other Slavs
fell upon him. Soon his corpse lay in the place where,
seventeen months before, Ibn Askeleja's had lain. Raised
to the throne by a conspiracy, by another conspiracy he had
lost both his sovereignty and his life.

[AUTHORITIES: Nuwairî, pp. 479–84; Ibn Khaldûn, f. 19; Ibn Hayyân
(ap. Ibn Bassâm, i. ff. 7–8); 'Abd al-Wâhid, pp. 28–30; Ibn al-
'Abbâr, pp. 159–60; Ibn al-Athîr (A.H. 366); Makkarî, i. 278;
Rodrigo de Toledo, Hist. Arabum, c. 32–5; Abbad., i. 244; Ibn al-
Khatîb (Art. on Zâwî, MS. G., f. 133).]

CHAPTER XV

THE SACK OF CORDOVA

UNDER a sovereign so feeble as Hishâm II, the Slavs were all-powerful. Wâdhih, who still held the post of Prime Minister, accordingly aimed at governing Spain after the manner of his patron Almanzor. Unluckily for him, circumstances had changed—and Wâdhih was not Almanzor. At first, however, he encountered no opposition in the Capital. Mahdî's head was carried through the streets without exciting a murmur, for none regretted the tyrant. Wâdhih's hopes that the Berbers would recognise the monarch on whom he had bestowed the throne, soon, however, proved chimerical. Madhî's head was sent to the Berbers and they were invited to submit to Hishâm; but so keen was their indignation, that Sulaimân had some difficulty in saving the lives of the envoys. Sulaimân himself shed tears at the sight of his uncle's head, which he embalmed and sent to 'Obaidallah, Mahdî's son, who was then at Toledo.

Disillusioned with regard to the Berbers, Wâdhih next discovered that he had foes within the city walls. Certain Omayyads, who could not brook Slav domination, and thought they might guard their own interests by advancing those of Sulaimân, secretly informed the latter that if he presented himself at the gates of the Capital on August 12, they would admit him. Sulaimân assented; but the plot was revealed to Wâdhih by Khairân and Anbar. The conspirators were arrested, and when Sulaimân, on the appointed day, appeared before the walls, he was vigorously attacked and compelled to retreat precipitately.

Trusting that the Berbers had been rendered more tractable by this rebuff, Wâdhih re-opened negotiations with them; his efforts, however, proved fruitless, and in the meanwhile Sulaimân appealed to his former ally, Sancho of Castile, offering to cede to him the fortresses captured by Almanzor. These may, or may not, have been those previously promised; at any rate the Count was enabled to enlarge his borders without the trouble of making an incursion into Andalusia.   Since the strongholds in question were not then in Sulaimân's power, but in Wâdhih's, Sancho informed the latter that if he did not give them up he would march with his Castilians to the assistance of the Berbers. The matter seemed to Wâdhih of such grave importance that he was unwilling to come to a decision on his own responsibility.   He therefore convoked the notables, and after laying Sancho's message before them, asked their opinion. The fear of seeing the Berbers reinforced by the Castilians stifled the sentiment of national honour among the notables, and they decided that the Count's demand should be granted. In August or September, 1010, Wâdhih therefore concluded a treaty with Sancho, and transferred to him, according to Arab writers, more than two hundred fortresses, amongst which Christian historians [1] explicitly include San Estevan, Coruña del Conde, Gormaz, and Osma.   The example was contagious.   Seeing that strong places could be obtained at the cost of a few trenchant threats, another Count made a similar requisition, backed by the announcement that he would join Sulaimân if it were not acceded to.   He could not be refused.   The Moslem empire, a prey to civil war and reduced to impotence, was thus crumbling piecemeal.   It may well be doubted whether the Cordovans still rejoiced over the fall of the 'Âmirids as they did on that fatal day when they hailed with short-sighted enthusiasm the success of the revolution; but, whatever their sentiments, they could never retrace their steps.   They must perforce bow the head before the enemies of their religion, accept any master imposed upon them by Slavs or Berbers, and submit to being plundered and maltreated by both parties.   In a word, the lot of the Cordovans was that of every nation which, without clearly defined aims, without the guidance of some exalted political or religious principle, blunders into the vortex of a revolution.

For the moment, however, it was not the citizens who were the chief sufferers from the Berbers' savagery.   After besieging Cordova for six weeks, the Africans turned aside and attacked Al-Zahrâ, which they captured after three days, thanks to the treason of an officer who opened to them one of the gates (November 4, 1010).   A massacre followed, and any uncertainty which the Cordovans may have felt

---

[1] *Ann. Compo.* and *Chron. Card.*

as to the fate destined for them by the Berbers, must have
been dispelled by the tragedy of Al-Zahrâ. The garrison
were butchered almost to the last man. The populace
sought sanctuary in the Mosque, but that proved no refuge
against the Africans, and men, women, and children were
indiscriminately slain. After pillaging Al-Zahrâ, the
Berbers set it on fire, and soon that town, one of the most
magnificent in Europe, became what Zâhira, whilom its
beautiful rival, was already—a heap of ruins.

Throughout the winter a part of the Berber army
pillaged the environs of Cordova, and intercepted all
supplies. Stripped of their possessions, the country-folk
flocked within the walls, and soon outnumbered the citizens,
but since the price of provisions had become excessive, it
was impracticable to supply them with food, and most
of them perished of want. The Government itself was
at the end of its resources; to obtain a little money Wâdhih
was even obliged to sell the greater part of Hakam's library.
Other bands of Africans harried the provinces. The
largest towns fell into their hands, and in most cases the
inhabitants met with the fate of the people of Al-Zahrâ.
Spain everywhere presented the most pitiful spectacle.
The villages were deserted, and a traveller might have
journeyed for days along what were a short while before
the most frequented routes without meeting a living being.

In the summer of 1011, distress in Spain, and especially
in Cordova, was even intensified. It seemed as though that
ill-starred city, devastated by pestilence, found morbid
delight in increasing its agony by civil discord. The
soldiers ascribed all their troubles to Wâdhih; and the Slav
general, Ibn Abî Wadâ'a, a personal enemy of the Minister,
fomented their discontent. Publicly insulted, and feeling
his position untenable, Wâdhih despatched one Ibn Bakr to
make proposals of peace to Sulaimân. This step excited
the liveliest indignation. When Ibn Bakr returned from
his interview with the anti-Khalif, and presented himself in
the council-chamber, the soldiers fell upon him and slew
him, in the presence of the Khalif and Wâdhih, before he
had time to communicate the reply which he had received.
The Minister then resolved to seek refuge among the
Berbers, but Ibn Abî Wadâ'a received information of his
design and thwarted it. Collecting his Slavs, he led them
into Wâdhih's palace: " Wretch," he cried, as he struck

him with his sword, "thou hast squandered the money we so sorely need! Thou wouldst betray us to the Berbers!" The soldiers speedily made an end of him, and in a few minutes Wâdhih's head was being borne through the streets, and the pillage of the houses of his adherents had begun: his body was cast where those of Mahdî and Ibn Askeleja already lay (October 16, 1011).

Another year and a half elapsed before their enemies broke in, and spared the Cordovans the task of continuing their internecine strife. In the interval Ibn Abî Wadâ'a ruled the town with a rod of iron. The ecclesiastics lent him their aid, by declaring the war against the Berbers a holy one. The besieged gained some successes. In May, 1012, an illustrious Berber fell into their hands. This was Hobâsa, a nephew of Zâwî. Striking right and left, he had forced himself into a mêlée, when his saddle-girth became unbuckled, and as he stooped to readjust it a Christian Slav unhorsed him with his spear, and he was immediately slain by the other Slavs. His brother Habbûs tried to snatch the body from the foe, but after a desperate fight he was repulsed. The Slavs carried Hobâsa's head in triumph to the palace, leaving his body to the insults of the populace, who after mutilating it, and dragging it through the streets, committed it to the flames. The Berbers were infuriated. "We will avenge our captain!" they cried: "and when the blood of the last Cordovan is shed, our vengeance will not be slaked!" They therefore redoubled their efforts; but despair lent superhuman energy to the Cordovans, and under Ibn Abî Wadâ'a they made so vigorous a sortie that they compelled the enemy to raise the siege. They even drove the Berbers from Seville, but could not prevent them from seizing Calatrava, soon afterwards to reappear before the walls of the Capital. In spite of the Cordovans' desperate resistance, the Berbers succeeded in filling up the trench, and this placed them in possession of the eastern quarter of the city. Once more fortune momentarily favoured the Cordovans, for they expelled the enemy from the vantage-ground they had gained: but this was their last success. On Sunday, April 19, 1012, the Berbers entered the city by the Secunda gate, opened to them by an officer they had suborned.

Cordova expiated its stubborn resistance in torrents of blood. The Slavs in despair sought hiding-places, and

the Berbers, with savage yells, ransacked every street.
Pillaging, ravishing, slaying—they overran the city. The
most inoffensive citizens fell victims to their blind fury.
Here lay the venerable Sa'îd ibn Mundhir, who had been
prior of the Great Mosque since the days of Hakam II and
was renowned for his virtue and piety; there lay the hapless
Merwân, scion of the noble family of the Beni Hodair, who
had been crazed by unrequited love. The learned Ibn al-
Faradî,[1] author of an erudite biographical dictionary, and
Kady of Valencia under Mahdî, met a like fate. The wish
uttered in a moment of religious enthusiasm was fulfilled—
his was a martyr's death. The victims were too numerous
to be counted. Soon lurid flames lit up the dreadful scene.
The fairest palaces were consumed. "I have at last learned,"
wrote Ibn Hazm later, "the condition of my splendid
mansion in the Bilât-Mughîth. A refugee from Cordova
has told me that it is a heap of ruins. I also know, alas!
the fate of my wives. Some are in the tomb; some are
vagrants in distant lands."

On the second day after the capture of the city, Sulaimân
proceeded to the Khalif's palace. All the Cordovans who
had been so fortunate as to escape the swords of the
Berbers were drawn up to greet him. Though their souls
were harrowed by the frightful scenes which they had
witnessed, they roused themselves to cry "Long live the
Khalif!" Sulaimân appraised this factitious enthusiasm at
its true value. "With their lips they wish me long life,"
said he, quoting an ancient poet, "but at their hands my
death would be speedy!"

On arriving at the palace, Sulaimân summoned Hishâm
II before him. "Traitor," he exclaimed, "didst thou not
abdicate in my favour, and didst thou not promise never
again to lay claim to the throne? Why hast thou broken
thy word?" "Alas!" replied the miserable man, clasping
his hands; "thou knowest that I am the thrall of others;
I do but what I am bid. Spare me, I entreat thee, for I
declare anew that I abdicate, and appoint thee my successor!"

The Berbers at first settled in Secunda; but three
months later all the Cordovans, except those who dwelt in
the eastern suburb and in the quarter called the Old Town,

---

[1] Abú 'l-Walid 'Abdallah Ibn al-Faradî, born at Cordova 962. See C. Huart,
Arabic Literature (1903), pp. 203–4.

were sentenced to exile, and their property was forfeited to the victors, who thereupon occupied the houses which had escaped destruction.

[AUTHORITIES: Nuwairî, pp. 484–6; Ibn al-Athîr (A.H. 400); Ibn Hayyân (ap. Ibn Bassâm, i. 8); Rodrigo de Toledo, c. 36–9; Makkarî, i. 250, 546; Ibn Hazm (*On Love*), ff. 38, 87–8, 96, 102, 106; Ibn al-Khatîb (Art. on Hobâsa, MS. G.), f. 124; Ibn Bassâm, i. 161; iii. 1 *sq.*; Ibn al-'Abbâr, p. 164; 'Abd al-Wâhid, p. 28.]

CHAPTER XVI

THE HAMMÛDITES

SINCE the commencement of the civil war many Governors had asserted their independence, and the capture of Cordova by the Berbers struck a final blow at the unity of the Empire. The Slav generals took possession of the larger towns in the East; the Berber chieftains, to whom the 'Âmirids had given fiefs or provinces to govern, also enjoyed complete independence; and the few Arab families that were still powerful enough to assert their rights ignored the new Khalif—whose authority was therefore limited to five considerable cities, namely, Cordova, Seville, Niebla, Oksonoba, and Beja.

There seemed little likelihood of political change. The Berbers were eager to enjoy the wealth acquired by the sack of the Capital and many other towns, and Sulaimân himself, though he had been compelled to wage war for four years, was not of a bellicose disposition. By a strange anomaly, the head of the savage hordes which had devastated the Empire was just, mild, and generous. He loved literature, he composed excellent verse; to women he paid delicate homage and showed chivalrous gallantry. His chief desire was to preserve, as far as he could, the calm which succeeded the tempest. Unluckily he had incurred much unpopularity through the cruelties of his troops, which he had witnessed but could not check—for his men acknowledged his command only on condition that their freedom of action was unfettered. In the eyes of the Andalusians he was a lawless and impious infidel; a usurper placed upon the throne by the Berbers and the Christians of the North—two peoples whom they held in aversion—and when the Khalif had the imprudence to threaten sundry towns that he would treat them as he had treated Cordova if they refused to acknowledge him, his manifesto was received with a chorus of maledictions.

"To your Solomon may God show no mercy!" exclaimed a poet; "How far different is he from the Solomon of whom the Scriptures tell. The one put the devils in fetters; but the other hath let them loose, and in

his name they go to and fro in the land with rapine and murder. I have
sworn to bury my sword in the hearts of the tyrants, and to restore to
Religion her lost glory! Strange sight! A descendant of 'Abd Shams
hath become a Berber, and is crowned in spite of the nobles. Never will
I obey these monsters! The sword shall be arbiter : if they fall, life hath
joys in store for me; and if it be my lot to perish, I shall at least be
delivered from the sight of their crimes ! "

Such were the sentiments of the Andalusians, as well as
of the Slavs, who in the public prayers still inserted the
name of Hishâm II, although Sulaimân had begged them
to substitute his own, assuring them that he would demand
no other act of homage. Yet it was by no means certain
that Hishâm still lived. The most contradictory rumours
were current with regard to him. Some declared that
Sulaimân had put him to death; others, that he had
immured him in a dungeon. The latter assertion met with
most belief, for on the execution of a deposed monarch by
a usurper the dead body was customarily exhibited to the
people of the Capital—and no one had seen Hishâm's corpse.
The Slavs therefore continued to fight in Hishâm's name.
Khairân was their most prominent leader. A client of
Almanzor—who had appointed him Governor of Almeria—
he had taken to flight when the Berbers entered Cordova,
but when pursued he had turned to bay. Abandoned by
his men, and covered with wounds, he was left for dead upon
the field. He revived, however, and made his way back to
Cordova, where he was harboured by a friend who belonged
to the victorious party. When his wounds were healed,
Khairân, supplied with money by his host, was able to
make his way eastwards. Many Slavs and Andalusians
flocked to his banner, and after a siege of twenty days he
captured Almeria. One of Sulaimân's generals, moreover,
had proved his powerful ally. This was 'Alî ibn Hammûd.
He was descended from the Prophet's son-in-law, but since
his family had been settled in Africa for two centuries they
had become Berberized, and he spoke Arabic imperfectly.
As Governor of Ceuta and Tangier, while his elder brother
Kâsim was Governor of Algeciras, 'Alî was almost independent; but his ambition was not satisfied—a throne alone
would content it. He accordingly resolved to make an
alliance with the Slavs, and approached Khairân. To gain
his ends he invented a fantastic fable. He averred that
Hishâm II had read in a book of prophecies, that after the
fall of the Omayyads an 'Alid, the initial of whose name

was *ain*, should reign over Spain. He further declared that Hishâm, after the capture of Cordova, had sent him a message in these words: " I have a presentiment that the usurper will put me to death: I therefore name you my successor, and let yours be the task of avenging me!" Overjoyed at gaining such an auxiliary and convinced that Hishâm was alive, Khairân unhesitatingly accepted this story; and while 'Alî consented to replace Hishâm on the throne if he yet lived, Khairân agreed to recognise 'Alî if the contrary should prove the case.

These preliminaries settled, 'Alî crossed the Straits, and demanded from 'Âmir ibn Futûh, the Governor, the surrender of Malaga. 'Âmir, as client of an Omayyad client, and therefore already disposed to make common cause with the Slavs, had personal grievances against the Berbers, for one of their chiefs had deprived him of Ronda. He therefore yielded upon 'Alî's summons, and 'Alî joined Khairân at Almuñecar, whence they set out against Cordova.

'Alî relied not only on the Slavs, but on a large part of the Berbers. The latter, as a whole, attached little importance to Sulaimân. They had proclaimed him Khalif, because, at the moment, a pretender was wanted, and he happened to be available; but for their tastes he was too tender-hearted, and since he was devoid of military talent—the only kind they appreciated—they despised him. 'Alî's bravery, on the other hand, inspired them with respect, and they looked on him as a fellow-countryman. Zâwî, Governor of Granada, the most powerful of their chieftains—who had placed Sulaimân on the throne—had fostered a bitter hatred against the Omayyads, since the head of his father Zîrî, who had fallen in Africa fighting against partisans of that dynasty, had been affixed to the walls of the Castle at Cordova, where it remained until he and his men captured and pillaged the town. This was an unpardonable insult. He therefore declared for 'Alî as soon as the latter raised the standard of revolt. Zâwî's example powerfully influenced the other Berbers. Those sent by Sulaimân against his rival allowed themselves to be beaten. " Emir," said a Berber general, " if you wish for victory, you yourself must lead." He consented; but on nearing the enemy's camp, he was led thither on his mule, and handed over to his adversary.

On Sunday, July 1, 1016, 'Alî and his allies entered the Capital. The first care of Khairân and the other Slavs was to search for Hishâm. To 'Alî's great relief their search

proved fruitless. 'Alî then asked Sulaimân, in the presence
of the Viziers and ministers of religion, what had become
of Hishâm. "He is dead," replied Sulaimân curtly. "In
that case," replied Alî, "point out his sepulchre." Sulaimân
indicated a tomb; it was opened, and 'Alî asked a servant of
Hishâm's whether the corpse within it was his master's. The
servant, who, we may be sure, knew that Hishâm still lived,
but who had been intimidated by 'Alî, replied affirmatively,
and pointed out a black tooth in the jaw of the corpse, by
way of identification. His testimony was confirmed by
others, who wished to ingratiate themselves with 'Alî, or
feared his displeasure. The Slavs were, therefore, obliged
to admit that their legitimate monarch was no more, and to
recognise 'Alî as his successor. 'Alî then ordered Sulaimân,
as well as his brother and father, to be put to death. But
as the latter was being led to execution, 'Alî said to him:
"You have killed Hishâm, then?" "Nay," replied the
pious septuagenarian, who, absorbed in religious exercises,
had taken no part in political events; "as God is my
witness, we have not slain Hishâm. He is still alive,
and . . ." Before he could utter another word, 'Alî, who
feared dangerous revelations, made a sign to the headsman,
and the blade fell. The alleged corpse of Hishâm II was
then reinterred with regal pomp.

Was that monarch really dead? Party feuds have thrown
a thick and almost impenetrable veil over this question. It
is certain that Hishâm never reappeared, and that the person
afterwards passed off for him was an impostor. But, on the
other hand, it was never proved that Hishâm was slain by
Sulaimân or died a natural death during that prince's reign,
and the Omayyad clients who had known him declared that
the body disinterred by 'Alî was not his. It is true that
Sulaimân had averred before the notables of Cordova that
Hishâm was no more; but his testimony seems to us to be
untrustworthy, and 'Alî may have encouraged him to believe
that the declaration would save his life. Sulaimân, it must
be remembered, was by no means bloodthirsty, and it is not
to be supposed that he would commit a crime from which
even the ferocious Mahdî had recoiled. It may be pointed
out, also, that if Hishâm had really died during his reign
Sulaimân would have exposed his corpse to the Cordovans,
as custom and self-interest demanded. The Omayyad clients
urge that he despised the Cordovans too much to do so;
but they forget that he did not despise the Slavs, that he

did his utmost to get himself recognised by them, and that
he could have found no better way than by convincing them
of Hishâm's death. Finally, we have the testimony of
Sulaimân's aged father, who despite his son's assertion, took
God to witness that Hishâm still lived. Would this devout
old man have lied just as he was about to appear before the
tribunal of the Eternal? It seems improbable.

These considerations tend to the belief that there was
some truth in the tales of the women and eunuchs of the
seraglio. They declared that Hishâm had contrived to
escape from the palace during Sulaimân's reign, and that
after hiding in Cordova, and earning his bread as a common
labourer, he fled to Asia. Was the escape made with
Sulaimân's connivance? Did Hishâm swear to disturb him
no more? Did they remain in communication with one
another? Such are questions suggested by the words of
Sulaimân's father; but no positive answers can be given
to them. It does not, however, seem improbable that
Hishâm, weary of hearing his name used as a war-cry by
ambitious men who had not left him even the shadow of
power, sought an asylum in some obscure corner of Asia,
and there ended in peaceful seclusion a life which had been
full of pain and sorrow. Be this as it may, 'Alî now reigned,
and a more prosperous epoch seemed dawning. Although
half a Berber, the founder of the Hammûdite dynasty, from
the very first, showed favour to the Andalusians. He
listened attentively to the songs of their poets—which he
scarcely understood—granted audience to all who desired
it, and rigorously suppressed the Berbers' extortions. He
punished inexorably the slightest offences against property.
One day, for instance, he met a Berber carrying a basket of
grapes on his saddle. The Khalif stopped him, and asked
him how the fruit had come into his possession. The horseman, surprised at the question, replied carelessly: " The
grapes were to my liking, so I took them." His pilfering
cost him his life. 'Alî even contemplated a measure of the
most generous scope; namely, that of restoring to the Cordovans all that had been taken from them during the civil
war. Unluckily for the citizens, Khairân's ambition forced
upon his master a sudden change of policy.

Khairân at first had served the Khalif loyally. In his
province he had arrested and punished those who intrigued
in favour of the Omayyads, and if he had continued to
support 'Alî's cause, peace would soon have been re-estab-

lished. But he aimed at playing Almanzor's part, and recognising that 'Alî was not a man to content himself with playing that of Hishâm II, he conceived the project of restoring the former dynasty, without prejudice to his own virtual sovereignty. He therefore sought for a pretender, and about 1017, he hit upon one, in the person of a great-grandson of 'Abd-er-Rahmân III, who bore his ancestor's name, and then lived at Valencia. Many Andalusians promised their support. Among them was Mundhir, Governor of Zaragoza—one of the Beni Hâshim—who marched southwards, accompanied by his ally Raymond, Count of Barcelona. Thus betrayed by those whom he had befriended, and seeing that the citizens also desired the restoration of the Omayyads, 'Alî found himself obliged to behave with severity to those whom he had hitherto protected, and to throw himself into the arms of the Berbers whom he had ruled harshly. He therefore once more gave the latter leave to treat Cordova as a conquered town, and set the example himself. To raise money, he imposed additional taxes, and having arrested many notables—including Ibn Jahwar, a leading member of the Council of State—he did not release them until they had been mulcted in immense sums. He added insult to injustice, for as the notables emerged from the prison and their servants brought them their mules, 'Alî exclaimed: "Let them walk; and let the mules be taken to my stables." Even the property of the mosques, bequeathed to them by the devout, was not respected. By the instrumentality of a base Fakih, one Ibn al-Jaiyâr, 'Alî forced the custodians to deliver it up. Terror reigned at Cordova. The city swarmed with agents of police, spies, and informers. Justice was no longer done. While 'Alî played the protector to the Andalusians, they had been treated with partiality in the law-courts, but the Judges, clinging to office, now paid no attention to complaints against the Berbers, however well-founded. Many other persons sold themselves to the monarch. "Half the inhabitants," writes a contemporary historian, "spy upon the other half." The streets were deserted; no sooner was a luckless suspect seen than he was thrust into prison. Those who evaded arrest hid themselves in cellars and stole out by night to buy food. In his anger against the Andalusians, 'Alî even swore to destroy the Capital, after exiling or exterminating the populace. Death absolved him from his oath. In November, 1017, he had set out against the insurgents, but on reaching Guadix heavy rains had obliged him to retreat. It was now April, 1018, and learning that the allies had reached Jaen, he ordered a grand review on the 17th, before taking the field. But on the day appointed the soldiers waited for him in vain, and when the officers proceeded to the palace to ascertain the cause of his absence, they found that he had been assassinated in his bath.

The crime had been committed by three Slavs of the palace, who had been in the service of the Omayyads. They had no personal grudge against the monarch, whose favour and confidence they enjoyed, nor did it appear that they had been suborned by Khairân or the Cordovans. When arrested and condemned to death, they persistently denied that their crime had been suggested to them. It seems clear that they slew their master to rid their country of a ruler whose tyranny had become unendurable.

At any rate, 'Alî's death caused great joy in the Capital. Yet it did not bring about the fall of the Hammûdites. 'Alî left two sons—the elder of whom, Yahyâ, was Governor of Ceuta—as well as his brother, then Governor of Seville. Some of the Berbers wished to confer the crown upon Yahyâ, but others thought Kâsim more eligible, since he was at hand. The latter party prevailed, and six days after his brother's death, Kâsim entered the Capital, and the oath of allegiance to him was taken.

Khairân and Mundhir, for their part, had convoked an assembly of all the chiefs on whom they could rely, for April 30. The Council, which was numerous and included many ecclesiastics, resolved that the Khalifate should be elective, and ratified the election of 'Abd-er-Rahmân IV, who assumed the title of Mortadha. They then marched on Granada. On reaching the city, Mortadha invited Zâwî, in a very courteous letter, to recognise him as Khalif. After hearing the letter read, Zâwî ordered his secretary to endorse upon it Sura 109 of the Koran, as follows :

> " O ye unbelievers !
> I worship not that which ye worship.
> And ye do not worship that which I worship ;
> I shall never worship that which ye worship,
> Neither will ye worship that which I worship,
> To you be your religion ; to me my religion."

On receiving this reply, Mortadha sent Zâwî another letter. It was a menacing one, and contained these words :

" I march against you with a Christian host, and all the bravest sons of Andalusia. What canst thou do?" The letter ended with this verse:

" Happy will be the fate of those who are on our side; but miserable that of our adversaries!"

Zâwî replied by quoting Sura 102, as follows:

> "The desire of increasing riches occupieth you,
> Till ye come to the grave.[1]
> Nay! but in the end ye shall know—
> Nay! once more, in the end ye shall know your folly.
> Nay! would that ye knew it with knowledge of certainty!
> Surely ye shall see hell-fire.
> Then shall ye surely see it with the eye of certainty;
> Then shall ye on that day be taken to task concerning pleasures."

Exasperated by this retort, the Khalif determined to have recourse to arms.

Khairân and Mundhir, however, soon learnt that Mortadha was not the kind of sovereign they desired. The rights of the Omayyads concerned them but little, and if they took up arms for one of the family, it was only on condition that they held the reins of government. Mortadha was too proud to play such a part; the mere shadow of power did not content him, and instead of conforming to his generals' wishes, he intended to rule them. They therefore resolved to play the traitor, and promised Zâwî that they would desert the Khalif when the battle was joined. They, however, procrastinated, and desultory fighting ensued for several days. Zâwî then reminded Khairân of his promise. " We have delayed its fulfilment," replied Khairân, " to give you a just idea of our strength and courage; if Mortadha could have gained our hearts, the victory would have already been his. But to-morrow we abandon him."

Next morning Khairân and Mundhir did indeed turn their backs upon the foe, to the deep indignation of many of their officers. Among these was Sulaimân ibn Hûd, in command of Mundhir's Christian troops, who instead of joining in the retreat, rallied his men. Mundhir, as he passed by, cried out: " Save thyself, wretched man! Thinkest thou I can stay for thee?" " Alas!" exclaimed Sulaimân; " we are ruined and disgraced through thee!" Nevertheless, seeing that resistance was impossible, he followed his master. Mortadha, forsaken by the bulk of his army, fought with the

---

[1] Cf. note in Sale's translation.

courage of despair, and managed to extricate himself. He
escaped to Guadix, beyond the frontier of Granada, but was
there assassinated by Khairân's emissaries.

Khairân expiated, by the ruin of his own party, his
cowardly and infamous treason. The Slavs were no longer
able to muster an army, and their opponents, the Berbers,
were henceforth masters of Andalusia. Meanwhile Cordova
was comparatively prosperous, and as contented as it could
be under alien domination. The rule of the sword had
almost ceased; a milder and more regular administration
succeeded it. Kâsim loved peace and repose; he did not
harass the Cordovans with fresh exactions. To wipe out the
memory of former dissensions, he sent for Khairân and was
reconciled to him; on another Slav, Zuhair lord of Murcia,
he conferred the fiefs of Jaen, Calatrava, and Baeza. Kâsim's
orthodoxy, however, was not above suspicion: it was
whispered that he was a Shî'ite. But whatever his real
opinions may have been, he never tried to impose them on
others; he never even spoke of them, and did not meddle
with ecclesiastical affairs. Thanks to this prince's moderation the Hammûdite dynasty seemed likely to endure. It
is true that the people of the Capital had little affection for
it, but in course of time they would probably have consoled
themselves for the loss of their former masters, if circumstances over which they had no control had not revived
fading aspirations.

Mistrusting the Berbers, Kâsim sought support elsewhere.
The Berbers had at their disposal a great number of negro
slaves. Kâsim bought them, procured others from Africa,
formed them into regiments, and entrusted important posts
to their leaders. By this proceeding he irritated the Berbers,
and his nephew Yahyâ utilised their discontent in his own
interest. He sent them a letter, in the course of which he
said: "My uncle has disinherited me, and he has done you
grievous wrong in conferring on your slaves offices which are
yours by right. Place me on my father's throne, and I will
restore to you your dignities and dismiss the negroes." As
might have been expected, the Berbers promised him their
aid. Yahyâ therefore crossed the Straits with his troops and
landed at Malaga, of which place his brother Idrîs, who made
common cause with him, was Governor. While there he received a letter from Khairân—ever ready to support a pretender, but tacitly reserving the right to plot against him if
he were successful. Khairân reminded Yahyâ of what he

had done for 'Alî, and offered his services. Idrîs advised the
rejection of the offer. "Khairân," he said, "is perfidious;
he will deceive us." "I am sure of it," replied Yahyâ;
"but we will take care that he does us no harm." He
therefore wrote to the lord of Almeria, accepting his services,
and then set out for Cordova. His uncle deemed it prudent
not to await him, and fled, on the night of August 11 or 12,
1021, to Seville, with only five horsemen. A month later
Yahyâ entered Cordova. His reign was a short one. The
negroes hastened to rejoin Kâsim, many Andalusian officers
did the like, and soon Yahyâ found himself deserted even by
many of the Berbers, who were offended at his arrogance.
His position thus became so perilous that he momentarily
feared to be arrested in his palace. He resolved to seek
safety, and fled by night to Malaga. Kâsim returned to the
Capital, and on February 12, 1023, was proclaimed Khalif
for the second time. But his power rested on no solid basis,
and speedily diminished. In Africa, Idrîs, then Governor of
Ceuta, seized the town of Tangier—which the Khalif had
carefully fortified, with a view to withdrawing thither in the
event of affairs going ill on his side of the Straits. In Spain
Yahyâ had taken possession of Algeciras, which sheltered
Kâsim's wife, as well as his treasures. Even in the Capital
the Khalif had only his negroes to rely upon.

Encouraged by the state of affairs, the Cordovans, who
had taken but a languid interest in the struggle between
uncle and nephew, grew restless. The idea of casting off
the Berber yoke was ingrained in their hearts, and a rumour
circulated that a member of the family of Omayya would
ere long appear and claim the throne. Kâsim took fright,
and as no particular Omayyad had been named, he ordered
all who could be found to be imprisoned. Some concealed
themselves among the scum of the city, others in the country,
but Kâsim's precautions did not prevent the revolution from
breaking out. Exasperated by the Berbers, the Cordovans
took up arms on July 31, 1023. After a desperate struggle
the opposing parties patched up a peace, or rather a truce,
promising to treat one another with respect. But the truce
was of short duration, although Kâsim tried to prolong it
by assumed condescension to the people. On Friday,
September 6, after divine service, the cry of "To arms!"
was raised on all sides, and the Cordovans forthwith expelled Kâsim and the Berbers from the city, but not from
the suburbs. Kâsim pitched his camp to the west of the

Capital and commenced a siege which lasted for more than fifty days. The rebels stubbornly defended themselves, but when food began to run low, they asked the besiegers to allow them to quit the city with their wives and children. Kâsim refused terms, and the Cordovans then adopted a course dictated by despair. They pulled down a gateway, and on Thursday, October 31, they sallied forth in a body with such impetuous fury that the enemy fled before them in utter confusion. Kâsim's officers retired to their fiefs : he himself sought safety at Seville ; but that city, encouraged by the Cordovans' example, shut its gates, and proclaimed itself a republic. He then threw himself into Xeres ; but Yahyâ besieged him there and forced him to surrender. Kâsim had played out his part. Yahyâ, who had dragged him to Malaga, loaded with chains, swore to kill him ; but his scruples for a long time prevented him from keeping his oath. In a dream his father appeared to him, and cried : "Slay not Kâsim, I adjure thee ! When I was yet a child he showed me kindness, and though he was my elder brother, he claimed not the throne." Often, nevertheless, during some drinking-bout Yahyâ determined to put him to death ; but he always yielded to the arguments of his boon-companions, who pointed out that his uncle, being a prisoner, was harmless. Kâsim remained immured in a castle in the province of Malaga for thirteen years ; but in 1036 Yahyâ heard that he had tried to incite the garrison to revolt. "What !" he cried, "doth the old man still cherish ambitions ? It is enough ! " and he ordered him to be strangled.

The Cordovans, having regained their independence, determined to place an Omayyad on the throne—not, however, by violence, but with due formality. In November, 1023, they held a convention. The Viziers put forward three candidates, namely Sulaimân, son of 'Abd-er-Rahmân IV (Mortadha)—'Abd-er-Rahmân, brother of Mahdî—and Mohammed ibn al-Irâkî. They were so convinced that Sulaimân—whose name stood at the head of the list—would be elected, that the Secretary of State, Ahmad ibn Bord, had drawn up the Act of Investiture in that candidate's name.

The Viziers had, however, overrated their own influence, and greatly under-estimated that of the supporters of Mahdî's brother. 'Abd-er-Rahmân, then twenty-two years of age, had been exiled by the Hammûdites, and had secretly returned to the Capital not long before the election. He had witnessed the rising of the Cordovans against the Berbers, and had upon that occasion tried in vain to form a party favourable to his succession. The Viziers who organized the revolt were unfavourable to his claims, and threw his emissaries into prison, where they still lay. They had tried to arrest 'Abd-er-Rahmân himself; but when they drew up the list of candidates, they thought it best to insert his name, to avoid giving offence to certain of their fellow-citizens. They were, however, far from suspecting that the prince would be a formidable competitor, and classed him with Mohammed ibn al-Irâkî, who enjoyed no popularity whatever.

Believing themselves on firm ground, the Viziers invited the nobles, the soldiers, and the populace to proceed to the election of a Khalif in the Great Mosque, on December 1. On the day appointed Sulaimân was the first to present himself, accompanied by the Vizier 'Abdallah ibn Mokhâmis. Sulaimân was splendidly apparelled, and his countenance was radiant with joy, for he was confident that the popular choice would fall upon him. His friends advanced to meet him, and bade him be seated on a dais which had been erected for him. Shortly afterwards, 'Abd-er-Rahmân entered the Mosque by another door. He was surrounded by a multitude of soldiers and workmen, who, as soon as they had passed the threshold, acclaimed him Khalif, making the Mosque re-echo with stentorian shouts. The Viziers, in their surprise, were dumbfounded—and, in any case, they could not have been heard for the tumult. They accordingly resigned themselves to accepting 'Abd-er-Rahmân as Khalif, and Sulaimân—yet more astonished and discomfited —perforce followed their example. He was led to 'Abd-er-Rahmân, whose hand he kissed, and who bid him sit by his side. The third candidate, Mohammed ibn Irâkî, also took the oath of allegiance; the Secretary then erased from the Act of Investiture Sulaimân's name, and substituted that of 'Abd-er-Rahmân, who assumed the title of Mostadhir.

[AUTHORITIES: Ibn Hayyân, f. 128; ap. Ibn Bassâm, i. 6–7, 9, 22–4, 120–2, 127–9; iii. 5, 141; Makkarî, i. 102, 280, 315–19; 'Abd al-Wâhid, pp. 35–8, 45; Ibn al-Athîr (A.H. 407); Nuwairî, pp. 486–490; Ibn al-Khatîb (Art. on Alî ibn-Hammûd, MS. E.); Ibn al-'Abbâr, pp. 160–1; Abbad., i. 222; ii. 214; Ibn Hazm (Dozy, Catalogue, i. 225).]

CHAPTER XVII

'ABD-ER-RAHMÂN V AND IBN HAZM

THE historian of a calamitous epoch, and of a people rent and agonised by civil wars, sometimes longs to avert his gaze from the strife of factions and its attendant bloodshed, in order to soothe the imagination for a while in the realms of fancy, amidst ideals of innocence and peace. Let us therefore linger for a brief space over the poems with which pure and ingenuous love inspired the youthful 'Abd-er-Rahmân V and his Vizier Ibn Hazm. Their verses exhale a perfume of youth, artlessness, and joy; the allurement of their pure accents is irresistible in the midst of universal devastation—the song of a nightingale heard amidst a tempest.

When scarcely past his childhood, 'Abd-er-Rahmân had passionately loved his cousin Habîba,[1] daughter of the Khalif Sulaimân. But his sighs were vain. Sulaimân's widow opposed the marriage and gave the youthful suitor to understand that he must bide his time. His wounded pride and thwarted longings thereupon found vent in the following verses :

" Endless are the pretexts for refusal, and against them my pride revolts ! In their blindness her family would force her to reject me ; but can the moon be refused to the sun? How can Habîba's mother, who knoweth my worth, frown upon me as a son-in-law ?

" For I love her—that fair and innocent daughter of the house of 'Abd Shams, who liveth secluded in her parents' palace. I have sworn to be her slave for life, and my heart shall be her dowry.

" As a hawk swoopeth upon a dove which spreadeth her wings, so dart I when I behold her, that dove of the 'Abd Shams—I who am sprung from the same noble stock.

" How fair is my beloved ! Her hands in their whiteness flout the radiance of the Pleiades, and the sheen of her bosom is the envy of the dawn.

" How long a fast hast thou imposed upon my love, oh, my beloved ! When wilt thou suffer me to break it ?

" It is beneath thy roof that I seek the remedy for all my ills—over that roof, may Allah shower his blessings ! It is there that my aching heart would find solace ; it is there that the fire which consumes me would be quenched !

---

[1] "The beloved."

" If thou rejectest me, my cousin, thou wilt reject—I swear it—a lover who is thy equal by birth, and whose eyes are dimmed by the ardour with which thou inspirest him !

" But I despair not of winning her one day, and thus shall I attain the height of my glory ; for I can wield the lance when the black horses are red with blood.   I render honour to the stranger within my gates ; I load with benefits the wretched who appeal to my generosity.   Which of her kinsfolk excelleth me in desert ? Who is my equal in renown ? Mine are the qualities needful to please her—youth, courtesy, tenderness and eloquence."

We know nothing of Habîba's sentiments towards her wooer, for Arab writers have left but a shadowy outline of this fair and flitting apparition, whom the imagination would fain picture more definitely.   She appears, however, not to have been insensible to 'Abd-er-Rahmân's homage.   Meeting him one day, she lowered her eyes before the prince's ardent gaze, and in blushing confusion forgot to return his salute.   'Abd-er-Rahmân, misinterpreting her modest timidity as coldness, composed these verses on the occasion :

" Greeting to her who deigneth not a word to me ! Greeting to the lovely gazelle whose glances are arrows piercing my heart ! Never, alas ! doth she send me her image to soothe the tumult of my dreams ! Knowest thou not—thou whose name is so sweet to utter—that I love thee unspeakably, and that I would be to thee the most faithful lover in the world ? "

'Abd-er-Rahmân, however, does not seem to have won Habîba's hand.   He was, indeed, as a rule unfortunate in his amours.   It is true that another damsel was not unkind to him, but she broke her plighted troth, as these lines witness :

" Ah ! weary are the hours since thou preferredst my rival ! O graceful gazelle—breaker of vows and faithless one—hast thou forgotten the nights when we lay alone among the roses ?   One shawl covered us ; as pearls on a necklace we lay ; entwined like the branches of trees, we twain were but one, while the golden stars glittered above us in the blue vault of heaven ! "

The youthful 'Abd-er-Rahmân had a friend like him in character and disposition : this was 'Alî Ibn Hazm, his Prime Minister.   Ibn Hazm's ancestors, who lived in the province of Niebla, had been Christians until his great-grandfather, Hazm, embraced Islamism ; but, ashamed of his origin, and wishing to conceal it, Hazm denied his ancestry. 'Alî's father, Ahmad (who had been Vizier under Almanzor), had set him the example ; alleging his descent from a Persian freedman of Yazîd, brother of the first Omayyad

Khalif, Mu'âwiya, he expressed profound contempt for the religion of his ancestors.[1]

"Human Superstition," remarks Ibn Hazm in his *Book of Religions and Sects*,[2] "need never excite our astonishment. The most numerous and civilized nations are thralls to it. Take, for example, the Christians. So great is their multitude that God alone can number them ; and they can boast of illustrious philosophers and sagacious princes. Nevertheless, they believe that one is three and three are one ; that one of the three is the father, another the son, and the third a spirit—that the father is the son, and that he is not the son —that a man is God, and that he is not God—that the Messiah is in all respects God, and yet that he is not the same as God—that he has existed from all eternity, and yet was created. A sect of theirs, known as the Jacobites[3]— numbered by hundreds of thousands—even believe that the Creator was scourged, buffeted, crucified and slain, and that for three whole days the Universe was without a ruler!"

These sarcasms, be it observed, are not those of a sceptic, but of a zealous Moslem. In religion Ibn Hazm followed the doctrines of the Zâhirites,[4] a sect which clung firmly to the letter of the sacred text, and branded decision by mere analogy—that is, the employment of human reason in interpreting the canon—as an invention of the Evil One. In politics, Ibn Hazm was a supporter of the legitimate dynasty —of which he had become a client by virtue of his false pedigree—and the Omayyads had no more faithful, devoted, and zealous follower. When their cause seemed irrevocably lost, when 'Alî ibn Hammûd occupied the throne, and even Khairân, chief of the Slavs, had submitted to him, Ibn Hazm had been one of those whose courage did not fail. Surrounded by enemies and spies, he nevertheless continued to intrigue and conspire, for, being an enthusiast, in his eyes prudence was cowardice. Khairân discovered his proceedings, and after throwing him into prison for several months to expiate his unseasonable zeal, he procured his exile. Ibn Hazm thereupon sought the hospitality of the Governor of Aznalcazar, not far from Seville, and was there when the news came that the Omayyad 'Abd-er-Rahmân IV had been proclaimed Khalif at Valencia. Ibn Hazm immedi-

[1] See Nicholson, *Lit. Hist. of the Arabs* (1907), pp. 426 *sq.*
[2] Kitâbu 'l-Milal wa-'l-Nihal.
[3] See p. 536 *n.*
[4] "Literalists."

ately embarked to tender his services, and fought valiantly
in the battle which Mortadha lost through the treachery of
his pretended friends; then, falling into the hands of the
victorious Berbers, he did not regain his liberty for some
time.

Ibn Hazm was ultimately to be hailed as the most
learned man of his age, and the most fertile writer that
Spain ever produced.[1] But in his earlier days he was
pre-eminently a poet, and one of the most graceful poets
of Moslem Spain. He was still of an age blessed with
illusions, for he was only eight years older than his young
sovereign. He too had had his romance—a simple one,
indeed, but he has recorded it so frankly, so artlessly, yet
with so much charm, that we cannot resist reproducing the
narrative. (Here and there we have omitted certain strained
metaphors, embellishments, and spangles, which in the eyes
of an Arab give inimitable literary grace, but which to the
more sober Western taste are barely tolerable.)

"In my father's palace there lived a damsel who had
been brought up under its roof. At the age of sixteen she
was peerless among women for beauty, intelligence, modesty,
and gentleness. Jesting and flattery wearied her, and her
words were few. While none dared to woo her, her loveliness overcame every heart: though proud, and chary of her
favours, she was more alluring than the most refined coquette.
Sedate and caring little for frivolous amusements, she
touched the lute to perfection.

"I was very young in those days, and all my thoughts
were of her. Sometimes I heard her speak, but always
when others were by, and for two years I sought an opportunity of conversing alone with her. One day an entertain-
ment, of a kind frequent in the palaces of the great, was
given at our house, and to it the ladies of our family, and
of our clients and chief dependants were invited. After
spending a part of the day within the palace, the ladies
proceeded to a belvedere affording a glorious prospect of
Cordova and its suburbs, and placed themselves where the
trees of the garden did not obstruct the view. I joined
them, and drew near to the embrasure at which *she* stood;
but when she saw me at her side she tripped gracefully to
another niche. I followed her; she again eluded me. She
well knew my sentiments towards her, for women have more

---

[1] See Nicholson, *op. cit.*, p. 426.

2 o

skill in divining love felt for them than the Bedawy travel-
ling by night has in marking his track; fortunately the
other ladies suspected nothing, for they were too much
occupied in seeking the fairest prospects to pay attention to
me. The company then descended into the gardens, and
those who were privileged by age and position begged the
idol of my heart to sing somewhat. Taking up her lute,
and attuning it with a modesty which, in my eyes, redoubled
her charms, she thereupon sang these verses by 'Abbâs, son
of Ahnaf:[1]

> " ' I have no thoughts save for my sun—the willowy and lissom maiden
> whom I saw vanish behind the dark walls of the palace. Is she human or
> a shade? She is more than woman; but if she hath all the beauty, she
> hath none of the malignity of a *jinni*. Her countenance is a pearl; her
> form, a narcissus; her breath, perfume—she is an emanation of pure light.
> Clad in an amber robe, walking with inconceivable lightness, she might
> tread on things the most fragile, and break them not!'

" While she sang this, it was not the cords of the lute,
but my heart-strings, that she struck with the plectrum.
Never hath that exquisite day faded from my memory; it
will linger therein on my deathbed. But since that day I
never heard that sweet voice again.
" In my rhymes I said:

> " ' Blame her not if she avoideth thee: she deserveth not thy reproaches.
> She is fair as a gazelle, or as the moon; but the gazelle is timid, and no
> mortal may attain to the moon. . . . Thou deprivest me of hearing thy
> sweet voice, and thou wilt not suffer mine eyes to drink in thy beauty.
> Absorbed in devotions, thy thoughts are fixed on God; thou hast none for
> mortal man. How happy that 'Abbâs whose verses thou singest! And
> yet if that great poet heard thee, he would be sad, he would envy thee as
> his vanquisher, for thy lips imbue his words with a pathos beyond his art!'

" Three days after Mahdî had been declared Khalif, we
quitted our new palace in the suburb of Zâhira, on the east
of Cordova, and returned to our former abode in the western
suburb, Balât-Moghith, but for reasons I need not dilate
upon, the damsel did not accompany us. On the accession
of Hishâm II we fell under the displeasure of those then in
power; they extorted immense sums from us, and cast us
into prison, and on regaining our liberty we were obliged to
go into hiding. Civil war followed. There were none who
did not suffer from it, but our family more than all. My

---

[1] See C. Huart, *Arabic Literature* (1903), p. 78.

father died on Saturday, June 21, 1012, and we were left
in evil plight.   One day when I was attending the funeral
of a kinsman, I recognised the maiden among the mourners.
Good reason had I for sorrow on that day! Misfortune
threatened me on all sides, and yet, as my eyes fell on her,
the present with all its woes seemed to roll away as though
by enchantment: she recalled the past—the fading memories
of halcyon days, of dawning love—and for a little space
youth and happiness seemed to return.   But, alas, for how
brief a moment! Then the grim realities of the present
flowed in upon my soul, and my sorrow, heightened by the
pangs of hopeless love, grew more bitter.   I composed these
verses on the occasion :

> "' She laments a dead man, whom all respected ; but he that still liveth
> hath more need of her tears.   Strange!   She weepeth for one who died
> an easy natural death, and she hath no pity for him whom she tortureth
> in despair!'

"Not long afterwards, when the Berbers had seized the
Capital, a decree of exile was issued against us, and we
quitted Cordova in July, 1013.   Five years passed by without my seeing the damsel.   At length, on my return to
Cordova in February, 1018, I went to lodge with one of
my kinsfolk, and there I beheld her.   But so greatly was
she changed that I scarce recognised her, and I had to be
assured that it was she.   The flower that I had erstwhile
gazed upon in ecstasy, and that all would have plucked if
respect had not restrained them, was now withered.   Nurtured under our roof in luxury, she had been suddenly cast
out to seek her bread with bitter toil.   Alas! women are
tender blossoms; as soon as they are neglected they fade :
their beauty cannot endure, as can the comeliness of a man,
the burning sun, the scorching blast, the inclemency of the
seasons, or bare neglect.   And yet, being what she was, she
would still have made me the happiest of all men had she
vouchsafed to me one tender word ; but she remained as
cold and indifferent to me as of yore.   Little by little this
coldness began to detach me from her ; the loss of her beauty
did the rest.   I never reproached her—and I do not reproach
her now.   I have no right to do so.   Of what can I complain?   I might have complained if she had coquetted with
me ; but she never gave me a gleam of hope, or promised
me aught."

In the foregoing narrative there are evidences of a

delicacy of sentiment unusual among Arabs, who prefer
graces that allure, eyes that anticipate, the sigh that en-
courages.   Ibn Hazm's love-dream is doubtless not devoid of
a sensuous element—for his regrets are alleviated when their
object is changed for the worse—but it comprises also
spiritual attraction, chivalrous esteem and enthusiasm, and
it charms by a calm, modest beauty, full of tender dignity.
But it must be borne in mind that this writer—the chastest,
and, we had almost said, the most Christian of Moslem
poets—was not an Arab of pure blood. Great-grandson
of a Spanish Christian, he had not entirely lost the modes
of thought and feeling characteristic of his ancestors.   In
vain did such orientalized Spaniards repudiate their descent
—in vain did they invoke, not Christ but Mohammed, and
assail their former co-religionists with sarcasms—in their
innermost nature there lingered a delicate and spiritual
element which was not Arabian.

[AUTHORITIES: Ibn al-ʿAbbâr, pp. 165–6; Ibn Bassâm, i. ff. 11–12 ;
    Makkarî, i. p. 284; Dozy, *Catalogue*, i. 225, 227, 230; Ibn Hazm,
    Tauq al hamáma, ff. 99–102; (*Bk. of Religions*), ii. f. 227.]

CHAPTER XVIII

THE FALL OF THE KHALIFATE

SCARCELY seven weeks had elapsed since 'Abd-er-Rahmân's election, and Ibn Hazm's appointment as *hâjib*, before the young Khalif was dead, and the Prime Minister had for ever relinquished worldly ambitions, to seek forgetfulness of the past in study, solitude, and prayer. Neither can be reproached with having introduced into affairs of State the levity and caprice too often popularly attributed to poets; on the contrary, both may be credited with great administrative aptitude. Nurtured in the rough school of misfortune and exile, they had early acquired a knowledge of human nature, as well as political acumen. But they were surrounded with many and various dangers. 'Abd-er-Rahmân had only the younger nobles to rely upon. Besides 'Alî Ibn Hazm, his usual counsellors were 'Abd al-Wahhâb ibn Hazm ('Alî's cousin), and Abû 'Âmir ibn Shohaid. These were talented men, but they offended strict Moslems by the laxity of their religious views. The older nobles had favoured Sulaimân's candidature, and on his rejection by the majority they intrigued so openly in his favour that 'Abd-er-Rahmân was obliged to arrest them. Thoughtful people approved of this necessary step; but it ruffled the aristocracy. The monarch also laid himself open to reproach for imprisoning his two rivals. They were, it is true, treated courteously, but they were confined to the palace. On the other hand, since public misfortunes had closed nearly all the avenues of labour, there were multitudes of unemployed workmen, all prepared to demolish the existing fabric of society. Unfortunately these anarchical cohorts had a leader—one Mohammed, an Omayyad. When the elective assemblies met he had hoped that the choice might fall on himself. Mohammed's name, however, was not even mentioned—a fact little to be wondered at, since he was an uneducated man, of slender natural abilities, and his only pleasures were gluttony and debauchery. But his vanity was immense, and when he learned that he had been wholly ignored, and that the throne had been conferred on a young man, his wrath knew no bounds. He accordingly made use of the influence which he possessed over the working-classes, who took his boorishness for urbanity and with whom he was on terms of such close intimacy that one Ahmad ibn Khâlid, a weaver, was his dearest friend. Zealously and ably seconded by this man, Mohammed incited the workmen to visions of plunder and havoc, and laid the train for a formidable revolt.

At first there seemed no reason to fear a coalition of the populace and the arrested nobles, since they had supported different candidates, but on Sulaimân's death the patricians joined hands with the demagogues. One of the former, Ibn Imrân, acted as intermediary. With unsuspecting good nature 'Abd-er-Rahmân, though warned, had set him at liberty. "If Ibn Imrân," said one of the Khalif's friends to him, "takes a single step outside his prison he will cut off a year of your life." He was, indeed, a dangerous man. He succeeded at his first attempt in gaining over the officers of the guard, for they were just then out of humour with the Khalif. Two days before, a Berber battalion had arrived at Cordova to offer their services to the monarch, and the latter, conscious of the need of troops in his perilous position, accepted their offer. This had aroused the jealousy of the guard, who, incited by Ibn Imrân, indulged in open complaints : " We vanquished the Berbers, and drove them out, and now the man whom we placed on the throne aims at bringing them back into the city and subjecting us once more to their detested rule." The populace, who only waited for a signal to rise, were willing converts to rebellion, and at a moment when 'Abd-er-Rahmân suspected nothing, a mob burst into the palace and set the imprisoned nobles free. The unfortunate Khalif, realizing at once that his life was at stake, asked the advice of his Viziers. Fearing for their own lives, they were deliberating on their best course of action, when the guards told them they need have no fear if they would abandon 'Abd-er-Rahmân to his fate. Most of the Viziers succumbed to the instinct of self-preservation, and one by one they stole away from the monarch. They were, however, soon to discover the value of the guards' promises, for several, including the prefect of the city, were slain as they were leaving the palace by the Gate of the Baths.

'Abd-er-Rahmân himself, mounting his horse, sought flight by the same gateway. But the guards obstructed his passage, threatening him with their spears and reviling him.

He retraced his steps, and dismounting, entered the bath-room; then, stripping to his tunic, he crept into a flue.

Meanwhile the populace and the guards were hunting down the Berbers mercilessly. The poor wretches were massacred wherever they were found, in the palace, the bath, or the mosque. The women of the Khalif's harem were divided by lot amongst the pretorians, who took them to their homes. Mohammed had triumphed. Proclaimed Khalif in the very room where the dethroned monarch lay hid, he returned to the great hall and seated himself upon the throne, surrounded by the guards and the mob. His position, however, was precarious so long as his predecessor lived. He therefore ordered search to be made everywhere for 'Abd-er-Rahmân, who was at last discovered and put to death (January 18, 1024).

Mohammed took the title of Al-Mustakfi. He courted popularity by distributing money and honours to all who would, but the wrath of the middle-class as well as of the nobles was aroused when he appointed his friend, the weaver, Prime Minister. The Khalif's reign was a brief one. He proved, as might have been expected, a bad ruler. Learning that there was a plot against him, he threw many of his family into prison. One of them was even strangled by his orders, an act which caused fierce indignation in Cordova. He also arrested his predecessor's principal counsellors, among them the two Ibn Hazms, while to avoid similar treatment Abû 'Âmir ibn Shohaid and many others quitted the Capital, and betaking themselves to the Hammûdite Yahyâ, at Malaga, urged him to put an end to the anarchy rife at Cordova. Their efforts were not wholly fruitless. It became known at Cordova that Yahyâ was preparing to attack the city, and a riot broke out (May, 1025). Moham-med's Vizier, the former weaver, was stabbed to death with knives, and the mob, in its frenzy, did not cease to mangle his corpse until it was cold. Mohammed was surrounded in his palace, and his guards exclaimed: " God knows that we have done all in our power to maintain thee on the throne, but we now see it to be impossible. Yahyâ threatens us; we must march against him; and we fear that evil may befall thee when we are gone. We counsel thee to leave the city secretly." Seeing that all was lost, Mohammed resolved to follow their advice. Assuming the guise of a singing-girl, and wearing a veil, he stole from the palace and the city, with two women. He sought to hide his shame in an obscure village on the frontier, where he was at last poisoned by an officer, who was too deeply compromised not to follow him, but who grew weary of being bound to an outlaw.

For six months Cordova was without a ruler. The city was governed, after a fashion, by a Council of State, but this régime was necessarily unstable. The time was not ripe for such a form of government; the old world was falling in ruins, but the new was yet but a dream. In public opinion a monarchy was still the only form of government by which order could be secured. But where was a sovereign to be found? Among the Omayyads? The attempt had already been made: in 'Abd-er-Rahmân V the best prince of that house had been chosen, and utter failure had resulted. To preserve the peace, to hold in check a populace, ever restless and excitable, ever ready to plunder and murder, a prince was needed who had foreign troops at his disposal, and the Omayyads had none. It was therefore determined to offer the throne to Yahyâ the Hammûdite, against whom there was little cause for ill-feeling, and it would appear that this design was not due to disaffected conspirators, as an Arab writer has declared,[1] but to the party of order, who saw no other means of safety. Negotiations were opened with Yahyâ at Malaga. He accepted the Cordovans' offer, but with cold indifference. He mistrusted the ingrained fickleness of those who made it, and was well aware that he was only looked upon as a last resource. He confined himself, therefore, to sending some troops to Cordova under a Berber general (November, 1025).

The event showed that Yahyâ was well advised. The citizens soon kicked against African domination, and lent an eager ear to emissaries from the Slav chieftains of the East —Khairân of Almeria, and Mojehid of Denia—who told them that if they desired liberty the Slavs would come to their aid. This was no empty promise. In May, 1026, when all had been put in train, the two princes marched on the Capital with a strong force, while the populace simultaneously rose, expelled Yahyâ's Governor, and killed many of his soldiers. The gates were then thrown open to Khairân and Mojehid, but when it came to establishing a Government, the two princes fell out, and Khairân, fearing treachery on the part of his ally, returned in all haste to Almeria (June 12).

---

[1] Homaidi, followed by other Arab chroniclers.

Mojehid remained some time longer in the Capital, but ultimately quitted it without restoring the monarchy. After his departure the Council of State resolved to try to accomplish what sad experience should have taught them to be impossible. An Omayyad prince, thrown, without the support of mercenaries, between two irreconcilable factions, must inevitably succumb either to a popular revolt or to a patrician conspiracy. To restore stable government the recall of the Omayyads was therefore a precarious device, but it was the only one which could be suggested. Abu 'l-Hazm ibn Jahwar, the most influential member of the Council, especially favoured the idea. He therefore consulted with the frontier chieftains, who ostensibly belonged to either the Omayyad or the Slav party, but who, in truth, were united only by a profound hatred of the Berbers. After long negotiations some of these chiefs fell in with the proposal— probably because they felt sure of its failure—and it was agreed that the throne should be offered to Hishâm, elder brother of 'Abd-er-Rahmân IV. This prince resided at Alpuente, whither he had fled after his brother's murder. In April, 1027, the Cordovans took the oath of allegiance to him, but nearly three years passed before all difficulties were surmounted, and during this time Hishâm III, surnamed Motadd,[1] wandered from town to town, since many chiefs barred his way to the Capital. At last the Cordovans heard that he was about to enter the city. The Council made preparations to receive him regally, but before all was ready, the news came (December 18, 1029) that Hishâm was already approaching. The troops marched out to meet him, and the city rang with shouts of joy. Crowds thronged the streets through which the prince would make his progress, and all were on tip-toe to view a magnificent and truly royal procession. They were disappointed. Hishâm was mounted on a sorry and meanly caparisoned nag, and wore plain apparel ill-suited to the dignity of a Khalif. He therefore made no very favourable impression ; yet he was greeted with noisy demonstrations of joy by those who hoped that disorders were at an end and that just and resolute government was at hand.

Hishâm III was ill-adapted to realize such hopes. He was a well-meaning man, but irresolute and indolent, and a lover of good cheer. On the day after his arrival the patricians were able to convince themselves that their choice

---

[1] Or Mu'tamid, according to some writers.

had not been a happy one. A great audience was held in the throne-room and all the officials were presented to the Khalif; but, unaccustomed to receptions and set speeches, the old man only managed to stammer a few words, and one of the ministers had to speak in his name. When the poets recited the odes composed in honour of his accession, he could find no gracious word of acknowledgment, and scarcely seemed to understand their verses.

The Khalif's début thus dispelled all illusions, and matters grew worse when, after a little while, he appointed Hakam ibn Sa'îd Prime Minister. Hakam, who was a client of the 'Âmirids, had exercised the calling of a weaver in Cordova, where he made Hishâm's acquaintance—for the Omayyad princes often formed politic intimacies among the lower classes. During the civil war Hakam had served as a soldier, and since he was wanting neither in courage nor military talents, he rose rapidly in rank and gained the esteem of the frontier chieftains under whom he served. After Hishâm had been proclaimed Khalif, Hakam presented himself, and recalling their former friendship, ingratiated himself so effectually that he soon gained the ascendancy. On becoming Prime Minister, it was his first care to see that the Khalif's table was laden with the choicest dainties and the richest wines; he surrounded him with singing-girls and dancers, and tried, in a word, to make his master's existence as pleasant as possible. The weak-minded Hishâm, indifferent to power, and only too happy to be relieved of business that wearied him, cheerfully abandoned the helm to Hakam.

The Prime Minister found the treasury empty. To meet current expenses revenues larger than the laws allowed were urgently needed. How could they be raised? To impose new taxes, as he was doubtless aware, would ensure his unpopularity. The Minister therefore had recourse to various expedients—not wholly honourable, but dictated by necessity. Discovering certain valuables which the sons of Muzaffar the 'Âmirid had deposited with their friends, he confiscated them, and compelled the principal merchants to purchase them at an exorbitant price. He also forced them to buy the lead and iron-work of the palaces demolished during the civil war. But the money thus acquired did not suffice, and Hakam had recourse to that Ibn al-Jaiyar, a hated and disreputable Fakih, who had on a previous occasion suggested to the Khalif 'Alî ibn Hammûd effectual, though discreditable, means of filling the treasury. He now contrived to procure Hakam a considerable revenue at the expense of the Mosques. This fraud leaked out, and excited much murmuring among the Cordovans, and especially the Fakihs. Nevertheless, not long before, the Fakihs who sat in the tribunal had accepted an increase in their salaries, well knowing that the necessary funds were provided out of illegal taxes. Hakam, therefore, naturally indignant at their hypocrisy, launched a stinging manifesto against them. Abû 'Âmir ibn Shohaid, who drew it up, read it publicly, in the palace and in the mosque (June, 1030). Bitterly offended, the Fakihs tried to communicate their anger to the people, but since the masses seem to have had no particular grievance, they did not succeed. The Government redoubled its rigour. A Vizier detected in a conspiracy was executed, and Ibn Shohaid urged a persecution of the " big hats," as he called them. " Heed not the declamations of this miserly crew," he exclaims in a poem addressed to the Khalif; " let them be hunted down; leave to my basilisk tongue the task of exposing them !"

If Hakam had merely had the theologians to deal with he could have held his own, for they were not then influential enough to injure him; but he had much more dangerous enemies: almost all the nobles were hostile to him. His lowly origin was an ineradicable stain in the eyes of the patricians. They regarded him, not as a soldier of fortune, but as a weaver, and they ranked him with the Prime Minister of Hakam II. There was, in truth, a great difference between the two men: the one had been a mere artisan, the other had spent the best years of his life in camps, or at the courts of frontier princes. The nobles were not scrupulous as to the means by which the treasury was filled, and they would readily have pardoned in a man of their own caste the financial operations to which the Minister had been driven; but since he was a plebeian, they denounced them as soon as they reached their ears, and used them to gratify their hatred. The policy of the nobles was, however, detrimental to their self-interest. At first Hakam had evinced no animosity towards them, and he had not discarded them deliberately—for instance he had made the patrician Ibn Shohaid his friend and confidant; but when he found that they only responded to his advances with disdain—when he found among them nothing but illwill, repugnance, and open hostility—his susceptibilities were touched, and he sought for officials among the plebeians. Those upon whom he conferred office were sure beforehand of the reprobation of the nobility, who did not fail to declare that the Minister appointed none but "callow young weavers, irreligious rascals who thought of nothing but wine, flowers, and truffles, who exercised their wit at the expense of worthy citizens, and derided the unfortunate who sought justice at their hands." Hakam himself they declared a shallow intriguer, a timid officer—a capable horseman and nothing more. They were perhaps blinded by their hatred; at any rate, the means they adopted to overthrow the object of their aversion were of the vilest kind.

They first tried to stir up a riot among the populace by declaring that the stagnation in trade—really due to public calamities—resulted from the dues imposed by the Minister upon many commodities. Such harangues bore fruit, and a band of men promised the nobles to attack the Minister's dwelling; but Hakam, warned in time, quitted his own palace and installed himself within the Khalif's; he then abolished the objectionable imposts, and addressed a long manifesto to the people, explaining that the duties had been imposed to satisfy the pressing needs of the treasury, but that in future he would try to dispense with them. The popular discontent having subsided, the nobles adopted another line of conduct. Hakam placed but little confidence in the Andalusian troops—who were devoted to the patricians—and tried to raise some companies of Berbers. The Andalusians complained, and the nobles took care to foment their grievances; but Hakam, perceiving their design, took effectual measures to preserve discipline among the soldiers, and punished the ringleaders by withholding their pay. The patricians next endeavoured to lead the Minister into disgrace with Hishâm. They were again unsuccessful; Hakam had more influence than they over the weak monarch, and they were prohibited from entering the palace. Ibn Jahwar alone, President of the Council, had some power over the Khalif, who regarded him with mingled respect and gratitude, for it was to him that he owed his throne, or rather his luxurious idleness. All Hakam's efforts to drive Ibn Jahwar from office were unsuccessful; he was not, however, discouraged, and never ceased to urge his dismissal upon the monarch, hoping ultimately to overcome his scruples. Ibn Jahwar was aware of this, and perhaps thought that he was losing ground. Henceforth his mind was made up;

an end must be made not only of the Minister but of the monarchy, and the Council of State must be supreme. His colleagues readily fell in with the project; but how were they to gain adherents? There lay the true difficulty; plenty of people would go any length to dethrone Hishâm III, but no one outside the Council seems to have dreamed of substituting an oligarchy for a monarchy, so deeply were monarchical ideas engrained in all minds. The Councillors thought it expedient, therefore, to conceal their true design, and feigning to aim merely at substituting another Khalif for Hishâm III, they entered into negotiations with a kinsman of his, Omayya by name, a rash and ambitious man, possessed of little foresight. The Councillors led him to understand that if he put himself at the head of an insurrection, the throne would be his. Not suspecting that he was being used as a mere tool, to be thrown aside as soon as it had served its purpose, the young prince received their overtures effusively, and since he was open-handed, he easily gained over the soldiers, whose pay had been withheld. In December, 1031, these men lay in ambush, fell upon Hakam as he left the palace, and assassinated him before he had time to draw his sword; they then cut off his head, and after washing it in a fishmonger's tub—for blood and mire had made it unrecognisable—they stuck it at the end of a lance. Omayya then directed the movements of the soldiers and the mob that had joined them, while Hishâm, dismayed by the horrible yells with which his palace re-echoed, ascended a lofty tower, accompanied by the women of his harem and four Slavs.

"What would you with me?" he cried to the insurgents, who had already entered the palace. "I have done you no ill! If you have any grievance, lay it before my Vizier; he will do you justice!"

"Behold thy Vizier!" came the shout from below, and Hishâm saw at the end of a lance a horribly mutilated head. "Behold the head of the villain to whom thou deliveredst thy people, thou poltroon!"

While Hishâm tried to appease the savage mob that only answered him with insults and abuse, another band broke into the women's apartments, whence they took everything worth carrying away, and where they found some new chains, which it was averred were intended for the nobles by Hakam. Omayya egged on the pillagers: "Help yourselves to these riches, my friends, all are yours! And

then ascend the tower and slay yonder wretch for me!"
An attempt to scale the tower was made, but it was too
high. Hishâm called for aid from the citizens who had
taken no part in the plundering; but there was no response.

Omayya, convinced that the Viziers were about to
recognise him as Khalif, proceeded to the great hall. Seated
on Hishâm's divan, and surrounded by the principal rioters,
on whom he had already bestowed offices, he issued his
orders as though actually Khalif. "We fear for thy life,"
exclaimed a bystander, "for good fortune seems to have
abandoned thy family!" "It matters not," replied Omayya.
"Let me be enthroned to-day and slain to-morrow!" The
ambitious youth had no inkling of what was taking place in
Ibn Jahwar's house.

Upon the outbreak of the riot, the President of the
Council had summoned his colleagues to confer with them
on the steps next to be taken, and when they had come to
a decision, they trooped to the palace, escorted by their
clients and servants, all well armed. "Let this plundering
cease!" they cried: "we will answer for Hishâm's abdication." Whether the multitude were awed by the presence
of these dignitaries, or feared an encounter with the escort,
or simply because there was nothing left worth plundering,
order was gradually restored. "Descend from the tower!"
cried the Viziers to Hishâm: "you must abdicate, but your
life will be spared." Very reluctantly Hishâm was obliged
to trust himself in their hands, for the tower contained no
provisions. He therefore descended, and was conducted by
the Viziers, with his wives, into a kind of vault forming
part of the Great Mosque. "I would rather be cast into
the sea than suffer such tribulations," he exclaimed on the
way. "Do what you will to me, but spare my wives, I
beseech you!"

At nightfall the Viziers summoned the principal inhabitants of Cordova to the Mosque to discuss Hishâm's
fate. It was resolved to intern him in a fortress without
delay. Certain sheiks were deputed to inform the captive
of this decision.

On entering the vault a pitiful sight met their eyes.
They found Hishâm crouching on the stone floor, surrounded
by his weeping wives in scanty attire and with dishevelled
hair. With despair in his eyes he was trying to warm in
his bosom his only daughter, whom he passionately loved.
The poor child, as yet too young to understand her father's

misfortune, shivered in the damp and chilly air of the noisome dungeon, for the night was bitterly cold—she was moreover almost dead with hunger, for, whether through carelessness or by a refinement of cruelty, no food had been supplied to the miserable prisoners. One of the sheiks addressed the ex-Khalif: "We have come, my lord," he said, "to announce that the Viziers and notables, assembled in the Mosque, have determined that . . ." "Yes! Yes!" interrupted Hishâm, "I bow to their decision, whatever it may be, but let me have a morsel of bread, I pray you, to give to this poor child who is dying of hunger!" Deeply touched, the sheiks could not refrain from tears. The food was brought, and the spokesman took up the thread of his communication: "My lord, it has been decided that at daybreak you shall be taken to a fortress, there to be imprisoned."

"Be it so," replied Hishâm, in sorrowful resignation. "I have but one favour to ask ; grant us a light, for the darkness of this dreadful place unnerves us."

On the morrow, as soon as Hishâm had quitted the town, the Viziers issued a proclamation to the Cordovans that the Khalifate was abolished for ever, and that the Council of State had assumed the reins of government. They then proceeded to the palace. Omayya was still there. He relied implicitly on their secret promises, and had summoned the officials in order that they might take the oath of allegiance. He was soon to be undeceived. The Viziers reproached the officials and soldiers for so hastily acknowledging a mere adventurer, without awaiting the decision of the notables. "The notables," declared Ibn Jahwar, "have abolished the monarchy, with the approval of the people. Take heed, soldiers, that ye stir not up civil strife; bear in mind the benefits that ye have received from us, and look for still greater ones if ye show yourselves well-disposed." Then turning to the officers, he said, "Arrest Omayya : lead him forth from the palace, and then conduct him beyond the frontier of our territory."

The order was immediately executed. Omayya, beside himself with rage, vowed vengeance against the perfidious Viziers who, after deluding him with false hopes, drove him out like a criminal, and he tried to enlist the sympathies of the officers, but since they were accustomed to obey the Council, his lavish promises were as useless as his threats and abuse. His ultimate fate is doubtful. For some time nothing was heard of him. He then aimed at returning to

Cordova, and some say that he was in consequence secretly assassinated by order of the patricians.

The luckless Hishâm escaped from the castle in which he was immured to the town of Lerida, then in the power of Sulaimân ibn Hûd. A contemporary writer tells us that, either through forgetfulness or in disdain, the Senate—for such we may henceforth call the Council of State—had neglected to make him sign an act of abdication; neither had they made him declare, before witnesses, that he was incapable of reigning and that the people were absolved from their allegiance, as is usual when a prince is dethroned. He was in fact unheeded and forgotten, and when he died five years later (December, 1036), his death was scarcely referred to in Cordova; it was even of less interest to the rest of Spain.

[AUTHORITIES: Ibn Bassâm, i. 82; Ibn Hayyân (*ap.* Ibn Bassâm, i. ff. 9–11, 114–15, 157; iii. ff. 139–43); Ibn al-Athîr; Makkarî, i. 319–320; 'Abd al-Wâhid, pp. 38–41; Rodrigo de Toledo, c. 44.]

BOOK IV

THE PETTY TYRANTS

CHAPTER I

THE KADY OF SEVILLE

FOR several years the provinces of Moslem Spain endured an independence which had been thrust upon them. Everywhere the public mind was troubled; the future was contemplated with dismay and the past recalled with regret. The foreign military commanders alone had profited by the disintegration of the empire. The Berber generals shared the South; the Slavs were masters of the East; the rest of the land had fallen into the hands either of upstarts, or of a few noble families who had by some chance survived the blows dealt the aristocracy by 'Abd-er-Rahmân III and Almanzor. Finally, the two chief cities, Cordova and Seville, had adopted a republican form of government.

The Hammûdites were only nominally the chiefs of the Berber party. While they claimed rights over all Arab Spain, they actually possessed the city of Malaga and its territory. The most powerful of their vassals were the princes of Granada—Zâwî, who made Granada the capital,[1] and his nephew and successor Habbûs. There were, besides, Berber princes at Carmona, Moron, and Ronda. The Aftasides who reigned at Badajoz were of the same race; but they posed as Arabs, and occupied a somewhat isolated position.

Of the Slavs, the most prominent were Khairân, prince of Almeria; Zuhair, who succeeded him in 1028; and Mojehid, prince of the Balearic Isles and Denia. The last named—the greatest pirate of his day—was as much renowned for his raids on Sardinia and the coast of Italy, as for his patronage of men of letters. Other Slavs were for a time rulers of Valencia, but in 1021, 'Abd al-'Azîz, grandson of Almanzor,[2] became its King. At Zaragoza, a noble Arab family, the Beni Hûd, acquired the sovereignty on the death of Mundhir in 1039.

Lastly, not to mention a number of petty States, the kingdom of Toledo still existed. One Ya'îsh reigned there

---

[1] Elvira had previously been the capital, but this town having suffered severely during the Civil War, its inhabitants migrated to Granada in 1010.

[2] And son of 'Abd-er-Rahmân Sanchol.

till 1036, when the Beni Dhu 'n-Nûn—an ancient Berber family who had assisted in the conquest of Spain in the eighth century —seized the throne.

At Cordova, on the abolition of the Khalifate, the principal inhabitants resolved to entrust the executive power to Ibn Jahwar, whose ability was universally acknowledged. He at first refused the proffered dignity, but yielded to the importunity of the Assembly on condition that he should be granted, as colleagues, two members of the Senate who were his kinsmen—Mohammed ibn 'Abbâs and 'Abd al-'Azîz ibn Hasan. The Assembly in acceding to his request stipulated that his coadjutors should be advisory only.

The First Consul ruled the Republic with wisdom and justice. The Cordovans no longer had to complain of the brutality of the Berbers, for one of Ibn Jahwar's first acts was to dismiss them; he retained only the Beni Iforen, upon whom he could rely, and replaced the others by a National Guard. Ostensibly he maintained republican institutions. When he was asked a boon, he would reply : " It is not in my power : the matter concerns the Senate ; I am merely their agent." If an official letter was addressed to him personally, he would refuse to take cognisance of it, saying that it should have been addressed to the Viziers. Before coming to a decision he invariably consulted the Senate. He never assumed princely airs, and instead of keeping state in the Khalifal palace, he continued to occupy his own modest residence. And yet, in reality, his power was limitless, for the Senate never opposed his views. He was of scrupulous honesty, and would not allow the public treasure to be kept under his roof, but entrusted it to the keeping of the most honourable citizens. He was thrifty, not to say miserly, and thus doubled his fortune and became the richest man in Cordova; but his love of money never tempted him to a breach of trust. He never ceased, moreover, from his efforts to renew public prosperity. He sought to enter into friendly relations with all the neighbouring States, and with such success that before long commerce and manufactures enjoyed the security they so greatly needed. The price of commodities fell, and Cordova welcomed a multitude of new inhabitants, who rebuilt some of the quarters demolished or burnt by the Berbers when the city was sacked. But nothing could restore the former Capital of the Khalifate to its political supremacy. The pre-eminence henceforth lay with Seville, and it is with the fortunes of that city that we shall now be chiefly concerned.

The fortunes of Seville had been for many years linked with those of Cordova.   Like the Capital, she had submitted successively to Omayyad and Hammûdite sovereigns, but to the revolt of 1028 at Cordova there was a counterstroke at Seville.   The Cordovan insurgents expelled Kâsim the Hammûdite from their territories, and that prince sought refuge at Seville, which was the residence of his two sons and was garrisoned by Berbers under Mohammed ibn Zîrî, of the tribe of Iforen.   Kâsim thereupon ordered the Sevillans to evacuate a thousand houses for the accommodation of his troops.   This order caused much discontent, the more so since Kâsim's beggarly soldiers had the reputation of being arrant thieves.   Cordova had shown the Sevillans the possibility of throwing off the yoke, and Seville was tempted to follow the example of the Capital.   Dread of the Berber garrison, however, restrained the citizens; but the Kady, Abu 'l-Kâsim Mohammed, one of the Beni 'Abbâd, succeeded in winning over the commander of the garrison.   He assured him that he might easily become lord of Seville, and Ibn Zîrî thereupon promised his aid.   The Kady next concluded an alliance with the Berber commandant of Carmona, and the Sevillans, assisted by the garrison, took up arms against the sons of Kâsim and surrounded their palace.   Kâsim arriving before the gates of Seville found them closed.   He tried to cajole the populace by promises, but without success, and since his sons were in great danger, he at last undertook to evacuate Sevillan territory provided that they and his property were restored to him.   The Sevillans consented, and on Kâsim's withdrawal they seized the first opportunity of expelling the Berber garrison.

The city having thus recovered its liberty, the patricians set to work to provide it with a government.   They were, however, by no means at ease with regard to the consequences of the revolt: they dreaded the reappearance of the angry Hammûdites, who would not fail to punish the ringleaders. None of them, therefore, would assume responsibility for what had passed, and they unanimously laid it upon the shoulders of the Kady, whose wealth they envied—indeed they looked forward with secret pleasure to its confiscation. They therefore offered the supreme authority to the Kady; but, whatever his ambition, he was too prudent to accept it just then.   He was not of illustrious origin.   He was im-

mensely rich—possessing a third part of the Sevillan territory
—and he was held in high esteem for his talents and his
knowledge; but his family had not long ranked among the
high nobility, and he was well aware that unless he had
soldiers at his call—and he had none—the proud and exclusive aristocracy of Seville would soon assail him as a
parvenu. Such indeed he was. It is true that later, when
the 'Abbâdids were about to re-establish the throne of the
Khalifs for their own ends, they claimed descent from the
ancient Lakhmite kings, who had reigned in Hîra during
" The Ignorance," and the hungry poets of their court never
lost an opportunity of celebrating so illustrious an origin;
but there was nothing to justify this claim, which neither
the 'Abbâdids nor their parasites could substantiate. All
that the family had in common with the kings of Hîra was
its connection with the Yemenite tribe of Lakhm; but the
branch of that tribe whence the 'Abbâdids sprang had never
dwelt in Hîra; its home was at Arîsh, on the frontiers of
Egypt and Syria, in the district of Emesa,[1] and the 'Abbâdids, far from being able to link their genealogy to that of
the kings of Hîra, could not trace it farther back then Noaim,
father of Itâf. This Itâf landed in Spain with Balj, as
captain of a regiment from Emesa, and his men having been
granted lands near Seville, he himself settled in the village
of Yaumîn in the district of Tocina, on the banks of the
Guadalquiver. After seven upright, thrifty and industrious
generations the family gradually emerged from its obscurity.
Ismâ'îl, father of our Kady, was the first to give it fame, and
to write, as it were, the name of the Beni 'Abbâd or 'Abbâdids,[2] in the " Golden Book " of the Sevillan nobility. At
once theologian, lawyer and soldier, he had commanded a
regiment of the guard under Hishâm II, and had been
successively Imâm of the Great Mosque at Cordova and
Kady of Seville. Renowned for his learning, his sagacity,
his prudent counsels, and the firmness of his character, he
was no less remarkable for his probity; for in the midst of
general corruption, he had never accepted a gift from the
Khalif or his ministers. His liberality was boundless, and
the exiled Cordovans had experienced his lavish hospitality.
All these qualities earned him the title of the noblest man
of the West. He died in 1019, not long before the epoch of
which we are now treating.

[1] *Cf.* Caussin, iii. pp. 212, 422.
[2] Abbâd was Ismâ'îl's great-great-grandfather.

Ismâ'îl's son, Abu 'l-Kâsim Mohammed, was perhaps intellectually his father's equal: morally, he was not. Self-seeking and ambitious, his first act had been one of in-gratitude. Upon his father's death he had hoped to succeed him as Kady, but another candidate had been preferred. He accordingly appealed to Kâsim ibn Hammûd, and by that prince's intervention obtained the coveted post. We have already seen how he requited this kindness.

The patricians of Seville, however, offered him the Governorship; but divining their motives, he replied that he could not accept the office, honourable though it was, unless in conjunction with certain persons, whom he named, as coadjutors. These persons, he added, would be his Viziers and his colleagues, and he would come to no decision without consultation with them. The Sevillans were reluctantly obliged to accept these conditions, for the Kady firmly re-fused to rule alone. He was then requested to name his colleagues. He nominated the heads of certain patrician families, such as Hauzanî and Ibn Hajjâj, as well as others who must be regarded as his creatures, or at any rate his partisans, such as Mohammed ibn Yarîm, of the tribe of Alhân, and Abû Bakr Zobaidî, the famous scholar who had been tutor to Hishâm II. The Kady's first care was to procure troops. The high pay which he promised attracted to his standard many soldiers—Arabs, Berbers, and others—and he also bought a number of slaves who were instructed in the use of arms. An expedition which he made in the North—probably in conjunction with other princes—enabled him to increase this nucleus of an army. Upon this occasion he besieged two castles to the north of Viseu, which stood facing one another on rocks divided by a ravine, and were known as the Two Brothers,[1] whence is derived the present name of Alafoens. They belonged to Spanish Christians, whose ancestors had made a treaty with Mûsâ ibn Nusayr when that general conquered Viseu, but who, at the time we are now speaking of, seem to have been subject neither to the King of Leon nor to a Moslem prince. The Kady seized these two castles and compelled three hundred of their defenders to enter his service.[2] He now had five hundred horsemen at his disposal.

---

[1] Ar. al-akhawén or al-akhowén, the Ar. guttural kh becoming f in Spanish and Portuguese.

[2] Sisenand, mentioned by the monk of Silos, who, after quitting Motadhid's service for that of Fernando I, became Governor of Coimbra, seems to have been a Christian of Alafoens.

His force was therefore sufficient to make raids on his neighbours' territories, though not yet large enough to defend Seville against a serious attack—as he discovered in 1027. In that year the Hammûdite Khalif Yahyâ ibn ʿAlî and the Berber lord of Carmona, Mohammed ibn ʿAbdallah, laid siege to Seville. Too weak to make a long resistance, the Sevillans opened negotiations with Yahyâ. They declared their willingness to acknowledge his sovereignty—provided the Berbers did not enter the city. Yahyâ consented, but required as hostages some young patricians to answer with their lives for the good faith of the Sevillans. This demand spread consternation throughout the city; no noble would hand over his son to the Berbers, to be slain on the merest suspicion. The Kady alone did not hesitate; he offered his son ʿAbbâd to Yahyâ, and the Khalif, knowing the great influence enjoyed by the Kady, was content with a single hostage.

This act of devotedness added to the Kady's popularity, and having nothing more to fear from the nobles or the Khalif—whose sovereignty he had formally recognised—he thought that the time had come for him to reign alone. Having already dismissed from the Council patricians such as Ibn Hajjâj and Hauzanî, he had now but two colleagues, Zobaidî and Ibn Yarîm. He dismissed them both, sending Zobaidî into exile.[1] As his Prime Minister he chose a plebeian, one Habîb, from the suburbs of Seville—an unprincipled man, but active, intelligent, and wholly devoted to his master's interests.

The Kady determined to extend his territories by annexing Beja. This town, which had suffered much in the ninth century at the hands of Arabs and Renegades, had lately been sacked and partly destroyed by the Berbers, who, pillaging and burning, had overrun the district. The Kady designed to rebuild it, but the prince of Badajoz, ʿAbdallah ibn Aftas, hearing of this, sent troops thither, under his son Mohammed—who succeeded him under the name of Muzaffar—and they were already in possession of Beja when Ismâʿîl, son of the Kady, appeared before the gates, with the army of Seville and that of the lord of Carmona, his father's ally. He commenced a siege, and sent his cavalry to plunder the villages between Evora and the sea. In spite of the reinforcements which he had received from Ibn

---

[1] Zobaidî first went to Kairwân and then to Almeria, where he became Kady.

Taifûr, lord of Mertola, Mohammed the Aftasid was defeated: after losing the flower of his army, he fell into the enemies' hands and was sent to Carmona.

Emboldened by their successes, the Kady and his ally made raids, not only into the territory of Badajoz, but also into that of Cordova, compelling the government of the latter city to enlist the services of Berbers from Sidona. After some time, however, an armistice was arranged, and Mohammed the Aftasid was liberated by the Kady's consent (March, 1030). In announcing his release, the lord of Carmona advised him to visit Seville and thank the Kady; but Mohammed had such deep aversion for the latter that he replied: "I would rather remain your prisoner than acknowledge an obligation to that man. If I am not indebted to you alone for my liberation, but must also thank the Kady of Seville, I will remain where I am." The lord of Carmona respected his sentiments, and had him escorted to Badajoz with the honours due to his rank.

Four years later, in 1034, 'Abdallah the Aftasid revenged his reverses in a way that did him but little credit. He granted permission to the Kady to pass through his territories with a force intended for a raid in the kingdom of Leon, but when Ismâ'îl had entered a defile not far from the frontier of Leon, he was attacked unexpectedly by 'Abdallah's troops. Many Sevillan soldiers were slain, and others were cut down in flight by the Leonese horsemen. Ismâ'îl himself escaped with a handful of troops; but while making their way to Lisbon, the north-western outpost of his father's dominions, they had to endure terrible privations.

Henceforth the Kady was the mortal foe of the prince of Badajoz; we know nothing, however, of the details of their conflict, and the war was certainly less important in its results for Moslem Spain than was another event now to be related.

The Kady, as we have seen, had recognised the sovereignty of the Hammûdite Khalif, Yahyâ ibn 'Alî. For some time this recognition had been ineffectual; the Kady reigned uncontrolled at Seville, since Yahyâ was too weak to exercise his rights. By degrees this state of affairs changed. Yahyâ rallied to his cause nearly all the Berber chiefs; he consequently became the actual, and not merely the nominal, leader of the whole African party, and having established his head-quarters at Carmona—whence he had driven out Mohammed ibn 'Abdallah—he threatened Cordova and Seville simultaneously.

The imminence of the danger inspired the Kady with an idea which would have been noble and patriotic if it had not been largely dictated by personal ambition. To prevent the now united Berbers from reconquering their lost territories, a coalition of Arabs and Slavs under one leader was imperative; this was the only means of saving the country from a return of calamities. The Kady accordingly planned a great league, embracing all enemies of the Africans—and of this league he intended to be chief. He was not blind to the obstacles in his path; he knew that the suspicions of the Slav princes, the Arab nobles, and the Senators of Cordova, would be aroused and their pride wounded, if he tried to set himself at their head; but he would not be discouraged; and—powerfully aided by circumstances, as will be seen—he to some extent carried out his project.

It has been already related that the luckless Khalif Hishâm II escaped from his palace during the reign of Sulaimân, and in all probability died in Asia, unheeded and unknown. The populace, however, since they still felt a strong attachment for the Omayyad dynasty, which had given them glory and prosperity, refused to acknowledge the monarch's death, and drank in every wild rumour current regarding him. Circumstantial accounts of his mode of life in Asia were not lacking. At first—so ran one story—Hishâm went to Mecca, taking with him a wallet full of money and jewels. He was robbed by the Emir's negro guards, and had been for two days without food, when a potter, touched with compassion, asked him if he could knead clay. Hishâm replied, at random, that he could. "Then," said the potter, "if you will enter my service you shall have a dirhem and a loaf daily." "With all my heart!" exclaimed Hishâm, "but first give me the bread, for I have fasted for two days." For some time the Khalif, though an indolent workman, earned his living as a potter, but eventually, sick of the drudgery, he joined a caravan bound for Palestine. He reached Jerusalem destitute. One day as he was wandering in the streets he halted opposite the shop of a matmaker, who was at work. "Why dost thou regard me so earnestly?" asked the mat-maker; "dost thou know the trade?" "Alas, no!" muttered Hishâm, turning away; "for I am starving." "Yet stay," said the workman; "you can fetch me rushes, and I will pay you for your services."

Hishâm gratefully accepted the offer, and after a while became skilled in making mats. Several years elapsed, and in 1033 Hishâm returned to Spain. He appeared first at Malaga, then at Almeria—in 1035—and soon afterwards, expelled by Prince Zuhair from his dominions, he settled at Calatrava.

This story, though eagerly adopted by the credulous, seems wholly undeserving of credit. The fact is that when Yahyâ menaced Seville and Cordova, there was a mat-maker in Calatrava, named Khalaf, who bore a striking resemblance to Hishâm; but there is no evidence that he was the ex-Khalif, while the historians Ibn Hayyân and Ibn Hazm, although—as Omayyad clients—it would have been to their interest to recognise the pretended Hishâm, energetically denounce what they term a rank imposture. Khalaf, however, was ambitious. Having often heard of his resemblance to Hishâm, he announced that he was, in fact, that monarch. He was not a native of Calatrava, and his fellow-citizens believed him. They went further: they acknowledged him as their sovereign, and rose in revolt against their lord, Ismâʿîl ibn Dhu 'n-Nûn, prince of Toledo. The prince thereupon laid siege to the town. The defenders soon yielded, and after expelling the pretended Hishâm, returned to their former allegiance.

Khalaf's part, however, was not yet played out; it was, indeed, only just begun. The Kady of Seville speedily realized the use he might make of this supposed reappearance of Hishâm II. It was nothing to him whether the man were Hishâm or not; so long as the resemblance was close enough to warrant the recognition of Khalaf as the ex-monarch on reasonable grounds, a league against the Berbers could be organized in his name, of which league the Kady, as the Khalif's Prime Minister, would, of course, be the moving spirit. The Kady accordingly invited Khalaf to Seville, promising his support as soon as his identity was confirmed. The mat-maker needed no pressing; and on reaching Seville the Kady showed him to the women of Hishâm's seraglio. Knowing what was required of them, they almost unanimously declared the man to be really the ex-Khalif. The Kady—relying on their testimony—thereupon informed the Senate of Cordova, as well as the Arab and Slav lords, that Hishâm II was under his roof, and urged them to take up arms on that monarch's behalf. This step was entirely successful. Hishâm's

sovereignty was acknowledged by Mohammed ibn 'Abdallah
—the dethroned prince of Carmona, then at Seville; by
'Abd al-'Azîz, prince of Valencia; by Mojehid, prince of
Denia and the Balearic Isles, and by the lord of Tortosa.
At Cordova the populace hailed the reappearance of Hishâm
with enthusiasm. The President of the Republic—Abu
'l-Hazm ibn Jahwar—who was less credulous and moreover
jealous of his own authority, was not himself duped. He
believed, however, that he could not resist the people's will,
he saw the need of uniting Arabs and Slavs under one
leader, and he feared an attack on Cordova by the Berbers.
He therefore allowed his fellow-citizens to renew their oath
of allegiance to Hishâm II (November, 1035).

Yahyâ, while the Arabs and Slavs were thus arming
against him, besieged Seville and ravaged its territory,
determined to wreak bitter vengeance on the crafty Kady.
But he was surrounded by traitors. The Berbers of
Carmona, compelled to serve under Yahyâ's banner, were
loyal at heart to their former lord, with whom they kept up
relations, and in October, 1035, some of them secretly
visited Seville. There they told the Kady and Mohammed
ibn 'Abdallah that Yahyâ could be easily taken by surprise,
seeing that he was seldom sober. The Kady and his ally
profited by the hint. Ismâ'îl, the Kady's son, set out at
the head of the Sevillan army, with Mohammed. At
nightfall they placed the main body of the troops in
ambush, and sent a squadron towards Carmona in the hope
of luring Yahyâ outside the walls.

Yahyâ was carousing when he heard of the Sevillan's
approach. Leaping from his sofa, he cried: " What good
fortune ! Ibn 'Abbâd comes to visit me ! Arm yourselves !
To horse ! " He was obeyed, and soon emerged from the
city with three hundred horsemen. Heated with wine, he
flung himself upon the enemy, without marshalling his
men, amidst darkness which rendered objects almost indis-
tinguishable. Though somewhat disconcerted by this
impetuous attack, the Sevillans made a vigorous resistance, and when compelled to fall back withdrew towards
Ismâ'îl's ambuscade. Yahyâ was lost. Ismâ'îl charged his
opponents, at the head of the Christians of Alafoens, and
routed them. Yahyâ was killed, and most of his soldiers
would have shared his fate, if Mohammed ibn 'Abdallah
had not entreated Ismâ'îl to spare them. " Nearly all of

them," he urged, "are Berbers of Carmona, compelled to serve, unwillingly, a hated usurper." Ismâ'îl yielded to his request, and the pursuit was stayed. Mohammed immediately galloped to Carmona to regain possession of his principality. Yahyâ's negroes, who held the gateways, tried to keep him out; but Mohammed, aided by the citizens, broke in through a breach. Entering Yahyâ's palace, he divided the inmates of the harem amongst his sons, and seized all the prince's treasures (November, 1035).[1]

The news of Yahyâ's death caused unspeakable joy at Seville and Carmona. The Kady, on hearing it, fell on his knees, with all those who stood by, and rendered thanks to heaven. Fear of the Hammûdites was for the moment at an end. Idrîs, Yahyâ's brother, was indeed proclaimed Khalif at Malaga; but he needed time to win over the Berber chiefs, by promises and concessions, and he was unable even to reduce Algeciras, where his cousin Mohammed had been proclaimed Khalif by the negroes. Believing, therefore, that circumstances were favourable, the Kady wished to install himself, with the pretended Hishâm, in the Khalifal palace at Cordova. But Ibn Jahwar was not inclined to resign the Consulship. He convinced the citizens that the alleged Khalif was an impostor; the name of Hishâm II was omitted from the public prayers, and when the Kady arrived before the city gates he found them shut. Not having a force adequate for the reduction of so strong a place he retired. He next resolved to turn his arms against the only Slav prince who had refused to acknowledge Hishâm II—Zuhair of Almeria. Since the Khalif Kâsim, wishing to conciliate the Âmirids, had given him many fiefs, Zuhair had usually made common cause with the Hammûdites, and when Idrîs was proclaimed Khalif, he immediately recognised him.

Menaced by the Kady, Zuhair allied himself with Habbûs of Granada, and when the Sevillan army took the field he marched against it with the combined forces and repulsed the enemy.

The Kady had clearly overrated his strength, and he now feared lest the armies of Almeria and Granada might

[1] Some chroniclers give the date as A.H. 429 instead of A.H. 427. But that the latter is correct is shown by Ibn Hayyàn, who quotes the narrative of a Berber soldier of Carmona who took part in the combat in which Yahyâ fell.

take the offensive and invade the territory of Seville. But Fortune, as usual smiling upon him, decreed that one of these adversaries should rid him of the other.

[AUTHORITIES: Ibn Bassâm, i. ff. 81–2, 129, 157; 'Abd al-Wâhid, pp. 37–38, 42–3, 45, 65; *Abbad.*, i. 220–5, 234, 381 *sq.*; ii. 7, 32–4, 127–8, 173, 208, 216; Ibn Khaldûn, ff. 22, 25.]

CHAPTER II

SAMUEL HA-LEVI AND IBN 'ABBÂS

TWO remarkable men, who hated one another with a
deadly hatred, were at this time ruling over Almeria
and Granada respectively. These were the Arab Ibn
'Abbâs and the Jew Samuel.

Rabbi Samuel Ha-Levi[1] was a native of Cordova,
where he studied the Talmud under Rabbi Hanokh, the
spiritual chief of the Jewish community. He also applied
himself, with much success, to Arabic literature and almost
all the sciences cultivated in those days. For a long time
he was withal a dealer in spices, first at Cordova, and afterwards at Malaga, whither he migrated on the capture of
the Capital by Sulaimân's Berbers. From this humble
condition a happy chance extricated him.

Samuel's shop was situated near a castle belonging to
Abu 'l-Kâsim ibn al-Arîf, Vizier of Habbûs, King of
Granada. The inmates of the castle often had occasion
to write to their master, and being illiterate, employed the
Jew as their secretary. The resulting letters excited the
Vizier's admiration, for they were composed in a polished
style, and were artistically bedecked with the fairest flowers
of Arab rhetoric. On visiting Malaga, Ibn al-Arîf was
therefore desirous to become acquainted with the writer,
and sent for the Jew. "A shop is no place for you," said
the Vizier: "You are fitted to ornament a court: if you
will, you shall be my secretary." Samuel accordingly
accompanied the Vizier to Granada, and Ibn al-Arîf's
esteem for him was much increased when, in conversation
on political subjects, the Jew displayed a rare knowledge
of men and matters, and a marvellous keenness of insight.
"When Samuel gave counsel," wrote a Jewish historian,
"the voice of God was heard." This was fortunate for
the Vizier, who always followed his advice. Upon his
deathbed, Ibn al-Arîf said to the King, who stood beside

---

[1] A.D. 1038-1073. His Arabic name was Ismâ'îl ibn Naghdâla. See Dozy,
Introd. à la Chron. d'Ibn Adhârí, p. 84 n.

him pondering how to replace the impending loss of his faithful Minister, " Of late, Sire, I have not advised you of my own initiative but through the inspiration of my secretary, Samuel the Jew. Pay heed to him, and may he be to you a father and a minister : follow all his advice, and God will be your helper." King Habbûs accordingly welcomed Samuel to his palace, and the Jew became his secretary and counsellor.[1]

In no other Moslem State, probably, did a Jew ever govern directly and openly as Vizier and Chancellor. It is true that Jews often held important positions under Moslem sovereigns, who were especially glad to entrust them with financial administration : but Musulman toleration did not often brook the appointment of a Jew as Prime Minister. At Granada alone, indeed, was such a thing possible. Israelites were so numerous there that it was known as " The City of the Jews," and since they were wealthy and influential, they often took an active part in politics. In Granada they had found, if not the Promised Land, at least manna in the desert, and the rock of Horeb. There was, moreover, another reason for Samuel's promotion. It was by no means easy for a king of Granada to select a *hâjib*, since neither an Arab nor a Berber could be suitably entrusted with that important post. In those days a Minister must be a scholar, able to compose letters fit for the eyes of foreign princes, and written with studied elegance in rhymed prose. The King of Granada attached peculiar importance to such talents. As a parvenu apes the airs of men of breeding, so the King, being a semi-barbarian, took infinite pains to conceal the fact. He prided himself upon his scholarship, and even claimed for the Sinheja, to whom he belonged, an Arab rather than a Berber origin. It was therefore necessary for him to appoint a *hâjib* inferior in no respect to any of his neighbours' ministers. But where was such an one to be found ? The Berbers could fight, they could sack and burn cities, but they could not write correctly a single line in the language of the Koran. As for the Arabs, who in submitting to the regal yoke trembled with rage and shame—not one of them could be relied on. To deceive and betray their master would be with them a point of honour. In these circumstances, a Jew such as Samuel—who, by the testimony of learned

---

[1] *Journ. asiat.*, Ser. IV., xvi. pp. 203-4.

Arabs, was versed in all the niceties of their tongue, and who, though zealous for his own faith, did not scruple when writing to Moslems to employ their conventional religious phraseology [1]—was a veritable treasure. The king's choice was, indeed, approved by the Arabs themselves. Notwithstanding their prejudices against Israelites, they could not but admit Samuel's commanding genius. His erudition was, in fact, both wide and deep. He was a mathematician, a logician, and an astronomer,[2] besides being familiar with seven languages.[3] To poets and scholars he showed great liberality. Those whom he loaded with favours did not stint their panegyrics, and the poet Monfatil even addressed to him the following verses—quoted by Moslem writers with pious horror :

"Oh thou who unitest in thy person all the virtues of which others possess but a part: thou who hast unchained captive Generosity—thou art as far above the most liberal men of East and West as gold is above copper! Could men but distinguish truth from falsehood they would touch but thy fingers with their lips. Instead of seeking to please the Eternal by kissing the Black Stone at Mecca, they would kiss thy hands, the dispensers of happiness. Through thee, I have obtained here below my heart's desire ; and I trust that through thee, I shall attain it in realms above. In thy presence I openly profess the religion which ordaineth the Sabbath—and when I am among my own people I profess it in secret."

The Arabs were nevertheless unable to appraise at their true value the services rendered by Samuel to Hebrew literature. These were far from inconsiderable. He published, in Hebrew, an introduction to the Talmud, and twenty-two works on Grammar, of which the most elaborate and remarkable was the *Book of Riches*, preferred by a competent judge — a Jew who flourished in the twelfth century—above all other grammatical treatises. He was also a poet, and wrote paraphrases of the Psalms, Proverbs, and Ecclesiastes. Teeming as they were with allusions, Arab proverbs, sentences borrowed from the philosophers, and singular expressions from sacred poets, these poems were very abstruse—even the most learned Jews could only gather their meaning with the aid of a commentary ;[4] but since subtleties and pedantries were then as common in Hebrew literature as in the Arabic on which it was modelled, such obscurity was accounted a merit rather than a defect.

Samuel watched with paternal solicitude over the young

---

[1] See Dozy, *op. cit.*, p. 97.
[2] *Ibid.*, pp. 96–7.
[3] *Journ. asiat.*, Ser. IV., xvi. p. 209 *n*.
[4] *Journ. asiat.*, pp. 222–4.

Jewish students, and if they were poor he provided generously for their needs. He employed scribes to copy the
Mishna and the Talmud, and presented these transcripts to
scholars who were too poor to buy them. His benevolence
was not confined to his brethren of Spain. In Africa, in
Sicily, at Jerusalem, at Baghdad—indeed, everywhere—the
Jews could reckon on his bounty,[1] and his brethren of the
principality of Granada, as a token of their esteem and
gratitude, conferred on Ha-Levi, in 1027, the title of
Naghíd, or Prince in Israel. As a statesman, he employed
his keen and penetrating intellect with firmness and consummate prudence. Usually he spoke little and pondered
much—a precious quality in a diplomatist. He could turn
passing events to advantage with wonderful skill; he read
the characters and passions of men, and knew how to sway
them through their vices. Further, he was a polished man
of the world. In the splendid halls of the Alhambra he
was so completely at his ease that it might have been
supposed that he had been nurtured in luxury. No one
conversed with such propriety and tact, or could flatter
more delicately; no one on occasion was more cordial and
affable, no one more captivating by his eloquence or persuasive by his arguments. And with all this, he lacked one
characteristic common in those whom a sudden turn of
Fortune's wheel has raised to wealth and dignity—he had
none of an upstart's arrogance, nor of the fatuous pride of
the wealthy parvenu. Kindly and urbane in his demeanour,
he displayed that innate dignity which is wholly free from
self-assertion. Far from being ashamed of his former lowly
condition, he boasted of it, and by his candour silenced even
his detractors.[2]

The Vizier of Zuhair of Almeria, Ibn 'Abbâs, was a no
less remarkable man. It was said that he was unrivalled in
four respects—namely in epistolary skill, wealth, avarice,
and vanity. His riches were indeed almost fabulous. His
fortune was estimated at five hundred thousand ducats.[3]
His palace was furnished with princely magnificence and
crowded with servants; in it were five hundred singing-
girls of rare beauty; and—still more to be admired—an
immense library, which contained four hundred thousand
volumes, without counting innumerable pamphlets. Nothing
seemed wanting to the happiness of this favourite of fortune.

---

[1] *Journ. asiat.*, p. 209.   [2] See Dozy, *op. cit.*, pp. 96–7.
[3] About £1,400,000 in present value.

He was handsome and still young, for he was scarcely thirty years old; he came of a noble family, sprung from the ancient stock of the Defenders of the Prophet; he swam in gold, and moreover, since he was well educated, prompt in retort, and correct and elegant in his diction, he enjoyed high literary repute. Unfortunately, he was victim to an infatuation—his presumption knew no bounds, and made him innumerable enemies. The Cordovans specially detested him, for when he had once visited their city with Zuhair he had treated with the utmost disdain men eminent for their birth or talents, and on departing had declared: "I have met with nothing but empty purses and empty heads!"[1] His arrogance, in fact, almost amounted to insanity. "Were all men my slaves," he declared in his verses, "my soul would not be content. It would fain mount above the stars, and then would long to ascend yet higher!" He had also composed this verse, which he was perpetually quoting, especially when playing chess:

"Misfortune ever sleepeth soundly when I pass by: he is forbidden to cast a dart at me, and awaketh not!".

This insolent defiance of fate excited universal indignation at Almeria, and a daring poet voiced public opinion by substituting for the second half of the distich words which proved prophetic:

"But Destiny, who is sleepless, will one day come and awake him!"

As an Arab of pure blood, Ibn 'Abbâs hated the Berbers and despised the Jews. Perhaps he did not actually wish his master to join the Arab-Slav league, for in that case Zuhair would be thrown into the shade by its head, the Kady of Seville; but he was still more unwilling to see him allied to a Berber, whose Minister was a Jew whom he detested, and who reciprocated his hatred. In concert with Ibn Bakanna, Vizier of the Hammûdites of Malaga, Ibn 'Abbâs had tried at first to overthrow Samuel, and with this object he had fruitlessly calumniated him. He then endeavoured to bring about dissension between Zuhair and the King of Granada, by inducing the former to lend aid to Mohammed of Carmona, an enemy of Habbûs, and in this he had succeeded.

In June, 1038, Habbûs died, leaving two sons—the elder

---

[1] Ar. *sâïl* and *jâhil*, "beggars and dolts."

Bâdîs, and the younger, Bologguîn. The Berbers and some of the Jews wished to confer the throne on the latter; but the other Jews, including Samuel, inclined to Bâdîs, as did the Arabs. Civil war would have broken out, had not Bologguîn spontaneously renounced his candidature, and after he had taken the oath to his brother, his partisans had no choice but to follow his example.[1]

The new prince did all he could to renew the alliance with the lord of Almeria, and the latter declared that all could be arranged at an interview. Accompanied by a numerous and brilliant escort, Zuhair set out, and arrived unexpectedly before the gates of Granada without having asked permission to cross the frontier. Bâdîs was greatly irritated by this unconventional conduct; but he received the prince of Almeria with due honour, entertained his retinue sumptuously, and conferred many gifts upon them.

The negotiations, however, came to nothing; neither the princes nor their ministers[2] could come to an agreement. Zuhair, moreover, who was under the influence of Ibn 'Abbâs, assumed an offensive tone of superiority towards Bâdîs. The King of Granada was meditating the punishment of the prince of Almeria for his insolence, when one of his officers—also named Bologguîn—undertook to make one last attempt at reconciliation. He therefore visited Ibn 'Abbâs by night and said: "Fear the wrath of God. It is thou who standest in the way of a reconciliation, for thy master is swayed by thee. When we acted in concert we were successful in every enterprise, and were envied by all. Renew then our alliance! The only obstacle is the support thou renderest to Mohammed of Carmona. Abandon that prince to his fate, as our Emir stipulates, and all will be well." Ibn 'Abbâs made a reply which was at once patronising and disdainful, and when the Berber tried to touch his heart by embracing him and shedding tears, he added: "Spare yourself these emotions and swelling words, for they do not affect me. What I told you yesterday I tell you to-day—that if you and yours do not accede to our wishes, I will see that you repent it." Bologguîn, exasperated by these words, exclaimed: "Is that the answer I am to take to the Council?" "Assuredly!" replied Ibn 'Abbâs; "and if you prefer to attribute to me phrases still more forcible, you are welcome to do so?"

---

[1] *Journ. asiat.*, Ser. IV., xvi. pp. 206–8.   [2] Samuel had retained his post.

Shedding tears of rage, Bologguîn presented himself before Bâdîs and the Council. Then, after reporting his conversation with the Vizier, he cried : " Kinhejites ! that man's arrogance is unendurable ! Arise, and crush him to the earth, or your homes will no longer be your own ! " The councillors of Granada shared his anger, but none was more indignant than Bologguîn, brother of Bâdîs : he urged the latter to take instant steps to punish the Almerians, and this Bâdîs promised to do.

In returning to his territories, Zuhair would have to traverse several defiles and to cross a bridge whence a neighbouring village derived its name of Alpuente. Bâdîs ordered this bridge to be cut, and the defiles to be occupied by troops. Nevertheless, since he felt less anger than his brother against Zuhair, and did not yet wholly despair of winning back his father's friend to kindlier sentiments, he resolved to warn him secretly of his peril. For this purpose he employed as intermediary a Berber officer serving in the Almerian army. This officer visited Zuhair during the night, and said : " Believe me, my lord, when I warn you that you would to-morrow find difficulties in your path. I advise you, therefore, to set out instantly : you will thus, perhaps, be able to traverse the defiles before the troops from Granada have had time to occupy them, and if they pursue you, you will be enabled to give them battle in the plain or take refuge in one of your fortresses." This advice seemed reasonable to Zuhair, but Ibn 'Abbâs, who was present, cried : " Fear makes him speak thus ! " " What ! " retorted the officer, " sayest thou that of me ? I, who have taken part in twenty battles, whilst thou hast never seen a fight ! Thou wilt find that the event will prove me right ! " And he flung out of the room in a rage.

The enemies of Ibn 'Abbâs—who, as we have seen, were numerous—have asserted that he rejected the Berber's advice, not because he thought it bad, but because he desired Zuhair's death. Ibn 'Abbâs, they say, aimed at the sovereignty of Almeria ; he therefore hoped that Zuhair would be slain by the men of Granada, trusting that he himself might find safety in flight, and on reaching Almeria be proclaimed prince. There was perhaps some truth in this, for we shall see later on that Ibn 'Abbâs boasted to Bâdîs of having led Zuhair into a trap ; but, be this as it may, Zuhair found himself surrounded next morning (August 3, 1038) by the Granadan army.

His soldiers were dismayed, but he himself did not lose his presence of mind. He therefore drew up in battle array his negro infantry, to the number of five hundred, and his Andalusians; he then ordered his lieutenant, Hudhail, to charge the enemy at the head of the Slav cavalry. Hudhail obeyed, but the combat had scarcely commenced before he was dismounted—either by a spear-thrust, or in consequence of his horse stumbling—whereupon the cavalry fled in great confusion. At the same moment Zuhair was betrayed by his negroes, in whom he had put perfect confidence: they went over to the enemy after seizing the armoury. Only the Andalusians remained, and since they—unsoldierlike, as usual—had no thought but for flight, Zuhair, seeing the day was lost, joined them. Since the bridge at Alpuente had been destroyed, and the defiles were occupied by the enemy, the fugitives were obliged to seek refuge in the mountains. Most of them were cut down by the Granadans, who gave no quarter; others were dashed to pieces at the foot of savage precipices, and among the latter was Zuhair.

All the civil functionaries were made prisoners, Bâdîs having ordered their lives to be spared. Among them was Ibn 'Abbâs. He believed he had nothing to fear, and the fate of his books alone caused him anxiety. " My God ! " he cried; " what will become of my baggage ? " and turning to the soldiers who were conducting him to Bâdîs, he added: " Bid your master take great care of my baggage, lest it suffer any damage, for it contains books of inestimable value." On coming into Bâdîs' presence, he said with a smile: " Confess that I have served thee well, since I have delivered those dogs into thy hands ! " and he pointed to the prisoners. " Do me, therefore, a favour in thy turn," he added, " and give orders that my books are to be respected, for they are nearest to my heart." As he spoke, the Almerian prisoners darted furious glances at him, and one of them, a captain,[1] exclaimed to Bâdîs: " My lord, I entreat you, by Him who gave you the victory, not to let that wretch escape who betrayed our master ! He alone is responsible for what has happened, and could I but witness his punishment, joyfully would I lose my head the moment after ! " At these words Bâdîs smiled good-naturedly, and ordered the captain to be released. No other soldier's life was, however, spared; all the rest paid the penalty of death.

[1] Ibn Shabîb by name.

Ibn 'Abbâs, on the other hand, was the only civilian who
was not set at liberty. The haughty Vizier was at last face
to face with that *Misfortune* whom he had defied in his
insane pride, and he saw accomplished the Almerian poet's
prediction. He was confined in a dungeon in the Alhambra,
loaded with fetters weighing forty pounds. He knew that
Bâdîs was greatly incensed with him, and that Samuel
sought his death. Yet a spark of hope remained in his
breast; Bâdis, to whom he had offered thirty thousand
ducats as the price of his deliverance, had replied that he
would think the matter over, and nearly two months had
elapsed without a decision being arrived at. Conflicting
influences, in fact, had been agitating the Court of Granada :
on the one hand the Cordovan ambassador asked for the
liberation of all the prisoners, especially Ibn 'Abbâs : while
Abu 'l-Ahwâz Man ibn Somâdih, ambassador and brother-
in-law of the 'Âmirid 'Abd al-'Azîz of Valencia, urged
Bâdîs to execute the prisoners without exception — Ibn
'Abbâs first of all. 'Abd al-'Azîz was in fact eager to take
possession of the principality of Almeria, on the pretext
that it devolved on him by right—Zuhair having been a
client of his family—and he feared that if Ibn 'Abbâs and
the rest were set at liberty they might dispute his authority.
Bâdîs himself vacillated ; cupidity and the desire of revenge
struggled for the mastery; but one evening, when riding
with his brother Bologguîn, he mentioned the offer made
by Ibn 'Abbâs, and asked his advice. " If you accept that
man's gold," replied Bologguîn, " and set him at liberty, he
will stir up a war against you which will cost you double
his ransom. I advise you to put him to death without
delay."

On returning from his ride, Bâdîs sent for his prisoner,
and reproached him sternly for the wrongs he had done.
Ibn 'Abbâs endured the long invective with resignation,
and when the king had made an end, he cried : " My lord,
I pray you, show me compassion, deliver me from my
afflictions ! " " Thou shalt be delivered this very day,"
replied the prince ; and seeing a gleam of hope light up
his prisoner's haggard countenance he was silent for a few
moments. Then with a bitter smile he continued : " But
in the place whither thou goest thy afflictions will be yet
more bitter ! " Bâdîs then spoke a few words to Bologguîn
in the Berber tongue, which Ibn 'Abbâs did not understand,
but the last words which the prince had addressed to him,

his menacing smile, and his fierce demeanour, told the
prisoner but too clearly that his last hour had come.
Falling on his knees, he cried, " Prince, spare my life, I
entreat thee ! Have pity on my wives and children ! It
is not thirty thousand ducats that I will give you—it is
sixty thousand ; but in God's name, spare my life."

Bâdîs listened in silence ; then poising his javelin, he
plunged it into the speaker's breast. His brother Bologguîn
and his Chamberlain 'Alî ibn al-Karawî followed his example ;
but Ibn 'Abbâs, shrieking for mercy from his murderers,
did not succumb until he had received seventeen wounds
(September 24, 1038).

It was not long before Granada learnt that the wealthy
and arrogant Ibn 'Abbâs was no more. The Africans rejoiced, but no one received the news with livelier satisfaction than Samuel. He had now but one dangerous enemy
left—Ibn Bakanna—and a presentiment assured him that
this last opponent would soon perish. Israelites, as well as
Arabs, believed that sometimes during the night-watches
spirit-voices might be heard prophetic of the future, and
one night Samuel, as he slept, heard a voice reciting three
Hebrew verses to the following effect :

"Ibn 'Abbâs is already dead, with his trusted friends ; to God be
praise ! Hallowed be His name ! The other Minister, who plotted with
him, will be brought low and bruised like tares. What avail their threats,
their enmity and their might ? Hallowed be the name of God !"[1]

We shall find that a few years later, Samuel saw this
prediction fulfilled ; so true it is that both hatred and love
sometimes impart strange prescience of the future.

[1] *Journ. asiat.*, Ser. IV., xvi. p. 212.

[AUTHORITIES : Ibn Bassâm, i. ff. 122, 171–5, 200 ; Râzî, p. 37 ; *Abbad.*,
ii. p. 34 ; Al Makkarî, ii. pp. 359–60 ; Ibn al-Khatîb (MS. G.), ff.
51–2, 134–5.]

CHAPTER III

ABU 'L-FOTÛH

IN ridding himself of Zuhair, Bâdîs had involuntarily rendered eminent service to the coalition that recognised Hishâm as Khalif. The 'Âmirid 'Abd al-'Azîz of Valencia, who, as we have seen, had seized the principality of Almeria, was not in a condition, it is true, to render assistance to his ally, the Kady of Seville—for he soon had to defend himself against Mojehid of Denia, who regarded with no favourable eye the enlargement of his neighbour's territories [1]—but the Kady at all events was relieved from fear of war with Almeria, and could consequently give his whole attention to offensive operations against the Berbers—beginning with Mohammed of Carmona, with whom he was at variance. Meanwhile, he entered into correspondence with a faction at Granada, and endeavoured to foment a revolt there. Many Granadans were discontented with Bâdîs. At the outset of his reign he had been a prince of some promise; but by degrees he had shown himself cruel, treacherous, bloodthirsty, and shamefully addicted to drunkenness. Complaints and murmurings preluded a conspiracy. The leader in the plot was an adventurer named Abu 'l-Fotûh. Born far away from Spain, of an Arab family settled in the Jurjân—the ancient Hyrcania—he had studied literature, philosophy and astronomy under the most famous professors at Baghdad. He was not only a scholar, but a skilled horseman and a gallant soldier: he appreciated a mettle-some steed or a keen sword-blade no less than a fine poem or a profound philosophical treatise. Abu 'l-Fotûh landed in Spain in 1015, apparently to seek his fortune, and spent some time at the court of Mojehid of Denia. There he sometimes conversed on literature with that learned prince, or worked at his Commentary on the grammatical treatise called the *Jomal;* at other times he fought by the prince's side in Sardinia; often, too, he would ponder over abstruse

---

[1] 'Abd al-'Azîz quitted Almeria about 1041, after entrusting the government to his brother-in-law Abu 'l-Ahwâz Man. *Recherches,* i. 241.

questions of philosophy, or seek to learn the future from the stars. He afterwards proceeded to Zaragoza, the residence of Mundhir, where he was at first cordially treated by that prince, who entrusted him with the education of his son; but, as our Arab authority justly though tritely remarks, "times change and men with them," and Mundhir one day informed the tutor that his services were no longer required, and that he might therefore leave Zaragoza. Abu 'l-Fotûh next settled in Granada, where he delivered a course of lectures on ancient poetry, especially on the anthology known as the *Hamâsa;* [1] but he found time for something else: knowing that Bâdîs had many enemies, he excited the ambition of Yazîr, the king's cousin, by assuring him that the stars declared that Bâdîs would be dethroned, and that his cousin would reign for thirty years. He thus contrived to hatch a plot, but Bâdîs having discovered it before it was mature, Yazîr and his fellow-conspirators had scarcely time to save themselves by flight. They sought refuge with the Kady of Seville—doubtless their accomplice, though it is impossible to say how far he was involved.

Meanwhile, the Kady had attacked Mohammed of Carmona, and his army—commanded as usual by his son Ismâ'îl—had already won brilliant successes: Ossuna and Ecija had been compelled to surrender; Carmona itself was besieged. Reduced to the last extremity, Mohammed sought help from Idrîs of Malaga and from Bâdîs. Both responded to his appeal; Idrîs, who was sick, sent troops under the command of his Minister Ibn Bakanna; Bâdîs led his own men. The two armies having united, Ismâ'îl, full of confidence in the number and quality of his force, immediately offered battle to his opponents, but Bâdîs and Ibn Bakanna — seeing, or supposing, that the enemy were numerically superior—would not accept it, and without giving another thought to the lord of Carmona, left him to his fate, and made for Granada and Malaga respectively. Ismâ'îl immediately pursued the Granadans. Fortunately for Bâdîs, Ibn Bakanna had parted company with him barely an hour before, and on being urgently sent for, returned in hot haste. The two armies, having effected a junction near Ecija, then awaited the enemy in good order.

The Sevillans, believing that they had to deal with a

---

[1] For an account of the *Hamâsa* (of Abû Tammâm) see R. A. Nicholson, *Lit. Hist. of the Arabs* (1907), pp. 129-30. It has been translated into German by F. Rückert.

retreating foe, were disagreeably surprised when they came
in contact with two armies in battle array. Demoralised
by this unexpected predicament, the first encounter threw
them into confusion. Ismâ'îl in vain tried to rally his
men : a victim to his own valour, he was the first to fall.
The Sevillans thereupon thought only of saving their own
lives.

Bâdîs, master of the field after so easy a victory, pitched
his camp near the gates of Ecija, and he was not a little
surprised to see Abu 'l-Fotûh approach and fling himself
at his feet. Affection for his family had spurred him on.
He had been obliged to quit Granada in such haste that
his wife and children had perforce been left behind. He
knew that Bâdîs had had them arrested by the negro Kodâm,
his "Tristan l'Ermite,"[1] and that Kodâm had imprisoned
them at Almuñecar. Now Abu 'l-Fotûh passionately loved
his wife, a young and beautiful Andalusian, and his affection
for their children, a son and a daughter, was also unbounded.
Life without them was worthless, and fearing, above all,
lest Bâdîs should wreak vengeance for his crime on their
beloved heads, he now came to sue for pardon. He was
aware of the tyrant's implacable and bloodthirsty disposition,
but trusted that he would not now be remorseless, since
he had shown clemency to Abû Rîsh who had also been a
conspirator. Kneeling before the prince, the suppliant cried :
" Have mercy upon me, my lord ! I swear to thee that I
am innocent ! " " Darest thou present thyself before me ? "
cried Bâdîs, his eyes flaming with anger : " Thou hast sown
discord in my family, and now thou declarest thyself innocent ! Thinkest thou I can be thus easily hoodwinked ? "

" For the love of God, have mercy, my good lord ! Remember how thou tookest me under thy protection, and
how, an exile from my native land, I am misfortune's thrall.
Impute not to me thy kinsman's crime ; I had no part nor
lot in it ! That I fled with him is true ; but it was because
our intimacy was known to thee, and I dreaded punishment
as his accomplice. I kneel before thee. If it pleaseth thee,
I will even confess a crime of which I am guiltless, so that
I may gain pardon. Treat me as befitteth a great king—
a monarch too exalted to feel malice against a poor wretch
like me—and restore me to my family ! "

" Of a truth I will treat thee, if it be God's will, accord-

---

[1] The provost of Louis XI of France, notorious for his cruelty.

ing to thy deserts. Return to Granada; thou wilt find thy
family there, and when I arrive I will settle thy affairs."

Reassured by these words, the ambiguity of which he
did not at the time perceive, Abu 'l-Fotûh set out for
Granada, escorted by two horsemen : but as they approached
the city, Kodâm carried out his master's orders. The
prisoner was seized by the Provost-marshal's minions, who,
after shaving his head, placed him on a camel. A negro
of herculean strength mounted behind him and proceeded
to buffet him without intermission. In this way Abu 'l-Fotûh
was led through the streets, to be finally thrown into a
narrow dungeon with one of his accomplices, a Berber taken
prisoner at Ecija.

Several days elapsed. Bâdîs had returned, but had come
to no decision with regard to his prisoner. This time it was
Bologguîn, the instigator of Ibn 'Abbâs' death, who delayed
the fatal sentence. For some reason, he took an interest
in the scholar and maintained his innocence, defending him
so warmly that Bâdîs, unwilling to offend his brother, hesitated. But one day, when Bologguîn was engaged in a
drunken orgy—no uncommon incident for either brother—
Bâdîs sent for Abu 'l-Fotûh and his fellow-prisoner. After
venting a torrent of abuse on the former, the king continued :
" Thy stars have been of no avail, liar that thou art! Didst
thou not promise thine Emir—that poor imbecile, thy dupe
—that he would soon ascend my throne, and reign for thirty
years ? Why didst thou not cast thine own horoscope ?
Thou mightest have saved thyself from dire misfortune. Thy
life, wretch, is now in my hands !"

Abu 'l-Fotûh made no reply. While hope remained
of seeing his adored wife and children once more, he had
abased himself to supplication and falsehoods; but now—
convinced that nothing could bend this savage and treacherous tyrant—all the pride, courage, and energy of his character returned. His eyes fixed on the ground, a scornful
smile upon his lips, he preserved a dignified silence. This
calm and serene demeanour filled up the measure of the
tyrant's wrath. Foaming with rage, Bâdîs started from his
throne, and drawing his sword plunged it into his victim's
heart. Abu 'l-Fotûh received the fatal blow without a
shudder or a groan, and his courage drew from Bâdîs himself an involuntary cry of admiration. Then, turning to
Barhûn, one of his slaves, the king said : " Decapitate this
corpse, and affix the head to a stake. Bury the body beside

that of Ibn 'Abbâs. Let my two enemies lie side by side until the Day of Judgment. And now, soldier, it is thy turn. Draw near ! "

The Berber, to whom these words were addressed, was a prey to unspeakable anguish, and trembled in every limb. Falling on his knees he struggled to exculpate himself, and implored the prince to spare his life. " Wretch ! " exclaimed Bâdîs : " hast thou no sense of shame ? The scholar that lies there, in whom some fear might have been excusable, suffered death with heroic courage, as thou hast seen ; he deigned not to open his lips, and dost thou—a veteran soldier—who countest thyself a brave man, display this cowardice ? May God have no pity on thee ! " In another moment the Berber's head had fallen (October 20, 1039). Abu 'l-Fotûh was duly interred beside Ibn 'Abbâs. The regrets of the intellectual and lettered part of Granadan society followed him to the grave, and in passing the spot where his remains rested, the Arab, condemned to endure in silence an alien and barbarous yoke, would often mutter : " Ah, what incomparable scholars were those whose bones lie there ! God alone is immortal ! Hallowed and glorified be His name ! "

[AUTHORITIES : *Abbad.,* i. 51 ; ii. 33–4, 207, 217 ; Ibn al-Khatîb (MS. G.), ff. 114–15 ; 'Abd al-Wâhid, pp. 44, 65.]

CHAPTER IV

MALAGA

THE bloodthirsty tyrant of Granada became more and more predominant in his party. It is true that he still formally recognised the suzerainty of the Hammûdites of Malaga—feeble princes, subservient to their ministers, but prone to removing rivals by dagger or poison. Without a thought of controlling their powerful vassals, they deemed themselves happy if they contrived to make some show of ruling peacefully over Malaga, Tangier and Ceuta.

There was, moreover, a profound difference between the two Courts of Granada and Malaga. At the former there were none but Berbers, or men who, like the Jew Samuel, always acted in the interest of the Berbers. A remarkable solidarity was the result. At the Court of Malaga, on the other hand, there were also Slavs, and sooner or later the jealousies, rivalries and hatreds, which had contributed so much to the overthrow of the Omayyads, began to show themselves.

The Khalif Idrîs I, who lay on a bed of sickness when he sent troops against the Sevillans, expired two days after receiving the head of Ismâ'îl, who had been killed at the battle of Ecija. A struggle ensued between Ibn Bakanna, the Berber, and Najâ, the Slav minister. The former wished to confer the crown on Yahyâ, the elder son of Idrîs, in the belief that power would thus devolve upon himself. The Slav opposed the scheme. As Prime Minister of the African provinces, he there proclaimed Hasan ibn Yahyâ—cousin of the other claimant—Khalif, and made preparations to cross the Straits. The Berber Minister, less bold and determined, was intimidated by Najâ's menacing attitude. Unable to make up his mind whether to resist or yield, he neglected the necessary precautions, and one day he saw the African fleet casting anchor in the roadstead of Malaga. He fled in all haste to Comares, with his candidate. Hasan, master of the Capital, assured him of pardon if he would return. The

Berber trusted him, and paid for his credulity with his
life. The prophetic dream of the Jew Samuel had come
true. A little later Hasan's rival was also put to death.
Najâ was, perhaps, as some historians have maintained,
the sole instigator of this crime; but Hasan paid the
penalty for it. He was poisoned by his wife, sister of the
unfortunate Yahyâ.

It seemed to Najâ that he had played the part of
Minister long enough. Having therefore put to death
Hasan's son—a mere boy—and thrown his brother Idrîs
into prison, he boldly offered himself to the Berbers as
their sovereign, and sought to cajole them with dazzling
promises. Although deeply indignant at his incredible
audacity and sacrilegious ambition—for they had an almost
superstitious veneration for the descendants of the Prophet
—the Berbers determined to wait for a more favourable
moment to punish him. They therefore swore fealty.

Najâ thereupon announced his intention of wresting
Algeciras from the reigning Hammûdite, Mohammed. He
took the field, but in his first encounters with the enemy
he became aware that his Berbers fought tamely, and that
he could not rely upon them. In prudence, therefore,
he ordered a retreat. He intended to exile the suspected
Berbers on his return to the Capital, to win over the rest
by bribery, and to surround himself with as many Slavs
as possible. But his bitterest enemies were either informed
of his design or guessed it, and as the army was passing
through a narrow defile they fell upon the usurper and
killed him (February 5, 1043).

Whilst the greatest confusion reigned among the troops
—the Berbers shouting for joy, and the Slavs fleeing
lest they should share their chief's fate—two of the assassins
galloped at full speed to Malaga, and entering the town
cried: "Good news! the usurper is no more!" then
throwing themselves upon Najâ's lieutenant, they murdered
him. Idrîs, Hasan's brother, was forthwith released from
prison and proclaimed Khalif.

The Slavs had played out their part at Malaga; but
peace, for a moment restored, was of no long duration.
Idrîs II was by no means a great man, but he was kind
and charitable, and never weary of scattering his bounties.
If it had rested only with him, all would have been happy.
He recalled the exiles from every quarter, and restored
their property to them; he would never listen to an

informer; each day he distributed five hundred ducats among the poor. His sympathy for the lower orders, with whom he loved to converse, contrasted singularly with the luxury, the ostentation, and the punctilious etiquette of his Court. The Hammûdites, as descendants of the Prophet's son-in-law, were regarded by their subjects almost as demi-gods. To maintain an illusion so favourable to their authority, they rarely showed themselves in public, and surrounded themselves with mystery. Idrîs himself, in spite of his simple tastes, did not swerve from the ceremonial established by his predecessors; a curtain shut him off from those with whom he conversed—but since he was good-nature itself, he sometimes forgot his part. One day, for instance, a poet from Lisbon recited an ode in praise of his liberality and noble ancestry. "Whilst other folk," he said, in his fantastic phraseology, "have been made of water and of dust, the descendants of the Prophet have been made wholly of pure water, the water of justice and piety. The gift of prophecy descended upon their ancestor, and the angel Gabriel, unseen by us, hovers above their heads. The countenance of Idrîs, Commander of the Faithful, resembles the rising sun, which dazzles with its rays the eyes of all beholders! Ah, my prince, would that we could gaze upon thee and bask in thy radiance— emanation from the glory which surrounds the Lord of the Universe!" "Draw back the curtain, Chamberlain!" cried the Khalif, who could never refuse a request. More fortunate than Jupiter's luckless leman who fell victim to her curiosity, the poet could contemplate at his leisure the person of his divinity, which, if it did not blaze with baleful glory, at any rate bore the impress of kindness and good-nature. Perhaps the spectacle was more pleasing to the poet than if it had been effulgent with the blinding rays of which he had spoken in his verses. It is at least certain that he received a sumptuous gift and withdrew well satisfied.

Unluckily for the dignity and stability of the State, Idrîs combined with great good-nature extreme weakness of character. He could not, or dared not say "No!" Bâdîs and other chiefs could always obtain a castle, or what not, for the asking. One day Bâdîs demanded the surrender of Idrîs' Vizier, who had had the misfortune to displease him. "Alas! my friend," said Idrîs to his Minister: "Here is a letter from the King of Granada, in which he requests me to hand you over to him.   I am deeply grieved, but I dare not refuse him."   "Do, then, what is required of you," replied the worthy Vizier, an old adherent of the clan : "God will grant me strength to meet my fate with resignation and courage."   On reaching Granada he was executed.

Such feebleness irritated the Berbers, who were already mortified by the sympathy shown by Idrîs to the lower orders—his socialistic tendencies, as they would now be termed — and the negroes were especially exasperated. Accustomed to be ruled with the lash, the sword and the gibbet, they despised a master who never pronounced sentence of death.   Discontent therefore already ran high when the Governor of the Castle of Airos[1] gave the signal for revolt.   As custodian of Idrîs' two cousins, he set them at liberty and proclaimed the elder, Mohammed, Khalif. The negroes, who formed the garrison of the citadel of Malaga, thereupon mutinied, and invited Mohammed to join them.   But the townsfolk would not abandon their benevolent and beloved prince in his hour of danger.   With much courage they flocked to him and loudly demanded arms, assuring him that if they were granted, the negroes should not hold the castle for another hour.   Idrîs thanked them for their devotion, but refused their offer.   "Return to your homes," he said, "for I would not have a single life lost on my account."   Mohammed therefore entered the Capital, and Idrîs was transferred to the prison of Airos. They had simply changed places (A.D. 1046-7).

The new Khalif resembled, not his predecessor, but his own mother—an Amazon who loved the life of camps, to watch the preparations for a battle or the progress of a siege, and to stimulate by eloquence, or largesse, the soldiers' courage.   Mohammed was brave to rashness ; but he was also an inexorable disciplinarian, and if Idrîs had lacked energy, his successor—as the promoters of the revolution soon discovered—possessed too much.   It was the old story of the frogs who asked Jupiter for a king.   Like La Fontaine's "marshy folk," Berbers and negroes soon found reason to curse the formidable stork and regret the peaceful log.   A plot was formed ; the conspirators opened negotiations with the Governor of Airos, and easily persuaded him to acknowledge Idrîs II as Khalif and to set him at liberty.

---

[1] Situation unknown.

This time Idrîs did not recoil from the idea of civil war; the tedium of a dungeon had outworn his scruples; but Mohammed, instigated by his mother, resisted his opponents so vigorously that they laid down their arms. Before making submission, however, they deported Idrîs in safety to Africa, where two Berber freedmen held sway—Sakôt and Rizk-allâh, Governors of Ceuta and Tangier respectively. Idrîs was received with great respect, and his name was inserted in the public prayers; but the Governors did not entrust him with any actual authority; jealous of their own power, they guarded him strictly, prevented him from showing himself in public, and forbade anyone to enter his presence. Certain Berber lords, however, contrived an interview with him, and said: "These two slaves treat you as a captive, and prevent you from exercising sovereignty. Empower us to do so, and we will set you free." But Idrîs, mild and submissive as ever, refused their offer; in the simplicity of his heart he went further, and related to the Governors what had passed. The lords implicated were promptly banished; but fearing lest Idrîs on some future occasion might lend an ear to malcontents, Sakôt and Rizk-allâh sent him back to Spain, without however ceasing to recognise him as Khalif in the public prayers. Idrîs sought refuge with the Berber chief of Ronda.[1]

Meanwhile the malcontents of Malaga had enlisted the aid of Bâdîs, who indeed went so far as to declare war on Mohammed, but was soon reconciled to him. The prince of Algeciras, also named Mohammed, was then declared Khalif. There were therefore at that time four Commanders of the Faithful—the false Hishâm II at Seville, Mohammed at Malaga, another Mohammed at Algeciras, and, finally, Idrîs II. Two of these had no vestige of real power; the others were princes of small importance, mere kinglets, and the abuse of the title of Khalif was the more ridiculous since in its true acceptance it implied sovereignty of all Islam.

The prince of Algeciras failed in his attempt. Abandoned by those who had called him to the throne, he fled to his own country, and died soon afterwards of shame and grief (A.D. 1048-9).

Four or five years later Mohammed of Malaga also died. One of his nephews unsuccessfully aspired to the throne as

---

[1] Or at Comares, according to Ibn Khaldûn.

Idrîs III. This time the worthy Idrîs II was restored, and destiny having ceased to persecute him, he reigned in peace until, in 1055, he too paid the debt of nature.

Another Hammûdite aimed at succeeding him, but Bâdîs frustrated his hopes. The King of Granada, now the virtual head of the Berbers, would have no more Khalifs; he resolved to make an end of the Hammûdite line and to incorporate the principality of Malaga with his own realm. This he did without much difficulty. The Arabs, it is true, did not willingly submit; but having won over the most influential of them, such as the Vizier-Kady Abû 'Abdallah Judâmî, Bâdîs heeded little the murmurs of the rest. As for the Berbers, since they had realized the feebleness of their princes, and the necessity of a close union with their brethren at Granada if they hoped to hold their own against the Arabs who were gaining ground daily in the South-west—they rather favoured the designs of Bâdîs than thwarted them. The King of Granada thus became master of Malaga, and all the Hammûdites were exiled. They had yet a part to play in Africa, but in Spain they had finally quitted the stage.

[AUTHORITIES: Ibn Bassâm, i. f. 224; Ibn al-Khatîb (MS. G.), f. 107; 'Abd al-Wâhid, ff. 45–9; Ibn Khaldûn, ff. 22–3; Makkarî, i. pp. 132, 282–4; Homaidî, *Dict. Biog.*]

CHAPTER V

AL-MU'TADID

IN order not to interrupt our rapid sketch of the history of Malaga, we have somewhat anticipated the course of events; and since we now propose to glance at the progress made by the Arab party during this interval, we must go back a few years.

On the death of the Kady of Seville, at the end of January, 1042, his son 'Abbâd, then twenty-six years old, succeeded him as *hâjib* of the pretended Hishâm II. 'Abbâd is best known in history as al-Mu'tadid, and though he did not adopt this surname until later, it will be convenient thus to designate him from the outset.

The new chief of the Arabs of the South-west was one of the most striking personalities ever produced in the green old age of a civilization. He was in every respect a worthy rival of Bâdîs, the leader of the opposing party.

Suspicious, vindictive, perfidious, tyrannical, and cruel as his adversary, and, like him, addicted to drunkenness, Mu'tadid surpassed him in licentiousness. Capricious and sensual by disposition, his appetites were insatiable. No prince possessed so numerous a harem as his: it is said that eight hundred maidens passed through its doors.

In spite of a general resemblance, the characters of the two princes were, however, not wholly alike. Bâdîs was almost a barbarian; he scorned refinement and intellectual graces. No poets frequented the halls of the Alhambra; its lord, indeed, who habitually spoke Berber, would scarcely have understood their odes. Mu'tadid, on the other hand, had been carefully educated; he could not, it is true, claim to be a scholar; he was not deeply read, but since he was endowed with fine discrimination and a retentive memory, his culture excelled that of the average man of the world. Mu'tadid's poems, which apart from their literary merit are of interest as furnishing a clue to his character, gained for him among his contemporaries a reputation as a capable versifier. He was a patron of literature and art. He

paid poets handsomely for a whiff of incense. He had a
passion for building splendid palaces. He made his slender
erudition subservient even to his tyranny—taking as his
model that Khalif of Baghdad whose title he had adopted,
while Bâdîs probably did not know at what epoch the
former Mu‘tadid had lived.[1]   While both princes were
wine-bibbers, Bâdîs made himself grossly and shamelessly
drunk, like a boor or a trooper. But Mu‘tadid, always a
gentleman and a man of the world, did nothing without
grace, and imported good taste and distinction, of a kind,
even into his orgies; while indulging in deep potations, he
and his boon-companions improvised bacchanalian ditties
distinguished by incongruous refinement and delicacy of
diction. His powerful constitution lent itself equally to
pleasure and toil: an unbridled sensualist and an untiring
worker, he passed from the indulgence of fevered passions
to the drudgery of business. He loved to fatigue himself
with the duties of sovereignty; but after superhuman
efforts to make up for the time lost in pleasures, fresh
debauchery was necessary to renew his strength. And—
strange anomaly!—the tyrant before whose fierce glance
the beauties of his harem quailed, addressed to some of
them verses of refined gallantry and winning sweetness.

Bâdîs and Mu‘tadid, therefore, differed as a barbarian
villain differs from a civilized villain; and all things considered, the barbarian was the least profoundly depraved
of the two. Bâdîs displayed a certain brutal frankness even
in crime; Mu‘tadid was inscrutable, even to his closest
friends. While his penetrating glance never failed to read
the inmost thoughts of others, no play of expression, no
tone of his voice betrayed his own. The prince of Granada
risked his life on many a battlefield; the prince of Seville,
although continually engaged in warfare, and by no means
lacking in courage, led his troops in the field but once or
twice; usually, as an Arab historian puts it, he traced out,
at the bottom of his den, the plans of campaign for his
generals. Bâdîs' stratagems were clumsy and easily baffled;
but those of Mu‘tadid—subtle and well-devised—seldom
failed. A story has been related illustrative of his craftiness, which perhaps deserves to be retold.

While waging war against Carmona, Mu‘tadid maintained a secret correspondence with an Arab in that town,

---

[1] Reigned A.D. 892–902.

who kept him informed of the movements and plans of the
Berbers. In order that their letters should not be intercepted, nor the intrigue even suspected, the utmost caution
was, of course, necessary. Now Mu'tadid, according to a
plan concerted with his spy, one day summoning to his
palace a peasant from the suburbs, a simple and guileless
man, said to him: " Doff that worthless cloak of thine, and
put on this jubbah.¹ It is a fine one, as you see, and I will
give it thee if thou doest what I am about to tell thee."
The peasant overjoyed, put on the jubbah—little suspecting
that the lining of the garment concealed a letter from
Mu'tadid to the spy—and promised faithfully to carry out
whatever orders the prince might give him. " It is well,"
replied Mu'tadid: " This is what thou must do; take the
road to Carmona; when thou drawest near the town cut
some sticks and bind them into a faggot. Then enter the
gates and place thyself where the woodcutters congregate, but
sell not thy bundle until thou art offered five dirhems for it."
The peasant, wholly ignorant of the motive of these
strange instructions, hastened to obey them. He therefore
set out for Carmona, and duly proceeded to make his faggot;
but since he was unused to the work, and, as the proverb
says, " there are faggots and faggots," he reached the town
with a scanty bundle of straggling branches, and took up a
position in the market. " What is the price of this faggot?"
asked a passer-by. " Five dirhems, and no less; take it or
leave it," replied the peasant. " It is of ebony, doubtless!"
said his interrogator, laughing in his face. " Nay!" said
another bystander, " it is of bamboo!" The amateur wood-
cutter became the object of unmerciful banter; but towards
evening Mu'tadid's spy approached him, and asking the
price of the faggot, at once bought it, adding: " Put the
wood on thy shoulder and carry it to my house. I will
lead the way." On reaching his destination, the peasant
flung down his load, and having received the five dirhems
made for the door. " Whither art thou going at this late
hour?" asked the master of the house. " Out of the city,"
replied the peasant, " for I do not live here." " Thou must
not think of such a thing! Knowest thou not that there
are robbers by the way? Stay here; I can give you shelter
and a meal; and you can proceed homewards early in the
morning."

¹ A long outer garment, similar to the caftan, but open in front and with
shorter sleeves.

The peasant gratefully accepted the offer, and a hearty supper soon banished from his mind the raillery of which he had been the butt. When the meal was over, he informed his host, in answer to an inquiry, that he lived in the suburbs of Seville. "Thou art indeed stout-hearted to have ventured hither!" was the reply; "Thou must have heard of the cruelty of our Berbers, and how they make short work of their victims. Some weighty business must have brought thee hither." "Nay! but a man must earn his living—and who would take the trouble to maltreat a poor harmless peasant like me?"

The conversation continued until the peasant grew drowsy, and having been conducted to his sleeping-place, flung himself down without removing his garments. "Take off your jubbah," said his host; "the night is warm, and you will be the more refreshed." The peasant did so, and was soon fast asleep.

The spy then ripped open the lining of the cloak, found Mu'tadid's letter, read it, and replacing it by a hastily written reply, sewed up the lining and replaced the jubbah where the peasant had thrown it. The latter, rising betimes, set out for Seville, after thanking the citizen for his kindly hospitality.

On his return, he presented himself before Mu'tadid and recounted his adventures. "I am well pleased with you," said the prince graciously, "and you deserve a reward. Give me back that jubbah, and take this complete suit of apparel as a gift." The peasant, beside himself with joy, took the fine clothes offered him, and told his friends and neighbours, with much glee, that the prince had presented him with a robe of honour, as though he had been a dignitary of the highest importance. That he had acted as courier extraordinary, and bearer of despatches so momentous that they would have cost him his life if the Berbers had found them upon him, he never had the least suspicion.

The crafty prince of Seville was indeed fertile in expedients and artifices of all kinds; he had to his hand a whole arsenal of devices. Woe to him who incurred his wrath: useless was it for such an one to seek safety in another land; the prince's vengeance would track him to the ends of the earth. It is related that a blind man had been deprived by Mu'tadid of the greater part of his property; he himself spent the residue, and then in utter destitution journeyed as a mendicant to Mecca. There he ceased not publicly to

MS-V

curse the tyrant who had reduced him to beggary. Mu'tadid
heard of this, and sending for one of his subjects who was
about to make pilgrimage to Mecca, entrusted him with a
casket containing gold pieces smeared with a deadly poison.
" On reaching Mecca," said the prince, " deliver this casket
to your blind fellow-citizen. Give him greeting and tell
him that this is a gift from me ; but take heed that you
open it not." When the pilgrim arrived at Mecca, he duly
presented himself before the blind man with Mu'tadid's gift.
" By Allah ! " cried the unfortunate man ; " it rings when
shaken ! There is gold within ! But how comes it that
Mu'tadid ruins me at Seville, and enriches me in Arabia ? "
" Princes have strange caprices," was the pilgrim's reply :
" or, mayhap, Mu'tadid feels remorse at some injustice which
he did thee. But that concerns me not ; I have executed
my commission. Take then this gift, which seems an unexpected boon."

" Such, of a truth, it is ! " replied the blind man ;
" accept a thousand thanks for thy pains, and assure the
prince of my gratitude."

With his treasure under his arm, the poor wretch
hastened, as fast as his blindness permitted, to his hovel,
and carefully locking the door, with eager fingers tore open
the casket. It is said that there is nothing more intoxicating for a man who has been by a happy chance suddenly
enriched after a long struggle with poverty, than to feast
his eyes on a heap of gold, and suffer them to gloat on
the entrancing glitter of the coins. The blind Sevillan was
incapable of this delight ; for him, touch and hearing took
the place of sight, and transported with ecstasy, he clutched
the precious coins, he bathed his hands in them, he let
them run through his fingers, he rang them, counted them,
kissed them. The poison worked ; ere nightfall the miserable man was a corpse.

Though Bâdîs and Mu'tadid were both cruel ruffians,
distinctions may be drawn between them even in that
character. While the former in paroxysms of blind fury
frequently slew his victims with his own hand, Mu'tadid
seldom trenched upon the domain of the executioner ; but
although he did not care to soil his aristocratic hands with
blood, his hatred was more tenacious and implacable than his
rival's. Bâdîs, when his enemy was dead, was satisfied, and his
rage quickly abated ; he would impale the head of his victim
on a stake, as was customary, but there the matter ended.

The prince of Seville's hatred, on the other hand, was an insatiable passion : his victims were pursued by it after their death ; he loved to whet his savage appetite by gloating over their mutilated remains. Following the example of the Khalif Mahdî, he caused flowers to be planted in the skulls of his enemies, and set them in the court of his palace. A label attached to each bore the name of its former owner. He often took pleasure in visiting what he called his "garden." But the parterre did not contain the heads most precious in his sight, namely, those of princes whom he had conquered : these were preserved with great care in a coffer beneath his palace.

And yet this monster of cruelty was in his own eyes the best of princes—a Titus created expressly for the benefit of the human race :

"If it is Thy will, O God," he exclaims in poetic fervour, "that felicity should be the lot of mortals, suffer me to reign over Arabs and barbarians alike ; for never have I strayed from the right way, never have I treated my subjects save as becometh a generous and magnanimous prince. I have ever shielded them from the aggressor, and turned aside the calamity that threatened them !"

[AUTHORITIES : *Abbad.*, i. pp. 243–5 ; ii. 48, 52 ; 'Abd al-Wâhid, pp. 67–70 ; Ibn Bassâm, i. f. 109.]

MU'TADID'S first step was to rid himself of Habîb, his father's Vizier and confidant, by putting him to death; he then turned his arms against the Berbers—especially his neighbours of Carmona. There were personal grounds for his hatred of these Africans. He believed that, if not thwarted, they would dethrone him or his descendants, for his astrologers had predicted that his dynasty would be brought low by men who were not natives of Spain. Mu'tadid accordingly strained every nerve to extirpate the Berbers. The resulting war was a tedious one; for though Mohammed, prince of Carmona, fell into an ambush and was killed (A.D. 1042-3), hostilities were continued under his son and successor, Ishâk.

Meanwhile Mu'tadid was extending his borders on the west. In 1044 he wrested Mertola from Ibn Taifûr. He next attacked Ibn Yahyâ, lord of Niebla. The latter was was not a Berber, but an Arab: when, however, an extension of his territory was in question, Mu'tadid was not fastidious. Closely pressed, Ibn Yahyâ threw himself into the arms of the Berbers. Muzaffar of Badajoz came to his assistance, repulsed Mu'tadid, and set to work to form a strong league against Seville, comprising Bâdîs, Mohammed of Malaga, and Mohammed of Algeciras. Abu 'l-Walîd ibn Jahwar, who, in 1043, had succeeded his father as President of the Republic of Cordova, did all he could to bring about a reconciliation between the opponents, but in vain ; his envoys were ignored.

The Berbers planned a march on Seville as soon as the armies had effected a junction. But Mu'tadid baffled them. Taking advantage of the absence of Muzaffar—who had not made due provision for the defence of his own frontiers—he laid waste the territories of Badajoz ; then, contrary to his wont, placing himself at the head of his army, he marched against Niebla, attacked the enemy in a defile near the city gates, and drove many of them into the Tinto; Muzaffar, however, rallied his troops to the attack, and forced Mu'tadid to retreat.

Muzaffar then rejoined his allies; but while they were engaged in ravaging the district of Seville, Ibn Yahyâ deserted his party, having been induced to form an alliance with Mu'tadid. Muzaffar punished the turncoat by confiscating the money which the latter had entrusted to him, and by devastating the district of Niebla. Ibn Yahyâ accordingly appealed to his new ally for help. Mu'tadid attacked the troops of Badajoz, lured them into an ambush, and defeated them. Not content with this success, he sent his son Ismâ'îl to lay waste the environs of Evora.

To repel the invaders, the King of Badajoz mustered every man capable of bearing arms, and, with a reinforcement from his ally Ishâk of Carmona, set out against the enemy. In vain did the Berbers of Carmona try to dissuade him. "You know not," they said, "how vast the Sevillan army is; but we have received information from Seville, and have ourselves seen Mu'tadid's troops." Their warnings fell on deaf ears. But the headstrong Muzaffar's rashness cost him dear. He sustained a terrible defeat, with a loss of at least three thousand men. Among the dead lay the prince of Carmona, who had commanded his father's troops: his head was presented to Mu'tadid, who placed it in his coffer beside that of the young prince's grandfather.

For a long time Badajoz presented a melancholy spectacle. The shops were closed, the markets deserted: the flower of her populace had perished on that fatal day. To crown her misfortunes, the Sevillans completed the destruction of the crops, so that the country around was soon in the grip of famine. Muzaffar was helpless. Abandoned by his allies, to whom he appealed in vain, he was condemned to eat his heart in helpless inactivity at Badajoz. But, unbending in his pride, he would not hear of reconciliation, though his victorious foe did not actually refuse Ibn Jahwar's mediation. Muzaffar even feigned to be indifferent to his losses, and sent an emissary to Cordova to buy some singing-girls. Such commodities were at that time scarce, and after some difficulty, only two, of mediocre ability, could be found. This whim on the part of the King of Badajoz excited some surprise. He was known to be a staid and studious man whose heart was not set upon singing-girls: it seemed strange, moreover, that he should have chosen a time for buying them when his realm was a scene of dire desolation. But when his motives leaked out astonishment ceased. Muzaffar had learned that, at the sale of the property of a recently deceased Cordovan Vizier, Mu'tadid had bought a renowned songstress, and it was to show that he could turn his attention to singing-girls with as much detachment of mind as his adversary, that he made his own purchase.

Ibn Jahwar, however, did not relax his efforts to bring about a reconciliation, and in July, 1051, they were crowned with success, for on that date Muzaffar and Mu'tadid concluded peace after protracted negotiations.

Mu'tadid thereupon turned his forces against Ibn Yahyâ of Niebla, who now had only his own resources to rely upon. The expedition proved a mere military promenade. Conscious of his weakness, Ibn Yahyâ made no attempt at defence, but set out for Cordova with the intention of ending his days in that city. Mu'tadid courteously sent him a squadron as an escort.

'Abd al-'Azîz the Bakrite, the prince then reigning over Huelva and the little island of Saltes, soon became aware that his turn had come. In the hope, however, of saving somewhat from the shipwreck, he wrote to Mu'tadid, congratulating him on his recent conquests, reminding him of the friendly relations which had always subsisted between their families, avowing himself his vassal, and offering him Huelva, on condition that he might retain Saltes. Mu'tadid accepted his offer, and on pretence of desiring an interview with the prince, set out for Huelva. But 'Abd al-'Azîz deemed it prudent not to await his guest, and hastened with his treasure to Saltes. Mu'tadid returned to Seville, after taking possession of Huelva, and leaving there one of his captains, with orders to prevent 'Abd al-'Azîz from quitting the island and any one else from landing on it. When informed of these measures 'Abd al-'Azîz adopted the prudent course of parleying with Mu'tadid's lieutenant, and he eventually sold his ships and munitions of war to the prince of Seville for six thousand ducats, at the same time obtaining permission to proceed to Cordova. The treacherous Mu'tadid intended to entrap him on his journey, and rob him of his money, but 'Abd al-'Azîz penetrated his design, and, thanks to an escort granted him by the prince of Carmona, reached Cordova unmolested.

Mu'tadid's next objective was the little principality of Silves, also governed by an Arab family, the Beni Muzaina,

whose ancestors had long possessed wide domains in that
part of the Peninsula, and had held important posts from
the days of the Omayyads.

Resolved to die rather than surrender, the prince of Silves
defended himself with the courage of despair. But the
Sevillan army—under the nominal command of Mohammed,
son of Mu'tadid, then barely thirteen years of age—conducted
the siege with no less vigour, and Silves was at length
stormed.[1] Ibn Muzaina vainly sought death where the combat
was fiercest; but Mu'tadid spared his life and merely exiled
him.   Then, conferring on his son Mohammed the government of Silves, the prince turned his arms against the town
of Santa Maria, situated on the Cape still bearing that name.
The Sultan Sulaimân had granted it as a fief to one Sa'îd
ibn Hârûn, of Merida—whose ancestry is unrecorded, and
who probably was neither Berber nor Arab, since men whose
descent was unknown to Arab chroniclers were usually
Spaniards.   On Sulaimân's death, Ibn Hârûn declared himself independent, and at his death his son Mohammed had
succeeded him.   The latter when attacked by the Sevillans
made but a brief resistance.

Mu'tadid united the district of Santa Maria to that of
Silves, and placed both under the governorship of his son
(A.D. 1052).

By these rapid conquests the principality of Seville was
greatly extended on the western side. Its expansion was,
however, still resisted towards the south, where the Berber
princes held sway. Most of these were then at peace with
Mu'tadid, and even recognised his suzerainty, or rather that
of the so-called Hishâm II. Mu'tadid, however, was by no
means content with this shadowy power; it was his intention
to exterminate the princes and seize their dominions; but
he proceeded cautiously, being unwilling to plunge into
so bold an enterprise until his success was assured by deep-
laid intrigues.

After the conquest of Silves he accordingly paid unexpected visits, accompanied by only two attendants, to two
of his vassals, Ibn Nûh, lord of Moron, and Ibn Abî Korra,
lord of Ronda. Considering the hatred with which he was
regarded by the Berbers, it seemed surprising that he should
thus place himself at their mercy; but Mu'tadid did not

---

[1] A.D. 1051 or 1052: for the storming must have taken place after the conquest
of Niebla and Huelva (A.H. 443), and before that of Santa Maria (A.H. 444). Cf.
Abbad., i. 252; ii. 123, 210.

lack courage, and in spite of his habitual perfidiousness he relied on the good faith of others. At Moron he was received with every mark of respect. Ibn Nûh assured him of the delight caused by his unexpected visit, entertained him with sumptuous hospitality, and renewed his assurances of fealty. But Mu'tadid had not come to bandy compliments or to hear professions of amity; his was a very different object. He came to discover how the land lay, and to win over, if possible, some personages of weight. He soon saw that the Arab population yearned to throw off the Berber yoke, and that when the time came, he could count on their support. With the aid of the gold and precious stones with which his attendants were provided, he even succeeded in corrupting several of the Berber officers, while the unsuspecting Ibn Nûh had no inkling of such intrigues.

Fully satisfied with the results of his visit, Mu'tadid extended his journey to Ronda. He was there received with equal honour, and his machinations met with equal, or perhaps greater, success, for the Arabs of Ronda were even more eager than those of Moron to free themselves from Berber domination—the Beni Abî Korra being, it would appear, harder masters than the Beni Nûh. Mu'tadid was therefore able to lay the train for a formidable conspiracy, ready to blaze into a revolt at the first signal.

Nevertheless he came near to paying for his rash enterprise with his life. One day, after a banquet, at which the wine had not been spared, he felt drowsiness stealing over him. "I feel weary," he said to his host, "and would fain repose; but let not that interrupt your merry-making; a brief sleep will refresh me, and I will then resume my place at the board." "As your lordship pleases," replied Ibn Abî Korra, conducting him to a couch.

In about half an hour, when Mu'tadid seemed to have sunk into a profound slumber, a Berber officer claimed the attention of the company, on the ground that he had somewhat of importance to deliver. Silence having been obtained, he proceeded in a low voice: "It seems to me that we have a fat ram here which offers its throat to the knife. This is a stroke of good fortune which we could never have dreamed of. Had we given all the gold in Andalusia for that man, it would have profited us nothing, and now he puts himself into our hands. He is a fiend incarnate; you all know it, and when he is dead no one will dispute with us the possession of this country."

A silence fell upon the revellers; but inquiring glances supplied the place of words, and since the idea of assassinating one whom they both feared and hated, and whose crafty wiles were known to them all, was only too attractive to men hardened in crime from their earliest days, their swarthy countenances displayed neither surprise nor repugnance. One alone, more loyal than the rest, felt his blood boil at the thought of treachery so infamous. This was Mu'âdh ibn Abî Korra, a kinsman of the lord of Ronda. His eyes flashing with generous indignation, he rose and said in a low but earnest voice: "In God's name, let us not do this deed! That man came hither trusting in our loyalty; his conduct shows that he believes us incapable of betraying him, and honour demands that we justify his confidence. What will our brethren of other tribes say when they learn that we violated the sacred rights of hospitality—that we murdered our guest? Accursed of God be he that doeth this deed!"

The Berbers were moved by these generous words. In reminding them so earnestly of the duties of hospitality Mu'âdh had thrilled that chord in their hearts which is seldom touched in vain among Eastern races.

Meanwhile, Mu'tadid, while he seemed to slumber, was acutely awake. In an agony of dread he listened to all that passed. Then, reassured by the effect of Mu'âdh's words, he feigned to arouse himself from sleep and rose to resume his seat at the table. The company started to their feet, and kissed him respectfully upon the forehead. Their embraces were the more effusive, since their consciences pricked them for having thought for an instant of speeding their guest to another world.

"My friends," said the prince, "I must shortly return to Seville; and now, on the eve of my departure, I cannot assure you too heartily how deeply your hospitality has touched me. I desire to present you with a few trifling tokens of my gratitude, though unfortunately the store of gifts which my servants carry with them is almost exhausted. But let paper and ink be brought to me, and let each of you tell me his name and mention his chief object of desire— robes of honour, money, horses, damsels, slaves, or what-not —and on my return to my capital, let him send thither a servant to receive the gift set apart for him."

The whole company eagerly fell in with the prince's wishes, and when Mu'tadid had reached Seville the

messengers of the Berbers flocked thither, afterwards returning to Ronda with splendid gifts for their masters.

The best possible relations now ostensibly existed between Mu'tadid and the Berbers; old animosities seemed
forgotten, and in their place a close alliance and cordial
friendship had sprung up. Six months later Mu'tadid
invited the lords of Ronda and Moron to a banquet, in
token, as he said, of his gratitude for their recent courtesy.
He also sent an invitation to Ibn Khazrûn, lord of Arcos
and Xeres, and at the time appointed the three Berbers
arrived at Seville (A.D. 1053).

Mu'tadid accorded them a magnificent reception, and,
as was customary, offered them, together with the chief
members of their retinues, the refreshment of a bath. On
some pretext, however, he requested Mu'âdh to remain
with him.

About sixty Berbers repaired to the building indicated
by the prince. After divesting themselves of their garments
in the vestibule, they entered the bathroom. This, as is
usual in Moslem countries, was built of stone lined with
marble, and surmounted by a cupola pierced with windows
glazed with ground-glass. The baths were of marble, while
flues, connected with a furnace and penetrating the walls,
maintained a high temperature throughout.

While the Berbers were luxuriating in the pleasures of
the bath, they heard a slight sound, as of masons at work,
but to this they paid little heed. After a while, however,
the heat gradually became oppressive, and they tried to
open the door. To their horror and despair they found the
doorway walled up. Every aperture had been closed.
They all perished of suffocation.[1]

Mu'âdh, after long awaiting the return of his companions,
grew uneasy, and ventured to ask Mu'tadid what delayed
them. The prince told him the truth, and seeing profound
terror depicted in the young man's face, added: "Fear
nothing. Thy kinsfolk and friends deserved to die, since
they dared to contemplate the thought of assassinating me.
I was awake and heard all. I shall never forget thy noble
words. It is to thee that I owe my life. Choose, then:
either remain here and share all my wealth, or, if thou wilt,
return to Ronda, whither thou shalt be escorted, laden with
rich gifts."

---

[1] An Aghlabite prince had rid himself in a similar manner of many of his
eunuchs and guards. *Cf.* Ibn Adhàri, i. 127.

" Alas! my lord," replied Mu'âdh, in a tone of profound dejection; " how can I return to Ronda, where everything will remind me of my loss ? "

" Remain, then, at Seville," said the prince, " and thou shalt have no cause for complaint." Then, addressing one of his attendants, he added : " See that a palace is immediately prepared for Mu'âdh's use. Let a thousand pieces of gold, ten horses, thirty damsels, and ten slaves be conveyed thither. I grant thee, moreover," he continued, turning to Mu'âdh, " a yearly emolument of twelve thousand ducats."

Mu'âdh therefore took up his residence at Seville, where he lived in princely opulence. Mu'tadid sent him daily some costly or beautiful gift, gave him a command in the Sevillan army, and when he consulted his Viziers upon affairs of state, the place of honour was always allotted to the preserver of his life.

Having deposited the heads of the Berber lords in the grim coffer on which he loved to feast his eyes, Mu'tadid despatched troops to seize Moron, Arcos, Xeres, Ronda, and other towns. Aided by the Arab population, and by the traitors who had sold themselves to Mu'tadid, the army had an easy task. The capture of Ronda, where Abû Nasr had succeeded his father, seemed likely to be a matter of some difficulty, for it stood on a lofty mountain, and, surrounded by precipices, passed for impregnable. But the Arabs rose *en masse* against the Berbers, and butchered them with indiscriminate savagery. Abû Nasr himself perished as he vainly sought safety in flight, for in climbing a wall, his foot slipped, and he was precipitated into the abyss below.[1]

The capture of Ronda greatly delighted the prince of Seville, and he immediately set to work to make the town stronger than ever. On the completion of the new fortifications he proceeded to inspect them, and in an access of joy and pride, composed this rhapsody :

"O Ronda! fairest jewel of my realm, never before didst thou boast such strength! The swords and spears of my valiant warriors have won thee for me : to me do thy inhabitants look up as their protector and their lord! Ah, that my life may endure, for then will mine adversaries' days

---

[1] The principal facts are given by Ibn Bassâm, who, however, makes two or three errors. Nuwairi gives Carmona instead of Ronda. (Cf. *Abbad.*, i. 250–1 ; ii. 129–30, 210, 214–15 ; also *Introd. à la Chron. d'Ibn Adhârí*, p. 86.)

be cut short! To keep myself well-breathed never will I cease to wage war upon them. Whole battalions have I put to the sword; the heads of my enemies, threaded like pearls, hang like a necklace on the gateway of my palace."

[AUTHORITIES: *Abbad.*, i. pp. 242, 247–9, 251–3; ii. 14, 60, 123, 209–11, 216; Ibn Bassâm, i. ff. 99, 108–9; ii. Art. on Ibn 'Ammâr; Ibn al-'Abbâr, pp. 50–1.]

CHAPTER VII

AL-MU'TADID (*continued*)

WHILE Mu'tadid, elated by success, indulged in extravagant transports of joy, Bâdîs fell a prey to ever-increasing anxiety. On hearing of the terrible fate that had befallen the Berber lords, he rent his clothes and roared with grief and anger. Then, when it became known that in an outburst of patriotic indignation all the Arab population of Ronda had risen like one man to massacre their oppressors, the gloomiest presentiments tortured his suspicious heart. How could he be sure that his own Arab subjects were not also in league with the 'Abbâdid against his throne and his life? This fear pursued him day and night, and goaded him to madness. Sometimes in a frenzy of rage, he ejaculated curses and inveighed against all the world; at other times, racked with fears and oppressed with gloomy forebodings, he preserved a mournful silence and drooped like a tree blasted by the lightning. And then—strange and menacing presage!—Bâdîs no longer had recourse to the wine-cup.

He was secretly maturing a horrible scheme. So long as there were Arabs in his dominions, he could never be safe for a moment; prudence, he thought, bade him exterminate them. He planned the deed for the approaching Friday, when all would be assembled in the Mosque. Since, however, Bâdîs did nothing without consulting his Minister, he informed Samuel of his design, adding that he was firmly resolved to carry it out, whether the Vizier approved of it or not. The Jew thought ill of the scheme, and tried to dissuade the prince, begging him to pause and reflect on the consequences of such an action. "Suppose," he said, "that all is carried out as you wish; suppose that you exterminate the Arabs, regardless of the danger of the attempt; do you think that those in the rest of Spain will ignore the disaster which has befallen their compatriots? Think you that they will quietly remain in their homes? Assuredly not! I see them in their fury rushing to arms :

I behold foes innumerable as the waves of the sea pouring
in upon you, and their scimitars flashing above your head!"
But Bâdîs was impervious to prudence and common sense.
He enjoined secrecy upon Samuel and made the necessary
preparations, issuing orders that on Friday the troops were
to parade fully armed, on the pretext that they were to be
inspected.

Samuel, meanwhile, did not remain idle; by means of
certain women of their acquaintance, he warned the principal
Arabs not to visit the Mosque on the ensuing Friday, but
to conceal themselves. The Arabs were thus put on their
guard, and on the appointed day the congregation in the
Mosque consisted merely of a few plebeians. Furious at
the failure of his design, Bâdîs sent for Samuel and reproached him with divulging the secret. The Vizier denied
having done so, and added: "It is easy to explain why the
Arabs did not attend the service. Since you paraded the
troops without any apparent reason, in a time of peace,
suspicions were naturally aroused. Instead of being angry,
you should render thanks to God: the Arabs guessed your
intention, they might have risen against you, and yet they
did not stir. Reflect coolly upon the matter, my lord; the
time will come, when you will agree with me." Perhaps
Bâdîs in his blindness would have even then persisted in his
obstinacy, but on a Berber sheik approving of the arguments advanced by Samuel, he admitted that he had been
in the wrong. He therefore dismissed the idea of exterminating his Arab subjects, but at the urgent solicitation of
the fugitives from Moron, Arcos, Xeres, and Ronda, who
had sought refuge at Granada, he determined to punish the
treacherous enemy of his race, and invaded the Sevillan
territory at the head of his own troops and the refugees.
The details of this war have not come down to us, but there
is reason to believe that it was a sanguinary struggle; for,
while the Africans were inflamed by a desire to avenge the
death of their compatriots, the Granadans were an object of
keener hatred to the Arabs than were the other Berbers.
They were looked upon as infidels, and enemies of Islam,
since they had a Jewish Vizier. "With thy sword thou
hast chastised a people who were no better than Jews,
though they call themselves Berbers!" So sang the Sevillan
poets when they celebrated Mu'tadid's victories. In the
eyes of the Sevillans war against the Granadans was a *jihâd*,
and so stubborn was their resistance that the invaders were

repulsed. The refugees were much to be pitied. Forbidden
to return to their homes by Mu'tadid, and forbidden to
remain at Granada by Bâdîs, they were compelled to cross
the Straits to seek subsistence. They landed near Ceuta,
but Sakôt, lord of that town, would have nothing to do with
them. Thus repelled on every side, at a time when a famine
was ravaging Africa, they almost all perished of hunger.

Mu'tadid then turned his arms against the Hammûdite
Kâsim, lord of Algeciras. He was the weakest of all the
Berber princes, and was soon compelled to sue for peace.
Mu'tadid permitted him to reside at Cordova (A.D. 1058).

On the completion of this new conquest, Mu'tadid considered that the time had come to drop the curtain upon
the comedy which, following his father's example, he had
thus far played, and to admit that the pretended Hishâm II
was dead. The reasons which had induced Abu 'l-Kâsim to
shield himself under the name of this monarch were no
longer valid. It was now universally recognised that a
revival of the old régime was impossible, and that the
Khalifate had fallen, never to rise again. Experience had
dissipated all illusions which may have lingered on this subject. The mat-maker of Calatrava had therefore become
an entirely useless personage. It may be that this man,
who showed himself neither to the people nor to the court,
had been long dead ; it may be that Mu'tadid, grown weary
of him, had slain him—as some chroniclers have asserted.
Only conjectures can be hazarded on this subject, for the
prince of Seville, when he chose, could veil his actions in
impenetrable mystery. What is certain is that in 1059
he summoned the principal inhabitants of his Capital, and
informed them that the Khalif Hishâm had succumbed, some
time before, to a stroke of paralysis. He added that prudence had dictated that this event should not be announced
publicly, during active warfare, but now that peace reigned,
the danger of divulging the fact had passed. He then
ordered the mortal remains of the mat-maker of Calatrava
to be interred with royal honours, and in his capacity of
hâjib he attended the obsequies on foot, and without his
tailesân : [1] he also informed his allies in the East of the
Khalif's death, and invited them to elect another monarch.
Naturally, no one thought of taking such a step. Mu'tadid
then, it is said, announced that the Khalif had in his will

---

[1] A kind of veil, covering the head and shoulders.

appointed him Emir of all Spain. All Mu'tadid's efforts
were henceforth directed to the attainment of this position,
and he determined to seize the former Capital of the monarchy. He was destined, however, to meet with a terrible
disappointment.

His troops had already made several raids on Cordovan
territory, when, in 1063,[1] he ordered his eldest son, Ismâ'îl,
the commander of his army, to occupy the half-ruined town
of Al-Zahrâ. Ismâ'îl demurred. For some time he had
been out of humour with Mu'tadid. He complained of
his father's harshness and tyrannical temper ; he declared
that he had often been exposed to great danger for lack of
a full complement of troops when there was a battle to be
fought or a fortress to be besieged. An ambitious adventurer fanned Ismâ'îl's discontent. This was Abû 'Abdallah
Bizilyânî, who had migrated from Malaga when that town
was captured by Bâdîs. Desiring to become *hâjib* at any
cost—under whom, or where, he cared not—this intriguer
had endeavoured to imbue Ismâ'îl with the idea of rebelling
against his father and setting up elsewhere—at Algeciras
for instance—an independent principality. Bizilyânî had
succeeded only too well : Ismâ'îl's irritation at the moment
when he received orders to proceed against Al-Zahrâ needed
but a trifling fillip to bring it to a climax, and unfortunately
Mu'tadid again refused to supply his son with additional
troops. Ismâ'îl in vain pointed out that with the small
force at his disposal he could not cope with such a state as
Cordova, and that if Bâdîs came to the assistance of the
Cordovans—which he could scarcely fail to do, since he was
their ally—the Sevillan force would be between two fires.
Mu'tadid turned a deaf ear to these expostulations—in his
rage calling his son a coward—and deeds nearly took the
place of words : " If thou delayest to obey me," he cried,
" thy head is forfeit ! "

Mortified and indignant, Ismâ'îl set out, and Bizilyânî,
whom he consulted, easily persuaded him that the moment
had arrived for carrying out the project so often discussed
between them. At two days' journey from Seville, Ismâ'îl
accordingly informed his officers that he had received a
letter from his father, enjoining him to return, on business
of much importance. Then, accompanied by Bizilyânî and
some thirty mounted guards, he galloped in hot haste to

[1] A.H. 455.

Seville.　Mu'tadid was not in the city, but at his castle of Zâhir, on the opposite bank of the river, and Ismâ'îl found the citadel of Seville weakly guarded.　He seized it during the night, loaded mules with his father's treasures, and to prevent any one from crossing the river and bearing the news to Zâhir, he sunk the craft moored below the citadel; then, taking with him his mother and the other ladies of the seraglio, he set out for Algeciras.

Notwithstanding, however, the care he had taken to prevent any rumour of his exploit from reaching his father's ears, the latter was informed of it by a trooper of his son's retinue, who disapproved of what had been done and swam his horse across the Guadalquiver.　Mu'tadid immediately ordered detachments of cavalry to scour the country, and sent messengers to the Governors of his fortresses.　The warnings were delivered in good time, and Ismâ'îl found the gates of every fortress shut against him.　Fearing lest the Castellans should combine to attack him, he implored the protection of Hassâdî, Governor of a castle situated on the summit of a hill on the borders of the district of Sidona. Hassâdî consented on condition that Ismâ'îl remained at the foot of the hill, and then, descending with his soldiers, counselled the young prince to be reconciled with his father, at the same time offering his mediation.　Seeing that his scheme had completely failed, Ismâ'îl yielded.　Hassâdî thereupon allowed him to enter the castle, with all the honour due to his rank, and at once wrote to Mu'tadid.　The letter declared that Ismâ'îl, repenting of his folly, entreated his father's forgiveness.　A reply was promptly received from Mu'tadid, and proved reassuring, for the prince expressed his willingness to pardon his son.

Ismâ'îl immediately returned to Seville.　His father left him in the enjoyment of all his property, but kept him strictly guarded, and beheaded Bizilyânî and his accomplices. Ismâ'îl himself, who knew but too well his father's duplicity, believed his pardon only a snare.　His mind was made up.　Suborning his guards and some slaves, he assembled them by night, gave them wine to stimulate their courage, and with them scaled a part of the palace which seemed open to surprise.　He hoped to find his father asleep, and determined to kill him.　Suddenly Mu'tadid appeared at the head of his body-guard.　The conspirators instantly fled.　Ismâ'îl contrived to surmount the city wall, but the soldiers rushing in pursuit, took him prisoner.　Frenzied with rage, his father dragged him within the palace, and dismissing all the attendants, slew him with his own hand. Mu'tadid then wreaked his vengeance on Ismâ'îl's accomplices, friends, servants, and even on the women of his harem. Hands, feet, and noses were cut off, and executions both public and private followed.

When his anger had cooled, the gloomy tyrant fell a prey to sorrow and despair. The son who had rebelled against him, who had sought his life, who had robbed him of his treasure and even of his wives, was doubtless very guilty, but it was in vain that he dwelt upon this thought; he could not forget how dearly he had loved him—for, with all his ruthlessness, the tyrant had a tender affection for his family. In that prudent son, wise in counsel, intrepid on the field of battle, he had seen the stay of his premature old age, and the continuator of his work. And now with his own hand he had shattered his fondest hopes.

"On the third day after this dreadful catastrophe," writes a Sevillan vizier, "I entered the presence-chamber with my colleagues. Mu'tadid's countenance was terrible to look upon; we trembled with fear, and as we saluted him we could scarce stammer a few words. The prince with a piercing glance measured us from head to foot; then roaring like a lion, he cried: 'Wretches! wherefore are ye silent? Ye gloat in your hearts over my misfortunes! Begone from my sight!'"

Perhaps for the first time that fierce spirit, that iron will, found itself broken; that apparently invulnerable heart had received a wound which time might slowly heal, but of which the scar would remain for ever. For the moment— leaving the Republic of Cordova at peace, and in mingled joy and surprise at her respite—he relinquished his vast projects; but they slowly revived, and Malaga reawakened his ambition.

After being thralls for several years to the tyranny of Bâdîs, the Arabs of Malaga daily cursed their oppressor, and it was to the prince of Seville that they looked for deliverance. They knew that he also was a tyrant, but of two autocrats they preferred him who was of their own race. They therefore came to an understanding with Mu'tadid, and hatched a plot. Bâdîs himself favoured their designs by his carelessness, for, sunk in almost ceaseless intoxication, he only concerned himself with affairs of state at rare intervals. On the day appointed, a general and irresistible

rebellion broke out in the Capital and in twenty-five fortresses; while simultaneously the Sevillan troops, commanded by al-Mu'tamid, son of Mu'tadid, crossed the
frontier to aid the insurgents. Taken unawares, the Berbers
were put to the sword; those who succeeded in escaping
owed their safety to the promptitude of their flight, and in
less than a week the whole principality was in the hands of
the prince of Seville. The castle of Malaga, garrisoned by
negroes, was the only stronghold which had not yet surrendered. Strongly fortified, and standing on the summit
of a mountain, it might hold out for a long time, and it was
feared that Bâdîs might profit by the delay and come to the
assistance of the besieged. Such at least was the opinion
of the insurrectionary leaders; they therefore advised
Mu'tamid to press forward the siege of the castle, to be
vigilant, and not to trust implicitly the Berbers who formed
so large a part of his army. This advice was prudent, but
Mu'tamid disregarded it. Indolent and unsuspicious, he
gave himself up to be feasted by the populace, who were
charmed by his affability, and he lent too ready an ear to
the Berber officers, who being in secret sympathy with
Bâdîs, and faithless to their commander, assured him that
the castle would soon surrender. The other soldiers, suspecting no danger, were off their guard and lost in self-
indulgence.

This carelessness was fatal. The negroes of the castle
found means of informing Bâdîs that it would be easy to
surprise the Sevillan army, and the Granadan troops were
soon on the march. They crossed the mountains so rapidly
and secretly that they entered Malaga before Mu'tamid
even suspected their approach. The Granadans had no
fighting to do; their task was merely that of cutting the
throats of unarmed and half-intoxicated soldiers. Mu'tamid
escaped to Ronda, but all the principality was once more
made subject to Bâdîs.

Mu'tadid's wrath may be imagined when he learnt that
by his son's culpable negligence, he had lost an army and
a splendid principality! Ordering Mu'tamid to be kept
prisoner at Ronda, the tyrant, forgetful of the remorse
which the murder of his eldest son had caused him, now
thirsted to inflict the death penalty upon Ismâ'îl's brother.

Ignorant of the intensity of his father's rage, Mu'tamid
sent him poems full of adroit flatteries. He eulogized his
generosity and clemency; he endeavoured to console him

by recounting his former successes. "What brilliant victories hast thou not gained," he wrote, "victories that future ages shall recall; travellers have spread thy fame in far-off lands, and when the Arabs of the Desert assemble in the moonlight to tell of knightly deeds, it is thine alone that they relate." Mu'tamid tried to exculpate himself by throwing all the blame upon the treacherous Berbers; he painted in the liveliest colours the grief that his failure had caused him. "My soul trembles, my voice and my sight fail me. All colour has faded from my cheeks, and yet I am not sick; my hair is white, although I am yet young. Henceforth nothing gives me pleasure; the wine-cup and the lute have no attraction for me; damsels whether coy or alluring have lost their empire over my heart. This is not fanaticism. No ascetic am I; nay, I feel the impetuous blood of youth still coursing through my veins; but all that could give me pleasure now would be to gain your forgiveness, and to thrust my spear through your enemies' hearts."

Mu'tadid softened by degrees, partly influenced by his son's verses—for he was very sensitive to good poetry—and partly by the prayers of a pious hermit of Ronda. He therefore permitted Mu'tamid to return to Seville, and was reconciled to him. But Malaga was irretrievably lost: henceforth Bâdîs was too much on the alert to give Mu'tadid another chance of a *coup de main*. It may also be assumed that the inexorable King of Granada, who always journeyed with headsmen in his train, punished by fire, sword, and dungeon the unfortunate wretches who had dared to rebel against him, and thus cooled the ardour of malcontents.

In the midst of all their woes, however, they had one consolation, and that a keen one—for with their hatred of oppression a spice of religious fanaticism was blended—the consolation, namely, of knowing that Jewish influence at the court of Granada was at an end.

On the death of Samuel, his son Joseph had succeeded him. The latter was an able and well-educated man, but he had not his father's art of earning condonation for the loftiness of his position by the modesty of his demeanour. He loved princely ostentation, and when he rode beside Bâdîs, monarch and minister were apparelled with equal magnificence. Joseph, indeed, was more kingly than the king. He completely dominated Bâdîs—who was, in truth, seldom sober—and to prevent the prince from making any attempt to deprive him of power, he surrounded Bâdîs with spies who reported his lightest word. Joseph was only nominally a Jew. It was said that he held neither the faith of his ancestors nor any other—despising them all. It does not appear that he openly attacked Judaism, but he declared publicly that the Prophet's religion was absurd, and he turned many a verse of the Koran into ridicule.

By his pride, his arrogance, his irreligion and his contempt of justice, Joseph had offended Arabs, Berbers and Jews alike. Numerous were the crimes imputed to him, and among a crowd of enemies an Arab Fakih, Abû Ishâk of Elvira,[1] was the most prominent. After sowing his wild oats this man had endeavoured to obtain a position at Court suitable to his birth ; but he had been thwarted by Joseph, who banished him. Abû Ishâk then turned Fakih, and full of hatred against Joseph, he launched the following virulent poem against the Jews in general:

"Go, my messenger, go and relate these words to all the Sinhejites— the full moons and lions of our days—these words of a man who loveth them, who pitieth them, and who believeth that he would fail in his religious duties if he did not give them salutary counsels :

"Your master hath done a deed at which his ill-wishers rejoice : though he could choose a minister among believers, he hath chosen an infidel! Through this minister, the Jews, contemptible outcasts, have become great lords, and their pride and arrogance know no bounds. When they least expected it they have obtained their heart's desire; they have attained the highest honours, so that the vilest ape among these unbelievers to-day reckons among his menials a multitude of pious and devout Moslems. And all this not by any efforts of their own. Nay! he who hath raised them so high is a man of our own religion! Ah, why did he not follow the example set him by devout princes of the days gone by? Why did he not humble the Jews and treat them as the vilest of mortals? Then in droves they would have led among us a vagabond life, the target of our aversion and disdain; then they would not have treated our nobles with arrogance and our saints with scorn; then would not these vile creatures have sat by our side and ridden with the nobles of our court.

"O Bâdîs, thou art a sagacious man, and thy conjectures are very sooth ; how then wast thou blind to the evil which would be done by these demons who lift up their horns in thy dominions? How couldst thou show affection for those bastards who have made thee odious in men's sight? How canst thou hope to establish thy power when these wretches pull down what thou buildest up? How canst thou place such confidence in a villain, and make him thy familiar friend? Hast thou forgotten how that the Almighty hath said in his Book that we should have no fellowship with the ungodly? Take not such men for thy ministers, but abandon

---

[1] A Todjibite ; died A.D. 1066. Cf. *Recherches* (1881), i. pp. 282–94.

them to curses, for the whole earth crieth out against them—ere long will it quake and we shall all perish. Turn thine eyes to other lands and behold how the Jews are treated as dogs, and kept apart. Wherefore dost thou alone take another course, thou, O prince beloved of thy people, descended from a line of kings, thou who surpassest thy contemporaries even as thine ancestors surpassed theirs?

" I came to Granada, and there I beheld the Jews reigning. They had parcelled out the provinces and the capital between them: everywhere one of these accursed ruled. They collected the taxes, they made good cheer, they were sumptuously clad, while your garments, O Moslems, were old and worn-out. All the secrets of the state were known to them; yet is it folly to put trust in traitors! While believers ate the bread of poverty, they dined delicately in the palace. They have supplanted you in your master's favour, O Moslems, and will you not oppose them? Will you suffer them? They slaughter oxen and sheep in our markets, and you eat without scruple the flesh of beasts unclean in their eyes![1] The chief of these apes hath adorned his mansion with incrustations of marble, and hath made fountains whence limpid waters flow; and while we stand waiting at the gate he scoffs at us and our religion. Great God! what disgrace! If I were to say that he is as rich as thou art, O my king, I should speak truth. Ah, hasten to slay him, and offer him up as a burnt-offering! Sacrifice him, for he is a fat ram! spare not his kinsfolk and his friends, for they too have heaped up great riches. Take their wealth; thou who hast more right to it than they. Think not that it would be treachery to slay them! Nay, but true treachery is it to suffer them to sit in high places. They have broken their covenant with us; who then would dare to blame thee if thou punishest the perjurers? How can we thrive if we live in the shade and the Jews dazzle us with the glory of their pride? Compared with them we are despised, and it might be deemed that we are the wicked and they are the righteous! Suffer them no longer to entreat us thus, for thou must answer to us for their conduct. Bear in mind that one day thou must render account to the Eternal for thy treatment of us, his chosen people, for whom is laid up everlasting felicity!' "

This poem had little effect upon Bâdîs, who reposed limitless confidence in Joseph, but it had a profound effect among the Berbers. They swore to compass the Jew's destruction, and the ring-leaders of the conspiracy spread abroad a rumour that Joseph had sold himself to Mu'tasim, King of Almeria, with whom the Granadans were then at war. When others, less credulous and less blinded by passion, asked what reason Joseph could possibly have for betraying a prince whom he entirely controlled, it was replied that when the Jew had compassed the death of Bâdîs and had handed over his dominions to Mu'tasim, he would also rid himself of the latter and mount the throne. It is scarcely necessary to say that this was mere calumny. The fact is that the Berbers wanted a pretext for overthrowing Joseph

---

[1] See *Recherches* (1881), pp. 288, lxxxi.

and plundering the Jews, upon whose wealth they had long cast greedy eyes. Believing that they had at last found such a pretext, they raised a riot and attacked the royal palace where Joseph had taken refuge. To escape their blind fury Joseph hid himself in a charcoal cellar, where he blackened himself as a disguise; but he was discovered, put to death, and fastened to a cross. The Granadans then proceeded to massacre the other Jews and plunder their dwellings, about four thousand persons falling victims to their fanatical hatred (December 30, 1066).

[AUTHORITIES : *Abbad.*, i. 51–4, 249–50, 253–9, 301–2 ; ii. 6, 60, 63–5. 207, 210 ; 'Abd al-Wâhid, pp. 66, 80 ; Ibn Khâkân, *Kaláyid*, i. 177 ; Ibn Khaldûn, f. 23 ; Ibn Bassâm, i. ff. 200–1 ; Dozy, *Introd. à la Chron. d'Ibn-Adhárí*, pp. 80–102.]

CHAPTER VIII

DEATH OF MU'TADID

THE rest of Moslem Spain was not less disturbed than the South; everywhere a fierce struggle for the fragments of the Khalifate was in progress; and now a flood was rising in the North which threatened to overwhelm all the Moslem States in the Peninsula.

For half a century the Christian Kings had been too much occupied with their own troubles to assume the offensive; but, about 1055, a change had taken place. Fernando I, King of Castile and Leon, at length found himself able to throw all his forces against the Saracens, who, it was obvious, were not in a condition to resist him. Fortune at length favoured the Christians; they possessed what their enemies lacked—a warlike spirit and religious enthusiasm. Fernando's conquests were therefore rapid and brilliant. He wrenched from Muzaffar, Badajoz, Viseu and Lamego (A.D. 1057), took from the King of Zaragoza the fortresses south of the Douro, made a formidable raid into the territory of Mamûn of Toledo, and advanced as far as Alcala de Henares. The inhabitants of this town informed their sovereign that if he did not hasten to their assistance they must surrender. Too weak to repulse the enemy, Mamûn adopted the most prudent course: presenting himself before Fernando he offered the king an immense quantity of gold, silver and precious stones, and, following the example of the rulers of Badajoz and Zaragoza, acknowledged himself his vassal and tributary.

Mu'tadid's turn then came. In 1063 Fernando burned the villages in the territory of Seville, and such was the impotence of the Moslem States, that Mu'tadid—although he was indisputably the most powerful sovereign in Andalusia —deemed it prudent to follow Mamûn's example. He therefore visited the Christian camp, offered splendid gifts to Fernando, and begged the king to spare his realm. Fernando seems not to have fathomed the craft and cruelty of the man with whom he was dealing. White hair and a

wrinkled forehead gave Mu'tadid a venerable aspect, though
he was not more than forty-seven years old; the cares and
toils of ambition, excesses, and perhaps remorse, had prematurely aged him.[1] It is, therefore, scarcely surprising
that the King of Castile was touched by his entreaties; but
thinking it advisable to take counsel with the nobles and
bishops of his kingdom, he summoned them to debate upon
the conditions which should be imposed on Mu'tadid.   The
assembly decided that the King of Seville should undertake
to pay an annual tribute, and deliver up to envoys whom
Fernando would send for the purpose, the body of S. Justa[2]
—a virgin and martyr under the Roman persecution.   Mu'tadid having accepted these terms, Fernando withdrew his
army, and, on returning to Leon, sent Alvitus,[3] bishop of
the Capital, and Ordoño, bishop of Astorga, to Seville.

These prelates had a twofold task to perform; namely,
to convey the Saint's remains to Leon, and to settle the
details of the tribute.   Unfortunately their endeavours to
discover S. Justa's relics were fruitless.   " It is evident, my
brethren," said Alvitus to his colleagues, " that unless divine
mercy comes to our aid, we shall return disappointed from
our arduous journey.   Let us, then, implore of God, during
three days of fasting and prayer, that He will vouchsafe to
reveal to us the hidden treasure that we seek."   The
Christians accordingly spent three days in supplication and
fasting, much to the detriment of the health of Alvitus,
who was ailing when he reached Seville.   On the morning
of the fourth day Alvitus called together his companions,
and thus addressed them : " Dearly beloved, let us return
heartfelt thanks to God, who, of His mercy, hath vouchsafed
that our journey should not be fruitless.   Heaven forbids
us, it is true, to take hence the remains of the blessed Justa,
but you shall bear with you to your country, a gift not less
precious—the body of the blessed Isidore, who wore the
episcopal mitre in this city, and who by his words and works
glorified all Spain.   I desired, my brethren, to watch and
pray throughout all the night that is past, but as I sat
oppressed by fatigue sleep overcame me.   A venerable figure

---

[1] The monk of Silos calls him " grandævus."

[2] SS. Justa and Rufina, patron saints of Seville, refused to sell earthen vessels
to be used in sacrifices to idols, and broke the image of Venus. Tradition relates
that the tower of the Giralda when twisted by an earthquake was set straight by
these saints. Cf. *Acta Sanct.*, July 19.

[3] Whom Ibn Khaldûn makes " King of Castile."   See *Recherches* (1881),
i. 104 *n*.

clad in the vestments of a bishop stood before me. ' I
know,' said he, ' wherefore thou and thy companions have
come hither; but since it is not in accordance with the
Divine Will that this city should be mortified by the departure of S. Justa, and since God, in His infinite mercy, nevertheless willeth not that thy companions should go empty
away, He giveth them my body.' ' Who, then, art thou
who speakest to me?' I asked. ' I am the Doctor of
Spain,' he replied, ' and formerly I was chief of the priests
of this city:[1] I am Isidore.' With these words he vanished,
and awaking I prayed God that if this vision was from Him,
He would vouchsafe that it should visit me three times.
Twice more the vision returned; twice more the old man
spoke the same words, and the third time he pointed out
the place where his body lies, striking the ground thrice
with his staff, and adding; ' Here, here, here, shalt thou
find my body; and that thou mayst know that no vain phantom speaketh with thee, a sign shall be given thee: as soon
as my bones are taken from the ground an incurable malady
will seize thee, and quitting thy mortal body, thou shalt
join us, crowned with the crown of the just.' And with
these words the vision faded."

Alvitus and his companions then proceeded to Mu'tadid's
palace, related the vision, and requested his permission to
remove the body of S. Isidore instead of that of S. Justa.
The bishop's narrative must have made a strange impression upon the prince. A sceptic and a mocker, Mu'tadid
held all religions in equal disdain, and believed in two
things only—astrology and wine.[2] He nevertheless listened
with imperturbable gravity to the bishop's long harangue,
and when it was ended, he exclaimed, in accents of profound
sorrow : " Alas, if I give thee Isidore, what is left to me ?
Nevertheless, God's will be done. Never could I refuse
aught to one so venerable. Seek, then, the body of Isidore
and bear it away, heedless of my regrets." The crafty Arab
saw how he could turn to account the piety of the Christians,
a weakness at which he laughed in his sleeve. Now that
he had a tribute to pay, he realized that if he feigned to
attach a high value to relics—if he did not allow them to

---

[1] S. Isidore (Isidorus Hispalensis), "Beatissimus Doctor Hispaniarum," died
A.D. 626. His body lay in the Cathedral between those of his brother, S. Leander,
and his sister, S. Florentina. See *Acta Sanct.*, April 4.

[2] In a poem which he composed at the hour of morning prayer, he wrote :
" Drink at the dawn of day ! This is a religious dogma: he who believeth it not
is a pagan."

be wrung from him save, so to speak, in self-defence, they might be made extremely useful.   He resolved to act like a debtor who, when pressed to liquidate his debt, proffers as part payment some worthless *curio* which he induces his creditor to accept as a rare antique of extraordinary value.   And so he played his part, for when the bishop of Astorga—whose colleague Alvitus was now dead—was on the point of setting out for Seville with Isidore's remains, Mu'tamid met the cortege, threw upon the sarcophagus a covering of brocade adorned with arabesques of exquisite workmanship, and with deep sighs, exclaimed: " Art thou then about to leave us, O venerable Isidore? Thou knowest how close was the friendship that united us ! " [1]

The following year, 1064, was a disastrous one for the Moslems.   Coimbra surrendered to Fernando after a siege of six months.[2]   By the terms of the capitulation, more than five thousand defenders of the town were handed over to the victor ; the rest were driven from their homes with barely enough money for their journey.   Nor was this all : the Moslems dwelling between the Douro and the Mondego were banished from the country.   Fernando then turned his arms against the kingdom of Valencia, over which the weak and indolent 'Abd al-Malik, who had succeeded his father 'Abd al-'Azîz in 1061, then reigned.   Siege was laid to the capital, but the Castilians, seeing that it would be difficult to storm, had recourse to a stratagem to deprive it of its defenders.   They made a feint of retiring, and the Valencians sallied forth in pursuit, clad in festal attire—so sure did they make of victory.   Their rashness cost them dear.   Near Paterna, on the left of the road leading from Valencia to Murcia, they were unexpectedly attacked by the Castilians.   Most of the Valencians were slain, and their king owed his safety only to the speed of his horse.   The capture of the fortress of Barbastro,[3] one of the most important strongholds in the North-east, was also a grievous blow. It fell into the hands of an army of Normans,[4] and the vanquished met with a terrible fate.   The garrison surrendered

---

[1] The monk of Silos relates the account of this embassy on the personal authority of the companions of Alvitus.

[2] See Ribeiro, *Dissert. chronol. e criticas.*

[3] Between Lerida and Zaragoza.

[4] Commanded, according to Ibn Hayyân, by "the commander of the cavalry of Rome"—*Kâïd Khail Rômia* (or *Rôma*). This seems to have been Guillaume de Montreuil, who was in the service of Pope Alexander II (1061–1073). For a full discussion, see *Recherches* (1881), ii. pp. 350–3.

on the condition that their lives should be spared, but on emerging from the town, they were almost all massacred. The inhabitants were no better treated. They too had obtained an amnesty, and were preparing to quit the town, when the commander of the Christians, disquieted by their numbers, ordered his troops to thin the ranks of the fugitives. The carnage which ensued did not cease until six thousand victims had perished. He then ordered all house-holders to return to the city with their wives and children. They obeyed, and then the Normans divided the spoil. "Each knight who received a house for his share," writes a contemporary Arab author, "received in addition all that it contained—women, children, and money; and the master of the house was his thrall. The householder was subjected to tortures of every kind, to reveal treasure alleged to be concealed. Sometimes the Moslem expired under these torments, and this of a truth was his good fortune; for if he survived, worse pains were in store for him, seeing that the infidels, by a refinement of cruelty, took delight in violating the wives and daughters of the prisoners before the eyes of their husbands and fathers. Loaded with fetters, the miser-able men were forced to be present at these horrible scenes, sobbing and heart-broken." Fortunate it was for the Moslems that the Normans soon quitted Spain, to enjoy in their own country the immense riches which they had amassed. Only a weak garrison was left at Barbastro,[1] and Muktadir of Zaragoza, after receiving from Mu'tadid a reinforcement of five hundred horsemen, took advantage of this fact to recapture the town in the spring of the following year (1065).

Fernando, however, did not relax his efforts to regain possession of Valencia, and although the king of that town had been reinforced by his father-in-law, Mamûn of Toledo, he found himself in a perilous plight, when Fernando fell ill, and was obliged to return to Leon. 'Abd al-Malik, however, had no great cause for congratulation, for in November he was dethroned and imprisoned in a fortress by his father-in-law, who incorporated Valencia with his own territories.

Soon afterwards, death delivered the Moslems from their most formidable adversary. Brave, pious, and virtuous, Fernando had been a model king: a saintly death crowned his noble life. On arriving at Leon (Saturday, December 24),

---

[1] 1500 horse and 2000 foot, according to Ibn Hayyân : *Recherches* (1881), ii. 345.

he immediately resorted for prayer to the church which he had dedicated to S. Isidore, convinced that the moment was at hand when his body would be laid at rest within its walls. After taking some hours of repose in his palace, he returned at night to the church, where the priests were celebrating with solemn chants the festival of the birth of Christ, and when they intoned, according to the liturgy of Toledo, the last nocturn of the Matins,[1] the *Advenit nobis*, the king mingled his feeble voice with theirs. At early dawn he asked them to say Mass, and having received the Eucharist, he was conducted back to his couch with difficulty, supported by his attendants.

On the morning of the morrow, Fernando was arrayed in his kingly robes and borne back to the church, where he knelt before the altar, and, laying down his royal mantle and crown, exclaimed in a clear voice : " Thine are the kingdom and the power, O Lord ! Thou art King of kings ; Thine is the dominion over the heavens and the earth. To Thee I render back that which Thou gavest, and which I have governed during Thy divine pleasure. Receive, I pray Thee, my soul delivered from the abyss of this world." Lying prostrate upon the pavement, he implored forgiveness of his sins, received the extreme unction at the hands of a bishop, and then, clad in sackcloth, and with ashes on his head, awaited death with an expression of faith and resignation. On the next day, Tuesday, at the hour of *Sexte* he yielded his soul to God, seeming to fall asleep with a calm and smiling countenance.

Shortly afterwards another death took place ; not that of a saint. Mu'tadid of Seville expired on Saturday, February 28, 1069. Two years before, he had incorporated Carmona with his kingdom, and a little later had laid the guilt of another murder upon his soul by stabbing with his own hand a Sevillan patrician, Abû Hafs Hauzanî. Mu'tadid's mind during the closing years of his life was a prey to gloomy presentiments. It was not that he feared that the throne which he had established by craft and treachery would succumb to the attacks of the Castilians ; the prediction of his astrologers, already referred to—that his dynasty would be overthrown by men not born in the Peninsula— directed his apprehensions elsewhere. For long he had believed that these strangers were his neighbours, the

---

[1] A service beginning at midnight.

Berbers; but he had no sooner exterminated them and flattered himself that he had arrested the judgment of the stars, than he began to suspect that he had been mistaken. On the other side of the Straits, a vast host of barbarians, summoned from their native deserts by a kind of prophet, was marching to the conquest of Africa with the rapidity and enthusiasm of the early Moslems. In these fanatics— whom the Spaniards named Almoravides [1]—Mu'tadid saw the future conquerors of Spain, and no arguments could dissipate the fears with which they inspired him. One day when he was reading again and again a letter which he had received from Sakôt, prince of Ceuta, informing him that the advance-guard of the Almoravides had encamped in the plain of Morocco, one of his Viziers exclaimed : " Why should this news cause you uneasiness, my lord ? Truly that same plain of Morocco is a fine place to dwell in, compared with our glorious Seville! What if these barbarians have en-camped there ? Between us and them there lie deserts and great armies, and the waves of the sea." " I am convinced," replied Mu'tadid, " that one day they will come hither; and it may be that thou wilt live to see it. Write instantly to the Governor of Algeciras, order him to strengthen the fortifications of Gibraltar, bid him be on his guard and watch with the utmost vigilance events on the other side of the Straits." Then fixing his gaze on his sons, he added: " Who can tell upon which of us the threatened blow will fall ? On you or on me ? " " Father," cried Mu'tamid, " may God spare thee at my expense! Let Him visit me with all the misfortunes, whatever they may be, which He destined for thee ! "

Five days before his death, feeling depressed in body and mind, Mu'tadid sent for one of his singers, a Sicilian, and bade him sing—it mattered not what. The prince had determined to regard as a presage the words of the song chosen. The singer happened to select one of those sweet yet melancholy ditties in which Arabic literature is so rich, beginning thus :

" Enjoy thy life while thou mayest, for soon it will be ended !
Mingle therefore wine with pure water, my beloved, and bring it hither ! "

Of this song he sang five verses, so that by a singular

[1] More correctly, "the Moravides," Ar. *al-Murâbitûn*, "those consecrated to the service of God," whence the modern " Marabouts."

but well-authenticated coincidence the number indicated that of Mu'tadid's remaining days.

Two days later (Thursday, February 26), the death of a daughter whom he adored—for as has been stated, his affection for his children, despite his cruelty, was profound—inflicted a bitter wound. On the evening of Friday he attended the funeral, almost heart-broken. When the ceremony was at an end, he complained of a violent pain in his head. A hemorrhage followed, which nearly choked him. His physician wished to bleed him, but Mu'tadid—an unruly patient—bade him wait until the next day. The delay hastened his death, for on the morrow, Saturday, the hemorrhage was renewed with greater violence, and after becoming speechless, Mu'tadid expired.

His son Mu'tamid, whose romantic career remains to be related, succeeded him.

[AUTHORITIES: Mon. Sil., c. 87, 89–93, 95–100, 105–6; *Chron. Compo.*, p. 327; *Chron Compl.*, pp. 317–18; *Abbad.*, i. 246, 251–2; ii. 61–2, 216, 219–20; Ibn Bassâm (MS. G.), last leaf; Makkarî, i. 111; ii. 748–9; 'Abd al-Wâhid, p. 70.]

CHAPTER IX

MUʿTAMID AND IBN ʿAMMÂR

BORN in 1040, Muʿtamid, at the age of only eleven or twelve, had been appointed by his father Governor of Huelva. Not long afterwards he nominally commanded the Sevillan army besieging Silves, and there he became acquainted with an adventurer, only nine years older than himself, who was destined powerfully to influence his career.

The name of this adventurer was Ibn ʿAmmâr. Born in a village near Silves, of poor and obscure Arab parents, he had commenced his education by studying literature at Silves [1] and Cordova; he then led a wandering life in Spain, earning his bread by composing panegyrics for all who could pay for them; for although poets of repute would have scorned to compose poems for any save princes and viziers, this indigent young man, unknown and ill-clad, who aroused mingled merriment and pity by his gabardine and skull-cap,[2] thought himself lucky if some wealthy *parvenu* deigned to throw him a few crumbs in exchange for verses which were not without merit. One day he reached Silves in dire distress, not knowing how to obtain provender for his mule, his faithful companion in privation. Fortunately he remembered a citizen able to assist him, if he would—a rich merchant of the town, who, though uncultured, had vanity enough to appreciate an adulatory ode. The poor poet wrote one, and sent it to his prospective patron, informing him of his distress. The gratified merchant sent the poet a sack of barley. Ibn ʿAmmâr on receiving so paltry a gift, thought that the merchant might at least have filled the sack with wheat; but the barley was a boon, and it will be seen in the sequel that the poet did not fail to show his gratitude to his benefactor.

Before long Ibn ʿAmmâr's poetic talent became known, and procured him the honour of an introduction to Muʿtamid.

---

[1] Or Shilb (in Portugal).
[2] Usually worn under the turban. See E. W. Lane, *Modern Egyptians*, ch. i.

He at once took the Prince's fancy, and since they were both lovers of pleasure, of adventures of every kind, and, above all, of good poetry, an intimate friendship was soon established between them. Accordingly, when Silves had been captured, and Muʿtamid had been appointed its Governor, he promptly created a Vizierate for his friend and entrusted him with the administration of the province.

The memory of those happy days spent at Silves, that enchanted spot where every one was a poet,[1] and which is still called the "Paradise of Portugal," never faded from Muʿtamid's mind. Love had not yet found a way into his heart; lively fancies sometimes possessed his imagination, but they vanished without leaving a lasting impress. For him it was a time of enthusiastic friendship, and to this sentiment he innocently abandoned himself with all the ardour of his years. Ibn ʿAmmâr, not having been brought up like the Prince in wealth and luxury, but having, on the contrary, been familiar from his earliest days with struggles, cruel disappointments, and poverty, had an imagination less fresh, less joyous, less youthful; he could not refrain from a vein of irony; on many points he was a sceptic. One Friday the two friends were proceeding to the mosque, when Muʿtamid, hearing the muezzin announcing the hour of prayer, improvised a verse, asking Ibn ʿAmmâr to add another rhyming with it: "Hark! the muezzin announceth the hour of prayer!" "And trusteth that therefore God will forgive him his many sins!" added Ibn ʿAmmâr. "May he find happiness, since he beareth witness to the truth!" continued the Prince; "Provided that he believeth in his heart that which his tongue uttereth!" retorted the Vizier with a smile.

It was a strange fact, but explicable when it is remembered how early he had learnt to know and mistrust men, that Ibn ʿAmmâr doubted even the limitless tenderness of the young Prince's friendship. Do what he would, he could not banish dark presentiments which invaded his soul—especially at carousals, for he was moody over his cups. In connection with this subject, an incident is related which, though a very singular one, seems authentic, since it rests on the best possible evidence, namely that of

---

[1] "Almost every peasant could improvise," Kazwînî, *Âthâru 'l-Bilâd*, ed. Wüstenfeld (1848), ii. 364. *Cf.* Nicholson, *Lit. Hist. of the Arabs* (1907), p. 416.

Mu'tamid and Ibn 'Ammâr themselves.[1]   One day, the
story runs, Mu'tamid invited Ibn 'Ammâr to supper.
After an evening of more than wonted revelry, when the
other guests had withdrawn, the Prince begged the Vizier not
to leave him : the latter obeyed, and soon they both yielded
to slumber. Ibn 'Ammâr had not long been asleep before
he heard a voice saying: "Unhappy man, one day he will
slay thee!" The Vizier started up in a fright : but after
seeking to banish from his mind these dark imaginings,
which he attributed to the fumes of wine, he at length
again fell asleep. For the second and the third time he heard
the same ominous words. Convinced that the warning was
supernatural, he could endure the situation no longer,
and rising noiselessly, he wrapped himself in a mat and
crouched in a corner of the porch, determined to escape
as soon as the gates were opened, and then to gain a sea-port
and embark for Africa.

Mu'tamid, however, on awaking and missing his
friend, uttered a cry of alarm which aroused the attendants.
The palace was ransacked for the missing Vizier. Mu'tamid
himself directed the search. Wishing to ascertain whether
the door had been opened, he entered the porch where Ibn
'Ammâr was concealed. The latter betrayed himself by
an involuntary movement beneath the mat which covered
him. "What stirs beneath that mat?" cried Mu'tamid,
and as the servants ran up Ibn 'Ammâr emerged, a truly
pitiful object, scantily clad, trembling in every limb, and
with downcast eyes blushing for shame.

Seeing him, Mu'tamid burst into tears. "Oh, Abû
Bakr!" he cried, "why dost thou act thus?" Then,
seeing that his friend continued to tremble, he led him
gently into his chamber and tried to draw from him the
secret of his strange conduct. For a long time his attempts
were fruitless. A prey to a violent nervous paroxysm, due
partly to fear and partly to the absurdity of his position, Ibn
'Ammâr laughed and wept by turns. At length, growing
calmer, he confessed all. Mu'tamid merely ridiculed his
avowal. "Dear friend," said he, clasping his hand affectionately, "the fumes of wine clouded thy brain, and thou hadst
a nightmare—'twas nothing more! Dost thou think it could
ever enter my heart to slay thee—thee, my life and my
soul? Nay, that would be suicide! And now dismiss

[1] 'Abd al-Wâhid gives it in Ibn 'Ammâr's words, and Ibn Bassâm as he had
heard it from several Sevillan Viziers who had heard Mu'tamid relate it.

these ugly dreams from thy mind, and speak of them
no more." "Ibn 'Ammâr," says an Arab historian, "succeeded in forgetting this adventure; and yet, when many
days and nights had rolled by, that which we shall recount
later, happened."

The two friends, when they were not at Silves, spent
their time at Seville, where they gave themselves up to
the enjoyment of all the pleasures afforded by that brilliant
and delightful capital. They often sallied forth in disguise
to the "Silver Field,"[1] on the banks of the Guadalquiver,
whither the populace, men and women, resorted for amusements. There it was that Mu'tamid met for the first time
her who was destined to be his life-long companion. Strol-
ling one evening with the Vizier in the "Silver Field," a
breeze happened to ruffle the surface of the river, and
Mu'tamid improvised this verse, challenging Ibn 'Ammâr
to add another:

"Lo, 'neath the gentle breeze the water is changed to a breast-plate!"

But as Ibn 'Ammâr pondered for a moment, a young
woman standing near them instantly supplied the anti-
phony:

"Armour glorious, indeed, for the warrior—were it but frozen!"

Astonished to hear the damsel improvise more promptly
than Ibn 'Ammâr, who was renowned for his talent in
that art, Mu'tamid regarded her attentively. Struck by
her beauty, he beckoned to a eunuch who followed his
master at some distance, and bade him conduct the im-
provisatrice to the palace, whither he hastened to return.
When the girl had been ushered into Mu'tamid's presence
he demanded her name and calling. "My name is I'timâd,"
she replied, "but I am usually known as Rumaykiyya, for
I am Rumayk's slave, and I am a mule-driver." "Art
thou married?" "No, my Prince." "That is well, for
I shall purchase thee and marry thee myself."[2] So long
as he lived Mu'tamid's love for Rumaykiyya knew no
change. In the Prince's eyes she lacked no endearing quality.
She has sometimes been compared to Wallâda, of Cordova,
the Sappho of her day.[3] The comparison, however, cannot

[1] "Pradera de plata."
[2] It was not until after his marriage that the Prince assumed the name of
Mu'tamid, which is formed from the same root as I'timâd.
[3] Daughter of the Omayyad Khalif Al-Mustakfi (†1025).

be wholly justified. Rumaykiyya could not rival Wallâda in learning; but she was not her inferior in sparkling conversation, prompt and brilliant repartees, quaint and mirthful sallies—and she perhaps surpassed her in natural and childlike grace, playfulness and roguishness. Her whims and caprices were the mingled delight and despair of her husband, who perforce humoured them at all costs, for nothing could induce her to relinquish whatever she had set her heart upon. Once, in the month of February, she watched, through a window in the palace of Cordova, falling snow-flakes, a rare spectacle in a country where the rigours of winter are scarcely known. Suddenly she burst into tears. Her husband tenderly inquired what ailed her. " What aileth me? " she replied between her sobs : " Thou art a barbarian, a tyrant, a monster! See how beautiful is the snow, how gently cling the soft flakes to the branches of the trees. And yet, ungrateful as thou art, thou never even thinkest of providing this lovely sight for me each winter; or of taking me to a land where the snow ever falleth!" "Yield not to despair, dear heart!" replied the Prince, wiping away the tears which trickled down her cheeks, " Thou shalt have snow each winter, even here; I promise it!"

Forthwith he ordered the Sierra of Cordova to be planted with almonds, that the white flowers of those beautiful trees which bloom as soon as the frosts of winter have passed away, might serve as a substitute for the snow-flakes so much admired by Rumaykiyya.[1]

On another occasion she saw some poor women treading out with their bare feet clay for brick-making. Again she burst into tears, and exclaimed to her husband: " Ah! how unhappy I have been since the day when you snatched me from the life of joyous freedom which I led in my cottage, and shut me up in a gloomy palace, loaded with the heavy chains of ceremony! Behold those women on the river bank! Would that, like them, I could knead the clay with my bare feet: but, alas! condemned by thee to be a wealthy Sultana, I cannot!" "Nay, but thou shalt!" replied the Prince with a smile.

Forthwith he descended into the court-yard of the palace, and ordered great quantities of sugar, spices, and perfumed essences of every kind to be brought thither;

---

[1] *El Conde Lucanor*, c. 14.

then, when the court-yard was filled with these precious
ingredients, he had the whole mass moistened with rose-
water, and kneaded into a pulpy mass. When all was
ready, the Prince exclaimed to Rumaykiyya, "Descend
into the court with thy train, I beg you; the clay is ready
for kneading!" The Sultana and her attendants descended,
and with bare feet indulged in a wild frolic in the aromatic
quagmire.

This was an expensive diversion, and Mu'tamid, upon
occasion, recalled the incident to the memory of his
capricious wife. One day when the Prince found it impossible to grant some extravagant demand, she cried:
"Ah! have I not cause for complaint? Assuredly I am
the most miserable of women! God knoweth that thou
hast never done the least thing to please me!" "Not
even on that day when thou troddest out the clay?" asked
Mu'tamid, in a plaintive voice. Rumaykiyya blushed and
did not pursue the subject.

It must be admitted that the ministers of religion never
pronounced the name of this sprightly Sultana without
devout horror. They regarded her as the great obstacle
to the conversion of her husband, who was, so they said,
dragged by her into a vortex of pleasures and luxury; and
if the mosques were deserted on Fridays, they imputed
the fault to her. Rumaykiyya laughed at their clamour;
in her heedless gaiety she little suspected that one day
these men would become formidable foes.

Notwithstanding his infatuation for his wife, Mu'tamid
still allotted a large share of his affection to Ibn 'Ammâr.
Once when staying with his friend far away from Rumaykiyya, he sent her the following acrostic:

Invisible to my eyes, thou art ever present to my heart.
Thy happiness I desire to be infinite, as are my sighs, my tears, and
    my sleepless nights!
Impatient of the bridle when other women seek to guide me, thou
    makest me submissive to thy lightest wishes.
My desire each moment is to be at thy side. Speedily may it be
    fulfilled!
Ah! my heart's darling, think of me, and forget me not, however long
    my absence!
Dearest of names! I have written it, I have now traced that delicious
    word—I'TIMÂD!

He ended the letter with these words: "Soon I shall see
thee again—if Allah and Ibn 'Ammâr permit!"

When Ibn 'Ammâr was informed of this final phrase, he addressed these verses to his friend:

"Ah! my Prince, I have no other desire than to do thy will; thou leadest me as the dazzling lightning on a dark night guideth the traveller. Wouldst thou return to her who is so dear to thee? Enter a swift shallop—I will follow thee; or leap into thy saddle—I still will follow thee. When by divine protection thou re-enterest the court of thy palace, suffer me to return to my abode, and without staying to ungird thy sword, throw thyself at the feet of the fair one with the golden girdle; then, recovering the lost days, thou wilt embrace her, and fold her to thy breast, while thy lips and hers murmur sweet words, as the birds welcome the dawn with their melodious songs!"

While friendship and love thus shared his heart, the young Prince led a life of felicity. Suddenly there was a catastrophe: his father banished Ibn 'Ammâr. This was a thunderbolt for the two friends; but what could they do? Mu'tadid's resolutions, once formed, were unshakable. Ibn 'Ammâr spent the dreary years of his exile in the North, and chiefly at Zaragoza, until Mu'tamid, at the age of twenty-nine, succeeded his father.[1] The Prince hastened to recall the friend of his youth, and asked him to select for himself the office he would prefer. Ibn 'Ammâr chose the Governorship of his native province. While regretting his removal to so great a distance, Mu'tamid nevertheless acceded to his request; but as his friend bade him farewell, the delightful memories of his sojourn at Silves, and those early emotions which had left no bitterness in his heart recurred to him, and he poured forth the following improvisation:

"Greet at Silves, O Abû Bakr, the beloved spots which thou knowest, and ask them if they still preserve my memory. Greet above all Sharâjîb, that fair palace whose halls are filled with lions [2] and dazzling beauties, so that it seemeth now a lions' den, and now a seraglio, and tell it that a youthful knight pines here burning with desire to see it once more. Ah, what nights have I spent there, beside a youthful beauty with slender waist and comely limbs. How often have damsels fair and dusky pierced my heart with their soft glances, as though their eyes had been swords and spears! What nights, too, have I passed in the glade beside the river with the fair songstress whose bracelet resembles the crescent moon! She fired me in divers ways—with her glances, with the wine she offered me, and with her kisses. Then, when she played a martial air upon her lute, methought I heard the clash of swords, and felt stirred with warlike

---

[1] The tradition that Ibn 'Ammâr returned to Court during Mu'tadid's lifetime seems less probable.
[2] As statues and bas-reliefs.

ardour. Sweetest moment of all, when casting aside her robe, she stood before me slender and supple as an osier branch! 'Lo, the bud,' I cried, 'hath unfolded and disclosed the flower!'"[1]

Ibn 'Ammâr entered Silves with a brilliant escort and with pomp such as Mu'tamid himself, when he was Governor of the province, had never displayed; but he atoned for this outburst of pride by a noble act of gratitude, for having ascertained that the merchant who had befriended him when he was a poor wandering poet still lived, he sent him a sack filled with silver pieces. This sack was that which the merchant had sent him filled with barley, and which Ibn 'Ammâr had carefully preserved. He did not, however, conceal from his former benefactor the circumstance that he had thought his gift a somewhat shabby one, for he sent him this message:

"If thou hadst sent this sack to me filled with wheat, I would have returned it brimming with gold."

Ibn 'Ammâr did not remain long at Silves. Unable to live without him, Mu'tamid appointed him Prime Minister, and recalled him to the Court.

---

[1] *Cf.* Shelley, *The Sensitive Plant*, pt. i.

[AUTHORITIES: 'Abd al-Wâhid, pp. 77, 79–83; *Abbad.*, i. 39, 84, 384; ii. 68–9, 88, 120, 151–3, 225–6, 234; Ibn Bassâm, ii. 98, 113.]

CHAPTER X

MU‘TAMID

SINCE both Mu‘tamid and his Minister loved poetry above all things, the Court of Seville naturally became the resort of the best poets of the day. It was, however, useless for mere poetasters to seek their fortunes there, for the Prince was a severe critic, who scrutinized every poem presented to him and weighed every phrase and syllable; but to men of real talent his generosity knew no bounds. One day he heard these verses recited :

"Verily observance of promises is a rare virtue ! Where shall we find the man who keepeth faith, or heedeth the words of his lips? Such a man is fabulous as the gryphon, or as the tale that a poet once was given a thousand ducats ! "

"Whose verses are these?" asked the Prince. "'Abd al-Jalîl's," was the reply. "What!" cried Mu‘tamid; "Doth a servant of mine, and one who is no mean poet to boot, call a gift of a thousand ducats fabulous?" and before long 'Abd al-Jalîl's incredible legend became veracious history.

On another occasion, as the Prince was conversing with a Sicilian poet who had come to Seville after the conquest of his country by Roger of Normandy,[1] a quantity of gold pieces fresh from the mint were brought to him. He handed two purses of these to the Sicilian, but the poet, not content with the gift—splendid though it was—cast covetous eyes on an amber statuette encrusted with pearls, representing a camel, which stood near. "My lord," he said, "your gift is magnificent—but it is heavy; methinks I shall need a camel to bear it to my house!" "The camel is thine," replied Mu‘tamid, with a smile.

Mu‘tamid, indeed, appreciated true genius of any kind —even for highway robbery, as the story of "Grey Falcon" testifies. Grey Falcon—he is known by no other name—

---

[1] Roger I (Roger Guiscard), with his brother Robert Guiscard, conquered Sicily (1060–77). He assumed the title of Count of Sicily about 1071.

was the most notorious robber of the day, the terror and
the scourge of the whole country. At last he was laid by
the heels, and condemned to crucifixion on the highway—
that the peasants might see that justice had been done.
The heat, however, being oppressive, there were but few
wayfarers on the day of his punishment. His wife and
children, weeping bitterly, clung to the foot of the cross
to which he had been affixed. "Alas!" they cried, "when
thou art no more, we shall perish of hunger!" Now Grey
Falcon had a very compassionate heart, and the thought
of his family suffering want troubled him sorely. Just then
a foreign chapman rode up on a mule laden with cloth and
other wares for sale in the neighbouring villages.

"Sir!" cried Grey Falcon, "I am, as you see, in a
woeful plight, but it is in your power to render me a great
service, not without benefit to yourself." "Name it," replied the chapman. "You see that well yonder?" "Surely."
"You must know, then, that when I blundered into the
hands of the accursed alguazils, I had just deposited a hundred ducats in that well—which happens to be dry. If you
will have the great kindness to get the money out, half of
it shall be yours. My wife and children will hold the mule
in the meanwhile."

Lured by the hope of gain, the chapman took a cord,
and fastening it to the well-head, lowered himself to the
bottom.

"Quick!" cried Grey Falcon to his wife: "Cut the
cord, take the mule, and flee in all haste with the children!"
His injunctions were instantly obeyed. The merchant yelled
like a madman, but the countryside was almost deserted,
and some time elapsed before a passer-by came to his aid ;
even then, since his would-be rescuer could not extricate
him single-handed, they had to await the arrival of further
assistance. When he had emerged from his subterranean
prison, the chapman explained to his liberators the cause
of his misadventure, and heaped many imprecations on the
robber who had so abominably cheated him. The story
quickly spread through the city and reached Mu'tamid's
ears. The prince ordered Grey Falcon to be detached from
the cross and brought to him. When the robber entered
the presence-chamber, Mu'tamid exclaimed: "Thou art
surely the most hardened scoundrel living, since even the
prospect of death could not wean thee from thy evil wiles!"
"Ah, my Prince," replied the brigand, "if you but knew the

delights of robbery, you would throw your royal mantle to
the winds and take to the road!"

"Impudent rascal!" cried Muʻtamid, with a burst of
laughter: "But, now," he continued, "let us talk seriously.
If I grant thee thy life, set thee at liberty, enable thee to
earn an honest living, and pay thee wages sufficient for thy
needs, wilt thou mend thy ways and abandon thy detestable trade?"

"To save his life, my lord, a man will do much—even
reform. Thou shalt have no reason to find fault with me."

Grey Falcon kept his word. Appointed commandant
of police, he henceforth inspired as much terror among his
former colleagues as previously among the country-folk.

Muʻtamid led a life of pleasure, without being over-
solicitous about affairs of State. In one of his poems he
insists that, "To live soberly, is not to live at all!" Much
of his time was occupied in feasting, and since he wished to
be renowned for his gallantry, the rest was devoted to the
youthful beauties of his harem. It was not that his love
for Rumaykiyya had cooled; on the contrary, it was ardent
as ever; but—since, by that strange code of love which ob-
tains in Moslem lands, transient caprices are not counted
as infidelities—if he paid homage now and again to other
ladies, Rumaykiyya, unchallenged queen of her husband's
heart, found nothing amiss in the circumstance.

The fair Amanda was bewitching, and when he pledged
her, the Prince found an added bouquet in his wine. Luna
was his companion when he studied the ancient poets, or
composed verses of his own; and if the sun peered indis-
creetly into the study, she was there to intercept his rays,
for, as the Prince remarked, "the Moon alone can eclipse
the Sun." More prudish and wayward, Margarita had
caprices at times; and when she was waspish Muʻtamid
took infinite pains to appease her. Once when he had incurred her displeasure, he wrote to her to exculpate himself.
"The Pearl" replied, but without placing her name at the
head of the letter, as custom dictated. "Alas! I am still
unforgiven!" cried the Prince; "for where is her signature?
She knows that I adore that name of hers, but such is her
anger that she will not write it. 'When he sees it,' she
says, ' he will kiss it!'[1] So, by Allah, he shall not see it!'"

And what a tender nurse was "The Fay!" The Prince

---

[1] *Cf.* Pope, *Eloisa to Abelard*, 7 *sq.*

prayed Allah to make him a life-long invalid, so that he might not cease to see that "gazelle with ruby lips" beside his pillow!

It would, however, be a mistake to infer that Mu'tamid wholly neglected to carry on the work initiated by his father and grandfather. Though he lacked their ambition, he nevertheless succeeded where they had striven in vain. For in the second year of his reign he united Cordova to his kingdom.

His father, it is true, had paved the way, and circumstances were exceptionally propitious. Six years before—in 1064—the aged President of the Republic, Abu 'l-Walîd ibn Jahwar, had resigned his office in favour of his two sons, 'Abd-er-Rahmân and 'Abd al-Malik. To the elder he entrusted the finances and general administration, and to the younger—his favourite—the military command. The latter son eclipsed his elder brother; but for a time all went well, under the influence of the able Vizier Ibn as-Sakkâ. This statesman inspired respect in all the avowed or covert enemies of the Republic—even in Mu'tadid, who realized that to attain his ends the Vizier must be overthrown. He therefore endeavoured to make him an object of suspicion to 'Abd al-Malik, and succeeded. Ibn as-Sakkâ was put to death, with disastrous consequences to the State. Most of the officers and soldiers, who had been much attached to the Vizier, resigned, while 'Abd al-Malik rendered himself hateful to the citizens by mingled harshness and indifference. He seems, moreover, to have gradually abolished all that remained of republican institutions.

'Abd al-Malik's power was therefore already tottering when, in the autumn of 1070, Mamûn of Toledo laid siege to Cordova. Possessing scarcely any troops—his cavalry had been reduced to two hundred men, and they could not be relied upon—'Abd al-Malik called upon Mu'tamid for assistance. Mu'tamid in response sent him strong reinforcements, and the Toledan army was forced to withdraw. But this was of no advantage to 'Abd al-Malik; for the leaders of the Sevillan troops, acting under secret instructions, agreed with the Cordovans to wrest the power from him and confer it upon the King of Seville. The plot was hatched without the slightest suspicion being aroused in 'Abd al-Malik's mind. On the morning of the seventh day after Mamûn's departure, he was on the point of leaving the palace to bid farewell to the Sevillans, who had announced their intention of setting out on that day, when seditious

2 U

cries fell upon his ears, and he saw the palace surrounded
by his so-called allies and the populace. He was immediately arrested, with his father and all his family.

Mu'tamid was proclaimed lord of Cordova, and the
Beni Jahwar were imprisoned in the Isle of Saltes; but the
aged Abu 'l-Walîd only survived his misfortune forty days.

The royal poet writes of this conquest as though it
were that of a somewhat haughty beauty:

"I have won at the first onset the hand of the lovely Cordova; that
brave Amazon who with sword and spear repelled all those who sought her
in marriage. And now we celebrate our nuptials in her palace, while the
other monarchs, my baffled rivals, weep tears of rage and tremble with fear.
With good reason do ye tremble, despicable foemen! for soon will the
lion spring upon you."

Mamûn, however, did not consider himself defeated; on
the contrary, he determined to be master of Cordova at
any cost. With his ally, Alfonso VI, he raided the vicinity
of the city, but was repulsed by the youthful Governor
'Abbâd, son of Mu'tamid and Rumaykiyya. Ibn Okâsha
next resolved to gain possession of the coveted city. He
was a fierce and bloodthirsty man—a former bandit of the
mountains—but he was not without talents, and knew
Cordova well, having already played a part in its politics.
Appointed Governor of a fortress, he set to work to start a
conspiracy within the city, and found it an easy task, for
discontent was rife among the citizens. 'Abbâd had, it is
true, raised fair hopes, but since he was too young to rule
personally, the authority had been vested in the Commandant of the garrison, Mohammed, son of Martin—of
Christian descent, as it would seem. Now this man, though
a good soldier, was cruel and vicious. The Cordovans detested
him, and many of them did not scruple to enter into relations with Ibn Okâsha. The latter, however, did not succeed
in wholly concealing his designs. An officer discovered that
the ex-brigand often came by night to the city gates and
held highly suspicious interviews with the soldiers of the
garrison. The fact was reported to 'Abbâd, but the prince
attached little importance to the matter, and sent the officer
to Mohammed, son of Martin. The latter referred him to
the subalterns. In fact, every one shifted the responsibility
to another's shoulders, and nothing was done.

Ibn Okâsha, however, remained on the alert, and in
January, 1075, a very dark and stormy night gave him the
opportunity of entering the town, with his men, unperceived.

They reached 'Abbâd's palace, and finding it unguarded, were on the point of breaking open the door, when the prince, awakened by the porter, ran up with a handful of slaves and soldiers and barred the way. In spite of his extreme youth he defended himself like a lion, and had cleared the vestibule of the foe, when his foot slipped, and, falling, he was instantly despatched by one of the assailants. His body was left in the street half naked, for, suddenly awakened, 'Abbâd had not had time to don his garments.

Ibn Okâsha then led his men to the house of the Commandant, who was so little expecting an attack that he was watching a dance of Almahs. Lacking 'Abbâd's bravery, he hid himself when he heard the clash of weapons in the courtyard, but his retreat was speedily discovered and he was despatched.

At dawn of day, as Ibn Okâsha was hastening from house to house, endeavouring to induce the nobles to make common cause with him, an imâm, on his way to the mosque, passed by 'Abbâd's palace. His eyes fell upon a body, naked and lifeless, which lay before it. Recognising, not without difficulty, the mud-stained corpse as that of the young prince, he piously performed a last act of homage, covering it with his cloak. He had scarcely departed before Ibn Okâsha came up, surrounded by that crowd which in great cities frantically applauds every revolution. By his orders 'Abbâd's head was severed from the body, and borne through the streets on a spear. At this sight the soldiers of the garrison threw down their arms and fled. Ibn Okâsha then assembled the Cordovans in the Great Mosque and bade them take the oath of allegiance to Mamûn. Although many of them were sincerely attached to Mu'tamid, so widespread was the reign of terror, that not a man disobeyed. A few days later, Mamûn arrived in person. He showed himself deeply grateful to Ibn Okâsha, loading him with honours and appearing to place implicit confidence in him. But in his heart Mamûn feared and hated this ex-brigand, hardened in crime, who, he knew, would assassinate him, if need be, as coolly as he had slain the young 'Abbâd. He accordingly sought eagerly for some pretext, or opportunity, of ridding his kingdom of so dangerous a subject. Mamûn did not, however, conceal his design from his courtiers, for one day, as Ibn Okâsha left the presence, the Prince heaved a sigh, and flushing with anger, muttered some ominous words; and when, a little later, a friend of Ibn Okâsha ventured to say a word in favour of the latter, Mamûn exclaimed: " Hold thy peace ! He who respecteth not the life of princes, is not fitted to serve them ! "

In the sixth month of his residence at Cordova—June, 1075—Mamûn died, poisoned. One of his courtiers was accused of the crime, but it is difficult to believe that Ibn Okâsha was not privy to it.

Meanwhile Mu'tamid had been overwhelmed with grief when the tidings reached Seville of the twofold calamity— the loss of Cordova, and the death of his first-born son whom he loved to idolatry ! Yet the dominant emotion in his noble heart was not grief nor the thirst for vengeance, but a sentiment of profound gratitude to the imâm who had so tenderly covered 'Abbâd's corpse with his cloak. The prince lamented that he could not reward him, and did not even know his name, but borrowing a verse composed by a poet of old on a similar occasion, he cried : " Alas ! he that covered my son with his mantle is a stranger to me, yet I know him for a noble and generous man ! "

For three years the efforts made by Mu'tamid to recover Cordova and avenge his son's death were fruitless, but at length, on Tuesday, September 4, 1078, the city was stormed. As Mu'tamid entered by one gate, Ibn Okâsha fled by another ; but he was pursued by cavalry, who over-took him. Knowing that he could look for no mercy at the hands of a father whose son he had murdered, the former brigand resolved at least to sell his life dearly, and charged his enemies like an infuriated bull ; but he was overwhelmed by superior numbers. By Mu'tamid's orders his body was crucified beside a dog's, and the conquest of Cordova was speedily followed by the subjugation of all the Toledan territories between the Guadalquiver and the Guadiana.

These were brilliant successes, but there was another side to the shield. Compared with the other Andalusian tyrants, Mu'tamid was a powerful prince ; and yet, like them, he was a tributary. His first suzerain had been Garcia, King of Galicia, third son of Fernando, but Alfonso VI had occupied this position since coming into possession of the realms of his two brothers, Sancho and Garcia. Now Alfonso was an extremely unpleasant suzerain : not content with a yearly tribute, he threatened from time to time to seize the states of his Arab vassals. On one occasion he in-vaded Sevillan territory at the head of a large army. Inde-

scribable consternation reigned among the Moslems, who
were too weak to defend themselves. The Prime Minister,
Ibn 'Ammâr, alone did not despair. He did not rely upon
the Sevillan troops—it would indeed have been futile to pit
them against the Christian army—but he was acquainted
with Alfonso, whose Court he had often visited, and knew
him to be ambitious, yet as easily managed as an Arab, by
anyone who humoured his tastes and foibles. It was upon
Alfonso's weakness, therefore, that Ibn 'Ammâr resolved to
work, and instead of organizing armed resistance he ordered
a chess-board to be made of workmanship so exquisite that
no king possessed its equal. The men were of ebony and
sandal-wood inlaid with gold. Provided with this work of
art, he visited, under some pretext, Alfonso's camp, and
was courteously received—for Ibn 'Ammâr was one of the
few Moslems whom the King held in esteem. One day
Ibn 'Ammâr showed his chess-board to a Castilian noble
who stood high in Alfonso's favour. The noble described
it to the King, and the latter asked Ibn 'Ammâr whether
he was a skilled chess-player. " My friends consider that I
play a good game," replied the Minister. " I am told that
you possess a beautiful chess-board." " It is true, Sire."
" May I see it ? " " Assuredly ; but on one condition—
that we play a game, and that if you win, the board is
yours, but if you are vanquished, I have the right to
demand what I will." " Be it so." The board was
brought, and Alfonso, amazed at the beauty and delicacy
of the workmanship, crossed himself and exclaimed :
" Marvellous ! I should never have imagined that a chess-
board could be made with such art ! " After feasting his
eyes on it, he added : " What were the conditions you
proposed ? " Ibn 'Ammâr repeated them. " Nay ! " cried
the King, " never will I play for an unknown stake ; you
might make a request which I could not grant." " As
you will, Sire," replied Ibn 'Ammâr coldly, and he ordered
the attendants to take the board back to his tent. The
interview was at an end ; but Ibn 'Ammâr was not a man
to be easily disheartened. In strict confidence he informed several Castilian nobles what he intended to demand of Alfonso if he won the game, and promised them
large sums if they would assist him. Greedy for gold,
and reassured as to Ibn 'Ammâr's designs, they consented
to perform their part, and when Alfonso—who was consumed with the desire of possessing such a marvel—con-

sulted the nobles on the subject, they replied: "If you win, Sire, you will be the owner of a treasure which every king will envy; and if you lose, what, after all, can this Arab demand? If he makes an extravagant request, are we not here, and cannot we bring him to reason?" Alfonso yielded to their arguments, and requested Ibn 'Ammâr to return, with his wondrous chess-board. "I accept your conditions," said the King; "let us begin the game." "With great pleasure," replied Ibn 'Ammâr; "but let us strictly observe the rules, and let witnesses named by me be present." The King consented, and when the Castilian nobles specified by Ibn 'Ammâr arrived the game began. Alfonso was beaten.

"I have won the right to ask of you what I will?" said Ibn 'Ammâr. The King assented. "I ask you to lead your army back to your own country!" Alfonso turned pale. He strode up and down the hall in fevered excitement, seated himself, and again sprang to his feet. "I am trapped!" he at length exclaimed to his nobles: "And ye are the cause of it! I feared some such request from this man; but ye reassured me, and bade me make my mind easy: and now I reap the fruit of your abominable advice!" Then, after a few moments of silence, the King added: "After all, why should I adhere to this condition? I throw it to the winds! I shall continue my advance!" "Sire," said the Castilians, "that would be a breach of honour: you, the mightiest king in Christendom, are surely incapable of breaking your word."

Alfonso at length grew calmer. "Well," he said, "I shall keep my word; but to compensate for my discomfiture, I shall exact at least a double tribute this year."

"You shall receive it, Sire," replied Ibn 'Ammâr. The Minister immediately took steps to provide the King with the money he demanded, and Seville, threatened by an alarming invasion, was relieved from her fears by the skill and tenacity of her Prime Minister.[1]

[1] About 1466, Boabdil al-Zagal played a game of chess with Pedro Fajardo, Governor of Lorca, the stakes being respectively Almeria and Lorca. Boabdil won, but his opponent baulked him of his prize. Cascalès, *Discursos históricos de Murcia*, f. 118.

[AUTHORITIES: *Abbad.*, i. 46–8, 322–4, 388, 391–2; ii. 16, 30, 35, 89, 146, 148, 222, 224–5; 'Abd al-Wâhid, pp. 72–3, 83–5, 90; Ibn Khaldûn, p. 25; Ibn Bassâm, i. ff. 158–60 (citing Ibn Hayyân); Ibn al-Kasîra (*ap.* Ibn al-Khatîb, MS. P., f. 51); Lucas de Tuy, p. 100; *Chron. Compo.*, p. 327.]

CHAPTER XI

THE FALL OF IBN 'AMMÂR

NOT content with having preserved the kingdom of Seville, Ibn 'Ammâr schemed to enlarge its borders. The principality of Murcia especially had attractions for his ambition. At one time it had formed part of Zuhair's dominions, and it was afterwards attached to the kingdom of Valencia; but at the period we have now reached it was independent. The reigning prince was Abû 'Abd-er-Rahmân ibn Tâhir, an Arab of the tribe of Kais. He was immensely rich—owning half the country—he was moreover a man of enlightened intellect, but his army was scanty, and his principality would prove an easy prey. Ibn 'Ammâr became aware of this when, in 1078, he passed through Murcia to visit, for an unrecorded reason, the Count of Barcelona, Raymond Berenger II, surnamed "Tow-head" from his abundant locks. Ibn 'Ammâr then took the opportunity to enter into friendly relations with certain Murcian nobles who were dissatisfied with Ibn Tâhir, or who, at any rate, were ready to betray him for a consideration, and on reaching Raymond's court the Vizier offered the Count ten thousand ducats if he would aid him in conquering Murcia. The Count accepted the proposal, and as a guarantee for the execution of the treaty, entrusted his nephew to Ibn 'Ammâr. For his part, the Vizier promised that if the money was not forthcoming by the date fixed, Mu'tamid's son, Rashîd, who commanded the Sevillan army, should serve as a hostage. Mu'tamid, however, was ignorant of this clause of the treaty, which Ibn 'Ammâr, convinced that the money would arrive in time, thought would not become applicable.

The Sevillan troops took the field in concert with those of Raymond, and attacked the principality of Murcia, but since Mu'tamid, with habitual carelessness, had let the stipulated date pass by, the Count suspected that Ibn 'Ammâr had deceived him, and arrested the Vizier as well as Rashîd. The Sevillan soldiers tried to liberate them, but were repulsed and forced to retreat.

Mu'tamid was at the time on his way to Murcia,

accompanied by the Count's nephew ; but since he marched slowly, he had only reached the bank of the Guadiana-menor, which he could not cross since it was in flood, when fugitives from his army appeared on the opposite bank. Among them were two horsemen to whom Ibn 'Ammâr had given instructions. They urged their horses into the stream, and crossing it, informed Mu'tamid of the deplorable events which had happened. They added that Ibn 'Ammâr hoped soon to be set at liberty, and begged Mu'tamid, in his name, to remain where he was. Mu'tamid did not take this advice. Dismayed at the news, and uneasy about his son's fate, he withdrew to Jaen, after putting the Count's nephew in fetters.

Ten days later, Ibn 'Ammâr, who had been released, arrived near Jaen ; but fearing Mu'tamid's wrath, he did not venture to enter his presence, and sent him these verses :

"Shall I be swayed by my own forebodings, or shall I lend an ear to my comrades' counsel ? Shall I execute my design, or remain here with my escort ? When I obey the promptings of my heart, I advance, sure to find the arms of my friend open to welcome me ; but cold reason makes me retrace my steps. Friendship drags me on, but the memory of my fault restrains me. Strange are the decrees of destiny! Who could have predicted that the day would come when I should be happier far from thee than at thy side ? I fear thee, because thou hast the right to deprive me of life—I trust in thee, because I love thee with all my heart. Have pity on him whose affection thou knowest to be immutable, and whose only merit is loving thee sincerely. I have done naught to give a handle to those who are envious of me, nothing which argues negligence or rashness on my part; but thou hast exposed me to a terrible calamity; thou hast blunted my sword—nay, thou hast broken it. Of a truth if I did not recall the numberless bounties thou hast bestowed upon me, like rain on the branches of trees, I should not thus yield myself a prey to torments, and I should not say that the fault was mine. On my knees I implore' thy clemency, I entreat thy pardon ; but were I blasted by the bitter north-wind of thy displeasure, I should cry, ' O Zephyr refreshing to my heart!' ''

Mu'tamid, who must have been aware that the fault was his own, could not resist Ibn 'Ammâr's appeal, and replied thus :

"Come, and once more take thy place at my side ! Come without fear, for honours await thee, and not reproaches. Know that I love thee too much to distress thee ; naught can be more pleasing to me than to see thee happy. When thou comest, thou will find me, as ever, ready to pardon the offender, and clement towards my friends. I shall treat thee with kindness as of yore, and I shall pardon thy fault, if fault there be ; for the Eternal hath not implanted in me a hard heart, and it is not my wont to forget an old and sacred friendship."

Reassured by these words, Ibn 'Ammâr flew to his sovereign's feet. The two friends decided to offer the Count his nephew's liberty, and the ten thousand ducats to which he was entitled, provided that Rashîd was set free. But Raymond was not content with the stipulated sum; he demanded thirty thousand ducats. Since Mu'tamid had not so much money available, he had the amount coined with a large admixture of alloy. Fortunately, the Count did not discover the fraud until Rashîd had been released.

In spite of the failure of his first attempt, Ibn 'Ammâr did not cease to covet Murcia. He declared that he had received very encouraging letters from some of the Murcian nobles, and succeeded in persuading Mu'tamid to let him besiege the city with the Sevillan army.

On reaching Cordova he halted for twenty-four hours, to add the cavalry in that city to his troops. He spent the night with Fath [1] the Governor, and so enchanted was he with Fath's witty and sparkling conversation, that when a eunuch came to announce that day was breaking, he improvised this couplet:

" Begone, thou fool! For me the whole night hath been dawn!
Could it be aught else, with Fath as my companion ? "

Proceeding on his march, he drew near to a castle [2] which still bore the name of Balj, the chief of the Syrian Arabs in the eighth century, and of which an Arab belonging to Balj's tribe—that of the Koshair—was Governor. This Arab, Ibn Rashîk by name, came to meet the Vizier, and begged him to repose in his castle. Ibn 'Ammâr accepted the invitation. The castellan entertained him magnificently, and omitted no means of enlisting his goodwill. He was only too successful. Ibn 'Ammâr at once reposed confidence in him; never had it been more misplaced.

Accompanied by his new friend, the Vizier set out to besiege Murcia. Mula speedily surrendered. This was a severe blow to the Murcians, for their supplies came through that district. Ibn 'Ammâr therefore felt confident that the city would soon capitulate, and entrusting Mula to the care of Ibn Rashîk, with whom he left a detachment of cavalry, he returned to Seville with the rest of the army. After his arrival he received letters from his lieutenant, to

---

[1] A son of Mu'tamid. [2] Perhaps Velez Rubio.

the effect that Murcia was devastated by famine, and that the principal citizens, to whom he had offered lucrative posts, had agreed to assist the besiegers. "To-morrow, or the day after," said Ibn 'Ammâr, "we shall hear that Murcia has fallen." He was right: the gates were treacherously opened to Ibn Rashîk; Ibn Tâhir was thrown into prison, and all the Murcians swore allegiance to Mu'tamid.

As soon as Ibn 'Ammâr, to his great joy, had heard this news, he asked Mu'tamid's permission to visit the conquered city. Mu'tamid granted it without hesitation. Thereupon the Vizier, wishing to reward the Murcians lavishly, procured a large number of horses and mules from the royal stables, and borrowing others from his friends, to the number of two hundred in all, he loaded them with costly products of the loom, and set out on his march with flying banners and tuck of drum. In each town which he passed through he replenished the public treasury. His entry into Murcia was a triumphal procession. On the morrow he held an audience and assumed royal airs—wearing a tall head-dress, such as his master was wont to don on formal occasions, and writing at the foot of petitions presented to him: "Be it so: if God willeth!" without mention of Mu'tamid's name.

Conduct so presumptuous smacked of treason: Mu'tamid, at any rate, thought so. But his emotion was rather one of profound sorrow and discouragement than of anger: he saw the dream in which he had indulged for twenty-five years suddenly fading. The instincts of his heart had been deceitful. Ibn 'Ammâr's friendship, his protestations of disinterestedness, of immutable devotion—all were falsehood and hypocrisy! The Vizier, however, was perhaps less culpable than he appeared in his master's eyes. His vanity, it is true, was excessive and ridiculous, but it is far from certain that he contemplated rebellion against his benefactor. Of a less ardent and impressionable character than Mu'tamid, the Vizier had not fully reciprocated his sovereign's enthusiastic and passionate friendship. And yet he had a real affection for the king, as the verses which he sent in reply to Mu'tamid's reproaches testify:

"Nay, thou deceivest thyself when thou declarest that the vicissitudes of fortune have changed me! The love which I bear towards my aged mother, Shams, is less ardent than that which I feel for thee. Dear friend, how cometh it that thy loving-kindness doth not shine on me, as lightning pierceth the darkness of night? Why doth not one kind word come to refresh me like a gentle breeze? I suspect that infamous men, whom I

well know, have conspired to poison our amity. Canst thou thus draw back
thy hand after a friendship of twenty-five years ?—years of unalloyed happiness, which have sped without yielding thee any cause of complaint against
me, and during which I have done no ill deed ? Wilt thou thus draw back
thy hand, and leave me a prey to the talons of destiny ? What am I but
thy obedient and submissive slave ? Ponder awhile ; be not hasty ; oft-
times he who hasteneth stumbleth, while he who walketh heedfully
reacheth his goal. Ah ! thou will think of me when the links which
unite us are snapped, and none but false and self-seeking friends are left
to thee ! Thou wilt seek for me when there is none at hand to give thee
good counsel, and when I am not there to serve as a whetstone to other's
wits."

A single hour of unreserved conversation would, perhaps, have dissipated Mu'tamid's misgivings, and reconciled
two friends whose natures were so sympathetic. But,
alas ! the Prince and the Vizier were far asunder, and the
latter had at Seville a crowd of enemies who were only too
eager to calumniate him, to blacken him in the monarch's eyes,
and to put a malicious interpretation upon his most trivial
acts and words. The " infamous men " of whom Ibn 'Ammâr
spoke in his poem—and of whom the most conspicuous was
Abû Bakr ibn Zaidûn,[1] then the most influential courtier—
had indeed so worked upon Mu'tamid's mind that he had
already conceived doubts of Ibn 'Ammâr's fidelity when the
Vizier bade him farewell on starting for Murcia. It must be
added that Ibn 'Ammâr had no less dangerous an enemy
in Ibn 'Abd al-'Azîz, prince of Valencia and a friend of Ibn
Tâhir.

On reaching Murcia, Ibn 'Ammâr had intended to treat
Ibn Tâhir with all courtesy. He accordingly sent him an
assortment of robes of honour in order that he might please his
fancy ; but Ibn Tâhir, whose naturally caustic humour was
embittered by the loss of his principality, replied to Ibn
'Ammâr's messenger : " Tell your master that I do but ask
of him a gabardine and a skull-cap." Ibn 'Ammâr received
this reply when surrounded by his courtiers, and bit his lip
in anger. " I understand the meaning of these words," he
said at length : " that was the costume I wore when, poor
and obscure, I recited my verses to him." Nor did he
pardon Ibn Tâhir for this bitter wound to his pride.
Changing his intentions, he imprisoned him in the fortress
of Monteagudo.[2] Yielding to the solicitations of Ibn 'Abd
al-'Azîz, Mu'tamid, however, sent orders to his Vizier to

---

[1] Son of the poet Abû 'l-Walîd ibn Zaidûn.
[2] A league from Murcia : the ruins of the ancient castle still exist.

release Ibn Tâhir. This order was disregarded. The prisoner, nevertheless, succeeded in escaping, by the help of 'Abd al-'Azîz, and took up his abode in Valencia. Ibn 'Ammâr was highly enraged, and composed a poem inciting the Valencians to revolt against their prince. It contained the following passage:

"Oh, inhabitants of Valencia, rise like one man against the Beni 'Abd al-'Azîz! Proclaim your just grievances, and choose you another king—a king who can defend you against your enemies! Be he Mohammed or Ahmad,[1] he must be better than the Vizier who hath disgraced your city, like a shameless husband who maketh his own wife a harlot! He hath harboured a man rejected by his own subjects. He hath brought a bird of ill omen into your midst; he hath given you as fellow-citizen a man vile and infamous. Ah! I must cleanse that brow which a girl without a bracelet, a debased slave, hath buffeted. Thinkest thou that thou canst escape the vengeance of one who slackeneth not in pursuit of his foe even when the night showeth no stars? By what crafty wiliness canst thou escape the avenging hands of a brave warrior of the Beni 'Ammâr, who is followed by a forest of spears? Soon shalt thou see him approach with an unnumbered host! Valencians! I give you sage counsel: march in your might against that palace which concealeth so many infamies within its walls; seize the treasures of its vaults; level it with the ground; let its ruins alone testify that it once existed!"

Mu'tamid, who was already much incensed with Ibn 'Ammâr, thus parodied this effusion:

"By what crafty wiliness canst thou escape the avenging hands of a brave warrior of the Beni 'Ammâr: of the men who but yesterday prostrated themselves in unutterable baseness at the feet of every lord, of every prince, of every monarch: who deemed themselves happy when they received from their masters a morsel a little larger than did the other menials: who, as vile executioners, beheaded criminals, and who are exalted from the basest condition to the highest dignities?"

These verses vastly pleased Ibn 'Abd al-'Azîz. Ibn Ammâr himself tried to stifle his wrath, but, choked with anger, launched a yet more scathing lampoon against Mu'tamid, Rumaykiyya, and the 'Abbâdids in general. The adventurer born in a hovel, whom Mu'tamid's generosity had raised from nonentity, dared to reproach the 'Abbâdids with having been merely obscure husbandmen of the hamlet of Jaumîn—"that capital of the universe," as he called it with bitter irony.

"Thou hast chosen among the daughters of the people," he continued, "Rumayk's slave, whom her master would gladly have given for a yearling camel. She hath borne thee wantons for daughters, and

---

[1] "Whoever he may be."

puny dwarfs that shame thee for sons. Mu'tamid! I will blaze abroad thy
dishonour: I will rend the veil that covereth thy sins! Ay, in emulation
of the knights of old, thou defendest thy villages, and yet, wittol, thou art
complaisant when thy wives are faithless!"

Some remaining sense of shame prevented Ibn 'Ammâr
from showing these verses—composed, as they were, in a
frenzy of rage—to any except his most intimate friends;
but among these was a rich Eastern Jew, in whom he
reposed complete confidence, little thinking that he was
an agent of Ibn 'Abd al-'Azîz. The Jew easily contrived
to procure a copy of the satire, in Ibn 'Ammâr's own
writing, and sent it to the prince of Valencia. The latter
immediately sent a letter, enclosing the satire, to Mu'tamid
by means of a carrier pigeon.

Henceforth reconciliation was impossible. Neither
Mu'tamid, nor Rumaykiyya, nor their sons could forgive
Ibn 'Ammâr such scurrilous abuse. But the King of
Seville was under no necessity of punishing his Vizier;
others undertook that duty. In his heedless self-indulgence
Ibn 'Ammâr did not perceive that Ibn Rashîk, aided by
the prince of Valencia, was playing the traitor, and when
at last his eyes were opened, it was too late. Egged on
by Ibn Rashîk, the soldiers clamoured for their arrears of
pay, and since Ibn 'Ammâr could not satisfy them, they
threatened to hand him over to Mu'tamid. Shuddering at
this menace, he saved himself by a hasty flight.

He sought refuge with Alfonso, in the hope that that
monarch would aid him in reconquering Murcia. But he
was mistaken. Alfonso had been influenced by Ibn Rashîk's
splendid gifts, and replied to Ibn 'Ammâr: "You tell me
a mere tale of robbery; how one robber was robbed by
another, who in his turn was robbed by a third!"[1] When
he found that he could hope for nothing at Leon, Ibn
'Ammâr proceeded to Zaragoza, where he entered Muktadir's
service. But this court, much less brilliant than that of
Seville, he found completely uncongenial. He therefore
proceeded to Lerida, where Muzaffar, a brother of Muktadir,
reigned. He was warmly welcomed, but since he found
Lerida even more dreary than Zaragoza, he returned to
the latter city, where Mû'tamin had succeeded his father
Muktadir.[2] Ibn 'Ammâr seemed destined to perish of
ennui, which hung like a black cloud over the present and

---

[1] Mu'tamid, Ibn 'Ammâr and Ibn Rashîk respectively.   [2] October, 1081.

the future; he therefore hailed with delight an opportunity of escaping from idleness. A castellan of his acquaintance was in rebellion. Ibn 'Ammâr promised Mû'tamin to reduce him to obedience, and set out with a small escort. On reaching the foot of the mountain on which the castle stood, he asked the rebel to receive him with two attendants only. The castellan, unsuspiciously, granted his request. " When you see me clasp the Governor's hand," said Ibn 'Ammâr to his two servants, Jâbir and Hâdî, " plunge your swords into his heart." The castellan was slain, his soldiers were granted quarter, and Mû'tamin was highly pleased with the service which Ibn 'Ammâr had rendered him. Soon afterwards the latter thought he saw another opportunity of gratifying the feverish activity which consumed him. He planned the acquisition of Segura for Mû'tamin. Perched upon the summit of an almost inaccessible crag, this fortress had maintained its independence when Muktadir had seized the territories of 'Alî, prince of Denia, and a son of the latter, named Sirâj-ud-Daula, had held it for some time; but he had recently died, and the Beni Sohail, who had been the guardians of his children, wished to sell Segura to a neighbouring prince. Ibn 'Ammâr promised Mû'tamin to obtain the fortress for him as he secured the other castle. He set out with a few troops, and asked the Beni Sohail to grant him an interview. They consented, but instead of luring them into his trap, Ibn 'Ammâr, who had given them offence when he reigned in Murcia, was himself ensnared. The approaches to Segura were defended by so precipitous a slope that to effect an entrance it was necessary to climb hand over hand. On reaching this dangerous spot, with Jâbir and Hâdî, his indispensable companions in every dangerous enterprise, Ibn 'Ammâr was the first to clamber up; but as soon as his feet touched level ground, the soldiers of the garrison seized him, and shouting to his two servants, bade them run for their lives if they did not wish to be shot down with arrows. There was no need to repeat the warning, and scampering down the rock the servants informed the Zaragozan soldiers that Ibn 'Ammâr had been taken prisoner. Well assured that any attempt to rescue him would be fruitless, the troops marched home.

Having thrown Ibn 'Ammâr into a dungeon, the Beni Sohail determined to sell him to the highest bidder. This proved to be Mu'tamid, who purchased him together with

the castle of Segura, and the prince’s son Râzî was instructed to bring the prisoner to Cordova.   The unfortunate
Vizier entered the city fettered and mounted on a baggage
mule, between two sacks of straw.   Mu‘tamid overwhelmed
him with reproaches, and showing him the vindictive satire,
asked him if he recognised his own writing.   The prisoner,
who could scarcely stand upright under his ponderous chains,
remained silent, with downcast eyes; but when the prince
had ended his long invective, the Vizier replied : “ I deny
nothing, my lord, of what you have said ; of what use would
it be for me to deny it, when even lifeless things would
testify to the truth of your words ?   I have erred, I have
grievously insulted you—yet pardon me ! ”   “ That which
thou hast done is unpardonable,” replied Mu‘tamid.

The ladies whom he had outraged in his satire took their
revenge by assailing him with biting mockeries.   At Seville
he had to endure afresh the insults of the crowd.   His imprisonment, however, was protracted, and this circumstance
gave him hope.   He knew, moreover, that several personages of importance, including Prince Rashîd, had spoken or
written on his behalf.   He did not cease to stimulate the
zeal of these allies by his verses, till Mu‘tamid grew weary
of the interminable petitions addressed to him, and forbade
any more writing materials to be given to the prisoner ; but
the Vizier implored him to let him have, only once more,
paper, ink and a reed, and his request having been granted,
he composed a long poem to be handed to the King in the
evening, while he sat at a banquet.   When the guests had
departed, Mu‘tamid read the verses, was touched, and summoned Ibn ‘Ammâr to his apartment, where he once more
reproached him with his ingratitude.   At first, Ibn ‘Ammâr,
choked with sobs, could scarcely reply, but recovering little
by little, he recalled with so much eloquence the happiness
which they had formerly enjoyed together that Mu‘tamid,
who was deeply moved, seemed softened—perhaps half vanquished—and addressed a few reassuring words to him, but
no formal pardon.   Unfortunately—and no misfortune is so
bitter as one which darkens the dawn of hope—Ibn ‘Ammâr
strangely misunderstood Mu‘tamid’s feelings towards him.
The alternations of anger and compassion which he had
witnessed, he had interpreted erroneously.   Mu‘tamid doubtless still felt for him a shred of his former affection, but
there was a wide gulf between regret and pardon.   This is
what Ibn ‘Ammâr did not understand.   On re-entering his

prison he dwelt upon his approaching return to fortune, and, unable to restrain the joy with which his heart overflowed, he sent Rashîd a letter announcing the happy issue of his conversation with the monarch. Rashîd was not alone when this letter reached him, and as he read it his Vizier 'Îsâ cast a rapid and furtive glance at the document, which sufficed to inform him of its tenour. Either through mere garrulity, or because he had no love for Ibn 'Ammâr, 'Îsâ noised abroad the matter, and it soon reached the ears of Abû Bakr ibn Zaidûn, embellished with exaggerations which are lost to us, but which must have been of a very scandalous nature, since an Arab historian observes that he passes them over in silence rather than soil his book with them. Ibn Zaidûn passed the night in anguish; for him Ibn 'Ammâr's rehabilitation would mean disgrace—perhaps death. On the morrow, uncertain what course to adopt, he remained in his house instead of repairing, as usual, to the palace. Mu'tamid sent for him, and greeted him with his accustomed friendliness, so that Ibn Zaidûn became sure that the situation was not so perilous as he had supposed. Accordingly, when the King inquired the cause of his delay, Ibn Zaidûn replied that he feared he had fallen into disgrace: he went on to relate how the King's conversation with Ibn 'Ammâr was known to all the Court; how the return of the ex-Vizier to power was momentarily expected; how his friend and compatriot Ibn Salâm, Prefect of the City, had already prepared splendid apartments for his reception in his own house, until his palaces should be restored to him; and of course he did not omit one of the calumnies which had been spread abroad.

Mu'tamid was beside himself with rage. Even if what had passed between himself and his prisoner had not been distorted by hatred, he would have been indignant at Ibn 'Ammâr's fatuous presumption in taking a few kindly words as a pledge that he was to be set at liberty and restored to power. "Go, ask Ibn 'Ammâr," he said to a eunuch, "by what means he divulged the conversation which I had with him last evening?" The eunuch speedily returned. "Ibn 'Ammâr," he said, "denies having spoken to anyone." "But he may have written!" replied Mu'tamid; "I gave him two sheets of paper: on one he wrote a poem which he sent to me; what has he done with the other? Go, and ask him that question."

The eunuch returning said: "Ibn 'Ammâr avers that

he used the other sheet for a draft of the poem." "If so," replied Mu'tamid, "let him give you the draft." Ibn 'Ammâr could no longer deny the truth. "I wrote to Prince Rashîd," he said penitently, "to inform him of the King's promise."

At this avowal, the blood of his terrible father, that vulture ever ready to swoop upon the prey and assuage his rage in its vitals, surged through Mu'tamid's veins. Grasping the first weapon that lay to hand—a splendid battle-axe given him by Alfonso—he mounted in a few strides the stairs which led to the chamber where Ibn 'Ammâr was confined.

As his glance met the monarch's flashing eyes, Ibn 'Ammâr trembled. He knew that his last hour had come. Dragging his chains he fell at Mu'tamid's feet, and covered them with kisses and tears; but the King, inaccessible to pity, struck his prisoner again and again with the battle-axe, until his blows fell upon a cold corpse.

Such was the tragic end of Ibn 'Ammâr. Throughout Arab Spain it caused a profound impression, which, however, was not of long duration, for grave events which took place at Toledo, and the advance of the Castilian army, soon diverted men's thoughts into other channels.

[AUTHORITIES: Ibn al-'Abbâr, pp. 186–9; *Abbad.*, ii. 36, 86–7, 91–4, 103–119; Ibn Bassâm, ii. (Art. on Ibn 'Ammâr); 'Abd al-Wâhid, pp. 85–90.]

2 x

CHAPTER XII

ALFONSO VI—BATTLE OF ZALLÂKA

THE Emperor Alfonso VI—King of Leon, Castile, Galicia and Navarre—was firmly resolved to conquer the whole Peninsula; nor did he lack the power to carry out his intention. He had, however, no wish to act hastily, and could afford to bide his time: for he was meanwhile steadily amassing the sinews of war—the surest means of attaining the object of his ambition. He crushed the treasuries of the Moslem kinglets as in a wine-press, till they poured forth gold.

The feeblest of all his tributaries was, perhaps, Kâdir, King of Toledo. Brought up in effeminacy, this prince was the puppet of his eunuchs and the laughing-stock of his neighbours, who vied with one another in fleecing him. Alfonso seemed his only protector. It was to the Emperor, therefore, that Kâdir turned when he could no longer control his subjects, who were weary of his rule. Alfonso expressed his readiness to furnish troops, but asked an immense sum for his services. Kâdir summoned the principal citizens and demanded the money from them. They refused it. " I swear," cried the King, " that if ye do not instantly provide me with this sum, I will deliver your children into the hands of Alfonso!" " Nay, rather will we drive thee out!" was the reply. The Toledans thereupon transferred their allegiance to Mutawakkil of Badajoz, and Kâdir fled from the city by night. He again implored Alfonso to render him assistance. " I will besiege Toledo," replied the Emperor, in effect, " and reinstate you on the throne; but you must give me all the gold you have carried away, and in pledge of further payments you must assign me certain fortresses." Kâdir submitted to these conditions, and hostilities against Toledo commenced in 1080.

This war had lasted for two years, when the Emperor sent his usual embassy, consisting of several knights, to Mu'tamid, to demand the annual tribute. The envoys were accompanied by a Jew, Ben-Shâlib[1] by name, who was empowered to receive the money—for at that period

---

[1] Or, simply Shâlib, according to Nuwairi.

Jews frequently acted as intermediaries between Moslems and Christians.

When the envoys had pitched their tents outside the city, the tribute-money was conveyed to them by a deputation of Mu'tamid's officers, headed by the Prime Minister, Abû Bakr ibn Zaidûn. A part of the money, however, was of debased coinage, since Mu'tamid had been unable to raise the required sum, although he had levied a special tax for the purpose. As soon as the Jew saw the base pieces, he exclaimed: "Think you that I am such a simpleton as to accept counterfeit money? I take nothing but pure gold—and, next year, towns."

When these words were reported to Mu'tamid, he was highly incensed. "Fetch me the Jew and his colleagues!" he cried to his soldiers. The order was obeyed, and when the envoys had been brought to the palace, Mu'tamid ordered the Christians to be imprisoned, and the Jew to be crucified.

"Have mercy!" cried the Jew, lately so arrogant, but now trembling in every limb, "and I will give you my weight in gold!"

"By Allah!" replied Mu'tamid, "if thou wert to offer me all Spain and Mauritania for your ransom I would not accept them!" And the Jew was crucified.[1]

On learning what had occurred, Alfonso swore by the Trinity and all the saints that he would exact a signal and terrible vengeance. "I will lay waste the infidel's dominions with warriors numerous as the hairs of my head, and I will not halt until I reach the Straits of Gibraltar!" Since, however, the Emperor could not abandon to their fate the Castilian knights who languished in the dungeons of Seville, he was obliged to ask Mu'tamid to name the conditions on which he would release them. The Emir demanded the restitution of Almodovar,[2] and upon being granted possession of this town, set the prisoners at liberty. Scarcely had they returned home when Alfonso executed his threat. He pillaged and burned the villages of the Axarafe, slew or enslaved all Moslems who had not found time to take refuge in some stronghold, besieged Seville for three days, and ravaged the province of Sidona. On reaching the shore near Tarifa the Emperor rode his horse into the surf, and cried: "I have reached the furthest

---

[1] This version of the story rests on the authority of Ibn al-labbâna, a poet of Mu'tamid's court. The *Raudh al-mitâr*, relied upon by Makkari, seems to be the work of a more recent copyist of Asiatic traditions.

[2] Pelagius of Oviedo (c. 11) includes this among the towns captured by Alfonso.

extremity of Spain!" Having thus fulfilled his vow, and gratified his vanity, he marched his army back to Toledan territory (A.D. 1082).

There, too, his arms were victorious, and Mutawakkil having been obliged to evacuate the country, the inhabitants of the Capital grudgingly opened their gates to Kâdir (1084). Kâdir levied an immense contribution upon the citizens, and offered it to the Emperor. Alfonso declared the sum insufficient. Kâdir thereupon begged for some delay, and this was granted, subject to his ceding additional fortresses as a pledge: he could not but consent; his heritage was vanishing piecemeal, his resources were at an end, but he knew that the sword of the terrible Alfonso hung above his head, and that at the first sign of contumacy it would fall. And so he gave him gold, and then more gold —and fortresses, and then more fortresses: to satisfy the Emperor he oppressed his subjects and ultimately depopulated his kingdom, for in desperation the Toledans emigrated in shoals, and settled in the territories of the King of Zaragoza. Yet Kâdir's efforts were fruitless; his extortions served only to whet Alfonso's appetite; and the Emperor, when his victim swore that he was penniless, proceeded to devastate the environs of Toledo. For a little while Kâdir still clung to his tottering throne, but at length he relaxed his hold. As Alfonso had anticipated, he offered to cede Toledo, making, however, certain stipulations, of which the chief were: that Alfonso should afford protection to the lives and property of the Toledans, who should not be forbidden to emigrate; that they should be subjected only to a fixed poll-tax; that they should retain the Great Mosque; and, that Kâdir should be granted Valencia.

The Emperor accepted these conditions, and on May 25, 1085, he entered the ancient capital of the Visigothic kingdom. Henceforth the arrogance of Alfonso was only paralleled by the abject servility of the Moslem princes. Almost all of them hastened to send the Emperor congratulatory embassies, offering him gifts, and assuring him that they looked upon themselves as his tax-collectors. Alfonso, the "Lord of the Two Faiths," as he termed himself in his letters, took no pains to conceal his contempt for the Moslems. Hosâm ad-daula, the lord of Albarrazin, came personally to offer him a superb present. Just then an ape was amusing the Emperor by its antics. "Take this beast in return for thy gift!" said Alfonso disdainfully: and the

Moslem, far from showing resentment, regarded the ape as a pledge of friendship and as a testimony that his territories were safe.

After the annexation of Toledo, Valencia's turn came. In that city the two sons of Ibn 'Abd al-'Azîz were contending for power, while a third faction wished to give Valencia to the King of Zaragoza, and a fourth, to Kâdir. Kâdir's party prevailed: his claim could, indeed, scarcely be resisted, backed as it was by a Castilian army under the command of the famous soldier Alvar Fañez. But the Valencians would have to maintain these troops, at the daily cost of six hundred gold pieces. It was useless for his new subjects to assure Kâdir that he did not need this army, since they were loyal. He was not so simpleminded as to trust them; knowing that the citizens hated him, and that his rivals had not abandoned their hopes, he kept his Castilians. To pay them he imposed a special tax upon the city and its territory, and wrung heavy contributions from the nobles.[1] Nevertheless, in spite of his despotic imposts, Kâdir, pressed by Alvar Fañez for arrears of pay, at length found himself at the end of his resources. He accordingly proposed to the Castilians that they should settle in his kingdom after being provided with extensive domains. They consented, but entrusting the cultivation of their lands to serfs, continued to make forays in the surrounding country. Their numbers were increased by the dregs of the Arab population. A multitude of slaves, convicts, and vagabonds, many of whom had abjured Islamism, enrolled themselves under their banners, and soon these bands became infamous for their cruelties. They murdered men, violated women, and would sell a Moslem prisoner for a jar of wine, a loaf of bread, or a pound of fish. When a prisoner would not, or could not, pay ransom, they would cut out his tongue, put out his eyes, and cause him to be torn to pieces by mastiffs.

Valencia was, therefore, practically Alfonso's. Kâdir was nominally its King, but most of its territory was in the hands of the Castilians, and Alfonso had but to speak the word to incorporate it with his empire. Zaragoza also seemed lost. Alfonso besieged it, and made a vow to capture it. At the further extremity of Spain, one of Alfonso's lieutenants, Garcia Ximenez, had installed himself with a body of horsemen, in the castle of Aledo, not far

---

[1] Including the sons of Ibn 'Abd al-'Aziz. *Recherches* (1881), ii. 121.

from Lorca, and made incessant raids into Almeria. Nor
was Granada spared, for in the spring of 1085, the Castilians
advanced to the village of Nibar, a league to the east of
Granada, and gave battle to the Moslems. In every quarter
dangers threatened, and blank despondency prevailed. The
Moslems dared not attack the Christians even with a
superiority of five to one. A body of four hundred Almerians
—picked men—were put to flight by eighty Castilians. It
was clear that if the Arabs of Spain were left to their own
resources, only two alternatives would be open to them—to
submit to the Emperor, or to emigrate. Many of them had
indeed made up their minds to adopt the latter course.
"Set out upon your journey, O Andalusians," exclaims a
poet, "for to remain here is madness!" Nevertheless,
emigration was an extreme measure, and the Arabs were
loath to adopt it. All was not yet lost, and help might yet
be obtained from Africa. It was thither that the more
sanguine looked for salvation. A suggestion was made that
the Bedawin of Ifrîkia should be appealed to; but it was
objected that they were as remarkable for their barbarity as
for their valour, and that if they landed in Spain they would
be likely to pillage the Moslems instead of fighting the
Christians. The Almoravides were then thought of. These
were the Berbers of the Sahara, who were for the first time
playing a part on the world's stage. Recently converted
to Islamism by a missionary from Sijilmesa, they had
made rapid conquests, and at the epoch we have now
reached, their vast empire extended from the Senegal to
Algiers. The idea of calling in the aid of the Almoravides
appealed chiefly to the religious. The princes, on the other
hand, for a long time hesitated. Some of them, such as
Mu'tamid and Mutawakkil, kept up a correspondence with
Yûsuf ibn Tâshifîn, King of the Almoravides, and they had
more than once gone so far as to seek his aid against the
Christians; but the Andalusian princes as a whole had little
sympathy with the chief of the barbarous and fanatical
warriors of the Sahara, regarding him rather as a dangerous
rival than an ally. But the daily waxing peril rendered it
necessary to grasp the only remaining means of safety.
Such at least was Mu'tamid's opinion, and when his eldest
son, Rashîd, pointed out the danger of introducing the
Almoravides into Spain, he replied: "That is true; but I
have no desire to be branded by my descendants as the man
who delivered Andalusia a prey to the infidels; I am loath

to have my name cursed in every Moslem pulpit; and, for my part, I would rather be a camel-driver in Africa than a swineherd in Castile."

Mu'tamid, having made up his mind, requested his neighbours, Mutawakkil of Badajoz and 'Abdallah of Granada,[1] to act in concert with him, and to nominate their Kadies as envoys. Abû Ishâk ibn Mokânâ and Abû Ja'far Kolai'î, the Kadies of Badajoz and Granada respectively, accordingly arrived at Seville. The Kady of Cordova, Ibn Adham, and the Vizier Abû Bakr ibn Zaidûn were associated with them, and these four embarked at Algeciras on their mission to Yûsuf. They were authorized to invite him, each in his sovereign's name, to land in Spain with an army, but the request was coupled with certain conditions of which no record remains; we only know that Yûsuf took an oath not to seize the states of any of the Andalusian princes. It then became necessary to determine the place of Yûsuf's landing. Ibn Zaidûn proposed Gibraltar; but Yûsuf preferred Algeciras, and suggested that that town should be ceded to him. Mu'tamid's Vizier replied that he was not authorized to comply with this request. Thereupon Yûsuf treated the envoys coldly, and gave them evasive and ambiguous replies; so that on leaving him they were uncertain which course he would adopt: he had neither promised nor refused to come.

The resulting perplexity of the princes was, however, soon removed in an unpleasant manner, and their previous suspicions were confirmed. Yûsuf, who undertook few enterprises without consulting the Fakihs, asked their advice, and they declared that it was his duty to fight the Castilians, and further, that if Algeciras were not given him he should take it. Armed with this *fetwa*, Yûsuf ordered a large force to embark at Ceuta in a fleet of a hundred vessels, and Algeciras soon found itself encompassed by an army clamouring for provisions and demanding the surrender of the town. Râzî, the commandant of Algeciras, was sorely perplexed by this unlooked-for emergency. He did not withhold provisions from the Almoravides, but at the same time he prepared to meet force with force. Meanwhile he sent a letter to his father, by carrier-pigeon, asking for instructions. Mu'tamid replied promptly; he quickly realized that he had gone too far to withdraw, in spite of Yûsuf's dishonourable conduct, and that he must put a

---

[1] On the death of Bâdîs, in 1073, his territories were divided between his two grandsons, 'Abdallah and Temîm—the first receiving Granada, and the second Malaga.

good face on the matter. He therefore ordered his son to evacuate Algeciras and retire to Ronda. Meanwhile fresh troops sailed from Ceuta, and at last Yûsuf himself landed at Algeciras. He immediately strengthened the fortifications of the town, stocked it with munitions of war and stores of food, and provided it with an adequate garrison. Then he set out for Seville with his main army. Mu'tamid rode out to greet him, surrounded by the chief dignitaries of the State. When they met, the King attempted to kiss Yûsuf's hand, but the latter prevented him, and embraced him affectionately. The customary gifts were not forgotten, and those offered by Mu'tamid were so lavish that Yûsuf was able to give somewhat to every soldier in his army, and conceived a lofty idea of the riches of Spain. The army halted near Seville, and the two grandsons of Bâdîs—'Abdallah of Granada and Temîm of Malaga—there joined the Almoravides, the former with three hundred, and the latter with two hundred horse. Mu'tasim of Almeria sent a regiment of cavalry under the command of one of his sons, with an expression of regret that the threatening attitude of the Christians of Aledo prevented him from appearing in person.

Eight days later the army set out for Badajoz, where it was joined by Mutawakkil and his troops. The combined forces then advanced on Toledo, but had not proceeded far before they came in touch with the enemy.

Alfonso was still besieging Zaragoza when he heard that the Almoravides had landed in Spain. Believing the King of Zaragoza to be unaware of the arrival of the Africans, the Emperor offered to raise the siege, on payment of a large indemnity. But Musta'în, who had learned the great news, refused to pay a single dirhem. Alfonso then fell back on Toledo, after ordering Alvar Fañez and his other lieutenants to join him there with their troops. As soon as his army, in which there were many French knights, had assembled, Alfonso set out, determined to assume the offensive. He encountered the Almoravides and their allies not far from Badajoz, near a place called Zallâka by the Moslems, and Sacralias by the Christians. Scarcely had his camp been pitched before he received a letter from Yûsuf, inviting him either to embrace Islamism or pay tribute, and threatening war if he refused. Alfonso was highly indignant at this message. He therefore ordered one of his Arab scribes to reply to the effect that since the Moslems had been tributary to him for many years, he paid no heed

to such insulting propositions, adding that he had a large
army which enabled him to punish the presumption of his
enemies.   On the receipt of this letter at the Moslem
Chancellery, an Andalusian immediately wrote a reply, but
Yûsuf found this composition too verbose, and endorsing
the Emperor's letter with the simple words : " *What will
happen thou shalt see!* " sent it back to Alfonso.[1]

The day of battle had now to be fixed, as was customary
at that period, and on Thursday, October 22, 1086, Alfonso
sent this message to the Moslems : " To-morrow is your
holy-day, and Sunday is ours : I propose, therefore, that we
join battle the day after to-morrow." [2]   Yûsuf agreed to
the   suggestion,   but   Mu'tamid   suspected   trickery,   and
since he would have to bear the brunt of a sudden attack
—for the Andalusians formed the advance-guard, while
the Almoravides were in the rear, concealed by the mountains—he took precautions against a surprise and sent light
horse to watch the movements of the enemy.   He felt
uneasy, and ceaselessly consulted his astrologer.   A critical
moment had arrived.   The fate of Spain hung upon the issue
of the forthcoming battle, and the Castilians were numerically superior.   The Moslems, indeed, believed the Christian
forces to number fifty or sixty thousand men, while they
themselves were not more than twenty thousand strong.

At dawn of day Mu'tamid saw his fears realized : his
scouts warned him of the approach of the Christians.   His
position was very perilous, for he ran the chance of being
annihilated before the Almoravides could come up ; he
therefore summoned Yûsuf to come to his support with
all his troops, or at least to send a strong reinforcement.
But Yûsuf was in no hurry.   He had formed a plan of
battle to which he intended to adhere, and so little did he
concern himself about the fate of the Andalusians that
he exclaimed : " What if these men are massacred ?   They
are all our enemies ! "   Thus abandoned to their own
resources, most of the Andalusians fled : the Sevillans alone,
encouraged by the example of the King—who although
wounded in the face and hand displayed superb courage—
valiantly stood their ground until at length an Almoravide
division came to their support.   Henceforth the combat
was less unequal ; nevertheless the Sevillans were amazed

---

[1] The Khalif Hârûn al-Rashid had sent a somewhat similar reply to the
Emperor Nicephorus.
[2] Some chroniclers aver that Monday was the day proposed, out of regard to
the Jewish Sabbath.

to see their opponents suddenly in full retreat, for the reinforcement had not been large enough to permit them to dream of victory. What had happened was this: Yûsuf on seeing the Castilian army engaged with the Andalusians determined to attack it in the rear. He accordingly sent in support of Mu'tamid a force sufficient to save him from annihilation, and then, making a *détour*, fell with his main body upon Alfonso's camp. There he inflicted frightful carnage upon the troops left to protect it, and having set fire to the camp he charged the Castilian rear-guard, driving a crowd of fugitives before him. Alfonso thus found himself hemmed in, and since the army attacking his rear was more numerous than that which faced him, he was compelled to turn his main body against the former. A desperate conflict ensued. The camp was alternately captured and recaptured, while Yûsuf rode amidst his men crying: " Courage, Moslems! Before you are the enemies of God! Paradise awaits those who fall in the fight!"

The Andalusians who had taken to flight now rallied and came to Mu'tamid's assistance. On the other side Yûsuf flung against the Castilians his negro guards, whom he held in reserve, and who did terrible execution. One of them even cut his way to Alfonso and wounded him in the thigh with a dagger. As night fell, the victory, so hotly contested, at last lay with the Moslems; most of the Christians lay dead or wounded on the battlefield, others took to flight, and Alfonso, escorted by only five hundred horse, with difficulty escaped (October 23, 1086).

This brilliant victory, however, did not yield all the fruits which might have been expected. Yûsuf had intended to penetrate into the enemy's country, but he abandoned this design on hearing of the death of his eldest son, whom he had left sick at Ceuta. He contented himself, therefore, with placing under Mu'tamid's command a division of three thousand men, and returned to Africa with the rest of his army.[1]

---

[1] The accounts of the battle of Zallàka given by the Latin chroniclers are very meagre : Arab historians, on the other hand, are diffuse but inconsistent on the subject.

[AUTHORITIES: *Abbad.*, i. 169, 175; ii. 8, 17–23, 27, 37–8, 174–5, 187–9, 191–3, 231, 238–9; *Kartás*, pp. 92, 109; Rodr. de Toledo, vi. 23; Ibn Khaldûn, *Hist. des Berb.*, ii. 77 (trans.); Ibn Khallikân, xii. 16; Ibn al-Khatîb, MS. E. (Art. on Mokâtil); Makkarî, ii. 672; 'Abd al-Wâhid, pp. 91, 93.]

CHAPTER XIII

YÛSUF IBN TÂSHIFÎN

THE arrival of the Almoravides in Spain had compelled the Castilians to evacuate the kingdom of Valencia and to raise the siege of Zaragoza. Alfonso's defeat at Zallâka had cost him many of his best soldiers—according to Moslem chroniclers he lost on that occasion ten thousand or even twenty-four thousand men. The Andalusian princes, moreover, were relieved from their shameful obligation to pay Alfonso an annual tribute, and the West—where the fortresses were henceforth defended by the soldiers whom Yûsuf had supplied to Muʻtamid—had nothing to fear from the attacks of the Emperor. These were, indeed, tangible benefits, and the Andalusians had good reason for rejoicing. The whole land rang with cries of joy ; the name of Yûsuf was on all men's lips ; his piety, his valour, his military talents, were everywhere extolled ; he was hailed as the saviour of Andalusia and of Islam ; he was proclaimed the greatest soldier of the age. The Fakihs especially never wearied in singing his praises. In their eyes Yûsuf was more than a hero : he was a man ordained of God.

And yet, important and brilliant as the victory had been, it was by no means decisive. The Castilians, at any rate, refused to regard it in that light. In spite of the defeats which they had sustained they did not despair of regaining their lost ground. They admitted that an attack against Badajoz and Seville would be too hazardous, but the east of Andalusia was vulnerable, and might easily be devastated, if not conquered. The petty principalities of the East— Valencia, Murcia, Lorca, Almeria—were the weakest States in the Peninsula, and the Castilians occupied a very strong position in their midst which completely dominated them. This was the fortress of Aledo—of which the ruins still exist[1]—between Murcia and Lorca. Situated on a very precipitous mountain, and able to accommodate a garrison of twelve or thirteen thousand men, Aledo was regarded as impregnable. Thence it was that the Castilians sallied

---

[1] K. Baedeker, *Spain and Portugal* (1908), p. 319.

forth to make raids upon the surrounding districts. They even besieged Almeria, Lorca, and Murcia, and it seemed probable, that if measures were not taken for their defence these towns would fall into the hands of the enemy.

Mu'tamid recognised the magnitude of the danger which threatened Andalusia on the east, and that his personal interests were also affected. Murcia and Lorca, the two towns most exposed to attack, belonged to him—the first of right, and the second virtually, since its king, Ibn al-Yasa, feeling unable to resist the Castilians of Aledo single-handed, had recognised Mu'tamid as his sovereign in the hope of being aided by him. At Murcia, Ibn Rashîk still reigned, and Mu'tamid yearned to punish that rebel. Having therefore determined to make an expedition into the East with the double object of checking the forays of the Christians and reducing Ibn Rashîk to submission, the Sevillan monarch united his own troops with those lent him by Yûsuf and set out for Lorca.

On reaching that town he learned that a squadron of three hundred Castilians was in the neighbourhood. He therefore ordered his son Râzî to attack them with three thousand Sevillan horsemen. Râzî, however, who loved literature better than warfare, excused himself on the plea of illness. Highly incensed at this refusal, Mu'tamid then entrusted the command to another of his sons, Mu'tadd. Once more was the superiority of Castilians over Andalusians illustrated. Although they outnumbered their foes in the ratio of ten to one, the Sevillans were disgracefully defeated.

Nor were Mu'tamid's attempts to reduce Murcia more successful. Ibn Rashîk contrived to secure the sympathies of the Almoravides in the Sevillan army, and Mu'tamid was obliged to return to his capital without having gained a single advantage.

It had thus become evident that the battle of Zallâka had left the Andalusians as incapable of self-defence as they had been before that victory, and that if Yûsuf did not once more come to their rescue they must finally succumb. Yûsuf's palace was therefore besieged by Fakihs and notables from Valencia, Murcia, Lorca, and Baza. The Valencians had a grievance against Rodrigo el Campeador (The Cid), who posed as Kâdir's protector after compelling him to pay a monthly subsidy of six thousand ducats, and who laid waste the country round under the pretext of subjugating rebels;[1] the inhabitants of the other towns were eloquent upon the outrages committed by the Castilians of Aledo, and all were agreed that if Yûsuf did not come to their aid, Andalusia would inevitably become a prey to the Christians. Their entreaties, however, seem to have had but little effect upon the Moroccan monarch. Yûsuf promised, it is true, to cross the Straits at a favourable season of the year; but he made no serious preparations, and hinted, if he did not openly declare, that he awaited a direct appeal from the princes. This Mu'tamid resolved to make. The suspicions which he had nursed with regard to Yûsuf's secret intentions, had been gradually dissipated, or at least weakened. Except in occupying Algeciras, the African monarch had done nothing to wound the susceptibilities of the Andalusian princes or justify their apprehensions; on the contrary, he had often declared that though before seeing Andalusia he had formed an exalted idea of the beauty and wealth of the country, the reality had disappointed him. Mu'tamid, therefore, was reassured, and since the danger which threatened his country was undoubtedly very great, he determined to pay Yûsuf a visit.

The Almoravide greeted him with the utmost respect and cordiality, at the same time assuring him that he need not have come personally, but that a letter would have received a prompt reply. "I have come," said Mu'tamid, "to tell you that we are exposed to a grave danger. Aledo lies in the heart of our country, it is impossible for us to wrest it from the Christians, and if you can do so, you will render an immense service to religion. You have already been our deliverer; save us once more." "I can but make the attempt," replied Yûsuf, and when Mu'tamid had returned to Seville, the Almoravide hastened his military preparations. When all was ready, he crossed the Straits with his troops, landed at Algeciras in the spring of 1090, and effecting a junction with Mu'tamid, invited the Andalusian princes to march with them to besiege Aledo. Temîm of Malaga, 'Abdallah of Granada, Mu'tasim of Almeria, Ibn Rashîk of Murcia, and some minor potentates, responded to the summons and the siege began. The engines of war were constructed by Murcian carpenters and masons, and it was agreed that the Emirs should each in turn attack the fortress for a day. Little

---

[1] Cf. *Recherches* (1881), ii. p. 128.

progress, however, was made: the defenders of Aledo,
who numbered thirteen thousand, including a thousand
horse, repelled all assaults with vigour, and the fortress
proved so strong that the Moslems, after vain attempts to
carry it by storm, resolved to starve out the garrison.

Meanwhile the besiegers were less concerned about
the siege than about their own self-interests. The camp
became a hot-bed of intrigue. Yûsuf's ambitions were
stimulated in new directions. That monarch had not been
sincere in saying that Spain had not answered his expectations. He thought it, in truth, the most desirable of all
lands, and whether through mere love of conquest, or for
nobler motives—for he had the interests of religion unfeignedly at heart—he longed to become its master. Nor
was this desire difficult of realization. Many Andalusians
believed that in union with the Almoravide empire lay
the only hope of saving their country. It is true that such
was not the opinion of the upper classes of society. In
the eyes of men of culture, Yûsuf, whose knowledge of
Arabic was elementary, was a churl and a barbarian, and
it must be admitted that he had given many proofs of
his lack of education. When Mu'tamid, for instance,
asked him whether he understood the poems recited before
him by the Sevillan poets, Yûsuf replied: "All I understood was that their composers were in need of bread."
Again, on his return to Africa he had received from
Mu'tamid a letter in which these two lines were quoted
from a famous poem which Abu 'l-Walîd ibn Zaidûn,[1] the
Tibullus of Andalusia, had addressed to his inamorata
Wallâda:[2] "Whilst thou art far from me, the desire of
seeing thee consumes my heart and I weep floods of tears.
Now my days are black, yet not long ago thou madest
my nights white." "Doth the king wish me to send him
black damsels as well as white ones?" asked Yûsuf. It
was then explained to him that "black" signified "gloomy,"
in poetic phraseology, and that by "white" "clear and
serene" was meant. "How beautiful!" exclaimed Yûsuf:
"Tell the king that I have a headache whenever he is out
of my sight!" In a land of scholars, like Andalusia, such
shortcomings were unpardonable. Men of letters, moreover, were quite content with their position, and desired
no change. The courts of the petty tyrants were so many

---

[1] The father of Mu'tamid's Vizier (A.D. 1003–1071).
[2] See p. 665 supra.

Academies, and literary men were spoiled children of the princes who lavished luxuries upon them. Nor had the representatives of free-thought any reason for complaint. Thanks to the protection afforded to them by most of the princes, they could for the first time write or say what seemed good to them, without fear of being stoned or burnt. They, therefore, had less reason than any class to desire the rule of the Almoravides, which would infallibly mean ecclesiastical domination.

If, however, Yûsuf could count upon but few adherents among the upper and better-educated classes, the masses were on his side. Discontent was rife, and not without reason. Almost every considerable town had its Court—an expensive luxury, for most of the emirs were wildly extravagant. It was not as though the populace purchased peace and safety at a high price. The princes, on the contrary, were usually too weak to protect their subjects even from their Moslem neighbours, much less from the Christians. There was therefore neither tranquillity nor security for life and property. Such a state of things was clearly insufferable, and it was but natural that the working classes wished to see it ended. But hitherto no chance of escape from these conditions had presented itself. Vague cravings after revolt were rife, and verses such as these by Somaisir, a Granadan poet,[1] were eagerly listened to:

"What is it, O Kings, that ye dare to do? Ye deliver Islam to its enemies, and put not forth a hand to save. To rebel against you is a duty, since ye make common cause with the Christians. To rid ourselves of your rule is no crime, for ye have rid yourselves of the authority of the Prophet."

Yet since rebellion would only have made matters worse, there was nothing for it but to cultivate patience, as the same poet pointed out:

"We put our trust in you, O Kings, but ye have falsified our hopes; to you we looked for deliverance, but we looked in vain! Patience! Time will work great changes. To the wise a word sufficeth!"

But now an insurrection seemed feasible, since a just, powerful, and illustrious monarch had arrived in Spain who had already gained a brilliant victory over the Christians and who would doubtless gain many more. Surely he was sent by Providence to restore Andalusia to greatness and prosperity. Submission to such a monarch would clearly

---

[1] For an account of Somaisir, see *Recherches* (1881), i. pp. 259-61.

be the best course, for it would at once relieve the populace of innumerable vexatious taxes. Had not Yûsuf abolished in his own territories all imposts which were not prescribed in the Koran ? And there was a general impression that he would do likewise in Spain.

Thus reasoned the people, and in some respects not unjustly : but they forgot that the government could not for long be carried on without the taxes the abolishment of which they craved ; that Andalusia as the ally of Morocco exposed itself to the countershock of revolutions which might break out in that empire ; that Almoravide domination would imply the rule of foreigners ; and, lastly, that Yûsuf's soldiers belonged to a race always detested in Spain, and being ill-disciplined, might turn out to be very inconvenient guests. The desire of change was, moreover, much more keenly felt in some States than in others. In Granada it was the unanimous wish of all the population, Arab and Andalusian, who had never ceased to curse the tyrannical Berbers ; but in Mu'tamid's territories there were not so many malcontents ; and in Almeria there were scarcely any —for the reigning prince was very popular ; he was pious, just, and clement ; he treated his people with paternal kindness, and was a ruler endowed with the most attractive virtues.

Almost everywhere, however, Yûsuf had as supporters the ministers of religion and of the law. These were his most active and devoted auxiliaries, for it was they who had most to lose if the Christians triumphed, and on the other hand they had little cause to love princes who, occupied with profane studies or immersed in pleasures, made light of them, would scarcely listen to their sermons, and openly patronised the philosophers. Yûsuf, on the contrary, who was a model of devoutness, who never failed to consult the divines on affairs of State, and to follow the advice they tendered him, claimed their sympathy and affection. They knew, or at least guessed, that he was sorely tempted to dethrone the Andalusian princes for his own aggrandisement. Yet they thought of nothing except how to stimulate his ambitions, and make him believe that they were sanctioned by religion.

One of the most active of these agitators was the Kady of Granada, Abû Ja'far Kolai'î. Being of Arab origin, he hated the Berber oppressors of his country. His efforts to conceal his sentiments were unsuccessful. By a secret instinct Bâdîs had come to look upon him as the probable agent of the downfall of his dynasty, and he had often intended to put him to death; but, in the phrase of an Arab historian, "God fettered the hands of the tyrant, that the decrees of destiny might be accomplished." Now the Kady was with the army which was besieging Aledo, and had many private conferences with Yûsuf, for it may be remembered that he was one of the ambassadors who, four years before, had invited the Almoravide to come to the aid of the Andalusians. The object of these interviews may easily be guessed. Yûsuf had scruples of conscience and the Kady sought to overcome them. He therefore pointed out that the Andalusian Fakihs could absolve him from his oath; that it would be easy to obtain from them a *fetwa* enumerating the shortcomings and misdeeds of the princes, and that the conclusion could hence be drawn that they had forfeited their right to the thrones they occupied.

The arguments of this Kady—one of those most renowned for wisdom and piety—made a great impression on Yûsuf's mind; on the other hand conversations which he had had with Mu'tasim, King of Almeria, had inspired him with a profound aversion for the most powerful of all the Andalusian princes.

Mu'tasim, as has been seen, was an excellent prince; but kind-hearted as he usually was, there was one man whom he hated, namely Mu'tamid. This hatred seems to have arisen from petty jealousy rather than from any real grievances, but it was none the less bitter, and although Mu'tasim was ostensibly reconciled with the King of Seville, he tried to ruin him in the estimation of the African monarch, whose favour he had gained by unworthy means. Mu'tamid, who suspected nothing of this intrigue, talked freely with Mu'tasim when alone with him, and one day when the prince of Almeria expressed his uneasiness at Yûsuf's prolonged sojourn in Andalusia, Mu'tamid replied, in a spirit of southern boastfulness, "Doubtless this man is making a long stay in our country; but when he wearies me, I shall have but to lift a finger, and on the morrow he and his soldiers depart. You seem to fear that he will do us some injury; but of what account is this despicable prince or his soldiers? In their own country they were famished beggars; wishing to do them a good turn we invited them to Spain that they might eat their fill; when they are satisfied we

will send them back whence they came." Such words
became in Mu'tasim's hands, terrible weapons. He reported them to Yûsuf, who flew into a violent rage, and
what had been a vague project in his mind became a fixed
and irrevocable determination. Mu'tasim had triumphed,
but little had he foreseen the consequences; "he had not
foreseen," as an Arab historian aptly put it, "that into the
well which he had dug for him whom he hated, he himself
would fall, nor that by the sword which he had made to
leap from its scabbard he would perish."

Such lack of foresight was, indeed, common to all the
Andalusian princes. They mutually accused one another
before Yûsuf; they made the Almoravide umpire in their
quarrels; and while the prince of Almeria tried to ruin the
ruler of Seville, the latter endeavoured to overthrow the
prince of Murcia, Ibn Rashîk. With that object he did
not cease to remind Yûsuf that Ibn Rashîk had been
Alfonso's ally; that he had rendered great services to the
Christians of Aledo; and that apparently he was still doing
so. Then, asserting his rights over Murcia, he demanded
that the traitor who had deprived him of that town should
be delivered up to him. Yûsuf ordered the Fakihs to
investigate the matter, and when they had decided in
Mu'tamid's favour, Yûsuf caused Ibn Rashîk to be arrested
and handed over to the ruler of Seville, forbidding the latter,
however, to put him to death. This arrest had untoward
consequences, for the irritated Murcians quitted the camp,
and refused henceforth to supply the army with the workmen and provisions of which they had need.

The besiegers therefore found themselves in a very
mortifying plight—which now that winter was approaching
threatened disaster—when it became known that Alfonso
was marching to the relief of the fortress with eighteen
thousand men. Yûsuf at first resolved to meet him in the
Sierra de Tirieza (to the west of Totana), and there give
battle; but he soon changed his plan and retired upon
Lorca. He declared that he feared that the Andalusians
would take to flight again, as they did at Zallâka, and, further,
he was convinced that Aledo was no longer capable of defence, and that the Castilians would be obliged to evacuate
it. His opinion proved to be well founded; Alfonso, finding the fortifications in ruins and the garrison reduced to
about a hundred men, burnt Aledo and conveyed its defenders to Castile.

The object of the campaign had therefore been attained, but ingloriously, for Yûsuf had besieged Aledo fruitlessly for four months, and his retreat upon Alfonso's approach savoured of a flight. The Fakihs, however, took care that his popularity should not suffer. They declared that if the Almoravide had not on this occasion gained a success comparable with his brilliant victory of four years ago, the fault lay with the Andalusian princes, who by their intrigues, jealousies, and interminable quarrels prevented the great soldier from achieving the successes which he would have gained had he been in sole command. The Fakihs, indeed, became more active than ever, and for a good reason, for since their schemes had become known to the princes they began to run serious risks. The Kady of Granada, Abû Ja'far Kolai'î, discovered this to his cost. Whilst in camp his sovereign, whose tent adjoined his own, had got wind of his secret interviews with Yûsuf, and had guessed their import. The presence of Yûsuf, however, intimidated the Emir, and he did not dare at the time to adopt rigorous measures against the conspirators; but on his return to Granada he sent for the Kady, reproached him with treason, and ordered his guards to put him to death. Fortunately for Abû Ja'far, 'Abdallah's mother threw herself at her son's feet and conjured him to spare so devout a man, and since 'Abdallah was usually ruled by his mother, he reprieved the Kady, but imprisoned him in a room in the castle. The Kady, who knew that he was surrounded by superstitious persons, began to recite prayers and verses from the Koran. His ringing and powerful voice resounded throughout the palace. Everyone listened to his pious ejaculations; every sound was hushed lest the prisoner should be disturbed, and it was dinned into the prince's ears that God would inflict on him a terrible punishment if he did not immediately release this model of piety and devoutness. None was more zealous than 'Abdallah's mother, and by mingled threats and entreaties she at last persuaded her son to release the prisoner. But the lesson he had received warned the Kady not to remain at Granada. During the darkness of night he escaped to Alcala, and thence proceeded to Cordova. Henceforth he had nothing to fear, and nursed his desire for revenge. He accordingly wrote to Yûsuf, depicting in vivid colours the ill-treatment to which he had been subjected, and urging him not to postpone the execution of the project which they had so often discussed. At the same time he communicated with the other Andalusian Kadies and Fakihs, calling upon them for a *fetwa* denouncing the princes in general, and the two grandsons of Bâdîs in particular. The Kadies and Fakihs had no hesitation in declaring that the princes of Granada and Malaga had forfeited their rights by their many misdeeds, and especially by the brutal manner in which the elder of the two had treated his Kady; but not venturing to pass so severe a judgment on the other princes, they contented themselves with presenting a petition to Yûsuf setting forth that it was his duty to call upon all the Andalusian princes to adhere to the law and to demand no other taxes than those prescribed in the Koran.

Armed with these two *fetwas*, Yûsuf commanded the princes to abolish statute labour and imposts with which they oppressed their subjects, and set out towards Granada with a division of his army, ordering three other divisions to follow him. He did not actually declare war against 'Abdallah, so that the prince could only guess his intentions. 'Abdallah's terror was extreme. In no respect did he resemble his grandfather, the ignorant but energetic Bâdîs. He had a smattering of learning, expressed himself passably in Arabic, even composed verses, and wrote so beautiful a hand, that a copy of the Koran in his writing was for a long time preserved at Granada. But he was pusillanimous, effeminate, indolent, incapable—a man for whom women had no attraction, who trembled at the sight of a sword, and so infirm of purpose that he sought advice from everybody. At this juncture, 'Abdallah, assembling his Council, first asked the opinion of the aged Mu'ammil, who had done good service for his grandfather. Mu'ammil tried to reassure him by declaring that Yûsuf had no hostile intentions, and advised him to show his confidence in the monarch by going forth to meet him. Then, seeing that this advice was not palatable to 'Abdallah and that the prince had a leaning towards assuming the defensive, Mu'ammil endeavoured to point out the impossibility of resisting the Almoravides. In this he was right, for 'Abdallah had but few troops, and mistrusting his best general, the Berber Mokâtil el Royo,[1] he had banished him. All the older councillors of the court agreed with Mu'ammil; but 'Abdallah had misgivings with regard to the old man's loyalty, and was even inclined to regard him

---

[1] "The ruddy-faced."

as an accomplice of the perfidious Abû Ja'far, at whose escape he reproached Mu'ammil with conniving. His suspicions were not wholly baseless. It is not certainly known whether he was really acting in Yûsuf's interests, but it is certain that that monarch, who appreciated Mu'ammil's talents, counted on his support. 'Abdallah therefore regarded Mu'ammil's counsel as a snare, and since his young favourites assured him that Yûsuf certainly came with evil intentions, he announced that he had decided to meet force with force, and loaded Mu'ammil and his friends with threats and reproaches. This was imprudent, for he thus alienated them wholly and almost drove them into Yûsuf's arms. Quitting Granada during the night, they proceeded to Loxa, and seizing that town proclaimed the sovereignty there of the king of the Almoravides. The troops sent against them by 'Abdallah, however, forced them to surrender and brought them back to Granada, where they were led through the streets like the vilest criminals. Thanks to Yûsuf's intervention they were nevertheless set at liberty. The African monarch peremptorily ordered the prince of Granada to release them, and since the latter did not yet positively know Yûsuf's intentions he dared not disobey. But while 'Abdallah yet tried to prevent an open rupture, he actively prepared for war. He despatched courier after courier to Alfonso praying him to come to his assistance, and by a lavish expenditure of gold he enrolled in the army a large number of tradesmen, weavers, and artisans of various kinds. His efforts were fruitless. Alfonso did not respond to his appeal, the Granadans were disaffected, they awaited the arrival of the Almoravides impatiently, and each day a number of citizens quitted the town to join them. In such circumstances resistance was impossible. 'Abdallah realized this, and on Sunday, November 10, 1090, when Yûsuf had arrived within eight miles of Granada, he once more summoned his Council. The assembly declared that he must not think of defence, and 'Abdallah's mother, who was present and who, we are assured, had conceived the extravagant idea that Yûsuf might marry her, addressed her son thus: " My son, there is only one course open to thee. Go and greet the Almoravide; he is thy cousin,[1] and he will treat thee honourably." 'Abdallah therefore set out, accompanied by his mother and a splendid retinue.

---

[1] *i.e.* " he is a Berber as thou art."

The Slav guards marched first, and an escort of Christian horsemen surrounded the prince's person. All the soldiers wore turbans of the finest cotton, and were mounted upon splendid chargers caparisoned with brocade. On arriving in Yûsuf's presence 'Abdallah dismounted, and entreated his forgiveness if he had had the misfortune to displease him. Yûsuf graciously assured him that any grievances he might have had against him were forgotten, and begged him to take possession of a tent which he indicated, where he should be treated with all the respect due to his rank. But as soon as 'Abdallah had set his foot within the tent he found himself fettered.

Soon afterwards the principal inhabitants of the city arrived in the camp. Yûsuf welcomed them cordially, assuring them that they had nothing to fear, but would be the gainers by the impending change of dynasty. And in fact when they had taken the oath of allegiance he issued an edict abolishing all the taxes not prescribed by the Koran. The Almoravide then entered the city amidst the enthusiastic shouts of the people, and alighted at the palace to inspect the treasures which it contained and which had been amassed by Bâdîs. These were astonishing and innumerable; the halls were adorned with hangings and carpets of immense value; everywhere emeralds, rubies, diamonds, pearls, vases of crystal, gold, or silver dazzled the sight. A single chaplet consisted of four hundred pearls, each of which was valued at a hundred ducats. The Almoravide was astounded by such treasures; before entering Granada he had declared that they belonged to him, but since his ambition exceeded his cupidity, he thought fit to display his generosity by dividing them among his officers without keeping anything for himself. It was, however, known that the palace contained more wealth than met the eye, and that 'Abdallah's mother had buried many precious objects. She was forced to reveal the hiding-places, and since it was suspected that she had not made full· disclosure Yûsuf ordered Mu'ammil—whom he had appointed Steward of the Palace and of the Crown Lands —to excavate the foundations and even the sewers of the edifice.

These events would have furnished a reasonable excuse to the Andalusian princes for breaking entirely with Yûsuf. But they did nothing of the kind. On the contrary, Mu'tamid and Mutawakkil repaired to Granada to congratulate the

Almoravide, and Mu'tasim sent his son 'Obaidallah as his
representative. With inexplicable blindness Mu'tamid
flattered himself with the hope that Yûsuf would cede
Granada to his son Râzî, in compensation for having seized
Algeciras. No one who deemed the African capable of
ceding territory knew that potentate! Yûsuf soon showed
him the gravity of the error. He received the Emirs
with icy coldness, and his only response to Mu'tamid's hint
concerning Granada was to throw Mu'tasim's son into prison.
Such conduct could not fail to open the eyes of the princes.
Mu'tamid became greatly disquieted. " We committed a
grievous error," he said, "in inviting this man to our country ;
he will give us to drink of the cup which 'Abdallah has
been compelled to drain." Then, on the pretext that they
had received tidings that the Castilians were once more
threatening their frontiers, the two princes requested permission to withdraw, and having obtained it, hastened to
their own States ; they then advised the other Emirs to
concert measures for defending themselves against the
Almoravide, whose plans were now patent to all. This step
was crowned with success. The Emirs banded themselves
together not to supply the Almoravides with troops or
provisions, and they further decided to form an alliance
with Alfonso.

Yûsuf himself returned to Algeciras, intending to sail
for Africa and leave to his generals the odious task of
dethroning the Andalusian princes. On his way he wrested
the little principality of Malaga from Temîm, 'Abdallah's
brother, a wholly insignificant prince, and warned the
Fakihs that the decisive moment had come for the issue of
a very explicit *fetwa*. This was speedily forthcoming. It
declared that the Andalusian princes were impious profli-
gates ; that by their bad example they had corrupted the
people and made them indifferent to sacred things—witness
their slackness in attendance at divine service ; that they
had levied illegal taxes, and had maintained them in spite
of Yûsuf's prohibition ; that, as a climax to their iniquities,
they had allied themselves with the King of Castile, an
implacable foe of the true faith ; and that, consequently,
they were incapable of reigning any longer over Moslems ;
that Yûsuf was absolved from all pledges he had made to
them, and that it was not only his right but his duty to
dethrone them without delay. " We take it upon ourselves,"
they said in conclusion, "to answer before God for this

decision. If we err, we consent to pay the penalty in another world, and we declare that you, Emir of the Moslems, are not responsible therefor; but we firmly believe that the Andalusian princes, if you leave them in peace, will deliver our land to the infidels, and in that case you must account to God for your inaction."

Such was the tenour of this memorable *fetwa*, which also contained accusations aimed at particular princes. Even Rumaykiyya was named in it; she was accused of having dragged her husband into a vortex of dissipation, and of being the chief cause of the decadence of religion.

The *fetwa* was of the highest value to Yûsuf, but to endow it with still greater authority, he procured its approval by his African Fakihs, and then sent it to the most eminent doctors of Egypt and Asia in order that they might confirm the opinions of the Western divines. The Eastern ecclesiastics might well have avowed themselves incompetent to meddle with matters of which they knew nothing; but they did quite otherwise: their pride was agreeably flattered by the idea that there was a country where men of their profession disposed of thrones, and the most renowned among them—the great Ghazâlî at their head—did not hesitate to express their entire approval of the Andalusian Fakihs' decision. They moreover addressed letters of counsel to Yûsuf, urging him to govern justly and not to stray from the right path—in other words to follow always the counsels of theologians.

[AUTHORITIES: *Abbad.*, i. pp. 172–5; ii. pp. 9, 23–7, 39, 120–1, 131–2, 151, 179–80, 199–204, 211, 221; 'Abd al-Wâhid, pp. 92, 94–7; Ibn Bassâm, i. 230; Ibn al-Khatîb (MS. G.), ff. 16–17; (MS. E.) Arts. on Abû Ja'far Kolai'î, Mukatil, Ibn Bologguîn and Mu'ammil; Ibn Khallikân, fasc. xii. pp. 25–6; Ibn Khaldûn, *Hist. des Berb.*, ii. pp. 79–82 (transl.); *Kartâs*, p. 99.]

CHAPTER XIV

THE RULE OF THE ALMORAVIDES

THE character of the struggle now commencing might
have been foreseen: it was to be a war of sieges rather
than of battles. The opposing forces prepared respectively
to attack strongholds and to defend them. The Almoravide army, of which Sîr ibn Abî Bakr, a kinsman of Yûsuf's,
was generalissimo, was formed into several divisions, one
of which besieged Almeria while the others operated against
Mu'tamid's fortresses. Of the latter, Tarifa fell in December,
1090. Soon afterwards, so rapid was their advance, Yûsuf's
troops had commenced the siege of Cordova, where Fath,
surnamed Mamûn—a son of Mu'tamid—was in command.
The former capital of the Khalifate did not make a long
resistance; its own citizens delivered it up to the Almoravides. Fath tried to cut his way through foes and traitors
but was overwhelmed by numbers. His head was cut off
and carried through the streets, on a spear, in triumph
(March 26, 1091). Carmona was taken on May 10, and
the siege of Seville then began. Two armies marched
against that city; one encamped on the east and the other
on the west. The Guadalquiver flowed between the latter
force and the town, which on that side was defended by a
fleet. Mu'tamid's position had therefore become critical.
One hope alone remained to him; he counted on the help
of Alfonso, to whom he had made the most lavish promises
conditionally on his coming to his assistance. Alfonso
agreed to do so, and kept his word, sending Alvar Fañez
into Andalusia with a large force. But unfortunately for
Mu'tamid, Alfonso's general was defeated near Almodovar
by a detachment sent against him by Sîr. The news of
this disaster was a thunderbolt to the King of Seville. Yet
he did not despair; his courage was sustained by the predictions and dreams of his astrologer. So long as the prog-
nostics remained favourable Mu'tamid believed that some
miracle would save him, but when they became inauspicious
and hinted of an approaching end—of a lion springing upon

his prey—he gave way to profound despondency, and resigned
the conduct of the defence to his son Rashîd.

Meanwhile the malcontents who desired to deliver up
the city to the enemy did not cease from their endeavours
to excite a revolt. They were well known to Mu'tamid,
who could have put them to death—as indeed he was
advised—but he was loath to end his reign with an act
of such severity, and contented himself with setting a
watch over them. Such vigilance, however, was ineffectual,
for the traitors found means of communicating with the
enemy, aided them in making a breach, and through this
breach, on Tuesday, September 2, some of the Almoravides
made their way into the city. On hearing what had
happened Mu'tamid seized a sword, and without waiting
for breastplate or shield, he sprang into his saddle and
charged the assailants with a few devoted horsemen. An
Almoravide hurled a spear at him: the weapon passed
beneath his arm and grazed his tunic. Thereupon, seizing
his sword in both hands, Mu'tamid hewed his antagonist
in twain, and forced the rest of the foe to seek safety in
precipitate flight. The breach was quickly repaired, but
the peril, though averted for the moment, was speedily
renewed. In the afternoon the Almoravides succeeded in
burning the fleet, a loss which struck terror into the besieged, for they were well aware that the destruction of
the ships made the city untenable, and that a general
assault was only postponed until the arrival of Sîr with
reinforcements. Self-preservation was now the citizens'
only thought. Some endeavoured to swim the river, some
dropped from the ramparts, some even crept into the sewers.
Meanwhile Sîr had arrived, and on Sunday, September 7,
the assault was delivered. The soldiers posted on the walls
defended themselves bravely, but they were overwhelmed
by superior numbers, and the Almoravides broke into the
city, which soon became a scene of rapine and excesses of
all kinds. In their greed the victors even stripped the
Sevillans naked.

Mu'tamid remained in his palace. His wives wept;
his friends urged him to surrender. He refused, for he
feared—not death, which he had faced too often to dread—
but some degrading punishment. He embodied his thoughts
in these verses:

"When my tears cease to flow, and a calm steals over my troubled heart,
I hear voices crying 'Yield! that is true wisdom!' But I reply, 'Poison

would be a sweeter draught to me than such a cup of shame!' Though
the barbarians wrest from me my realm, and my soldiers forsake me, my
courage and my pride remain steadfast. When I fell upon the foe, I
scorned a breastplate, I encountered them unarmed; hoping for death,
I flung myself into the fray; but, alas, my hour had not yet come!'"

Resolved once more to seek the death which seemed to
elude him, he rallied his guard; together they charged in
desperation upon an Almoravide battalion which had penetrated the palace, drove them out, and hurled them into
the river. His son Mâlik fell during the combat, but
Mu'tamid himself received no hurt. Returning to the
palace, the thought of suicide passed through his mind,
but he dismissed it as an offence in the eyes of God, and
at length decided to surrender. At nightfall he sent his
son Rashîd to Sîr, hoping to be granted terms. His hope
was deceived. Rashîd in vain begged for an audience: he
was informed that his father must surrender unconditionally.
Mu'tamid then bowed to the inevitable. Bidding farewell
to his family, and to his weeping companions in arms, he
submitted with his son Rashîd to the Almoravides. The
castle was pillaged, and Mu'tamid was informed that the
lives of himself and his family would be spared only on
condition that he ordered his two sons, Râzî and Mu'tadd—
who were commandants of Ronda and Mertola respectively
—to surrender promptly to the besieging Almoravide
troops. Mu'tamid consented, and knowing that his two
sons were as stout-hearted as himself, he entreated them,
in the most affecting terms, to obey his injunctions, since
in that way only could the lives of their mother, brothers,
and sisters be saved. Rumaykiyya joined her entreaties
to Mu'tamid's, for she too feared lest her sons might refuse
to surrender. Nor was that fear baseless. Râzî especially,
though touched by the fate which would await his family
if he persisted in defending Ronda, could scarcely bring
himself to obey, for he felt able to hold out indefinitely.
Guerûr, the general in charge of the siege, kept at a distance,
not daring to approach that eagle's nest on a precipitous
mountain, and despairing to capture it by force of arms.
At length, however, filial affection won the day; Râzî
consented to parley, and having obtained favourable terms,
opened the gates of his fortress to the Almoravides. But
Guerûr infamously broke his word, and to punish Râzî for
his obstinate defence, procured his assassination. Mu'tadd,
who capitulated sooner, met with a fate less hard; but

even in his case the treaty was violated, for his property, which it had secured to him, was confiscated.

The capture of Seville hastened the reduction of Almeria. Mu'tasim, on his deathbed, had advised his eldest son 'Izz al-daula, to seek refuge in the court of the lords of Bujayah[1] as soon as Seville fell. 'Izz al-daula respected his father's last wishes, and the Almoravides soon entered Almeria in triumph.[2] Soon afterwards Murcia, Denia, and Xativa fell into their hands. They then turned their attention to Badajoz. During the siege of Seville Mutawakkil attempted to stave off ruin by forming an alliance with the Almoravides, and went so far, it is said, as to aid them in the capture of Mu'tamid's capital : but later, when his nominal allies began to devastate his frontiers, he threw himself into Alfonso's arms and purchased that monarch's protection at the price of Lisbon, Cintra, and Santarem. This step proved unpopular, and some of his subjects made overtures to the Almoravides. Sîr, who had been appointed governor of Seville, accordingly despatched an army against Mutawakkil at the beginning of 1094, and the conquest of the kingdom, including the capital, was effected with such ease and rapidity that Alfonso had not time to come to the aid of his ally. Mutawakkil himself was made prisoner, upon the storming of the citadel of Badajoz, where he had sought safety with his family. Sîr compelled him, by torture, to reveal his hidden treasures, and then announced that he was to be taken to Seville with his two sons Fadl and 'Abbâs. Such, however, was not Sîr's real intention ; on the contrary, he had determined to make an end of these princes, but since he feared that their execution, if it took place in Badajoz, might have a bad effect, he instructed the officer commanding the escort to despatch them when out of sight of the city. After journeying for some distance, the captain, therefore, ordered Mutawakkil and his sons to prepare for death. The unfortunate prince made no appeal for mercy to his executioners—this, he well knew, would be useless—he begged only that his sons should be the first to die; for, according to Moslem ideas, sin may be redeemed by suffering. His request was granted, and when he had seen the heads of his two children fall, he knelt down in a last prayer; but ere he had finished it, the soldiers pierced him with their spears.

---

[1] The modern Bougie.   [2] At the end of 1091 : *Recherches* (1881), i. 272.

In 1102 the Almoravides took possession of Valencia, a city which eight years before had been captured by the Cid. During his life-time they had tried in vain to wrest it from him, and after his death (1099), his widow Ximena held it for yet two years; but Alfonso, to whom she had appealed for aid, considered that Valencia was too far distant to be defended by him against the "Saracens" for long, and decided to abandon it: the Castilians, however, in evacuating the city set fire to it, leaving for the Almoravides only a heap of ruins.

Only two States of Moslem Spain now remained to be reduced by the Almoravides—Zaragoza, ruled by Musta'în, a member of the Beni Hûd, and La Sahla, which belonged to the Beni Razîn. The latter acknowledged Yûsuf's sovereignty but were nevertheless deposed. Musta'în, who had gained the goodwill of the Almoravides by magnificent gifts, was more fortunate, and retained the throne during his life-time; but upon his death (January 24, 1110) a change took place. The inhabitants of Zaragoza refused allegiance to his son and successor 'Imâd al-daula unless he would dismiss all the Christian soldiers in his army. This was a hard condition, for the Christians had formed the flower of the Zaragozan army for a century past, and if 'Imâd al-daula dismissed them, his fall would be inevitable, since his subjects wished for nothing better than to yield themselves to the Almoravides. The prince, however, was compelled to make the required promise, and when he had fulfilled it, his subjects immediately communicated with 'Alî, Yûsuf's son, who now reigned— his father having died three years before—and pointed out that since the Christian troops had been disbanded the kingdom lay open to him. On hearing of this intrigue, 'Imâd al-daula once more enrolled the Christians. This step brought the resentment of his subjects to a climax. They informed 'Alî of what had happened, and begged him for help. 'Alî inquired of the Fakihs of Morocco whether it was permissible for him to intervene, and on receiving an affirmative reply he ordered the Governor of Valencia to take possession of Zaragoza. The order was executed without difficulty, for 'Imâd al-daula, who thought himself no longer safe in his capital, evacuated it and threw himself into the fortress of Rueda.[1] Before his departure

---

[1] Which he held until his death in 1130. Ten years later his son and successor, Saif al-daula, ceded the fortress to Alfonso VII.

he sent 'Alî a touching letter, entreating him, by the friendship which had subsisted between their fathers, to spare
his State, since he had done nothing to deserve 'Alî's
hostility. 'Alî was the more impressed by this letter since
his father, on his deathbed, had enjoined him to live at
peace with the Beni Hûd; he therefore countermanded the
order he had sent to the Governor of Valencia; but it
was too late—the Almoravides were already in Zaragoza.

All Moslem Spain was therefore now united under
the sceptre of the King of Morocco; the desire of the
people and the Fakihs was gratified, and the latter at
any rate had no reason to regret the revolution. We must
revert to the time of the Visigoths to find an example of
a clergy as powerful as the Moslem divines under the
Almoravides. The three princes of that house who reigned
successively over Andalusia—Yûsuf, 'Alî (1106–1143), and
Tâshifîn (1143–1145)—were extremely devout; they held
all Fakihs in honour, and did nothing without their approval. But the palm of piety must rest with 'Alî. He
was never meant by nature for a throne, but for a life of
placid meditation, in a monastery or a desert hermitage.
He spent his days in prayer and fasting. The Fakihs
naturally rejoiced at having such a monarch; they swayed
him as they would, they seized the administration, they
dispensed offices and honours, they amassed vast wealth—
in a word, they reaped the fruits they had hoped for from
Almoravide domination, and the harvest exceeded their
anticipations. But if the event had justified their expectations it had also justified the fears of those who desired
to be ruled neither by ecclesiastics nor barbarians from
Morocco and the Sahara. Scholars, poets, philosophers, all
had bitter grievances. It is true that many men of letters
who had served in the chanceries of the Andalusian princes
obtained posts under their new masters; but they found
themselves out of place amongst an uncongenial crowd
of fanatical priests and uncouth soldiers; far different had
been the Courts they had been accustomed to. Even
among those who, to earn their bread, flattered the
Almoravide lords and dedicated books to them, a certain
melancholy was noticeable, and deep regret for the lettered
princes who had passed for ever. Some of them at times
felt an irresistible impulse to vent their wrath—as for
instance a secretary who was ordered by the monarch to
address a reproof to the Valencian army for being defeated

by the King of Aragon, and who showed his antipathy
by decorating his letter with such phrases as these:
"Cowards, poltroons that flee at the sight of a single horseman! Ye should be given ewes to milk rather than horses
to ride. Ye are ripe for condign punishment; the Sahara
awaits the offscourings of Spain!" It is scarcely necessary
to say that such language did not meet with the monarch's
approval, and the secretary was dismissed. Poets found
but few patrons; they deplored the decline of taste and
cursed the barbarian invaders. A few of them eked out
a precarious livelihood by composing panegyrics of the
Fakihs, for the latter, with all their piety, were not exempt
from vanity, of which their head, Ibn Hamdîn, Kady of
Cordova, had a large share. Claiming to belong to the
Arab nobility and assuming princely airs, he was gratified
by such verses as these: "Speak not of the glories of
Baghdad, nor of the beauty of China or of Persia: in all the
world no city can compare with Cordova, and no man can
rival Ibn Hamdîn." But the Fakihs, without excepting
Ibn Hamdîn—who was the richest citizen in Cordova—
were excessively parsimonious,[1] and self-respecting poets
who loved their art had no inducement to sing their
praises. Poverty was therefore their lot. Ibn Bakî, a
delightful poet, one of the best that Andalusia had produced, wandered hungry from town to town. "I live
among you, my fellow-countrymen," he laments, "in
poverty and distress, and had I preserved my self-respect,
I should have long ago departed. Your gardens yield no
fruit, your skies no rain. Yet I have merit, and if Andalusia rejects me, 'Irâk will welcome me. To seek to live
by poetic talent here is madness; for the land containeth
none but doltish and miserly upstarts." One consolation
alone remained to the poets—to lampoon the powers that
were; to aim envenomed satires at the Fakihs—"hypocrites, wolves that skulk in the darkness, and piously
devour all men's goods." But this was dangerous, for the
Fakihs had the means of punishing their traducers. Philosophy, it need scarcely be said, was a prohibited science.
Mâlik ibn Wohaib, of Seville, had the imprudence to study
it; but finding that his life was in danger, he renounced
it and devoted himself to Theology and Canon Law. He

---

[1] "The end of the world approaches," said the poet Ibn al-Binnî, "for Ibn
Hamdîn promises us payment. The stars are still as far from our grasp as is
his money."

had no reason to regret this step, for he became the monarch's friend and confidant; nevertheless, his youthful error was never wholly condoned, and an enemy wrote: "The Court of 'Alî, grandson of Tâshifîn, would be pure and spotless if the Devil had not contrived to introduce thither Mâlik ibn Wohaib." The intolerance of the Fakihs passed all bounds, and was equalled by the narrowness of their views. Little versed in the study of the Koran and the Traditions of the Prophet, they relied solely on the writings of the Mâlikites, which they regarded as binding and infallible. Their Theology, in fact, consisted in a minute knowledge of Canon Law. In vain did more enlightened theologians protest against this exclusive predilection for books and dogmas of secondary importance: the Fakihs replied by persecuting their critics, and branding them as impious and schismatical. The work which the celebrated Ghazâlî [1] had published in the East under the title of *The Revival of Religious Science* caused great scandal in Andalusia. Yet it was not a heterodox book. Ghazâlî, dissatisfied with every system of philosophy, at first leaned to scepticism; but mere negations brought him little solace, and he plunged into mysticism, becoming henceforth the sworn foe of philosophy. He declares in the book alluded to that philosophy is only of use in defending revealed religion against innovators and heretics; in a time of lively faith, he declared, it was superfluous. Natural Science should be wholly eschewed, if its study tended to shake the foundations of belief. The religion he preached was personal and passionate—a religion of the heart—and he energetically attacked contemporary theologians, who, content with mere externals, concerned themselves solely with questions of legality, useful only in adjusting the petty disputes of the lower orders. This was touching the Andalusian Fakihs on the raw, and they screamed loudly. The Kady of Cordova, Ibn Hamdîn, declared that any man who read Ghazâlî's book was an infidel ripe for damnation, and he drew up a *fetwa* condemning all copies of the book to the flames. This *fetwa*, signed by the Fakihs of Cordova, was formally approved by 'Alî. Ghazâlî's book was accordingly burnt in Cordova and all the other cities of the Empire, and possession of

---

[1] The best account of al-Ghazâli is that given by D. B. Macdonald, in *The Journal of the American Oriental Society*, vol. xx. (1899), pp. 122 *sqq.* See Nicholson, *Lit. Hist. of the Arabs* (1907), p. 382.

a copy was interdicted on pain of death and confiscation of
property.

Under such a régime the lot of those who were not
Moslems was, of course, intolerable. A Cordovan Fakih,
for instance, thought he had hit upon an excellent mode
of forcing the Jews to embrace Islamism. He alleged that
he had discovered among Ibn Masarra's papers a tradition
that the Jews had solemnly promised Mohammed to become Moslems at the end of the fifth century after the
Hijra, if the expected Messiah had not previously appeared.
Literary history was evidently not the Fakih's strong point,
or he would have been careful to find the tradition elsewhere than in the papers of a far from orthodox philosopher.
But his colleagues were not critical, and Yûsuf himself,
who was then in Spain, proceeded to Lucena—a town exclusively Jewish [1]—and summoned the Jews to fulfil the
promise made by their ancestors. Great was the consternation of the Jews of Lucena, but, happily for them, there
was a way of escape. After all, it was not their conscience
or their faith that was aimed at; they were reckoned the
richest Jews in the Mohammedan world, and the Government looked to them to supply the deficit caused in the
treasury by the abolition of illegal taxes. Of this fact they
were all aware, and they begged the Kady of Cordova to
intercede with Yûsuf on their behalf. Ibn Hamdîn was
not deaf to their entreaties, and advocated their cause
before the monarch; that he did so gratuitously is more
than doubtful, but his appeal was successful. The sum
demanded by the King was indeed enormous; but in the
circumstances the Jews must have been thankful to escape
with only a pecuniary loss.

The Christians, or Mozarabs as they were called,
suffered still more: the Fakihs and the populace fostered
against them a yet more envenomed hatred. In most
towns they formed but a small community: but in the
province of Granada they were still numerous, and near
the capital they possessed a beautiful church, which had
been built about A.D. 600 by Gudila, a Gothic noble. This
church was an offence to the Fakihs. Basing their action,
probably, on the authority of the Khalif 'Omar II, who
had desired to leave standing not a church nor chapel,

---

[1] Fifteen miles S.W. of Polei. The suburb was mainly inhabited by Moslems;
but the town itself, which was surrounded by a wall and moat, was held by Jews
alone, who refused admission to Moslems. See Idrisi, ii. p. 54.

ion. Yûsuf having given his approval, the sacred edifice
was levelled with the ground (A.D. 1099). Other churches
seem to have met with a similar fate; and the Fakihs
treated the Mozarabs so oppressively that the latter at
length appealed to Alfonso the Battler, King of Aragon,
to deliver them from their intolerable burdens. Alfonso
acceded to their request. In September, 1125, he set out
with four thousand knights[2] and their men-at-arms, all
sworn on the Gospels not to desert one another. Alfonso
did not, however, achieve the result he aimed at. It is true
that he ravaged Andalusia for more than a year, advanced
to the gates of Cordova, and won a great victory at Arnisol,
S.W. of Lucena; but the ultimate object of the expedition
had been the capture of Granada, and this was not effected.
Upon the withdrawal of the Aragonese army, the Moslems
cruelly avenged themselves on the Mozarabs. Ten thousand
of the Christians were already out of their reach, for,
knowing the fate in store for them, they had obtained permission from Alfonso to settle in his territories; but
many who still remained were deprived of their property,
maltreated in endless ways, thrown into prison or put to
death. The majority, however, were transported to Africa,
and endured terrible sufferings, ultimately settling in the
vicinity of Saleh and Mequinez (A.D. 1126). This deportation was carried out in virtue of a decree which the Kady
Ibn Rushd—grandfather of the famous Averroes—had procured from 'Alî. Eleven years later a second expulsion
of the Mozarabs took place, and very few were left in
Andalusia.

Many classes therefore found the new Government harsh
and tyrannical. Yet the Christians, the Jews, the more
liberal Moslem ecclesiastics, philosophers, poets and men
of letters, even in the aggregate formed a minority of the
nation. This minority was indisputably an important one,
which could not be ignored, comprising as it did nearly all
men of talent, but it did not represent the bulk of the
populace. What the latter expected may be thus formu-
lated: Internal tranquillity, security against external foes,
diminished taxes, and increased prosperity. It may be
admitted that these hopes were realized during the reign

[1] See *Journ. asiat.*, ser. iv. t. xviii. p. 513.
[2] Among them, Gaston, Vicomte de Bearn, Pedro, Bp. of Zaragoza, and Stephen,
Bp. of Huesca; *Recherches* (1881), i. 353.

of Yûsuf and the early years of that of his successor.
Public order was maintained ; the trade routes were secure ;
and the Castilians were so effectually kept in awe that they
did not venture to make raids into Andalusia.   Neither,
at first, did the Government raise illegal taxes—for, as we
have seen, the Jews supplied the deficiencies in the Moslem
treasury. The statement of one chronicler to the effect
that no extraordinary impost was resorted to cannot,
however, be accepted, for it is certain that at least on one
occasion Yûsuf tried to levy a war-tax—a *ma'ûna* or aid,
as it was called. The Almerians, who had never shown much
partiality for the Almoravides, refused to pay it, and the Kady
of the city, Abû 'Abdallah ibn al-Farrâ,[1] replied thus to
Yûsuf's reprimand : " You blame me, Sire, because I would
not compel my fellow-citizens to pay the *ma'ûna*, and tell
me that its legality—in the opinion of the Kadies and Fakihs
of Morocco and Andalusia—rests upon the example of
'Omar, Companion of the Prophet, who was buried beside
him, and whose justice has never been impugned. I reply,
Emir of the Moslems, that you are not a Companion of the
Prophet, that you will not be buried by his side, that I am
not aware that your justice has never been impugned, and
that if the Kadies and Fakihs rank you with 'Omar, they
will have to answer before God for their audacity. 'Omar,
moreover, did not demand the contribution in question until
he had sworn in the mosque that not a dirhem remained in
the treasury ; if you can do the like you will have the right
to call for an aid ; if not, you have no right.   Greeting ! "
We cannot tell whether this outspoken criticism influenced
Yûsuf, but it seems certain that under 'Alî illegal taxes
were reimposed to some extent, for a chronicler mentions
that certain Christians were employed by that prince to
collect the *maghram*, a word commonly used to denote
imposts not prescribed in the Koran.[2]   But in any case, the
taxation was lower than it had been under the Andalusian
princes, and that fact, coupled with general tranquillity,
made for the public welfare. A high level of prosperity,
indeed, was attained : bread was cheap, and vegetables
could be obtained for next to nothing.
      The people as a whole were therefore not disappointed

---

[1] Killed at the battle of Cutanda, near Daroca, in 1120.
[2] According to the trustworthy geographer Idrîsî, the Almoravides levied taxes,
at all events in the capital, on nearly all commodities. (Ed. Dozy and de Goeje,
1866, p. 70 of text.)

—unless they had hoped that the Almoravides would gain decisive victories over the Christians and restore Moslem Spain to the splendour and might she had enjoyed under 'Abd-er-Rahmân III, Hakam II, and Almanzor. Yet circumstances had been favourable for conquests. After the death of Alfonso VI, in 1109, Christian Spain was for long a prey to civil war; but the Almoravides did not grasp the opportunity. All their efforts to capture Toledo were fruitless; they seized some towns of secondary importance, but such successes were counterbalanced by the loss of Zaragoza (A.D. 1118).

The beneficial results of the revolution were, after all, transient. Administrators, generals, and soldiers deteriorated with surprising rapidity. Yûsuf's generals when they landed in Spain, though illiterate, were pious, brave, honest, and inured to the simple and frugal life of the Desert. But enriched by the gifts which Yûsuf had showered upon them, they speedily lost their virtues, and henceforth devoted themselves to the undisturbed enjoyment of their wealth. Andalusian civilization had been to them a novel spectacle: ashamed of their barbarism, they began to ape the princes whom they had dethroned; but their uncouth attempts at assimilating the taste and refinement of the Andalusians proved, as might have been expected, grotesque failures.

They posed as patrons of literature, and were fain to be adulated in poems and dedications; but all their strivings after culture were clumsy and tasteless; they remained semi-barbarians, and imitated successfully only the worst features of Andalusian civilization. 'Alî's brother-in-law, Abû Bakr ibn Ibrâhîm, successively Governor of Granada and Zaragoza, was a type of the generals who endeavoured, without much success, to Andalusianize themselves, if the expression is permissible. Born in the Sahara, he had been brought up in the austere principles of his kinsfolk; but at Zaragoza he forgot his early training, and took as his models those convivial monarchs the Beni Hûd; and when he drank amongst his boon-companions, he wore a crown and royal robes. The Beni Hûd, moreover, had been patrons of philosophy—two of them, Muktadir and Mû'tamin, had even written on that science—and Abû Bakr must needs follow their example; so, heedless of what his brother-in-law and the Fakihs might say, he chose for his friend and adviser a man whose name was mentioned with horror by the faithful, a man who disbelieved in the Koran and all revelation—the famous philosopher Avempace.[1] So indignant were his troops, that many of them deserted him. But the soldiers themselves, despite their orthodoxy, became no less degenerate than their officers. Insolence towards the Andalusians and pusillanimity in the field became their chief characteristics. So great was their cowardice that 'Alî was obliged to overcome his aversion for Christians and enrol those whom his admiral, Ibn Maimûn—a veritable man-hunter—brought him from Galicia, Catalonia, Italy, and the Byzantine Empire;[2] and yet the Almoravides treated Andalusia as a conquered country, and seized whatever they pleased—men's property or wives. The Government was helpless. Its feebleness was pitiful. The Fakihs deputed their authority to women, or at least shared it with them. 'Alî was dominated by his wife Kamar; other ladies swayed high dignitaries at their pleasure, and by gratifying their greed complete liberty of action might be purchased. Even brigands could count upon impunity if they were able to purchase the protection of these ladies. Official posts were in the gift of women, and were usually filled by the most incompetent men. The whole administration, in fact, became contemptible and ridiculous. The army and the people derided it when it revoked to-day orders given yesterday; nobles began to aspire to the throne, declaring that they could rule far better than the feeble 'Alî, who could only fast and pray.

As the crowning calamity, a terrible insurrection broke out in Africa (1121). Fanaticized by an ambitious reformer, Ibn Tûmart, who claimed to be the Mahdî predicted by Mohammed, the barbarous tribes of the Atlas, calling themselves the Almohades, took up arms against the Almoravides. For the tottering dynasty this blow was fatal. With the exception of the Christians, the Almoravide troops were so demoralised that they usually fled as soon as the enemy was in sight. The Government, in extremities, sought to prolong its miserable existence by withdrawing all troops, with arms and munitions of war, from Andalusia. The Christians seized the opportunity thus presented to them. In 1125, Alfonso the Battler, King of Aragon, ravaged Andalusia, as we have seen, for more than a year. In 1133, Alfonso VII, of Castile—who, like his grandfather

---

[1] 'Abû Bakr Ibn al-Sâ'igh Ibn Bâjja, died 1138. See C. Huart, *Hist. of Arabic Literature* (1903), p. 288.
[2] These *Roum* were almost equivalent to the former *Slavs*.

Alfonso VI, styled himself Emperor—carried fire and sword
through the districts of Cordova, Seville, and Carmona, pillaged and burned Xeres, and, in emulation of his grandsire,
penetrated to what was then called the Tower of Cadiz,
namely the Pillars of Hercules.[1] Five years later he devastated the environs of Jaen, Baeza, Ubeda, and Andujar.
In 1143 the turn of Cordova, Seville, and Carmona came
again. In the following year the whole of Andalusia was
overrun from Calatrava to Almeria.

After a brief period of prosperity, the inhabitants of
Andalusia had therefore gained, by the revolution which
they had hailed with enthusiasm, the following results : an
impotent and corrupt government ; a cowardly, undisciplined, and brutal soldiery ; a despicable executive—for
the towns teemed with thieves, and the country with
brigands ; almost complete stagnation of trade and commerce ; dearness and scarcity of food ; and, finally, more
frequent invasions than they had ever before endured. All
their hopes were dashed, and they cursed the Almoravides,
whom previously they had welcomed as the saviours of
their faith and country. In 1121 the Cordovans rose
against their garrison—who had committed with impunity all
kinds of excesses—expelled these barbarians, and plundered
their houses. Thereupon 'Alî descended upon Andalusia
with a cloud of Africans ; never had so vast an army landed
in Spain. Then the Cordovans, with the courage of despair,
resolved to defend themselves. They shut their gates and
barricaded their streets. But the conflict would have been
too unequal, and the Fakihs interposed to prevent bloodshed. On this occasion, laying aside their usual servility,
they took the part of the citizens against the Government.
They issued a *fetwa* declaring that the revolt of the Cordovans was justifiable, since they had only taken up arms
in self-defence. 'Alî, as usual, yielded to the Fakihs, and,
after some parleying, the Cordovans agreed to pay compensation for the losses they had inflicted. In other
towns discontent daily increased, and although the past
had not been brilliant it was looked upon with regret when
compared with the insufferable gloom of the present.
These feelings are expressed in the message sent by the
Sevillans, in 1133, to Saif al-daula, son of the last King of
Zaragoza, who was serving in the army of Alfonso VII,
then at their gates : " Appeal to the King of the Christians ;

---

[1] See *Recherches* (1881), ii. 312.

with his aid, deliver us from the yoke of the Almoravides. When we are free we will pay the King a larger tribute than our fathers ever paid his, and thou and thy sons shall reign over us." Eleven years later, when the Empire was crumbling in every part, words such as these were heard in the streets and the mosques: " The Almoravides have sucked the very marrow from our bones! Where are our goods, our wives, our children? Let us rise and slay our oppressors!" But others said: "Let us first ally ourselves with the Emperor of Leon, and pay him a tribute as of yore. All means of deliverance from the Almoravides are good!" The blessing of heaven was invoked on this project; the Andalusians rose like one man to massacre their oppressors—led by the Kadies and Fakihs, for gratitude is rarely included among ecclesiastical virtues.

It is no part of our task to relate the history of this revolution, nor of the conquest of Spain by the Almohades, who had overthrown the Almoravides in Morocco. We undertook to describe the rise and progress of independent Andalusia, and if in this rapid sketch of its fate as a province of an alien empire we have transgressed the limits of our subject, it is because it seemed necessary to show that Andalusia in delivering herself to the Almoravides procured no happiness, and that the day came when she even regretted those native princes whom she had calumniated, abandoned, and betrayed in the hour of danger.

The story of Mu'tamid's captivity yet remains to be told.

[AUTHORITIES: 'Abd al-Wâhid, pp. 98–101, 114, 122–4, 127–8, 132–3, 148; *Abbad.*, i. 54–9, 303–4, 356; ii. 42, 44, 68, 178, 204–5, 227–8; *Kartás*, pp. 100–1, 104, 108; *Ann. Toled.*, ii. 404; *Chron. Lusit.*, pp. 326, 419; *Ann. Compl.*, p. 317; Ibn al-'Abbâr, pp. 182, 225; *Holal*, ff. 30–1, 33–6, 39, 41, 52, 62, 58–9; Makkarî, i. 229; ii. 262–3, 303–4, 322–3, 360–1, 472, 590, 729; *Chron. Adef.*, c. 13–16, 45–6, 60, 64, 82, 88–9, 91, 94; Ibn Abî-Usaibi'a (Art. on Avempace); Ibn Khallikân, fasc. xii. pp. 17–18; Ibn al-Khatîb (MS. G.), ff. 98–100; Ibn Khâkân, *Kalayid* (Art. on Avempace).]

CHAPTER XV

MU'TAMID IN EXILE

WHATEVER virtues Yûsuf may have possessed—and the Fakihs averred that they were numerous—magnanimity towards the vanquished was not one of them. His treatment of the captive Andalusian princes was both mean and cruel. It is true that the two grandsons of Bâdîs had little to complain of: they were set at liberty on condition that they did not quit Morocco, and received so handsome an allowance that 'Abdallah was enabled to leave a considerable fortune to his children. But Yûsuf had a partiality for these two princes; they were of his own race, and he had nothing to fear from incompetent men who, moreover, flattered him. Far different had been the lot of the other princes: we have already recounted the fate of Râzî, Mutawakkil, Fadl, and 'Abbâs—that of Mu'tamid, although his life was spared, was no less deplorable.

After the capture of Seville the deportation of Mu'tamid to Tangier had been decreed. When he set sail with his wives and many of his children, a vast crowd stood beside the Guadalquiver to bid him a last farewell. In one of his elegies the poet Ibn al-labbâna has thus described the scene :

"Overcome after a brave resistance, the princes were dragged to the vessel. Multitudes thronged the banks of the river; the women were unveiled, and their countenances were marred with grief. At the moment of parting what cries were uttered, what tears were shed! What now remains to us? Depart hence, O stranger! collect thy chattels, and make provision for thy journey, for the abode of generosity is deserted! Ye who would fain sojourn in this valley, be warned that the family ye seek hath departed, and that drought hath destroyed our harvest. And thou, O knight with thy glittering retinue, lay down thy useless arms, for the lion hath already opened his jaws to devour thee!"

When Mu'tamid had reached Tangier, where he remained for several days, the poet Husrî, who then lived there, and who had formerly resided at the court of Seville, sent him some poems which he had composed in his praise. Among these pieces one alone was new, and in this Husrî craved a gift, although he must have known that Mu'tamid had none to bestow. The ex-king of Seville had indeed saved from his riches but thirty-six ducats; these he had hidden in his shoes, and they were stained by his bleeding feet; but such was his generosity that he did not hesitate to sacrifice this last resource: he wrapped the coins in a scrap of paper, and, enclosing a few verses apologizing for so paltry a gift, he sent them to Husrî. That shameless beggar had not even the courtesy to thank the exile, and when other rhymesters of Tangiers heard that Mu'tamid still had money to spend, they flocked to him with their doggerel. Alas! they went empty away, and it was upon this occasion that he wrote:

"The poets of Tangier and of all Mauritania have bestirred themselves to rhyme, and would fain receive rewards at the hands of the captive. Rather is it for him to ask an alms of them. Can such things be? If an innate sense of shame and hereditary pride checked him not, he who formerly scattered his gold lavishly among those who appealed to his generosity would rival them in importunity."

From Tangier Mu'tamid was taken to Mequinez. On the way he met a procession proceeding to the mosque to pray for rain, and he improvised these verses:

"When folk who were about to implore heaven for rain met me, I exclaimed, 'My tears will supply the place of showers!' 'Thou sayest truth,' they replied; 'thy tears would suffice—but they are mingled with blood!'"

Mu'tamid remained at Mequinez for several months, and was then transferred, by Yûsuf's orders, to Aghmât, a town not far from Morocco. On his way thither, his son Rashîd, who for some unexplained reason had fallen under his displeasure, sent his father these verses to pacify him:

"Rival of the kindly rain, lord of generosity, protector of men! The greatest boon thou couldst bestow upon me would be to permit me for a moment to behold the light of thy countenance, which in its glory supplies the place of torches by night, and of the sun by day!"

Mu'tamid replied thus:

"I was the rival of the kindly rain, the lord of generosity, and the protector of men, when my right hand scattered gifts on the day of benefactions, and slew the foe on the day of battle, while my left hand curbed the war-horse terrified by the rattle of the spears. But now I am in thraldom and misery; I am become like a desecrated shrine, or a bird with broken wings. No longer can I respond to the appeal of the poor and the oppressed. The light of my countenance is bedimmed by sorrow; my cares banish all cheerful thoughts; to-day men who formerly sought my presence turn away their faces from me."

At Aghmât the prisoner dragged out a pitiful existence. The Government from time to time ordered his chains to be removed, or replaced, but otherwise wholly neglected him. He lived with his family in utter destitution. His wife and daughters earned a bare subsistence by spinning. In poesy alone did the prince find consolation. Once when he saw through the narrow window of his dungeon a flock of those swift birds called by the Arabs *katâ*—a kind of partridge—he expressed his feelings thus :

" I shed tears when I saw fleeting across the sky a covey of katâ; they were free, they knew not prisons and fetters. It was not for envy that I wept; it was because I desired to be free as they; could I but go wheresoever I would, no longer would my heart be oppressed with sorrow, nor should I bewail the loss of my children. Happy birds! They are not separated from one another; they know not the grief of being torn from their family, nor what it means to pass the night in agony after the bolts of the prison door have grated in their sockets. God careth for their little ones; as for mine, they perish of thirst and lack of shelter! "

In his poems he also recalled his bygone greatness, the splendid palaces which had been the witnesses of his happiness, and his sons who had been massacred. On the festival of the " Breaking of the Fast " he composed these verses :

" In days gone by the festivals made thee joyous, but sad is the festival which findeth thee a captive at Aghmât. Thou seest thy daughters clothed in rags and dying of hunger ; they spin for a pittance, for they are destitute. Worn with fatigue, and with downcast eyes, they come to embrace thee. They walk bare-footed in the mire of the streets, who once trod on musk and camphor![1] Their hollow cheeks, furrowed with tears, attest their poverty. . . . Just as on the occasion of this sad festival —God grant that thou mayest never see another!—thou hast broken thy fast, so has thy heart broken hers: thy sorrow, long restrained, bursts forth afresh. Yesterday, when thou spakest the word all men obeyed ; now thou art at the beck of others. Kings who glory in their greatness are the dupes of a vain dream! "

For the unhappy Rumaykiyya so hard a life was unendurable : she fell dangerously ill. Mu'tamid's grief was intensified by the fact that there was no one at Aghmât to minister to her wants. Fortunately, however, the famous Avenzoar[2]—who during the last years of Mu'tamid's reign had been court physician, and to whom the king had restored the property that Mu'tamid had confiscated from his grandfather—was then in Morocco. Mu'tamid therefore wrote to the physician, begging him to visit Rumaykiyya. Avenzoar

---

[1] Cf. *supra*, p. 666.   [2] Abu 'l-'Alâ Ibn Zuhr.

promised to come, and since in his letter he had wished Mu'tamid long life, the latter when thanking him enclosed the following verses :

"Thou wishest me a long life; but how can a prisoner desire it? Is not death preferable to a life which incessantly bringeth fresh torments? Others may desire length of days, because they hope for happiness; my sole hope is death. Could I wish to see my daughters bare-footed and in rags? They are now the menials of him who was wont to herald my approach when I rode forth, to thrust aside the folk who impeded me, to control them when they thronged the court-yard of my palace, to gallop on my right hand or on my left when I reviewed my troops, and see that no soldier quitted the ranks.[1] Nevertheless thy kindly prayer hath touched my heart. May God reward thee, Abu 'l-'Alâ! I know not when my desire will be accomplished, but I am consoled by reflecting that all things in this world have an end."

From time to time Mu'tamid was solaced by the letters and visits of poets upon whom he had once showered his bounty. Many of them journeyed to Aghmât—amongst others, Abû Mohammed Hijârî, who for a single poem had received a sum which enabled him to become a merchant and earn a competence as long as he lived. In conversation with him Mu'tamid admitted that he had erred in summoning Yûsuf to Andalusia. "In so doing," he said, "I dug my own grave." When the poet bade the prisoner farewell, on returning to Almeria, where he then dwelt, Mu'tamid wished to confer a gift upon him, notwithstanding his poverty; but Hijârî refused it delicately in two improvised verses :

"I swear that I can accept naught from thee, who art suffering so cruel and undeserved a fate. Thy gifts in the past suffice, though thou rememberest them not."

Mu'tamid's closest and most faithful friend was Ibn al-labbâna, and one day, on visiting Aghmât, the poet brought good news from Andalusia, to the effect that the minds of thinking men were agitated, and that the patricians, who had never desired the rule of Yûsuf, were conspiring with the object of replacing Mu'tamid on the throne. Ibn al-labbâna's report was true; great discontent prevailed, as we have seen, among the upper classes, and the government soon became aware of this fact. They took precautions, and arrested many suspects, especially at Malaga; but the conspirators in that town—led by Ibn Khalaf, a much re-

---

[1] Among the women who brought flax to be spun by Mu'tamid's daughters was a daughter of the ex-king's *arîf*, or usher.

spected noble—escaped from their prison by night, and seized the castle of Montemayor.[1] Soon ʻAbd al-Jabbâr, a son of Muʻtamid, who had remained in Andulasia, and whom the people mistook for Râzî—who had been assassinated at Ronda—joined them. He was hailed as leader, and all seemed going well. A Moroccan war-ship, which had stranded near the castle, supplied them with provisions and munitions of war. Algeciras and Arcos declared for the conspirators, and in 1095 ʻAbd al-Jabbâr made the latter town a base for raids, which he pushed to the gates of the former capital of the kingdom.

The news of his son's insurrection at first greatly perturbed Muʻtamid. The rashness of the enterprise alarmed him; he feared that ʻAbd al-Jabbâr would meet with the fate which had befallen many of his brothers. But fear soon gave place to hope; he caught glimpses of the possibility of reascending his throne, and he did not conceal these hopes from his friends. In writing to the poet Ibn Hamdîs, who had returned to Mahdia after visiting the exile, Muʻtamid, for instance, sent him a poem beginning thus:

"The pulpit in the mosque and the throne in the palace lament the captive whom destiny hath cast upon the shores of Africa,"

and containing this passage:

"Oh, that I might be assured that I shall see once more my pleasance and my lake in that fair land where grow the olive-trees, where the moan of doves is heard, and the sweet warblings of song-birds!"

Ibn al-labbâna fostered these hopes. On the eve of his return to Andalusia he had received from Muʻtamid twenty ducats and two pieces of cloth: he returned the gift, and among the verses he sent upon the occasion were these:

"Have patience for a little while! Soon thou wilt crown my happiness, for thou wilt reascend the throne. On the day that thou enterest thy palace thou wilt raise me to the highest honours. Thou wilt then surpass the son of Merwân in generosity, and I shall surpass Jarîr [2] in talent. Prepare to shed thy beams once more: an eclipse of the moon is transient."

Muʻtamid accordingly yet lived in hope, and this in spite of his being loaded afresh with chains by order of Yûsuf, who was heedful of the warning, attributed to a rhetorician of the day, that "when the whelp growls the onset of the lion is near." Nor was his hope ill-founded: ʻAbd al-

---

[1] Near Marbella, now a *despoblado*, or uninhabited place.
[2] † 728 A.D.; court-poet of Hajjâj, Governor of ʻIrâk; a famous satirist.

Jabbâr's party was numerous, and it inspired the government with grave uneasiness; for two years it threatened, and it was not put down until the moment of Mu'tamid's death, after a long illness, at the age of fifty-five (1095).[1]

The ex-king of Seville was buried in the cemetery at Aghmât. Some time afterwards, on the festival of the Breaking of the Fast, the Andalusian poet Ibn 'Abd as-Samad made a sevenfold circuit of his tomb, as pilgrims encircle the Ka'ba; then he knelt, kissed the earth which covered the remains of his benefactor, and recited an elegy. Touched by his example, the crowd also circumambulated the tomb, uttering loud lamentations.

"All men love Mu'tamid," writes an historian of the thirteenth century; "all men feel pity for him, and he is still lamented." He was, indeed, the most popular of all the Andalusian princes. His liberality, his bravery, his chivalry, endeared him to the cultured in succeeding generations; the compassionate were touched by his unparalleled misfortunes; the populace were captivated by his romantic adventures; and as a poet he was admired even by the Bedawin, who as judges of poetic diction were regarded as severer and more competent critics than the townsfolk.

Early in the twelfth century, a Sevillan, journeying through the Desert, reached an encampment of Lakhmite Bedawin. Approaching a tent, he sought hospitality from its owner; the latter, delighted to exercise a virtue so highly rated by his nation, cordially welcomed him. The traveller had remained for two or three days with his host, when one night, after seeking sleep in vain, he stepped out of the tent to enjoy the gentle breeze. It was a serene and lovely night. In a sky of azure, sprinkled with stars, the moon rose slowly in all her majesty, illuminating the solemn desert in its silence and repose till it shone like a vast mirror. The spectacle recalled to the Sevillan a poem composed by his former sovereign, and he began to recite it:

"As the night threw her shadow over the earth like a mighty veil, I drank by the light of torches wine which sparkled in the goblet, when lo! of a sudden, while Orion was high in the heaven, the Moon shone forth. She seemed a glorious queen, gazing forth over the loveliness of nature, beneath Orion as her canopy. One by one the stars appeared in glittering rivalry; ever the glory grew, and amidst the throng hung the Pleiades like the banner of their queen."

---

[1] The revolt began in 1093; two years later 'Abd al-Jabbâr entered Arcos. He was there besieged by Sir, Governor of Seville. 'Abd al-Jabbâr was killed by an arrow, but his party did not surrender for some time.

" As she above, so am I below, surrounded by valiant warriors and the lovely damsels of my harem, whose tresses rival the darkness of the night, while the gleaming goblets are my stars. Let us quaff, my friends, let us quaff the juice of the grape, while these fair ones chant melodiously to the music of the lute."

The Sevillan then recited a long poem composed by Mu'tamid to appease the wrath of his father, which had been aroused by reason of the disaster due to his son's negligence at Malaga. He had scarcely ended when the hangings of the nearest tent were drawn aside, and a man whose venerable aspect would in itself have marked him as the sheik, appeared before him, and addressed him with that elegance of diction and purity of accent for which the Bedawin have always been renowned, and of which they are extremely proud.

"Tell me, O citizen—upon whom may the blessing of God light—whose are these poems, limpid as a brook, fresh as a meadow newly sprinkled by a shower,—now tender and sweet as the voice of a maiden with a necklace of gold, anon full and sonorous as the cry of a young camel?"

"They were composed by a king who reigned in Andalusia, named Ibn 'Abbâd," replied the traveller.

"Doubtless," continued the sheik, "this king ruled over a narrow realm, and could therefore consecrate all his hours to poesy; for a man with many occupations hath not leisure to create verses such as those." "Pardon me; the king was ruler of a great people." "Can you tell me the tribe to which he belonged?" "Assuredly; he was of the Beni Lakhm." "The Beni Lakhm! My own tribe!" And overjoyed at having discovered a new source of fame for his clan, the chief, in an outburst of enthusiasm, shouted in a resounding voice: "Arise! arise! tribesmen! Arise in haste!"

In a moment the camp was astir, and the Bedawin came flocking around their chief. Seeing them assembled, the sheik addressed them thus: "Listen to that which I have just heard, and implant in your memory that which is engraven in mine; for it is a title of glory to you all, an honour of which you have the right to be proud. Citizen, once more, I pray thee, recite our cousin's poems."

When the Sevillan had complied with this request, and all the Bedawin had applauded the verses as enthusiastically as had their chief, the latter related to them what he had been about to tell the stranger, on the subject of the origin

of the Beni ‘Abbâd, their kinsfolk and connexions— how
they too were of the blood of a Lakhmite family that in
former days traversed the Desert with their camels, and
pitched their tents where the sands separate Egypt from
Syria; then he went on to speak of Mu‘tamid, a poet by turns
tender and sublime, a brave soldier, and the mighty monarch
of Seville.   When he had made an end, the Bedawin, intoxicated with joy and pride, leaped to their saddles and
indulged in a brilliant *fantazia*[1] which lasted till dawn.
Then the chief chose twenty of his best camels and presented them to the stranger.   Others followed his example
in proportion to their means, and before the sun had wholly
risen the Sevillan was in possession of a hundred camels.
After having caressed, feasted, and honoured him in every
way, these generous sons of the Desert would scarcely let
the traveller go when the time for his departure arrived,
so dear to them had become one who could recite the poems
of their kinsman the royal poet.

Some two centuries and a half later, when Moslem
Spain, formerly so sceptical, had grown devout, a pilgrim
with staff and rosary was journeying through the kingdom
of Morocco to converse with pious hermits and visit the
holy places.   This pilgrim was the celebrated Ibn al-Khatîb,
Prime Minister of the King of Granada.   On reaching
the little town of Aghmât he sought out the cemetery,
where reposed Mu‘tamid and his wife within a hillock
overgrown with lotus.   At the sight of the two neglected
tombs, dilapidated with age, the Vizier could not restrain
his tears, and improvised these verses :

" I am at Aghmât in fulfilment of a pious duty, to kneel, namely, at
thy tomb ! Ah ! why was it not granted me to know thee living and to
hymn thy glory ? Thou who surpassedst all kings in generosity, and
shinedst like a torch in the darkness of the night! Let me at least
respectfully salute thy tomb ! The swelling ground meetly distinguishes
it ; thou wert exalted over other men while thou livedst, and thou liest
now above those who sleep their eternal sleep at thy feet. Sultan among
the living ! Sultan among the dead ! The ages that have passed never
beheld thy equal, and never, I trow, will the ages yet to come see a king
like thee ! "

Mu‘tamid, nevertheless, cannot be ranked among great
rulers.   Reigning over a people enervated by luxury and
living only for pleasure, such he could scarcely have become

---

[1] For a description of a *fantazia*, see C. R. Conder, *Tent Work in Palestine*
(1885), p. 346.

even if his natural indolence and that love of mere beauty which is at once the bane and the delight of the artistic temperament, had allowed him. But assuredly no other monarch ever possessed so sensitive and poetic a soul. For him the most trivial and transient events of life instantly clothed themselves in a poetic form, and his biography, or at any rate his intellectual history, could be constructed from his poems—intimate revelations of his heart, where are reflected the joys and sorrows which the sunshine and clouds of each passing day brought with them. Moreover, he had the good fortune to be the last Spanish-born king, who represented worthily, nay, brilliantly, a nationality and culture which succumbed, or barely survived, under the dominion of barbarian invaders. His memory was cherished as the youngest-born of that numerous family of poet-princes who held sway in Andalusia. More than any other he was lamented—perhaps to the oblivion of all others—with something of the tender regret inspired by the last blossom of the rose, the last calm days of dying autumn, the last rays of the setting sun.

[AUTHORITIES : Ibn al-Khatîb (MS. E.), Art. on Ibn Bologguîn ; *Abbad.*, i. 40, 59–68, 71, 306, 310–14, 319–20, 366, 383 ; ii. 63, 66–7, 71–4, 147–9, 175, 222–3, 228–9, 232 ; 'Abd al-Wâhid, pp. 101–2, 109 ; Makkarî, ii. 293.]

CHRONOLOGICAL TABLES OF THE MOSLEM PRINCES OF THE ELEVENTH CENTURY

SEVILLE. *The 'Abbádids.*

Abu 'l-Kâsim Mohammed (I) ibn Ismâ'îl (the Kady) .	1023–1042
Abû 'Amr 'Abbâd ibn Mohammed, *al-Mu'tadid* . .	1042–1069
Abu 'l-Kâsim Mohammed (II) ibn-Abbâd, *al-Mu'tamid* .	1069–1091

CORDOVA. *The Beni-Jahwar.*

Abu 'l-Hazm Jahwar ibn Mohammed ibn Jahwar . .	1031–1043
Abu 'l-Walîd Mohammed ibn Jahwar	1043–1064
'Abd al-Malik ibn Mohammed	1064–1070

(Cordova annexed to the Kingdom of Seville.)

MALAGA. *The Hammúdites.*

Hammùd
|
'Alî (the Khalif)
|

Yahyâ (Khalif)   Idris I (1)

Idris II (4, 7) Hasan (3) Yahyâ (2) Mohammed I (5) Hasan Mohammed II (8)

Yahyâ   Idrîs III (6)

1. Idrîs I	1035–1039
2. Yahyâ	1039
3. Hasan	1039–1041
Najâ (the Slav)	1041–1043
4. Idrîs II	1043–1047
5. Mohammed I	1047–1053
6. Idrîs III	1053
7. Idrîs II (again)	1053–1055
8. Mohammed II	1055–1057

(Malaga annexed to the Kingdom of Granada.)

ALGECIRAS. *The Hammúdites.*

Mohammed, son of the Khalif Kâsim ibn Hammûd	1035–1048 (9)
Kâsim (his son)	1048 (9)–1058

(Algeciras annexed to the Kingdom of Seville.)

GRANADA. *The Beni Zîrî.*

Zâwî ibn Zîrî	to 1019
Habbûs	1019–1038
Bâdîs	1038–1073
'Abdallah	1073–1090

CARMONA. *The Beni Birzel.*

[According to Ibn Khaldûn, *cf. Abbad.* ii. p. 216.]
Ishâk.
'Abdallah (his son).

Mohammed ibn 'Abdallah	to 1042 (3)
Al-'Azîz Mustadhir	1042 (3)–1067

[According to Ibn Hayyân, *apud* Ibn Bassâm, i. f. 78]

Ibn 'Abdallah (*i.e.* Mohammed ibn 'Abdallah) ruled Carmona while Hishâm III reigned at Cordova . [1029–1031]

[And according to the same writer (*ibid.* f. 109), who is more trustworthy than Ibn Khaldûn, Ibn 'Abdallah had for his successor] Ishâk (his son), who was reigning in 1050

[Ibn al-'Abbâr seems to be in error in asserting that Ibn 'Abdallah was still living in 1051: cf. *Recherches,* 1st ed., i. p. 286.]

RONDA.

Abû Nûr ibn Abî Korra	1014 (5)–1053
Abû Nasr (his son)	1053
(Ronda annexed to the Kingdom of Seville.)	

MORON.

Nûh	1013 (4)–1041 (2)
Abû Menâd Mohammed (his son)	1041 (2)–1053
(Moron annexed to the Kingdom of Seville.)	

ARCOS.

Ibn Khazrûn	to 1053
(Arcos annexed to the Kingdom of Seville.)	

HUELVA. *The Bakrites.*

Abû Zayd Mohammed ibn Ayyûb	from 1011 (2)
Abu 'l-Mu'sab 'Abd al-'Azîz	to 1051
(Huelva annexed to the Kingdom of Seville.)	

NIEBLA. *The Beni Yahyâ.*

Abu 'l-'Abbâs Ahmad ibn Yahyâ Yahsobî . . 1023–1041 (2)
Mohammed, his brother.
Fath ibn Khalaf ibn Yahyâ, nephew of the preceding . to 1051
    (Niebla annexed to the Kingdom of Seville.)
[Ibn al-Abbar, (cf. *Recherches*, 1st ed., i. 287) gives the
    last Prince of Niebla the name of Yahyâ ibn Ahmad
    ibn Yahyâ; but Ibn Khaldûn (*Abbad*. ii. 211) is here
    followed. Ibn Hayyân (*apud* Ibn Bassâm, i. f. 108)
    names him Fath ibn Yahyâ.]

SILVES. *The Beni Mozain.*

Abû Bakr Mohammed ibn Sa'îd ibn Mozain . . . 1028–1050
Abu 'l-Asbagh 'Îsâ . . . . . . to 1051 (2)
    (Silves annexed to the Kingdom of Seville.)

SANTA-MARIA DE ALGARVE.

Abû 'Othmân Sa'îd ibn Hârûn 1016–1043
Mohammed, his son 1043–1052
    (Santa-Maria annexed to the Kingdom of Seville.)

MERTOLA.

Ibn Taifûr . . . . to 1044
    (Mertola annexed to the Kingdom of Seville.)

BADAJOZ.

Sâbûr.

(*The Aftasides.*)

Abû Mohammed 'Abdallah ibn Mohammed ibn Maslama,
    al-Mansûr I.
Abû Bakr Mohammed, *Muzaffar* . . . . . to 1068
Yahyâ, *al-Mansûr II.*
'Omar, *al-Mutawakkil* . . . . . . to 1094

TOLEDO.

Yaîsh ibn Mohammed ibn Yaîsh . . . . to 1036

(*The Beni Dhu 'n-Nûn.*)

Ismâ'îl, *al-Zâfir* 1036–1043 (4)
    [See *Recherches* (1881), i. 238 *n.*]
Abu 'l-Hasan Yahyâ, *al-Ma'mûn* . . . . 1043 (4)–1075
Yahyâ ibn Ismâ'îl ibn Yahyâ, *al-Kâdir* . . . 1075–1085

ZARAGOZA.

Mundhir ibn Yahyâ, the Todjîbite . . . . . to 1039

(*The Beni Húd.*)

Abû Ayyûb Sulaimân ibn Mohammed, *al-Musta'în I*	1039–1046 (7)
Ahmad, *Muktadir*	1046 (7)–1081
Yûsuf, *Mútamin*	1081–1085
Ahmad, *al-Musta'în II*	1085–1110
'Abd al-Malik 'Imâd ad-dawla	1110

LA SAHLA (*Capital, Albarrazin.*)

(*The Beni Razín.*)

Abû Mohammed Hudhail I, ibn Khalaf ibn Lope ibn
Razîn . . . . from 1011
Abû Merwân 'Abd al-Malik I, ibn Khalaf, his brother;
Abû Mohammed Hudhail II 'Izz ad-dawla, son of the
preceding.
Abû Merwân 'Abd al-Malik II, Hosâm ad-dawla . . to 1103
Yahyâ.

ALPUENTE. (*The Beni Kâsim.*)

'Abdallah I, ibn Kâsim the Fihrite, Nidhâm ad-dawla .	to 1030
Mohammed Yumn ad-dawla	
Ahmad Adhud ad-dawla	to 1048 (9)
'Abdallah II, Janâh ad-dawla, brother of the preceding	1048 (9)–1092

VALENCIA.

The Slavs Mobârak and Muzaffar.
The Slav Lebîb, Lord of Tortosa.

'Abd al-'Azîz, *al-Mansûr*	1021–1061
'Abd al-Malik, *al-Muzaffar*	1061–1065
(Valencia united to Toledo.)	
Ma'mûn (of Toledo)	1065–1075
(Valencia separated from Toledo.)	
Abû Bakr ibn 'Abd al-'Azîz	1075–1085
The Kady 'Othmân, his son	1085
Kâdir (ex-king of Toledo)	1085–1092
(Valencia becomes a Republic.)	
Ibn Jahhâf, *President*	1092–1094

DENIA.

Abu 'l-jaish Mujahid Muwaffak . . .	to 1044 (5)
'Alî Ikbâl ad-dawla	1044 (5)–1076
(Dethroned by Muktadir of Zaragoza. Denia united to the Kingdom of Zaragoza.)	

Muktadir (of Zaragoza) 1076–1081
    (Muktadir divides his realm between his two sons, one
        of whom, known as the *hájib* Mundhir, receives
        Lerida, Tortosa, and Denia.)
The *hájib* Mundhir 1081–1091
    His son, under the guardianship of the Beni Betir.

MURCIA.

Khairân (of Almeria) . . . . . . 1016 (7)–1028
Zuhair (of Almeria) 1028–1038
'Abd al-' Azîz, *al-Mansûr* (of Valencia) 1038–1061
'Abd al-Malik, *al-Muzaffar* (of Valencia). . . . 1061–1065
Under these three princes Abû Bakr Ahmad ibn Tâhir is
    Governor of Murcia; he dies 1063
His son, Abu 'Abd-er-Rahmân Mohammed, succeeds him 1063–1078
Mu'tamid (of Seville).
Ibn Ammâr.
Ibn Rashîk . . . . to 1090

ALMERIA.

Khairân . . . . to 1028
Zuhair 1028–1038
'Abd al-'Azîz al-Mansûr (of Valencia) 1038–1041

(*The Beni Somádih.*)

Abu 'l-Ahwâz Man 1041–1051
Mohammed Mu'tasim 1051–1091
'Izz ad-dawla 1091

AUTHORITIES

THE following list will serve for the precise identification of the authorities cited above in an abbreviated form. The editions of printed books are indicated, and the Catalogue Nos. of manuscripts in public collections. The notes enclosed in square brackets have been added by the translator.

ABBAD. Scriptorum Arabum loci de Abbadidis . . . editi a R. Dozy. Leyden, 1846. [Completed, in 3 vols., in 1863.]

'ABD AL-WÂHID. Abdu'l-Wâhid al-Marrâkoshî; The History of the Almohades, &c. . . . edited . . . by R. Dozy. Leyden, 1847. [A translation, by E. Fagnan, was published at Algiers in 1893.]

ABÛ'L-MAHÂSIN. Abû'l-Mahâsin Ibn Tagri Bardii Annales . . . Ed. par T. G. J. Juynboll et B. F. Mathes. Leyden, 1852–61. [Ar. *Nujum al-Zâhira*, "The Shining Stars"; a history of Egypt under the Arabs. French transl. by C. A. C. Barbier de Meynard, 1884.]

AGHÂNÎ. Alii Ispahanensis Liber Cantilenarum magnus . . . [Ed.] J. G. L. Kosegarten. Greifswald, 1840. [The *Kitâb al-Aghânî*, "Book of Songs," by Abû'l-Faraj al-Isfahânî, has been published at Bûlâk (1868), in 20 vols., and a supplementary vol., (ed. by R. E. Brünnow), at Leyden, 1888.]

AHMAD IBN ABÎ YA'KÛB. *Kitâb al-Buldân;* MS. of M. Muchlinski, of St. Petersburg. (Cf. Specimen e literis orientalibus exhibens Kitâbo 'l-Boldân auctore Ahmed ibn abî Jaqûb, noto nomine Al-Jaqubîi, ed. A. W. Th. Juynboll. Leyden, 1861.)

AKHBAR MAJMÛ'AT. Paris MS., anc. fonds, No. 706. [In 1867 the text was publ. at Madrid, with a Spanish transl. by E. L. y Alcántara: see also Dozy's *Recherches* (1881), i. 40, and his *Introd. à la Chron. d'Ibn-Adhârî*, pp. 10–12.]

ALVAR. (Alvaro); *Vita Eulogii*, in *Esp. sagr.*, x. 420–481; *Epistolæ*, in *Esp. sagr.*, xi. 81–218; *Indiculus luminosus*, in *Esp. sagr.*, xi. 219–275.

ANN. COMPL. *Annales Complutenses*, in *Esp. sagr.*, xxiii. 310–314.

ANN. COMPO. *Annales Compostellani*, in *Esp. sagr.*, xxiii. 317–324.

AN. TOL. *Anales Toledanos*, in *Esp. sagr.*, xxiii. 358–362.

'ARÎB. Histoire de l'Afrique et de l'Espagne intitulée al-Bayâno 'l-Mogrib, par Ibn-Adhârî . . . et fragments de la chronique d'Arîb . . . par R. Dozy, Leyde, 1848–51. ['Arîb ibn Sa'd, al-Kurtubî.]

AUTHORITIES

BALÂDHURÎ. Leyden MS. [Ahmad ibn Yahyâ al-Balâdhurî.]

BASRÎ. "The Fotooh al-Shâm," being an account of the Moslim conquests in Syria, by . . . . . Mohammad bin 'Abd Allah Al-Azdî Al-Baçri . . . Ed. by Ensign W. N. Lees, Calcutta, 1854. (*Bibliotheca Indica,* vol. xvi.)

BERGANZA. Francisco de Berganza; *Antiguedades de España.* Madrid, 1719–21.

CATALOGUE. *Catalogus Codicum Orientalium Bibl. Acad. Lugd. Batav.* . . . R. P. A. Dozy. Leyden, 1851.

CAUSSIN. A. P. Caussin de Perceval, *Essai sur l'histoire des Arabes, avant l'Islamisme.* Paris, 1817–8.

CHRON. ADEF. *Chronica de Alfonso VII,* in *Esp. sagr.,* xxi. 307–409.

CHRON. ALB. *Chronicon Albeldense,* in *Esp. sagr.,* xiii. 417–464.

CHRON. BURG. *Chronicon Burgense,* in *Esp. sagr.,* xxiii. 307–310.

CHRON. CARD. *Chronicon de Cardeña,* in *Esp. sagr.,* xxiii. 370–380.

CHRON. COMPL. *Chronicon Complutense,* in *Esp. sagr.,* xxiii. 315–317.

CHRON. COMPO. *Chronicon Compostellanum,* in *Esp. sagr.,* xxiii.

CHRON. CONIMB. *Chronicon Conimbricense,* in *Esp. sagr.,* xxiii. 329–355.

CHRON. IRI. *Chronicon Iriense,* in *Esp. sagr.,* xx. 598–608.

CHRON. LUSIT. *Chronicon Lusitanum,* in *Esp. sagr.,* xiv. 402–419.

ESP. SAGR. España sagrada, Theatro Geographico-Historico de la Iglesia de España. Segunda edicion. Madrid, 1754–1850 [1879]. (Ed. by H. Florez and others.)

EULOG. The works of Eulogius as contained in Schottus, *Hispaniæ Illustratæ,* vol. iv. [They are also comprised in Migne, *Patrol. Curs. Compl.,* vols. cxv.–cxvi.]

FÂKIHÎ. (History of Mecca), Leyden MS., No. 463. See *Catalogue,* ii. p. 170. [Abû 'Abdallah, al-Fâkihî.]

HAMÂSA. Hamasae Carmina . . . Ed. G. G. Freytag. Bonn, 1828–51. [The *Hamâsa* of Abu Tammâm Habîb ibn Aus; an important Anthology.]

HAMÂSA BUHT. [The Hamâsa of Al-Buhturî.] Leyden MS. [unique].

HIST. COMPO. *Historia Compostellana,* in *Esp. sagr.,* xx.

HOLAL. (History of Morocco), Leyden MS., No. 24. Cf. *Abbad.* ii. pp. 182 *sq.*, and *Catalogue,* ii. p. 185.

HOMAIDÎ. (Biographical Dictionary); Oxford MS., Hunt. 464.

IBN ABÎ USAIBI'A. (Biographies of Physicians); a copy of relevant part of Paris MS. (No. 673 suppl. ar.), with variants from Oxford MSS. (Hunt. 171, and Pocock, 356). [This work, the '*Uyûn al-anbâ*, was publ. at Königsberg by A. Müller in 1884.]

IBN ADHÂRÎ. See '*Aríb.*

IBN AL-'ABBÂR. In *Notices,* q.v. [The *Hullat al-siyarâ* of Abû 'Abdallah Ibn al-'Abbâr.]

IBN AL-ATHÎR. Paris MS. (from copy in possession of M. Tornberg). [The *Kitâbu al-Kâmil fi'l-ta'ríkh,* "Complete Chronology," of Abu 'l Hasan 'Alî 'Izz al-din Ibn al-Athîr; publ. by Tornberg, 1851–76.]

IBN AL-KHATÎB. (*Al-ihâta fî ta'ríkhi Gharnâta,* and its abridgment : *Markaz al-ihâta bi-odabâi Gharnâta.*) B. Berlin MS.; E. Escorial MS.; G. MS. in possession of M. de Gayangos; P. Paris MS. See *Abbad.* ii. pp. 169–172, and *Recherches* (2nd ed.), i. pp. 293–4.

IBN AL-KÛTIYYA. Paris MS., No. 706. (See Dozy, *Introd. à la Chron. d'Ibn-Adhârí,* pp. 28–30). [The *Ta'ríkh al-Andalus,* a history of Spain under the Arabs until A.D. 893.]

IBN BADRÛN. Commentaire historique sur le poème d'Ibn-Abdoun (par Ibn Badroun). . . . R. Dozy; Leyde, 1846. [Abû Marwân 'Abdal-Malik Ibn Badrûn : Ibn 'Abdûn's ode refers to the fall of the Aftasides.]

IBN BASSÂM. *Dhakhíra,* Vol. I., MS. in possession of M. Jules Mohl; Vol. II., Oxford MS. (No. 749 Catal. Uri); Vol. III., Gotha MS. (No. 266) collated with MS. in possession of M. de Gayangos in the case of passages of Ibn Hayyân quoted by Ibn Bassâm. See *Abbad.* i. pp. 189 *sq.*, and *Journ. asiat.* fév.-mars, 1861.

IBN BATÛTA. *Voyages d'Ibn-Batoutah.* . . . C. Defrémery et B. R. Sanguinetti, Paris, 1853, etc.

IBN HABÎB. See *Ta'ríkh.*

IBN HAYYÂN. Oxford MS., Bodl. 509 (Nicoll's Catal., No. 137). See also Ibn Bassâm. [Abû Merwân Ibn Hayyân, whose great historical work is almost entirely lost.]

IBN HAZM. (Treatise on Religions), Leyden MS., No. 480.—(Treatise on Love), Leyden MS., No. 927. [Abû Muhammad 'Alî ibn Hazm : the two works are respectively the *Kitâb al-milal wa'l-nihal* (History of Religious and Philosophical Sects), and the *Tauq al-hamâma* (The Dove's Necklace), an erotic anthology.]

Ibn Khâkân. *Matmah al-anfus*, London and St. Petersburg MSS. *Kalâ'id al-'Ikyân wa-mahâsin al-A'yân*, Leyden MSS. (Nos. 306 and 35.) [The latter work, "Necklaces of pure Gold and Beauties of the Great," has been translated by E. Bourgade.]

Ibn Khaldûn. *Prolegomena*, edited by E. Quatremère, in the *Notices et extraits des manuscrits de la Bibl. imp.* (vols. xvi., xvii., xviii.): (*History of the Eastern Omayyads*), Leyden MS., ii. No. 1350: (*History of Spain*), Paris MS. (No 742-4 suppl. ar.) and Leyden MS. (iv. No. 1350): (*History of the Berbers*) edited, and translated by MacGuckin de Slane. [Abû Zaid 'Abdal-Rahmân Ibn Khaldûn, 1332-1406.]

Ibn Kutaiba. Ibn Coteiba's Handbuch der Geschichte . . . herausgegeben von F. Wüstenfeld ; Göttingen, 1850.

Idat. Chron. *Idatii Episcopi Chronicon*, in *Esp. sagr.* iv. 345-427.

Idrîsî. *Géographie d'Édrisi, traduite . . . par P. A. Jaubert*, Paris, 1836-40. [The *Nuzhat al-mushtâk*, of Abû 'Abdallah al-Sharîf al-Idrîsî, 1099-1154.]

Isid. *Isidori Pacensis Episcopi Chronicon*, in *Esp. sagr.*, viii. 282-325 [Cf. *Recherches* (1881), i. pp. 2 *sq.*]

Isid. Sev. *Divi Isidori Hispal. Episcopi Historia de Regibus Gothorum*, in *Esp. sagr.*, vi. 482-525.

Istakhrî. Liber Climatum, . . . ad similitudinem Cod. Gothani . . . exprimendum curavit J. H. Moeller, Gothæ, 1839. [Abû Ishâk al-Farîsî, born at Persepolis (Istakhr).]

Kartâs. *Annales Regum Mauretaniæ ab Abu-l-Hasan Ali ben-Abdallah ibn-abi-Zer' Fesano conscripti*, ed. Tornberg, Upsala, 1846.

Kazwînî. Kosmographie, ed. F. Wüstenfeld, Göttingen, 1847-8. [The *Athâru 'l-Bilâd* of Zakarîyyâ Ibn Mohammed al-Kazwînî.]

Khoshanî. (History of the Kadies of Cordova), Oxford MS. (Nicoll's Catalogue, No. 127).

Llorente. Juan Antonio Llorente ; *Noticias históricas de las tres Provincias Vascongadas* . . . Madrid, 1806-8.

Lucas. (Lucas, Bp. of Tuy), *Chronicon Mundi . . . usque ad Eram 1274*. In *Hispaniæ illustratæ* (F. Schottus), vol. iv.

Makkarî. Analectes sur l'histoire et la littérature des Arabes d'Espagne . . . Publ. par R. Dozy, G. Dugat, L. Krehl et W. Wright. Leyde, 1855-61. [This is the introductory portion of the important history of Moslem Spain by Ahmad ibn Mohammed al-Tilimsânî al-Makkarî (*c.* 1590-1632). Other parts, rearranged, were translated by Pascual de Gayangos, under the title of "History of the Mohammedan Dynasties in Spain." London, 1840-3.]

Mas'ûdî. *Murûj al-Dhahab.* ["The Golden Meadows."] Leyden MSS., Nos. 127 and 537d. ['Alî ibn Husain's great historical work, of which the above is an epitome, is lost. The *M. al-D.* has been translated by A. Sprenger (*Or. Transl. Fund, 1841*).]

Meyá. Manuscript of Meyá, in the *Memorias de la Academia de la Historia,* t. iv.

Mon. Sil. *Monachi Silensis Chronicon,* in *Esp. sagr.,* xvii. 270–330.

Mubarrad. *Kâmil,* Leyden MS. No. 587. See *Catalogue,* i. pp. 204–5. [Mohammed ibn Yazîd al-Azdî al-Mubarrad.]

Nawawî. The Biographical Dictionary of illustrious men . . . by Abu Zakariya Yahya El-Nawawi . . . edited . . . by F. Wüstenfeld. Göttingen, 1842–5. [The *Tahdhíb al-Asmâ,* "Correction of Proper Names."]

Notices. Notices sur quelques manuscrits arabes, par R. Dozy. Leyde, 1847–51.

Nuwairî. (History of Spain.) The pages of the Leyden MS., No. 2 h, are cited, but the superior Paris MS., No. 645, has been collated.

Paul. Emerit. Pauli Diaconi Emeritensis De vita P. P. Emeritensium, in *Esp. sagr.,* xiv. 459–475.

Pelag. Pelagius of Oviedo; in *Esp. sagr.,* xiv.

Raihân. *Raihan al-Albâb,* Leyden MS., No. 415. See *Catalogue,* i. 268–9.

Râzî. *Cronica del Moro Rasis,* in Mem. de la Academia de la Historia, t. viii. See Dozy, *Introd. à la Chron. d'Ibn-Adhârî,* pp. 24–5. [Based on the work of Ahmad ibn Mohammed al-Râzî of Cordova.]

Recherches. Recherches sur l'histoire et la littérature de l'Espagne pendant le moyen âge, par R. Dozy: 3me éd., Leyde, 1881.

Rodr. de Tol. Rodrigo of Toledo, *De Rebus Hispanicis,* in A. F. Schottus, *Hispaniæ Illustratæ,* vol. ii. (The best ed. of his *Hist. Arabum* is contained in *Elmacini Historia Saracenica,* ed. Erpenius.)

Sa'îd of Toledo. Extract from his *Tabakât al-omam;* Leyden MS., No. 159.

Samhûdî. Paris MS., No. 753 bis. [Nûr al-dîn al-Samhûdî; his *Hist. of Medina* was epitomised by Wüstenfeld, Göttingen, 1873.]

Samp. *Chronicon de Sampiro,* in *Esp. sagr.,* xiv. 419–457.

Sams. *Samsonis Abbatis Cordubensis Apologeticus,* in *Esp. sagr.,* xi. 325–516.

Sebast. *Sebastiani Chronicon,* in *Esp. sagr.,* xiii. 475–489.

SHARASTÂNÎ. The Book of Religious and Philosophic Sects, by Muhammad al-Sharastâni. . . . Ed. by W. Cureton, London, 1842–6. [Abu 'l-Fath al-Sharastânî; his work bears the same name as Ibn Hazm's, *q.v.*]

SOTA. Francisco de Sota : *Chronica de los principes de Asturias y Cantabria.* Madrid, 1681.

SUYÛTÎ. Ta'rîkh al-Khulafâ. The History of the Khaliphs, by Aboo al-Fadhl 'Abd al-Rahmân Jalal al-Dîn bin Abî Bakr al-Soyooti. Ed. by W. N. Lees and Mawlawi 'Abd al-Haqq. Calcutta, 1856. [An English translation, by Maj. H. S. Jarret (1881), is given in *Bibliotheca Indica*, vol. lxxxvii.]

TABARÎ. Tabaristanensis Annales . . . regum atque legatorum Dei. . . . Ed. J. G. L. Kosegarten, Greifswald, 1831–53. [The "Annals" of Mohammed ibn Jarîr al-Tabarî have been edited by De Goeje and others, Leyden, 1879–1898.]

TA'RÎKH IBN HABÎB. Oxford MS. (Nicoll's Catalogue, No. 12). See *Recherches*, i. pp. 32 *sqq.*

VITA BEATÆ VIRGINIS ARGENTEÆ. In *Esp. sagr.*, x. 475.

VITA JOHANNIS GORZIENSIS. In Pertz, *Monumenta Germanica (Scriptores)*, vol. iv.

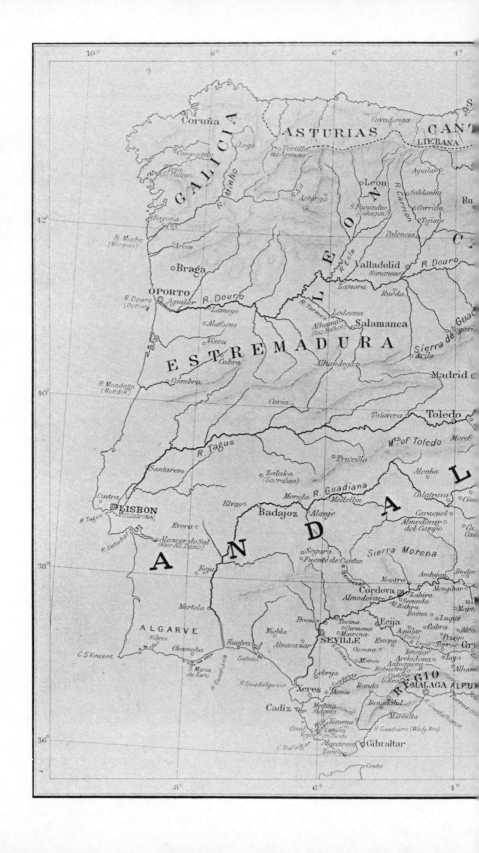

THE
IBERIAN PENINSULA
(711 A.D. to 1144 A.D.)
To illustrate
"SPANISH ISLAM"

English Miles

0 10 20   40   60   80   100   120

INDEX

The abbreviation " b." is used for " ibn " (son of), except at the beginning of a name. All words expressing relationship are ignored in the alphabetical arrangement, as also is the definite article " al," when not initial.

A

Abadsolomes. *See* Leovigild
Abân, son of Mu'âwiya, 161
'Abbâd, ancestor of Ismâ'îl, 598 *n.*
'Abbâd (Mu'tadid). *See* Mu'tadid
'Abbâd, son of Mu'tamid, 674 ; murder of, 675
'Abbâdids, origin of the, 598
'Abbâs b. Ahnaf, 578
'Abbâs b. Firnâs, poet, 304 *n.*
'Abbas, al-, uncle of Mohammed, 12 *n.*
'Abbâs, son of Mutawakkil, 716
'Abbâsids, The, usurpation of, 161 ; diminished power of, 423
Abda, daughter of Hishâm, 161
'Abdallah, Sultan, 322–3 ; shows favour to Spaniards, 324
'Abdallah, King of Granada, 695–6 ; at Aledo, 701 ; 707 ; character of, 708 ; is made captive by Yûsuf, 709-10 ; 728
'Abdallah b. 'Abbâs, 38, 47
'Abdallah b. 'Abd al-Malik, Govr. of Moron, 195–6
'Abdallah, son of 'Abd-er-Rahmân I, 281 ; character of, 295 ; 296
'Abdallah b. al-Aftas, Prince of Badajoz, 600 ; his treachery, 601
'Abdallah, father of Almanzor, 458 *n.*, 459
'Abdallah, son of Almanzor, 506 ; plots against his father, 507–8 ; executed, 508
'Abdallah b. 'Amr, 196
'Abdallah b. Ash'ath, 346
'Abdallah, " Flintheart," takes Zamora, 497 ; plots against Almanzor, 507 ; escapes, 508 ; captivity of, 509-10
'Abdallah b. Hajjâj, captures Carmona, 342 ; assassinated, 349
'Abdallah b. Handhala, at Tiberias, 51, 53 ; at Harra, 59 ; death of, 60
'Abdallah, descendant of Hudhayfa, 98 *sq.*
'Abdallah al-Kaddah (Fâtimid Khalif). *See* 'Obaidallah
'Abdallah b. Maymûn, 403–5
'Abdallah b. Mohammed. *See* Shakyâ
'Abdallah, son of Mohammed b. Lope, 382
'Abdallah b. Mokhâmis, 573

'Abdallah b. Motî, 56 ; at Harra, 58 ; flight of, 60
'Abdallah b. 'Omar, opposes Ibn Zubair, 48
Abdallah b. Omayya, 287, 300
Abdallah, son of Sa'd, son of Abû Sarh, 29
'Abdallah b. Zubair, 43 ; at Mecca, 44 ; his panegyric of Husain, 47 ; his interview with Ibn Idhâh, 49–50 ; 64, 72–3 ; welcomes the Khârejites, 83 ; death of, 95–6
'Abd al-'Azîz b. 'Abdallah b. Asîd, 106
'Abd al-'Azîz, grandson of Almanzor, King of Valencia, 595 ; acknowledges Khalaf, 604 ; 615 ; 617 ; death of, 657
'Abd al-'Azîz, the Bakrite, 636
'Abd al-'Azîz b. Hasan, 596
'Abd al-'Azîz, son of Merwan, 101, 103 ; defeated by Khârejites, 107 ; Govr. of Egypt, 117
'Abd al-'Azîz, son of Mûsâ, 236
'Abd al-Ghâfir, brother of Jad, 347
'Abd al-Hamîd (b. Basîl), 395
'Abd al-Jabbâr, 732, 733 *n.*
'Abd al-Jalîl, poet, 670
Abdallah, father of Mohammed, 12 *n.*
'Abd al-Malik, captor of Carteya, 231, 458-9
'Abd al-Malik b. Abî 'l-Jawâd, 352
'Abd al-Malik (Muzaffar), son of Almanzor, 506 ; made *hâjib*, 511 ; commands troops in Africa, 520 ; last interview with his father, 523 ; his prosperous rule, 534 ; death of, 538–9 ; sons of, 586
'Abd al-Malik b. Habîb, prophecy of, 408, 410
'Abd al-Malik (Ibn Jahwar), 673
'Abd al-Malik, son of Katan, Govr. of Spain, 138 ; his hatred of the Syrians, *ib.* ; seeks their aid, 140 ; 141–2 ; slain, 143
'Abd al-Malik b. Merwân, 58 ; besieges Kirckesia, 90 ; subdues 'Irâk, 91–2 ; appoints Hajjâj commander, 94–5 ; 103–5 ; appoints Muhallab, 109 ; death of, 115
'Abd al-Malik b. Mundhir, conspiracy of, 488–9 ; crucified, 490
'Abd al-Malik (Muzaffar), King of Valencia, 657–8

3 B